The Shape of the Writings

Siphrut
Literature and Theology of the Hebrew Scriptures

Editorial Board

1. *A Severe Mercy: Sin and Its Remedy in the Old Testament*, by Mark J. Boda
2. *Chosen and Unchosen: Conceptions of Election in the Pentateuch and Jewish-Christian Interpretation*, by Joel N. Lohr
3. *Genesis and the Moses Story: Israel's Dual Origins in the Hebrew Bible*, by Konrad Schmid
4. *The Land of Canaan and the Destiny of Israel: Theologies of Territory in the Hebrew Bible*, by David Frankel
5. *Jacob and the Divine Trickster: A Theology of Deception and YHWH's Fidelity to the Ancestral Promise in the Jacob Cycle*, by John E. Anderson
6. *Esther: The Outer Narrative and the Hidden Reading*, by Jonathan Grossman
7. *From Fratricide to Forgiveness: The Language and Ethics of Anger in Genesis*, by Matthew R. Schlimm
8. *The Rhetoric of Remembrance: An Investigation of the "Fathers" in Deuteronomy*, by Jerry Hwang
9. *In the Beginning: Essays on Creation Motifs in the Bible and the Ancient Near East*, by Bernard F. Batto
10. *Run, David, Run! An Investigation of the Theological Speech Acts of David's Departure and Return (2 Samuel 14–20)*, by Steven T. Mann
11. *From the Depths of Despair to the Promise of Presence: A Rhetorical Reading of the Book of Joel*, by Joel Barker
12. *Forming God: Divine Anthropomorphism in the Pentateuch*, by Anne Katherine Knafl
13. *Standing in the Breach: An Old Testament Theology and Spirituality of Intercessory Prayer*, by Michael Widmer
14. *What Kind of God? Collected Essays of Terence E. Fretheim*, edited by Michael J. Chan and Brent A. Strawn
15. *The "Image of God" in the Garden of Eden: The Creation of Humankind in Genesis 2:5–3:24 in Light of the* mīs pî pīt pî *and* wpt-r *Rituals of Mesopotamia and Ancient Egypt*, by Catherine L. McDowell
16. *The Shape of the Writings*, edited by Julius Steinberg and Timothy J. Stone
17. *A Message from the Great King: Reading Malachi in Light of Ancient Persian Royal Messenger Texts from the Time of Xerxes*, by R. Michael Fox
18. *"See and Read All These Words": The Concept of the Written in the Book of Jeremiah*, by Chad L. Eggleston

The Shape of the Writings

edited by
Julius Steinberg and Timothy J. Stone
with the assistance of Rachel Marie Stone

Winona Lake, Indiana
EISENBRAUNS
2015

Library of Congress Cataloging-in-Publication Data

The shape of the Writings / edited by Julius Steinberg and Timothy J.
Stone ; with the assistance of Rachel Marie Stone.
    pages cm.—(Siphrut : literature and theology of the Hebrew
    Scriptures ; 16)
    Includes bibliographical references and index.
    ISBN 978-1-57506-373-7 (hardback : alk. paper)
    1. Bible. Hagiographa—Criticism, interpretation, etc.   2. Bible.
Hagiographa—Theology.   I. Steinberg, Julius, 1972– editor.
    BS1308.S53   2015
    223'.06—dc23
                           2015024198

Contents

Preface

This book examines the significance of the different arrangements of the Writings in the Hebrew canon, which is a field of research that is mostly uncharted territory. Some readers may suppose that a preface should sink a few signs solidly into the ground to guide them through this unfamiliar territory. This practice would allow readers to skip from one section to another in an effort to mine the book quickly for desirable nuggets to use in their own research. However, readers who do this either jump quickly to a few desired locations or travel through the entire landscape at excessive speed. Both of these approaches, we fear, will fail to appreciate the diverse dialogue in the following pages, or worse, caricature the unfamiliar terrain from the safe distance of one's preconceived notions. The table of contents contains enough information to be a sufficient yet underdetermined guide. Furthermore, in titling this volume *The Shape of the Writings*, we were not making it our goal to mold a rigid shape but to present essays that add a question mark to the end of the title without dismissing the topic altogether.

After the contributors' essays, we are providing space for responses from well-established scholars—for serious critique that also extends and deepens the dialogue. If the approaches in the volume are valuable, then the ideas will need to be revised, altered, and perhaps in some cases, abandoned. We encourage readers to view these responses at the end of the volume as furthering the discussion rather than shutting it down.

We have provided a breadth of perspectives and have ensured that most of the books in the Writings are treated in one way or another, yet there remain significant gaps. The discussion in these pages is also incomplete because it is part of other conversations. This is, of course, true of any book, but much in the following pages summarizes or presents specific examples from larger and more-detailed works in both German and English. This has the advantage and convenience of bringing together the shortened form of lengthy arguments; the disadvantage is that it threatens to flatten nuanced positions once they have been unmoored from larger contexts and possibly convey the illusion that one has heard everything essential. Instead, we view this book as opening the door to a room where one can listen to a discussion that may reveal another series of doors that he or she can open if so inclined. We encourage doubtful, critical, and curious readers to follow the footnotes.

As volume editors, we want to express our gratitude to all the authors and reviewers who contributed to this collection. We want to thank Daniel

Jander and Stefan Thiemert, who assisted in translating the German articles and worked on the bibliographical references. We also express our gratitude to Jim Eisenbraun for including our volume in the Siphrut series, and to his staff, including Beverly McCoy, whose careful editorial hand improved the volume in numerous ways.

This book is dedicated to the late Brevard Childs and to the late Erich Zenger, each of whom in his own way left an indelible mark on the field of Old Testament studies and prepared the soil for projects like this to take root.

—JULIUS STEINBERG
—TIMOTHY J. STONE and RACHEL MARIE STONE

Abbreviations

General

A.D.	Anno Domino
b.	Babylonian Talmud
B.C.(E.)	Before Christ / Before the Common Era
C.E.	Common Era
ch(s).	chapter(s)
ChrH	Chronistic History/Historian
DtrH	Deuteronomistic History/Historian
ed.	edited by / edition
ET	English translation
FS	Festschrift
HB	Hebrew Bible
JPS	Jewish Publication Society version of the Bible
LXX	Septuagint
m.	Mishnah
MT	Masoretic Text
NIV	New International Version of the Bible
NJPS	New Jewish Publication Society version of the Bible
n(n).	note(s)
no(s).	number(s)
NRSV	New Revised Standard Version of the Bible
NT	New Testament
OT	Old Testament
p(p).	page(s)
repr.	reprint/reprinted by
SBL	Society of Biblical Literature
t.	Tosefta
TNK/TaNaK	Tanak (acronym for Torah, Nebiʾim, and Ketubim)
trans.	translated by
v(v).	verse(s)
vol(s).	volume(s)
y.	Jerusalem (Yerushalayim) Talmud

Reference Works

AB	Anchor Bible
ABD	*Anchor Bible Dictionary*. Edited by David N. Freedman et al. 6 vols. New York: Doubleday, 1992
AJBI	*Annual of the Japanese Biblical Institute*
ATANT	Abhandlungen zur Theologie des Alten und Neuen Testaments
ATD	Das Alte Testament Deutsch
BBB	Bonner biblische Beiträge
BBR	*Bulletin for Biblical Research*
BETL	Bibliotheca Ephemeridum Theologicarum Lovaniensium

Bib	*Biblica*
BibInt	*Biblical Interpretation*
BibS	Biblische Studien
BJRL	*Bulletin of the John Rylands Library*
BJS	Brown Judaic Studies
BKAT	Biblischer Kommentar Altes Testament
BN	*Biblische Notizen*
BSac	*Bibliotheca Sacra*
BWANT	Beiträge zur Wissenschaft vom Alten und Neuen Testament
BZAW	Beihefte zur Zeitschrift für die Alttestamentliche Wissenschaft
CBQ	*Catholic Biblical Quarterly*
DBAT	*Dielheimer Blätter zum Alten Testament*
DBSup	*Dictionnaire de la Bible: Supplément.* Edited by Louis Pirot and André Robert. Paris: Letouzey & Ané, 1928–
DSD	*Dead Sea Discoveries*
EncJud	Skolnik, Fred, and Michael Berenbaum, eds. *Enclopedia Judaica.* 2nd ed. 22 vols. Detroit: Macmillan, 2007
ER	*Encyclopedia of Religion.* Edited by M. Eliade. 16 vols. New York: Macmillan, 1987
ExpTim	*Expository Times*
FAT	Forschungen zum Alten Testament
FOTL	Forms of the Old Testament Literature
FRLANT	Forschungen zur Religion und Literatur des Alten und Neuen Testaments
HAT	Handbuch zum Alten Testament
HBS	Herders Biblische Studien
HBT	*Horizons in Biblical Theology*
HThKAT	Herders Theologischer Kommentar
HTS	Harvard Theological Studies
HUCA	*Hebrew Union College Annual*
Int	*Interpretation*
ISBE	*International Standard Bible Encyclopedia.* Edited by Geoffrey W. Bromiley. 4 vols. Grand Rapids, MI: Eerdmans, 1979–88
JANES	*Journal of the Ancient Near Eastern Society*
JBL	*Journal of Biblical Literature*
JBQ	*Jewish Bible Quarterly*
JBTh	Jahrbuch für Biblische Theologie
JETS	*Journal of the Evangelical Theological Society*
JSOT	*Journal for the Study of the Old Testament*
JSOTSup	Journal for the Study of the Old Testament, Supplement Series
JSP	*Journal for the Study of the Pseudepigrapha*
JSS	*Journal of Semitic Studies*
JTI	*Journal of Theological Interpretation*
JTS	*Journal of Theological Studies*
Jud	*Judaica*
KAT	Kommentar zum Alten Testament
LHBOTS	Library of Hebrew Bible/Old Testament Studies
NCB	New Century Bible
NEB	Neue Echter Bibel
NedTT	*Nederlands theologisch tijdschrift*

NIB	*The New Interpreter's Bible.* Edited by Leander E. Keck. 12 vols. Nashville: Abingdon, 1994–2004
NICNT	New International Commentary on the New Testament
NICOT	New International Commentary on the Old Testament
NKZ	*Neue kirchliche Zeitschrift*
NovTSup	Novum Testamentum, Supplements
NTT	*Nork Teologisk Tidsskrift*
OBO	Orbis Biblicus et Orientalis
OTE	*Old Testament Essays*
OTG	Old Testament Guides
OTL	Old Testament Library
PG	Patrologia Graeca [= *Patrologiae Cursus Completus*: Series Graeca]. Edited by Jacques-Paul Migne. 162 vols. Paris: Lutetiae, 1857–86
RB	*Revue Biblique*
SBB	Stuttgarter Biblische Beiträge
SBLDS	Society of Biblical Literature Dissertaion Series
SBLMS	Society of Biblical Literature Monograph Series
SBLSP	Society of Biblical Literature Seminar Papers
SBLSymS	Society of Biblical Literature Symposium Series
SBS	Stuttgarter Bibelstudien
STDJ	Studies on the Texts of the Desert of Judah
STI	Studies in Theological Interpretation
TDNT	*Theological Dictionary of the New Testament.* Edited by G. Kittel and G. Friedrich. Translated by G. W. Bromiley. 10 vols. Grand Rapids, MI: Eerdmans, 1964–76
TDOT	*Theological Dictionary of the Old Testament.* Edited by G. J. Botterweck and H. Ringgren. Translated by J. T. Willis et al. 8 vols. Grand Rapids, MI: Eerdmans, 1974–2006
ThTo	*Theology Today*
ThWAT	*Theologisches Wörterbuch zum Alten Testament.* Edited by G. Johannes Botterweck and Helmer Ringgren. Stuttgart: Kohlhammer, 1970–
TOTC	Tyndale Old Testament Commentaries
TP	*Theologie und Philosophie*
TRE	*Theologische Realenzyklopädie.* Edited by Gerhard Krause and Gerhard Müller. Berlin: de Gruyter, 1977–
TRev	*Theologische Revue*
TTZ	*Trierer Theologische Zeitschrift*
TynBul	*Tyndale Bulletin*
TZ	*Theologische Zeitschrift*
VT	*Vetus Testamentum*
VTSup	Vetus Testamentum Supplements
WBC	Word Biblical Commentary
WMANT	Wissenschaftliche Monographien zum Alten und Neuen Testament
WUNT	Wissenschaftliche Untersuchungen zum Neuen Testament
ZAW	*Zeitschrift für die alttestamentliche Wissenschaft*
ZBK	Zürcher Bibelkommentare
ZTK	*Zeitschrift für Theologie und Kirche*

The Historical Formation of the Writings in Antiquity

JULIUS STEINBERG AND TIMOTHY J. STONE

Over the past few decades, scholarly interest in the Old Testament canon has moved the topic from its place at the end of many introductions to a new position as a topic of central concern. On the one hand, there is fresh interest in the historical development of the canon, especially after the demise of the classic three-stage theory associated with Herbert Ryle.[1] As older models eroded, newer approaches were set out by, among others, Sid Leiman, Roger Beckwith, John Barton, Lee McDonald, and Peter Brandt.[2] On the other hand, the canonical approach championed by Brevard Childs and to a lesser extent James Sanders brought to the fore issues and questions regarding the hermeneutical implications of canon and the canonical process.

This is not to say, however, that a new consensus has arisen. What is more, despite intense interest and a large number of publications on the subject, in the Anglo-American world the contours of the canon debate have not significantly changed over the past 25 years.[3] To be sure, positions have been refined, and the discussion has acquired greater nuancing,

---

1. H. Ryle, *The Canon of the Old Testament: An Essay on the Gradual Growth and Formation of the Hebrew Canon of Scripture* (2nd ed.; London: Macmillan, 1895); for a summary, see Timothy J. Stone, *The Compilational History of the Megilloth: Canon, Contoured Intertextuality and Meaning in the Writings* (FAT 2/59; Tübingen: Mohr Siebeck, 2013) 34–35; and Julius Steinberg, *Die Ketuvim: Ihr Aufbau und ihre Botschaft* (BBB 152; Hamburg: Philo, 2006) 58–69.

2. Sid Z. Leiman, *The Canonization of Hebrew Scripture: The Talmudic and Midrashic Evidence* (Transactions of the Connecticut Academy of Arts and Sciences 47; Hamden, CT: Archon, 1976); Roger T. Beckwith, *The Old Testament Canon of the New Testament Church and Its Background in Early Judaism* (Grand Rapids, MI: Eerdmans, 1985); John Barton, *Oracles of God: Perceptions of Ancient Prophecy in Israel after the Exile* (London: Darton, Longman and Todd, 1986); Lee M. McDonald, *The Biblical Canon* (Peabody, MA: Hendrickson, 2007); Peter Brandt, *Endgestalten des Kanons: Das Arrangement der Schriften Israels in der jüdischen und christlichen Bibel* (BBB 131; Berlin: Philo, 2001).

3. The respective views of Barton, *Oracles*, published in 1986, and Beckwith, *OT Canon*, published in 1985, sum up the major lines of the debate, and these lines have only moved slightly since the publication of these two volumes. Barton admits as much in the preface to the 2nd ed. of *Oracles* (2007) vii. Regarding the OT canon, the publication of *The Canon Debate* (ed. L. M. McDonald and J. A. Sanders; Peabody, MA: Hendrickson, 2002) did not significantly alter earlier discussions. For more on this, see Stone, *Megilloth*, 34–45.

but the two prominent positions remain in trenchant opposition to each other. The first argues that the canon was closed sometime before the Christian era and that its tripartite arrangement is not a historical accident but, rather, the result of purposeful design. The second view holds that the Law as well as a wide swath of religious literature without definite bounds (which included but was not limited to the Prophets and the Psalms) circulated as Scripture before the Christian era; only later were some of these books lost or rejected in differing degrees by Jews and Christians. Inherent in the second view, though not central, is the logical implication that the arrangement of the Old Testament/Hebrew Bible, with the exception of the Law and possibly the Former Prophets, is of little or no significance, since the historical gap between the literature's development and the canon's shape has cut the two asunder.

Despite the past 25 years of research, substantive dialogue between these two camps has not been a hallmark of the discussion; instead, both sides have become more entrenched.[4] In 2002, the publication of The Canon Debate purported to present a debate, and the time was ripe for conversation across the lines of the debate, but the book did not live up to its title; only one side of the debate was included in the volume.[5] The lack of dialogue is nothing new: in the 1980s, in response to James Barr's argument that Jude cites 1 Enoch as Scripture, Brevard Childs, without argument, flatly asserted that Jude does not cite it as Scripture.[6] Later, Childs admitted that he and Barr were like "ships passing in the night."[7] These are but two examples and, although they do not represent the nature of the whole discussion, they nevertheless point to the inescapable fact that the canon debate has reached an impasse, with both sides in need of engaging the substance of the other's arguments.

In the German discussion, the opinions are likewise divided, although the boundaries are set up a little differently. First, there is a small but growing group of scholars interested in canonical hermeneutics.[8] Their work

---

4. The debate has been acrimonious at times as illustrated by Barton's review of Beckwith's *Old Testament Canon*.

5. The article by Steven Mason, "Josephus and His Twenty-Two Book Canon," 110–27, is the exception that proves the rule in this case. The book (*The Canon Debate*), edited by Lee McDonald and James Sanders, does contain a number of outstanding articles defending a position that McDonald has argued in favor of for years—with two revised and expanded versions of his original thesis written in the early 1980s. None of these works conceded ground to his opponents, but instead, as his book grew to almost 600 pages, old trenches were dug deeper and fortified, even though modified slightly.

6. Brevard Childs, *Biblical Theology of the Old and New Testaments: Theological Reflection on the Christian Bible* (Minneapolis: Fortress, 1993) 62.

7. Daniel Driver, *Brevard Childs, Biblical Theologian* (FAT 2/46; Tübingen: Mohr Siebeck, 2010) 213.

8. For an overview, see, for example, Christoph Dohmen and Manfred Oeming, *Biblischer Kanon: Warum und Wozu?* (Quaestiones disputatae 137; Freiburg: Herder, 1992) 11–26; Christoph Dohmen, "Der biblische Kanon in der Diskussion," *TRev* 6 (1995) 451–60;

focuses on the multiple forms of the canon throughout history[9] and on reader-oriented approaches to the canon,[10] rather than with the quest for historical origins and intentions. Therefore, the historical questions tend not to be as heated as they are in the Anglo-American realm. Second, there remains a majority of scholars who favor the classic "historical-critical" approach and reject canonical hermeneutics due to its alleged dogmatism and ahistorical stance. Third, yet another group of scholars integrates questions of canonical hermeneutics into historic-genetic approaches.[11]

In this essay, we evaluate the historical evidence concerning the formation of the Writings. We will not presume neutrality—though our exact positions differ in substantial ways from one another[12]—but our goal is to set forth the contours of the debate in such a fashion that each side, hopefully, will be able to say that we faithfully represented both the spirit and the letter of their approach before we set out our own position. It is not possible to present every position or even many of the nuances of the two primary positions. Instead, we will outline several but by no means all of the key issues that have proven so divisive. There will be no attempt to reference all the scholars who have taken part in this debate; instead, a few prominent voices will be employed to represent positions that have been echoed by many others. The goal of this simple approach is to put clearly into focus the contours of the canon debate for those already involved in the discussion as well as for those who are unfamiliar with its sometimes very complicated dynamics. If this were an essay on the OT canon as a whole, it would take on different proportions, but because this work focuses on the Writings, our discussion will be concentrated on issues directly related to either the formation or the shape of the Writings.

First, regarding the formation of the collection, we explore in this essay the closure of the Hebrew canon and evidence for its tripartite structure, specifically probing the prologue to Ben Sira, the Dead Sea Scrolls, the New Testament (Luke 11:49–51; 24:44), Josephus, and 4 Ezra. Central to this discussion is a historically informed and nuanced definition of canon and the

---

idem and Thomas Söding, eds., *Eine Bibel – Zwei Testamente: Positionen biblischer Theologie* (Uni-Taschenbücher 1893; Paderborn: Schöningh, 1995); Jörg Barthel, "Die kanonhermeneutische Debatte seit Gerhard von Rad: Anmerkungen zu neueren Entwürfen," in *Kanonhermeneutik: Vom Lesen und Verstehen der christlichen Bibel* (ed. Bernd Janowski; Theologie Interdisziplinär 1; Neukirchen-Vluyn: Neukirchener Verlag, 2007) 1–26.

9. E.g., Brandt, *Endgestalten* (and see his essay in the present volume); Thomas Hieke, ed., *Formen des Kanons: Studien zu Ausprägungen des biblischen Kanons von der Antike bis zum 19. Jh.* (SBS 228; Stuttgart: Katholisches Bibelwerk, 2013).

10. E.g., Georg Steins, *Die 'Bindung Isaaks' im Kanon (Gen 22): Grundlagen und Programm einer kanonisch-intertextuellen Lektüre* (HBS 20; Freiburg: Herder, 1999).

11. E.g., Frank-Lothar Hossfeld and Erich Zenger, "Neue und alte Wege der Psalmenexegese: Antworten auf die Fragen von M. Millard und R. Rendtorff," *BibInt* 4 (1996) 332–45. See also their essay in the present volume.

12. Our respective positions can be seen in more detail: Stone, *Megilloth*; Steinberg, *Ketuvim*.

canonical process. Second, regarding the collection of the Writings, we explore the collection's shape and the variety of orders for the collection. Core issues are the possible conceptions of ancient forms of arrangement prior to the invention of the codex and the evidence in the OT itself of a purposeful arrangement; the talmudic order found in b. B. Bat. 14b and its possible criteria for arrangement; the Masoretic order as found in the Leningrad Codex and the related issue of the liturgical development of the Megillot.

The Closure of the Hebrew Canon and Evidence for Its Tripartite Structure

"Canon" and "Canonical Process": On Method and Definitions

Confusion over the meaning of the term *canon* and the canonical process and, in turn, the relationship of each to the other continues to complicate and hinder the canon debate. Despite calls for precision and the construction of several decent proposals to remedy the problem, the canon debate has often failed to find common ground from which to pursue various findings, with the result that conclusions are said to be different because the proposals began with different sets of core definitions. It is easy for researchers who are new to the discussion and those already engaged in the debate to get lost in the sea of competing proposals and the very different and thus very confusing ways in which scholars employ terms such as *canon, canonical process,* and *canonical consciousness.*[13] McDonald provides a summary of scholarly approaches, and in the following discussion we use his definitions as a starting point for exploring the topic in more depth.

McDonald begins by distinguishing between canon 1 and canon 2.[14] *Canon 1* designates an authoritative source—either oral or written—while *canon 2* refers to a fixed or delimited collection of authoritative books. The key distinction between the two canons is the idea that there are authoritative sources that either never became or are not yet part of a fixed collection. The most common way that scholars employ this term is by referring to a number of authoritative books (canon 1), which included many of the books that would later be in the Hebrew Bible and others such as 1 Enoch or Ben Sira, but they had not yet become part of a fixed collection (canon 2). Many of the books were on their way to becoming canon 2, such as Esther and Ezekiel but, during the 1st century C.E. and before, they only had the status of canon 1. Other books, such as Ben Sira and 1 Enoch, had a canon 1 status but never achieved a canon 2 status, at least not in Judaism. Sundberg and then Barton make a similar distinction between Scripture without definite boundaries (canon 1) and a fixed or delimited collection

---

13. This was Barr's chief contention with Childs's body of work.
14. He borrows these terms from Sheppard. See McDonald, *Biblical Canon,* 55.

in which only the books in the collection are authoritative and no others (canon 2).[15] When the collection is considered to be merely "Scripture" (canon 1), it means that books can be added and taken away from the collection, since the borders are porous; when they turn into a canon, it means that no books can be taken out of the collection or added to it. It is akin to the difference between modern dating (canon 1) and marriage without the option of divorce (canon 2).

Ulrich labels these two aspects of the discussion differently, calling canon 1 "the canonical process" and canon 2, "canon." Ulrich has a precise definition of *canon*: "the final, fixed, and closed list of the books of Scriptures that are officially and permanently accepted as supremely authoritative by a faith tradition, in conscious contradistinction from those books that are not accepted."[16] Furthermore, Ulrich argues that the canonical process includes every aspect of the literature's development, from inception until the books are officially canonized, and should be sharply distinguished from canon.

Childs, by contrast, does not hold to a strong distinction between the canonical process and the canon or between Scripture and canon. For Childs, the canon can be open and grow while still having relatively stable borders.[17] The sharp distinction between the canonical process (canon 1) and a delimited canon (canon 2) cuts asunder the fundamental connection, for Childs, between the formation and fixation of the canon. Decisions about the latter are intimately connected to the former and, according to Childs, are not qualitatively different.[18] For McDonald and Barton, the Hebrew canon looks like a collection of potted plants, the number of which fluctuates as pots are moved in and (mostly) out of the garden (canon 1) until, one day, the gardener decides to put up a fence and lock the gate so that no pots can be moved either in or out. Childs's conception is quite different. For him, the Hebrew canon looks like a grove of trees that have grown up together in a complex symbiotic relationship (canon 1) until they finally reach maturity (canon 2). In other words, for McDonald and Barton, the fixing or scope of the canon is late, possibly very late, so its limits *could not* be organically connected to the formation of the literature *as a collection*. The idea that the Hebrew literature grew and took shape during the canonical process *as a well-formed collection*, with the exception of the Law (and possibly the Deuternomistic History), is logically excluded from this

---

15. Barton, *Oracles*, 56; Albert C. Sundberg, *The Old Testament of the Early Church* (HTS 20; Cambridge: Harvard University Press, 1964).

16. Eugene Ulrich, "The Notion and Definition of Canon," in *The Canon Debate* (ed. Lee M. McDonald and James A. Sanders; Peabody, MA: Hendrickson, 2002) 31.

17. Brevard Childs, *Introduction to the Old Testament as Scripture* (Minneapolis: Fortress, 1979) 50–68.

18. Ibid., 59.

model since, apart from the Law, there was only a large amount of religious literature without a definite shape, so that most books only later became canonical (canon 2) *as individual books.*

There are a number of things at stake here, and many nuances could be explored at great length, but the canon 1 and canon 2 approach has done more to obfuscate than reveal the historical situation. Childs's confusing use of canon terminology, while pointing in what we view to be the right direction, has done little to alleviate the problem.[19] In our judgment, there are four crucial issues.

First, the debate continues to claim that different definitions of canon have caused a great deal of the confusion, but this is mostly a red herring.[20] The concept of a fixed canon, a delimited canon, is not the area of confusion. And the problem is not, as is sometimes claimed, that narrow definitions of canon (canon 2) have progressively pushed the date back (sometimes into nonexistence) for the closing of the canon.[21] The problem is the form or kind of evidence that is deemed appropriate to support these claims. One instance will suffice to illustrate the problem. Ulrich's definition of canon added to the idea of a delimited collection by including the notions that it should be a "list of the books" "officially" "accepted" "in conscious contradistinction" from books that were rejected. Even though derived from dictionary definitions, this delimiting would sufficiently describe the historical situation if one were looking for the *concept* of a closed list of books. Ulrich, however, wants evidence in the *form* of a list, in this case a catalog or codex. Moreover, his insistence on the canon's being officially and consciously closed strongly implies the need for a council imbued with the authority to make such judgments.

Barton, for instance, objects to the idea of applying the word *canon* in this period precisely because it implies "some authoritative body endowed with the power to include some books and exclude others."[22] We have no knowledge of either a catalog or a council prior to the 1st century C.E., so Ulrich, among others, concludes that there is no canon (canon 2) in this period.[23] What goes unstated in the argument is that there is no catalog or council following the 1st century C.E. in Judaism either.

In the history of the church, by contrast, one can take this definition to its logical conclusion by referring to the 4th and 5th centuries C.E.—the time of the great codices, which all contain different lists of books—as the period of canonization, or even later in history by declar-

---

19. See Barr's continual and penetrating critique of Childs in this area.
20. McDonald, *Biblical Canon*, 57.
21. Leiman, *Canonization*, 11–14.
22. Barton, *Oracles*, 63.
23. Eugene Ulrich, "The Canonical Process, Textual Criticism, and the Latter Stages in the Composition of the Bible," in *"Shaʿarei Talmon": Studies in the Bible, Qumran, and the Ancient Near East Presented to Shemaryahu Talmon* (Winona Lake, IN: Eisenbrauns, 1992) 275.

ing the Council of Trent as the time when concrete evidence for canon 2 can be spoken of without anachronism.[24] Is there any evidence of the concept of a delimited collection of texts in the 1st century C.E.? In the discussion below, it is our contention that Josephus and 4 Ezra both provide different yet solid evidence for a delimited collection, even if these works are not accompanied by evidence of an official list propagated by an authoritative council.[25]

Second, as McDonald reminds us, it is vital "to distinguish disagreements about the canon between different parties from uncertainty about the canon within those parties."[26] In other words, is it possible that one group adheres to a delimited collection and another does not? If one group has a porous, undefined collection of texts, it does not therefore follow that all groups in the period have the same conception. In the complex and extremely diverse world of the Second Temple period, this distinction is key. If Qumran had a different collection of sacred texts with or without porous borders, it does not necessarily follow that everyone in the 1st century shared these beliefs. The reverse is also true. The evidence of a delimited collection, as illustrated by Josephus, does not mean that all groups in the 1st century held to his position, but neither can his position be dismissed because not everyone held to it in the 1st century. This distinction is essential.

McDonald, however, does not follow his own advice when he attempts to undermine the testimony of Josephus by attributing little or no significance to him because there is no "*universally* accepted closed biblical canon in the first century C.E."[27] Here, the definition of canon has been expanded to include universal scope, but this is a *non sequitur*. Canons, in the 1st century or any other, have never enjoyed universal scope. Discrediting the evidence of a delimited collection in the 1st century by this means is like claiming that horses do not exist in the 1st century because there is no evidence of unicorns in the same period. Since one of these species never existed, to claim that its absence also means that the other never existed is a logical fallacy. Conceptions of open collections of Scripture without definite boundaries do not reveal that there is no canon in the 1st century C.E.; rather, to use the terminology of the debate, they reveal that some groups hold to canon 1 and others to canon 2.

Third, the presence of authoritative texts outside the boundaries of a group's delimited collection (canon 2) does not automatically mean that this group adhered to canon 1. It is conceivable that a group possessed

---

24. Lee M. McDonald, *The Formation of the Christian Biblical Canon* (rev. ed.; Peabody, MA: Hendrickson, 1995) 150. For more on this, see Stone, *Megilloth*, 46–47.

25. A catalog and council of this sort are not only anachronistic to Judaism in this period but are completely without evidence in any century.

26. McDonald, *Biblical Canon*, 191.

27. Ibid., 156, italics his.

a closed, delimited collection of sacred texts yet treated others texts in addition to these with authority. As we will see in the case of 4 Ezra in the 1st century, *"There can be a fixed, clearly demarcated canon, in the midst of other"*[28] books that hold some degree of authority. Again, Josephus treats 1 Maccabees in the same way that he treats Judges, but he strongly professes a closed canon. It does not follow from the mere presence of authoritative books outside the bounds of the Hebrew canon that there is no fixed collection to which nothing can be added. One implication of this is that it should not be assumed that canon 1 precedes canon 2 so that, if given enough time, canon 1 will naturally lead to canon 2.[29] Certainly this may be the case, but it is not automatically so.

Again, in a faith community, as 4 Ezra demonstrates, one may see signs of both canon 1 and canon 2 concurrently. If *canon* means authority only, defined as it is in the current discussion in some nebulous and general manner, then in Jewish and Christian circles there is never a delimited collection (canon 2).[30] Again, pointing this out in the 1st century without noticing that it is similar in the 6th century and today is to oversimplify the way in which canons function authoritatively in faith communities. Of course, this adds complexity to the discussion, but to describe the historical situation accurately requires nuance.

Our definition of canon, then, is *a fixed or delimited collection of texts received and recognized as sacred (authoritative) by a faith community*. It is important to remember that this canon is not universally held, and even among the faith community that accepts it there will be occasional disagreements over which books are in and which are out. Nor does it automatically follow that the canon is the only source of authority. The group may have a number of sources of authority, but these sources cannot be added to the canon even if the community feels the freedom to place these sources of

---

28. Stone, *Megilloth*, 71, italics original.

29. E.g., McDonald, *Biblical Canon*, 57. This is one area in which equating canon 1 with canonical process and canon 2 with a delimited canon fails because canonical process and canon cannot occur concurrently.

30. There certainly are different degrees of authority in the Second Temple period. The current discussion has made little attempt at nuance here. It is still an open question whether there is an official versus functional authority dynamic or different language needs to be used to describe the various degrees of authority or whether distinctions of this sort are anachronistic. What is the relationship between the authority of the Law to the rest of the Hebrew Bible or the Hebrew Bible to the Talmud or the Old Testament to the New or Ben Sira to Proverbs? These are not easy questions to answer. Mapping the relationship between canons and other sources of authority today would be extremely difficult and complicated, and we guess that there would be many different results. In this essay, although we do not move this discussion forward, we still maintain that there is evidence of belief in a delimited or fixed canon at the same time that other sources hold some degree of authority. Timothy Lim, *The Formation of the Jewish Canon* (New Haven, CT: Yale University Press, 2013), has the most nuanced discussion of the varying degrees of a textual authority in the period under consideration.

authority *alongside* the canon. The Talmud would be an example of this in Judaism,[31] and the growing number of texts of the New Testament, in the early church. Neither of these additional sources of authority by itself indicates that the boundaries of the Hebrew canon are porous.

Fourth, it should be admitted openly that we have no sources that directly address the canonical process. What we know must be inferred from comparative studies and from the texts contained in the Hebrew Bible. Defining the canonical process as every aspect of the literature's development before canonization helps only in distinguishing it from canon. This is far too general a definition; it only describes the situation in negative terms and misses the heart of the canonical process. In our view, the canon and the canonical process are organically related in terms of both *the scope and the shape* of the final collection. With Childs, we agree that the "formation of the canon was not a late extrinsic validation of a corpus of writings, but involved a series of decisions deeply affecting the shape of the books."[32]

We want to emphasize, in a way Childs did not,[33] that the formation of the canon (canonical process) involved a series of decisions that also affected the shape or structure of the canon. Through a complex process, *individual books* were rendered authoritative for future generations, but at the same time (not necessarily later), these individual books were composed, redacted, and compiled based on their interrelationship within a nascent collection.[34] Without question, the various ways in which books are related to other books is complex and multifaceted. For this reason, it is better to leave specifics out of the definition of the canonical process, but in the essays in this volume there should be ample, specific illustrations of the way that books were shaped vis-à-vis other books and in relation to their place within the shape of a collection.[35]

An analogy of a cathedral may help one better understand our position. The canon is like a great cathedral in which the various buildings on the grounds are constructed over a very long period, often by different hands and according to different plans, but each is done at least in part in relationship to one or more of the other structures. Some old buildings are torn down to make room for new ones, even as other old structures are refashioned according to new purposes. If one looks closely, there are

---

31. See David Kraemer, "The Formation of the Rabbinic Canon: Authority and Boundaries," *JBL* 110 (1991) 613–630.

32. Childs, *OT as Scripture*, 59.

33. He does mention this aspect of the canonical process, but he does not emphasize it until his last publication.

34. On the crucial nature of textual interrelatedness, see esp. Stephen Chapman, "The Canon Debate: What It Is and Why It Matters," *JTI* 4 (2010) 273–94; Georg Steins, "Der Bibelkanon als Denkmal und Text: Zu einigen methodologischen Aspekten kanonischer Schriftauslegung," in *The Biblical Canons* (ed. J. M. Auwers and H. J. de Jonge; BETL 163; Leuven: Leuven University Press, 2003) 180.

35. For more on this, see Stone, *Megilloth*, 10–17.

signs that some old doors and windows have been filled with new stones to make walls, and some other old walls have been cut to make way for new entrances. There are architectural designs from various periods and no overall scheme that unites the entire building, but they nevertheless rightly belong together.[36]

Assessing the Sources

When assessing the historical sources, therefore, one should be precise about what follows from them and what does not. As argued above, the explanatory model applied to the canon should not be based on a simple linear, uniform development. Rather, one should take into account the idea that the historical process may have been quite complex and diverse among different groups in Judaism and in Christianity. As a result, the observation that some of the *Christian* church fathers from the 3rd century C.E. rejected the book of Esther should not be used as evidence that the *Jewish* canon was still "open" during this period.[37] Likewise, the reference to a tripartite canon in Ben Sira's prologue in the 2nd century B.C.E. does not conclusively prove that all groups within Judaism agreed on the tripartite structure at this time. Again, there is probably no linear historical development from sources that number the books of the canon as 24 and those that number it as 22. Both ways of counting may have existed side by side.[38]

In addition, the relationship between the labels for the canon and the number of books included should be carefully nuanced to avoid oversimplification. For example, in the NT the Scriptures are often referred to as "Moses and the Prophets." Some conclude from this that the Writings were not yet canonical during this period.[39] This would be an anachronistic interpretation of the word "Prophet," however, because it reads later specific implications of the labels "Torah, Prophets, and Writings" back into older sources. Rather, the formula should be rendered "Moses and the other inspired writers," which may allude to the two levels of graded authority within the canon but is otherwise a just a common term referring to the Jewish Bible as a whole without necessarily making any point regarding the extent of books or some specific internal structure.[40] In the later literature, one and the same canon may be called "Torah," "Torah and Prophets," or "Torah, Prophets, and Writings"—the choice of the formula depending on the author's communicative

---

36. This idea of the canon as a cathedral is taken from Dohmen and Oeming, *Biblischer Kanon*, 96.

37. Contra McDonald, *Formation*, 108.

38. Against a linear model, as in Andrew Steinmann, *The Oracles of God: The Old Testament Canon* (St. Louis: Concordia Academic, 1999) 186–95.

39. On this position and its rejection, see Barton, *Oracles*, 35–44.

40. Stephen Chapman, *The Law and the Prophets: A Study in Old Testament Canon Formation* (FAT 27; Tübingen: Mohr, 2000) 269. See the discussion on the NT evidence, pp. 22–26 below.

purposes as well as on historical conventions of the period.[41] Another *non sequitur* is the idea that a variation in naming would suggest an open canon while a fixed expression would always go with a fixed collection. Rather, we must ask whether there is a specific collection in view on which the author and addressee(s) agree. A clue to this may be the use of the definite article.

Again, the fact that some of the biblical books have been disputed from time to time does not in all circumstances necessitate the notion that the canon is "open." Rather, it can be the established nature of the canon that provokes disagreement.[42] Luther's rejection of the Letter of James may serve as an example. Therefore, one should be careful not to overstate one's case when drawing conclusions from the rabbinic discussions on the subject.[43]

The Book of Ben Sira and Its Prologue

The first source to be examined is the book of Ben Sira and the prologue to its Greek translation that was crafted by his grandson. The source is considered an important witness to the history of the biblical canon in pre-Christian times. In the prologue, the Holy Scriptures of Israel are named three times, each time using a three-part formula:

V. 1: διὰ τοῦ νόμου	καὶ τῶν προφητῶν	καὶ τῶν ἄλλων τῶν κατ᾽ αὐτοὺς ἠκολουθηκότων
V. 3: τοῦ νόμου	καὶ τῶν προφητῶν	καὶ τῶν ἄλλων πατρίων βιβλίων
V. 7: αὐτὸς ὅ νόμος	καὶ αἱ προφητεῖαι	καὶ τὰ λοιπὰ τῶν βιβλιῶν
V. 1: through the Law	and the Prophets	and the others that follow them
V. 3: of the Law	and the Prophets	and the other books of the fathers
V. 7: the law itself	and the prophecies	and the remaining books

While the first and second elements of the formula are almost identical in all three instances, the third one varies, albeit using more or less synonymous expressions.

From the context, it is likely that the passage speaks about the Holy Writings of the Jews. There is an obvious closeness of the expressions used for the collections of the Hebrew Bible as *Torah, Prophets, and Writings* to the names we know from the Talmud and later tradition. Therefore, several

---

41. Regarding the relationship between canon designations and canon structures, see Steinberg, *Ketuvim*, 167–72.

42. See Beckwith, *OT Canon*, 275.

43. See Peter R. Ackroyd, "The Open Canon," in *Studies in the Religious Tradition of the Old Testament* (London: SCM, 1987) 222–23; Beckwith, *OT Canon*, 318–23; Leiman, *Canonization*, 132; Georg Steins, "Torabindung und Kanonabschluß: Zur Entstehung und kanonischen Funktion der Chronikbücher," in *Die Tora als Kanon für Juden und Christen* (ed. Erich Zenger; HBS 10; Freiburg: Herder, 1996) 248; S. Talmon, "Heiliges Schrifttum und kanonische Bücher aus jüdischer Sicht: Überlegungen zur Ausbildung der Grösse 'Die Schrift' im Judentum," in *Mitte der Schrift? Ein jüdisch-christliches Gespräch—Texte des Berner Symposions vom 6.–12. Januar 1985* (ed. Martin Klopfenstein, Ulrich Luz, Shemaryahu Talmon, and Emanuel Tov; Judaica et Christiana 11; Bern: Peter Lang, 1987) 78–79; Günter Stemberger, "Jabne und der Kanon," *JBTh* 3 (1988) esp. p. 173.

scholars assume that the Ben Sira prologue is, in fact, the first source evidencing the three-part formula for describing the Hebrew Bible.[44]

Barton, however, gives a different evaluation. In his view, the Scriptures are entirely encompassed by the formula "the Law and the Prophets." The third group of texts refers to literature in general but not to texts that belong among Israel's Scriptures.[45] This idea may be surprising unless one places it in the context of Barton's larger argument. Barton points to the fact that, in virtually all of the older sources, especially the NT and the Mishnah, the Scriptures are referred to with the two-part formula "the Law and the Prophets." He avers that the three-part formula—and even the very idea of a structured canon with a definite number of books—is a late phenomenon.

Regardless of how one thinks about Barton's overall approach, with regard to his interpretation of Ben Sira's prologue, we do not view his interpretation as the most likely. Repeating the three-part formula three separate times in such a short passage suggests a common parlance,[46] which gives the strong impression that the third group regularly belongs with the other two. The use of the definite article in reference to all three sections indicates that each group is considered to be part of the same whole.[47] The other books explicitly "follow" the Law and the Prophets (v. 1); the word "remaining" certainly does not refer to any remaining books that were known in the time of Ben Sira but, rather, to those that remain *of the sacred collection* in addition to the Law and the Prophets. All three collections are likewise accredited to the one authoritative tradition of the "fathers" (v. 3).[48] Therefore, we hold that the Ben Sira prologue witnesses to a three-part canon around 130 B.C.E.[49]

---

44. E.g., Otto Kaiser, *Einleitung in das Alte Testament: Eine Einführung in ihre Ergebnisse und Probleme* (5th ed.; Gütersloh: Mohn, 1984) 408; Roger T. Beckwith, "A Modern Theory of the Old Testament Canon," *VT* 49 (1991) 388; Bernd J. Diebner, "Erwägungen zum Prozeß der Sammlung des dritten Teils der antik-jüdischen (hebräischen) Bibel, der Ketuvim," *DBAT* 21 (1985) 181, 191–92; Stephen G. Dempster, "From Many Texts to One: The Formation of the Hebrew Bible," in *The World of the Arameans*, vol. 1: *Biblical Studies in Honour of Paul-Eugène Dion* (ed. P. M. Daviau, John W. Wevers, and Michael Weigl; JSOTSup 324; Sheffield: Sheffield Academic Press, 2001) 29–30; Max L. Margolis, *The Hebrew Scriptures in the Making* (repr., Philadelphia: Jewish Publication Society, 1948) 15–16; A. van der Kooij and K. van der Toorn, eds., *Canonization and Decanonization: Papers Presented to the International Conference of the Leiden Institute for the Study of Religions (LISOR), Held at Leiden, 9–10 January 1997* (Studies in the History of Religions 82; Leiden: Brill, 1997) 23–24.

45. Barton, *Oracles*, 47; followed, e.g., by F. F. Bruce, *The Canon of Scripture* (Leicester: Inter-Varsity, 1988) 31.

46. Georg Steins, *Die Chronik als kanonisches Abschlussphänomen: Studien zur Entstehung und Theologie von 1/2 Chronik* (BBB 93; Weinheim: Athenäum, 1995) 512.

47. Van der Kooij, "Canonization," 23; John W. Miller, *The Origins of the Bible: Rethinking Canon History* (New York: Paulist Press, 1994) 8.

48. Van der Kooij, "Canonization," 23–24.

49. The conclusion of Stone, *Megilloth*, 50–51 is more modest, even though he argues that Ben Sira may give us some idea of the canonical subdivisions of the canon; however, this point cannot be inferred from Sir 39:1–3.

Andrew Steinmann takes another approach to the issue. He argues that the third collection cannot relate to the later Writings since Ben Sira uses books from the Prophets and the Writings side by side without distinction.[50] The same can be said, however, about the distinction between Torah and Prophets, as Steinmann himself states a few pages earlier.[51]

If Ben Sira knew of a tripartite canon, as Steinmann argues, the third division could only have contained the wisdom books, as presented in Sir 39:1.[52] However, Sir 39:1–3 does not provide a canonical structure but a list of seven genres of biblical literature.[53] In our view, it is hardly possible from Ben Sira's use of biblical books to infer a canonical structure.[54]

The evidence from the prologue challenges the model of a linear development of the collection from a two-part designation to a three-part designation. Instead, both ways of naming the collection probably existed side by side—either in different groups within Judaism or as different ways of referring to the collection, depending on the communicative needs of the moment. Other evidence for the coexistence of both is the tripartite organization reflected in b. B. Bat. 14b, which stems, as far as we know, from the time of the Mishnah. In the Mishnah, dipartite references prevail.

According to a common view, the Hebrew canon could not have been closed around 130 B.C.E. Therefore, several scholars argue that the canon was not closed in the period when Ben Sira's prologue was written. Two primary arguments have been put forward.

First, some contend that the grandson placed the book by his grandfather on the same level as the other writings in the Hebrew Bible.[55] Therefore, the prologue would testify to a "canon in the making." We, however, interpret the prologue differently. In our view, by designating the books as the writings of the "fathers" and thus old and authoritative, the prologue distinguishes the biblical books from Ben Sira's new work.[56] Ben Sira is

---

The date can be inferred from information given in the prologue and is generally accepted. For a discussion of the controversial view of Bernd J. Diebner, "Mein Großvater Jesus," *DBAT* 16 (1982) 1– 37, see Steinberg, *Ketuvim*, 158 n. 183; and the essay by Steins in the current volume.

50. Steinmann, *Oracles*, 54.

51. Ibid., 36.

52. Ibid., 54.

53. As Steinmann himself states in ibid., 36.

54. Cf. Theodore N. Swanson, *The Closing of the Collection of Holy Scriptures: A Study in the History of the Canonization of the Old Testament* (Nashville: Vanderbilt University Press, 1970) 100–103. But see n. 49 above.

55. E.g., Odil Hannes Steck, "Der Kanon des hebräischen Alten Testaments: Historische Materialien für eine ökumenische Perspektive," in *Vernunft des Glaubens: Wissenschaftliche Theologie und kirchliche Lehre: FS W. Pannenberg* (ed. Jan Rohls and Gunther Wenz; Göttingen: Vandenhoeck & Ruprecht, 1988) 242; John J. Collins, "Before the Canon: Scriptures in Second Temple Judaism," in *Old Testament Interpretation: Past, Present, and Future—Essays in Honor of Gene M. Tucker* (ed. James L. Mays, David L. Petersen, and Kent H. Richards; Edinburgh: T. & T. Clark; Nashville: Abingdon, 1995) 231; Swanson, *Closing*, 125.

56. E.g., Beckwith, *OT Canon*, 111; Miller, *Origins of the Bible*, 4.

presented as a work drawing from the Scriptures and directing its readers toward Scripture but is not itself part of Scripture.

Second, several scholars argue that the canonical division of the Writings was not yet closed since a slightly different formula describes the third section in each instance.[57] But does variation in terminology generally suggest an open canon or, conversely, does a fixed expression suggest a fixed collection? Suppose the writer had the technical term *Ketubim* in mind and needed to paraphrase it for his Greek-speaking readers. Since all books are "written," the term could easily be misunderstood, since it is general rather than specific, and thus it needed to be explained that this term refers to "the other writings that belong to the sacred collection." In our view, this is the reason behind the varied and expanded terminology for the third section in the prologue.[58]

The definite article is used in all three variants, which probably refers to the Writings. By employing the definite article, the author informs his readers that he is referring to a defined collection of books. Since the book is addressed not to an individual but to the public faith-community, this probably means that a publicly defined collection is in view.

In the body of Ben Sira, there is evidence concerning the extent of the Scriptures during this period (written around 180 B.C.E.). Ben Sira refers or alludes to most of the books of the later Jewish Bible. There is not evidence for all the books found in the Writings. There may be several reasons for this. One would be the extent of Scripture around 180 B.C.E.; another would be Ben Sira's specific point of view as a teacher of Torah wisdom. Perhaps one should distinguish between the collection of sacred texts in Ben Sira and the collection addressed in the prologue, especially when a Maccabean dating of Daniel in its present form is taken into consideration. Therefore, no definite assessment can be made regarding the extent of the Writings around 180 and/or 130 B.C.E.[59]

We conclude that the prologue to Ben Sira testifies to a tripartite canon of Scripture. The designations given to the three parts probably correspond to the later TaNaK structure.[60] The naming of the third division varies, which is probably due to the general nature of the term "writings." Apart from this, the third canonical division may be fixed. The exact number of

---

57. E.g., Kaiser, *Einleitung*, 408; Joseph Blenkinsopp, *Prophecy and Canon: A Contribution to the Study of Jewish Origins* (Notre Dame, IN: University of Notre Dame Press, 1977) 125–26; G. W. Anderson, "Canonical and Non-Canonical," in *The Cambridge History of the Bible*, vol. 1: *From the Beginnings to Jerome* (Cambridge: Cambridge University Press, 1970) 129; Hans Peter Rüger, "Das Werden des christlichen Alten Testaments," *JBTh* 3 (1988) 176. Swanson, *Closing*, 128–30, even expands the argument to the second canonical division, because of the variation προφητῶν/προφητεῖαι.

58. Steins, *Chronik als Abschlussphänomen*, 512; idem, "Torabindung und Kanonabschluss," 247–48.

59. For more on this from a different perspective, see Stone, *Megilloth*, 49–51.

60. But see n. 49 above.

books in the collection cannot be derived from the source. Whether the prologue mirrors the position of all Judaism or merely some group within Judaism, we are unable to determine.

The Dead Sea Scrolls

Many different issues have been the subject of research with regard to the Dead Sea Scrolls and the formation of the Hebrew canon,[61] but two are essential and have been the source of disagreement: (1) the books that were considered authoritative and (2) whether this collection of scrolls represented the view of Jews in general or only of the group that deposited them in the caves. In the following discussion, only representative voices will be examined.

James VanderKam offers three categories to use in establishing textual authority at Qumran: (1) whether a book was cited as an authority, (2) whether a work's self-conception was that it contained divine authority (often God's direct speech), and (3) whether a work had a commentary written on it.[62] Apart from the books that are now found in the Hebrew Bible, according to VanderKam, Jubilees, 1 Enoch, and the Temple Scroll were considered authoritative at Qumran. Each of these books strongly claims to be divine revelation. Fifteen copies of Jubilees and 20 copies of 1 Enoch were discovered; this places these books slightly behind the Psalms and Isaiah in terms of copies. Jubilees is cited twice with an authoritative formula, while 1 Enoch (or at least The Book of the Watchers) was clearly an influential text for the community.[63]

---

61. For instance, was their collection of authoritative literature bipartite or tripartite? There has been much speculation about whether 4QMMT (4Q394–399) contains a reference to a tripartite collection, but this issue has largely been settled. See Eugene Ulrich, "The Non-attestation of a Tripartite Canon in 4QMMT," *CBQ* 65 (2003) 202–14, in which he argues—persuasively, in our view—that the text is too difficult to reconstruct with any degree of confidence. Moreover, if the tripartite reconstruction is valid, there still remains the issue of whether or not the reference to David is a way of referring to the Psalms, which in turn is a way to refer to the Writings. In our view, so many suppositions fall under their own weight. On this issue, see Stone, *Megilloth*, 57. Cf. Lim, *Jewish Canon*, 131, who concludes that the sectarian scrolls were bipartite. Another issue that could be discussed in relation to the Dead Sea Scrolls and the canon is the stabilization of the Hebrew text, but if one could determine when the text was stabilized, then it is still not clear among those involved in the canon debate what implications this should have for the closure of the canon. Childs, *Biblical Theology*, 61, argues that the stabilization the text must follow its canonization, but Eugene Ulrich, *The Dead Sea Scrolls and the Origins of the Bible* (Studies in the Dead Sea Scrolls and Related Literature; Leiden: Brill, 1999) 57–59, to the contrary, posits that the textual form of the book can vary after it is canonized because it is not textual forms that are canonized but books. For more on this issue, see the comments of Stone, *Megilloth*, 51–59.

62. James C. VanderKam, *The Dead Sea Scrolls Today* (2nd ed.; Grand Rapids, MI: Eerdmans, 2010) 187.

63. Ibid., 191–93. VanderKam lists two additional references in which the book of Jubilees is alluded to, but neither one is introduced with a citation formula.

Lim offers a different perspective. According to him, Jubilees and some of the other texts had a graded degree of authority, such as the pesherim (authoritative commentaries on books in the Hebrew canon) and 1 Enoch, but their authority was not identical to the books that they considered Scripture.[64] Lim does not mention numbers of scroll copies as evidence of a book's authority[65] and states, "it should be clear at the outset that a book's claim of authority by itself is insufficient."[66] Regarding Jubilees, Lim argues that the book is an authoritative interpretation of the Torah of Moses and thus is secondary to the Torah, but it still maintains a degree of authority.[67] In fact, as a *perush*, it is secondary, but for the community, it may well have been "more authoritative."[68] Jubilees should be understood as an authoritative explanation or *perush* of the Torah, and Lim interprets the reference to Jubilees in the Damascus Document (CD) in the same manner. CD 16:2–3 states the following: "As for the exact determination of their times to which Israel turned a blind eye, behold it is strictly defined in the Book of the Division of the Times into Their Jubilees and Weeks."[69] All agree that this is a reference to the book of Jubilees, and that it is connected to the Torah of Moses.

VanderKam claims that this reference indicates that Jubilees and the Torah of Moses are of equal authority.[70] Lim, on the other hand, notes that the reference, while not a direct quotation, is probably taken from Jub. 1:4.[71] CD uses Jubilees as a "legal explanation" of the Torah, and thus one is instructed in CD to bind oneself to the Torah but not to the "book of Jubilees as such."[72] Jubilees accords itself the same kind of authority as the Torah of Moses, but it is unlikely that CD considered Jubilees to have the same authority as the Torah.

Lim concludes that the quotations from biblical books at Qumran (or books later to be included in the canon) had a "formal primacy" and "authoritative status" during the 1st century B.C.E. that the community recognized and that was "widely recognized among Jews generally."[73] The commentaries or pesherim, however, were considered authoritative for the community since, in them, the Teacher of Righteous mediated the will of

---

64. Lim, *Jewish Canon*, 119–47.
65. Ibid., 132, except possibly here, because Lim notes that the multiple copies of Jubilees confirm its importance as a pesher of Torah.
66. Ibid., 131.
67. Ibid., 132.
68. Ibid., 139.
69. Translations of all ancient texts in this essay are ours.
70. VanderKam, *Scrolls Today*, 191. For a similar perspective on the Dead Sea Scrolls that in large part is dependent on VanderKam's various writings on the subject, see McDonald, *Biblical Canon*, 126–36.
71. Lim, *Jewish Canon*, 132.
72. Ibid.
73. Ibid., 139.

God directly to the community.[74] In fact, these secondary explanations probably had a functional authority that surpassed that of the biblical books.[75] Lim then summarizes the idea that "authoritative Scripture" has a conceptual advantage over "canon" because authoritative Scripture "admits patterns other than the relationship between the traditional biblical text and their interpretations."[76] This appears to be the case for Lim because the sectarians—meaning the Qumran community—did not "have a notion of a closed list of authoritative books" and because there is no clear demarcation of authority between the biblical books and the other documents such as Jubilees and the pesherim.[77]

Beckwith's approach is very different from VanderKam's and Lim's. He lists the books from within the Hebrew canon that were cited authoritatively at Qumran and does not think that Jubilees was cited as Scripture; nor were any other books outside the canon.[78] After listing which books are cited with an authoritative formula or cited as divine or prophetic texts, and which books are the subject of pesherim (commentaries), he posits that the fact that "Qumran texts on the priestly courses maintain the twenty-four courses of 1 Chr 24, whereas twenty-six course would have fitted much better into their calendar of exactly fifty-two weeks," suggests that Chronicles was "canonical."[79]

Before we can assess these three perspectives, we must present the evidence regarding the way that books in the biblical canon were regarded. This information is generally not disputed, but it is necessary for contextualizing our position. Texts were probably not added to Qumran after 125 B.C.E., and among their texts there is evidence of every book found in the Hebrew Bible with the exception of Esther. This book's absence has been explained as both intentional[80] and as the unintentional result of the vagaries of preservation over such a long period of time.[81] According to VanderKam and Beckwith, the five books of the Torah and all the books of the Prophets, the Psalms, and Daniel are the subject of commentaries, interpretive scrolls, or rewritten Scripture. In addition, most of these books are cited with authoritative formulas (the exceptions being Judges, 1 and

---

74. Cf. Adam van der Woude, "Fifty Years of Qumran Research," in *The Dead Sea Scrolls after Fifty Years* (ed. Peter W. Flint and James C. VanderKam; Boston: Brill, 1999) 1–45, esp. p. 43.

75. Lim, *Jewish Canon*, 139.

76. Ibid., 146.

77. Ibid., 146–47.

78. Beckwith, *OT Canon*, 364; idem, "Formation of the Hebrew Bible," in *Mikra: Text, Translation, Reading and Interpretation of the Hebrew Bible in Ancient Judaism and Early Christianity* (ed. M. J. Mulder; Minneapolis: Fortress, 1990) 47.

79. Ibid.

80. For a quick survey of the various options, see Stone, *Megilloth*, 56.

81. Frank M. Cross, *From Epic to Canon: History and Literature in Ancient Israel* (Baltimore: Johns Hopkins University Press, 1998) 225.

2 Kings, Jeremiah, and five of the Twelve Minor Prophets). The only remaining books not cited with an authoritative formula are Job, Ruth, the Song of Songs, Ecclesiastes, Lamentations, Esther, Ezra/Nehemiah, and 1 and 2 Chronicles.[82]

With this overview of scholarly approaches to Scripture at Qumran in place, we turn to our evaluation of the situation. We concur with Lim's analysis of the *graded textual* authority of Jubilees and that it probably had a functional authority greater than the biblical books. This may also be the case for other books, especially 1 Enoch, the Temple Scroll, and the commentaries. We do not see any clear evidence that texts outside the Hebrew canon were cited in the *same manner* as books within the Hebrew canon (with the possible exception of Jubilees).[83] VanderKam challenges this notion, but Lim, in a qualified manner, defends this assessment. Lim concludes that the term "authoritative Scripture" has conceptual advantages over the term "canon" for Qumran, as mentioned above, but we object to the reasons leading him to this conclusion. His primary reason for conceptualizing matters in this way is the fact that Qumran's graded levels of textual authority do not fit into the "traditional" mold of a biblical text that is more authoritative than its various interpretations. As Lim argued, the interpretation, although different in authority, may be more authoritative and, thus, the term "authoritative Scripture," with its flexible idea of authority, is preferable to the term "canon."

This assessment is questionable on two grounds. First, this may be the traditional understanding for Protestants, but it is far less clear whether this is the dominant position in all of church history. Within Jewish tradition, the authority of the biblical text in relation to its interpretations is by no means clear. Often it appears that the interpretation has a functional authority greater than that of the biblical text. The Mishnah and the Talmud, for instance, are both authoritative in Judaism, and the relationship of this authority to the Hebrew Bible is not always clear, since it has been suggested that the Oral Torah's functional authority can be greater than the Hebrew canon.[84] Our goal is not to decide these debates or give a definitive position of our own but to observe that the relationship between Scripture and authoritative tradition at Qumran is not without significant analogies in the Judeo-Christian tradition.

---

82. VanderKam, *Scrolls Today*, 188–89; Beckwith, "Formation," 47.

83. For the exception in the case of Jubilees, see Stone, *Megilloth*, 56, and his discussion of 4Q228 1 I 9. Lim's analysis, however, has persuaded us that this citation is probably better understood within the larger context of the way in which Jubilees was most often understood as an authoritative explication of the Torah of Moses rather than an independent authority.

84. On this contested issue, see Jacob Neusner, *Midrash in Context: Exegesis in Formative Judaism* (Philadelphia: Fortress, 1983); idem, *The Foundations of Judaism: Method, Teleology, Doctrine* (3 vols.; Philadelphia: Fortress, 1983–85); idem, *Torah: From Scroll to Symbol in Formative Judaism* (Philadelphia: Fortress, 1885); Kraemer, "Rabbinic Canon," 613–30.

Second, Lim has convincingly demonstrated that the books in the canon were treated differently from books outside the canon at Qumran, even though the issue of authority between them is complicated. We therefore do not understand why the concept of "canon" is not *conceptually superior* to that of "authoritative Scripture," since it provides more coherent conceptual categories for understanding how books can be *both* authoritative (albeit in different ways) and *distinct*. Why would biblical books be consistently cited in a different manner from other works if they were not delimited or at least separate in some way? In neither the Jewish nor the Christian tradition, if an interpretation is considered more functionally authoritative does it follow that the contours of the canon are redrawn to incorporate this new authority. Instead, this authority often comes to stand alongside or after/above the canon. Authority by itself, as we have said before is, in our view, too broad a brush with which to paint the historical situation clearly.

This leads us also to object to Beckwith's argument that Chronicles is considered canonical because it appears to have influenced texts on the priestly courses at Qumran. If Beckwith were consistent, influence would then equal canonical status, which means he would surely have to include Jubilees and the Book of the Watchers in 1 Enoch within the canon. This same line of reasoning undercuts VanderKam's position. The number of copies of a book at Qumran can be explained in a variety of ways, but if it does correspond to a book's worth in the community, it does not necessarily follow that it was canonical, since functional authority in the community appears to have meant that a book was more significant than a canonical book. Nor does the influence of the Book of the Watchers mean that it was canonical, since books could be influential without being biblical, as Lim has demonstrated. Furthermore, influence and the number of copies of a book are not part of VanderKam's criteria for establishing authoritative books at Qumran. Lim has rightly criticized the notion that a book's self-understanding as divine speech is not the same as the community's concept of it, as mentioned above. Lim's analysis renders problematic each of VanderKam's arguments.

Lim does not address, however, the implications of a book's own self-understanding of being divine speech or of the use of pseudonymity at Qumran. The presence of texts that *protest strongly* and *self-consciously* in their favor as being divine, such as the Temple Scroll, and the proliferation of pseudonymous works, such as 1 Enoch, may indicate, not that the canon is open but that the canonical period has come to an end. Strong protestations of being the direct speech of God in a manner not found among biblical books reveals a self-conscious awareness of the canonical status of other works. Before the canon is closed, there is no need to make such strong claims. Like 4 Ezra, these attempts to be considered authoritative by claiming to be better than canonical books should be examined critically.[85]

---

85. See the discussion about 4 Ezra.

The abundance of pseudonymous works in the 2nd and 1st centuries B.C.E. indicates this same sort of self-conscious reaching for things out of one's grasp. This accords well with the notion of a prophetic era that came to an end in the Persian period,[86] which these books were striving to become a part of not by continuing the prophetic tradition but by being better than it (direct divine speech) or feeling the need to place themselves fictionally in the ancient context (pseudonymity).

Finally, if one were to include Jubilees, 1 Enoch, and the Temple Scroll among the scriptural books, this would still not be evidence of a wide religious literature without definite bounds. This collection of texts, whether with or without porous borders, would be *smaller* than the Hebrew canon since it would *exclude ten* books found the canon while only *adding three*.

This brings our discussion to the second essential issue: did the Qumran collection distinguish the sect, or was it probably the same set as was known and used by most Jews? Answering this question is very difficult because we have no direct evidence concerning the deposit of the Scrolls in the caves.[87] Nor do we possess a similar deposit of texts from the temple in Jerusalem (or anywhere else, for that matter) during this period of history with which to compare the scrolls. These two factors render any final conclusion doubtful. That said, there is a general consensus that the best theory identifies the community with the Essenes. This argument has been made many times and made well, so there is no need to rehearse the details again.

The basics of the argument can be summed up in three points. First, Pliny the Elder (23–79 C.E.) in his *Natural History* places the Essenes geographically on the western side of the Dead Sea, somewhere between the sea's northern end and En-Gedi. This geographical location fits well with the location of the discovery of the Scrolls. Second, the Essenes shared basically the same beliefs on spitting, the afterlife, determinism, property, meals, and bodily functions as are found in the Scrolls. Third, there are no signs of dissonance between the Essenes and the Qumran community. In other words, what we know of them matches the Essenes without any glaring differences. Thus, it is likely that the scrolls beside the Dead Sea belonged to a group of Essenes.[88]

Since it is likely that they were a sectarian group, it is possible that they possessed a different set of sacred texts from other groups in the 1st century

---

86. For a summary and a nuanced defense of the traditional understanding of the cessation of prophecy, see Stephen Cook, *On the Question of the "Cessation of Prophecy" in Ancient Judaism* (Texts and Studies in Ancient Judaism 145; Tübingen: Mohr Siebeck, 2011).

87. This fact leads Emanuel Tov, *Textual Criticism of the Hebrew Bible* (Minneapolis: Fortress, 1992) 117; and James A. Sanders, "Canon: Hebrew Bible," *ABD* 6.837–52, to be cautious about findings from Qumran.

88. VanderKam, *Scrolls Today*, 99–114. See these pages for additional arguments in favor of VanderKam's thesis.

C.E. Ulrich argues, however, that the Scrolls do not contain sectarian variants, and thus they represent the "Scriptures of Second Temple Judaism." This is an argument from silence that Ulrich supports by comparing the character of variants in the Samaritan Pentateuch. According to Ulrich, there are no signs in the Scrolls that texts have been altered deliberately to match a sectarian agenda, such as for instance when the Samaritans changed the text from "Mount Ebal" to "Mount Gerizim" in order to support their own sacred practices.[89] This may indicate, as Ulrich has argued, that the Scrolls are the Scriptures of Second Temple Judaism, which means for Ulrich that there were other texts in addition to those found in the OT/HB that were considered Scripture. As we have seen in the foregoing discussion, however, it is not clear that the community to which the Scrolls belonged did in fact have a different set of holy texts to which there were no definite boundaries. In addition, Lim's conclusion that the commentaries and the other texts mentioned above functioned in a more authoritative manner for the community than other texts found in the OT (what Ulrich would say later become the OT/HB), would render it unnecessary to alter texts to fit a sectarian agenda. Moreover, the comparison fails with the Samaritans because at Qumran they believed that prophecy had not ceased in the time of Ezra or even before with Moses so that individuals, like the Teacher of Righteousness, could still function as the mouthpiece of God.[90] If, on the other hand, Ulrich is correct and the Scrolls do represent the state of Scripture in Second Temple Judaism, then one must find a way to account for the evidence against this view in Josephus and 4 Ezra, each of which indicate that there was a closed list of books.[91]

In sum, we are left with three options regarding the nature of sacred texts at Qumran.[92] First, the residents had a collection of sacred texts with porous borders that characterized the situation throughout the Second Temple period. There was no fixed collection of sacred texts. Second, they had a collection of sacred texts with porous borders, but it did not represent the situation during this period, since other communities may have had different collections of sacred texts (the Samaritans are an obvious, clearly sectarian example) and possibly different conceptions of sacred

---

89. Eugene Ulrich, "The Absence of 'Sectarian Variants' in the Jewish Scriptural Scrolls Found at Qumran," in *The Bible as a Book: The Hebrew Bible and the Judaean Desert Discoveries* (ed. Edward Herbert and Emanuel Tov; London: British Library, 2002) 179–95; idem, "The Qumran Biblical Scrolls: The Scriptures of Late Second Temple Judaism," in *The Dead Sea Scrolls in Their Historical Context* (ed. Timothy Lim et al.; Edinburgh: T. & T. Clark, 2000) 67–87.

90. James C. VanderKam, "Authoritative Literature in the Dead Sea Scrolls," *DSD* 5 (1998) 401.

91. See the discussion on this below.

92. There is, of course, a fourth option, but no one to our knowledge argues this position: the community of the Dead Sea Scrolls had a closed canon, while other groups in the period did not.

texts, which may have led some of them to possess a closed canon. We think that this was the case with the OT/HB with at least some groups, if not mainstream Judaism. In other words, some groups had a collection of sacred Scripture and others of a canon, to use the language of the debate. Thus, during this period, no one conception of sacred texts existed. Third, Qumran possessed a fixed canon to which other literature, much of which was an interpretation of canonical texts, functioned for the community in a more authoritative way than the texts in the canon. Most of Second Temple Judaism shared this canon, and some groups shared their view that prophecy was ongoing (the early Christians are one example), while others did not. In our judgment, the third option is the most likely, but the second is also a strong possibility.

The Use of Texts in the New Testament

One could take the issue of the use of texts in the New Testament in many directions,[93] but we will discuss two: one predominates, and the other is pertinent to the structure or shape of the OT canon. The first question is which texts are referenced and in what way—that is, are they cited as Scripture or merely alluded to—in the NT? The second issue is the evidence for a tripartite structure to the Hebrew canon. Much ink has been spilled on these issues, and many factors large and small are outside the scope of the following discussion.

It is generally agreed that a reference to a text does not necessarily mean that it is Scripture. Paul's citation of Epimenides in Acts 17:28 in his discussion on Mars Hill, for instance, does not mean that he considered the quotation to be sacred. There is no agreement, however, about whether the NT implies a canon or the opposite. Many but not all of the books of the OT by any means are cited with scriptural formulas such as, "it is written" or this "fulfills the words of. . . ." The NT cites books from the Law and the Prophets more frequently than books from the Writings, and among individual books, Deuteronomy, Isaiah, and the Psalter are the most quoted. All the books of the OT are alluded to in the NT with the exception of Ruth, Song of Songs, and Esther (according to Beckwith),[94] and possibly Judges, Ecclesiastes, Lamentations, and Ezra/Nehemiah (according to others).[95] What is clear to almost everyone is that citation of or allusion to OT texts in the NT does not by itself reveal or determine the boundaries of

---

93. We want to make it clear that it would be better to examine all citations and allusions in Second Temple Judaism rather than in the NT alone, but this has been the scholarly paradigm, and we will not challenge it here. At any rate, the same issues brought up in this section appear when one looks at a wider selection of literature during this period. For a helpful, if somewhat one-sided (he does not discuss 1 Enoch), examination of citations, see Beckwith, "Formation," 45–49.

94. Ibid., 48.

95. Allusion is an elusive category, and one could debate two or three of the books listed here. For more on this topic, see Stone, *Megilloth*, 59.

the canon. McDonald rightly cautions that citation of a book or lack of it in the NT should not be the "sole basis for canonicity."[96] None of this is hotly debated. What is debated is the degree of NT allusions to books outside the Hebrew Bible and, in particular, Jude's citation of 1 Enoch.

McDonald has argued for a very large number of allusions to texts outside the boundaries of the Hebrew Bible; his book has a 13-page appendix listing all of them.[97] For McDonald (following Sundberg's early argument), what the cumulative evidence "confirms, of course, is that the biblical canon of the early Christian community was still in a fluid state during the time of Jesus' ministry and later, when most of the canonical Christian literature was produced."[98] Daniel Harrington observes that McDonald's list appears to be impressive but concludes that, in almost every case, no direct dependence can be found.[99] Lim, responding to Sundburg's argument regarding Paul's supposed use of sources, concludes that some of the texts cited postdate Paul and then only share a similar thought or expression while, for those that predate Paul's writings, the evidence for direct "dependence is not compelling."[100] Lim goes on to identify Paul's canon with the Pharisees' and state that it was "emerging" but not yet "closed."[101] Lim articulates well a common warning regarding scriptural citations in the NT. "The authors of the New Testament took for granted what they regarded as authoritative scripture." And thus they were not concerned to define the extent of their canon.[102] The evidence is circumstantial and depends to a large extent on the agendas and literary techniques of the authors of the NT.[103]

The citation of 1 Enoch in Jude has also been hotly debated. As mentioned in the introduction, Barr says that Jude cites 1 Enoch (or at least The

---

96. McDonald, *Biblical Canon*, 98.

97. Ibid., 452–64. Cf. Sundberg, *OT of Early Church*, 54–55.

98. McDonald, *Biblical Canon*, 197. Some of McDonald's evidence in context consists of the many citations to extracanonical literature by the early Church Fathers. We do not dispute that the early Church Fathers, on occasion, cited a text with the same formula as texts from the canon.

99. Daniel S. J. Harrington, "The Old Testament Apocrypha in the Early Church and Today," in *The Canon Debate* (ed. Lee Martin McDonald and James A. Sanders; Peabody, MA: Hendrickson, 2002), 200–201.

100. Lim, *Jewish Canon*, 169.

101. Ibid., 177.

102. Ibid., 156, 173. McDonald, *Biblical Canon*, 194, approvingly cites Stuhlmacher, "Old Testament Apocrypha," 12, who states, "Nowhere in the New Testament writings can any special interest in the canonical delimitation and fixing of the Holy Scriptures be detected." This is supposed to negate the view that the NT authors had a fixed canon, but if they did, their position was assumed and therefore did not need to be stated explicitly. The lack of special interest in this topic probably points in the other direction since, if there was a general collection of sacred texts without any clear borders, then one would expect to find at least a few skirmishes over the borders.

103. For more on this, see Stone, *Megilloth*, 59–63.

Book of the Watchers) as Scripture, while Childs states flatly that he does not. Jeremy Hultin has recently summed up the vital evidence, concluding that both Jews and Christians in the 1st century C.E. considered 1 Enoch to be Scripture and that it was rejected by both groups only later.[104] We find Hultin's argument persuasive regarding the Christian evidence and concede that the book was influential in Judaism, but we can find no evidence—unless one counts Jude as a Jewish source—that 1 Enoch was considered to be Scripture in Jewish circles.[105] We think it is very likely that Jude *does* consider 1 Enoch to be Scripture, since he refers explicitly to 1 En. 1:9 as a *prophecy*. Barton has convincingly argued that referring to a text in this manner means that one considers it to be Scripture.[106]

Other NT authors use the exact same language to refer to authoritative texts (Matt 11:13; 15:7; 1 Pet 1:10; 2 Pet 1:21). This may mean that our view of the canon is flawed, but we think it is more likely that the citation is the exception that proves the rule. In view of the *proportion* of the evidence, most NT writers—maybe all except the author of Jude—cite texts from the Hebrew canon a great number of times in comparison with the one citation from 1 Enoch. Nor do we think it is surprising, in view of the different positions on authoritative literature that probably existed in the 1st century C.E., that at least some of this diversity was found among the early Christians. We think that the NT is highly suggestive, but if the case could be decided absolutely for or against an assumed canon in the NT, then this conclusion would still not be decisive for the Hebrew canon since the Christian use of the OT does not *determine* its shape or authority.

The second, less-discussed issue among scholars is the possible evidence that the canon was tripartite and, in conjunction with this, ended with the book of Chronicles. The most common expression used to refer to the OT is "law and prophets" (e.g., Matt 7:12) or something similar such as "Moses and the prophets" (e.g., Luke 16:13). As Barton has demonstrated, these phrases and similar ones can refer to books from the Law, Prophets, and Writings. For Barton, the Law is the first five books, but the Prophets compose a large category, possibly as large as the "Greek Bible" that has undefined borders.[107]

This is probably the wrong conclusion to draw from the fact that books from all three divisions of the canon can be referred to in this manner, since there is not one example in the NT or anywhere else in Jewish sources

---

104. Jeremy Hultin, "Jude's Citation of 1 Enoch," in *Jewish and Christian Scriptures: The Function of "Canonical" and "Non-Canonical" Religious Texts* (ed. James H. Charlesworth and Lee Martin McDonald; Jewish and Christian Texts 7; London: T. & T. Clark, 2010) 114. Cf. Stone, *Megilloth*, 61–64.

105. The book was highly regarded at Qumran, but even there it is not clear that it was considered Scripture. Cf. Stone, *Megilloth*, 62–63.

106. Barton, *Oracles*, 1–95.

107. For a summary of Barton's position, see Stone, *Megilloth*, 36–37.

in the Second Temple period where this formula refers to books *outside* the Hebrew Bible. In our view, it is more likely that this formula is a way of referring to the *whole* canon and may but does not necessarily indicate anything about particular divisions in the canon. As Chapman has concluded, "Law and Prophets" may "have been used as an umbrella term for the totality of scripture."[108]

Beckwith, however, has made much of the tripartite reference to the OT in Luke 24:44. Here, Jesus says that things have taken place in the way that they have because everything written in the "law of Moses and the prophets and the Psalms must be fulfilled." "The Psalms," according to Beckwith, is a shorthand way to refer to all of the Writings, since it begins the collection in the talmudic order found in b. B. Bat. 14b, with Ruth only serving as a brief introduction.[109] Why Ruth should be so easily passed over is complete conjecture on Beckwith's part; the only solid evidence for the Psalms' being a way to refer to the Writings as a whole does not appear until the 10th century C.E.[110]

McDonald holds that Beckwith's conclusion is in "considerable doubt" but goes on to say that Luke 24:44 refers (since the Psalms are important by themselves) to the "early beginning of a three-part biblical canon that had not yet developed." The Psalms are given a special place alongside a "widely recognized two-part biblical collection called the Law and Prophets."[111] We agree with McDonald that Beckwith has made too much of this passage, but we also think that the same holds for McDonald. In the context of Luke 24, it is far more likely that Luke adds the Psalms to the common designation in order to stress that the *totality* of Scripture has been fulfilled. Luke's tripartite reference, then, should not be aligned with any particular structure of the canon.

Beckwith also contends that Luke 11:49–51 (// Matt 23:34–36) indicates that Chronicles is the last book of the OT, since Jesus refers to the blood of Abel in Genesis 4 and to the blood of Zechariah in 2 Chronicles 24. In this way, Jesus' reference is to the first and last books of the canon as found in the talmudic order.[112] There is more than a little confusion over the identity of the prophet Zechariah and whether or not Luke is in fact referring to the Zechariah who is murdered in 2 Chronicles 24, but the details of that discussion are beyond the scope of this current essay.[113] In our view, it is

---

108. Chapman, *Law and Prophets*, 269.

109. Beckwith, *OT Canon*, 211–15.

110. Ibid.

111. McDonald, *Biblical Canon*, 93.

112. Beckwith, *OT Canon*, 211–22.

113. See ibid.; H. G. L. Peels, "The Blood from Abel to Zechariah (Matthew 23:35; Luke 11:50f.) and the Canon of the Old Testament," *ZAW* 113 (2001) 583–601; and Lim, *Jewish Canon*, 157–62, for different perspectives on this issue. Lim does not seem to grasp Beckwith's argument when he states that Zechariah would not have been the last murdered since Uriah, the son of Shemaiah, in Jer 26:20–23 was the last murdered chronologically.

likely that he is referring to the Zechariah in 2 Chronicles, but H. G. L. Peels argues that the two deaths are connected because the victims were both innocent, and the call for retribution was never fulfilled.[114] This argument makes Jesus's words meaningful without reference to the canon. Moreover, if Chronicles was the first book of the Writings as found in the Leningrad Codex, then it would still be the last canonical murder in the OT of one of Israel's righteous. In our view, Beckwith's argument is possible, but it presupposes rather than proves Chronicles' canonical location.

In sum, the overwhelming use of texts in the NT is from the Hebrew Bible with the exception of 1 Enoch in Jude, which in our judgment indicates that most NT authors presupposed the Hebrew canon in a relatively stable shape.[115] The large number of supposed allusions to other books outside the Hebrew canon is not persuasive. The NT evidence alone, however, is not decisive for identifying the canon or its structure.

Josephus, **Against Apion**

Another crucial piece of evidence regarding the canon—as is generally agreed among scholars—is the testimony of Josephus in *Against Apion*. The pertinent passage is as follows:

> Among us there are not thousands of books in disagreement and conflict with each other, but only *twenty-two books*, containing the record of all time, which are rightly trusted. *Five of these are the books of Moses*, which contain both the law and the tradition from the birth of humanity up to his death; this is a period of a little less than 3,000 years. From the death of Moses until Artaxerxes, king of the Persians after Xerxes, *the prophets after Moses wrote* the history of what took place in their own times *in thirteen books*; the *remaining four books* contain hymns to God and instructions for people on life. From Artaxerxes up to our own time every event has been recorded, but this is not judged worthy of the same trust, since the exact line of succession of the prophets did not continue. (*Ag. Ap.* 1.38–41)[116]

Three primary issues have occupied scholarly discussions of this text: first is whether Josephus's position on the canon is trustworthy and whether it belongs exclusively to the Pharisees or to a wider section of Judaism; second, which books belong to the count of 22; and third, what the structure of Josephus's collection is.

This aids Beckwith's argument, since he is not the last murdered chronologically but canonically, based on the talmudic order.

114. Peels, "Abel to Zechariah."

115. This is a judgment about the scope of the OT canon, not the state of the various textual witnesses to the individual books in this period.

116. Josephus, *Against Apion* (trans. John Barclay; Translation and Commentary 10; Leiden: Brill, 2007) 29–30.

Josephus understands the sacred texts of Israel to be a closed list of books. These books are ancient and were closed when prophecy ceased (or, rather, the chain of prophecy was broken; there could still be prophets) in Israel; thus, after the time of Artaxerxes, no books could be admitted to this collection. Scholars generally agree that this was the view of Josephus,[117] but there is a dispute about the trustworthiness of his testimony since *Against Apion* is a polemical work. Josephus was using this passage in particular to show that his history was better than Greek history precisely because he had a unified, trustworthy source, the 22 books, while his opponents had a myriad of contradictory books. Both McDonald and Barton, among others, argue that the work is "polemical," "obviously apologetic" in tone, and propaganda aimed at the "pagan intellectuals of his day."[118] All would probably agree that Josephus was prone to exaggeration, but McDonald and Barton distrust Josephus's view of the canon and consider him to be out of step with his contemporaries, since "no one had yet begun to think in such terms."[119]

To support this claim, McDonald cites Qumran's freedom to add or subtract from sacred texts, which "suggests that there was no *universally* accepted closed biblical canon in the first century C.E."[120] He goes on to suppose that there must not have been a canon that every Jew was aware of or else Melito, at the end of the 2nd century C.E., would not have needed to travel to Jerusalem (probably) to discover the extent of the biblical texts since he could have "simply crossed the street" to ask one of the Jews in the large synagogue in Sardis. Barton also cites Qumran's use of texts to discredit Josephus, noting that the community "prized Ecclesiasticus as highly as Proverbs, and Tobit as highly as Ruth or Daniel."[121] Josephus himself does not adhere to his own "theoretical canon," according to Barton, since he uses 1 Esdras and the Additions to Esther, and refers to the Sibylline Oracles as the "records of the ancient prophets."[122] In this interpretation, it is certainly possible that Josephus's view of the canon represents

---

117. However, see Barton, *Oracles*, 59, in which he states that Josephus does not claim that *"no other book could conceivably be found* that would meet the criterion of prophetic authorship" (italics original). This is not essential to Barton's argument, but it is in our view a highly improbable supposition that runs counter to the tenor of Josephus's view since the very concept that these ancient prophecies are not complete is the direct opposite of his point.

118. McDonald, *Biblical Canon*, 154–56, holds this view and cites several other scholars with the same perspective. Barton, *Oracles*, 58.

119. Ibid. Cf. McDonald, *Biblical Canon*, 156.

120. Ibid.

121. Barton, *Oracles*, 58–59.

122. Ibid., 62. Here, Barton is referring to *Ant.* 11.216–19.

only the view of the Pharisees, but even among the Pharisees this view was not uniformly accepted.[123]

In contrast to this approach, Steve Mason argues that Josephus should not be viewed as a Pharisee or an apologist for the group.[124] If Josephus's identification with the Pharisees is questionable, then the only grounds for limiting his view of the canon to this one group is the conclusion that other groups in this period had different conceptions of sacred texts since, by his own testimony, Josephus says nothing of the Pharisees' canon but claims that his view is the view of all Jews and has been for long ages. This may be an exaggeration because there were clearly other Jewish groups that did not adhere to this canon, as we see in the case of Jude's citation of 1 Enoch and 4 Ezra. It may, on the other hand, simply be standard rhetoric for a majority position. Lim concludes that, "if Josephus meant that most Jews in his present time at the end of the first century C.E. agreed on the canon, then that would have been a credible generalization."[125] While not directly addressing Barton or McDonald, Mason argues that Josephus holds to a closed canon yet willingly makes major alteration to these canonical sources. He writes:

> It is fair to say that if we lacked the *Against Apion*, Josephus himself would offer the clearest case for an open canon. But we do have the *Against Apion*, in which this same Josephus most emphatically, not to say matter-of-factly, insists that the Judean records have long since been completed in twenty-two volumes. Plainly, then, the circumstantial evidence of Josephus' own "Bible" in *Antiquites* does not mean what it might seem to mean at first: it does not, after all, imply an open canon.[126]

According to Mason, Josephus's "example removes the force from appeals to circumstantial evidence as proof that the Dead Sea Scrolls' authors or Philo or Ben Sira had an open canon."[127] Mason's conclusion undercuts the

---

123. McDonald, *Biblical Canon*, 157–58, adheres to this position and cites several scholars who posit that Josephus's canon only represents the view of the Pharisees. Cf. Lim, *Jewish Canon*, 45–49.

124. Steve Mason, *Flavius Josephus on the Pharisees: A Composition-Critical Study* (Leiden: Brill, 1991) 356.

125. Lim, *Jewish Canon*, 49. Cf. Carr, *Writing*, 251, who reverses his earlier position in "Community," 53, and contends that it would be incorrect to dismiss Josephus's view due to his alleged polemical aims. David M. Carr, "Canonization in the Context of Community: An Outline for the Formation of the Tanakh and the Christian Bible," in *A Gift of God in Due Season: Essays on Scripture and Community in Honor of James A. Sanders* (ed. Richard D. Weis and David M. Carr; LHBOTS; Sheffield: Sheffield Academic Press, 1996) 53; and idem, *Writing on the Tablet of the Heart: Origins of Scripture and Literature* (Oxford: Oxford University Press, 2005) 251.

126. Steve Mason and R. A. Kraft, "Josephus on Canon and Scripture," in *Hebrew Bible/Old Testament: The History of Its Interpretation* (ed. Magne Sæbø; 5 vols.; Göttingen: Vandenhoeck & Ruprecht, 1996–2015) 1/1.217–35, esp. p. 234.

127. Mason, "Josephus," 125.

arguments of both Barton and McDonald regarding Qumran. As we argued above, a methodological distinction must be made between the appreciation and use of books by a certain community and their concept of canon.

We do not think it is likely that Josephus's canon enjoyed universal acceptance, nor do we think it only represents the canon of the Pharisees. We do think it is possible that Qumran may have had a different concept of sacred literature. Both McDonald and Barton use a sect to discredit Josephus, but is there a way to collaborate his testimony regarding a position that could be considered mainstream? In our view, 4 Ezra, written at almost the same time as *Against Apion*, confirms the position of Josephus, not as out of step with his contemporaries but, rather, as representative of them (on this, see below). Furthermore, if Josephus were fabricating things for polemical reasons, one would expect that we would later discover his falsehood, but remarkably, this lie comes true since the 22-book collection is known to Jerome and Origen. It is likely that Josephus's collection is identical to the current Hebrew Bible, but more on this below. Since another witness confirms Josephus's position,[128] and later evidence matches it exactly, we see no reason not to trust his testimony, even if it is slightly exaggerated.

The second major scholarly question is this: which books belong to Josephus's count of 22? There is no debate about which books belong to the 5 books of Moses, but scholars differ on the 17 remaining books divided into the 13 prophetic books and the 4 books of hymns and instructions. Beckwith, based on Josephus's use of texts in his *Antiquities*, argues that all the books of the Hebrews are here listed with the possible exception of either Ecclesiastes or the Song of Songs.[129] With greater assurance, Leiman concludes that this collection contains exactly the same books as found later in the Hebrew Bible.[130] McDonald criticizes Leiman for drawing such strong conclusions. He says, "Nothing here justifies Leiman's identification of the books in Josephus's list with the books that finally obtained [significance] in the Jewish Bible." He is working "backward in anachronistic fashion" from later evidence, according to McDonald.[131] He goes on to cite Ziony Zevit approvingly, who excludes Isaiah, Jeremiah, Ezekiel, the Twelve, the Song of Songs, and Lamentations from Josephus's collection by counting 1 and 2 Samuel and 1 and 2 Kings and 1 and 2 Chronicles as two books

---

128. His position on a prophetic age was also not idiosyncratic but widespread. On this, see Barton, *Oracles*, 59–60. Cf. Stone, *Megilloth*, 74–75.

129. Beckwith, "Formation," 50–51. Lim, *Jewish Canon*, 45, makes it appear that Beckwith only made an educated guess regarding the books in the Hebrew canon, but this misrepresents his position.

130. Leiman, *Canonization*, 32–33. Beckwith's analysis is not consistent on this issue, however. See his *OT Canon*, 78–80, in which Job is the book that may be excluded.

131. McDonald, *Biblical Canon*, 153.

each and Ezra and Nehemiah as two books.[132] How can these different perspectives be evaluated?

First, dividing Samuel, Kings, Chronicles, and Ezra/Nehemiah into different books is a Christian practice, which according to McDonald's standard of judgment is also anachronistic. However one adds up the books in his collection, it will of necessity be based on later sources. For many people, this is seen as problematic, but it need not be if the sources are relatively close in time and plausibly fit earlier evidence. Second, there is no way to know for certain which books belonged to Josephus's collection, but, observing Josephus's use of biblical books in his *Antiquities* and considering widespread conventions of counting the biblical books, we think it is likely that his collection matches the current Hebrew Bible's precisely.[133] The 13 prophetic books probably but not necessarily contained Joshua, Judges with Ruth (counted as one book), Samuel, Kings, Chronicles, Daniel, Ezra/Nehemiah (one book), Esther, Isaiah, Jeremiah with Lamentations (counted as one book), Ezekiel, and the Twelve (one book). Job was included in this section because the book was considered to be historical.[134] The 4 remaining books would then be Psalms, Proverbs, Ecclesiastes, and the Song of Songs. As Lim and many others have demonstrated, both Jerome and Origen observe that the Hebrews numbered the books at 22 by counting Judges and Ruth as one book and Jeremiah and Lamentations as one book.[135] This numbering scheme was identical with the number of letters in the Hebrew alphabet, and it matches exactly with numbering the Hebrew Bible at 24 books (according to the Greek alphabet) if Ruth and Lamentations are counted as separate books (for more on this, see the discussion below on 4 Ezra).

The third major issue is the structure of Josephus's collection. Is there a relationship between Josephus's division of the books into three groups and the TaNaK? Barton argues that this way of dividing the collection does not attest a tripartite canon since the division of the books of the Writings

---

132. Ziony Zevit, "The Second–Third Century Canonization of the Hebrew Bible and Its Influence on Christian Canonization," in *Canonization and Decanonization* (ed. A. van der Kooij and Karel van der Toorn; Leiden: Brill, 1998) 140 n. 20.

133. With Beckwith, *OT Canon*, 80; Steck, "Kanon des AT," 246; Steinmann, *Oracles*, 115–16; Rudolf Smend, *Die Entstehung des Alten Testaments* (Stuttgart: Kohlhammer, 1978) 14; van der Kooij, "Canonization," 20; cf. Diebner, "Sammlung der Ketuvim," 179.

134. Based on the *Antiquities*, Beckwith demonstrates that Josephus refers to all of the books mentioned above with the exception of Job. Therefore, one could argue that Job was left out, and Ruth was counted on its own, or that some other unknown book was part of Josephus's second group. However, it is also plausible that Josephus understood Job as a historical book and thus placed it in his second section but did not mention it in his *Antiquities*, because it was not part of the historical chain of events.

135. Lim, *Jewish Canon*, 47. Cf. Sid Leiman, "Josephus and the Canon of the Bible," in *Josephus, the Bible, and History* (ed. Louis Feldman and Gohei Hata; Leiden: Brill, 1989) 50–58, esp. p. 54; Beckwith, *OT Canon*, 235–40.

clearly does not match Josephus's scheme.[136] This appears to be a widely accepted position. Does this mean, however, that Josephus's scheme should be used as evidence that the tripartite canon of the TaNaK was not in existence yet? According to some, yes.[137] Barton goes on to suggest that the divisions are thematic; that the books are divided by "law, histories, hymns and precepts."[138] Mason's conclusions are similar. He states:

> Josephus' remarks in *Against Apion* 1.37–43 cannot be made to specify divisions within the first-century canon. His language is on a different plane. His most consistent ordering criterion is that of genre: Law, tradition, hymns, and advice. These genres do not correlate to the division of the Bible. They simply provide a means of elaborating for Gentile readers the various kinds of material to be found among the twenty-two volumes.[139]

If we consider again the purpose of *Against Apion*—Josephus was referring to the Bible in the sense of historical sources for his *Antiquities*—it is easy to understand that his way of reckoning needs to be understood in terms of historical/nonhistorical books rather than as canon divisions. As O. Steck writes: "The context of the statement in *Against Apion* clearly shows that Josephus is not presenting a tripartite canon, but rather an order mirroring his own purposes."[140]

If this is the case, and we think it is likely,[141] then Josephus does not provide evidence for the structure of the Jewish canon, and consequently he should not be used as a witness against its possible tripartite structure.

In sum, Josephus testifies to a closed canon of 22 books, which is probably identical to the Hebrew canon, though his arrangement of the collection is due to genre considerations rather than any formal structuring principle. It is likely that this canon was generally recognized among Jews in the 1st century C.E.

---

136. Barton, *Oracles*, 48.

137. Cross, *Epic to Canon*, 228. Cf. Swanson, *Canonization*, 376.

138. Barton, *Oracles*, 48.

139. Mason, "Josephus," 127.

140. "Der Kontext der c.Apionem-Aussage zeigt eindeutig, daß Josephus nicht eine dreigeteilte Kanonliste angibt, sondern einer eigenen Sachanordnung folgt" (Steck, "Kanon des AT," 247). Also Leiman, "Josephus and the Canon of the Bible," 55; again Mason and Kraft, "Josephus on Canon and Scriptures," 221, 234; Miller, *Origins of the Bible*, 7. As a counterposition, see, e.g., Bruce, *Canon of Scripture*, 33.

141. This is a common view, contra Lim, *Jewish Canon*, 46, who states that it is against the "prevailing scholarly consensus." Even John Barton, "Canons of the Old Testament" in *Texts in Context* (ed. A. D. H. Mayes; Oxford: Oxford University Press, 2000) 216 admits that this is a possibility. See also Carr, "Community," 52; Sundberg, *OT of Early Church*, 71; and Chapman, *Law and Prophets*, 273–74.

4 Ezra

In the canon debate, since there is a meager amount of primary information, it is vital to give proper proportion to the available evidence. 4 Ezra is a case in point since it is rarely given a prominent position in the debate and, when it is mentioned, it is usually only in passing.[142] It is our contention that 4 Ezra deserves a more important place in the debate. In the following discussion, we will survey various readings of 4 Ezra's contribution to the canon question and then present our own approach.

4 Ezra is a Jewish apocalyptic text containing seven visions and was most likely written sometime near the end of the 1st century C.E. The author takes on the pseudonymous name of "Ezra" in order to disguise his discussion of the destruction of the temple by the Romans in 70 C.E. by appearing to be reflecting on the destruction of the temple by the Babylonians. In the seventh apocalyptic vision, Ezra mentions 70 books reserved for the wise and 24 for public use. Ezra pleads with God to restore to Israel the law that was burned—presumably when the temple burned—and in answer to his prayer he is given wisdom, and his memory is miraculously restored. Over a period of 40 days, he dictates the law to five scribes, who write in characters that they do not understand. This is the literary context of the key text for our discussion. 4 Ezra 14:44–47 says:

> So during the forty days, ninety-four books were written. And when the forty days were ended, the Most High spoke to me, saying, "Make public the twenty-four books that you wrote first and let the worthy and unworthy read them; but keep the seventy that were written last, in order to give them to the wise among your people. For in them is the spring of understanding, the fountain of wisdom, and the river of knowledge." And I did so.

McDonald concludes that both collections are of equal authority and that one cannot be "certain" about which books are included in the 24 or the 70.[143] Since both groups of books were recovered through the work of the Spirit in the same manner, it is "easy to conclude that the seventy books were held in equally high regard as the twenty-four books." He

---

142. McDonald, *Biblical Canon*, only devotes about one page to analyzing this text (pp. 162–63) from his 240-page discussion of the Old Testament canon. By way of contrast, he devotes about 6 pages to his discussion of the use of 1 Enoch in Jude (pp. 105–11). See also Lim, *Jewish Canon*, who devotes about a page to 4 Ezra (pp. 49–50), and it does not contribute in any significant way to his conclusions. Childs does not discuss this text to our knowledge in any of his works. Beckwith, *Old Testament Canon*, only mentions this text in passing but later devotes a good portion of his rejoinder to Barton to discussing 4 Ezra in "Modern Theory," 385–95. Beckwith's short essay is not cited in McDonald's bibliography and, while Lim, *Jewish Canon*, cites Beckwith's article in his bibliography, he does not discuss it or cite it in the body of his work.

143. McDonald, *Biblical Canon*, 161–63.

goes on to argue that "there is no way to know for certain whether either collection" contained Ruth, Lamentations, Ezekiel, Daniel, Ecclesiastes, or the Song of Songs since these books were still among the disputed books, nor can one know for "certain" that the Wisdom of Solomon and Ben Sira were excluded from either collection. Thus, "One should be very careful about attributing to 4 Ezra a definition of canon that cannot be established."[144]

Barton, by contrast, observes that it is "generally agreed" that the 24 books are the same as those in the current Hebrew Bible. Barton finds it significant, however, that 4 Ezra places the 70 books "on a *higher* level" of authority than the 24 books.[145] The 24 books are readily available to everyone—even the unworthy—but only the 70 are reserved for the *wise*, which indicates their superior status. According to Barton, this text "by no means suggests a sacred canon" of 24 books in which the 70 works are "excluded as of inferior importance, but on the contrary a multiplicity of holy books of which only a few can be safely entrusted to all and sundry."[146] In more recent scholarship, Lim expresses this same view: "It is this seventy-book collection that has greater authority."[147] Barton concurs with McDonald that 4 Ezra does not support the notion of a closed canon during this period, but he disagrees that the 24 and the 70 are of equal authority. Also, in contrast to McDonald, Barton seems to agree with the majority of scholars that the 24 books are the same as the Hebrew Bible.[148]

Beckwith takes yet another approach to 4 Ezra. He argues that the intention of the text is to establish the 70's superior and, more importantly, secret status, but when read critically this indicates the superiority of the 24 books. According to Beckwith, the author of 4 Ezra is trying to establish the authority of his own work, which the author includes among the 70. 4 Ezra is "striving for the recognition of his pseudepigrapha against a public opinion which recognizes only the 24 canonical books."[149] This is the case because 4 Ezra demeans the 24 books by saying that even the *unworthy* can read them, while the 70 are reserved exclusively for the *wise*. If the 24 books were not a well-established collection, there would have been no reason for 4 Ezra to exclude his own work from them. The case is strong that the 24 books are a canonical collection, because he must make an "involuntary"

---

144. Ibid., 163.
145. Barton, *Oracles*, 64, italics original.
146. Ibid., 64–65.
147. Lim, *Jewish Canon*, 50.
148. This may seem confusing on the part of Barton, but he is being consistent with the way he has framed the whole issue and his definition of canon, in which the exclusion of all other books from the collection becomes the key. Here the 70 are not excluded from the 24, in Barton's view, but are made more important than the 24. In our reading, it is essential to note that the 24 books are presented as a separate collection from the 70 books.
149. Beckwith, "Modern Theory," 392.

and "grudging admission" that the 24 books are known to the public, while his own secretly recovered work is not.[150]

There are three main issues to discuss in light of these three different approaches to 4 Ezra. First, we agree with Barton and Beckwith that the 24 books are probably the same as those in the current Hebrew Bible.[151] Of course, one cannot know this for *certain*, to use McDonald's language, but we think the probability of this conclusion is rather high.[152] We object, however, to McDonald's rhetorical use of certainty to discredit the most likely conclusion. There probably are no certainties when doing historical research, so asserting that one cannot be certain about one issue or the meaning of a text reveals that one's epistemological understanding of historical investigation is lacking. Employing epistemological scales, as McDonald does, fails to give evidence its proper proportion in the discussion.

Second, we disagree with McDonald's conclusion that the 24 books and the 70 books should be considered equal in authority. Instead, we agree with Barton and Lim that the 70 are given a higher status than the 24, but we also want to acknowledge that this is the agenda of 4 Ezra and thus concur with Beckwith that this sort of reading takes the text at face value and is not sufficiently critical. As Stone has argued, the author of 4 Ezra uses the same language with which he described the 70 books to portray his own work (4 Ezra 12:36–38). The rhetoric of the author's attempt to establish the authority of his own writings makes the most sense against the background of a 24-book collection that is delimited and well known. Otherwise, there is no reason he would exclude his own book from the collection of 24 or even press for the acceptance of his own book within these categories.

According to Stone, this reveals something essential about the canon since there may be books with some degree of authority—the 70—alongside *"a fixed, clearly demarcated canon."*[153] This canon is not universally accepted, but at least in this very important case, even one who is attempting to give other books a higher status recognizes its presence. Stone concludes, "*4 Ezra* reveals the *traditional* status of a fixed canon in the public square of Judaism by his dismissive use and yet acknowledgement of 24 books in support of a 'superior' collection of secret knowledge not transmitted

---

150. Ibid.

151. For more details in support of this claim, see Stone, *Megilloth*, 70–72.

152. We would, however, disagree with Barton's contention that this collection is not closed since it is differentiated from the 70 books and there are many reasons (as we argue above) to conclude that, if the 24-book collection were in fact open, then the author of 4 Ezra would have attempted to include his book among them or might have approached the entire subject in a different manner.

153. Stone, *Megilloth*, 71. Italics original.

through open tradition."[154] It is vital to note that this view does not dismiss the possibility of other collections of sacred texts, whether delimited or open, in the 1st century among Jews. It proposes, instead, that it is appropriate to argue that this canon is recognized across most of Judaism, even in the midst of the vast diversity of Jewish groups that existed in the 1st century C.E.[155]

This is our understanding of 4 Ezra's contribution to the canon debate and, as a result, we think it should have a more prominent place in the discussion. In sum, when read critically, 4 Ezra reveals the presence of a closed collection of 24 books in mainstream Judaism. It also reveals that one can simultaneously be aware of this canon and yet consider other books to be authoritative. This way of numbering the books counts Ruth and Lamentations as individual books and in later sources is always connected to the tripartite divisions of the OT in which Ruth and Lamentations are considered among the Writings.

The Shape of the Writings

The books of the Bible have come down to us in many different arrangements. In the case of the Writings of the Jewish TaNaK, Beckwith and Brandt present about 30 orders without a grouped Megillot and about 90 orders that have the Megillot grouped.[156] Taking the Greek, Latin, and Syriac traditions into consideration, the diversity of arrangements increases even more: these traditions do not even know of the "Writings" collection in the strict sense (see Brandt's article in this volume). What are the issues that emerge from these data for canonical approaches, especially regarding the Writings?

First, the book order of the Leningrad Codex and *BHS*, respectively, should no longer be taken for granted as the starting point for addressing the question of order, as was done in older introductions and commentaries to the OT. Rather, the multiplicity of orders needs to be perceived and appreciated.

Second, the multiple orders do not necessarily lead to completely abandoning the questions of book order. To the contrary, it is rewarding for

---

154. Ibid., italics original. In many ways, Lim, *Jewish Canon*, 180, comes to this same conclusion. According to Lim, "By the end of the first century CE, there was a canon that *most* Jews accepted." Italics ours.

155. It is possible that this view only represented the canon of the Pharisees, as Lim, *Jewish Canon*, 179–80, has argued, and then only later, after Jewish power was consolidated under them, can one speak of *canon* without anachronism. Lim labels this the "majority canon" and argues that before this period "there were several collections of authoritative scriptures held by different groups" (p. 179). It is unclear in Lim's account if the Pharisaic canon actually closed (and was open to change until this time) in the 2nd century C.E. or if it only then became dominant, even though its contents remained, in all essentials, the same.

156. Beckwith, *OT Canon*, 452–57; Brandt, *Endgestalten*, 156–62.

canonical exegesis to probe the rationale behind the different orders as well as the hermeneutical effects that emerge when one reads the books in one or the other order.

Third, in our opinion, book orders do not stand next to each other unconnected and with equal status. Rather, they can be structured into families based on principles and traditions of arrangement. Late developments can be distinguished from early forms and individual variations from main strands of tradition. A well-known principle of textual criticism applies to the arrangement of books as well: orders *non numerantur sed ponderantur*. As a result, some orders or families can be found that are of overarching interest, due to their age, reasoning, or authority.

Fourth, although the quest for an "original" book order may be quixotic, reaching back into history is nevertheless of interest. A more "catholic" approach, cherishing the richness of tradition, and a more "protestant" approach, searching for the roots, can happily coexist side by side.

In doing the latter, however, a very basic objection arises. It is whether— or since when?—order played a role at all.

In the following, we will address this topic first, and after that assess two of the most important book orders from the Jewish TaNaK tradition: the order found in b. B. Bat. 14b and the order of the Leningrad Codex.

The Arrangement of Books in the Old Testament before the Appearance of Codices

It is commonly asserted but seldom argued that the very concept of a meaningful arrangement of books in the OT would be anachronistic for the Second Temple period or before, due to the simple fact that there was no technology for physically setting individual scrolls within a larger arrangement. The invention of the codex overcame this technological problem, which then made it necessary to consider the idea of book order. William Schniedewind represents the consensus view when he says, "The invention of the codex forced decisions to be made about the set order of the biblical books within the codex."[157] The invention of the codex is usually dated around 300 C.E., and then it became more and more popular among Christians in the following centuries.[158] Before this time, the very idea of order is not meaningful, while after the invention of the codex, order begins to "have a clear meaning," according to Barton.[159] There are three points we will make in response to this consensus.

First, the great codices of the 4th and 5th century C.E.—Vaticanus, Sinaiticus, and Alexandrinus—all differ in very significant ways from one

---

157. William Schniedewind, *How the Bible Became a Book* (Cambridge: Cambridge University Press, 2004) 196. Cf. Barton, *Oracles*, 83.

158. Brandt, *Endgestalten*, 58–62.

159. Barton, *Oracles*, 83.

another concerning the number and order of the books.[160] There are no signs within the arrangements of these codices that meaningful decisions had been made regarding the order of presentation. Moreover, the Jews did not adopt the codex until much later, since the earliest evidence we have for codices in Judaism is from the 9th or 10th century C.E.[161] B. B. Bat. 14b, which is usually dated to the 2nd century C.E., predates this practice by a considerable period of time within Judaism.[162] This text is concerned about the order of the Prophets and the Writings. Thus an order can, at least in this instance, be significant before the use of the codex.

Second, there is internal evidence in the OT that the sequence of the books was not arbitrary but meaningful. This is surely not in doubt for the Law or Torah, which were too large to be entirely written on one scroll. These first five books are almost always found together and in the same order in both Jewish and Christian tradition. Additionally, there are signs that they have been "tied together" at their seams by means of catchwords.[163] For instance, Genesis and Exodus are linked at their seams by the repetition of Joseph's death at the end of Genesis (50:26) and again at the beginning of Exodus (1:6). The same can be observed in the Former Prophets and the connection between the end of the Torah and the beginning of the Former Prophets.[164] It can also be plausibly argued that, at one point in the formation of the Genesis-to-2 Kings collection, Ruth was added between Judges and 1 Samuel by the use of catchwords or phrases that connect Ruth's seams to the end of Judges and beginning of 1 Samuel. The very unusual use of the verb "to take" wives (in Hebrew נשׂא) in Judg 21:23, rather than the usual verb to take a wife (in Hebrew לקח), and its repetition in Ruth 1:4 link the two books at their seams. Again, Ruth is linked to 1 Samuel by the repetition of the phrase "better to you than seven/ten sons," which is only found in Ruth 4:15 and 1 Sam 1:8 in the entire OT.[165]

One may suppose that these books, especially Genesis to 2 Kings are linked together because they present a *continuous history* of Israel, and thus this order is of little significance. One may continue to suppose that, even if order is significant here, there can be no comparison with other portions of the OT because the Genesis-to-2 Kings collection narrates a continual

---

160. McDonald, *Biblical Canon*, 442.

161. They probably had codices earlier than this, since they must have adopted the practice before this time: the creation of the Leningrad and Aleppo codices would have been the work of several generations of Masoretes.

162. Stone, *Megilloth*, 103.

163. The Twelve Minor Prophets and the Psalter each exhibit the same practice of knitting books or psalms together at their seams. On this, see the summary by Stone, *Megilloth*, 17–33.

164. For more on this in the Law and Former Prophets, see Konrad Schmid, *Genesis and the Moses Story* (trans. James Nogalski; Siphrut 3; Winona Lake, IN: Eisenbrauns, 2010) 23–29; Stone, *Megilloth*, 88–93.

165. See the essay by Stone in this volume.

story, while other portions of the OT do not.[166] There are several problems with this line of thinking. First, if this were the case, then there would be no conceivable reason to link the books together at their seams, since connecting the "natural sequence" would be superfluous. Second, the fact that Ruth can be included in this history reveals that there is more than one way to arrange the collection. It is not simply inevitable that these books were collected in this order for chronological reasons. Third, this continuous history is not the entire biblical story of Israel. If narrating a history of Israel were the primary reason that these books were arranged in this fashion, then why wasn't Ezra/Nehemiah placed after 2 Kings?

There are many possible answers to this question, and the reasons have been pursued at great length, but the answer is not vital to our argument here. However, the fact that the collection ends with 2 Kings and not with the return from exile does show that it was not simply intended to narrate a continuous story. The collection was meant to have a particular frame and shape. The order of Genesis to 2 Kings—with or without Ruth—was significant before the rise of the codex. It is therefore possible to posit a meaningfully arranged collection even without the technology of a codex. It is not necessary to discern the exact reasons behind this idea to know that it is, practically speaking, a real possibility.

Third, the temple archive is a plausible place to posit a (conceptually and technologically) meaningful arrangement of the sacred texts. There is no debate that a temple archive existed in Second Temple Judaism,[167] but there are disagreements about its significance and whether all of the books that are today included in the OT/HB could be found there. Beckwith has championed this view. He observes that the books of the OT were called holy at least by the end of the 1st century B.C.E.[168] He then goes on to observe that the "holiest place of the nation's religious life" was the temple and, since there is evidence in the OT, Josephus, 2 Macc 2:13–15, and rabbinic literature of its existence, then while it stood, the main test of a book's canonical status would have been whether it was "laid up in the Temple."[169] Based on Josephus, he concludes that the Law (*J.W.* 7.150; *Ant.* 3.38; 4.302–4) and Joshua (*Ant.* 5.61) were included in the archive. The use of the term "Fifth" in t. Kelim Baba Meši'a 5.8 refers to the Psalter, which in turn would have been a title for the Writings as a whole. In regard to individual books, in the Mishnah and other tannaitic writings there are references to the Psalms, Job, Proverbs, Daniel, Ezra, and Chron-

---

166. This is not an argument that I have encountered in scholarly writing but one that has appeared on several occasions in conversations on this topic.

167. See Stone, *Megilloth*, 84, and the many sources cited there.

168. Beckwith, *OT Canon*, 80–81.

169. Idem, "Formation," 41–44.

icles that indicate that the books could be found in this archive, according to Beckwith.[170]

Recently, Lim has challenged this proposal. Based on a close reading of 2 Macc 2:13–15, he concludes that Judas did not found a library, as did Nehemiah, but instead gathered together the books that had been damaged by the war, which was a collection of unspecified books.[171] Lim concedes that the Law was kept in the temple based on the testimony of Josephus but notes that he said "nothing about the rest of the prophets and the writings."[172] The reference to the term "Fifth" as a term to denote the whole of the Writings is doubtful. The term, instead, probably refers to the five books of Moses.[173] Lim does not address the other references that Beckwith cites in rabbinic literature regarding the books that were found in the temple. Lim concludes that there were scriptural scrolls deposited in the Jerusalem temple but that there is no evidence that it contained an "official" or "public" depository of scrolls.[174]

This is a particularly difficult area because of the lack of information at our disposal. The temple was destroyed, and its substantial role in Second Temple Judaism means, from a sociological and cultural perspective, that many of the specifics of its powerful influence went unstated. Despite this, we can say with some confidence that the temple was *the* central cultic institution and that it was a focal point across the vast diversity of Jewish groups in the period—Qumran excepted.[175] It is certainly possible that not all the books currently in the Hebrew Bible were present in this archive (since we do not have evidence stating explicitly which books were there), but we think this is unlikely. If the temple archive only had the sources for which we have explicit evidence, then we cannot say that it contained even Genesis, for instance, since the Law may refer to Scripture in general and not only to the Torah, exclusively. But, if we granted that the five books of Moses were in this archive and even Joshua, for which there seems to be good evidence, then we might still conclude, based on lack of evidence, that Isaiah, Jeremiah, and Ezekiel were not included. In our view, it is hard to imagine that the temple in Jerusalem did not contain these three books

---

170. Ibid., 43.

171. Lim, *Jewish Canon*, 114–17.

172. Ibid., 28.

173. Ibid.

174. Ibid., 117. There are a number of other details that could be included in this exchange such as the role of scribal correctors in the temple.

175. Karel van der Toorn, *Scribal Culture and the Making of the Hebrew Bible* (Cambridge: Harvard University Press, 2007) 236–47; McDonald, *Biblical Canon*, 114. Carr, *Writing*, 212–14; Philip R. Davies, *Scribes and Schools: The Canonization of the Hebrew Scriptures* (Louisville: Westminster John Knox, 1998) 178–82; Schniedewind, *Bible Became a Book*, 198–203; A. F. J. Klijn, "A Library of Scriptures in Jerusalem?" *Texte und Untersuchungen zur Geschichte der altchristlichen Literatur* 124 (1977) 265–72.

or for that matter the rest of the books in the Hebrew Bible, but this is not an issue that can be determined absolutely.

We concede with Lim that the term "Fifth" probably does not refer to the Psalter and certainly not to the Writings as a whole. However, we find his minimalist reading of 2 Maccabees to be questionable, as we do Beckwith's maximalist approach. Deciding between the two is not essential to our argument here.[176] We also do not know how to adjudicate between Beckwith's approach, in which a book's inclusion in the temple archive was the canonical standard, and Lim's approach that it was not an official collection. The term *official* is probably the wrong word to denote the situation, but we cannot see how the archive, in such a sacred place, would not have been highly *influential*.[177]

However, we want to discuss an issue that neither scholar considers. We want to entertain the idea that the sacred space of the temple may have provided a conceptual way for an arrangement of the scrolls to be possible and significant. The furniture and space of the temple was carefully arranged; the duties of the priest and where they could move were carefully circumscribed. It is unlikely that in such a sacred space the Holy Scriptures would not have been meticulously arranged, either in jars or on shelves or by another means. In the sacred space of the temple, where everything was put in its proper place, why wouldn't the sacred texts have been arranged with the utmost care? Again, this issue cannot be determined with any degree of probability, since the temple was destroyed but, in our view, it provides a plausible way for the collection and arrangement of the Hebrew Bible to make sense within the conceptual world of 1st-century Judaism.[178] If we are correct, in this context the arrangement of the scrolls would have been far more important than in a codex.

Regardless of one's conclusions regarding the function of the temple archive in respect to book arrangement, order was significant before the invention of the codex. There is ample evidence for this in b. B. Bat. 14b and in the Genesis-to-2 Kings collection. We have each argued, in various ways, for the significance of the order in the Writings,[179] and in this volume many of the essays explore this possibility.

B. Baba Batra 14b

As said above, from a reader's perspective, any historical book order of the Writings is worth studying with regard to its canon-hermeneutical implications. At the same time, one must admit that the results of the study

---

176. For a reading between these two extremes, see Stone, *Megilloth*, 85.

177. The way in which many synagogues tried to represent the features of the Jerusalem temple is but one important example of the temple's influence. On this, see ibid., 87.

178. For more on this, see ibid., 83–88.

179. See Steinberg, *Ketuvim;* and Stone, *Megilloth*.

will be more valuable and relevant if the order under consideration fulfills two criteria:

- Not only should the rationale for the order be based on formal principles of chronology, genre, and authorship, etc., but it should presumably take content and theology into consideration.[180]
- The order can be shown to have had a certain degree of prominence in the community of faith or some group of it.

Regarding these two criteria, the book order given in the Babylonian Talmud, tractate b. B. Bat. 14b is of particular significance.

Historical Relevance
Regarding Baba Batra's age, influence, and authority, the following can be stated:

1. The source is the oldest in the Jewish realm explicitly dealing with the order of biblical books. The tradition is identified as a baraita, which means it was reduced to writing around 200 C.E.[181]
2. The source itself refers back to the Rabbanan (Jewish authorities) and claims to present "the" order of the Prophets and Writings. According to Brandt, in the Jewish realm there are only two other orders that claim to be authoritative; both are from the late Middle Ages.[182]
3. Baba Batra is in agreement with the early evidence regarding the tripartite structure of the canon and the number of 24 books.[183]
4. The Megillot are not yet grouped. According to the standard position, which Steinberg also follows, the grouping of the Megillot (Ruth, Song, Ecclesiastes, Lamentations, and Esther) is a relatively

---

180. For example, in manuscipts of the LXX tradition, all sorts of narrative books are put in a chronological chain. When you read them continuously, you can see that some of the books are in fact made to be read in a chain (such as the five books of the Pentateuch), but others are not (for example, reading Chronicles after Kings or Esther after Nehemiah). Several scholars assume that the TaNaK order does more justice to the relationships among the books than the LXX tradition—for example, Roland E. Murphy, "Old Testament/Tanakh: Canon and Interpretation," in *Hebrew Bible or Old Testament? Studying the Bible in Judaism and Christianity* (ed. Roger Brooks and John J. Collins; Notre Dame, IN: University of Notre Dame Press, 1990) 13; Norbert Lohfink, "Eine Bibel – Zwei Testamente," in *Eine Bibel – Zwei Testamente: Positionen biblischer Theologie* (ed. Christoph Dohmen and Thomas Söding; Uni- Taschenbücher 1893; Paderborn: Schöningh, 1995) 79; Brandt, *Endgestalten*, 351. For a counterposition, see J. C. H. Lebram, "Aspekte der alttestamentlichen Kanonbildung," *VT* 18 (1968) 176.

181. See the detailed discussion in Hermann L. Strack and Günter Stemberger, *Einleitung in Talmud und Midrasch* (7th ed.; Munich: Beck, 1982) 127–42; also Beckwith, *OT Canon*, 122; 170 n. 28;

182. Brandt, *Endgestalten*, 149–50; see also his article in the present volume. Stone, as you will see, objects to this conclusion.

183. See on Ben Sira and 4 Ezra above.

late phenomenon that occurred only after the 6th century C.E.[184] Therefore, orders that do not have this group can be considered to have a higher probability of being original.

5. Baba Batra has had significant influence on most of the other orders that are extant in the Jewish tradition. It can be said to be the mother of the family of manuscripts without a grouped Megillot, and even the orders with grouped Megillot strongly correspond to Baba Batra's principles, except, of course, for the placement of the Megillot themselves.[185]

Again, no attempt is being made to make Baba Batra the "one order" or the "original" order. Nevertheless, one can clearly see its historical significance. Regarding the rationale for the arrangement, however, opinions differ.

Formal Principles of Arrangement?
The order of the Writings as given in b. B. Bat. 14b is:

Ruth–Ps–Job–Prov–Eccl–Song–Lam–Dan–Esth–Ezr/Neh–Chr.

Beckwith tries to explain the sequence from a combination of several formal principles.[186] He observes a division between narrative and non-narrative works: the narrative works are arranged according to chronology, and the non-narrative works according to decreasing size.[187] However, the actual sequence deviates from these principles at several points. For these exceptions, Beckwith offers additional explanations:[188]

1. Ruth is separated from the other narrative works. Explanation: Ruth was understood as an introduction to or preparation for Psalms and was therefore placed before it.
2. The order Ezra/Neh–Chr contradicts the principle of chronology. Explanation: Chronicles was understood as closing the Bible and was therefore placed at the end.
3. According to decreasing length, the sequence should read Lam–Song and not Song–Lam. Explanation: The three Solomonic books were formed as a block. Another explanation is given by Brandt: The "large" (Psalms, Job, Proverbs) and the "small" (Ecclesiastes, Song of Songs, Lamentations) Writings each form a block. In addition, the books of the "Solomonic trio" were kept together by placing Proverbs as the last of the "large" and Ecclesiastes and Song of Songs as the first two of the "small" Writings. Brandt derives the divisions

---

184. Brandt, *Endgestalten*, 129.
185. For the detailed argument, see Steinberg, *Ketuvim*, 144–51.
186. Beckwith, *OT Canon*, 199; 158–62.
187. This criterion is in effect, for example, in the mishnaic tractates. Beckwith, *OT Canon*, 161.
188. Ibid., 158, 162.

of "large" and "small" Writings from b. Ber. 57b; however, this section is not explicitly dealing with canonical sequence.[189]

Thus, the rules of arranging the books would have been rather complicated and formed a mixture of arguments based on form and content: a division into narrative and non-narrative works; the chronological ordering of three of the five narrative works; Ruth is understood as introducing Psalms, and Chronicles as closing the canon; and division of the non-narrative works into the groups of "large" and "small" Writings while keeping the Solomonic books together as a group. This means there are six different rules for organizing the 11 books, which is not a convincing approach in our opinion.

In view of these weaknesses, Beckwith offers a second interpretation: all books of the Writings are arranged chronologically with the one exception of Chronicles. Job, however, poses a problem, since it is placed after Ruth and Psalms. Admittedly, we must take into consideration Rabbi Nathan in b. B. Bat. 15b, who connects the *šewa* of Job 1:15 to 1 Kgs 10:1ff., thus assigning Job to the time of Solomon. R. Nathan's argument, however, is neither very convincing nor does it play a major role in rabbinic discourse. W. Riedel's analysis is more plausible. He sees a chronological order in the books from Job to Ezra/Nehemiah,[190] understanding Ruth+Psalms and Chronicles in the sense of a theological framework.

However, one could also ask: if chronology is the key, why, then, are Ruth, Chronicles, Ezra/Nehemiah, and Esther placed in the Writings at all? The very fact that the narrative works are distributed over the three canonical divisions, in our opinion, demonstrates that genre and chronology cannot be the primary key to the rationale of the TaNaK structure.

Therefore, the order of the Writings according to b. B. Bat. 14b cannot fully be explained by formal criteria.[191] Rather, at several places, arguments from content and theology were already suggesting themselves, especially regarding the framing books. This suggestion needs to be examined further.

Theological Principles of Ordering

Intertextual relationships between books can be determined in different ways and on various levels. Vital to Steinberg's approach[192] is a holistic way of dealing with the biblical books. As a first step, the literary character and theological message of each book are to be scrutinized by means of literary study. As a second step, the interrelationships between the books' messages are explored in the search for an overall structure in which each book

---

189. Brandt, *Endgestalten*, 152; cf. Beckwith, *OT Canon*, 162. See Stone, *Megilloth*, 109–10.

190. Riedel, "Kanon," 101–2; cf. Brandt, *Endgestalten*, 152.

191. As also Brandt (ibid., 153) admits, in view of the position of Chronicles.

192. Steinberg, *Ketuvim*, 75ff.

may possibly be understood as a part of the greater literary and theological whole.

Regarding the first step, Steinberg cannot reproduce his interpretations of the individual books in the confines of this essay. Instead, we must hope for some degree of agreement on the matter. Regarding the second step, Steinberg's interpretation (explanation) of the Talmudic sequence Ruth–Ps–Job–Prov–Eccl–Song–Lam–Dan–Esth–Ezr/Neh–Chr is as follows: First, we can observe that the three wisdom books—Job, Proverbs, and Ecclesiastes—appear next to each other. Second, we can determine a group of three historical books—namely, Daniel, Esther, and Ezra–Nehemiah—that deal with exile and restoration. The book of Chronicles does not belong to this group, since it does not fit chronologically. Third, in the middle between these two groups we find the books of Song of Songs and Lamentations. To relate these two books to each other is not very rewarding. It makes much more sense to see Song of Songs as a follow-up to Ecclesiastes, especially via the connection of the call to enjoy life. On the other hand, Lamentations, notwithstanding its poetic genre, forms a perfect introduction to the historical subcollection of books dealing with exile and restoration. Therefore, the arrangement may be read as two subcollections of four books each.

One subcollection is Job, Proverbs, Ecclesiastes, and Song of Songs, and the second is Lamentations, Daniel, Esther, Ezra/Nehemiah. The first subcollection relates to the sphere of the individual; the second relates to the sphere of politics and the nation. Interestingly, both subcollections begin with suffering and end with joy: Job and Lamentations are the two books of the Bible that devote themselves fully to the topic of suffering and sorrow, whereas Song of Songs and Ezra/Nehemiah represent topics of particular joy, which are love between man and woman on the personal level and the new beginning after the exile in the political realm. This is not to say that Ezra/Nehemiah is joyful from the first to the last verse. Nevertheless, the series Lam–Dan–Esth–Ezr/Neh stretches from the destruction of Jerusalem to its rebuilding, which gives this troublesome part of Israel's history a happy ending.

Fourth, before and after these two subcollections, there are the two large books of Psalms and Chronicles. They are both like a compendium in character regarding history and theology and can be said to form a framework around the two subcollections. Finally, we must consider the book of Ruth. In its position, it functions as an introduction and preparation not only to the Psalms (David) but also to all of the Writings (motif of exile and return).[193]

---

193. Regarding the hermeneutical importance of the "exile-and-return" model for the Hebrew Bible, see Hendrik J. Koorevaar, "The Torah Model as Original Macrostructure of the Hebrew Canon," *ZAW* 122 (2010) 64–80.

Framework
The "two houses": House of David / House of God
The Torah and the "two ways": turning to God / turning away from God

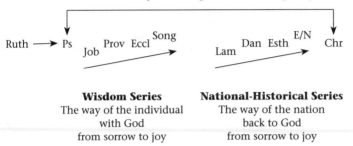

Wisdom Series   **National-Historical Series**
The way of the individual   The way of the nation
with God   back to God
from sorrow to joy   from sorrow to joy

The Rationale and the Variant Orders

Most of the extant orders without a grouped Megillot (there are 29 orders attested in about 50 manuscripts, which are mostly from medieval times)[194] more or less resemble the order of Baba Batra. Studying the variants, we can see that some sections of the sequence vary more than others. This gives us additional insights into which of the alleged criteria were decisive and which were less important. The discussion can only be summarized here.[195]

On the one hand, the formal criteria as given by Beckwith and Brandt would allow the two books of Psalms and Job to appear as either Ps–Job or Job–Ps, depending on how one dates Job. Despite the fact that Job is often connected to the time of the patriarchs, virtually none of the extant manuscripts chooses Job–Ps; other criteria must have been involved. Again, the formal criteria of Beckwith would allow the books of Chr and Ezr/Neh to appear as Chr–Ezr/Neh more than as Ezr/Neh–Chr. However, in only 2 of 51 instances does the order Chr–Ezr/Neh appear. Therefore, chronology does not seem vital.

On the other hand, Beckwith's criterion of decreasing length and Brandt's criterion of authorship would force Job always to appear before Proverbs. However, in a couple of instances, Job and Proverbs appear in the order Prov–Job. Again, from the criterion of chronology, Daniel should always appear before Esther. However, they appear in the order Esth–Dan in about one-third of the manuscripts. To be sure, one could date Daniel after Esther by referring to its prophetic sections. Thus, Daniel should be placed

---

194. Beckwith, *OT Canon*, 452–57; Brandt, *Endgestalten*, 156–58; see Steinberg's table 1 on pp. 168–169 of this volume.

195. For a detailed presentation, see Steinberg, *Ketuvim*, 132151.

after Ezra/Nehemiah or even at the end of the Writings—which, however, is never the case. The frequent sequence Esth–Dan–Ezr/Neh cannot be explained by chronology alone.

The formal rationale based on genre, chronology, and decreasing length is easily disrupted in several of the variants. Thus, these criteria do not seem to be as predominant as Beckwith and Brandt argue. Rather, it is the continuation of theological criteria that is evident, even in many of the variants.

Psalms continues to frame the collection in most manuscripts, which is probably the reason that it does not switch places with Job. In the same way, Chronicles is seen as a summarizing book, preventing it from being switched with Ezra/Nehemiah. Very often, Ruth is placed before the Psalms, which again cannot be explained from formal criteria. On the other hand, Job and Proverbs are often switched—and they can be switched without destroying the idea of a wisdom series: Proverbs is well fashioned as an alternative introductory book to the subcollection. Again, the positions of Daniel and Esther can be reversed without affecting the interpretation of the national-historical subcollection as spanning from the destruction until the restoration of political autonomy with either order (Lam–Dan–Esth–Ezr/Neh or Lam–Esth–Dan–Ezr/Neh). In sum, about 60% of the extant manuscripts (without Megillot grouped) can be interpreted from a theological angle in a way that is similar to the arguments given above for Baba Batra.

To be sure, there are variants that weaken the theological coherence as interpreted above. For example, in one of the manuscripts, Ezra/Nehemiah is placed after Chronicles, possibly with the purpose of correcting what seemed to be a chronological flaw. In some other cases, new and interesting arrangements occur—for instance, by placing Job in the middle of the national-historical subcollection (thus Lam–Esth–*Job*–Dan–Ezr/Neh), connecting the suffering of the individual to the story of the suffering nation, while at the same time reducing the wisdom subcollection to a proper "Solomonic" collection.

In a number of manuscripts, Chronicles stands at the beginning of the Writings rather than at the end. There, it still has a summarizing function for the two preceding canonical divisions. In some cases, Chronicles stands at the beginning and Ezra/Nehemiah at the end of the Writings, and thus they form a framework around the collection, which places the other books in the context of being on the verge of return from exile.

One may conclude, first, that even if there are only a few manuscripts that directly follow the sequence of b. B. Bat. 14b, many others do so with only slight variations. This demonstrates the prominence that b. B. Bat. 14b has had—not in the sense of a strict decree but in the sense of a beginning basis. Second, even though we do not have direct access to the intentions behind the arrangement presented in b. B. Bat. 14b, by observing sections of stability and of variety in the related manuscripts, we understand that the most prominent criteria are those of content and theology rather than form; that is, Psalms is a framing work at the beginning of the Writings, with regard to its importance and its comprehensive character, mostly preceded by Ruth as being a preparation to it; Chronicles' separation from the other narrative books and its framing position show an appreciation for its summarizing character. The three books of Ruth, Psalms, and Chronicles are in framing positions in almost all of the medieval manuscripts that do not group the Megillot. Also, the distinction between a wisdom subcollection (however, in different orders) and a national-historical subcollection (in different orders) is retained in about three-fourths of the witnesses.

The Leningrad Codex

Now that we have examined the talmudic order, it is time to look at the Masoretic order. This is not a subject that has been examined in the canon debate, so in the following section we will present our view, which can be investigated more thoroughly in our other publications.[196] The order of the books in the Masoretic tradition as found in the Cairo, Aleppo, and Leningrad codices, which are dated from the ninth to early eleventh centuries C.E., are as follows: Chronicles, Psalms, Job, Proverbs, Ruth, Song of Songs, Ecclesiastes, Lamentations, Esther, Daniel, and Ezra/Nehemiah. This is, as Stone argues, one of two ancient Jewish orders.[197] In this section, we examine the differences and similarities between the talmudic and MT orders in relation to their structural logic and then the MT order's association with the liturgical practice of reading the Megillot at the five major festivals in Judaism, since this development is usually given as evidence for the order's late date.

Talmud	Ruth	**Ps**	**Job**	**Prov**	Eccl	Song	*Lam*	*Dan*	*Esth*	E/N	Chr
MT	Chr	**Ps**	**Job**	**Prov**	Ruth	Song	Eccl	*Lam*	*Esth*	*Dan*	E/N

First, there are substantial differences between these two arrangements, but they should not be exaggerated, since the similarities are far greater. The following is only a sketch, which one can explore at greater length by following the sources in the footnotes.

The most striking difference is the position of Ruth after Proverbs rather than before the Psalter. Located in front of the Psalter, Ruth functions as an introduction to David in the Psalms. Ruth's location after Proverbs in the MT is anchored by strong textual connections to the very end of Proverbs.[198] Ruth does not have connections to the Song, in our view.

Chronicles is located first rather than last, but this difference is not major. One would expect the last book to join the collection to be located at

---

196. Steinberg, *Ketuvim*; and Stone, *Megilloth*.
197. Stone (ibid., 113–16) argues that the MT order predates the talmudic order.
198. See the article by Stone in this volume.

either end.[199] This may indicate that the book was not able to break apart existing subcollections (on this, see below regarding Ezra/Nehemiah and the national-historical subcollection). Its associations are strongest with Ezra/Nehemiah, and this connection is highlighted by each order. If it is last, it immediately follows Ezra/Nehemiah and, if first, it forms a bracket around the collection in conjunction with Ezra/Nehemiah.[200]

The MT locates Ecclesiastes, not after Proverbs as in the Talmud, but between the Song of Songs and Lamentations. In both orders, it follows Proverbs and is juxtaposed with the Song of Songs. This keeps the "Solomonic" books together, possibly because the prologue to Proverbs (1:1–7) and the epilogue to Ecclesiastes (12:9–14) were redacted to form brackets on the outer edges of a Solomonic/wisdom collection.[201] The basic logic of this redaction remains in place in both the talmudic and MT arrangements since, in both, Ecclesiastes either directly follows Proverbs or brackets the end of the collection, which includes Ruth and the Song of Songs. Ruth's inclusion in this subcollection of the MT fits with the "son of David" superscriptions in Prov 1:1 and Eccl 1:1.

In both the talmudic and MT arrangements, Psalms, Job, and Proverbs are in the same order (as indicated in bold in the chart above). Job has strong connections to Psalms (which are more intelligible if Job follows the Psalter)[202] and to Proverbs (which emphasizes the wisdom themes in both books).[203]

Again, in both orders, Lamentations, Esther, Daniel, and Ezra/Nehemiah (in italics above in the chart) are grouped together, though the order of Daniel and Esther is reversed in the talmudic arrangement (probably to fit chronological sensibilities).[204] Steinberg has labeled this a national-historical series. This subcollection moves from the anguish of the destruction of Jerusalem, through the exile in Esther and Daniel, to the joy (although mixed with tears) over the city's and temple's restoration in Ezra/Nehemiah. Esther has a few connections to the end of Lamentations and a number of strong connections to Daniel 1–6, especially Daniel 1.[205] This subcollection remains intact even though Chronicles is part of the Writings. The textual overlap between the end of Chronicles and beginning of Ezra, in combination with the historical progression of the books would lead one to think that Chronicles should precede Ezra/Nehemiah, but this

---

199. See Steins's and Koorevaar's articles in this volume.

200. Freedman, *Unity*, 76–77. Steinberg, *Ketuvim*, 146–47; 152–53.

201. For an examination of Ecclesiastes as part of a wisdom collection, see Steinberg, *Ketuvim*, 446–49; and for its possible redaction in conjunction with Proverbs, see Stone, *Megilloth*, 193–201.

202. See Kynes's article in this volume.

203. See Steinberg's essay in this volume. See Richard Schultz, "Unity or Diversity in Wisdom Theology? A Canonical and Covenantal Perspective," *TynBul* 48 (1997) 271–306.

204. Beckwith, *OT Canon*, 159–60.

205. For the details of this argument, see Stone, *Megilloth*, 140–81. See Steinberg's similar conclusions in *Ketuvim*, 449–50.

does not happen in either order. In our view, and this is of course speculative, this does not occur because the national-historical subcollection was already well established, and Chronicles' inclusion before Ezra/Nehemiah would break the collection apart.[206]

The similarities between these two arrangements far outweigh the differences, and the arrangement of both orders is not random.[207] Only Ruth's canonical context is substantially altered. This sketch posits neither one overall structure that organizes the Writings nor the idea that one theme unites them; instead, one can see that most books are in dialogue with at least one other book in the collection. Some themes, like wisdom, resonate across several books, but this does not extend to every book in the collection. The canonical shape of the collection foregrounds these relationships, so that one can better see Job's relationship with the Psalter, or Ruth's with Proverbs, or again, the way that Daniel frames the story of Esther. The nature of this dialogue is varied, with no two relationships the same. It is our contention that the Writings took their character as a collection over a long process in which books were shaped and located, in various degrees, by authors, redactors,[208] and compilers in order to highlight various relationships *between* books. This means that the books were not selected by some official council or group out of a wide religious literature without definite bounds. The collection grew until it ultimately fossilized. The canonical process is primarily one of growth to maturity rather than a process of trimming or rejecting other texts.

This bring us to the second, related issue of the MT order's association with reading the five books of the Megillot at the five major festivals in Judaism. In this practice, the Song of Songs is read at Passover, Ruth at Weeks, Lamentations at the Ninth of Ab, Ecclesiastes at Tabernacles, and Esther at Purim. The almost unanimous view is that the MT order is late, because it follows the liturgical reading in grouping the five Megillot together. Since this reading practice is a posttalmudic development, the order must also be dated to this period or later. The MT *rearranged* the talmudic order of books. Once made into a subcollection in the Writings, these five books were then rearranged again for chronological reasons.[209] Ruth, for instance, was moved from following the Song of Songs to preceding it, since Ruth is set in

---

206. One may object to this view, since it appears to be based on the last sentence of 2 Chronicles and the first of Ezra that the author/redactor of Chronicles meant for the book to precede Ezra/Nehemiah. In the view of Stone, however, this connection would serve the purpose of linking the two books over the span of the Writings as a whole in the MT, where they form a bracket around the entire collection, rather than linking the books in a contiguous manner (which is not found in the Jewish tradition or, for that matter, very often in the Greek tradition).

207. The number of possible arrangements for the 11 books is 39,916,800.

208. Regarding the idea of context-sensitive redactions of the individual Writings, Steinberg is rather hesitant.

209. Beckwith, *OT Canon*, 202–8. Cf. Childs, *OT as Scripture*, 501–2.

the days of the judges, before David, while the Song has strong associations with Solomon. This view has remained unchallenged for the past century.[210]

Stone offers six objections to this standard theory. First, the order of the Megillot does not follow the order of the liturgy. If the liturgy were responsible for their movement, then for them to be recast chronologically would be a step away from the reason that they were moved in the first place.

Second, this common theory does not explain why Chronicles would be moved from last place in the talmudic order to first place in the MT. It has no connection to the five festivals.

Third, it is likely that the reading of all five of the Megillot liturgically developed *after* the MT order. Esther and Lamentations (at least privately) were read liturgically during the talmudic period, and the posttalmudic minor tractate Soperim (14:3, 18) states that Ruth, the Song of Songs, Lamentations, and Esther were read liturgically, but there is no mention of Ecclesiastes. Dating this minor tractate is very difficult, but it probably should be dated between the 8th and 10th centuries C.E. The prayer book Mahzor Vitray, dated to 1208 C.E., provides the first evidence that Ecclesiastes joined the liturgy. The first complete evidence for the MT order is found in the Cairo and Aleppo codices, which can be dated to 896 and 925 C.E., respectively. If we date Soperim to the 10th century, then the practice of reading Ruth and the Song liturgically postdates the MT order. No matter what date we choose for Soperim, the first sign of the liturgical reading of Ecclesiastes occurs 300 years after the first evidence for the MT order. The MT order, then, predates this practice and thus cannot be the result of it.

Fourth, b. Ber. 57b lists four of the five Megillot in the order of Song of Songs, Ecclesiastes, Lamentations, and Esther. This is the same as the MT order, which predates Soperim 14 by several hundred years, even if one dates the minor tractate to 800 C.E.

Fifth, Esther and Lamentations fit well with their respective festivals, and Ruth and the Song less so (Song of Songs is strongly connected to Passover in the targum), while Ecclesiastes appears only superficially to be connected to Tabernacles. If these five books were already associated in the MT arrangement, then the reading of Esther and Lamentations would have been a first step that would naturally have led to the reading of the other three books. It is possible that their liturgical association was generated from their canonical association and not the reverse, as is so commonly argued.

Sixth, it seems unlikely that Ruth's place in the MT order after Proverbs is completely the result of chance. In the standard theory, Ruth was moved from before the Psalter into the Megillot to be part of the liturgy and then moved, yet again, for chronological reasons, to be placed at the head of the subcollection, which fortuitously placed it right after Proverbs. This series

---

210. For more details on this subject and the arguments presented here, see Stone, *Megilloth*, 105–11.

of moves excludes explanations that Ruth was placed by some late com-
piler after Proverbs for thematic reasons, since no such motivation is part of
the standard approach. Stone thinks it is more likely that the strong textual
and thematic connections between the very end of Proverbs and Ruth are
due to their canonical association.[211]

The historical situation is complex and our evidence incomplete, but in
the judgment of Stone the standard theory is questionable, which leads to
the possibility that, while the MT order comes into our purview in the late
8th century C.E., it had ancient roots.

Conclusion

We maintain that the Hebrew canon was closed in mainstream Judaism
considerably before the 1st century C.E., as seen primarily in the testimony
of Josephus and 4 Ezra, each of whom addresses canonical issues explicitly.
Although the two sources number the books differently, it is quite likely
that each collection contained the same books, since the two ways of numbering the books are known from other sources. The explicit nature of these
two texts should give them greater weight in proportion to circumstantial
evidence from Qumran and other quarters. There were other conceptions
of sacred texts in the 1st century C.E., possibly at Qumran, and also according to the author of Jude and the author of 4 Ezra—to name only three
examples. The Hebrew canon was not universally adhered to, but neither
was it only one position among a number of equally valid alternatives. The
large number of NT allusions to and scriptural citations from the OT canon
confirms this.

The shape of the canon is very difficult to discern during the Second
Temple period. The prologue to Ben Sira probably indicates that there was
a tripartite canon during this time, but whether it was exactly the same as
the talmudic or the masoretic collection is impossible to determine from
the available evidence. Despite strong proposals that the NT confirms a
tripartite canon, the evidence is far from clear. Almost everywhere, the NT
does seem to assume a complete collection of sacred literature, but again,
the exact shape of this collection cannot be determined from the evidence.

We argued that order was significant before the rise of codices, as demonstrated by the compilation practices that bound together the Law and
the Former Prophets. The temple archive in Jerusalem may have been a
place where sacred space gave physical shape to the arrangement of the
scrolls, possibly on shelves or in baskets. The holiness associated with the
temple space would have made the arrangement of the canon conceptually
possible, perhaps even vital, since everything in these spaces was arranged
with the utmost care. Two of the most important arrangements to examine
are the talmudic, found in b. B. Bat. 14b, and the masoretic, found in the

---

211. Ibid., 130–36.

Leningrad Codex. Both of us have examined each order in detail and found their shapes to be significant and related.

In our view, the received form of the canon—both in its tripartite structure and even in the arrangements of the books within these divisions—is organically linked to the canonical process. The canonical books "grew up" together much like a tree in the forest matures and takes shape in relation to those around it.

Our goal in this essay is not to bring an end to the canon debate but to help define the contours of the discussion and foster meaningful dialogue. We refer readers who are new to the debate to the following bibliography, not because it is exhaustive, but because we think it represents the various positions presented in this essay. Finally, it is vital to note that the paucity of the historical evidence for the formation of the Hebrew canon leaves much unexplained and any final appraisal in serious doubt. We think it is necessary to add a dimension to this debate by examining the books in the OT for signs of their compilation into well-ordered collections. This essay has only touched on this issue, but many of the other essays in this volume explore this issue in more depth.

Bibliography

Ackroyd, Peter R. "The Open Canon." Pp. 209–24 in *Studies in the Religious Tradition of the Old Testament*. London: SCM, 1987.

Anderson, G. W. "Canonical and Non-Canonical." Pp. 113–59 in *The Cambridge History of the Bible*, vol. 1: *From the Beginnings to Jerome*. Edited by P. R. Ackroyd and C. F. Evans. Cambridge: Cambridge University Press, 1970.

Barr, James. "Childs' Introduction to the Old Testament as Scripture." *JSOT* 16 (1980) 12–23.

Barthel, Jörg. "Die kanonhermeneutische Debatte seit Gerhard von Rad: Anmerkungen zu neueren Entwürfen." Pp. 1–26 in *Kanonhermeneutik: Vom Lesen und Verstehen der christlichen Bibel*. Edited by Bernd Janowski. Theologie Interdisziplinär 1. Neukirchen-Vluyn: Neukirchener Verlag, 2007.

Barton, John. "Canon and Old Testament Interpretation." Pp. 37–52 in *In Search of True Wisdom: Essays in Old Testament Interpretation in Honour of Ronald E. Clements*. Edited by Edward Ball. JSOTSup 300. Sheffield: Sheffield Academic Press, 2000.

———. "Canonical Approaches Ancient and Modern." Pp. 199–209 in *The Biblical Canons*. Edited by J. M. Auwers. BETL 163. Leuven: Leuven University Press, 2003.

———. "Canons of the Old Testament." Pp. 200–222 in *Texts in Context*. Edited by A. D. H. Mayes. Oxford: Oxford University Press, 2000.

———. *Holy Writings, Sacred Text: The Canon of Early Christianity*. Louisville: Westminster John Knox, 1998.

———. "The Old Testament Canon of the New Testament Church." Review of *The Old Testament Canon of the New Testament Church and Its Background in Early Judaism* by Roger T. Beckwith. *Theology* 90 (1987) 63–65.

———. *Oracles of God: Perceptions of Ancient Prophecy in Israel after the Exile*. London: Darton, Longman & Todd, 1986.

————. *Oracles of God: Perceptions of Ancient Prophecy in Israel after the Exile*. 2nd ed. Oxford: Oxford University Press, 2007.

————. *Reading the Old Testament: Method in Biblical Study*. Louisville: Westminster John Knox, 1996.

————. "The Significance of a Fixed Canon of the Hebrew Bible." Pp. 67–83 in *Hebrew Bible / Old Testament: The History of Its Interpretation—From the Beginnings to the Middle Ages*. Edited by Magne Sæbø. Göttingen: Vandenhoeck and Ruprecht, 1996.

Beckwith, Roger T. "Formation of the Hebrew Bible." Pp. 39–86 in *Mikra: Text, Translation, Reading and Interpretation of the Hebrew Bible in Ancient Judaism and Early Christianity*. Edited by M. J. Mulder. Minneapolis: Fortress, 1990.

————. "A Modern Theory of the Old Testament Canon." *VT* 49 (1991) 385–95.

————. *The Old Testament Canon of the New Testament Church and Its Background in Early Judaism*. London: SPCK, 1985.

Blau, L. "The Five Megillot." Pp. 429–51 in vol. 8 of *The Jewish Encyclopedia*. Edited by Isidore Singer and Cyrus Adler. New York: Funk & Wagnalls, 1912.

Blenkinsopp, Joseph. *Prophecy and Canon: A Contribution to the Study of Jewish Origins*. Notre Dame, IN: University of Notre Dame Press, 1977.

Brandt, Peter. *Endgestalten des Kanons: Das Arrangement der Schriften Israels in der jüdischen und christlichen Bibel*. BBB 31. Berlin: Philo, 2001.

Bruce, F. F. *The Canon of Scripture*. Leicester: Inter-Varsity, 1988.

Carr, David M. "Canonization in the Context of Community: An Outline for the Formation of the Tanakh and the Christian Bible." Pp. 22–64 in *A Gift of God in Due Season: Essays on Scripture and Community in Honor of James A. Sanders*. Edited by Richard D. Weis and David M. Carr. LHBOTS. Sheffield: Sheffield Academic Press, 1996.

————. *Writing on the Tablet of the Heart: Origins of Scripture and Literature*. Oxford: Oxford University Press, 2005.

Chapman, Stephen. "The Canon Debate: What It Is and Why It Matters." *JTI* 4 (2010) 273–94.

————. "A Canonical Approach to Old Testament Theology? Deuteronomy 34:10–12 and Malachi 3:22–24 as Programmatic Conclusions." *HBT* 25 (2003) 121–45.

————. *The Law and the Prophets: A Study in Old Testament Canon Formation*. FAT 27. Tübingen: Mohr, 2000.

Childs, Brevard. *Biblical Theology of the Old and New Testaments: Theological Reflection on the Christian Bible*. Minneapolis: Fortress, 1993.

————. *The Church's Guide for Reading Paul: The Canonical Shaping of the Pauline Corpus*. Grand Rapids, MI: Eerdmans, 2008.

————. *Introduction to the Old Testament as Scripture*. Minneapolis: Fortress, 1979.

Collins, John J. "Before the Canon: Scriptures in Second Temple Judaism." Pp. 225–41 in *Old Testament Interpretation: Past, Present, and Future—Essays in Honor of Gene M. Tucker*. Edited by James L. Mays, David L. Petersen, and Kent H. Richards. Edinburgh: T. & T. Clark, 1995.

Cook, Stephen. *On the Question of the "Cessation of Prophecy" in Ancient Judaism*. Texts and Studies in Ancient Judaism 145. Tübingen: Mohr Siebeck, 2011.

Cross, Frank M. "The Biblical Scrolls from Qumran and the Canonical Text." Pp. 67–75 in *The Bible and the Dead Sea Scrolls*. Edited by James H. Charlesworth. Waco, TX: Baylor University Press, 2006.

————. *From Epic to Canon: History and Literature in Ancient Israel.* Baltimore: Johns Hopkins University Press, 1998.

Davies, Philip R. *Scribes and Schools: The Canonization of the Hebrew Scriptures.* Louisville: Westminster John Knox, 1998.

Dempster, Stephen G. "An 'Extraordinary Fact': Torah and Temple and the Contours of the Hebrew Canon. Part 1/2." *TynBul* 48 (1997) 23–56, 191–218.

————. "From Many Texts to One: The Formation of the Hebrew Bible." Pp. 19–56 in *The World of the Aramaeans*, vol. 1: *Biblical Studies in Honour of Paul-Eugène Dion.* Edited by P. M. Daviau, John W. Wevers, and Michael Weigl. JSOTSup 324. Sheffield: Sheffield Academic Press, 2001.

Diebner, Bernd J. "Erwägungen zum Prozeß der Sammlung des dritten Teils der antik-jüdischen (hebräischen) Bibel, der Ketuvim." *DBAT* 21 (1985) 139–99.

————. "'Mein Großvater Jesus'." *DBAT* 16 (1982) 1–37.

Dohmen, Christoph. "Der biblische Kanon in der Diskussion." *TRev* 6 (1995) 451–60.

Dohmen, Christoph, and Manfred Oeming. *Biblischer Kanon: Warum und Wozu?* Quaestiones disputatae 137. Freiburg: Herder, 1992.

————. "Der Kanon des Alten Testaments." Pp. 277–97 in *Das Alte Testament als christliche Bibel in orthodoxer und westlicher Sicht.* Edited by Ivan Z. Dimitrov, James D. G. Dunn, Ulrich Luz, and Karl-Wilhelm Niebuhr. WUNT 174. Tübingen: Mohr Siebeck, 2004.

Dohmen, Christoph, and Thomas Söding, eds. *Eine Bibel – Zwei Testamente: Positionen biblischer Theologie.* Uni-Taschenbücher 1893. Paderborn: Schöningh, 1995.

Driver, Daniel. *Brevard Childs: Biblical Theologian.* FAT 2/46. Tübingen: Mohr Siebeck, 2010.

Freedman, David Noel. *The Unity of the Hebrew Bible.* Ann Arbor: University of Michigan Press, 1993.

Harrington, Daniel J. "The Old Testament Apocrypha in the Early Church and Today." Pp. 196–210 in *The Canon Debate.* Edited by Lee Martin McDonald and James A. Sanders. Peabody, MA: Hendrickson, 2002.

Harris, R. Laird. *Inspiration and Canonicity of the Scriptures: An Historical and Exegetical Study.* Grand Rapids, MI: Zondervan, 1995.

Hengel, Martin. *The Septuagint as Christian Scripture: Its Prehistory and the Problem of Its Canon.* Translated by Mark E. Biddle. Edinburgh: T. & T. Clark, 2002.

Hieke, Thomas, ed. *Formen des Kanons: Studien zu Ausprägungen des biblischen Kanons von der Antike bis zum 19. Jh.* SBS 228. Stuttgart: Katholisches Bibelwerk, 2013.

Hossfeld, Frank-Lothar, and Erich Zenger. "Neue und alte Wege der Psalmenexegese: Antworten auf die Fragen von M. Millard und R. Rendtorff." *BibInt* 4 (1996) 332–45.

Hultin, Jeremy. "Jude's Citation of 1 Enoch." Pp. 113–28 in *Jewish and Christian Scriptures: The Function of 'Canonical' and 'Non Canonical' Religious Texts.* Edited by James H. Charlesworth and Lee Martin McDonald. Jewish and Christian Texts 7. London: T. & T. Clark, 2010.

Josephus. *Against Apion.* Translated by John Barclay. Translation and Commentary 10. Leiden: Brill, 2007.

Kaiser, Otto. *Einleitung in das Alte Testament: Eine Einführung in ihre Ergebnisse und Probleme.* 5th ed. Gütersloh: Mohn, 1984.

Katz, Peter. "The Old Testament Canon in Palestine and Alexandria." Pp. 72–98 in *The Canon and the Masorah of the Hebrew Bible*. Edited by Sid Leiman. New York: Ktav, 1974.

Klijn, A. F. J. "A Library of Scriptures in Jerusalem?" *Texte und Untersuchungen zur Geschichte der altchristlichen Literatur* 124 (1977) 265–72.

Kooij, A. van der, and Karel van der Toorn, eds. *Canonization and Decanonization: Papers Presented to the International Conference of the Leiden Institute for the Study of Religions (LISOR), Held at Leiden, 9–10 January 1997*. Studies in the History of Religions 82. Leiden: Brill, 1997.

Koorevaar, Hendrik J. "The Torah Model as Original Macrostructure of the Hebrew Canon." *ZAW* 122 (2010) 64–80.

Kraemer, David. "The Formation of the Rabbinic Canon: Authority and Boundaries." *JBL* 110 (1991) 613–30.

Lebram, J. C. H. "Aspekte der alttestamentlichen Kanonbildung." *VT* 18 (1968) 173–89.

Leiman, Sid Z. *The Canonization of Hebrew Scripture: The Talmudic and Midrashic Evidence*. Transactions of the Connecticut Academy of Arts and Sciences 47. Hamden, CT: Archon, 1976.

———. "Josephus and the Canon of the Bible." Pp. 50–96 in *Josephus: The Bible and History*. Edited by Louis H. Feldman and Gohei Hata. Leiden: Brill, 1989.

Lim, Timothy. *The Formation of the Jewish Canon*. New Haven, CT: Yale University Press, 2013.

Lohfink, Norbert. "Eine Bibel – Zwei Testamente." Pp. 71–81 in *Eine Bibel – Zwei Testamente: Positionen biblischer Theologie*. Edited by Christoph Dohmen and Thomas Söding. Uni-Taschenbücher 1893. Paderborn: Schöningh, 1995.

Margolis, Max L. *The Hebrew Scriptures in the Making*. Repr., Philadelphia: Jewish Publication Society, 1948.

Mason, Steven. *Flavius Josephus on the Pharisees: A Composition-Critical Study*. Leiden: Brill, 1991.

———. "Josephus and His Twenty-Two Book Canon." Pp. 110–27 in *The Canon Debate*. Edited by Lee Martin McDonald and James A. Sanders. Peabody, MA: Hendrickson, 2002.

Mason, Steven, and R. A. Kraft. "Josephus on Canon and Scripture." Pp. 217–35 in *Hebrew Bible/Old Testament*, vol. 1/1: *The History of Its Interpretation*. Edited by Magne Sæbø. Göttingen: Vandenhoeck & Ruprecht, 1996.

McDonald, Lee M. *The Biblical Canon*. Peabody, MA: Hendrickson, 2007.

McDonald, Lee M., and James A. Sanders, eds. *The Canon Debate*. Peabody, MA: Hendrickson, 2008.

———. *The Formation of the Christian Biblical Canon*. Rev. ed. Peabody, MA: Hendrickson, 1995.

McDonough, Sean M. "'And David Was Old, Advanced in Years': 2 Samuel 24:18–25, 1 Kings 1, and Genesis 23–24." *VT* 49 (1999) 128–31.

Miller, John W. *The Origins of the Bible: Rethinking Canon History*. New York: Paulist Press, 1994.

Morgan, Donn F. *Between Text and Community*. Minneapolis: Fortress, 1990.

Murphy, Roland E. "Old Testament/Tanakh: Canon and Interpretation." Pp. 11–29 in *Hebrew Bible or Old Testament? Studying the Bible in Judaism and Christianity*. Edited by Roger Brooks and John J. Collins. Notre Dame, IN: University of Notre Dame Press, 1990.

Neusner, Jacob. *Midrash in Context: Exegesis in Formative Judaism,* vol. 1: *The Foundations of Judaism: Method, Teleology, Doctrine.* BJS 141. Philadelphia: Fortress, 1883.

———. *Torah: From Scroll to Symbol in Formative Judaism.* Philadelphia: Fortress, 1885.

Peels, H. G. L. "The Blood from Abel to Zechariah (Matthew 23:35; Luke 11:50f.) and the Canon of the Old Testament." *ZAW* 113 (2001) 583–601.

———. "The Qumran Biblical Scrolls: The Scriptures of Late Second Temple Judaism." Pp. 67–87 in *The Dead Sea Scrolls in Their Historical Context.* Edited by T. Lim. Edinburgh: T. & T. Clark, 2000.

Riedel, Wilhelm. *Alttestamentliche Untersuchungen.* Erstes Heft. Leipzig: Deichert, 1902.

Rüger, Hans Peter. "Das Werden des christlichen Alten Testaments." *JBTh* 3 (1988) 175–89.

Ryle, Herbert E. *The Canon of the Old Testament.* New York: Macmillan, 1892.

Sanders, James A. *Canon and Community.* Philadelphia: Fortress, 1984.

———. "Canon: Hebrew Bible." Pp. 837–52 in vol. 6 of *ABD.*

———. *From Sacred Story to Sacred Text.* Philadelphia: Fortress, 1987.

———. "Introduction." Pp. 3–18 in *The Canon Debate.* Edited by Lee Martin McDonald and James A. Sanders. Peabody, MA: Hendrickson, 2002.

———. "The Issue of Closer in the Canonical Process." Pp. 252–63 in *The Canon Debate.* Edited by Lee Martin McDonald and James A. Sanders. Peabody, MA: Hendrickson, 2002.

———. "The Old Testament Canon of the New Testament Church." *ThTo* 44 (1987) 131–34.

———. *Torah and Canon.* Eugene, OR: Wipf & Stock, 2000.

Schmid, Konrad. *Genesis and the Moses Story.* Translated by James Nogalski. Siphrut 3. Winona Lake, IN: Eisenbrauns, 2010.

Schniedewind, William. *How the Bible Became a Book.* Cambridge: Cambridge University Press, 2004.

Schultz, Richard. "Unity or Diversity in Wisdom Theology? A Canonical and Covenantal Perspective." *TynBul* 48 (1997) 271–306.

Seitz, Christopher. "The Canonical Approach and Theological Interpretation." Pp. 58–110 in *Canon and Biblical Interpretation.* Edited by Craig Bartholomew and Anthony Thiselton. Scripture and Hermeneutics 7. Grand Rapids, MI: Zondervan, 2006.

———. *The Goodly Fellowship of the Prophets: The Achievement of Association in Canon Formation.* Acadia Studies in Bible and Theology. Grand Rapids, MI: Baker Academic, 2009.

Sheppard, Gerald T. "Canon." Pp. 62–69 in vol. 3 of *The Encyclopedia of Religion.* Edited by Lindsey Jones. New York: Macmillan, 1987.

———. "Canonical Criticism." Pp. 861–66 in vol. 1 of *ABD.*

———. "Canonization: Hearing the Voice of the Same God through Historically Dissimilar Traditions." *Int* 37 (1982) 21–33.

———. *Future of the Bible: Beyond Liberalism and Literalism.* Toronto: United Church Publishing, 1990.

———. *Wisdom as a Hermeneutical Construct: A Study in the Sapientializing of the Old Testament.* BZAW 151. Berlin: de Gruyter, 1980.

Smend, Rudolf. *Die Entstehung des Alten Testaments.* Stuttgart: Kohlhammer, 1978.

Steck, Odil Hannes. "Der Kanon des hebräischen Alten Testaments: Historische Materialien für eine ökumenische Perspektive." Pp. 231–52 in *Vernunft des Glaubens: Wissenschaftliche Theologie und kirchliche Lehre: FS W. Pannenberg.* Edited by Jan Rohls and Gunther Wenz. Göttingen: Vandenhoeck & Ruprecht, 1988.

Steinberg, Julius. *Die Ketuvim: Ihr Aufbau und ihre Botschaft.* BBB 152. Hamburg: Philo, 2006.

Steinmann, Andrew. *The Oracles of God: The Old Testament Canon.* St. Louis: Concordia Academic, 1999.

Steins, Georg. "Der Bibelkanon als Denkmal und Text: Zu einigen methodologischen Aspekten kanonischer Schriftauslegung." Pp. 177–98 in *The Biblical Canons.* Edited by J. M. Auwers and H. J. de Jonge. BETL 163. Leuven: Leuven University Press, 2003.

———. "The Biblical Canon according to Lee McDonald: An Evaluation." *European Journal of Theology* 18 (2009) 55–64.

———. *Die 'Bindung Isaaks' im Kanon (Gen 22):* Grundlagen und Programm einer kanonisch-intertextuellen Lektüre. *Mit einer Spezialbibliographie zu Gen 22.* HBS 20. Freiburg: Herder, 1999.

———. *Die Chronik als kanonisches Abschlussphänomen: Studien zur Entstehung und Theologie von 1/2 Chronik.* BBB 93. Weinheim: Athenäum, 1995.

———. "Torabindung und Kanonabschluß: Zur Entstehung und kanonischen Funktion der Chronikbücher." Pp. 213–56 in *Die Tora als Kanon für Juden und Christen.* Edited by Erich Zenger. HBS 10. Freiburg: Herder, 1996.

Stemberger, Günter. "Jabne und der Kanon." *JBTh* 3 (1988) 163–74.

Stone, Timothy J. *The Compilational History of the Megilloth: Canon, Contoured Intertextuality and Meaning in the Writings.* FAT 2/59. Tübingen: Mohr Siebeck, 2013.

Strack, Hermann L., and Günter Stemberger. *Einleitung in Talmud und Midrasch.* 7th ed. Munich: Beck, 1982.

Stuhlmacher, Peter. "Old Testament Apocrypha and Pseudepigrapha for Understanding Jesus and Christology." Pp. 1–15 in *The Apocrypha in Ecumenical Perspective.* Edited by S. Meurer. Translated by P. Ellingworth. United Bible Societies Monograph Series 6. New York: United Bible Societies, 1991.

Sundberg, Albert C. "The Old Testament Canon of the New Testament Church." *Int* 42 (1988) 78–82.

———. *The Old Testament of the Early Church.* HTS 20. Cambridge: Harvard University Press, 1964.

———. "The Protestant Old Testament Canon: Should It Be Re-Examined?" *CBQ* 28 (1966) 194–203.

Swanson, Theodore N. *The Closing of the Collection of Holy Scriptures: A Study in the History of the Canonization of the Old Testament.* Nashville: Vanderbilt University Press, 1970.

Talmon, S. "Heiliges Schrifttum und kanonische Bücher aus jüdischer Sicht: Überlegungen zur Ausbildung der Grösse 'Die Schrift' im Judentum." Pp. 45–79 in *Mitte der Schrift? Ein jüdisch-christliches Gespräch. Texte des Berner Symposions vom 6.–12. Januar 1985.* Edited by M. Klopfenstein, U. Luz, S. Talmon, and E. Tov. Judaica et Christiana 11. Bern: Peter Lang, 1987.

Toorn, Karel van der. *Scribal Culture and the Making of the Hebrew Bible.* Cambridge: Harvard University Press, 2007.

Tov, Emanuel. "Groups of Biblical Texts Found at Qumran." Pp. 85–102 in *Time to Prepare the Way in the Wilderness*. Edited by Devorah Dimant and Lawrence H. Schiffman. STDJ 16. Leiden: Brill, 1995.

———. "The Interpretive Significance of a Fixed Text and Canon of the Hebrew and the Greek Bible." Pp. 49–66 in *Hebrew Bible/Old Testament: The History of Its Interpretation—From the Beginnings to the Middle Ages*. Edited by Magne Sæbø, Chris Brekelmans, and Menahem Haran. Göttingen: Vandenhoeck & Ruprecht, 1996.

———. "The Nature and Background of Harmonizations in Biblical Manuscripts." *JSOT* 31 (1985) 3–29.

———. *Scribal Practices and Approaches Reflected in the Texts Found in the Judean Desert*. STDJ 54. Leiden: Brill, 2004.

———. *Textual Criticism of the Hebrew Bible*. Minneapolis: Fortress, 1992.

Ulrich, Eugene. "The Absence of 'Sectarian Variants' in the Jewish Scriptural Scrolls Found at Qumran." Pp. 179–95 in *The Bible as a Book*. Edited by Edward Herbert and Emanuel Tov. London: British Library, 2002.

———. "The Canonical Process, Textual Criticism, and the Latter Stages in the Composition of the Bible." Pp. 267–91 in *"Sha'arei Talmon": Studies Presented to Shemaryahu Talmon*. Winona Lake, IN: Eisenbrauns, 1992.

———. *The Dead Sea Scrolls and the Origins of the Bible*. Studies in the Dead Sea Scrolls and Related Literature. Leiden: Brill, 1999.

———. "The Non-attestation of a Tripartite Canon in 4QMMT." *CBQ* 65 (2003) 202–14.

———. "The Notion and Definition of Canon." Pp. 21–35 in *The Canon Debate*. Edited by Lee M. McDonald and James A. Sanders. Peabody, MA: Hendrickson, 2002.

———. "Qumran and the Canon of the Old Testament." Pp. 57–80 in *The Biblical Canons*. Edited by J. M. Auwers and H. J. de Jonge. BETL 163. Leuven University Press, 2003.

———. "The Qumran Biblical Scrolls: The Scriptures of Late Second Temple Judaism." Pp. 67–87 in *The Dead Sea Scrolls in Their Historical Context*. Edited by Timothy Lim et al. Edinburgh: T. & T. Clark, 2000.

VanderKam, James C. "Authoritative Literature in the Dead Sea Scrolls." *DSD* 5 (1998) 382–402.

———. *The Dead Sea Scrolls Today*. Grand Rapids, MI: Eerdmans, 1994.

———. *The Dead Sea Scrolls Today*. 2nd ed. Grand Rapids, MI: Eerdmans, 2010.

Wilson, Gerald H. *The Editing of the Hebrew Psalter*. SBLDS 76. Chico, CA: Scholars Press, 1985.

———. "'The Words of the Wise': The Intent and Significance of Qoheleth 12:9–14." *JBL* 103 (1984) 175–92.

Wolfenson, L. B. "Implications of the Place of Ruth in Editions, Manuscripts, and Canons of the Old Testament." *HUCA* (1924) 151–78.

Woude, Adam van der. "Fifty Years of Qumran Research." Pp. 1–45 in *The Dead Sea Scrolls after Fifty Years*. Edited by Peter W. Flint and James C. VanderKam. Boston: Brill, 1999.

Zevit, Ziony. "The Second–Third Century Canonization of the Hebrew Bible and Its Influence on Christian Canonization." Pp. 133–66 in *Canonization and Decanonization*. Edited by A. van der Kooij and Karel van der Toorn. Leiden: Brill, 1998.

Final Forms of the Writings:
The Jewish and Christian Traditions

The search for canonical order[1] has gained increased interest during recent decades, thanks to the influence of the exegetical schools that give
priority to the "later" developmental stages of Scripture rather than to the
oldest units of tradition. The question of the correct order of the books of
the Bible is especially crucial for approaches concentrating on the final
form of the text (*Endtext-Lektüre*).

The concept of a "correct sequence," however, is an anachronism arising
from the book age that is just as inappropriate when applied to the time
before the first codices appeared as it is to the age of hyperlinked Internet
texts. The concept of "arrangement" is more appropriate for describing the
interrelatedness of individual texts to the whole. It involves more than
linear sequencing; it can include grouping (including hierarchical groupings) and circular arrangements as well. The linear arrangement of books,
whether in manuscript codex or printed form, is a straitjacket that time
and again has forced editors of Bible editions to solve the problem of the
order in a linear or sequential way. In this respect, an examination of manuscripts and Bible editions over the past two millennia yields two results:
the first is that editors solved the problem of linear ordering in multiple
ways. The second is, however, that the multitude of individual orders can
be shown to result from only a limited number of multidimensional arrangement traditions.[2]

These constants that—despite the freedom to arrange or rearrange the
books—seem to be historically unalterable may play an important role
regarding the question of the normative power of the arrangement. From
a systematic perspective, there is some perplexity about this issue: to what
degree can activities of editorial arrangement be seen as part of Scripture's
formation? Are they part of the holy writ to which nothing may be added
or taken away? Or can they be handled rather arbitrarily, like questions of
font size and cover design? And are editorial activities of the early time,
that is, the Second Temple period, more normative than later editorial

---

1. The present contribution is based on my dissertation of 2001 and does not consider research that has been done since then: Peter Brandt, *Endgestalten des Kanons: Das
Arrangement der Schriften Israels in der jüdischen und christlichen Bibel* (Berlin: Philo, 2001).
2. Ibid.

Table 1. *Online Jewish Bible Editions*

Online Edition of the Jewish Publication Society[a]	Biblia Hebraica Stuttgartensia	The Complete Jewish Bible with Rashi Commentary[b]
Chronicles		
Psalms	Psalms	Psalms
Job	Job	Proverbs
Proverbs	Proverbs	Job
Ruth	Ruth	Song of Songs
Song of Songs	Song of Songs	Ruth
Ecclesiastes	Ecclesiastes	Lamentations
Lamentations	Lamentations	Ecclesiastes
Esther	Esther	Esther
Daniel	Daniel	Daniel
Ezra/Nehemiah	Ezra/Nehemiah	Ezra/Nehemiah
	Chronicles	Chronicles

a. "A Hebrew-English Bible according to the Masoretic Text and the JPS 1917 Edition," 2005, http://www.mechon-mamre.org/p/pt/pt0.htm.

b. Can be found at http://www.chabad.org/library/bible_cdo/aid/63255/jewish/The-Bible-with-Rashi.htm.

activities? How could they be, if normativity also resulted from living recognition in the form of Scripture reading and everyday usage, rather than solely from an authoritative canonical decision? This issue is not developed here.[3] The point is that editors needed to solve the problem of arrangement for themselves. Scripture itself does not and could not provide the solution. However, the above-mentioned constants within the different arrangements should have functioned as a guide for the tradition-conscious editor.

The purpose of this contribution is to set out the evidence for the various arrangements of the Writings over the last two millenia. There are unsettling signs of relative arbitrariness but also signs of orderliness within the variety. The first section presents the arrangements of the Writings in Jewish Bibles. The second, shorter section traces the placement of the Writings in Christian arrangements, concentrating on what can be called the "principal form" of the Old Testament but also includes traditions that directly connect to Jewish prototypes.

In this article, I will set aside the issue of whether or not a tripartite canon was firmly established in the Second Temple period, which would

3. I discuss it from a Catholic-theological point of view and from a biblical-hermeneutical and systematic-theological perspective in ibid., 383–439.

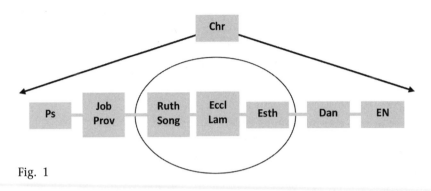

Fig. 1

mean that deviating Christian orders had to be understood as a conscious rejection of the Jewish canon.[4]

The Writings in Jewish Bibles

The Writings Today

Current Jewish Bibles contain a section of books labeled "Writings." This is the last of three subdivisions and comprises the following books: Psalms, Job, Proverbs, Ruth, Song of Songs, Ecclesiastes, Lamentations, Esther, Daniel, Ezra, Nehemiah, and Chronicles. This structure is found in critical editions such as *Biblia Hebraica Stuttgartensia* and is even reflected in current Jewish online Bible editions (see table 1).

Even at first glance, a few differences in the order of the books are evident:

- Chronicles can be placed at the beginning or at the end of the Writings.
- Job and Proverbs can be interchanged.
- Ruth and Song can be interchanged.
- Ecclesiastes and Lamentations can be interchanged.

Beyond these differences, the following primary arrangement emerges: Chronicles framed the Writings. Within this frame, we find a sequence consisting of three sections:

1. The books of Psalms, Job, and Proverbs, which are called the "Larger Ketubim"[5] or *Piwutim*, and are also referred to with the acronyms *emet* or *taʾam*[6]
2. The five festal scrolls (Megillot)
3. The sequence Daniel–Ezra/Nehemiah (see fig. 1 above).[7]

---

4. See my presentation of the state of the discussion in ibid., 57–124.

5. B. Soṭah 7b; Sipre Num. 5:19.

6. See Rudolf Mosis, "Eine neue 'Einleitung in das Alte Testament' und das christlich-jüdische Gespräch," *TTZ* 106 (1997) 235–36.

7. Here and in the following, the books of Ezra and Nehemiah will be abbreviated as EN, in order to do justice to the fact that these two books belong together historically.

In surveying the ancient textual witnesses, we will see that not all current orders have ancient roots. Some arrangements result from changes that occurred relatively late in the Bible's history. There is also evidence that different streams of tradition survived concurrently, influenced each other, and were further developed. On the other hand, some important arrangements have not survived—for instance, the so-called eastern Babylonian order.

While the order of the JPS Bible is based on the oldest complete manuscripts of the Jewish Bible (Leningrad Codex/Petropolitanus), the Complete Jewish Bible mirrors the order of the so-called Rabbinic Bible, which developed at a relatively late stage. *BHS* presents an interim solution in that it uses the Leningrad Codex/Petropolitanus but follows the Rabbinic Bible regarding the position of Chronicles.

That the current editions of Bibles presented here all have the Writings as a group of books on the largest structural level should not lead to the conclusion that this arrangement is the only one of significance. Alternative solutions found in manuscripts and printed editions must be considered as well, especially those having the Megillot as a group separated from the rest of the Writings.

For the transmission of the Bible, Jews used scrolls exclusively until the 5th or even the 8th century A.D.[8] In early times, each literary work was transmitted on an individual scroll, and the extent of the work determined the length of the scroll.[9] From Qumran, we know of scrolls containing the whole book of Psalms and of scrolls containing the book of the Twelve Prophets. Soon the capacity of the scrolls increased, and eventually, whole sections of the tripartite canon could be contained on a single scroll. However, complete Jewish Bibles are only handed down to us by way of a codex (beginning in the 10th century A.D.). Until the invention of printing, complete Bibles were rare, which is to say that the entire medieval manuscript tradition is characterized by collections of large scrolls and small codices.

This means that people discussed the order of the biblical books long before the physical prerequisites for the manufacturing of complete Bibles existed. Most prominent in the scholarly discussion is the order of biblical books issued in the talmudic baraita b. Baba Batra 14b. It may be referring to the way scrolls were stored in libraries[10] but may even point to the

---

8. In the secular realm, codices were used beginning in the 5th century. For biblical books, scrolls were used even longer. See Raphael Posner and Israel Ta-Shema, *The Hebrew Book: An Historical Survey* (Jerusalem: Leon Amiel, 1975) 22.

9. See Menahem Haran, "Archives, Libraries, and the Order of the Biblical Books," *JANES* 22 (1993) 51.

10. According to Nahum M. Sarna, "Bible: Canon," *EncJud* 4 (1971) 827–28.

manufacture of scrolls that contained more than one book—an established practice even in tannaitic times.[11]

TNK and Alternative Structures

The Writings as the Third Collection of the TNK

The TNK is the predominant form of the complete Jewish Bible and consists of the three sections Torah, Prophets, and Writings, in this exact sequence. The oldest codices, Aleppo and Petropolitanus, testify to this tripartite arrangement. Other manuscripts often contain one or two of the three divisions of the TNK.

With the advent of printing, the form of the TNK found its way into the first Rabbinic Bibles, at the beginning of the 16th century. The structure of the TNK is found in the First Rabbinic Bible of Felix Pratensis, Venice, Bomberg, 1516/17 (and its reprint as First Bomberg Quarto-Bible); the Second Rabbinic Bible of Jacob ben Chayyim, Venice, Bomberg 1524/25, which was also the first printed Masoretic Bible.[12] In my opinion, only beginning with the middle of the 18th century can the TNK order be said to be completely established, since only then did the Second Rabbinic Bible finally reach the status of a *textus receptus* compared with other printings.[13] Critical editions present the Scriptures only in TNK structure.[14]

While the TNK structure represents the most common form of the Jewish Bible, there are prominent counterproposals, which are discussed in the following sections.[15]

Separate Megillot

Megillot after the Pentateuch. The first printed complete Hebrew Bibles were the Soncino 1488, Naples 1491, Brescia 1494, and the second and

---

11. See Sid Z. Leiman, *The Canonization of Hebrew Scripture: The Talmudic and Midrashic Evidence* (Transactions of the Connecticut Academy of Arts and Sciences 47; Hamden: Archon, 1976) 162–63 n. 258, and 202 n. 644; Haran, "Archives."

12. See Louis Bernard Wolfenson, "Implications of the Place of the Book of Ruth in Editions, Manuscripts, and Canon of the Old Testament," *HUCA* 1 (1924) 154–55 n. 12.

13. See Jordan S. Penkower, "The Chapter Divisions in the 1525 Rabbinic Bible," *VT* 48 (1998) 350ff.

14. See the information in Emanuel Tov, *Textual Criticism of the Hebrew Bible* (Minneapolis: Augsburg Fortress, 1992) 3.

15. In addition, there are rare arrangements that are not discussed here: in the catalog of the Hebrew MSS in the Cambridge University Library (Stefan C. Reif, *Hebrew Manuscripts at Cambridge University Library: A Description and Introduction* [University of Cambridge Oriental Publication 52; Cambridge: Cambridge University Press, 1997), the rare order Torah–Ketubim–Nebiʾim is attested in the Bible Add. 3203 from the 14th/15th century. Besides, the MS Add. 652 consists only of the Pentateuch and Ketubim.

Only a few MSS attest deviation from the generally agreed-upon assignment of books into canonical divisions. For example, the Basel MS Kennicott 392 places Lamentations and Daniel among the Latter Prophets; the printed edition of Paris (Carolus Stephanus) 1555 puts Jeremiah in the Megillot: Song–Ruth–Lam–Jer–Eccl–Esth; and Cambridge Add. 1208.1 is a Prophets codex containing Ruth (14th–15th century).

third editions of the Bomberg Quarto Bible of 1521 and 1525. All of them placed the Megillot immediately after the Pentateuch. [16] According to Louis Bernard Wolfenson, the following must be added to the list: the fourth complete Hebrew Bible, Pesaro 1511–17, "the important folio edition of the Hebr. Bible by John Buxtorf, Sr., Basel, 1618–1619; and the excellent critical edition of Raphael Chayyim Basila . . . completed 1626 but not previously published, Mantua, 1742–1744." [17] In addition, there has been discussion about whether the first printing of the Pentateuch (Bologna 1482) had a supplement containing the Megillot. [18]

The tradition that places the Megillot after the Pentateuch seems to have arisen only with printing—or, at least, no manuscript with this arrangement is known. [19] Regarding the manuscript evidence collected in my *Endgestalten*, there are no manuscripts containing *only* the Megillot and hardly any manuscripts containing the Writings *without* the Megillot. [20] Only one manuscript contains the Pentateuch and the Megillot (BM Ar.Or.2).

In a way, placing the Megillot next to the Pentateuch in printed Bibles fits a strict, "radial" criterion, like spokes radiating from a central point. In other words, it is based on the different levels of popularity of the biblical Scriptures in the context of rabbinic exegesis: "The rabbis did not give the same attention to the whole Bible. . . . The biblical Scriptures most frequently considered are the Five Books of Moses and the five . . . Megillot. [. . . Other biblical] texts, however, are taken into view almost only in connection with the Pentateuch or the Megillot." [21]

However, we may assume that the attention of the rabbis correlated with a books' liturgical use. Admittedly, even the common TNK (with grouped Megillot inside the Ketubim) resulted from reorganization based on liturgical criteria, but in the Pentateuch–Megillot manuscripts, the liturgical criterion is more sweeping, since all of the biblical books that are read in their entirety are grouped together. The placement of the Megillot after the Torah has this purpose: "that the books which alone are read through their entirety during the annual cycle of reading of Scripture in the Synagogue may be kept conveniently together." [22]

Moreover, the textual witnesses discussed here share similarities with liturgical compilations: there are various types of liturgical manuscripts containing biblical texts that cannot be comprehensively presented here.

---

16. See Sarna, "Bible: Canon," 830.

17. Wolfenson, "Implications," 155 n. 13.

18. See ibid., n. 14.

19. See also ibid., 158 n. 19.

20. Exceptions are the ÖNB Hebr 5, BM Harl. 2427, Or 1478, Add. 15451.

21. Translated from Günter Stemberger, *Midrasch: Vom Umgang der Rabbinen mit der Bibel, Einführung – Texte – Erläuterungen* (Munich: Beck, 1989), 27.

22. Wolfenson, "Implications," 155.

However, a few aspects of their structure are presented here to demonstrate possible mutual dependencies.

Commonly, the liturgical compilations begin with the Pentateuch, which has continuous texts for synagogue readings; then, as a second block, the Haftarot (that is, selected passages from the Nebi'im that are read in the synagogue together with the Pentateuch); third, the Megillot (that is, the scrolls that are read through completely on festival days),[23] which are frequently followed by additional biblical[24] and liturgical texts. The Megillot can also be in the second position—that is, between the Pentateuch and the Haftarot.[25]

Thus, the biblical text of the liturgical manuscripts is reduced to all the passages needed for the liturgy. Where the order Pentateuch–Haftarot–Megillot is found, we have a liturgical extract from the TNK structure, and the relevant liturgical passages are taken successively from the three divisions of the canon. Where the order Pentateuch–Megillot–Haftarot is found, however, there are similarities with the special types of Bible discussed here. It is even possible that the printed Bibles containing the Megillot after the Pentateuch are late receptions of these sorts of liturgical manuscripts.[26]

Megillot as a Section of the First Part of the Canon.   Bibles with the Megillot after the Pentateuch have had more than a shadowy existence. In the year 1701, Johannes Hieronymus Imhoff described the phenomenon in his prologue to the (Christian) Ulenbergbibel, calling it "the Jewish Bible" and giving even more peculiarities of its structure:

> [The Jews] divided the first book of the Holy Scripture into five *quinquerniones*. The author of these books is without doubt Moses. To these the festal books are attached [Song–Ruth–Eccl–Lam–Esth]. The second part of the Old Testament comprises, according to the Jewish division, the old [former] prophets, which are the book of Joshua, the book of Judges, the two books of Samuel, and the two books of Kings; the third part contains the prophets Isaiah, Jeremiah, Ezekiel, but not David;[27] to these are added

---

23. But in clear contrast to the Torah and Haftarot reading: "The festal readings from the 'Megillot' are not liturgical readings in a strict sense. Likewise, Hagiographa readings for edifying purposes do not have the same quality." Johann Maier, "Schriftlesung in jüdischer Tradition," in *Streit am Tisch des Wortes? Zur Deutung und Bedeutung des Alten Testaments und seiner Verwendung in der Liturgie* (ed. Ansgar Franz; Pietas liturgica 8; St. Ottilien: EOS, 1997) 505 n. 2; translation mine.

24. Among the MSS of the British Museum, these are Job, Psalms, and parts of Isaiah and Jeremiah (Add. 10455; Add. 9401/02; Or 2451).

25. For the British Museum evidence, a comparison shows that in 11 cases the Haftarot are found in the second position (Add. 9403; 21160; 27167; 15283; Harl. 5773; Or 2286; 2350; 2348; 2364; 2451; 2786), and only in 8 cases are they in the third position (Add. 4709; 9400; 9401/02; 9404; 19776; 10455; 15282; Harl. 5706).

26. See my *Endgestalten*, 138.

27. David is probably mentioned because of a statement in the prologue that, "in Luke 16:29, the Psalms are counted among the Prophets."

the Twelve Minor Prophets. The fourth part is the book *Librorum Scripto-rum*, embracing the Psalms, the Proverbs of Solomon, the book of Job; af-ter this, the book of Daniel and, finally, the books of Esther,[28] Nehemiah, and Paralipomenon [Chronicles]. All these books are viewed as canonical by the Jews.[29]

According to Imhoff, the Jewish Bible is a collection consisting of four parts. The first part is the five books of the Torah (here seen as five parts of one book) *together with the five Megillot*. The division of the Prophets is, ac-cording to Imhoff, split into Former and Latter Prophets (a distinction that is indeed applied in the TNK but not on the largest structural level), and the rest of the Writings (without the Megillot) are combined into a single book, *Librorum Scriptorum*. This is especially remarkable since the books given here are precisely the books that are hardest to put together in a single book, due to their divergent nature and the fact that they are mostly understood as independent works. Thus, the Bible that Imhoff refers to is structured this way:

1. Torah–Megillot
2. Former Prophets
3. Latter Prophets
4. Writings minus the Megillot (*Librorum Scriptorum*)

An examination of the catalog of printed Bibles in the Museum of the British and Foreign Bible Society (BFBS) suggests that Imhoff had access to a copy of Bomberg's third Quarto Bible from the year 1528 (or an edition dependent on it). There, we find the four sections with separate superscrip-tions and, indeed, the Pentateuch and the Megillot with a joint super-scription. Unfortunately, the description in the catalog does not provide information about whether the title of the fourth part, *Librorum Scriptorum*,

---

28. Apparently, Imhoff made a mistake here: Esther was already mentioned in the Megillot; here, Ezra probaby is meant.

29. Translation is by the volume editors; Uwe Köster, *Studien zu den katholischen deutschen Bibelübersetzungen im 16., 17. und 18. Jahrhundert* (Reformationsgeschichtliche Studien und Texte 134; Münster: Aschendorff, 1995) 315; phrases in italics are from the original prologue. The German is as follows:

[Die Juden] haben das erste Buch der Heiligen Schrift in fünf quinquerniones ein-geteilt. Autor dieser Bücher ist ohne Zweifel Moses. Diesen werden die Festbücher beigefügt [Hld – Ruth – Koh – Klgl – Est]. Der zweite Teil des Alten Testaments um-faßt nach der Einteilung der Juden die alten Propheten, das Buch Josua, das Buch der Richter, die zwei Bücher Samuel und die zwei Bücher der Könige, der dritte Teil enthält die Propheten Jesaias, Jeremias, Hesekiel, nicht aber David; dazu kommen die zwölf kleinen Propheten. Der vierte Teil ist das Buch Librorum Scriptorum, das die Psalmen, die Sprüche Salomos, das Buch Hiob, danach das Buch Daniel und schließlich die Bücher Esther, Nehemia und Paralipomenon zusammenfaßt. Alle diese Bücher werden von den Juden als kanonisch angesehen.

uniquely denotes a *single* book in this instance.[30] Also in the Bible of Sebastian Muenster, Basel 1535, the separation of Former and Latter Prophets is clear: the two-volume edition arranges four sections as follows: 1st volume: (a) Pentateuch, (b) Former Prophets; 2nd volume: (a) Latter Prophets, (b) Writings, including Megillot, but at the end.[31] In the other editions, the divisions—if they are there—are arranged differently: the Pentateuch, Megillot, and Prophets each form a block.[32]

Megillot within the Pentateuch. Combining the Torah and Megillot in one section was a radical, new arrangement in some editions of the Rabbinic Bible which interspersed the books of the Megillot among the books of the Pentateuch.[33] The order was determined based on liturgical readings. In these editions, "each of the Megillot is interpolated after the book of the Pentateuch read at the season during which the festival to which it is assigned usually falls, thus disrupting the 'order' even of the *Torah*."[34] Wolfenson describes these editions in more detail:[35] according to him, the Song of Songs is placed after Leviticus because Leviticus is read around the time of Pesach, Ruth after Numbers (which is read around Shavuot), Lamentations and Ecclesiastes after Deuteronomy (9th of Ab, Sukkot), and Esther after Exodus (because of Purim). Since Sukkot falls on the last day of the Deuteronomy reading, Ecclesiastes and Lamentations need to be placed after Deuteronomy, and therefore Genesis remains without a Megillah. In the Rabbinic Bible Warsaw 1885, the books of the Pentateuch appear as individual volumes, with the related festal scrolls as appendixes.

Book Sequences

The next step of our investigation leads to the topic of arranging the books. The book sequences found in the manuscripts can be divided into two classes: those in which the books of the Megillot are dispersed and those in which the books of the Megillot are grouped. Both variants are frequent and have prominent textual witnesses.

To begin with a short overview, we will examine the manuscripts of the British Museum.[36] There, regarding the complete Bibles, we find a balanced result of distributed (five instances) and grouped (six instances) Megillot.

---

30. See Thomas H. Darlow and Horace F. Moule, *Historical Catalogue of the Printed Editions of Holy Scripture in the Library of the British and Foreign Bible Society*, vol. 2: *Polyglots and Languages Other Than English* (New York: Kraus, 1963), no. 5086.

31. See ibid., no. 5087.

32. See ibid., no. 5075: Soncino Bible 1488, with separate indexes for Pentateuch, Megillot, Prophets, and Writings, respectively; no. 5083: Pratensis Bible 1517, contains an analogous four-part division.

33. See Tov, *Textual Criticism*, 3.

34. John Barton, *Oracles of God: Perceptions of Ancient Prophecy in Israel after the Exile* (London: Darton, Longman & Todd, 1986) 84.

35. For the following, see Wolfenson, "Implications," 156 n. 14.

36. See my *Endgestalten*, 155.

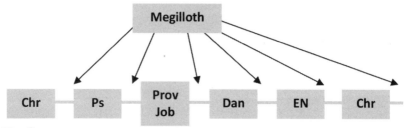

Fig. 2

Among incomplete Bibles, the ratio changes in favor of the variant with dispersed Megillot: while 12 manuscripts disperse the Megillot, 6 manuscripts group the collection of the Megillot. In addition, there are 3 manuscripts of the Writings without Megillot.[37]

Writings with Grouped Megillot
Sequence of the Books with Megillot Grouped. From 87 witnesses,[38] 80 match the system in fig. 2 above. The arrangement of these manuscripts can be described as the sequence Ps–Prov/Job–Dan–EN, to which Chronicles is added either at the beginning or at the end. Job and Proverbs stand next to each other, yet they can switch places.[39] The Megillot are inserted in arbitrary positions[40] or are altogether separate. Because of the two possible positions for Chronicles, the sequence could also be depicted as a circle. By transforming the circle into a linear arrangement, as a "starting point" either Chronicles or Psalms was chosen. However, the idea of a "circle canon"[41] is not compelling since none of the manuscripts of the Writings chooses a starting point other than Chronicles or Psalms. In addition, it is unclear in what Sitz im Leben such a circle would function, since the Writings (except for Psalms and the Megillot) do not fulfill a liturgical function.

Among the 80 representatives of the system, the most frequent insertion point for the Megillot is after the pair Proverbs/Job (44 instances). In this group, the order Chr–Ps–Job–Prov–Megillot–Dan–EN is attested as being the most frequent; there are important, old textual witnesses such as the Aleppo Codex from 925 and the Leningrad Codex/Petropolitanus B19a from 1009. The same order of biblical books is described in *Adath Deborim*

---

37. The absence of the Writings is explainable because the Megillot frequently appear as a section in liturgical compilations (17 cases).

38. As considered in my *Endgestalten*, 159–62.

39. The sequence of Prov–Job seems to be more frequent: 48 attestations / 17 variants in contrast to 38 attestations / 10 variants of Job–Prov.

40. In cases when Chronicles is located at the beginning of the Writings, the Megillot are never placed before it.

41. For such a conception, see Jack Miles, *God: A Biography* (New York: Simon & Schuster, 1995) 451–52.

("bee swarm"), a Hebrew compilation by Joseph of Constantinople from the year 1207. The order is generally held to be the Palestinian or western order of the Writings. In the introduction to the second Rabbinic Bible of Jacob ben Chayyim, this order is said to be "according to the Masora."

For his printed edition (1524–25), Jacob ben Chayyim admittedly chose a different order: Ps–Prov–Job–Megillot–Dan–EN–Chr. Among the 80 textual witnesses of the system described above, it is the second most-common variant, represented 11 times. It was chosen for the first printed edition of the Writings (Naples, 1486–87) as well as for the first Rabbinic Bible of Felix Pratensis (1516–17).

Sequence of the Megillot When Grouped Together. An examination of 114 textual witnesses[42] shows that two basic types are prevalent: Ruth–Song–Eccl–Lam–Esth (western or Palestinian order; see below) and Song–Ruth–Lam–Eccl–Esth (festal order).

The first type is found in 42 of the 114 witnesses, among them the Aleppo and Leningrad/Petropolitanus B19a codices. When complete Bibles group the five Megillot together, they do it largely in this order.[43]

The second type is often found in liturgical manuscripts and apparently was taken over from there into the important early printed editions. The order is based on the sequence of the feasts at which the Megillot were used for liturgical readings. Twenty-eight of the 114 textual witnesses evidence the festal order and often have a German background. Nine additional manuscripts provide evidence of the festal order beginning with Esther (8 MSS) or Ruth (1 MS).

Thus, three starting points for the festal cycle appear: normally, the textual witnesses have the Song of Songs as the first reading, since Pesach (Passover) is the first feast of the religious year. The other frequent variant begins with the Feast of Purim, and thus Esther is read. The corresponding manuscripts point to Germany and Spain, so one reason for this may have been the beginning point of the year in a Christian environment. Maybe, however, it was conceived from the ending: Sukkot is held to be the final feast in the Jewish festal year. The third documented starting point is Ruth, which is unique. Possibly, the purpose was the similarity with the chronological order of the Megillot, at least for the beginning. An order starting with the secular Jewish New Year has not been found. Figure 3 shows the cycle of the year with the festal readings. The festal order is not witnessed before the 11th century and seems to have gained more prevalence only in the 13th century.[44]

The Writings without Grouped Megillot

An analysis of 51 manuscript witnesses that have the Megillot dispersed over the Writings yields 30 different possible orders. They are documented

---

42. Brandt, *Endgestalten*, 164–71.
43. See ibid., 164.
44. See ibid., 169.

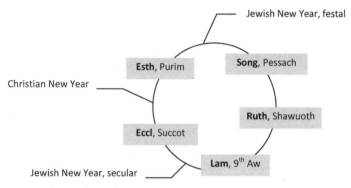

Fig. 3 (to be read clockwise)

in detail.[45] Twenty-nine of the 51 witnesses reflect an arrangement in which books and pairs of books are arranged according to the scheme in fig. 4. Only the inner order of each of the pairs may vary. Thus, when the books of the Megillot are dispersed throughout the Writings, there is a high probability that the order begins with Ruth, followed by the three "Larger Writings" Psalms and Job/Proverbs, before the three Megillot Ecclesiastes/ Song and Lamentations. After them follows the pair Daniel/Esther. The sequence ends with Ezra–Nehemiah and Chronicles.

The order attested most frequently (13 cases) is Ruth–Ps–Job–Prov–Eccl–Song–Lam–Dan–Esth–EN–Chr, which is the order of the Babylonian Talmud (according to b. B. Bat. 14b). The earliest manuscripts evidencing the talmudic order originate in the 12th century, the latest from the 15th century. No printed edition is among them.

The remaining 22 textual witnesses contain variants exceeding the scheme given above. Only 4 of them relocate Chronicles at the beginning. The final position of Chronicles seems to be one of the constants here.

Orders of the Writings and Their Rationale

As a conclusion to the section about the Jewish Bibles, I discuss the most prominent arrangements culled from analyses of the textual witnesses in relation to external sources and the rationale for their order.

Eastern order: Ruth–Ps–Job–Prov–Eccl–Song–Lam–Dan–Esth–EN–Chr

There is evidence for the talmudic order (b. B. Bat. 14b) at the beginning of the 10th century from the Babylonian region in the form of a Masoretic list of total numbers of verses.[46] Furthermore, the order is attested in a number

---

45. Ibid., 155–159.

46. See Hans Peter Rüger, "Ein Fragment der bisher ältesten hebräischen Bibelhandschrift mit babylonischer Punktation," *VT* 16 (1966) 67. The fragment under considera-

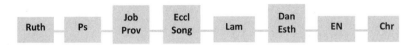

Fig. 4

of Bible manuscripts from the 12th to the 15th centuries. It is not found, however, in old printed editions. Neither does any recent Jewish Bible have the talmudic order. Obviously, efforts to bring liturgical arrangements back to the Bible have been too sweeping. Additionally, in *Adath Deborim* ("bee swarm"), a Hebrew compilation of Joseph of Constantinople in 1207, we find a polemic against Babylonian ordering traditions that placed Chronicles (or Esther) at the end.[47] This polemic probably prevented the Babylonian order from spreading any further.[48]

The eastern order is primarily structured by a chronological frame: with the historical sequence of David, Solomon, Jeremiah, the exile, and the postexilic time, the books of Psalms, Proverbs/Ecclesiastes/Song of Songs, Lamentations, Daniel, and Ezra–Nehemiah are solidified or fixed. The remaining positions appear to be chronological for the following reasons:

> Because of its Davidic genealogy, Ruth serves as an introduction to Psalms. The tight connection is expressed in b. B. Bat. 14b in the form of an "and," which is used only in certain places between the book titles. Roger Beckwith goes so far as to maintain that Ruth was understood to be part of a larger work, so that Psalms could be said to be the "first" book of the Writings even in this order.[49]

> Some of the rabbis believed that Job was a contemporary of the queen of Sheba (see b. B. Bat. 15b), and from this the location of Job between Psalms (David) and Proverbs (Solomon) immediately suggests itself.

---

tion is T-S. N-S 246.26:2 from the Cambridge University Library. It probably originates in the part of Persia where the Hebrew is pronounced in a Babylonian way (pp. 68–29). See the edited text on p. 69. It is interesting that the list is found after Neh 13:31, which hints that Nehemiah was the last book in the ms. This would be another case in which the order of the list and the actual book order in the ms deviate from each other.

47. In the English translation by Lipschütz, the text of *Adath Deborim* reads as follows:

> Know . . . that the Hagiographa are divided into 11 sections: Chronicles, Psalms, Job, Proverbs, Ruth, Song of Songs, Ecclesiastes, Lamentations, Esther, Daniel, Ezra. But the Babylonians have altered this order: some place Chronicles at the end of the volume; others place the Scroll of Esther at the end of the volume. Now, we intend to begin with the first of these books, Chronicles, according to the land of Israel; for this order is the right and true one; and all who copy the Holy Scriptures, in Babylonia and elsewhere, will return to this order.

Lazar Lipschütz, "Mishael ben Uzziel's Treatise on the Differences between Ben Asher and Ben Naphtali," *Textus* 2 (Supplement; 1962) 41. For the Hebrew, see Rüger, "Fragment," 69.

48. See my *Endgestalten*, 150; Roger T. Beckwith, *The Old Testament Canon of the New Testament Church and Its Background in Early Judaism* (London: SPCK, 1985) 201–3.

49. Ibid., 112.

Among the Scriptures with alleged Solomonic authorship, Ecclesiastes and the Song of Songs are connected by the above-mentioned "and" in some of the textual variants of b. B. Bat. 14b. At the same time, they are both "small Writings" according to b. Ber. 57b. Since the two small books are placed after Proverbs, the order of the Solomonic books does not correspond to the rabbinic saying (R. Jonathan) regarding the time of writing in Solomon's life: "[I]t was the rabbis who explained that the first [Song of Songs] was written in his youth, the second in his maturity [Proverbs], and the third [Ecclesiastes] in his old age, thus providing a sort of typology of the three ages of man."[50] For the sequence Prov–Eccl–Song, one can posit an arrangement according to decreasing length that makes it possible for Proverbs to be next to the other two "large Ketubim."[51]

The position of Esther before Ezra–Nehemiah has its roots in the rabbinic position that Esther lived before Ezra (b. B. Bat. 15a). In addition, the Ahasuerus in Esther could be identified with the Ahasuerus and Darius in Dan 9:1, who lived before Cyrus, with whom Ezra–Nehemiah begins. That this sort of misunderstanding was possible can be seen in LXX Dan 5:31; 9:1, where Darius is identified with Artaxerxes. From its intention, therefore, the order is historical, although EN–Esth seems to be historically more correct. An "and" between Esther and Daniel shows that the connection between these two books was thought to be stronger than their connection to Ezra–Nehemiah.

Most likely, the greatest difficulties were caused by the positioning of Chronicles, since it ranges from Adam until the return from exile. Aside from the idea that Chronicles was possibly written in order to close the canon (e.g., Georg Steins),[52] the final position suggests itself for several reasons: the order of the three large prophetic books, Jeremiah–Ezekiel–Isaiah, testifies that b. B. Bat. 14b tends to arrange books chronologically according to the book's ending. In addition, the example of the Solomonic books demonstrates that the common authorship of books suggested juxtaposition.[53] According to b. B. Bat. 15a, Ezra and Nehemiah wrote Chronicles. Correspondingly, the baraita connects Ezra–Nehemiah and Chronicles with an "*and.*" Why Chronicles was not therefore placed *before* Ezra–Nehemiah the arguments given so far cannot explain. Accord-

---

50. Daniel Boyarin, *Intertextuality and the Reading of Midrash* (Indiana Studies in Biblical Literature; Bloomington: Indiana University Press, 1990) 149 n. 14 about HldR 1.1. There, Rabbi Chija the Great proposes an alternative dating of the books in the sequence Proverbs, Ecclesiastes, and Song of Songs. The rabbis finally came to an agreement that Ecclesiastes should be considered the last work.

51. According to b. Ber. 57b.

52. See, for example, Georg Steins, *Die Chronik als kanonisches Abschlußphänomen* (BBB 93; Weinheim: Athenäum, 1995); and the articles by him and of H. Koorevaar in the present volume.

53. Solomon as author of Proverbs, Ecclesiastes, and Song of Songs, for example, in HldR 1.1.

ing to Beckwith, the intent was to have Chronicles be the final recapitulation.[54] This would be compatible with the ideas of Steins.

Western order: Chr–Ps–Job–Prov–Meg (Ruth–Song–Eccl–Lam–Esth)–Dan–EN

Compared with the eastern order, the position of Chronicles changed in the western order, and the Megillot appeared as a group. This order survived, appears even in recent editions, and is attested in important manuscripts. For example, in the Aleppo Codex we have an early and important textual witness for the grouping of the five festal scrolls as one entity inside the third part of the canon. But is this tradition considerably older than the 10th century? The Talmud does not conceive of the "five Megillot." Only Esther is referred to as a "Megillah" in the Talmud. Therefore, the final redaction of the Talmud poses as a *terminus a quo* for the grouping. Furthermore, one must ask when, exactly, the five books of Scripture were used for liturgical readings. In talmudic times, only Esther was read. The extracanonical Tractate Soperim from the middle of the 8th century (14.3:18; 18.4) provides evidence for the liturgical reading of Ruth, Song of Songs, and Lamentations as well. Ecclesiastes was probably added as the last book nearer to the 10th century.[55] In light of these data, the blunt dates given in literature on the subject are even more astonishing.[56]

The western order merits its designation from the origin of the textual witnesses but also from the ascriptions made by Joseph of Constantinople[57] and Mishael ben Uzziel ("order of the Syrians").[58] Joseph of Constantinople holds that the western order is the original and thus precedes the eastern order, which later influenced it. However, there is no compelling evidence for this.

Arrangements with the Megillot grouped together can be termed a "liturgical order,"[59] but additional criteria are needed. The framing books and the position of the Megillot in their place in the third division of the canon can be explained chronologically: Chronicles leads, drawing a line from Adam to David and Solomon, whose Scriptures (Psalms and Proverbs) follow, before the postexilic books of Daniel and Ezra–Nehemiah form a conclusion. Chronicles is therefore chronologically reckoned based on its beginning, not its ending. Since the Megillot were grouped, it was necessary to find a place where they could fit together as a block. The position between Proverbs and Daniel offered itself, since thereby three of the

---

54. Beckwith, *Old Testament Canon*, 158.
55. According to ibid., 202–3.
56. See an overview in my *Endgestalten*, 129.
57. See above, n. 47: "according to the land of Israel."
58. Mishael ben Uzziel, *Kitab al-Khilaf: the "Book of Differences" between Ben Asher und Ben Naphtali* (11th to 13th centuries), edited in Lipschütz, "Mishael ben Uzziel's Treatise."
59. See ibid., 209.

five Megillot would chronologically be in their right place, while Ruth and Esther as the framing Scriptures featured a flashback and a view forward. Already in the eastern order, the books of the Song of Songs, Ecclesiastes, and Lamentations formed the center. The books of Ruth and Esther were taken from their outer positions and moved near that center. As a result, the inner order of the Megillot reflects the sequence in the eastern order. Compare this with the talmudic order, in which Ecclesiastes and the Song of Songs are exchanged. This may be due to the tradition that Solomon wrote Ecclesiastes in his old age.[60]

Rabbinic Bible Order: Ps–Prov–Job–Meg (Song–Ruth–Lam–Eccl–Esth)–Dan–EN–Chr

The order of books in the Rabbinic Bible is a hybrid of the western and eastern orders. It is attested in about the turn of the 12th to the 13th century.[61] It agrees with the western orders regarding the grouping of the Megillot but with the eastern orders regarding the position of Chronicles. It differs from both in the order of Job–Proverbs and the internal sequence of the Megillot. Regarding the Megillot, the Rabbinic Bible follows the order of the feasts, because the Megillot had come to be read successively. Therefore, the Song of Songs and Ecclesiastes were moved apart from each other, thus breaking apart the small collection of Solomonic books. Furthermore, it was no longer necessary to place Proverbs at the end of the "large Ketubim." When one takes away the argument of Solomonic authorship as a criterion, it is unnecessary to connect Proverbs with the following books, which would then free Job to migrate after Proverbs based on the tradition that Job was a returnee from the exile.[62] Then, however, the question must be asked why Job was not placed between Daniel and Ezra–Nehemiah. Apparently, as a counterbalance, the block of the "Large Ketubim" was kept, which is also classified with the shorthand *ta'am* or *emet*.[63] Besides, the sequence Psalms–Proverbs–Job is that of b. Ber. 57b. Within the festal block, Ruth moves close to Lamentations, with an interesting effect: the origin and destruction of the Davidic Dynasty follow one another. Altogether, the arrangement of the Rabbinic Bibles is shaped by liturgical criteria more than other orders.

Regarding the issue of canonical reading, many questions remain open: Should we, against the relatively early witness of the Babylonian Talmud, follow a sequence of Scripture that conforms to today's editions? Should we, together with Mishael ben Uzziel, hold the western order to be the

---

60. Assumed by Beckwith, *Old Testament Canon*, 228 n. 54. See also above, n. 50. Wolfenson is more cautious ("Implications," 157): "What principle is followed in this arrangement it is impossible to say. Perhaps it is supposedly chronological order, based on the date of origin of the books."

61. Dating derived from the textual witnesses given in my *Endgestalten*.

62. With b. B. Bat. 15a.

63. See Mosis, "Einleitung," 235–36.

older and therefore original order? Should we even follow the later developments (liturgical orders, festal order of Megillot), since these were further developments of the canon by the responsible community? Should we pay attention at all to the sequence of books, since the Bible editors were so free and creative with them? Before I formulate some cautious suggestions regarding these issues, we first need to tackle the more complex situation within the Christian tradition.

The Books of the Writings in Christian Bibles

The history of the Old Testament in Christian Bibles shows an even greater variety of arrangements than in the Jewish tradition.[64] In these Bibles, the Writings are not grouped together, and only seldom are they placed at the end of the Old Testament. However, it is not always the Prophets that—according to the cliché—occupy the position directly preceding the transition to the New Testament. Regarding the reception of the Writings, it might well be interesting to track the diverse options for placing each of the Writings in Christian canon lists and Bibles, but there is not space here to explore this topic.[65]

The "Basic Form" of the OT

On the basis of an investigation of canon lists and textual witnesses, something like a core arrangement of the Old Testament can be identified that integrates countless possibilities for ordering, understanding each of them as a linear realization of a single "basic form."[66] This primary form, however, has such a high degree of abstraction that it cannot be conceived as a linear structure by itself.

The Overall Structure

The scaffolding of the "basic form" consists of three larger blocks, the historical, the Solomonic, and the prophetic books, and a series of individual Scriptures that are integrated according to various principles of structuring. The Jewish Writings largely fall into this last group, with the exception of Proverbs, Ecclesiastes, Song of Songs (Solomonic books), and Daniel and Lamentations (prophetic books).

When one transforms the structure into a linear codex, the problem arises how to arrange the Solomonic and the prophetic block. The orders chosen are either historical–prophetic–Solomonic books or—more often—historical–Solomonic–prophetic books (see fig. 5).

The remaining books of the OT appear in different places—mostly those whose authority was frequently disputed over the course of its canonical history (that is, the agreed-upon deutercanonical books Tobit, Judith,

---

64. For more details, see my *Endgestalten*, 172–346.
65. For this, see the register in ibid., 476–80.
66. Ibid., 352–53.

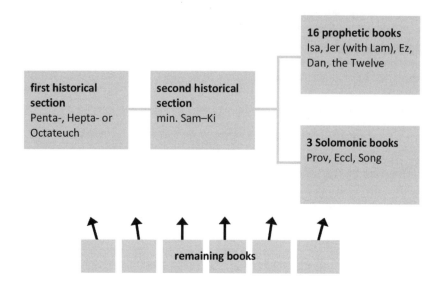

Fig. 5

1–2 Maccabees, Baruch, the Additions to Daniel and Esther, as well as the occasionally disputed books such as Esther, and the books that were only regionally accepted: Enoch, Jubilees, 3–4 Maccabees, and others) but also the undisputed books of Ruth, Chronicles, Job, Psalms, and Ezra–Nehemiah. These books were placed in the basic structure differently, according to whether the arrangement was based more on the criterion of genre, alleged historical order, or canonical ranking.

The internal arrangements of the groups were partly fixed. In the historical books, the order Pentateuch–Joshua–Judges–Samuel–Kings is standard: the internal order of the Pentateuch is most familiar, and Ruth often follows Judges. For the Solomonic books, the normal order is Proverbs–Ecclesiastes–Song of Songs, commonly followed by Wisdom–Sirach. The order of the Prophets varies more than these books, however. Aside from the permutation of Ezekiel and Daniel in many early witnesses, the placement of the Twelve Prophets differs following regional traditions.

Implementations

In table 2, three important codices are presented to demonstrate how the abstract principles given above were implemented: from the Greek tradition, Codex Alexandrinus (5th cent.), from the Latin tradition, Amiatinus (around 700), and from the Syriac, Ambrosianus (6th–7th cent.).

Typical structural elements of Christian Bibles are clearly recognizable here. As described above, the books of the Pentateuch appear at the be-

Table 2. *Order of Books in Three Codices Compared*

Alexandrinus	Amiatinus	Ambrosianus
Gen to Deut	Gen to Deut	Gen to Deut
		Job
Josh, Judg, Ruth	Josh, Judg, Ruth	Josh, Judg
Sam	Sam	Sam
		Ps
Kings	Kings	Kings
Chr	Chr	
	Ps	
	Prov	Prov
	Wis, Sir	
	Eccl, Song	Eccl, Song
The Twelve		
Isa	Isa	Isa
Jer, Bar, Lam, EpJer	Jer, Lam, Bar	Jer, Lam, Bar
Ezek	Ezek	Ezek
		The Twelve
Dan, Sus, Bel	Dan, Sus, Bel	Dan, Bel
	The Twelve	
	Job	
		Ruth, Sus
Esth, Tob, Jdt	Tob, Esth, Jdt	Esth, Jdt
		Sir, Chr, EpBar,[a] 4Ezr
1–2 Esdras	1–2 Esdras	EN
1–4 Macc	1–2 Macc	1–4 Macc
Ps, Job		
Prov, Eccl, Song		
Wis, Sir		

a. That is, the "Epistle of Baruch to the Nine and a Half Tribes," which now appears as an appendix to 2 Baruch (Syriac Apocalypse).

ginning of the Old Testament, followed by a varied number of historical books. At certain points, nonhistorical books are inserted, making the boundaries visible in the historical progression. The Ambrosianus inserts Job after Deuteronomy, thus clarifying the break that is possible after the Pentateuch in Christian Bibles. In other textual witnesses, a similar break is found after Ruth.[67] The block of the prophetic books in the strict sense is clearly recognizable in all three MSS. The internal order is fixed: Isaiah, Jeremiah (with additions), Ezekiel, and Daniel (with additions) form the foundation, to which the Twelve Prophets are added at different places in the traditions. In the Greek tradition, it is common to have the Twelve Minor Prophets at the head of the line; in the Latin tradition—as mediated by the Vulgate—they appear at the end. Syrian Christians mostly chose a position in the middle, after Ezekiel, or, more often, between Isaiah and Jeremiah.

The poetic books are grouped together as well, though the margins of the grouping are determined differently. For the Greek tradition, it is self-evident that around the Solomonic core of Proverbs, Ecclesiastes, and Song of Songs in most instances Wisdom and Sirach are grouped, because they are "Solomonic" books in a wider sense. Psalms and Job surround the resulting block as poetic books. In contrast, the Latin tradition does not include Job in this group, and the Syrian tradition shows the group reduced to its Solomonic core.

The variations in the arrangement of the block correspond to the scheme presented above: after the historical books come either the prophetic or the poetic books. In two of the three examples, the poetic books are placed before the prophetic books, but only in one case do the prophetic books appear before the poetic. This relationship is somewhat representative of the entirety of the manuscript evidence from a quantitative point of view.[68]

After the historical (including the Pentateuch), poetic, and prophetic groups are determined, a number of books remain. Of these, the first to be considered are the books that did not find a place in either the poetic or the prophetic sections. In Ambrosianus, Psalms and Job need to find a place as well as the Susanna narrative, since it is separated from Daniel. According to historical criteria, Job is placed after the Pentateuch (Moses as the alleged author of Job [see b. B. Bat. 15a] or Job as the Jobab of Gen 36:33–34 [see Job 42:17, LXX]), and the Psalter is placed between Samuel and Kings (lifetime of King David). Susanna together with Ruth, Judith, and Esther forms the common west Syrian group called the "Book (or 'books') of Women."[69]

---

67. Seen from the perspective of Jewish arrangements, the insertion of Ruth would already mark a break point. In Christian Bibles, however, Ruth was usually placed in the corpus of historical books.

68. Among the Greek MSS, both types balance each other; among the Latin MSS in the centuries before the Paris Bible, a similar relationship must be assumed. From the late Middle Ages onward, the MSS with the Prophets after the poetic books clearly predominate.

69. See my *Endgestalten*, 223ff.

Job is not counted as a poetic book in Amiatinus. This is due to an old Latin tradition that formed a group named the *historiarum*, which contained Job, Tobit, Esther, Judith, and Esdras and sometimes also the Maccabees and Chronicles.[70] In most cases, these "tales" are markedly separate from the historical books of Genesis to Kings, with no continuous flow of history intended.[71]

Codex Alexandrinus also demonstrates a tendency to separate the late historical books from the early ones and to place Esth–Jdt–Tob–Esdras–Macc far behind in the OT. In the Greek tradition, however, no common designation of such a group of books is known. In Codex Alexandrinus as well as in the Amiatus, these Scriptures are placed after the Prophets. Principally, many Christian arrangements concur by placing Tobit, Judith, and Esther next to each other. Their similar size and their edifying character are probably the leading factors.

This discussion explains the books in Codex Alexandrinus and Amiatinus but has not yet explained the placment of Sir–Chr–EpBar–4Ezra–EN–Macc in Ambrosianus. All of these were disputed books. Their placement at the end may be an indication of a radial arrangement—that is, the unimportant books follow the important. However, it can also indicate the late inclusion of these books among books already considered canonical. These considerations are meant to call attention to the possibility of interpreting the addition of disputed books: either synchronically, in the sense of spreading away from the core, or diachronically, in the sense of a secondary addition.

This thought leads to Luther's Bible, which as a paragon of Protestant Bibles arranged the disputed books as an attachment separated from the rest. Again it is possible to read the attachment synchronically or diachronically, either to accept a lower appreciation of the "Apocrypha" as a given, or to perceive in it the canonical history and to understand the books' separation as being a historical development. In table 3, the order in Luther's Bible is compared with that in the Paris Vulgate. It is easily discernible that the Luther Bible merely presents the Paris OT minus the "Apocrypha."

The Paris Vulgate corresponds remarkably to the canonical lists of the Greek fathers (Prophets between the poetic books and the late historical books)[72] as well as matching the needs of the Paris University.[73] Both aspects (connection to antiquity and academic usability) could well have driven its wide distribution. It not only had an impact on the Latin church (authorization by the councils of Florence and Trent) but also defined the frame in which the Luther Bible developed its new shape.

---

70. See ibid., 246–62.

71. See Rudolf Mosis, "Canonical Approach und Vielfalt des Kanon: Zu einer neuen Einleitung in das Alte Testament," *TTZ* 106 (1997) 50–53.

72. Frequently, Esther was the last book of the OT.

73. Brandt, *Endgestalten*, 299–304.

Table 3. *Two Orders Compared*

Paris Vulgate	Luther's Bible
Gen to Deut	Gen to Deut
Josh, Judg, Ruth	Josh, Judg, Ruth
Sam, Kings, Chr, Esdras	Sam, Kings, Chr, Esdras
Tob, Jdt	
Esth	Esth
Job, Ps, Prov, Eccl, Song	Job, Ps, Prov, Eccl, Song
Wis, Sir	
Isa, Jer, Lam	Isa, Jer, Lam
Bar	
Ezek, Dan, The Twelve	Ezek, Dan, The Twelve
Macc	
	Tob, Jdt, Wis, Sir
	Bar, Macc, DanA, EsthA

The separation of the Pentateuch by its section title from the block of the historical books is a rather unusual phenomenon. Admittedly, on the Catholic as well as on the Protestant side, we find attempts to define a separate block of the "Books of the Law" at the top level of the table. This is often connected to the approach of defining a general four-part structure of legal, historical, poetic, and prophetic books.

While the Pentateuch is kept separate in most of the canonical lists, in the manuscripts the Pentateuch often was not able to prevail against attempts to link it with Joshua and Judges in order to form a Heptateuch (Old Latin) or, with Ruth, to form an Octateuch (Greek and Vulgate). With this move, the viewpoint has changed from "Torah" to "history." An exception to this is the Ethiopian canon, which in *orit* ("eight-book Torah") unites the concept of an Octateuch with that of the Torah.[74]

Traditions Following Jewish Models

In the history of the Christian Bible, there are numerous arrangements of the Old Testament that correspond to Jewish models. To be sure, these traditions could not extend their influence to recent editions. Nevertheless, they will be discussed with regard to the question of the Writings' reception.

---

74. See my "Geflecht aus 81 Büchern: Zur variantenreichen Gestalt des äthiopischen Bibelkanons," *Aethiopica* 3 (2000) 79–115.

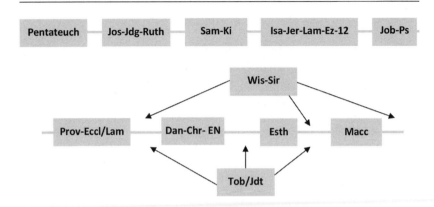

Fig. 6

The Latin Tradition Following Jerome

In the history of the Latin Bible, there are numerous witnesses to an arrangement of the OT books according to Jewish examples. Via Jerome and his structure in the *Prologus Galeatus,* they found their way into the West and persisted into the high Middle Ages. In these orders—except in the Greek and in many Oriental traditions—the Pentateuch is clearly demarcated as an individual block, and we can also see a collection of books mirroring the Jewish collection of the Writings.

In fig. 6, the various linear implementations of this arrangement that resulted from inserting "movable" books are made visual.[75] The following Old Testaments are organized according to the *ordines* of Jerome: the Teodulf Bibles, Codex Toletanus, and Complutensis 2. From the 11th century, the Lincoln Manuscript, Cathedral Library I (A.I.2) can be named. In the 12th century, the Bible of Stephan Harding (abbot of Cîteaux) matches the pattern. Other MSS (for example, Complutensis 3 and Metz 7) put the Wisdom books together but kept Daniel separate from the Prophets.

Again, the assumption that, generally, the Prophets were placed at the end of the OT must be debunked; it happens neither in the Latin nor in the Syriac tradition. Locating the Prophets last can only be observed in the Greek tradition; even here, the order depends more on canon lists than in actual Bibles, and only in some of these canon lists, because some books are classified as Prophets that would not normally be included based on the Western understanding—namely, Job, Esther, and Esdras.

---

75. See my *Endgestalten,* 278ff.

The Syriac Tradition of Beth Mawtabhe

Like the Latin tradition, the Syriac Bible was influenced by Jewish arrangements. So, despite all confessional differences, the separation of the Pentateuch remains a peculiarity of Syriac Bibles.

In eastern Syriac Nestorian Bibles, one finds clearly defined segments of the OT that, similar to the TNK, reflect different levels of canonicity and probably also liturgical use. In the Nestorian Bibles, five subsections can be discerned: (1) *Oreita* (Pentateuch), (2) *Beth Mawtabhe* (see below), (3) *Newiyye* (Prophets), (4) *Daweedha* (Psalms), (5) *Makwai* (disputed books). Mostly, the MSS contain only one of the subsections, occasionally with an extract from another subsection. "In contrast to the western Syriac Bible, the eastern Syrian is organized into blocks. Not the whole of the Bible stands in the foreground—there is no single MS of the whole Bible or even of the whole OT—but the . . . individual volumes."[76]

In this, the *Beth Mawtabhe* is a group of biblical books that can be characterized as something like the remains of the narrow eastern Syriac canon of Theodor of Mopsuestia (A.D. 350–428).[77] It encompasses all the books that remain after the well-defined blocks of the Pentateuch, the Prophets, and the Psalms have been set aside. Compared with these blocks, the *Beth Mawtabhe* contains books that are definitely considered to be of lower canonical rank.[78] The interpretation of the title *Beth Mawtabhe* is unclear. Ephräm Eising assumes a reading of it as a "repository of the sections," in the sense of "repository of the (remaining biblical) Scriptures."[79]

To be sure, the subsection only partly corresponds to the Writings, since *Beth Mawtabhe* contains the Former Prophets as well as some of the Writings. The lists of the Peshitta Institute show that the order of the books is relatively stable.[80] There is a later standard order of Josh–Judg–Sam–Kgs–Prov–Eccl–Ruth–Song–Sir–Job that followed an older order by placing Sirach between Proverbs and Ecclesiastes. This change took place between the 13th and the 15th centuries.

The comments of the Išoʾdad of Merv (second half of 9th cent.) played a key role in understanding the eastern Syriac canon. From these, we learn not only of the books rejected by Theodor but also of the structure of the Nestorian OT:[81]

76. Editors' translation; from Ephräm Burkhard Eising, *Zur Geschichte des Kanons der Heiligen Schrift in der ostsyrischen Kirche im ersten Jahrtausend*, 3 vols.: *I. Text; II. Tafeln; III. Anmerkungen* . . . (Ph.D. diss., Würzburg, 1972) 1.215.
77. See my *Endgestalten*, 228ff.
78. See ibid., 229.
79. Eising, *Geschichte des Kanons*, 1.215.
80. See the synopsis in: "Peshitta Institute Communications V," *VT* 17 (1967) 132.
81. See Eising, *Geschichte des Kanons*, 1.143.

1. The books that Theodor rejected in the OT are: Proverbs, Ecclesiastes, Song of Songs, Sirach, Ruth, and Job.[82]
2. The OT of Išoʾdad of Merv is structured as follows: (1) the Pentateuch under the title *Oreita* forms the first group; (2) the *Beth Mawtabhe* (Josh–Judg–Sam–Kgs–Prov–Sir–Eccl–Song–Ruth–Job) follows; (3) the third group is the Prophets (*Newiyye*: Isa–the Twelve–Jer–Ezek–Dan); and (4) the final group is the *Daweedha*, the Psalter of David.[83]

This structure reflects Theodor's canon: after subtracting the rejected books of the *Beth Mawtabhe*, the remaining books match the canon of Theodor precisely—including the specific placement of the Psalms after the Prophets.[84] According to Eising, the structure of Theodor's canon is as follows: the books of full canonical rank are the Pentateuch, Joshua, Judges, Samuel, Kings, Isaiah, Jeremiah, Ezekiel, Daniel, The Twelve, and Psalms; the noncanonical but esteemed books books follow: Proverbs, Sirach, Ecclesiastes, and Ruth.[85]

The Nestorian mss reflect the groups witnessed by Išoʾdad of Merv precisely and add another group where Scriptures of disputed rank are collected (*Makwai*). After the turn of the millennium, the *Makwai* were considered more-certainly to be part of the Bible.[86] During this time, the number of books was slowly increased to 10,[87] and a stable order was established: 1–3 Maccabees, 1–2 Chronicles, Ezra–Nehemiah, Wisdom, Judith, Esther, Susanna, Epistle of Jeremiah, EpBar, and Baruch.

Concluding Considerations

Over the millennia, editors have time and again shaped the textual surface of the Christian Old Testament differently. They put Scripture together into groups, they chose a specific sequence of the books inside the groups, and they arranged the groups in a certain linear arrangement. In this, the books attributed to the "Writings" in the Jewish Bibles seldom appear in a unified collection. A historical reason for this may be that the "Writings" were not yet considered a fixed canonical concept in those circles propagating the reception of the Jewish Bible in early Christianity.[88] As shown in the preceding section, there were indeed important editorial traditions that shaped a class of "Writings" referring to Jewish examples and placed it at

---

82. See ibid.
83. See ibid., 213.
84. See ibid., 190, 219.
85. See ibid., 168, II, 488ff, Tafel 44F.
86. See ibid., III, 340f n. 243.
87. See ibid., I, 265.
88. For discussion see my *Endgestalten*, 57–124.

the end of the OT, which is in accordance with the TNK structure. However, these traditions were not able to prevail in Christianity.

Regarding the question of canonical hermeneutics and the suitability of future editorial practice, it seems to be appropriate to the historical evidence to allow a certain plurality of arrangement and to appreciate the potential of several of the historically important orders for exegesis. Biblical editors should reflect on and substantiate their decision to hold to a particular order.

Bibliography

Barton, John. *Oracles of God: Perceptions of Ancient Prophecy in Israel after the Exile.* London: Darton, Longman & Todd, 1986.

Beckwith, Roger T. *The Old Testament Canon of the New Testament Church and Its Background in Early Judaism.* London: SPCK, 1985.

Boyarin, Daniel. *Intertextuality and the Reading of Midrash.* Indiana Studies in Biblical Literature. Bloomington: Indiana University Press, 1990.

Brandt, Peter. *Endgestalten des Kanons: Das Arrangement der Schriften Israels in der jüdischen und christlichen Bibel.* BBB 31. Berlin: Philo, 2001.

———. "Geflecht aus 81 Büchern: Zur variantenreichen Gestalt des äthiopischen Bibelkanons." *Aethiopica* 3 (2000) 79–115.

Darlow, Thomas H., and Horace F. Moule. *Historical Catalogue of the Printed Editions of Holy Scripture in the Library of the British and Foreign Bible Society,* vol. 2: *Polyglots and Languages Other Than English.* New York: Kraus, 1963.

Eising, Ephräm Burkhard. *Zur Geschichte des Kanons der Heiligen Schrift in der ostsyrischen Kirche im ersten Jahrtausend.* 3 vols.: *I. Text; II. Tafeln; III. Anmerkungen. . . .* Ph.D. diss. Würzburg, 1972.

Haran, Menahem. "Archives, Libraries, and the Order of the Biblical Books." *JANES* 22 (1993) 51–61.

Köster, Uwe. *Studien zu den katholischen deutschen Bibelübersetzungen im 16., 17. und 18. Jahrhundert.* Reformationsgeschichtliche Studien und Texte 134. Münster: Aschendorff, 1995.

Leiman, Sid Z. *The Canonization of Hebrew Scripture: The Talmudic and Midrashic Evidence.* Transactions of the Connecticut Academy of Arts and Sciences 47. Hamden: Archon, 1976.

Lipschütz, Lazar. "Mishael ben Uzziel's Treatise on the Differences between Ben Asher and Ben Naphtali." *Textus* 2 (supplement; 1962) 1–45.

Maier, Johann. "Schriftlesung in jüdischer Tradition." Pp. 505–59 in *Streit am Tisch des Wortes? Zur Deutung und Bedeutung des Alten Testaments und seiner Verwendung in der Liturgie.* Edited by Ansgar Franz. Pietas liturgica 8. St. Ottilien: EOS, 1997.

Miles, Jack. *God: A Biography.* New York: Simon & Schuster, 1995.

Mosis, Rudolf. "Canonical Approach und Vielfalt des Kanon: Zu einer neuen Einleitung in das Alte Testament." *TTZ* 106 (1997) 39–59.

———. "Eine neue 'Einleitung in das Alte Testament' und das christlich-jüdische Gespräch." *TTZ* 106 (1997) 232–40.

Penkower, Jordan S. "The Chapter Divisions in the 1525 Rabbinic Bible." *VT* 48 (1998) 350–74.

————. "Peshitta Institute Communications V." *VT* 17 (1967) 132–33.

Posner, Raphael, and Israel Ta-Shema. *The Hebrew Book: An Historical Survey.* Jerusalem: Leon Amiel, 1975.

Reif, Stefan C. *Hebrew Manuscripts at Cambridge University Library: A Description and Introduction.* University of Cambridge Oriental Publications 52. Cambridge: Cambridge University Press, 1997.

Rüger, Hans Peter. "Ein Fragment der bisher ältesten hebräischen Bibelhandschrift mit babylonischer Punktation." *VT* 16 (1966) 65–73.

Sarna, Nahum M. "Bible: Canon." *EncJud* 4 (1971) 816–32.

Steins, Georg. *Die Chronik als kanonisches Abschlußphänomen.* BBB 93. Weinheim: Athenäum, 1995.

Stemberger, Günter. *Midrasch: Vom Umgang der Rabbinen mit der Bibel, Einführung – Texte – Erläuterungen.* Munich: Beck, 1989.

Tov, Emanuel. *Textual Criticism of the Hebrew Bible.* Minneapolis: Augsburg Fortress, 1992.

Wolfenson, Louis Bernard. "Implications of the Place of the Book of Ruth in Editions, Manuscripts, and Canon of the Old Testament." *HUCA* 1 (1924) 151–78.

A Wandering Moabite: Ruth—A Book in Search of a Canonical Home

Stephen Dempster

Canon and Context

Knowledge of context is crucial for effective communication across cultures as well as within cultures. For example, "spitting" may be an act of disdain or a complement depending on the cultural context. A handshake can be an example of friendliness or forwardness. Similarly, within a particular culture, depending on the situational context, a person wielding a knife can be either a criminal or a surgeon.

Context is not only important for the interpretation of life, it is essential for the interpretation of texts. For example, consider the following text:

> Rocky slowly got up from the mat, planning his escape. He hesitated a moment and thought. Things were not going well. What bothered him most was being held, especially since the charge against him had been weak. He considered his present situation. The lock that held him was strong, but he thought he could break it.[1]

The text yields two fundamentally different meanings when provided with these different titles: "A Wrestler in a Tight Corner" and "A Prisoner Plans His Escape."[2] The different contexts presented by the titles lead to different meanings for the identity of Rocky and the main vocabulary of the text ("held," "charge," "lock," "break").

Knowledge of biblical context cannot be overstated as important for proper interpretation of the text of Scripture. Reading Ecclesiastes without its "orthodox" epilogue in 12:8–14 can result in a very different meaning.[3] The ending eliminates any semantic ambiguity that the previous text might convey. Similarly, the addition of a genealogical note to a text can transform

---

1. Gillian Brown and George Yule, *Discourse Analysis* (Cambridge: Cambridge University Press, 1983) 139.

2. Ibid.

3. "The prime legacy of source criticism in the interpretation of Ecclesiastes is this tendency to read the book without the epilogue. By comparison, in almost all pre-critical interpretation of Ecclesiastes the epilogue provides the interpretative key." See Craig G. Bartholomew, *Ecclesiastes* (Grand Rapids, MI: Baker Academic, 2009) 37.

it from a seemingly banal story of domestic life into a dramatically charged central act of salvation history.[4] Shorn of its canonical context The Song of Songs could easily be viewed as "pornographic."[5] In other texts, context is equally crucial for proper understanding. The narrator of 2 Samuel 6 places a statement about Michal's barrenness after her criticism of David's wild dance in front of the ark to suggest a cause-effect relationship. Saul's lethal jealousy is not limited to his person but also infects his daughter long after the death of her father.[6] Even the choice of diction is motivated by context, as the frequent reference to Bathsheba as "the wife of Uriah" in 2 Samuel 11–12 reveals, as well as the paucity of use of the title "king" referring to David.[7] Reading the stories of David's tragic demise in the ensuing chapters suggests that David has been the architect of his own fate. Indeed, reading texts in a certain sequence constrains meaning in the same way that the first person leaving the scene of a murder creates a certain impression of guilt.[8] Knowing this context is the difference between seeing "clues" versus seeing brute "facts."

When the literary context transcends the boundaries of the individual books of the Bible, its hermeneutical relevance is just as important. After all, the canon of Scripture is a more-global context that has been created out of many smaller texts. What a very different Bible it would be if Exodus and Genesis switched their positions or if Deuteronomy and Kings exchanged canonical locations. What would be the theological impact for Christians of placing the Old Testament after the New Testament? In the first case, world history would be subordinated to Israelite history rather than vice-versa. In the second, Deuteronomy would lose its pivotal role as a theological bridge between the previous books of the Torah and the

---

4. Ruth 4:18–22.

5. Perhaps this is the reason why the Song of Songs has been functionally "decanonized"—not used very much any longer. Its embedded context within the canon has been severed by historical criticism. In other words, theoretical "decanonization" has taken place before functional "decanonization." David Carr makes the point that, as the allegorical meaning shifted to the literal meaning in the nineteenth century, this led to far less use of the Song in the Church. Thus, "biblical scholarship's push for an exclusively literal approach . . . has transformed what was once a religious literary classic into a literary one . . . [thus leading to the conclusion that] the triumph of a critical approach can divest a text of its canonical function." Carr's argument for an "original non-theological intention" of the Song reveals his own reliance on the historical-critical methodology. David M. Carr, "The Song of Songs as a Microcosm of the Canonization and Decanonization Process," in *Canonization and Decanonization* (ed. A. van der Kooij and K. van der Toorn; Leiden: Brill, 1998) 185–86, 188.

6. See the discussion in Gabriel Josipovici, *The Book of God: A Response to the Bible* (New Haven, CT: Yale University Press, 1990) 22–23. While the author tries to stress the ambiguity of the grammar, the context eliminates any ambiguity.

7. 2 Sam 11:3, 11, 26; 12:9, 10, 15.

8. See the insightful observations by John H. Sailhamer, *Introduction to Old Testament Theology: A Canonical Approach* (Grand Rapids, MI: Zondervan, 1995) 251–52.

subsequent historical books. In the last example, the Old Testament would have the status of an appendix, or afterthought, providing information to shed light on the events disclosed in the New Testament, rather than as an essential root of development completed by the New Testament.[9]

But these possibilities of various sequences are not just a matter of hypothetical speculation. In a number of important instances, there are some concrete examples. For example, in the Greek tradition the book of Chronicles is given the title "The Remaining Things." This is probably because it followed Samuel–Kings in this canonical sequence, and it therefore was viewed as a supplement to the earlier narrative. But in an important Hebrew tradition, Chronicles serves to close the canon, where it functions as a historical recapitulation of and theological reflection on the entire Bible. In the one sequence, it functions as an appendix; in the other, it is a culminating conclusion![10]

Ruth, Context, and Meaning

The book of Ruth is one of the biblical books, the canonicity of which has rarely been in doubt, but the canonical context has been.[11] In the history of the canon, it has seemed to wander from place to place within the orders of the various canonical books. Did this wandering Moabite ever have an original canonical home?[12] How did it adapt to its new surroundings and contribute to them as it wandered from place to place in the country of the canon? How was it affected by its new locations?

One of the weaknesses of Brevard Childs's groundbreaking study of canon in *The Old Testament as Scripture*[13] was his seeming lack of concern for the order of individual books in the canon and the hermeneutical

---

9. Thus in the traditional arrangement with the Old Testament preceding the New Testament, Jesus is seen as the climax of Israel's history rather than just the savior of the world. For further thoughts on the importance of canonical context, see my "Exodus and Biblical Theology: On Moving into the Neighborhood with a New Name," *Southern Baptist Journal of Theology* 12 (2008) 6.

10. Georg Steins, *Die Chronik als kanonisches Abschlussphänomen: Studien zur Entstehung und Theologie von 1/2 Chronik* (Weinheim: Athenäum, 1995). For more on this view, see Steins's essay in the present volume.

11. From a statement in the Babylonian Talmud (b. Meg. 7a), some scholars have concluded that at one time Ruth's canonicity had been challenged, since its canonicity was affirmed with books whose canonicity was known to be disputed. Thus the book was "guilty by association." While theological problems caused by the content of the book probably led to this questioning, concerns of this rarely surfaced in the tradition (only this once). For the relevant discussion, see Roger T. Beckwith, *The Old Testament Canon of the New Testament Church* (Grand Rapids, MI: Eerdmans, 1985) 304–6.

12. David Jobling, "Ruth Finds a Home: Canon, Politics, Method," in *The New Literary Criticism and the Hebrew Bible* (ed. J. Cheryl Exum and David J. A. Clines; Sheffield: Continuum, 1993) 125–39.

13. Brevard S. Childs, *Introduction to the Old Testament as Scripture* (Philadelphia: Fortress, 1979).

relevance of such a sequence.[14] Although he wrote much about the context of the canon, it was clear in his work that he was concerned with establishing the importance of the final form of the individual canonical books.[15] This oversight was addressed in some of his later work.[16] But at the same time, in his most notable early study on canon for the book of Ruth, he did see the importance of a canonical context that transcends the book itself. He believed that it was difficult to ascertain an original canonical home for this book (that is, its canonical order), but he felt that a "far more fruitful avenue of investigation would be to explore the effect of a canonical ordering on the reading of the book and the differing theologies involved in the canonical arrangement of the Greek and Hebrew Bibles."[17]

While there has been little attention given to the impact of the arrangement of the canonical books on their meaning, some studies have shown that this can be a fruitful area for investigation. Walter Brueggemann's *Creative Word* and Claus Westermann's *Elements of an Old Testament Theology* have shown the significance of the major canonical divisions of the Hebrew Bible for issues of education and biblical theology, respectively.[18] In these studies, the various combinations of books are shown to be hermeneutically significant. As it is important to study the larger literary context of an individual book to understand the meaning of the book, it is important to study the larger literary horizon of a larger grouping of books that have been placed together in a larger text such as the canon. It may be that their grouping is simple aggregation in the form of an anthology, but this is a conclusion that will result from careful study. That the groupings are *not* simply aggregation is the conviction of three recent major studies.

The point of departure for Peter Brandt's massive study on canon is the following statement: "Die Bibel ist mehr als nur ein 'Bücherschrank', eine Sammlung selbständiger Einzelschriften, und das Arrangement der Schriften in der Bibel stellt einen Schlüssel bereit, um die Vielfalt der inhalte strukturiert zu lesen."[19] Similar is the essential thesis statement of Julius Steinberg's impressive monograph on the Ketubim: "Die Makrostruktur des Hebräischen Bibelkanons ist hermeneutisch signifikant. Mit dem Ort eines jeden Buches im literarischen Gesamtfüge weist sie diesem auch seinen Ort

---

14. Stephen G. Dempster, "An 'Extraordinary Fact': Torah and Temple and the Contours of the Hebrew Canon, Part 1," *TynBul* 48 (1997) 32. See also Walter Brueggemann, *The Creative Word* (4th ed.; Philadelphia: Fortress, 1982) 5.

15. See, for example, the pertinent comments by Timothy J. Stone, *The Compilational History of the Megilloth: Canon, Contoured Intertextuality and Meaning in the Writings* (Ph.D. diss., University of St. Andrews, 2010) 11–14.

16. Ibid., 13–14.

17. Childs, *Introduction*, 564.

18. Brueggemann, *The Creative Word*; Claus Westermann, *Elements of Old Testament Theology* (trans. Douglas W. Scott, Atlanta: John Knox, 1982).

19. Peter Brandt, *Endgestalten des Kanons: Das Arrangement der Schriften Israels in der jüdischen und christlichen Bibel* (Berlin: Philo, 2001) 16.

im theologischen Gesamtgefüge zu."[20] Timothy Stone's study of the Megillot in the context of the third division of the Hebrew Bible concludes that "the Writings' arrangement does not appear random, nor does 'anthology' seem to best describe its contents. Though diverse, the writings are more like a curated exhibition in which works of art are arranged carefully in relationship to one another."[21]

If one were to consider the place of the book of Ruth in the various editions of the Hebrew Bible during the first half of the second millennium C.E., there would be many different possibilities. But just as happens today, various editions of the Bible were made in the past for various reasons. Today there are parallel Bibles, chronological Bibles, one-year study Bibles, liturgical Bibles, devotional Bibles, archaeological study Bibles, women's Bibles, and some of these provide different arrangements of the books based on a difference of function. For instance, in Gideon New Testaments, the books of Psalms and Proverbs are often found in an appendix. This does not mean that the other books of the Old Testament were not considered important, but this arrangement has been made for practical and liturgical/devotional reasons. Similarly, there are editions featuring only the Gospels or Prophets. An individual from the future studying our century might conclude that canonical order was not important because of all the diversity. But that would be a mistake. Similarly, for the late medieval period, the diversity of order—particularly for the Writings—should not lead to the conclusion that canonical order was unimportant. For example, after a survey of the various locations of Ruth in the Hebrew manuscripts and editions of the Bible, L. B. Wolfenson observes:

> At first the position of Ruth and the arrangement of the Hagiographa as given in the Talmud was followed. When, however, it was convenient to depart from this order, there was evidently no scruple about doing this. There could, therefore, have been nothing about the Talmudic order which was considered sacred or even necessary and binding. It was merely the order of "our Rabbis," and any one else could have another order if he chose. Hence it is that the Masoretes departed from the order of "our Rabbis."[22]

Wolfenson reaches a false conclusion based on the evidence. Diversity need not preclude canonical order but may well have assumed it.[23] Because there was a certainty of order, there was freedom to experiment with various orders for various reasons, whether heuristic or liturgical. For example, there were some Hebrew Bibles in which five scrolls (Megillot) were united

---

20. Julius Steinberg, *Die Ketuvim: Ihr Aufbau und ihre Botschaft* (BBB 152; Hamburg: Philo, 2006) foreword, p. 7.

21. Stone, *Compilational History*, 188.

22. L. B. Wolfenson, "Implications of the Place of the Book of Ruth in Editions, Manuscripts, and Canon of the Old Testament," *HUCA* 1 (1924) 163.

23. See the perceptive comments by Steinberg, *Ketuvim*, 85.

because of their liturgical function on festival days: Song of Songs (Passover), Ruth (Weeks), Lamentations (Ninth of Ab), Ecclesiastes (Sukkot), Esther (Purim). Sometimes these five books were placed immediately after the Torah to form two collections of five for liturgical convenience, since these ten books were the only ones that were publicly read in the synagogue in their entirety during the course of a year.[24] Occasionally, they were even inserted into the Pentateuch, each matched with a corresponding book of the Torah.[25] But this fact in no way should be interpreted to conclude the irrelevance of an original canonical order.

The various locations, of course, led to multiple meanings based on the new contexts. Four examples from various traditions illustrate this point. In the Hebrew tradition, in which the liturgical reading of the scrolls is stressed, the content of the books as well as their small size made them particularly appropriate for being read on these occasions. The imagery of springtime in the Song of Songs contributed to its being read on Passover, just as the barley harvest imagery in Ruth linked it with the Feast of Weeks. The outpouring of grief in Lamentations was suitable for the commemoration of the destruction of the city of Jerusalem, while the emphasis on enjoying the fruits of work made Ecclesiastes appropriate for reading at the Feast of Sukkot (Tabernacles). Esther, of course, carried its own justification for the Festival of Purim. Some have suggested that one can detect a sort of allegory for human life with the order of some of the books: Songs, the youthful springtime; Ruth nearing middle age; and Ecclesiastes, old age and the enjoyment of the fruits of the harvest.[26] In the Masoretic Hebrew tradition, there is a shift from the more liturgical sequence of Songs, Ruth, Lamentations, Ecclesiastes, and Esther to the more chronological order of Ruth, Songs, Ecclesiastes, Lamentations, and Esther.

In one very early canonical list, possibly coming from Christian circles, there is the following sequence: Genesis, Exodus, Leviticus, Deuteronomy, Numbers, Ruth, Job, Judges."[27] This anomalous arrangement places Ruth between Numbers and Job.[28] Thus three books are placed beside each other that strikingly develop the theme of loss and restoration, or death and rebirth. In each, an old generation gives way to a new generation, with survivors from the old continuing.[29] In each, there is incredible loss yet inconceivable restoration. In each, there is mention of inheritance, particularly

24. Brandt, *Endgestalten*, 136–141.

25. Ibid., 140.

26. Irmtraud Fischer, *Rut* (HThKAT; Vienna: Herder, 2001) 101.

27. This is the Bryennios List. See J. P. Audet, "A Hebrew-Aramaic List of Books of the Old Testament in Greek Transcription," *JTS* 1 (1950) 135–54. This list has been variously dated from the early 2nd to the 4th century C.E.

28. To my knowledge, this list is unique.

29. In Numbers, the first generation of Israelites who experienced the exodus is replaced with a second generation. The survivors of the first generation are Joshua and Caleb. In Ruth, all the males from Elimelech's line die, and the survivors are the women, Naomi and Ruth. Job loses all his children, but they are replaced with a new generation.

of women: Zelophad's daughters, Naomi and Ruth, and Job's daughters. Important central players in each book—the exasperated Moses, the bereft Naomi, and the inconsolable Job—all seem like members of the same family.[30]

In another sequence, deriving from the Eastern Church in early Peshitta manuscripts in which some apocryphal books are included, Ruth is grouped with three other books dealing with women in a so-called Book of Women: Ruth, Susannah, Esther, and Judith.[31] These "books" are united because the main character in every one is female, and each of the women overcomes great odds to become a real heroine in Israel.

Finally, in the Greek tradition, Ruth appears in a more familiar place to modern readers, because it follows Judges. But sometimes in this position, it can terminate a narrative sequence beginning with Genesis before a new division of poetic books begins. The sequence from Genesis to Ruth is thus an Octateuch.[32] While it is not possible to ascertain all the reasons for this series,[33] no doubt Christian hermeneutical reasons were at least partially at work. That a division of books would begin with Genesis with all of its genealogies and end with the genealogy of David—the Old Testament Messiah—could hardly have been fortuitous. This would clearly link up this genealogy with the genealogy of David's greater Son that begins the Gospel of Matthew.[34] In one manuscript of the Ethiopic tradition, this messianic thrust became explicit because Ruth with its genealogy is placed as the last book of the Old Testament![35]

All of these various locations for the book of Ruth have created a certain meaning. New juxtapositions create new meanings. Old Testament theologian John Sailhamer describes this effect as "montage." Citing the work of the Russian filmmaker Sergei Eisenstein, he writes:

> [C]ompetent viewers always seek to understand the parts in the light of the whole. . . . When the materials within distinct "shot-pieces" are linked by juxtaposing them on the projector reel and thereby onto the screen, the viewer is forced to identify elements of both shots that is [*sic*] characteristic of a single theme or image. A montage thus actually forces the viewer of a film to construct a theme or an image of a theme. The

---

30. For example, some commentators have described Naomi as "Job's sister." See S. Spangenberg, "Constructing a Historical Context for the Ruth Novelette: Dovetailing the Views of J. A. Loader and R. Albertz," *OTE* 18 (2005) 345–55.

31. See the Milan Codex from the 6th–7th centuries C.E. and the Florence Codex from the 9th century. See Beckwith, *Old Testament Canon*, 196. Beckwith also notes that there is a similar sequence of three books, Ruth, Esther, and Judith, in the Latin Bobbio Missal dating to the 7th century (p. 226 n. 34). For the list, see Henry Barclay Swete, *An Introduction to the Old Testament in Greek: With an Appendix Containing the Letter of Aristeas* (1st ed.; Cambridge: Cambridge University Press, 2010) 213.

32. Brandt, *Endgestalten*, 201–4.

33. Ibid., 204.

34. Matt 1:1–18.

35. Fischer, *Rut*, 106.

same can be said of reading a canonical sequence such as is found in OT texts.[36]

Thus a book is understood a bit differently as a result of its new position in the Bible, and in this position a distinctive meaning has been created. But what about an original canonical order or canonical home for this wandering biblical book about a Moabite woman? What were the hermeneutical implications of such an original home and its major migrations?

The Search for a Canonical Home

The search for an original canonical home for this book has been undertaken by a few scholars, and they will be noted in due course. Most investigators agree that the migrations of the book have stemmed originally from two possible positions in the canon. These two positions can be documented and are to be identified with the Hebrew Bible and the Septuagint, or the Hebrew and Greek traditions. The Hebrew tradition locates the book in the third division of the Tanak, the Writings, while the Greek tradition locates it in the historical books between Judges and 1 Samuel. To be sure, the Greek tradition is probably not derived from a Christian tradition; it was adopted by Christians, but its roots are to be found in Judaism.

Hebrew Tradition

(1) The first order can be traced back to the Talmud and beyond that to at least the first century C.E. According to an early tradition cited in the Talmud, Ruth begins the third division of the Hebrew Bible:

> The order of the Hagiographa is Ruth and the Book of Psalms, Job and Proverbs, Ecclesiastes, Song of Songs, Lamentations, Daniel and the Scroll of Esther, Ezra and Chronicles. Now on the view that Job lived in the days of Moses, should not the book of Job come first?—We do not begin with a record of suffering. But Ruth also is a record of suffering?—It is a suffering with a sequel [of happiness], as R. Yohanan said: Why was her name called Ruth?—Because there issued from her David who replenished the Holy One, blessed be He, with hymns and praises.[37]

Since this text is a *baraita*, which is a saying from the rabbis that was not included in the Mishnah, it could date to anywhere from the middle of the 1st century C.E. to the end of the 2nd century. There is one clue that suggests the latest possible date for this baraita. A Rabbi Yohanan is said to have provided explanations for the order of a number of the books. This assumes an order that requires explanation, so this particular order, in which Ruth precedes Psalms as the first book of the Ketubim, can be regarded as being fixed before 100 C.E. since Yohanan's dates are 30–90 C.E.[38] Roger Beckwith in his study of the canon argued that this particular understand-

---

36. Sailhamer, *Old Testament Theology*, 252.
37. B. B. Bat. 14b (ET: I. Epstein, ed., *The Babylonian Talmud* [London: Soncino, 1961]).
38. This, of course, assumes the reliability of the tradition.

ing could be traced back as far as 150 B.C.E., when in his opinion the canon was organized and closed under the Maccabees.[39]

The fact that this particular order belongs to a closed canon of 24 books has independent confirmation in one important text, 4 Ezra 14. This book, which is dated near the end of the first century C.E., is trying to argue for a more inclusive canon but makes a telling distinction between 24 books that can be read in public and 70 in private. The 24 are clearly canonical books recognized by all.[40]

(2) A second order deriving from Jewish circles places Ruth following Proverbs. In this list, Chronicles precedes the Psalter, and Ruth is followed by Songs, Ecclesiastes, Lamentations, and Esther. This evidence is found in the Leningrad Codex, which dates to the early 11th century C.E. but certainly has earlier antecedents.[41]

Most scholars have argued that this must reflect a later arrangement from the first order mentioned above, since Ruth is grouped together to form the Megillot—five books that were associated as a group for liturgical reasons. Since liturgy was a later development in Judaism, this arrangement must also be later. The fact that the order found in this manuscript is not the standard, apparently later (calendrical) liturgical order (Songs, Ruth, Lamentations, Ecclesiastes, and Esther) has suggested to scholars that the standard order has been modified for chronological reasons in the Masoretic sequence.[42]

Recently, Timothy Stone has argued that the first Masoretic order was not primarily liturgical but preserved an ancient sequence.[43] Even though the books known later as the Megillot were grouped together, there were other, nonliturgical factors that generated this particular sequence—factors relating to what he has termed a "compilational" grammar. Later, when liturgical factors came into play for reading some of the books (Esther, Lamentations), others in close canonical contiguity were drawn into their liturgical orbit (Ruth, Songs, Lamentations). But originally, Stone argues, in the history of the canon there were efforts made to secure certain sequences through various techniques such as the use of catch-words,

---

39. Beckwith, *Old Testament Canon*.

40. Independent confirmation of the number can be found in saying #52 of the 2nd-century C.E. work The Gospel of Thomas, which suggests that the Old Testament is to be understood as 24 prophets. Possibly there is a similar reference to the 35 books of the Old Testament in The Shepherd of Hermas, The Twelve (minor prophets) being counted individually. In Hermas 101:16 there is a reference to the 35 stones of a foundation being God's prophets and ministers. I am indebted to Simon Gathercole (personal communication) for this reference.

41. One of which is certainly the Aleppo Codex, which dates about 80 years earlier. The Writings essentially begin with Song 3:11 and end with the end of Nehemiah. Ruth is missing, but it probably preceded Song of Songs and was preceded by Proverbs. Codex Cairensis comes from the same Tiberian tradition but, unfortunately, it only contains the second division of the Hebrew Bible. It dates to around 895 C.E.

42. Beckwith, *Old Testament Canon*, 210, 229 n. 76.

43. Stone, *Compilational History*, 64–97.

phrases, framing devices, superscriptions, linking motifs, and contrastive content.[44] Thus the ending of Proverbs 31 with its question "Who can find a virtuous woman?" is directly answered by the book of Ruth, in which Boaz addresses Ruth with the statement, "You are a virtuous woman!" John Sailhamer has made similar arguments for this particular arrangement of books, arguing that the sequence Ruth–Song–Ecclesiastes–Lamentations–Esther contains "the only books in the Hebrew canon which have a feminine singular subject throughout."[45]

Greek Tradition

Josephus provides the first evidence for an order in which Ruth is placed between Judges and Samuel, an arrangement that has become standard in modern Christian Bibles. Josephus's statement on canon is critical, since it attests to a 22-book, closed canon:

> Naturally, then, or rather necessarily—seeing that it is not open to anyone to write of their own accord, nor is there any disagreement present in what is written, but the prophets alone learned, by inspiration from God, what had happened in the distant and most ancient past and recorded plainly in their own time just as they occurred—among us there are not thousands of books in disagreement and conflict with each other, but only twenty-two books, containing the record of all time, which are rightly trusted. Five of these are the books of Moses, which contain both the laws and the tradition from the birth of humanity up to his death; this is a period of a little less than 3,000 years. From the death of Moses until Artaxerxes, king of the Persians after Xerxes, the prophets after Moses wrote the history of what took place in their own times in thirteen books; the remaining four books contain hymns to God and instruction for people on life. From Artaxerxes up to our own time every event has been recorded but this is not judged worthy of the same trust, since the exact line of succession of the prophets did not continue. It is in clear in practice how we approach our own writings. Although such a long time has now passed, no-one has dared to add, to take away, or to alter anything; and it is innate in every Judean right from birth, to regard them as decrees of God, to remain faithful to them and, if necessary, to die on their behalf. Thus, to date many have been seen, on many occasions, as prisoners of war suffering torture and all kinds of death in theaters for not letting slip a single word in contraventions of the laws and records associated with them.[46]

This description of 5 books of Moses, 13 books of prophecy, and 4 books of hymns and precepts does not explicitly name Ruth, but it seems to classify

---

44. Ibid., 9–30.

45. Sailhamer, *Old Testament Theology*, 214.

46. *Against Apion* 8.37–43 (ET: John M. G. Barclay, *Flavius Josephus: Translation and Commentary* [Leiden: Brill, 2006] 28–32).

books according to genre. From Josephus's study of the Bible—*The Antiquities*—it is clear that Judges was followed by Ruth.[47] Melito, who provides the earliest explicit Christian list of Old Testament books, dates to the last half of the 2nd century C.E. His list is preserved by Eusebius, and it claims to be based on Jewish sources. In this list, Ruth follows Judges and precedes Samuel.[48] Similarly, a tradition from the time of Origen seems to confirm this because he describes a 22-book canon of the Jews based on the number of letters in the Hebrew alphabet. Origen notes that the number 22 was reached by combining Ruth with Judges and Lamentations with Jeremiah.[49] This probably reflects the order that became the basis of the Septuagint. Moreover, about a century later, Jerome mentions two traditions among the Jews, an arrangement of 22 books like that described by Origen and an ordering of 24 in which Ruth and Lamentations are relocated to the Hagiographa.[50] Again the first number is important, because it is connected to the Hebrew alphabet. It is also noteworthy that the sequence Judges–Ruth–1 Samuel, which became dominant in the Greek tradition, has Hebrew and not Christian roots.

The Irrelevance of Sequence?

Before considering the question of the meaning generated by the above sequences and seeking to determine an original canonical home for Ruth, it is important to deal with an objection. A number of scholars claim that, before the invention of the large scroll or the codex, canonical sequence would have been irrelevant since each of the canonical books would have been on separate individual scrolls. It was only when books were included on the same larger scroll or placed in the same codex that sequence became important. Thus, there could be no "canonical montage" before the technological innovation of the codex. The new technology created a physical, linear sequence, which then would have had ramifications for meaning. Before this time, "the question of an original place of Ruth in the Canon is, therefore, quite useless and absurd, since there could have been no original

---

47. *Antiquities* 5.9.

48. Accordingly when I went East and came to the place where these things were preached and done, I learned accurately the books of the Old Testament, and send them to thee as written below. Their names are as follows: Of Moses, five books: Genesis, Exodus, Leviticus, Numbers, Deuteronomy, Jesus Nave, Judges, Ruth; of Kings, four books; of Chronicles, two; the Psalms of David, the Proverbs of Solomon, which is also Wisdom; Ecclesiastes, Song of Songs, Job; of Prophets, Isaiah, Jeremiah; of the twelve prophets, one book; Daniel, Ezekiel, Esdras. From which also I have made the extracts, dividing them into six books. (Eusebius, *Ecclesiastical History* 4.26:13–14, trans. Arthur Cushman McGiffert, in Philip Schaff and Henry Wace, eds., *Nicene and Post-Nicene Fathers*, 2nd Series, vol. 1 [Buffalo, NY: Christian Literature, 1890])

49. Eusebius, *Ecclesiastical History* 6.25: 2.

50. *Prologus Galeatus* ("Helmeted Preface" to Kings).

place with each book a separate volume, and the combination of one or more books of Scripture into one volume a very late procedure."[51]

This sort of view may be guilty of having assumptions that predetermine the evidence. There are many cases of multivolume works from before and after the invention of the codex. *Enuma Elish*, *The Epic of Gilgamesh*, and Herodotus's *Histories* come readily to mind before the invention,[52] and after, contemporary works such as Will Durant's 11-volume *Story of Civilization* and Karl Barth's 31-volume *Die kirchliche Dogmatik*. The fact that the conventionally published 3-volume *Lord of the Rings* is frequently nowadays published in a 1-volume form does not mean that order was once unimportant. Order and sequence are mental constructs first before they are realized in a material form. Before the larger scroll or codex, there certainly were other means to maintain the sequence of a multivolume collection. One way was to use other means, such as physical contiguity. Books in a particular grouping could be placed in a box together or inserted into ordered niches in a wall that functioned like an ancient version of bookshelves. There is ample evidence of both types of collections from the ancient world. But literary links could ensure the proper reading as well as identification tags in the form of incipits, colophons, or clay bullas.[53] Thus the opening of Exodus connects it to Genesis as does Leviticus to Exodus and Numbers to Leviticus, and Deuteronomy to Numbers as well as Joshua to Deuteronomy.[54] The idea that sequence is anachronistic does not square with the evidence of this integrated unity of the first nine books in the Hebrew Bible.

Many scholars assume that the reason that lists and concern for explicit order among canonical books were unimportant until relatively late in the history of the canonical process has to do with the late emergence of the concept of canon. But another reason lies closer at hand and is far more convincing. The desire to specify a fixed order in writing would have been unnecessary while the scrolls were being stored in the same sacred space. But when the sacred space was eliminated by the destruction of the temple,

---

51. Wolfenson, "Implications of the Place of Ruth," 174. See also James Barr, *Holy Scripture: Canon, Authority, Criticism* (Oxford: Oxford: Oxford University Press, 1983) 57. John Barton, *Oracles of God: Perceptions of Ancient Prophecy in Israel after the Exile* (Oxford: Oxford University Press, 2007) 83–91.

52. One also thinks of the works by Theophrastus (*De Causis Plantarum*, 8 vols.; and *Historia Plantarum*, 10 vols.) and Strabo (*Geography*, 17 vols.).

53. Stephen G. Dempster, "From Many Texts to One: The Formation of the Hebrew Bible," in *The World of the Aramaeans I: Biblical Studies in Honour of Paul-Eugene Dion* (ed. P. M. Michèle Daviau, John William Wevers, and Michael Weigl; Sheffield: Sheffield: Sheffield Academic Press, 2001) 49–51.

54. See, for example, Konrad Schmid, who argues persuasively, for example, through literary devices, grammar, content, and chronological factors that "the Genesis–2 Kings complex [9 books] is thus not merely a series of individual books whose content coincidentally fit together." Konrad Schmid, *Genesis and the Moses Story: Israel's Dual Origins in the Hebrew Bible* (Siphrut: Literature and Theology of the Hebrew Scriptures 3; Winona Lake, IN: Eisenbrauns, 2010) 1–2, 16ff., 26–29. See also my "Many Texts," 45–49.

the focus had to shift to the texts themselves. Andrew Steinmann describes this point concisely:

> Just as the Temple records of priestly lineage served as a definitive official collection of records, the books archived in the Temple as Scripture must have served as a definitive collection of those sacred books. The clear implication of this evidence is that before the fall of Jerusalem in AD 70 canonicity was determined by a book's admission to the archives of Scripture in the Temple, not by being part of a list of accepted books as in later times.[55]

Timothy Stone's recent study confirms Steinmann's point. Observing that meticulous precision and order was the hallmark of sacred space in the ancient world, never mind ancient Israel, Stone remarks:

> Imagine the temple without a collection of sacred documents or that they are haphazardly piled in a corner or on a shelf. In my judgment, this is unthinkable, whereas a temple collection gives a plausible answer to Kraft's doubts about canonical assumptions. In the cultural context of a temple collection, the boundaries and order of the canon may well be more—not less—important than they are today. To make lists of holy books while the temple remained standing would be superfluous. It is precisely this sacred *space*, and not some sacred *list,* that one would expect to be meaningful in the conceptual world of Judaism! Scholars' demand for a list may (ironically) betray an anachronistic appeal to the *formulation* of canons *as* lists in the second to fourth century C.E. in the church.[56]

"Canonical Montage"

1. Ruth before Psalms: David

In this particular order, the justification given by the citation in the Talmud provides a major reason for the meaning generated by the sequence. The tradition says that books dealing with judgment are balanced by works dealing with salvation. Thus, Ruth begins the Writings, and some other book does not. But it is clear from the explanation given in the baraita that books dealing with judgment are balanced by works dealing with salvation. Although Job is chronologically earlier, it is displaced by Ruth because Ruth ends on a positive note at the end with its announcement of the birth of David: "It is a suffering with a sequel [of happiness], as R. Yohanan said: Why was her name called Ruth?—Because there issued from her David who replenished the Holy One, blessed be He, with hymns and praises."[57] Although Job is a book of suffering that also ends on a positive note, it does

---

55. Andrew Steinmann, *The Oracles of God: The Old Testament Canon* (St. Louis: Concordia, 1999) 113. See also the insightful study by a historian: Donald Harman Akenson, *Surpassing Wonder: The Invention of the Bible and the Talmuds* (Chicago: University Of Chicago Press, 2001).

56. Stone, *Compilational History,* 70. For a popular version of this theory, see Akenson, *Surpassing Wonder.*

57. B. B. Bat. 14b (Soncino edition).

not have the same genealogical connection with the Psalms as does Ruth. This suggests that there is a hermeneutic at work that sees Ruth as an important prelude to the Psalter, David's book of praises.

What is the impact of reading the story of Ruth immediately before the Psalms? What is the meaning of this sequence that initiates the Writings? I have written about this before in other works,[58] but first to be noted is that Ruth in initial position in the Writings places David and his Gentile origins front and center in the final section of the Hebrew Bible.[59] Read in this way, the ubiquitous references to Bethlehem in Ruth become a lightning rod for Messianic hope with a universal scope. In the preceding prophetic message, David's hometown is clearly Bethlehem (1 Samuel 16), an eternal covenant has been made with him (2 Samuel 7), and Bethlehem has become the focus of a Davidic descendant whose domain will extend "to the ends of the earth" (Mic 5:1–3[2–4]). Ruth provides a "Messianic birth narrative" that compresses history, tying David to the patriarchal period, to the judges, and to the monarchy. The fact that this story concludes with his genealogy—which is the third and last ten-member genealogy in the Hebrew Bible—particularizes the global perspective of the previous two genealogies, sketching a genealogical trajectory reaching from Genesis 3 to the final division of the Hebrew Bible. The first of these genealogies began with Adam and ended with Noah, who provided salvation from the deluge (Genesis 5). The second genealogy led to Abram, who would bless the entire world through his descendants (Gen 11:10–26). The final genealogy culminates with David (Ruth 4:18–22).

The particular genealogical list with which the book of Ruth is concluded is signaled by the term: "These are the generations" (אֵלֶּה תּוֹלְדוֹת). This exact expression is only found 10 times in Genesis and once in Numbers.[60] It is probably significant that the 12th occurrence of this formula, the completion of the history of Israel, is found in Ruth. In some ways, David's birth is the capstone to the nation of Israel, because it will be through his line that the Messiah will come. Zvi Ron comments:

> The list of ancestors in Ruth was written as a ten-generation list to evoke these earlier lists and also to indicate that here a new epoch was beginning; the epoch of the Davidic monarchy. Just as Noah began the post-Flood world and Abraham the Israelite people in a new world divided into nations, David began the dynasty that will ultimately lead to messianic times under the Messiah son of David.[61]

---

58. Dempster, "Extraordinary Fact"; and idem, "Geography and Genealogy, Dominion and Dynasty: A Theology of the Hebrew Bible," in *Biblical Theology: Retrospect and Prospect* (ed. Scott J. Hafemann; Downers Grove, IL: InterVarsity, 2002) 79–80.

59. See further my "Extraordinary Fact"; "Geography and Genealogy, " 79–80.

60. Gen 2:4; 6:9; 10:1; 11:10, 27; 25:12, 19; 36:1, 9; 37:2; Num 3:1.

61. Zvi Ron, "The Geneaological List in the Book of Ruth: A Symbolic Approach," *JBQ* 38 (2010) 86.

In particular, this final genealogical note in Ruth led the rabbinic sages to the following conclusion: "The Rabbis understood that the Ruth list was written in a way that indicates that it represents the culmination of the cosmic saga of Genesis, the coming of the Messiah."[62] One rabbi even used this genealogy to explain the *plene* writing of the word David with a *yôd* in Chronicles. Because David was the 10th in the genealogy of Ruth and this had Messianic significance, whenever the name David was written in Chronicles, it signified the "complete David," the 10th one![63] Thus, beginning the third and final section of the canon with Ruth helps pick up themes from the rest of the biblical story, and it becomes a beacon for Messianic hope. It is not as if this provides an alternative version of history that can bypass the book of Samuel, but it functions also to supplement this history and to highlight some important information that the reader is aware of from the Torah and the Prophets: the genealogy of Tamar and the importance of Bethlehem.[64] By this time in a reading of the canonical story, Bethlehem (1 Samuel 16; Mic 5:1–3[2–4]) has become synonymous with hope for a ruler whose domain will reach "to the ends of the earth." Ruth thus provides a type of proto-messianic birth narrative originating at the threshing floor in Bethlehem for the founder of the Davidic Dynasty, to show his universal significance.[65]

The Psalter that follows Ruth in this canonical arrangement is David's book. The first two psalms present the blessedness of the individual who meditates on the Torah day and night and those who take refuge in Yahweh's coming universal King. David is the exemplar of the blessed man who meditates on the Torah day and night and who takes refuge in Yahweh. Although his great-grandfather Boaz has been viewed negatively by some commentators as a "blowhard" and an old man with "ulterior motives,"[66] it is nonetheless true that he has congratulated a Gentile woman for coming to Israel to take refuge under the wings of Yahweh and does indeed become those wings for her.[67] His great-grandson takes his advice, and his Torah meditation leads him to stress the importance of taking refuge in

---

62. Ibid., 87.

63. Ibid., 86.

64. For an alternative history, see David Jobling, *1 Samuel* (Berit Olam; Collegeville, MN: Liturgical Press, 1998). Jobling uses the terms "canonical alternative" and "short cut" to describe Ruth's function, particularly in its place before Samuel.

65. In the much larger context of the canon, perhaps there is a new Adam waking up from a deep sleep to find his new Eve, who will be the "mother" of David, another new Adam! See, for example, Peter Leithart, "When Gentile Meets Jew: A Christian Reading of Ruth and the Hebrew Scriptures," *Touchstone* 22 (2009) 20–24.

66. Linafelt, *Ruth*, 55ff. Such a view of Boaz is shortsighted and unable to grasp the grace that he experiences that night on the threshing floor. He sees clearly the meaning of Ruth's double *ḥesed*, that it is extended to those who cannot help themselves: Naomi, an old woman who almost views herself as dead (the first *ḥesed*), and an older man well past the springtime of youth and love (the second). For him, it is overwhelming (Ruth 3:10).

67. Ruth 2:12, 3:9. Boaz puts his theology into practice!

Yahweh—in fact, 13 times in the Psalms.[68] He is thus the embodiment of the blessed man in Psalm 1, who looks forward to the king who will rule the nations and direct the universal choir in praise of Yahweh. His Gentile birth emphasizes this universal dimension all the more—that is, "to the ends of the earth."[69] He is the hope of the *world!*

The beginning of the Writings, Ruth, ends with a genealogy, and the last book of the Writings, Chronicles, begins with a genealogy—in fact, nine chapters of them.[70] It is no coincidence that David is announced at the end of Ruth's ten-member genealogy and that, when the genealogies are completed in Chronicles, the text becomes completely occupied with David and his house, understood in both senses—family and temple.

Thus David and his importance are highlighted sharply by being placed before Psalms in this Hebrew Bible. Placing Ruth at the beginning of the Writings provided a frame for understanding the Writings and orienting them eschatologically: kingship and salvation. In a recent study of the Writings, Julius Steinberg points out that the Psalms and Chronicles function as bookends around the Writings (in the BHS-MT order), stressing the themes of Divine Kingship and Worship/Temple. In the canon under discussion, Ruth functions as an introduction announcing the birth of David, who will be the anointed one through whom God exercises his sovereignty over the earth.[71] Just as Boaz congratulates Ruth, a Gentile, for coming to Israel to take refuge under the wings of Yahweh, so the nations are urged to kiss the Son so that they might take refuge in him and be blessed.[72]

2. Ruth after Proverbs: Ruth and Woman Wisdom

In one canonical sequence, Ruth heads a list of the Megillot directly following the wisdom book of Proverbs. In this position, it functions to initiate a sequence of books that deal with an important wisdom theme, that of Woman Wisdom, who is introduced as a most important teacher for the young. Throughout Proverbs, she is featured as the one whose teaching must be imbibed, whose wares must be bought, whose food must be eaten. She is a true lover, who beckons youth into her newly built house to partake of her banquet of delights, as opposed to a whore who seeks to lure them into her den of death with her empty promises. The book concludes with a chapter devoted to pressing this teaching home. A royal mother teaches her royal son to avoid the wrong type of women at all cost, along with a profligate lifestyle (Prov 31:1–9). Added to this motherly advice is the famous acrostic poem about the proper type of woman to marry (Prov

---

68. Pss 3:1, 7:1, 18:1, 34:1, 5:11, 52:1, 54:1, 56:1, 57:1, 59:1, 60:1, 63:1, 142:1.

69. Ps 2:8. Note that Psalm 2 is the only place in Scripture where an Israelite ruler is referred to by the terms "Son of God," "Anointed One," and "King."

70. 1 Chronicles 1–9.

71. Steinberg, *Ketuvim*, 442–55.

72. Ruth 2:12; Ps 2:12. Notice the repetition of the verb חסה.

31:10–31). It is initiated by the words, "Who can find a virtuous woman?" and climaxed by "her works shall praise her in the gates" (31:21). Throughout the poem of praise, there is a litany of virtues: She is like a merchant ship coming from afar with her food (31:14); she rises in the middle of the night to get food for her family (31:15); she is not afraid of hard work (31:17, 27); her husband is known in the gates when he sits with the elders (31:23); *tôrăt ḥesed* is on her tongue (31:26); her children and husband declare her worth to be more valuable than any other woman's (31:29), and her works praise her in the city gates (31:31).

Many scholars have argued that such a woman is an idealization of Woman Wisdom and is not to be realized in any one person. But when Ruth follows Proverbs, one finds that a real-life Moabite widow is the perfect incarnation of this ideal. Ruth is decidedly not like the immoral woman who takes away the virtue of kings, but she adds to the virtue of Boaz, who, like her, is a person of virtue (2:1). In fact, Boaz declares her to be the woman of virtue who is so hard to find (3:11). She comes from afar (Moab), bringing food; she rises in the night to ensure the survival of her family by obtaining food for them (3:7, 8, 17); she is not afraid of hard work, rolling up her sleeves, and slaving in the fields throughout the day (2:7, 17); the man who becomes her husband is known to the elders in the city gates (4:1–11); and her request that Boaz marry her is but the expression of *tôrăt ḥesed* on her tongue (3:9–10). Her value to Naomi, her mother-in-law, is incomparable, surpassing even the worth of seven sons (4:15), while everyone in the gate of Bethlehem praises her as a woman of virtue (3:11).[73] Moreover, it is interesting that Woman Wisdom has not pursued a young man here but an old one, and together they have given life to the aged Naomi.

Thus reading Ruth after Proverbs shows that the ending of the one book is incarnated in the form of the hardworking, committed, woman of *ḥesed*, the widow Ruth. This Moabite widow is an example of what Lemuel's mother desired for her son's wife. She is a woman fit for a king. It is no wonder then that Ruth marries Boaz and produces a royal heir!

All the books of the Megillot that follow suggest (some more strongly than others) the realization of Wisdom and/or the feminine. The Song of Songs follows Ruth and it is the Song of Solomon, the renowned sage in Israel, pursuing and being wooed by his beloved. That this is reciprocal is shown by the fact—unique in the Hebrew Bible—that over half the verses of the book are written in the woman's own voice. Sage and Wisdom express their love for each other in erotic ways, evoking the eroticism of Wisdom pursuing youth in Proverbs. Some of these parallels have been conveniently summarized by Roland Murphy:

---

73. Many of the above parallels and more are noted by Stone, *Compilational History*, 112.

The essential point is this: the language and imagery used to describe the pursuit of Lady Wisdom are drawn from the experience of love. Although the Canticle speaks of the love between man and woman in the literal historical sense, it is by that very fact open to a wisdom interpretation. Wisdom is to be "found" (Prov. 3:13, 8:17, 35) just as one finds a good wife (Prov. 18:22, 31:10). In verses that are remarkably parallel Wisdom and wife are termed "favor from the Lord." The sage invites the youth to "get Wisdom," to love and embrace her (Prov. 4:6–8). The youth is to say, "Wisdom, you are my sister" (Prov. 7:4) just as the beloved in the Song of Songs is called "sister" (Cant. 4:9–5:1).[74]

It has even been suggested that a future birth is anticipated in the Song of Songs.[75]

The book of Ecclesiastes, which follows Song of Songs, is presented as the teaching of a sage whose name is the form of a feminine-singular participle, and "she" is envisioned as teaching throughout the book. This word occurs seven times and is used as an important part of the narrative frame of the book at the beginning, the center, and the end of the book. The word can be understood as simply a grammatical phenomenon, since the participle is normally conjugated with a masculine verb (Eccl 1:2; 12:8, 9, 10) or the context indicates it has a masculine reference (Eccl 1:1, 12).[76] But in the fourth and central use of the form in the book, it is conjugated with a feminine verb (Eccl 7:27).[77] In this notorious "misogynistic" passage, there is a remarkable statement about wisdom's being beyond the reach of humanity, and this coincides with the facts that a "[bad] woman" often leads to death, on the one hand,[78] and a good woman is hard to find. Read in the context of the previous books, the "misogyny" is instead an amplification of the beginning of Proverbs, which is filled with warnings for young men to avoid the embrace of Woman Folly,[79] and the ending of which contains the words of a king's mother, who is warning her son not to give his strength to such "women" but to look for the rare virtuous woman.[80] Thus, this grammatical form may be an example of intentional

---

74. Roland E. Murphy, *The Tree of Life: An Exploration of Biblical Wisdom Literature* (Grand Rapids, MI: Eerdmans, 2002) 106.

75. See Carlos Bovell, "Symmetry, Ruth and Canon," *JSOT* 28 (2003) 189–90.

76. The feminine participle functioning like this suggests that it has become a frozen form for a type of profession. See, for example, Neh 7:57, 59. See further Roger N. Whybray, *Ecclesiastes* (Sheffield: JSOT Press, 1989) 15–16.

77. Cf. ibid.

78. William P. Brown, *Ecclesiastes* (Interpretation; Louisville: John Knox Press, 2011) 83–84.

79. Ibid.

80. Prov 2:16–19; 5:2–11; 7:5–27; 9:13–18; 31:2–3, 10. Note the statement by Bartholomew: "With Proverbs in the background the most likely interpretation of this woman is as Lady Wisdom. As in Proverbs 31:10 so here: she is hard to find and more precious than jewels." Bartholomew, *Ecclesiastes*, 267. Bartholomew (ibid.), citing Wolters,

ambiguity in Ecclesiastes,[81] which may suggest that earlier interpreters were not far from the mark when they saw references to Solomon as well as Woman Wisdom being suggested by this form of the verb.[82] This would be particularly appropriate following Song of Songs, where Solomon and Wisdom embrace.[83]

The feminine element is continued in Lamentations, as the daughter of Jerusalem pours out her agony and grief over the judgment of the city and the nation. The feminine element in the first two chapters is particularly powerful. The once great city is now a widow (1:1), the once great princess, a slave (1:1). She is now a deserted lover (1:2), an abandoned sinner (1:8), naked and shameful (1:8), an unclean menstruant (1:16). The virgin daughter of Judah has been trampled down (1:15). The feminine forms predominate in the first two chapters, and ch. 4 with the personification of Jerusalem as a female is an important feature of the text.[84] While the personification of Zion as female connects this material to the Prophetic Literature, its dramatic use in Lamentations gives voice to the pain and grief of God's judgment.[85] Its inclusion in this wisdom setting points, like

---

notes that Hugo of St. Cher draws the parallel between Woman Wisdom in Ecclesiastes 7 and Proverbs 31.

81. Doug Ingram, *Ambiguity in Ecclesiastes* (London: Continuum, 2006) 85. One of the significant strengths of Ingram's argument is the threefold use of Qohelet's name with the verb "to say":

1:2   אָמַר קֹהֶלֶת
7:27   אָמְרָה קֹהֶלֶת
12:8   אָמַר הַקּוֹהֶלֶת

It is used uniquely in each occurrence, first with the feminine participle and the masculine verb, then with the feminine verb form, and finally, with the article attached to the participle. The feminine verb form and feminine participle are central. The translator of the LXX, of course, viewed the last letter on the Hebrew verb (*he*) as belonging to the next word (the participle) in 7:27. This suggests that there may be a scribal error in the MT. On the other hand, the larger pattern in the MT suggests intentionality, and the translation in the LXX is probably a misreading of the Hebrew, or an attempt to correct it.

82. E.g., Robert Jamieson, Andrew Robert Fausset, and David Brown, *A Commentary, Critical and Explanatory, on the Old and New Testaments* (Hartford, CT: Scranton, 1871) 403.

83. The use of this term may suggest that Wisdom points to the future for a resolution of the crisis caused by its inaccessibility. The teachings of Qohelet are "goads" from the "One Shepherd" (12:11). This title is only found in one other place in the Hebrew Bible, and there it refers to a new David who will come and restore Israel (Ezek 34:23, 37:24). I am indebted for these references to an unpublished paper by Lance Higginbotham, "Interpreting Ecclesiastes as Christian Scripture: A Proposal," November 2010. He directed me to the following paper: R. Perrin, "Messianism in the Narrative Frame of Ecclesiastes?" *RB* 108 (2001) 37–60.

84. "The personification of Jerusalem is a significant device within Lamentations. As a literary device it is most developed in chs. 1 and 2 and is present with diminished intensity in ch. 4." Elizabeth Boase, *The Fulfilment of Doom? The Dialogic Interaction between the Book of Lamentations and the Pre-exilic/Early Exilic Prophetic Literature* (New York: Continuum, 2006) 99.

85. Ibid., 104.

Qohelet, to the inscrutable nature of wisdom, particularly in light of this tremendous blow, which has resulted in the loss of everything Judah has held dear.

The anguished cry of a woman is continued in Esther, where it is a beautiful woman who exercises her ingenuity to save her people from disaster in exile. In contrast to a Gentile woman's using her wiles to marry a Hebrew man and save the line of Jesse, here is a Jewish woman who marries a Gentile king and saves her people as a result.[86] Thus, with its position following Proverbs, Ruth is the first of a number of books that develop the theme of wisdom and the feminine in diverse ways.[87]

3. Ruth after Judges: Kingship through ḥesed

In another canonical arrangement, Ruth provides a bridge between Judges and 1 Samuel.[88] As many scholars have indicated, this order suggests a counterbalance to the chaotic and corrupt picture at the end of the book of Judges.[89] The mass murder and rape at the end of that book show the political and moral anarchy in Israel. To be sure, this anarchy has been building to a climax with the practice of human sacrifice by Jepthah (Judg 11:39–40) and the sexual immorality of Samson (Judges 13–16). To this sordid state of affairs, the narrator adds two appendixes featuring the town of Bethlehem that plumb the depths of Israel's depravity. An Israelite from Ephraim makes an idol from stolen money to worship in his own personal chapel, and he hires a "mercenary" Levite from Bethlehem to be his priest (Judges 17). To this is added the sad story of another Levite, who gratifies the lust of a rapacious pack of human animals by yielding up his Bethlehemite concubine to their insatiable libido (Judges 19). Her gang rape suggests that Israel has fallen to a new low, even lower than the people of Sodom. Then her death leads to the virtual extirpation of a tribe of Israel, Benjamin, which is prevented by a mass kidnapping of young women and their forced marriage to their captors at a festival at Shiloh (Judges 19–21). This grim picture in Judges is typified by the fourfold refrain "There was no king in Israel" (Judg 17:6, 18:1, 19:1, 21:25) and the twofold "Every man did what was right in his own eyes" (Judg 17:6, 21:25). Israel is at a new

---

86. On the development of wisdom themes in Esther, see S. Talmon, "Wisdom in the Book of Esther," *VT* 13 (1963) 419–55.

87. Stone argues that the entire series is in the form of a chiasm, with Ruth and Song of Songs being the positive charges in the series, Lamentations and Esther being the negative counterparts, and Ecclesiastes being central. See Stone, *Compilational History*, 175–76.

88. Many scholars hold to a variant of this position in which Ruth is seen as a conclusion to Judges. See the bibliographical literature listed in Stone, *Compilational History*, 106 n. 9. A significant number of scholars see Ruth as providing a bridge between the two books. See, for example, Linafelt, *Ruth;* Katharine Doob Sakenfeld, *Ruth* (Interpretation; Louisville: Westminster John Knox, 1999). See also Stone, *Compilational History*, 103ff.

89. For a study of the contrast see ibid., 109.

low, which the words of the later Hosea could easily be describing: "There is no honesty and no goodness and no obedience of God in the land. False swearing, dishonesty and murder and theft and adultery are rife; crime follows upon crime" (Hos 4:2–3, JPS).

When Ruth follows this horrific description of Israel at the end of Judges, there is a point-by-point contrast. Ruth thus completes "a Bethlehem trilogy."[90] But in contrast to the previous two stories, here is a story where Bethlehem is redeemed. In fact it is a story of incredible faithfulness practiced by a Moabite widow in opposition to the faithlessness of the Israelites in Judges. Instead of a desertion of God in the face of death, she boldly proclaims undying faith in Israel's God. Instead of sexually illicit lust, she practices *ḥesed* in marriage in order to be faithful to her dead husband and to provide for her foreign mother-in-law.[91] Instead of lawless rape-marriages, "murder, and mayhem," to preserve the tribal name[92] there is concern for legality, decorum, and covenant in marriage in order to preserve a family name.[93] And most importantly, Ruth provides an answer to the refrains of kinglessness and lawlessness. "Ruth shows that in the days of the judges not every man did what was right in his own eyes"[94] and that behind the scenes the real king of Israel was working to introduce true kingship.

At the beginning of Ruth, a family from Bethlehem moves to Moab in search of food: Elimelech, Naomi, and their two sons Mahlon and Chilion. The father, whose name means "My God Is King," dies, and not long after this the two sons, now married to Moabite women, also die. Their destiny has been marked by their names, which mean "sickness and weakness." Naomi decides to head home when she hears that there is food again in Israel, but she feels that she may as well be dead as the rest of her family: her womb is dead, too old to bear children; she is empty and destitute. She changes her name from Naomi, meaning "Pleasant," to Marah, meaning "Bitter." Here in Ruth, the bleakness of Judges is continued but with a

---

90. Eugene Merrill, "The Book of Ruth: Narration and Shared Themes," *BSac* 142 (1985) 131.

91. There are some commentators who speculate that Ruth seduced Boaz on the threshing floor in ch. 3, and thus her behavior can hardly be a contrast to Judges. The "marriage" was thus consummated. See, for example, D. R. G. Beattie, "Ruth III," *JSOT* 5 (1978) 39–48. While it is possible to read between the lines in this chapter, and the language *is* sexually charged ("uncover the feet," "lie down," etc.), the *actual* lines of the text suggest that this is a matter of *ḥesed* first of all and then sex in the context of marriage (Ruth 4:13). The text indicates that both Boaz and Ruth are to be praised for controlling their passions in the interests of *ḥesed*. Boaz later tells Ruth "to lodge" with him and not "lie" with him—a word without a hint of sexual innuendo (3:13). See Edward F. Campbell, *Ruth* (1st ed.; AB 7; Garden City, NY: Doubleday, 1975) 131–34.

92. Sakenfeld, *Ruth*, 8.

93. Jobling, "Ruth Finds a Home," 133.

94. Phyllis Trible, "Ruth, Book of," *ABD* 5.846.

big difference. A Moabite woman, Ruth, practices *ḥesed* by returning with her mother-in-law, marrying an older Israelite kinsman-redeemer, and thus giving birth to a royal line that provides Israel with a king. Elimelech may be dead at the beginning of the book, but by its end David is alive. As Robert Bell puts it, "The reader should be asking, 'When will the Lord raise up a deliverer who will give Israel more than temporary rest from her troubles?' The last word of Ruth is David!"[95]

Thus the birth of David is announced well ahead of the unfolding of the book of Samuel but, if Samuel followed Ruth without this announcement, David's existence would be a type of "Messianic secret" kept as long as possible before he arrived.[96] With Ruth preceding Samuel, there is no such secret. And as the new story unfolds, the words of Naomi's friends regarding the value of her daughter-in-law, "Is she not worth more to you than seven sons," receive a resounding echo in the words of Elkanah to his wife Hannah, "Am I not worth more to you than ten sons" (Ruth 4:15; 1 Sam 1:8). Hannah's answer to prayer comes with the birth of a child who will become the one who anoints David to be king over Israel and eventually to preside over a new world order. Her prayer about Yahweh's filling the hungry and turning the full away echoes Yahweh's filling the emptiness of Naomi and Ruth in the book of Ruth![97] Similarly, Bethlehem of Judah becomes the place of future hope (David) and Gibeah of Benjamin a portent of disaster (Saul).[98]

An Original Home

Which of the three positions for Ruth above was original? Some scholars argue that there was no original position, because sequence was irrelevant, but this argument has already been found lacking.[99] Scholars have argued for each position as being original, and their basic positions are presented here.

---

95. Robert D. Bell, "The Book of Ruth: The Conclusion to Judges," *Biblical Viewpoint* 35 (2001) 3.

96. Jobling, *1 Samuel*, 107.

97. See Ruth 1:21, 4:15; 1 Sam 2:5. See Fischer, *Rut*, 110.

98. On the development of this theme in particular, see Stone, *Compilational History*, 105–8. See also:

> Along a quite different line, the question of Saul's origin raises ominous possibilities. His provenance from Gibeah calls to mind the hideous events related to that town in Judges 19–21. In the most literal way Saul is a product of the anarchy of the time of judges. He must be the offspring of the rape-marriages by which Gibeah and Benjamin were repopulated! Just as the book of Ruth stands in for the missing birth story of David, so Judges accounts for Saul's origin. The contrast between the two kings could hardly be more effective. (Jobling, *1 Samuel*, 67 n. 38)

99. See the discussion above and, in particular, Wolfenson, "Implications of the Place of Ruth."

Ruth before Psalms (Consensus)

The consensus is that the original home for Ruth was before Psalms. This is based on the following reasons: (1) It is the earliest attested Hebrew order. This is based on the argument that the grouping of Ruth with the Megillot was probably the first step in either a liturgical arrangement or a chronological adaptation of a liturgical order. Since there is no evidence for a liturgical practice of this sort in the Talmud, this order probably evolved between the 6th and 11th centuries C.E. According to most accounts, the liturgical sequence of the Megillot was later modified by a chronological arrangement.[100] (2) When one compares the Greek and Hebrew orders of the canon, it is more difficult to explain why a "demotion" took place (Ruth leaving the second division of the Prophets for the third division of the Writings) than a "promotion" (Ruth leaving the Writings for the Prophets).[101] (3) The genealogical ending of Ruth implies that David is already a well-known entity; otherwise, his naming becomes incomprehensible in the Judges–Ruth–Samuel sequence.[102] The announcement of his future birth would be an unprecedented occurrence in the sequence of Genesis to Kings. In my judgment, this is the Achilles heel of this particular arrangement. It is true that there is one parallel in the announcement of Josiah in 1 Kings 13, but this happens in the same book, and it is a *prediction* of his future reign—the announcement is clearly a prophecy (1 Kgs 13:2).[103] But the ending in Ruth assumes that David's existence is a well-known fact.

Ending a narrative with a genealogy is a striking anomaly unless it is somehow viewed as a new beginning.[104] The most appropriate context for

---

100. Contra Stone, who argues that the MT evidence is earlier than the liturgical sequence since it is found in the Cairo, Aleppo, and Leningrad codices. Thus he would argue that the liturgical sequence found in later codices is a later adaptation of the MT (*Compilational History*, 86–89).

101. Campbell, *Ruth*, 34–35.

102. Steinberg, *Ketuvim*, 128.

103. One could also argue that there is such a proleptic reference in the use of Agag in Num 24:7 (cf. 1 Samuel 15), but such a use is extremely rare.

104. Fischer argues that, in fact, genealogies conclude stories. She cites Gen 37:2 as an example of genealogical closure for the Jacob story. However, it functions there as the inception of the story of Jacob's sons! Similarly, when the words "these are the generations" occur, they initiate sections of Scripture with one possible exception (Gen 2:4). Even this text is more likely to be seen as beginning a section of text. See Fischer, *Rut*, 70. Irmtraud Fischer, "Der Männerstammbaum im Frauenbuch: Uberlegungen zum Schluss des Rutbuches (4,18–22)," in *"Ihr Völker alle, klatscht in die Hände!"* (FS E. Gerstenberger; ed. Rainer Kessler; Münster: LIT, 1997) 205. For the genealogy as having an introductory, titulary function, see S. Tengström, *Die Toledotformel* (Uppsala: CWK Gleerup, 1981) 17. Also note the following comment: "[T]he Hebrew phrase clearly and consistently structurally marks the beginning of new sections": J. W. Wright, "Genealogies," in *Dictionary of the Old Testament: Pentateuch* (ed. T. Desmond Alexander and David Weston Baker; Downers Grove, IL: InterVarsity, 2003) 346. See now the latest statement of the question: Matthew A. Thomas, *These Are the Generations: Identity, Covenant and the Toledot Formula* (London: T. & T. Clark, 2011).

Ruth 4:18–22	*1 Chr 2:4–15*
	4 His daughter-in-law Tamar also bore him Perez and Zerah. Judah's sons were five in all.
18 This is the line of *Perez*: Perez begot *Hezron*,	5 The sons of *Perez: Hezron* and Hamul.
	6 The sons of Zerah: Zimri, Ethan, Heman, Calcol, and Dara, five in all.
	7 The sons of Carmi: Achar, the troubler of Israel, who committed a trespass against the proscribed thing;
	8 and Ethan's son was Azariah.
19 *Hezron* begot *Ram*,	9 The sons of *Hezron* that were born to him: Jerahmeel, *Ram*, and Chelubai.
(1) *Ram begot Amminadab*, 20 (2) *Amminadab begot Nahshon*,	10 (1) *Ram begot Amminadab*, (2) *Amminadab begot Nahshon*, prince of the sons of Judah.
(3) *Nahshon begot Salmon*, 21 (4) *Salmon begot Boaz*, (5) *Boaz begot Obed*, 22 (6) *Obed begot Jesse*, (7) *Jesse begot* **David**.	11 (3) *Nahshon begot Salma*, (4) *Salma begot Boaz*, 12 (5) *Boaz begot Obed*, (6) *Obed begot Jesse*. 13 (7) *Jesse begot* Eliab his firstborn, Abinadab the second, Shimea the third, 14 Nethanel the fourth, Raddai the fifth, 15 Ozem the sixth, **David** the seventh.

Ruth's ending with a Davidic genealogy is the Psalms—as a suitable segue into the Psalter—David's book. There is not a compelling rationale for such an ending preceding the Song of Songs in the Masoretic sequence, particularly because the genealogy is probably dependent on Chronicles, as the following chart indicates:

What makes this especially interesting is that nowhere else in the Hebrew Bible do the names Salmah, Boaz, and Obed occur together besides these two places. Ruth is an adaptation of the longer genealogy in Chronicles with an interest in preserving a strict linear genealogy and also focusing on the number "seven." The last seven members of each genealogy appear verbatim with the exception of additional descriptions of members ("prince of the sons of Judah") and Jesse's first six sons. This focus on the number "seven" also highlights the statement about Ruth at the end of the book that she was worth more to Naomi than seven sons![105]

(4) The placement of Ruth between Judges and Samuel assumes a 22-book canon in which Ruth is an appendix to Judges, and Lamentations to

---

105. See Fischer, "Männerstammbaum," 204–5.

Jeremiah. It is much easier to explain how the canon could be contracted to the number 22 (based on the number of letters in the Hebrew alphabet) than how it could be expanded to 24. Thus, it probably was contracted to 22 in the Greek tradition, and it was easily done because of the subject matter of each book. This also would explain why another book of the Megillot, Esther, was placed with other historical books in the Greek tradition and why Lamentations was placed with Jeremiah.[106]

Ruth after Judges

The canonical arrangement with Ruth following Judges has been argued by a number of scholars, and its strongest argument is linguistic. Edward Campbell summarizes the evidence as follows:

> There is a series of verbal correspondences which, when taken together, may suggest a relationship between the two stories [Judges and Ruth]. Thus Judges 19:23 and Ruth 1:13 both use Hebrew *'al* as an independent negative, two of only six occurrences in the Old Testament. Judges 19:24 uses a suffix which must be analyzed as an archaic or dialectical feminine dual, comparable to the seven instances of this phenomenon in Ruth. Judges 20:24 uses *hinneh* as an expression of surprise, "lo and behold," in a manner recalling its use in Ruth 2:4 and 4:1. In Judges 19:6 and 33 the Levite and each of his hosts eat and drink until their hearts became "good" (merry). . . . This recalls the same idiom in the ambiguous circumstance of Ruth 3:7. . . . Finally in Judges 21:23 there occurs the only other pre-exilic use of the idiom "to take wives" using the verb *ns'*, besides the use in Ruth 1:4.[107]

Campbell and others would argue that, if this is an example of Deuteronomistic editing, it points to a very early canonical location in antiquity.[108]

Recently, Timothy Stone has made a strong case for a complex canonical process in which Ruth was originally anchored between Judges and Samuel, then was later edited into a canonical sequence between Proverbs and Song of Songs.[109] These and only these two orders of 22 books and 24 books were the earliest orders reflected in the Greek and Hebrew traditions. Then in the Hebrew tradition another, later move was made to place Ruth before Psalms in a more chronological arrangement in order to highlight Davidic authorship of the Psalter.

I cannot present Stone's argument in detail. He builds a case for a compilational, canonical grammar in which criteria are developed for understanding how canonical sequences were achieved in the Scriptures. As already

---

106. Note that the Greek form of the book, followed in the Vulgate and Peshitta, attributes authorship to Jeremiah. This was probably an inner Greek development based on the later canonical sequence, and it was transferred from there to the Latin and Syriac.

107. Campbell, *Ruth*, 35.

108. Ibid., 36.

109. Stone, *Compilational History*.

mentioned above, Stone seeks to establish a "compilational grammar" that was used by those involved in the canonical process to establish certain canonical sequences such as the grouping of psalms in the Psalter and the arrangement of prophetic books in The Twelve. In his analysis of these sequences, he observes catchphrases, superscriptions, framing devices and contrastive contents that enable him to have an objective means by which to establish other canonical sequences between books. On the basis of his research, he concludes that special catchphrases link the end of Judges with the beginning of Ruth, and the end of Ruth with the beginning of Samuel. Some of these have been noted before but not in the framework of Stone's methodology. Thus, a rare idiom used to indicate marriage appears conspicuously at the end of Judges and at the beginning of Ruth. Similarly, the only times that an identical grammatical, comparative expression is used to indicate the much higher value of a woman over sons is at the end of Ruth and the beginning of Samuel.[110]

In addition, Stone notes some of the contrastive content between Judges and Ruth and observes that the origins of Israel's first two kings are sharply brought into focus: Gibeah of Benjamin (Saul) and Bethlehem of Judah (David). This provides a smooth transition into the first book of Samuel. Noting also that a genealogy usually precedes a story rather than ending a story, Stone points out the fact that the genealogical ending of Ruth introduces the story of David in Samuel.

However, sometime later in the canonical process, Ruth was shifted to its position after Proverbs. This was done in order to continue the feminine focus on wisdom found in Proverbs. Canonical links were added at the end of Proverbs to forge the bond between the books. Thus, it is no accident that the ending of the book of Proverbs praises the virtuous woman in the gates and that this is exactly what Boaz says of Ruth. Ruth is thus the realization of Woman Wisdom.

According to Stone, then, these two orders are reflected in the early Greek and Hebrew traditions. Later within the Hebrew tradition, a different order was achieved by shifting Ruth to introduce the Psalter.[111] This reflects the evidence of the baraita in the Talmud.

While this view certainly has its merits, it needs to posit two canonical redactions that required textual changes: one that updated and changed the earlier one. Would this have been likely—that is, changing the text to provide for another canonical order—if it had already been done to secure the original order? The process was no doubt complex and one must assume that it took quite a long period of time, but it seems to suggest dis-

---

110. Ibid., 104. The marriage idiom is וַיִּשְׂאוּ נָשִׁים (Judg 21:23, Ruth 1:4), and the two comparative expressions are: הִיא טוֹבָה לָךְ מִשִּׁבְעָה בָּנִים (Ruth 4:15); הֲלוֹא אָנֹכִי טוֹב לָךְ מֵעֲשָׂרָה בָּנִים (1 Sam 1:8).

111. Stone does not give a specific date for this development but if pressed would argue for a time considerably before 100 C.E. (personal communication).

satisfaction with a previous canonical redaction—or ignorance of it—and an attempt to create another one. While this is possible, it seems unlikely. There are also clear editorial additions that function to provide a context for Ruth when none is required if it follows Judges. In fact, the beginning of Samuel reads seamlessly with the end of Judges, particularly because the frames of the final appendixes in Judges and the beginning of Samuel contain a reference to a man "from the hill country of Ephraim" (Judg 17:1, 19:1; 1 Sam 1:1). Thus, the beginning formula of Ruth, "It happened in the days when the judges judged," is a contextualizing statement for the book *because one is required.* Thus it would be far more fitting for this link to appear in a canonical context that was separated from the chronological sequence. The similar linguistic terminology, then, has more to do with seeking to describe the same temporal period or even being part of such a linguistic milieu. This particular perspective dovetails with the dominant critical view that Joshua–Kings is an edited unity, the so-called Deuteronomistic History.[112] Ruth is an obvious stylistic intrusion.[113] A birth story of David placed before the birth of Samuel is also an obvious semantic interruption.

The contextualizing insertion at the beginning of Ruth then links up with its genealogical ending, which many scholars believe is also an editorial addition. In the genealogy of Ruth 4:18–22, Boaz, the seventh on the list, is placed in the period of the Judges, thus showing chronological harmony. The fact that asyndeton is used in 4:17b ("And they called his name Obed—he was the father of Jesse, the father of David, and these are the generations of Perez . . . David") probably shows that this is an addition identifying the lineage of David with the more-complete genealogy to follow; it is an editorial remark that brings out the dramatic significance of the actions within the book. Thus, while being the only example of a genealogy to conclude a book, it is not just any genealogy but the genealogy that introduces the author of the next book as the one whose line will rule and bless the world. In other words, contrary to those who argue that the genealogy can be explained by the book itself, the peculiarity is removed if Ruth is seen as a contextual bridge to the next book, the Psalter.

It is a fact that the genealogical ending is quite similar to the genealogy of David found in Chronicles (1 Chr 2:5–15) and is probably dependent on it.[114] But Ruth 4:18–22 is an abbreviated version, stylized to fit the book of

---

112. Martin Noth, *Überlieferungsgeschichtliche Studien: Die sammelnden und bearbeitenden Geschichtswerke im Alten Testament* (2nd ed.; Tübingen: Max Niemeyer, 1957).

113. Stone makes the point that few scholars even think about including Ruth in this Deuteronomistic framework. He points out a few exceptions. See Stone, *Compilational History*, 111 n. 34. In my judgment, it seems more likely that the originally edited, canonical unity was secondarily edited to make room for Ruth in a new literary context that demanded a 22-book canon.

114. Erich Zenger, *Einleitung in das Alte Testament* (Stuttgart: Kohlhammer, 2008) 225. There are other authors who argue that the two genealogies are based on an independent

Ruth, with Perez (Tamar's son) in the initial position, Boaz in the important seventh location, and David in the tenth and final position. Thus these two genealogies at the end of the first book of the Writings and near the beginning of the last book of the Writings help clamp the last division of the Hebrew Bible together.[115] While Stone has shown good reasons for the placement of Ruth after Proverbs in the Writings in a secondary development, I think the evidence for canonical redaction creating verbal links is less persuasive; these links are created more as a result of placement than editing. In my judgment, the genealogical conclusion that uniquely ends the book of Ruth is a finely stitched seam knitting together David's birth narrative with his worship manual (the Psalter).

Ruth after Proverbs

There are few who argue that the sequence with Ruth after Proverbs was an original order because of the implied late development of the Megillot. But an early order is the implication of the work of John Sailhamer. He asks,

> Has contextuality in the shape of the OT text been intentionally determined? Was Ruth, for example, deliberately placed after Proverbs in the Hebrew Bible because of the link between the "virtuous woman" acrostic and Boaz's use of the same expression in Ruth 3:11? Or, Was the "virtuous woman" acrostic added to the book of Proverbs to provide a link for the attachment of the book of Ruth? The concept of contextuality does not propose to answer such questions. They are important questions but they go beyond the limits of the concept. Contextuality only raises the question of the effect of context on meaning, not the intent that lies behind it. The question of intentionality is addressed by means of the study of OT composition and redaction.[116]

But then in a footnote on the same page, he reveals his own view:

> It should be noted, for example, that each of the five books which follow Proverbs in the Hebrew Canon (Ruth, Song of Songs, Qoheleth, Lamentations, Esther) has a grammatically feminine singular subject: Ruth, the Shulamite, Qoheleth (fem. sing. noun), the daughter of Jerusalem, and Esther. These are the only books in the Hebrew Canon that have a feminine singular subject throughout. This suggests a conscious and intentional grouping of these books after the theme of wisdom as young woman in the book of Proverbs (cf. Prov. 8:31).[117]

---

source. Perhaps, but it is telling that these two genealogies contain the only reference to some of the names: Salma, Boaz, and Obed.

115. See also Hendrik J. Koorevaar, "Die Chronik als intendierter Abschluss des alttestamentlichen Kanons," *Jahrbuch für evangelikale Theologie* 11 (1997) 42–76 (English translation appears in the present volume).

116. Sailhamer, *Old Testament Theology*, 214–15.

117. Ibid., 214 n. 28.

The problem with this view is that, throughout his book, Sailhamer is using a Hebrew canon whose third division begins with Psalms. The Masoretic canon with its chronological arrangement of the Megillot has a third division that begins with Chronicles. This makes Sailhamer's acceptance of an intentional, early arrangement of the Megillot for wisdom reasons problematic because there is no early sequence of the Writings that begins with Chronicles.[118]

Stone's argument that canonical redaction was at work here in linking Proverbs with Ruth to secure the development of a feminine wisdom motif in the Megillot has been dealt with above. I think this arrangement would more likely have been created for some of the reasons he mentions, but later, as the penultimate step in a liturgical development.

Conclusion

Ruth's various positions in the Old Testament/Hebrew Bible show the impact of canonical context on the meaning of the book. In the drama of biblical history, Ruth was a wandering Moabite who found her way home to the nation of Israel. In canonical history, the book of Ruth for various reasons wandered from its original canonical home, enriching the history of interpretation by emphasizing the birth of kingship through *ḥesed* and by stressing the realization of Woman Wisdom in the ordinary daily events of life that had extraordinary significance. This in no way detracts from the significance of this book's original home, which showcased both David and his universal significance to bring the nations under the shadow of the divine wing: "Just as Noah began the post-Flood world and Abraham the Israelite people in a new world divided into nations, David began the dynasty that will ultimately lead to messianic times under the Messiah son of David."[119]

If the original home of Ruth was before Psalms, it is rather easy to explain why it was inserted between Judges and Samuel at a later time. Historical context, genre, and chronology to some degree "trumped" canonical context in the interests of making the number of books in the canon match the number of letters in the Hebrew alphabet. Later, for thematic reasons, stressing the importance of the wisdom motif in Ruth resulted in moving it from its place before the Psalter to the position following Proverbs.

Stone concludes from his study that "Ruth's compilational history reveals its deliberate and meaningful contextualization in multiple places during the canonical process. This may reveal that the search for an 'original' order—as well as the rejection of the significance of order if there are

---

118. This order appears in later manuscripts—for example, Or. 2201. See also orders 46, 54, 55, 56, 62, 64, 69, 70 in Beckwith, *Old Testament Canon*, 459–63. These all date to the 12th century C.E. and beyond.

119. Ron, "Geneaological List," 86.

multiple arrangements—may be misguided."[120] My own analysis would question this conclusion if the canonical process is limited to the period of the closure and arrangement of the canon. That other arrangements occurred with various meanings and for various reasons after the canonical process is certain. But Ruth's original home highlights the significance of David's birth to extend a welcome to the nations to join David in coming from Moab to Judah in "replenishing the Holy One, blessed be He, with hymns and praises."[121] My own analysis agrees with Stone's first statement, but questions his second. At the same time, it is clear that, to some degree, canonization allows for flexibility of arrangement in the interests of hermeneutical creativity.

---

120. Stone, *Compilational History*, 116.
121. B. B. Bat. 14b. Note Moshe Halberthal's comment that the closure of the canon gives birth to hermeneutical creativity rather than killing it: Moshe Halbertal, *People of the Book: Canon, Meaning, and Authority* (Cambridge: Harvard University Press, 1997) 32–40.

Bibliography

Akenson, Donald Harman. *Surpassing Wonder: The Invention of the Bible and the Talmuds*. Chicago: University of Chicago Press, 2001.

Audet, J. P. "A Hebrew-Aramaic List of Books of the Old Testament in Greek Transcription." *JTS* 1 (1950) 153–54.

Barr, James. *Holy Scripture: Canon, Authority, Criticism*. Oxford: Oxford University Press, 1983.

Bartholomew, Craig G. *Ecclesiastes*. Grand Rapids, MI: Baker Academic, 2009.

Barton, John. *Oracles of God: Perceptions of Ancient Prophecy in Israel after the Exile*. Oxford: Oxford University Press, 2007.

Beattie, D. R. G. "Ruth III." *JSOT* 5 (1978) 39–48.

Beckwith, Roger T. *The Old Testament Canon of the New Testament Church*. Grand Rapids, MI: Eerdmans, 1985.

Bell, Robert D. "The Book of Ruth: The Conclusion to Judges." *Biblical Viewpoint* 35 (2001) 1–4.

Boase, Elizabeth. *The Fulfilment of Doom? The Dialogic Interaction between the Book of Lamentations and the Pre-exilic/Early Exilic Prophetic Literature*. New York: Continuum, 2006.

Bovell, Carlos. "Symmetry, Ruth and Canon." *JSOT* 28 (2003) 175–91.

Brandt, Peter. *Endgestalten des Kanons: Das Arrangement der Schriften Israels in der jüdischen und christlichen Bibel*. BBB 31. Berlin: Philo, 2001.

Brown, Gillian, and George Yule. *Discourse Analysis*. Cambridge: Cambridge University Press, 1983.

Brown, William P. *Ecclesiastes*. Interpretation. Louisville: John Knox, 2011.

Brueggemann, Walter. *The Creative Word*. 4th ed. Philadelphia: Fortress, 1982.

Campbell, Edward F. *Ruth*. 1st ed. AB 7. Garden City, NY: Doubleday, 1975.

Carr, David M. "The Song of Songs as a Microcosm of the Canonization and Decanonization Process." Pp. 173–89 in *Canonization and Decanonization*. Edited by A. van der Kooij and Karel van der Toorn. Leiden: Brill, 1998.

Childs, Brevard S. *Introduction to the Old Testament as Scripture*. Philadelphia: Fortress, 1979.

Dempster, Stephen G. "Exodus and Biblical Theology: On Moving into the Neighborhood with a New Name." *Southern Baptist Journal of Theology* 12 (2008) 3–23. .

———. "An 'Extraordinary Fact': Torah and Temple and the Contours of the Hebrew Canon, Part 1." *TynBul* 48 (1997) 23–56

———. "From Many Texts to One: The Formation of the Hebrew Bible." Pp. 19–56 in *The World of the Arameans*, vol. 1: *Biblical Studies in Honour of Paul-Eugène Dion*. Edited by P. Michèle Daviau, John W. Wevers, and Michael Weigl. JSOTSup 324. Sheffield: Sheffield Academic Press, 2001.

———. "Geography and Genealogy, Dominion and Dynasty: A Theology of the Hebrew Bible." In *Biblical Theology: Retrospect and Prospect*. Edited by Scott J. Hafemann. Downers Grove, IL: InterVarsity, 2002.

Fischer, Irmtraud. "Der Männerstammbaum im Frauenbuch: Überlegungen zum Schluss des Rutbuches (4,18–22)." Pp. 195–213 in *"Ihr Völker alle, klatscht in die Hände!" Festschrift für Erhard S. Gerstenberger zum 65. Geburtstag*. Edited by Rainer Kessler et al. Münster: LIT, 1997.

———. *Rut*. HThKAT. Vienna: Herder, 2001.

Halbertal, Moshe. *People of the Book: Canon, Meaning, and Authority*. Cambridge: Harvard University Press, 1997.

Ingram, Doug. *Ambiguity in Ecclesiastes*. London: Continuum, 2006.

Jamieson, Robert, Andrew R. Fausset, and David Brown. *A Commentary, Critical and Explanatory, on the Old and New Testaments*. Hartford, CT: Scranton, 1871.

Jobling, David. *1 Samuel*. Berit Olam. Collegeville, MN: Liturgical Press, 1998.

———. "Ruth Finds a Home: Canon, Politics, Method." Pp. 125–39 in *The New Literary Criticism and the Hebrew Bible*. Edited by J. Cheryl Exum and David J. A. Clines. Sheffield: Continuum, 1993.

Josipovici, Gabriel. *The Book of God: A Response to the Bible*. New Haven, CT: Yale University Press, 1990.

Koorevaar, Hendrik J. "Die Chronik als intendierter Abschluss des alttestamentlichen Kanons." *Jahrbuch für evangelikale Theologie* 11 (1997) 42–76. [ET appears in the present volume.]

Leithart, Peter. "When Gentile Meets Jew: A Christian Reading of Ruth and the Hebrew Scriptures." *Touchstone* 22 (2009) 20–24.

Linafelt, Tod. *Ruth*. Berit Olam. Collegeville, MN: Liturgical Press, 1999.

Merrill, Eugene. "The Book of Ruth: Narration and Shared Themes." *BSac* 142 (1985) 130–41.

Murphy, Roland E. *The Tree of Life: An Exploration of Biblical Wisdom Literature*. Grand Rapids, MI: Eerdmans, 2002.

Noth, Martin. *Überlieferungsgeschichtliche Studien: Die sammelnden und bearbeitenden Geschichtswerke im Alten Testament*. 2nd ed. Tübingen: Max Niemeyer, 1957.

Perrin, R. "Messianism in the Narrative Frame of Ecclesiastes?" *RB* 108 (2001) 37–60.

Ron, Zvi. "The Geneaological List in the Book of Ruth: A Symbolic Approach." *JBQ* 38 (2010) 85–92.

Sailhamer, John H. *Introduction to Old Testament Theology: A Canonical Approach.* Grand Rapids, MI: Zondervan, 1995.

Sakenfeld, Katharine Doob. *Ruth.* Interpretation. Louisville: Westminster John Knox, 1999.

Schmid, Konrad. *Genesis and the Moses Story: Israel's Dual Origins in the Hebrew Bible.* Siphrut 3. Winona Lake, IN: Eisenbrauns, 2010.

Spangenberg, S. "Constructing a Historical Context for the Ruth Novelette: Dovetailing the Views of J. A. Loader and R. Albertz." *OTE* 18 (2005) 345–55.

Steinberg, Julius. *Die Ketuvim: Ihr Aufbau und ihre Botschaft.* BBB 152. Hamburg: Philo, 2006.

Steinmann, Andrew. *The Oracles of God: The Old Testament Canon.* St. Louis: Concordia, 1999.

Steins, Georg. *Die Chronik als kanonisches Abschlussphänomen: Studien zur Entstehung und Theologie von 1/2 Chronik.* Weinheim: Athenäum, 1995.

Stone, Timothy J. *The Compilational History of the Megilloth: Canon, Contoured Intertextuality and Meaning in the Writings.* Ph.D. Dissertation, University of St. Andrews, 2010.

Swete, Henry Barclay. *An Introduction to the Old Testament in Greek: With an Appendix Containing the Letter of Aristeas.* 1st ed. Cambridge: Cambridge University Press, 2010.

Talmon, S. "Wisdom in the Book of Esther." *VT* 13 (1963) 419–55.

Tengström, S. *Die Toledotformel.* Uppsala: CWK Gleerup, 1981.

Thomas, Matthew A. *These Are the Generations: Identity, Covenant and the Toledot Formula.* London: T. & T. Clark, 2011.

Trible, Phyllis. "Ruth, Book of." Pp. 842–47 in vol. 5 of *ABD.*

Westermann, Claus. *Elements of Old Testament Theology.* Translated by Douglas W. Scott. Atlanta: John Knox, 1982.

Whybray, Roger N. *Ecclesiastes.* Sheffield: JSOT Press, 1989.

Wolfenson, L. B. "Implications of the Place of Ruth in Editions, Manuscripts, and Canons of the Old Testament." *HUCA* (1924) 151–78.

Wright, J. W. "Genealogies." *Dictionary of the Old Testament: Pentateuch.* Edited by T. Desmond Alexander and David Weston Baker. Downers Grove, IL: InterVarsity, 2003.

Zenger, Erich, et al., eds. *Einleitung in das Alte Testament.* Stuttgart: Kohlhammer, 2008.

Thoughts on the "Davidization" of the Psalter

FRANK-LOTHAR HOSSFELD AND ERICH ZENGER

In his detailed discussion of messianic expectations in the Old Testament, Heinz-Josef Fabry emphasized its original messianic connection with the (Judean) king ideology: "In the Old Testament, kingship ideology bears the brunt for the later formation of the Messianic expectations. It consists of two sections relating to each other: the concept of God's kingship and the concept of the earthly king's being anointed as the representative of YHWH."[1] In particular, the Psalms have made the content of the title "Anointed of YHWH" distinctive: "The Old Testament literature of the Psalms has prepared this by incorporating and further developing the traditional king concept."[2] Thereby, H.-J. Fabry rightly refers to the Royal Psalms: "The Royal Psalms (Psalms 2; 18; 20; 21; 45; 72; 89; 101; 110; 132; 144) originate from an interest group that propagated expectations of a restorative dynastic king. The Psalms originally had in mind the king who was currently reigning and were made to refer to the coming ruler of the eschaton in the postexilic era."[3] The change in the concept of kingship in the Psalter prepares the way for the manifold concepts of Messiah in early Judaism and at Qumran, which Fabry then describes in detail. In the present essay, we want to pick up these ideas and relate the messianic expectations in the Psalter to the larger context of the "Davidization" of the Psalms that is typical in the Psalter.

The Developing Davidization of the Psalter

It is obvious that David, as a historical character as well as a prototypical character, represents a formative figure in the book of Psalms. This is based less on the scant evidence in the psalms themselves than on the meta-textual superscriptions, which assign 73 psalms to David (and

---

Authors' note: This essay was originally published as "Überlegungen zur Davidisierung des Psalters," in *Juda und Jerusalem in der Seleukidenzeit: Herrschaft – Widerstand – Identität* (FS H.-J. Fabry; ed. Ulrich Dahmen and Johannes Schnocks; BBB 159; Göttingen: Vandenhoeck & Ruprecht, 2010). ET of German quotations in this essay are by volume editors.

1. H.-J. Fabry and K. Scholtissek, *Der Messias* (NEB Themen 5; Würzburg: Echter-Verlag, 2002) 26.
2. Ibid., 27.
3. Ibid.

partially to biographical situations). They guide one to understand the psalms with these superscriptions as being connected to David.[4]

The process behind this observation can be summarized by the following statements, which represent our current position on the development of the Davidization of the Psalter:[5]

1. The Davidization of the Psalter as a whole was a complex process of growth that began in the Psalter itself and continued beyond it to the point when the book of Psalms was identified as the Psalms of David.
2. The first two Davidic psalters (Psalms 3–41, 51–70)[6] were the foundation or basis of the Davidization and at the same time the basis of the collection of psalm groups that grew until it became the entire Psalter.
3. The first Davidic psalter originated in the 6th century B.C.E. in Judah. The point of connection between the psalms being incorporated into the basic collection was the continuous perspective of the individual laments—that is, David's being saved from difficulties. One hint that the praying man should be identified as David is the frame around the large Royal Psalm 18 (see vv. 1 and 51), which is also the only psalm that is found both here and in the Davidic narrative (2 Samuel 22).
4. Groups of temple musicians such as the Asaphites and Korahites (and including the Ezrahites) took their own Davidic psalms with them into the Babylonian Exile. They added these psalms to the nascent form of the first Davidic psalter. They considered the bracketing function of David as a man of prayer and then revealed their connection to the first Davidic psalter by a similar means, the well-known tradition of double-Psalms 14 // 53 and 40:14–18 // 70. In addition, they developed the identification of the praying man in the first and second Davidic psalters with recourse to Ps 18:1, 51, and David's biography according to 1 and 2 Samuel. First, they added situational information from the life of David to eight psalms in the second Davidic psalter and to Ps 3:1 and 34:1 in the

---

4. B. Weber, "Psalm 78 als 'Mitte' des Psalters? Ein Versuch," *Bib* 88 (2007) 321.

5. Cf. E. Zenger, "Das Buch der Psalmen," in *Einleitung in das Alte Testament* (7th ed.; Stuttgart: Kohlhammer, 2008) 363–65 (Kompositions- und Redaktionsgeschichte des Psalters); F.-L. Hossfeld, "Der elohistische Psalter Ps 42–83: Entstehung und Programm," in *The Composition of the Book of Psalms* (ed. E. Zenger; BETL 238; Leuven: Leuven University Press, 2010) 199–214; idem, "David als exemplarischer Mensch: Literarische Biographie und Anthropologie am Beispiel Davids," in *Biblische Anthropologie: Neue Einsichten aus dem Alten Testament* (ed. C. Frevel; Quaestiones disputatae 237; Freiburg: Herder, 2010) 243–55.

6. In the book of Psalms, there are five collections of Davidic psalms, Psalms 3–41, 51–70 (51–72), 101–3, 108–10, and 138–45, which will be called the five Davidic psalters throughout this article.

first Davidic psalter. Second, they shaped the final collection of the second Davidic psalter, Psalms 69–71, into a prayer by a poor, conscience-stricken, suffering old man who committed his royal legacy to his son Solomon in a prayer at the end of his life, and who is identified in the unique colophon in Ps 72:20 as David, son of Jesse.

5. The heritage of Davidization in the first two Davidic books was passed along to the third (Psalms 101–3), fourth (Psalms 108–10), and fifth (Psalms 138–45) Davidic psalters. It was continued by assigning additional individual psalms to David (Psalm 86 and the Pilgrimage Psalms 122, 124, 131, and 133) and via further steps taken in the Septuagint as well as at Qumran, until the book was received as a whole as being the canonical "Psalms of David."

David's Imprint on the Whole Psalter

If one wants to approach the figure of David, it is reasonable to begin with the psalms themselves without the superscriptions. Within the psalms corpora, David is mentioned 6 times; 4 times he is explicitly made a subject of discussion:

- The final verse of Psalm 18 shows a purposeful self-identification of the praying man as David, which sets the course for the Davidization of the Psalter. David receives the titles "king" and "Anointed One." Moreover, he receives the promise of the enduring—that is, temporally unlimited—existence of his dynasty, which implies a future aspect. In content and language, this promise is close to the oracle of Nathan in 2 Sam 7:11b–16.
- Psalm 79, a historical psalm of Asaph that sits in the central position of Psalms 73–83, tells the history of Israel from the exodus until the fall of the Northern Kingdom and possibly further, until the salvation of Jerusalem in 701 B.C.E. (see Ps 78:66). It culminates in the election of the tribe of Judah (Southern Kingdom), Zion, and David as the royal shepherd.
- Psalm 89 reveals the conflict between God's promises in the Davidic covenant and the rejection or fall of the kingdom.[7] It deliberately raises the accusatory question about the validity of God's promises to David and therefore keeps the memory of David alive.
- Psalm 132 explicitly covers the achievements of David. According to this psalm, David founded the temple and the temple liturgy on Zion. YHWH answers with the (conditional) promise of the kingdom's revival at the consecrated place. The psalm affirms the restorative postexilic expectations.

---

7. Cf. J. Schnocks, "Verworfen hast du den Bunde mit deinem Knecht (Ps 89,40)," in *Für immer verbündet: Studien zur Bundestheologie der Bibel* (FS F.-L. Hossfeld; ed. C. Dohmen and C. Frevel; SBS 211; Stuttgart: Katholisches Bibelwerk, 2007) 195–202.

- David is further mentioned in Ps 122:5 (thrones of the House of David in Jerusalem) and 144:10 (deliverance of David, the servant of Yнwн—that is, the salvation of the later successors of David). Within the contexts of their collections, the Psalms of Ascent, and the fifth Davidic psalter, respectively, both verses have a meaning greater than just being sporadic allusions (see below).
- To these observations, one should add the 10 occurrences of the royal title "Anointed One." Five verses (Ps 18:51; 89:39, 52; 132:10, 17) belong to the Royal Psalms already mentioned. Four more verses confirm the importance of the *king* topic in the Royal Psalms: Ps 2:2 belongs to the basic psalm 2:1–9, which serves as an introduction to the so-called Messianic Psalms, Psalms 2–89, and probably for this reason was separated as an "orphan" from the first Davidic psalter. Ps 20:7 is an editorial intercession for the king and belongs to the third Royal Psalm. Ps 28:8 is an editorial statement of trust in God's support for the king followed by a prayer for the nation. In the same way, Ps 84:9–10 has been inserted as intercession for the king into the opening psalm of the second collection of Korah psalms. In Ps 105:15, the title is applied to the patriarchs, assigning to them a function derived from the royal title.

Approaching the topic from the occurrences of the name "David" and the texts relating to David by use of the title "Anointed One" naturally leads us to the 11 Royal Psalms that organize the framework of the Psalter:[8]

- The *first Royal Psalm* (Ps 2:1–9) is recognized as the preface to the Messianic psalter—situated as it is in conscious tension with the end of the Messianic psalter in Psalm 89, which could explain the obvious absence of assigning the psalm to David.
- The *second Royal Psalm* (Psalm 18), together with the *third and fourth Royal Psalms* (Psalms 20 and 21), forms an older center of the second collection (Psalms 15–24 in the first Davidic psalter), which was later superseded by the insertion of Psalm 19.
- The *fifth Royal Psalm* (Psalm 45) is a metaphorical wedding song on the marriage of the king to the king's daughter, Zion. It functions as a counterpoint to the nation's complaint in Psalm 44 and as a bridge and hermeneutical key to the triad of Zion Psalms 46–48.
- The *sixth Royal Psalm* (Psalm 72) appears at the end of the second Davidic psalter. Since the second Davidic psalter builds on the first, Psalm 72 also forms the end of David's biography kept up in the first

---

8. Cf. K.-P. Adam, *Der königliche Held: Die Entsprechung vom kämpfenden Gott und kämpfenden König in Ps 18* (WMANT 91; Neukirchen-Vluyn: Neukirchener Verlag, 2001); M. Leuenberger, *Konzeptionen des Königtums Gottes im Psalter: Untersuchung zu Komposition und Redaktion der theokratischen Bücher IV–V innerhalb des Psalters* (AThANT 83; Zurich: Theologischer Verlag, 2004); M. Saur, *Die Königspsalmen: Studien zur Entstehung und Theologie* (BZAW 340; Berlin: de Gruyter, 2004); F.-L. Hossfeld, "Messianische Texte des Psalters: Ein Überblick mit hermeneutischen Konsequenzen," in *Das AT als christliche Bibel in orthodoxer und westlicher Sicht: Zweite europäische orthodox-westliche Exegetenkonferenz im Rila-Kloster vom 8.–15. September 2001* (ed. Dimitrov I. Z. et al.; Tübingen: Mohr Siebeck, 2004) 307–24.

and second Davidic psalter (compare the final group of Psalms 69–71, 72 together with the Solomonic assignment and the colophon [see above]). Besides, at the end of the second book (Psalms 42–72), Psalm 72 is marked by a doxology, the *barukh*-formula of which is in line with the characteristics of the Elohistic psalter.

- The *seventh Royal Psalm* (Psalm 89) closes the Messianic psalter. Editorial notes on royal theology such as in Ps 20:7, 28:8–9, 61:7, 63:12, 89:9–10, which keep up interest in the question about the king in the previous collections, are absent after Psalm 89. At the same time, the psalm marks the end of the third book. With regard to the overall dynamic of the Psalter, which moves from complaint to praise, Psalm 89 appears at the accepted main caesura or watershed of the Psalter.

- The *eighth Royal Psalm* (Psalm 101) follows after the grand finale of the King Yʜwʜ Psalms in Psalm 100, which completes the collection of the King Yʜwʜ Psalms. In this sense, it answers the theocratic climax and hence carries on the basic question of the entire Psalter, which resonates in all Royal Psalms as well: How is the kingship of Yʜwʜ mediated in concrete history? Psalm 101 presents the prayer of a humble, provincial king who reigns from Jerusalem, the city of Yʜwʜ (v. 8), and lives near the temple. Assigning the psalm to David provides an autobiographical flair. "That David is given a say in Psalms 101 and 103 is nevertheless relevant to interpretation: the attitudes or experiences described in both psalms are in a way typical for the life of David. His example provides guidance on managing current situations of distress."[9] Consequently, Psalm 101 opens the triad of the third Davidic psalter, a sequence coherent in itself (Psalm 101: self-presentation of the king; Psalm 102: the king in difficulties; Psalm 103: thanks for salvation from sin and human weakness, addressed to Yʜwʜ, the creator and king of the world). The third Davidic psalter further develops the topic of the "divine and earthly kingdom" and considers David as a paradigm for the people.

- The *ninth Royal Psalm* (Psalm 110) completes the triad of the fourth Davidic psalter. After the introduction to the fifth book in Psalm 107, the people, who are returned and have been redeemed from exile, praise God's love and his saving deeds. The fourth Davidic psalter tackles the above-mentioned core issue of the Royal Psalms, the mediation and reification of God's kingship. The composite of Psalm 108 draws on the second Davidic psalter and renews the postexilic restorative hope of reestablishing David's reign over the land. King David becomes the speaker of the triad and hence the speaker representing the nation. In Psalm 109, he defends himself against false charges. Afterward, in Psalm 110 he receives the firm promise that Yʜwʜ, the ruler of the world, will enthrone him at his right hand.

---

9. J. Steinberg, *Die Ketuvim: Ihr Aufbau und ihre Botschaft* (BBB 152; Hamburg: Philo, 2006) 256. Steinberg does not speak of Psalm 102, whose title does not mention David, but whose title corresponds to the topic of Psalms 101 and 103 as quoted. Furthermore, the third Davidic psalter corresponds to the composition principle of the triad occuring in several instances.

- The *tenth Royal Psalm* (Psalm 132) belongs to the Psalms of Ascent, 120–34, and forms the third and last of the center psalms—Psalms 122, 127, and 132—of the three constitutive groups of five (120–24, 125–29, and 130–34).[10] Being assigned to David, Psalm 122 describes David as a prototypical pilgrim coming to Jerusalem, which is featured by the presence of the Temple (House of Yʜᴡʜ) and the Dynasty of David (House of David). Psalm 127 describes the doctrine of Solomon's wisdom concerning the peacefulness of the community in Jerusalem, which is blessed and recognized by Yʜᴡʜ. Similar to Psalm 122, the Royal Psalm 132 parallels the topics of the temple in relation to Zion and the Davidic Dynasty. It is a prayer for the Anointed One and successor of David, which refers back to David's vow and to the divine promise regarding the everlasting election of Zion. David is introduced as the founder of the temple with its liturgy, and Yʜᴡʜ warrants the existence of the Davidic Dynasty and the wealth of Jerusalem. Again, Royal Psalm 132 witnesses restorative, postexilic king expectations.
- The *final Royal Psalm* (Psalm 144) is the second-to-last psalm in the fifth Davidic psalter (Psalms 138–45). At one time, this collection completed the entire Psalter (Psalms 1–145), which was fashioned after the "five-part Torah of David."[11] The fifth Davidic psalter consists of eight individual prayers. In Psalm 144, the king is a single individual and at the same time the representative of the nation, as the concluding we-passage in vv. 12–15 shows. From the beginning, the fifth Davidic psalter is focused on the topic of kingship. In Psalm 138, the praying man, David, is the leader of the universal praise of the kings of the nations. In the final psalm (145), he takes over the same role. Psalm 144 can only be understood together with Psalm 145, the royal praise of the divine reign of Yʜᴡʜ in creation and history. Psalm 144 presents the king as a needy representative of Yʜᴡʜ, the king of the world. It does so by referring to the first Davidic psalter, especially to Royal Psalm 18. The earthly king appears in his lowliness and defines himself by comparison with older Royal Psalms by a sequence of negations: the king is not a cooperator with Yʜᴡʜ as in Psalm 18, he is no mediator of blessing as in Psalm 72, he is not the holder of majesty titles such as "king," "Anointed One," "shepherd," or "judge"; in contrast, among the people, the transient creatures, he is the *primus inter pares*.

Diachronic and Synchronic Observations on the Davidization of the Psalter

An inspection of the occurrences of "David" and "anointed" in the psalm corpora as well as of the structural framework of the Royal Psalms within the Psalter has shown the permanence, broad distribution, and charisma of David as a king, poet, and musician in the Psalter. In recent research on the

---

10. Cf. Steinberg, *Ketuvim*, 261–63; and F.-L. Hossfeld and E. Zenger, *Psalmen 101–150* (HThKAT; Freiburg: Herder, 2008) 403.

11. Cf. Zenger, "Buch der Psalmen," 365.

Psalms, the Royal Psalms have especially been recognized as the starting point for a historical investigation into the Psalms and the psalm groups. This is not by chance but, rather, relates to the core of the subject of kingship—namely, the question about how the kingship of Y<small>HWH</small> is mediated in creation and history (especially in the history of Israel).

R. G. Kratz traces the basic *historical development of the kingdom* over the lifetime of the Psalms by beginning with the doxologies and their arrangement into five books:

> Hence, the first two doxologies in 41:14 and 72:18–19 (with v. 20) lead to the monarchy under David and Solomon (72:1, 20).[12]

> The position of the doxologies in Ps 89:53 and 106:(47) 48 is undoubtedly inspired by the Chronicler's presentation and its transparency to the exilic/postexilic standards. At the same time, the order of the book suggests a"historical" trace. It begins with the founding era under David and Solomon (Psalms 2/3–41, 42–72), which is followed—in the sense of the doxological dividers!—by the era of the fall (Psalms 73–89, 90–106) of the monarchy (Psalm 89) and leading into, at least, a "70-year" (Ps 90:10) period of exile (Psalms 90–106), prefigured by Moses. In this period, the Davidic-Solomonic kingdom is handed over to Y<small>HWH</small> alone (Ps 74:12 in context; 93ff.; 103:22). From this time on, David himself completely loses his "historical" role, as in Ps 2–41, 42–72, and becomes merely an example of a pious individual.[13]

> Subsequent to the fourth and last doxology in 106:48 (with Psalm 107), another transition occurs, which is the transition from the fourth to the fifth book in Psalms 107–50. . . . These editorial doxologies link the two psalms, so that the plea of 106:47 is fulfilled in 107:2–3, thus beginning an era of restitution. The kingdom, which had been present in Psalms 3–72 and was lost in Psalms 73–106, returns and takes on a new form in the fifth book.[14]

Kratz presents, *grosso modo,* the historical and theological scheme of epochs behind the five books. He understands the interrelation of the historical and the paradigmatic meaning of each of the eras but does not apply this to the figure of David. In our opinion, from the beginning to the end of the Psalter, David continuously serves as a historical as well as a paradigmatic figure; he is the historical king and the typical man. However, it is also true that, wherever he appears in the Psalter, the reader is provoked to think of the history of the kingdom. Therefore, in each of the five Davidic psalters, at least one Royal Psalm is found in an accentuated position; overall,

---

12. R. G. Kratz, "Die Tora Davids: Psalm 1 und die doxologische Fünfteilung des Psalter," *ZTK* 93 (1996) 21.

13. Ibid., 22–23.

14. Ibid., 23–24; cf. Weber, "Psalm 78," 317 n. 32; as well as B. Janowski, "Ein Tempel aus Worten: Zur theologischen Architektur des Psalters," in *The Composition of the Book of Psalms* (ed. E. Zenger; BETL 238; Leuven: Leuven University Press, 2010) 279–308.

seven Royal Psalms are spread over five Davidic psalters (1st Davidic psalter: Psalms 18; 20; 21; 2nd Davidic psalter: Psalm 72; 3rd Davidic psalter: Psalm 101; 4th Davidic psalter: Psalm 110; 5th Davidic psalter: Psalm 144). The Psalter attests a change in the image of David, which will be considered now. Focusing on the midrash-like psalm titles, especially in the first and second Davidic collection (but see also Psalm 142), E. Zenger states:

> The image of David emerging here differs significantly from the image of David in Chronicles. In Chronicles, David appears neither as a praying man nor as a psalm singer but as a founder and organizer of the temple music, probably even as an inventor of instruments as well as someone who commissioned others to write psalms and perform them with music. The David of the psalm headings, however, occurs in no liturgical context (except Psalm 30). On the contrary: he is at "profane" places, he is a persecutor and sinner, he is threatened by his enemies and rescued from their hands, being under the special protection of YHWH—and documents this in the psalms that he himself recites. He prays *these* psalms neither in his "official" capacity as king nor by alluding to the *special* royal-theological basis of his nearness to God. At least in the psalms that refer to David's biographical situations in their headings, David is (anachronistically) a "layman." But even as *such*, David the man of prayer is identified as a common figure: "As David, so every man."[15]

This contrast between the "layman" David and the "officiate" David is a beginning place for asking about the change in the guiding image of kingship as reflected especially in the Royal Psalms including Psalm 78.

Regarding the fourth Davidic psalter, Psalms 108–10, Zenger characterizes the change in the king's image in the following way:

> The editors placed the following "David trilogy," Psalms 108–10, after Psalm 107 in order to present the vision of the restitution of Israel according to the model of a second Davidic era. The remembrance of the "historical" David and the territorial extent of his kingdom (Psalm 108) but also the subjection of his enemies, which was a gift of YHWH (Psalm 110), makes him into a prototypical figure of hope for the postexilic period. However, it is striking that his royal role (compared with Psalms 2, 18, 21, 45, 72, 89) is portrayed in a restrained way (he does not hold the kingly title but asks for the help of YHWH). Since the editors also ascribe Psalm 109, the prayer of a "poor and wretched man" (Ps 109:22), to David, this reduction of power becomes particularly obvious (regarding the "de-potentiation" of the king, see also Psalm 144).[16]

As shown above, Psalm 89 represents the crisis of the traditional image of the strong king (cf. vv. 26, 28). According to Psalm 89, at the main break

---

15. E. Zenger, "Der Psalter als Buch: Beobachtungen zu seiner Entstehung, Komposition und Funktion," in *Der Psalter in Judentum und Christentum* (ed. E. Zenger; HBS 18; Freiburg: Herder, 1998) 40–41.

16. Hossfeld and Zenger, *Psalmen 101–150*, 158.

in the Psalter, the image of the king changes from a strong to a weak king. This applied—in addition to Royal Psalms 110 and 144 mentioned above by Zenger—to the provincial king of Psalm 101 and the Anointed One of Psalm 132, who by contrast, acts liturgically and is focused on Zion. The image of the king adapts to the postexilic course of history, without being abandoned in the ongoing restoration.

Concordant with these observations, the so-called theocratic tendency (the combative enforcement of the kingdom of God on earth by YHWH himself) increases from Psalm 89 onward.[17] Psalm 101 keeps silent on foreign affairs. Psalm 110 continues the theocratic tendency:

> On the one hand, now the postexilic reality comes into view insofar as the "new" Davidide is attributed pontifical dignity and function; this corresponds to the image of David in Psalm 132. . . . Possibly this pontifical dimension of the kingdom is meant to relativize or to correct the military dimension dominating in the remaining part of the psalm. . . . YHWH and the king enforce their universal kingdom (cf. vv. 5–7). This happens, however, in such a way that YHWH is the true protagonist, who in the fight acts "at the right hand" of the king, as demonstrated in iconography as well.[18]

Like Psalm 101, Psalm 132 concentrates on Zion. The pontifical traits of the Davidic kingdom (see above) lead to no statements about military affairs. In Psalm 144, the humble servant of YHWH fights for his royal survival, not for rule over the nations. YHWH needs to subdue even his own people under him (v. 2 MT); he needs to release David from the henchmen of foreign occupational forces (vv. 7, 11) and save him from the evil sword (vv. 10, 11). YHWH alone achieves the major victories and deeds (Psalm 145). This change in the royal image must be considered well when one is speaking of the "Davidic-messianic tendencies" of the Psalter, or of "eschatological messianism," "proto-messianism," and so on. In addition, restorative interests must be taken into consideration, which expect "merely" a human king.

Heinz-Josef Fabry ascribed the Royal Psalms to an interest group that promoted hopes for a restorative, dynastic king (see above). Analogously, we ask: Who was behind the Davidization of the Psalter, behind the five Davidic psalters with their 73 ascriptions to David, not to speak of the Solomonic ascription, and the colophon in Ps 72:1, 20? Who supported the idea of recurring Royal Psalms and arranged them to control the overall structure of the Psalter? Who explicitly approached David or the Anointed

---

17. According to Psalm 89, *only* YHWH defeats the enemies. From Psalm 2 as proem of the psalter collection of 2–89* on, the earthly king follows the character of the royal hero less and less (Psalms 2, 18, 21, 45). Instead, the Psalms increasingly describe YHWH in this acting role. This can be seen in Psalm 74 (vv. 12–14) and is especially detailed in Psalm 89. In this latter psalm, Psalm 89, this *theocratic tendency* comes to its zenith. (Adam, *Der königliche Held*, 176)

18. Hossfeld and Zenger, *Psalmen 101–150*, 210.

One in the psalms corpora under consideration? This could not have been the court and temple singers of the Judaic royal court alone, who were deported to Babylon during the exile (cf. Psalm 137). As stated above, they— the Asaphites, Korahites, and Ezrahites—received the first and second Davidic psalters as a heritage and then revised it. At the same time, they published their own psalms under their own names, carried on the Davidic tradition (Psalm 78), and continued the tradition of distinctive theology (Psalms 2, 89; cf. the royal-theological notices) of the Royal Psalms. This points to a Davidic tradition that was already established for them to follow. In the fourth and fifth books of the Psalms, the number of psalms without a title increases, and no additional ascriptions to groups of temple singers appear, even though one can follow the traces of the temple singers, as the liturgical and structuring praise formulas show, or as a solitary psalm such as Psalm 137 reveals. Only the ascriptions to David continue in the fourth and fifth books of the psalms (Psalms 101–3, 108–10, 138–45), in the same way that the Royal Psalms and the references to David in the psalm texts are retained. Therefore, it is not appropriate to identify a monocausal ascription of the Davidization to a group of temple singers.

This is supported by an additional consideration. Regarding the different traditions in the Penta-, Hexa-, and Enneateuchs and the pillars of Deuteronomism and Priestly theology—their influence on the Psalter can be observed as well. This is not to deny further prophetic and wisdom influences. We have observed the closeness of the Asaphites to Deuteronomistic theology and their analysis of it—even outside the actual Asaph psalms (Psalms 18, 95, 103). Furthermore, we observe a Priestly redaction in the triad of the historical psalms, 104–6; we ascribe the pilgrimage psalter, 120–34, and the fifth Davidic psalter of 138–45 to Priestly circles; while in the fourth Davidic psalter, 108–10, as well as in the Passover Hallel of 113–18 and the final Hallel of 146–50, we discover compositions of the temple singers. If these findings are used for understanding the Davidization in a broader sense, then the Davidization was basically the common property of different groups related to King David and the temple. That is, at least two groups were continuously responsible for the transmission of the Psalms: the priests and the temple singers. The priests were exiled just as the temple singers were. In the exile, they continued to hold fast to the temple and King David. To support this, there is considerable evidence outside the Psalter, such as the book of Ezekiel, which gauged its dating system based on the year of deportation, 597 B.C.E.—the year when (in the eyes of the priests) the last Davidide, Jehoiachin, was deported with the gentry to Babylon. Ezekiel is the book that concludes with the grand temple vision (Ezekiel 40–48) and that, like the Psalter in the fourth and fifth books, persistently anticipates a restorative king, as Ezek 34:23–24 and 37:24–25 show. If the Davidization of the Psalter was common property, if the tradition was treasured by the priests and temple singers as well, an analogy imposes itself regarding the circle of the authors of Deuteronomy that is characterized by G. Braulik as follows:

> Miscellaneous information indicates that the author of Deuteronomy can be found in literary as well as theological and legally capable circles of the administrative elite of Jerusalem. They sustained a mainly cultic and politically oriented reform movement, which aimed to lead Israel back to its original identity. Thus it was the high priest Hilkiah and the chancellor Shaphan, the two most important officials of the king, who were mainly involved in finding the "Torah book" (2 Kings 22–23); later, the prophet Jeremiah was related to the family of Shaphan (especially with Gedaliah). In addition, the prose of Deuteronomy shows connections to a courtly style of speaking and to the language of wisdom literature, as it was probably used especially in the higher civil service.[19]

To sum up: the Davidization of the Psalter shows remarkably well the individuality as well as the interconnectedness of the Psalter in relation to other traditions and books of the OT and thus confirms the reputation of the Psalter as a "small library."

---

19. G. Braulik, "Das Buch Deuteronomium," in *Einleitung in das Alte Testament* (ed. E. Zenger et al.; 7th ed.; Stuttgart: Herder, 2008) 142.

Bibliography

Adam, K.-P. *Der königliche Held: Die Entsprechung vom kämpfenden Gott und kämpfenden König in Ps 18*. WMANT 91. Neukirchen-Vluyn: Neukirchener Verlag, 2001.

Braulik, G. "Das Buch Deuteronomium." Pp. 136–53 in *Einleitung in das Alte Testament*. Edited by E. Zenger et al. 7th ed. Stuttgart: Herder, 2008.

Fabry, H.-J., and K. Scholtissek. *Der Messias*. NEB Themen 5. Würzburg: Echter-Verlag, 2002.

Hossfeld, F.-L. "Der elohistische Psalter Ps 42–83: Entstehung und Programm." Pp. 199–214 in *The Composition of the Book of Psalms*. Edited by E. Zenger. BETL 238. Leuven: Leuven University Press, 2010.

———. "David als exemplarischer Mensch: Literarische Biographie und Anthropologie am Beispiel Davids." Pp. 243–55 in *Biblische Anthropologie: Neue Einsichten aus dem Alten Testament*. Edited by C. Frevel. Quaestiones disputatae 237. Freiburg: Herder, 2010.

———. "Messianische Texte des Psalters: Ein Überblick mit hermeneutischen Konsequenzen." Pp. 307–24 in *Das AT als christliche Bibel in orthodoxer und westlicher Sicht: Zweite europäische orthodox-westliche Exegetenkonferenz im Rila-Kloster vom 8.–15. September 2001*. Edited by I. Z. Dimitrov et al. Tübingen: Mohr Siebeck, 2004.

Hossfeld, F.-L., and E. Zenger. *Psalmen 101–150*. HThKAT. Freiburg: Herder, 2008.

Janowski, B. "Ein Tempel aus Worten: Zur theologischen Architektur des Psalters." Pp. 279–308 in *The Composition of the Book of Psalms*. Edited by E. Zenger. BETL 238. Leuven: Leuven University Press, 2010.

Kratz, R. G. "Die Tora Davids: Psalm 1 und die doxologische Fünfteilung des Psalter." *ZTK* 93 (1996) 1–34.

Leuenberger, M. *Konzeptionen des Königtums Gottes im Psalter: Untersuchung zu Komposition und Redaktion der theokratischen Bücher IV–V innerhalb des Psalters.* ATANT 83. Zurich: Theologischer Verlag, 2004.

Saur, M. *Die Königspsalmen: Studien zur Entstehung und Theologie.* BZAW 340. Berlin: de Gruyter, 2004.

Schnocks, J. "Verworfen hast du den Bunde mit deinem Knecht (Ps 89,40)." Pp. 195–202 in *Für immer verbündet: Studien zur Bundestheologie der Bibel.* FS F.-L. Hossfeld. Edited by C. Dohmen and C. Frevel. SBS 211. Stuttgart: Katholisches Bibelwerk, 2007.

Steinberg, J. *Die Ketuvim: Ihr Aufbau und ihre Botschaft.* BBB 152. Hamburg: Philo, 2006.

Weber, B. "Psalm 78 als 'Mitte' des Psalters? Ein Versuch." *Bib* 88 (2007) 305–25.

Zenger, E. "Das Buch der Psalmen." Pp. 348–70 in *Einleitung in das Alte Testament.* Edited by E. Zenger et al. 7th ed. Stuttgart: Kohlhammer, 2008.

———. "Der Psalter als Buch: Beobachtungen zu seiner Entstehung, Komposition und Funktion." Pp. 1–57 in *Der Psalter in Judentum und Christentum.* Edited by E. Zenger. HBS 18. Freiburg: Herder, 1998.

Reading Job following the Psalms

WILL KYNES

"There are no *texts*, but only relationships *between* texts."[1] Harold Bloom made this statement, describing his distinctive understanding of literary influence, but it concisely expresses a more general hermeneutical truth: texts cannot be understood in isolation; they must be read in dialogue with others, and which others are chosen necessarily affects their interpretation.[2] The book of Job is mainly read together with Proverbs and Ecclesiastes as a fellow member of the category "Wisdom Literature." As one of these Wisdom texts, Job tends to be contrasted with the retributory world view of Proverbs, associated with the skepticism of Ecclesiastes, and accredited with a sapiential concern for addressing philosophical problems presumed to be shared by both. There is an element of truth to all three of these insights; without it, they would not have become so well known. However, restricting Job to this interpretive context threatens to distort its interpretation since it has links at least as strong, if not stronger, with another book: the Psalms. Based on the nature of these connections, which involve characters, forms, and allusions, I suggest that the meaning of Job is not only found *between* the book and the Psalms but *following* the Psalms, since knowledge of the Psalms is a prerequisite for fully understanding Job.

If this is the case, then it attests the exegetical insight offered by the rabbinic tradition in b. B. Bat. 14b that placed Job immediately after the Psalms. Though the compilers of this list may not have intended the order to communicate a reading strategy for Job, the connections between the books and the way the author of Job manipulates them for rhetorical effect demonstrate that having Job follow the Psalms was certainly prescient, because reading Job through a psalmic lens brings new clarity to this often-obscure book. Thus, the purpose of this essay is not to base an interpretive approach to Job and the Psalms on the order in b. B. Bat. 14b or to suggest that this order should be considered normative but simply to argue that

---

1. H. Bloom, *A Map of Misreading* (Oxford: Oxford University Press, 1975) 3. Emphasis original.

2. Thus, John Barton observes that "unless we can read a text *as* something—unless we can assign it to some genre, however ill-defined and in need of subsequent refinement—we cannot really read it at all" (J. Barton, *Reading the Old Testament: Method in Biblical Study* [2nd ed.; London: Darton, Longman & Todd, 1996] 24). Putting a text in a genre is a way of choosing a group of works between which one interprets a text.

links between Job and the Psalms demonstrate the hermeneutical value of that order.[3] Three successive movements in the history of the interpretation of Job reveal three different ways that the Psalms may be drawn upon to enrich the book's interpretation: the precritical comparison with the character of David, the form-critical attention to the Job poet's "misuse" of forms, and recent intertextual readings of allusions to particular psalms.

"The Prayer of Job and David"

Interpreters have long recognized resonances between Job and the Psalms. When the Psalms were still attributed to David, several interpreters compared the protagonists of the two books. Rabbinic traditions include isolated comparisons of Job with David, along with other figures. For example, the distinctive cantillation in Job, Psalms, and Proverbs is explained by the fact that Job was humiliated and then restored to glory just as David and Solomon were dethroned temporarily.[4] Additionally, the midrash on Psalm 26 states, "Four are mentioned in Scripture as having been smitten," before giving a list of their responses, presumably in ascending order of virtue, from Job, who "rebelled" (Job 10:1–3, 13:23, 16:17–18), through Abraham, who laughed (Gen 17:17), and Hezekiah, who sought the LORD as his friend (Isa 38:2), to David, the prime example, who declared: "Why is the lash held back? Strike me again!" (Pss 26:2, 94:12).[5]

Ambrose provides a much more extensive interpretation of both Job and the Psalms in light of the connections between the experiences and personalities of their respective heroes in his *Prayer of Job and David*. The title itself testifies to his character-focused approach. Depicting the common response of these two men to suffering, Ambrose writes, "Many indeed have complained over human weakness and frailty, but the holy Job and holy David have done so in a fashion superior to the rest." However, he distinguishes the tone of their prayers. Job is "straightforward, forceful, sharp, and displays a loftier style, as one who has been provoked by severe

---

3. Though other orders for the Ketubim in Jewish tradition diverge from b. B. Bat. 14b at various points, they all put the Psalms before Job, most immediately before, with the exception of Jerome's report of a Jewish order, in which he lists the books chronologically, with the patriarchal setting of Job making it first; and Taschereau 17.18 from 1512 (J. Steinberg, *Die Ketuvim: Ihr Aufbau und ihre Botschaft* [BBB 152; Hamburg: Philo, 2006] 133, 137, 143, 152). Historically, in the Christian canonical orders for Greek and Latin Bibles, Job's location varied drastically. It was even occasionally placed among the historical books or with "apocryphal" texts such as Judith and Tobit. The order Job–Psalms–Proverbs of modern Christian Bibles was not normative. See Peter Brandt, *Endgestalten des Kanons: Das Arrangement der Schriften Israels in der jüdischen und christlichen Bibel* (BBB 131; Berlin: Philo, 2001).

4. L. Ginzberg, *The Legends of the Jews* (7 vols.; Baltimore: Johns Hopkins University Press, 1998) 5.390.

5. W. G. Braude, *The Midrash on Psalms* (2 vols.; Yale Judaica Series 13; New Haven, CT: Yale University Press, 1959) 1.357–58.

afflictions," whereas David is "ingratiating and calm and mild, of a gentler disposition."[6] Despite their differences in presentation, according to Ambrose, both make a similar argument, praying to God "on the grounds that God was forgetful of His own work and of the generosity and the grace that He had bestowed on man; He abandoned man, whom He had undertaken to protect and honor, and cast him out to destruction, feeble and wrecked by various weaknesses."[7]

Like Ambrose, John Calvin also takes an "exegetical turn of interpreting Job through the person of David."[8] In his *Sermons on Job*, he similarly notes that, in terms of affliction, "David had passed that way as well as Job. For he had endured great adversities to such a degree that it was like he had been forsaken of God."[9] For both, the most devastating torment was feeling God's hand heavy upon them (Job 6:8–14; Ps 32:4), and this suffering was magnified by the lack of comfort they received from their friends (Job 6:15–23; Ps 41:10).[10] References to David and his response to suffering are woven throughout Calvin's sermons on Job with such frequency and approval that it actually appears that David, not Job, is the true model that Calvin encourages his listeners to emulate.[11]

Calvin also shares with Ambrose the recognition of a difference in tone between the prayers of the two men, and he repeatedly uses David's example to correct Job.[12] Thus, commenting on Job's opening lament in ch. 3 in which Job curses the day of his birth, Calvin claims that "words escaped his mouth without advisement, by force of the misery that he endured." However, Calvin encourages his listeners not to follow Job's example but instead that of David in Psalm 22, who, after he has "made his moan" in the first verse, renders thanks to God and sings unto his name, as he remembers God's faithfulness to him from his mother's womb (v. 10).[13] Later, Calvin notes that, though Job and David both claim to have kept God's commands (Job 23:11–12; Ps 119), David also admits his guilt before God (Pss 130:3, 143:2), and thus humbly receives his righteousness as a gift, while Job uses his obedience as a means to attempt to go to do legal

---

6. Ambrose, "The Prayer of Job and David," in *Saint Ambrose: Seven Exegetical Works* (trans. Michael P. McHugh; Father of the Church 65; Washington, DC: Catholic University of America Press, 1971) 325–420, 389.

7. Ibid., 330.

8. S. E. Schreiner, "'Why Do the Wicked Live?' Job and David in Calvin's Sermons on Job," in *The Voice from the Whirlwind: Interpreting the Book of Job* (ed. L. G. Perdue and W. C. Gilpin; Nashville: Abingdon, 1992) 130.

9. J. Calvin, *Sermons on Job* (Edinburgh: Banner of Truth Trust, 1993); repr. of *Sermons on Job* (trans. Arthur Golding; London: George Bishop, 1574) 45. In quoting from these sermons, I have modernized the English from the 1574 translation.

10. Ibid., 108, 115. Golding's translation mistakenly lists Ps 14:10 as the second cross-reference.

11. Schreiner, "Why Do the Wicked Live?" 137.

12. Ibid.

13. Calvin, *Sermons on Job*, 52.

battle with God. Calvin claims that Job is therefore "grossly overseen in this behalf," but if he had acted like David, "his protestation would have been good and holy."[14]

Seen as a whole, these character-based connections observed between Job and a David constructed from the Psalms reflect a dialectical relationship between the two books in which the similarities between the experiences, and even the arguments, of the two protagonists highlight the contrast between the tones of their "prayers." Thus, in this synchronic comparison, in which the two texts are interpreted simultaneously, the shared struggle to respond to suffering comes to the fore, but Job's reaction is judged by the psalmic paradigm.

The Use (and Misuse) of Forms

With the rise of biblical criticism, this character-based comparison between the texts was largely abandoned, and, with the modern categorization of Job as a "Wisdom" book, the earlier emphasis on the proper faithful response to suffering was also eclipsed by the more abstract concerns of theodicy and the viability of the retributive principle.[15] However, connections between Job and the Psalms were not ignored altogether. The development of form criticism in the early 20th century offered new impetus for comparing Job with the Psalms. Though, by this time, the figure of David was rarely associated with the Psalter, this approach arrived at similar conclusions regarding the relationship between the two books. As a result, "psalmistic interpretations" of Job have become a consistent, albeit secondary feature of Job scholarship, focusing mainly on the resonances between the book and the lament form.[16]

The most prominent form-critical comparison between Job and the Psalms is Claus Westermann's *The Structure of the Book of Job*. He characterizes Job as a "dramatization" of the psalm of lament in which Job, the friends, and God correspond to the individual, the enemies, and God in the lament.[17] According to Westermann, the Job poet, standing within his tradition, "cannot express himself in other than already formed linguistic structures" and thus "dramatizes the lament by weaving together the

---

14. Ibid., 419.

15. See C. Westermann, *The Structure of the Book of Job: A Form-Critical Analysis* (trans. Charles A. Muenchow; Philadelphia: Fortress, 1981) 1.

16. My translation. See the survey in H.-P. Müller, *Das Hiobproblem: Seine Stellung und Entstehung im alten Orient und im Alten Testament* (3rd ed.; Erträge der Forschung 84; Darmstadt: Wissenschaftliche Buchgesellschaft, 1995) 82–91, 111–18.

17. Westermann, *Structure of the Book of Job*, 8. See A. Bentzen, *Introduction to the Old Testament* (2 vols.; Copenhagen: Gad, 1948–49) 1.182. For a similar comparison of Job and the implicit voices in the lament from a dialogical perspective, see C. Mandolfo, "A Generic Renegade: A Dialogic Reading of Job and Lament Psalms," in *Diachronic and Synchronic: Reading the Psalms in Real Time* (ed. J. S. Burnett; New York: T. & T. Clark, 2007) 45–63.

basic motifs of lamentation, motifs which were already ancient."[18] These "ancient" motifs are known to us primarily through the Psalms, so a comparison with texts from the Psalter drives Westermann's analysis. Though Westermann focuses on the lament, he also recognizes other psalmic forms in Job, such as praise[19] and wisdom.[20]

Georg Fohrer argues that the book of Job, deeply rooted in the traditional material and motifs of the Hebrew Bible (HB), picks up and uses traditions from across the canon to such a degree that only a few verses in the whole text lack reference to them.[21] He observes that laments and hymns appear most frequently.[22] According to Fohrer, the Job poet mixes forms throughout the speeches, often for purposes different from their original function.[23] Developing Fohrer's insight, Katharine Dell maintains that often the forms are "misused," thereby contributing to the skeptical tone she perceives in the book. She illustrates this pattern of misuse by comparing the forms in Job with the same forms as they appear elsewhere in the HB, with the majority coming from the Psalms.[24] For example, Dell claims that Job 3:11–26 is a misuse of a lament form because Job presents death as desirable instead of as the unwelcome outcome of God's wrath (e.g., Ps 88:4–5[3–4]).[25]

These form-critical comparisons of Job and texts across the HB, and particularly the Psalms, once again demonstrate a dialectic dialogue between Job and the Psalms. On the one hand, Job builds on the forms found in the Psalter. These paradigmatic forms of speech, which the Job poet imitates, are often misused or parodied by being put to a different purpose. Thus, again, similarity reveals difference. However, these interpretations introduce a diachronic, or at least sequential element into the comparison between Job and the Psalms, though it applies to the reader and not necessarily the author and is therefore more logical than chronological. For the author of Job to "dramatize" or "misuse" the forms found in the Psalms, he must have been aware of those forms. Because these scholars understand the author of Job to be interacting with the forms appearing in the Psalms and not necessarily the texts themselves, Job need not be written after the Psalms, but, since our knowledge of those forms comes primarily through reading the Psalms, we would miss this resonance if the Psalms did not

---

18. Westermann, *Structure of the Book of Job*, 32.

19. E.g., Job 7:17 // Psalm 8; Job 11:7–9 // Psalm 139 (Westermann, *Structure of the Book of Job*, 71–80).

20. See below, n. 33.

21. G. Fohrer, *Das Buch Hiob* (KAT 16; Gütersloh: Mohn, 1963) 48.

22. Fohrer, *Das Buch Hiob*, 50–51.

23. Ibid., 49–50; idem, "Form und Funktion in der Hiobdichtung," in *Studien zum Buche Hiob (1956–1979)* (BZAW 159; Berlin: de Gruyter, 1983) 60–77.

24. K. J. Dell, *The Book of Job as Sceptical Literature* (BZAW 197; Berlin: de Gruyter, 1991) 125–36.

25. Ibid., 125.

contribute to our preunderstanding of Job. Appreciating the Job poet's interaction with psalmic forms requires a sequential and not merely simultaneous approach—we must read Job *following* the Psalms.

From Paradigm to Parody

In the past quarter-century, a growing number of biblical scholars have turned their attention from generalized connections between forms to lexically specific allusions,[26] and Job scholarship testifies to this intertextual turn. Interaction with a developing HB is seen increasingly to be a vital aspect of the method and meaning of the book of Job, with scholars discovering allusions to various texts in the HB throughout the book.[27] Once again, the Psalms have emerged as a prominent component of this interpretive perspective on Job.

The most well-known and thoroughly discussed intertextual connection in Job is the "bitter parody" of Ps 8:5[4] in Job 7:17–18:

Job 7:17–18[28]

מָה־אֱנוֹשׁ כִּי תְגַדְּלֶנּוּ	What are human beings, that you make so much of them,
וְכִי־תָשִׁית אֵלָיו לִבֶּךָ:	that you set your mind on them,
וַתִּפְקְדֶנּוּ לִבְקָרִים	visit them every morning,
לִרְגָעִים תִּבְחָנֶנּוּ:	test them every moment?

Ps 8:5[4]

| מָה־אֱנוֹשׁ כִּי־תִזְכְּרֶנּוּ | What are human beings that you are mindful of them, |
| וּבֶן־אָדָם כִּי תִפְקְדֶנּוּ: | mortals that you care for them? |

The repetition of the phrase מה אנוש ("What are human beings?"), the common structure of both passages, and the recurrence of the verb פקד set in a context that reverses its meaning have led to a nearly unanimous consensus that Job is intentionally twisting the meaning of the psalm from a

---

26. Anthony Campbell has characterized form criticism's fall from favor this way: "Above all . . . the focus away from the present text into a surmised past accessible to a scholarly few was too burdened with subjectivity to survive in a generation focused on the present reality of what was possessed in the final text" (A. F. Campbell, "Form Criticism's Future," in *The Changing Face of Form Criticism for the Twenty-First Century* [ed. M. A. Sweeney and E. Ben Zvi; Grand Rapids, MI: Eerdmans, 2003] 22).

27. See, e.g., T. N. D. Mettinger, "Intertextuality: Allusion and Vertical Context Systems in Some Job Passages," in *Of Prophets' Visions and the Wisdom of Sages* (ed. H. A. McKay and D. J. A. Clines; JSOTSup 162; Sheffield: JSOT Press, 1993) 257–80; Y. Pyeon, *You Have Not Spoken What Is Right about Me: Intertextuality and the Book of Job* (Studies in Biblical Literature 45; New York: Peter Lang, 2003); L. S. Wilson, *The Book of Job: Judaism in the 2nd Century BCE: An Intertextual Reading* (Studies in Judaism; Lanham, MD: University Press of America, 2006); K. Schmid, "Innerbiblische Schriftdiskussion im Hiobbuch," in *Das Buch Hiob und seine Interpretationen: Beiträge zum Hiob-Symposium auf dem Monte Verità vom 14.–19. August 2005* (ed. T. Krüger et al.; ATANT 88; Zurich: Theologischer Verlag, 2007).

28. All biblical translations are from the NRSV.

hymn of praise for God's watchful care to a complaint against his overbearing attention.[29] As a parody, this connection between Job and the Psalms depends on evident similarities to signal the textual interplay and yet puts its emphasis on the antithetical relationship between the texts[30] and thus continues to testify to their dialectical relationship.

This parody is often interpreted as Job's skeptical rejection of Psalm 8 and the psalm's affirmation of God's care for humanity, whom God has exalted.[31] However, the broader context of the parody in the dialogue suggests that it makes more sense to see this as a "reaffirming" parody—Job presents the psalmic imagery antithetically, not to ridicule it, but to support his repeated accusations against God by demonstrating how the deity's current behavior toward him violates the psalmic paradigm.[32] Job uses the psalm to demand for himself the royal dignity that it proclaims God has bestowed on humankind,[33] and thus he does not reject the psalm or the God it depicts but pleads that the God he is now encountering conform to this paradigm. As Ambrose observed, Job prays, like the David of the laments, "on the grounds that God was forgetful of His own work and of the generosity and the grace that He had bestowed on man." As Christian Frevel argues, understood this way, the parody becomes a powerful rhetorical tool in Job's larger goal of gaining vindication before God.[34]

Eliphaz's response supports this interpretation:

---

29. For more on the linguistic indicators of this parody, see D. J. A. Clines, *Job* (2 vols.; WBC 17–18A; Nashville: Thomas Nelson, 1989–2006) 1.192; M. Fishbane, "The Book of Job and Inner-Biblical Discourse," in *The Voice from the Whirlwind* (ed. L. G. Perdue and W. C. Gilpin; Nashville: Abingdon, 1992) 87. For a dissenting voice, see R. C. Van Leeuwen, "Psalm 8.5 and Job 7.17–18: A Mistaken Scholarly Commonplace?" in *The World of the Aramaeans*, vol. 1: *Biblical Studies in Honour of Paul-Eugène Dion* (ed. P. M. Michèle Daviau et al.; JSOTSup 324; Sheffield: Sheffield Academic Press, 2001).

30. For antithetical allusion as the essential definition of parody, see my "Beat Your Parodies into Swords, and Your Parodied Books into Spears: A New Paradigm for Parody in the Hebrew Bible," *BibInt* 19 (2011) 290–91.

31. E.g., Dell, *Book of Job*, 126; Mettinger, "Intertextuality: Allusion and Vertical Context Systems," 267.

32. Kynes, "Beat Your Parodies into Swords," 303–6. Similarly, C. Frevel, "'Eine kleine Theologie der Menschenwürde': Ps 8 und seine Rezeption im Buch Ijob," in *Das Manna fällt auch heute noch: Beiträge zur Geschichte und Theologie des Alten, Ersten Testaments* (ed. F.-L. Hossfeld and L. Schwienhorst-Schönberger; HBS 44; Freiburg: Herder, 2004) 262.

33. See also Job's parody of Ps 8:6[5] in Job 19:9, in which he accuses God of stripping his "glory" (כבד) and tearing the "crown" (עטר) from his head, in contrast to the psalmist's affirmation that God has "crowned" (root: עטר) humanity with "glory" (כבד) and honor (Frevel, "Eine kleine Theologie," 264).

34. Ibid., 262. Michael Fishbane observes this type of appeal to earlier texts to remind God of his own nature and motivate the deity to intervene in the citation of the divine attribute formulary (Exod 34:6–7a) in Mic 7:18–20 and Psalms 103 and 109 (M. Fishbane, *Biblical Interpretation in Ancient Israel* [Oxford: Clarendon, 1985] 439).

Job 15:14

מָה־אֱנוֹשׁ כִּי־יִזְכֶּה   What are mortals, that they can be clean?

וְכִי־יִצְדַּק יְלוּד אִשָּׁה: or those born of woman, that they can be righteous?

Ps 8:5[4]

מָה־אֱנוֹשׁ כִּי־תִזְכְּרֶנּוּ   What are human beings that you are mindful of them,

וּבֶן־אָדָם כִּי תִפְקְדֶנּוּ:   mortals that you care for them?

Besides repeating the opening phrase and structure of Ps 8:5[4], Eliphaz indicates that he is alluding to the psalm as he responds to Job's parody of the verse by drawing on its surrounding context.[35] He continues, "God puts no trust even in his holy ones (קְדֹשָׁיו),[36] and the heavens (שָׁמַיִם) are not clean in his sight; how much less one who is abominable and corrupt, one who drinks iniquity like water!" (vv. 15–16). The psalmist had wondered at the exalted place God has given humans, considering their lowliness in comparison with the "heavens" (שָׁמַיִם) (vv. 4–5[3–4]) and the apparent inappropriateness of their place a little lower than the "heavenly beings" (אלהים; v. 6[5]).[37] Eliphaz, also contrasting humanity with the "heavens" and God's "holy ones,"[38] regards these comparisons as declarations of the lowly place of humankind instead of its exaltation and even as indications of moral impurity.[39] Michael Fishbane considers this a "caustic rejoinder"

---

35. Frevel argues that Eliphaz is not referring to Psalm 8 because his low view of humans conflicts with the exalted place given them in Psalm 8 (Frevel, "Eine kleine Theologie," 268). Similarly, H. Irsigler, *Vom Adamssohn zum Immanuel* (Arbeiten zu Text und Sprache im Alten Testament 58; St. Ottilien: EOS, 1997) 43. This overlooks the possibility, however, that Eliphaz may be interpreting the psalm's message in his own way as he alludes to it.

36. This is the *Qere*; the *Kethiv* is קדשו.

37. The NRSV translates אלהים in Ps 8:6[5] as "God." However, A. A. Anderson and Hans-Joachim Kraus, following the LXX, targum, Syriac version, and Vulgate, argue that "angels" or "heavenly beings" is a better translation (A. A. Anderson, *The Book of Psalms* [2 vols.; NCB; Grand Rapids, MI: Eerdmans, 1981] 1.103; H.-J. Kraus, *Psalms: A Continental Commentary* (trans. Hilton C. Oswald; 2 vols.; Minneapolis: Fortress, 1993) 1.183. For the "holy ones" in Job 15:16 as angels, see, e.g., Fohrer, *Das Buch Hiob*, 271; M. H. Pope, *Job* (3rd ed.; AB 15; Garden City, NY: Doubleday, 1973) 116. This corresponds to the similar statement in Eliphaz's first speech where he compares humans to God's "angels" (Job 4:18; מלאכים).

38. Gerald Janzen notes the parallel between Eliphaz's words and Ps 8:4[3] (J. G. Janzen, *Job* [Interpretation; Atlanta: John Knox, 1985] 117). See also J. Hempel, "Mensch und König: Studie zu Psalm 8 und Hiob," *Forschungen und Fortschritte 35* (1961) 123.

39. Bildad makes a similar point by returning to Psalm 8 once again in 25:5–6: "If even the moon is not bright and the stars are not pure in his sight, how much less a mortal, who is a maggot, and a human being, who is a worm!" He repeats the comparison to the moon and stars from Ps 8:4[3] and the parallel terms אנוש and בן־אדם from Ps 8:5[4] but, like Eliphaz, distorts the psalm's message into a declaration of human worthlessness. See W. Beyerlin, "Psalm 8: Chancen der Überlieferungskritik," *ZTK* 73 (1976) 18; Janzen, *Job*, 174, 176; H. Klein, "Zur Wirkungsgeschichte von Psalm 8," in *Konsequente Traditionsgeschichte: Festschrift für Klaus Baltzer zum 65. Geburtstag* (ed. R. Bartelmus, T. Krüger, and

to Job's earlier allusion to Ps 8:5[4], in which Eliphaz has "ironically re-established the original *traditum*" by answering the question of Ps 8:5[4] himself.[40] However, since Psalm 8 expresses an exalted view of humanity, Eliphaz is not reestablishing its message but twisting it into its opposite in order to support his argument. That Eliphaz presents the psalm negatively to respond to Job's parody of it further indicates that Job has actually ap-pealed to its positive message.

This sophisticated interaction with Psalm 8 in Job, which includes two further allusions (Job 19:9 // Ps 8:6[5];[41] Job 25:5–6 // Ps 8:4–5[3–4][42]), suggests that a number of the other parallels between Job and the Psalms may also be allusions intended to contribute to the debate among Job, the friends, and God.[43] Several of these possible allusions in Job's speeches also appear to be parodies in which Job transforms psalmic acclamation into divine accusation (e.g., Job 10:8–12 // Ps 139:13–16;[44] Job 12:13–25 // Psalm 107[45]). However, the friends also appear to allude to the Psalms, often the same ones as Job (e.g., Job 11:7–9 // Ps 139:7–10;[46] Job 5:16 // Ps 107:42[47]), but they seem to use them for a different purpose: to silence Job's com-plaints. In so doing, they provide an alternative response to suffering that expects the world to conform to a strict, retributive world view, leaving no room to challenge God to rectify injustice, because none can exist.[48] In so doing, they take to the extreme an alternative theme in the Psalms, one found in "wisdom" or "didactic" psalms, such as Psalm 37, which affirms

---

H. Utzschneider; OBO; Göttingen: Vandenhoeck & Ruprecht / Freiburg: Universitäts-Ver-lag, 1993) 188.

40. Fishbane, "The Book of Job and Inner-Biblical Discourse," 93.

41. See above, n. 33.

42. See above, n. 39.

43. For further discussion of allusions to the Psalms in the Job dialogue, see W. Kynes, *"My Psalm Has Turned into Weeping": Job's Dialogue with the Psalms* (BZAW 437; Berlin: de Gruyter, 2012).

44. Though William Brown claims that Joban dependency is "entirely possible," and "an equally valid case" can be made for Job's "deconstruction of Ps. 139" as for his parody of Psalm 8 in (Job) 7:17–18 because this dependence is "difficult to prove conclusively," he focuses on the rhetorical effects of the parallels instead. W. P. Brown, *"Creatio Corporis* and the Rhetoric of Defense in Job 10 and Psalm 139," in *God Who Creates* (FS S. Turner; ed. W. P. Brown and S. D. McBride Jr.; Grand Rapids, MI: Eerdmans, 2000) 122, 118 n. 33).

45. Clines, *Job*, 1.287, 297–304. He writes, "The connections with Ps 107 are so close and numerous that it seems right to term it a 'source' of the present hymn, in the way that Ps 8 was the 'source' of Job 7:17–18" (1.297).

46. Pyeon, *You Have Not Spoken*, 186–88.

47. R. Gordis, *The Book of Job: Commentary, New Translation, and Special Studies* (Mo-reshet 2; New York: Jewish Theological Seminary of America, 1978) 57.

48. Mandolfo argues that the friends take on the role of the "didactic voice" in the psalmic laments, which aims "to shore up faith in the face of contrary experiences" (Man-dolfo, "A Generic Renegade," 58).

God's justice and commands sufferers to "be still before the Lᴏʀᴅ, and wait patiently for him" (v. 7).[49]

This widespread dialogical interaction with the Psalms in Job would further testify to the profit of reading Job following the Psalms and would indicate an even more diachronic, sequential relationship between the texts because allusions require both the readers[50] and the author to be aware of the earlier texts. Without the readers' prior knowledge of the Psalms, they would miss these allusions and their significance would be lost, but without the author's prior knowledge of at least the psalms to which he alludes, these allusions would not even be possible.

Thus, when the characters of Job and the "David" who speaks in the Psalms are compared, their shared appeal to God in the midst of affliction becomes apparent, but Job's tone falls short of the psalmic paradigm. When Job takes up the forms of psalmic prayer, however, he often deliberately "misuses" those paradigms for addressing God.[51] And when Job alludes to the Psalms, he refers to them as paradigms for divine-human relationship to ground his accusations against God. The friends then try to reinterpret those paradigms in order to defend the deity. As a whole, through the "misuse" of forms and direct allusions, the book of Job pushes the psalmic patterns for relating to God—lament, praise, and even wisdom—to their limits in its author's apparent inquiry into whether psalmic piety (which earlier interpreters associated with the character of David) can withstand Job's superlative adversity. This supports the argument made by Westermann and several others that the book does not deal primarily with a theoretical "problem" but with an existential question as it explores the proper response to suffering.[52]

---

49. Parallels between Psalm 37 and Job include: v. 1 // 5:2; v. 2 // 14:2; v. 4 // 22:26 and 27:10; v. 5 // 21:31; v. 6 // 11:17; v. 10 // 8:22 and 24:24; v. 12 // 16:9; v. 19 // 5:19–20; v. 23 // 21:14; vv. 25, 28 // 4:7; v. 31 // 12:5 and 23:11; vv. 35–36 // 5:3. See G. H. B. Wright, *The Book of Job* (London: Williams & Norgate, 1883) 239. Most of these occur in the friends' speeches. Thus, Westermann proclaims, "Psalm 37 exhibits a whole array of parallels to the speeches of the friends (above all, to chap. 20)" (Westermann, *Structure of the Book of Job*, 87).

50. For this implication of the allusions in Job, see R. Heckl, *Hiob: Vom Gottesfürchtigen zum Repräsentanten Israels* (FAT 70; Tübingen: Mohr Siebeck, 2010) 64.

51. Frevel calls the Psalms the "paradigm on which the book of Job 'works,'" and claims that, without a knowledge of the Psalms, the book cannot be fully understood (Frevel, "Eine kleine Theologie," 257, 267, my translation).

52. Westermann, *Structure of the Book of Job*, 1–2. See also, P. Volz, *Weisheit: Das Buch Hiob, Sprüche und Jesus Sirach, Prediger* (Die Schriften des Alten Testaments; Göttingen: Vandenhoeck & Ruprecht, 1911) 25–26; F. Baumgärtel, *Der Hiobdialog: Aufriss und Deutung* (BWANT 61; Stuttgart: Kohlhammer, 1933) 187–88; Fohrer, *Das Buch Hiob*, 549; Heckl, *Hiob*, 205, 215.

Job between the Psalms and Wisdom

In his interpretation of the Ketubim according to the order given in b. B. Bat. 14b, Julius Steinberg expresses concerns with this view.[53] He observes that one's behavior in suffering is a direct consequence of one's understanding of the nature of suffering. *Verhalten* and *Verstehen* are indivisible. Instead of reading Job following the Psalms, Steinberg goes on to defend Job's place in the Wisdom Literature, reading the book primarily as the introduction to a series in b. B. Bat. 14b going from Job through Proverbs and Ecclesiastes to Song of Songs.[54] However, in my view, the ways in which Job resonates with and even presupposes the Psalms suggest that Steinberg offers more insight into the way the location of the book reflects its theological message when he notes this combination of response to and reflection on suffering in the book, since the former draws on the Psalms, and the latter resonates with the "Wisdom Literature." In fact, a similar argument could also be made for connections in characters, forms, and allusions between Job and Proverbs, though it would not be quite as strong. One of the rabbinic traditions mentioned earlier compares Job with Solomon; several common forms appear in both books, such as numerical sayings (e.g., Job 5:19–21; cf. Prov 30:18), proverbs (e.g., Job 8:11–12, 12:12–13, 17:5), and hymns to wisdom (e.g., Job 28; cf. Proverbs 8), though these forms are not predominant in Job;[55] and there are occasional possible allusions to specific Proverbs, as well (e.g., Job 15:7 // Prov 8:25; Job 18:5–6, 21:17 // Prov 13:9, 24:20).[56] Ivan Engnell remarks that, "from many points of view, it can be said that [Job] occupies a middle position between the

---

53. Steinberg, *Die Ketuvim*, 277.

54. Ibid., 454–55. In response to Hendrik Koorevaar, who sees Job and the Psalms connected primarily in the persons of Job and David as suffering "servants of the LORD," Steinberg argues that the material of the Psalter is so rich and extensive that relationships could be demonstrated between the Psalms and nearly each of the books in the Ketubim, and that, in fact, the collective message of the Psalms actually differs significantly from the book of Job. Steinberg does not explain exactly how he understands the messages of the two books to differ, and it is not clear to me that they do so in a way that would discount reading them in close connection, particularly when the other option is to read Job in conjunction with Proverbs, a book with which Job is widely seen to be at odds because of its differing view on retribution. In fact, Steinberg himself notes that, because the Psalter is made up largely of prayers, its message, at least in part, is to teach how one can search for a refuge in God through prayer (p. 268). As Job uses the forms and even the words of these prayers to address God in order to motivate the deity to respond to his cries for justice, he reflects this message. For Koorevaar's argument, see H. J. Koorevaar, *Wijsheidscanon 1: Rut, Psalmen, Job, Spreuken, Prediker, Hooglied* (Leuven: Evangelische Theologische Faculteit, 2003) 27.

55. Dell, *Book of Job*, 64–72.

56. E. Dhorme, *A Commentary on the Book of Job* (trans. Harold Knight; Nashville: Thomas Nelson, 1967) clxv–clxvi.

Psalms of Lament and the so-called Wisdom Literature."[57] This reflects the order of the Ketubim given in B. Bat. 14b, in which Job stands precisely in that middle position between the Psalms and "Wisdom Literature."

Conclusion

Although intertextual connections between Job and several other texts, including Proverbs and Ecclesiastes, offer insight into the book, the prominence of its links with the Psalms suggests that these resonances are a prime resource for interpreting the book. The rabbinic tradition that placed the Psalms before Job reflects this reading strategy, in which Israel's prayers become a lens through which to understand Job's struggle to hold onto faith in the midst of suffering. Thus, Job does not merely follow the Psalms in this traditional order, the book also follows the models for relationship with God that the Psalms depict, pressing them to their breaking point.

Reading Job after the Psalms, however, creates a "dialogical" relationship between the texts,[58] which also invites the Psalter to be read anew, its meaning filtered through its connections with Job. Not only does Job's interaction with individual psalms, such as Psalm 8, highlight tensions within them,[59] but, by alluding to psalms of various types, drawing on a variety of psalmic forms, and even having the characters embody the clash between lamenting and didactic voices in the Psalter, Job's interactions with the Psalms reveal the tensive diversity of the collection. And yet, the dramatic structure of Job also offers a means for holding these tensions together, as it moves, like the Psalter, from initial intense obedience (Job 1; cf. Psalm 1) through a dispute over God's חסד ("loyal love"), which dominates much of the book of Job and the Psalter (see, e.g., Psalms 25, 73), to praise in the divine speeches and Job's response and the Psalter's concluding doxology (Psalm 150).[60] Walter Brueggemann, who notes this similarity, warns that it should not be drawn too tightly and refrains from affirming that it is in-

---

57. I. Engnell, "The Figurative Language of the Old Testament," in *Critical Essays on the Old Testament* (trans. and ed. J. T. Willis; London: SPCK, 1970) 256. Similarly, C. Kuhl, "Neuere Literarkritik des Buches Hiob," *Theologische Rundschau* 21 (1953) 163–204; 257–317, esp. pp. 311–12.

58. For the "dialogical" nature of intertextuality, see S. Moyise, "Intertextuality and Biblical Studies: A Review," *Verbum et Ecclesia* 23 (2002) 424–25.

59. This accords with Fishbane's description of aggadic exegesis, which, he claims, is "not content to supplement gaps in the traditum, but characteristically draws forth latent and unsuspected meanings from it" (Fishbane, *Biblical Interpretation*, 283). Newsom claims that the Job poet "fragments and recombines motifs from traditional psalms of supplication, re-presenting them in ways that expose repressed aspects of their meaning" (C. A. Newsom, *The Book of Job: A Contest of Moral Imaginations* [Oxford: Oxford University Press, 2003] 131). As the allusions to Psalm 8 demonstrate, this technique is not restricted to psalms of supplication.

60. W. Brueggemann, "Bounded by Obedience and Praise: The Psalms as Canon," in *The Psalms and the Life of Faith* (ed. P. D. Miller; Minneapolis: Fortress, 1995) 211 n. 41.

tentional but cannot resist the observation that both texts "portray Israel's way with God that moves from obedience to praise."[61] Thus, *lectio continua* inspires *lectio alterna* as reading Job following the Psalms creates a hermeneutically generative reciprocal relationship *between* Job and the Psalms.

---

61. Ibid.

Bibliography

Ambrose. "The Prayer of Job and David." Pp. 325–420 in *Saint Ambrose: Seven Exegetical Works*. Translated by Michael P. McHugh. Fathers of the Church 65. Washington, DC: Catholic University of America Press, 1971.

Anderson, A. A. *The Book of Psalms*. 2 vols. NCB. Grand Rapids, MI: Eerdmans, 1981.

Barton, J. *Reading the Old Testament: Method in Biblical Study*. 2nd ed. London: Darton, Longman & Todd, 1996.

Baumgärtel, F. *Der Hiobdialog: Aufriss und Deutung*. BWANT 61. Stuttgart: Kohlhammer, 1933.

Bentzen, A. *Introduction to the Old Testament*. 2 vols. Copenhagen: Gad, 1948–49.

Beyerlin, W. "Psalm 8: Chancen der Überlieferungskritik." *ZTK* 73 (1976) 1–22.

Bloom, H. *A Map of Misreading*. Oxford: Oxford University Press, 1975.

Braude, W. G. *The Midrash on Psalms*. 2 vols. Yale Judaica Series 13. New Haven, CT: Yale University Press, 1959.

Brown, W. P. "*Creatio Corporis* and the Rhetoric of Defense in Job 10 and Psalm 139." Pp. 107–24 in *God Who Creates: Essays in Honor of Sibley Turner*. Edited by W. P. Brown and S. D. McBride Jr. Grand Rapids, MI: Eerdmans, 2000.

Brueggemann, W. "Bounded by Obedience and Praise: The Psalms as Canon." Pp. 189–213 in *The Psalms and the Life of Faith*. Edited by P. D. Miller. Minneapolis: Fortress, 1995.

Calvin, J. *Sermons on Job*. Edinburgh: Banner of Truth Trust, 1993. Reprint of *Sermons on Job*. Translated by Arthur Golding. London: Bishop, 1574.

Campbell, A. F. "Form Criticism's Future." Pp. 13–31 in *The Changing Face of Form Criticism for the Twenty-First Century*. Edited by M. A. Sweeney and E. Ben Zvi. Grand Rapids, MI: Eerdmans, 2003.

Clines, D. J. A. *Job*. 2 vols. WBC 17–18A. Nashville: Thomas Nelson, 1989–2006.

Dell, K. J. *The Book of Job as Sceptical Literature*. BZAW 197. Berlin: de Gruyter, 1991.

Dhorme, E. *A Commentary on the Book of Job*. Translated by H. Knight. Nashville: Thomas Nelson, 1967.

Engnell, I. "The Figurative Language of the Old Testament." Pp. 242–90 in *Critical Essays on the Old Testament*. Translated and edited by J. T. Willis. London: SPCK, 1970.

Fishbane, M. *Biblical Interpretation in Ancient Israel*. Oxford: Clarendon, 1985.

———. "The Book of Job and Inner-Biblical Discourse." Pp. 86–98 in *The Voice from the Whirlwind*. Edited by L. G. Perdue and W. C. Gilpin. Nashville: Abingdon, 1992.

Fohrer, G. *Das Buch Hiob.* KAT 16. Gütersloh: Mohn, 1963.

———. "Form und Funktion in der Hiobdichtung." Pp. 60–77 in *Studien zum Buche Hiob (1956–1979).* BZAW 159. Berlin: de Gruyter, 1983.

Frevel, C. "'Eine kleine Theologie der Menschenwürde': Ps 8 und seine Rezeption im Buch Ijob." Pp. 244–72 in *Das Manna fällt auch heute noch: Beiträge zur Geschichte und Theologie des Alten, Ersten Testaments.* Edited by F.-L. Hossfeld and L. Schwienhorst-Schönberger. HBS 44. Freiburg: Herder, 2004.

Ginzberg, L. *The Legends of the Jews.* 7 vols. Baltimore: Johns Hopkins University Press, 1998.

Gordis, R. *The Book of Job: Commentary, New Translation, and Special Studies.* Moreshet 2. New York: Jewish Theological Seminary of America, 1978.

Heckl, R. *Hiob: Vom Gottesfürchtigen zum Repräsentanten Israels.* FAT 70. Tübingen: Mohr Siebeck, 2010.

Hempel, J. "Mensch und König: Studie zu Psalm 8 und Hiob." *Forschungen und Fortschritte* 35 (1961) 119–23.

Irsigler, H. *Vom Adamssohn zum Immanuel.* Arbeiten zu Text und Sprache im Alten Testament 58. St. Ottilien: EOS, 1997.

Janzen, J. G. *Job.* Interpretation. Atlanta: John Knox, 1985.

Klein, H. "Zur Wirkungsgeschichte von Psalm 8." Pp. 183–98 in *Konsequente Traditionsgeschichte: Festschrift für Klaus Baltzer zum 65. Geburtstag.* Edited by R. Bartelmus, T. Krüger, and H. Utzschneider. OBO. Göttingen: Vandenhoeck & Ruprecht / Freiburg: Universitäts-Verlag, 1993.

Koorevaar, H. J. *Wijsheidscanon 1: Rut, Psalmen, Job, Spreuken, Prediker, Hooglied.* Leuven: Evangelische Theologische Faculteit, 2003.

Kraus, H.-J. *Psalms: A Continental Commentary.* Translated by H. C. Oswald. 2 vols. Minneapolis: Fortress, 1993.

Kuhl, C. "Neuere Literarkritik des Buches Hiob." *Theologische Rundschau* 21 (1953) 163–204; 257–317.

Kynes, W. "Beat Your Parodies into Swords, and Your Parodied Books into Spears: A New Paradigm for Parody in the Hebrew Bible." *BibInt* 19 (2011) 276–310.

———. *"My Psalm Has Turned into Weeping": Job's Dialogue with the Psalms.* BZAW 437. Berlin: de Gruyter, 2012.

Mandolfo, C. "A Generic Renegade: A Dialogic Reading of Job and Lament Psalms." Pp. 45–63 in *Diachronic and Synchronic: Reading the Psalms in Real Time.* Edited by J. S. Burnett. New York: T. & T. Clark, 2007.

Mettinger, T. N. D. "Intertextuality: Allusion and Vertical Context Systems in Some Job Passages." Pp. 257–80 in *Of Prophets' Visions and the Wisdom of Sages.* Edited by H. A. McKay and D. J. A. Clines. JSOTSup 162. Sheffield: JSOT Press, 1993.

Moyise, S. "Intertextuality and Biblical Studies: A Review." *Verbum et Ecclesia* 23 (2002) 418–31.

Müller, H.-P. *Das Hiobproblem: Seine Stellung und Entstehung im alten Orient und im Alten Testament.* 3rd ed. Erträge der Forschung 84. Darmstadt: Wissenschaftliche Buchgesellschaft, 1995.

Newsom, C. A. *The Book of Job: A Contest of Moral Imaginations.* Oxford: Oxford University Press, 2003.

Pope, M. H. *Job.* 3rd ed. AB 15. Garden City, NY: Doubleday, 1973.

Pyeon, Y. *You Have Not Spoken What Is Right about Me: Intertextuality and the Book of Job.* Studies in Biblical Literature 45. New York: Peter Lang, 2003.

Schmid, K. "Innerbiblische Schriftdiskussion im Hiobbuch." Pp. 241–61 in *Das Buch Hiob und seine Interpretationen: Beiträge zum Hiob-Symposium auf dem Monte Verità vom 14.–19. August 2005.* Edited by T. Krüger, M. Oeming, K. Schmid, and C. Uehlinger. ATANT 88. Zurich: Theologischer Verlag, 2007.

Schreiner, S. E. "'Why Do the Wicked Live?' Job and David in Calvin's Sermons on Job." Pp. 129–43 in *The Voice from the Whirlwind: Interpreting the Book of Job.* Edited by L. G. Perdue and W. C. Gilpin. Nashville: Abingdon, 1992.

Steinberg, J. *Die Ketuvim: Ihr Aufbau und ihre Botschaft.* BBB 152. Hamburg: Philo, 2006.

Van Leeuwen, R. C. "Psalm 8.5 and Job 7.17–18: A Mistaken Scholarly Commonplace?" Pp. 205–15 in *The World of the Aramaeans,* vol. 1: *Biblical Studies in Honour of Paul-Eugène Dion.* Edited by P. M. M. Daviau, J. W. Wevers, and M. Weigl. JSOTSup 324. Sheffield: Sheffield Academic Press, 2001.

Volz, P. *Weisheit: Das Buch Hiob, Sprüche und Jesus Sirach, Prediger.* Die Schriften des Alten Testaments. Göttingen: Vandenhoeck & Ruprecht, 1911.

Westermann, C. *The Structure of the Book of Job: A Form-Critical Analysis.* Translated by C. A. Muenchow. Philadelphia: Fortress, 1981.

Wilson, L. S. *The Book of Job: Judaism in the 2nd Century BCE: An Intertextual Reading.* Studies in Judaism. Lanham, MD: University Press of America, 2006.

Wright, G. H. B. *The Book of Job.* London: Williams & Norgate, 1883.

The Place of Wisdom Literature in an Old Testament Theology

A Thematic and Structural-Canonical Approach

JULIUS STEINBERG

The Task: Understanding OT Wisdom and Integrating It into OT Theology

OT Wisdom Literature presents scholars with two tasks: understanding the individual wisdom books and integrating them into an overall framework within a theology of the OT. Regarding the latter, two major problems arise:

1. Strong discrepancies can be observed between the wisdom books. They even seem to contradict each other at certain points. Was there nevertheless a common way of thinking behind them, a "Theology of Wisdom"? And if so, how can it be approached?
2. There seem to be only a few connections between the wisdom books and the rest of the OT. Despite this, is it possible to integrate wisdom into an OT Theology? How can this be achieved?

Approaches to OT theology use very different strategies for handling Wisdom Literature.[1] In most of the *chronological* or *historic-genetic approaches*, the chapter on wisdom is not part of the main body of the book but comes as an addition or appendix. An exception to this is Walter C. Kaiser's work,[2] which integrates wisdom into his chronological system by defining a "sapiential era," which was the time of Solomon and after. While this historical assignment can of course be argued for, history in my opinion is not the key that unlocks wisdom theology.

Topical approaches to OT theology that use key concepts to organize their material encounter similar problems. Central theological concepts in the Pentateuch and the historical books do not connect well to wisdom. H. D. Preuss, for example, uses the key concept of YHWH acting in history by

---

1. For a detailed review of the question how to integrate the various contents of the OT into a structure, see my book *Die Ketuvim: Ihr Aufbau und ihre Botschaft* (BBB 152; Hamburg: Philo, 2006) 19ff.
2. Walter C. Kaiser Jr., *Toward an Old Testament Theology* (Grand Rapids, MI: Zondervan, 1978) 46.

electing Israel in order to commune with the world.[3] He admits that the areas of creation and of wisdom are not covered by this conceptualization of the material and therefore deals with them in separate chapters.[4]

In older conceptions of OT theology, creation theology has often been neglected.[5] Claus Westermann, by contrast, gives it new esteem by presenting OT theology from a double center, "the saving God and history" and "the blessing God and creation."[6] Together with creation, wisdom can find its place within the overall framework. In an excursus, Westermann relates wisdom to the task of "tilling and keeping" the garden (Gen 2:15).[7] However, he does not elaborate on the topic, since in his opinion, wisdom does not deal with the interaction of God and humankind primarily and therefore is not a topic of Old Testament theology.[8]

Literary approaches to OT theology offer the possibility of unfolding the message of each book of the OT in its own right. Therefore, each of the wisdom books would receive its place. The problems, however, lie in the question of how to integrate each book's message into an overall framework. In respect to literary approaches to Wisdom Literature, this quote from James Barr is pertinent:

> If a Theology were to be written for every single book . . . would the sum of these be a Theology of the entire Bible? I have a feeling that it would not: for the most serious problems lie in the *interrelations* between books . . . not in the content of each one.[9]

A possible remedy to this problem is the use of dual approaches. For instance,[10] in Rolf Rendtorff's theology, each of the wisdom books receives its appropriate space in the first main section, where the OT is presented book by book. In the second section, the results are synthesized by way of a topical approach. Yet wisdom again proves to be a difficult topic. Rendtorff gives it a mere two pages (pp. 665–66), discussing only the tensions between the books. In this approach, wisdom offers no positive contribution to OT theology.

---

3. "Jнwнs erwählendes Geschichtshandeln an Israel zur Gemeinschaft mit seiner Welt, das zugleich ein dieses Volk (und die Völker) verpflichtendes Handeln ist." Horst Dietrich Preuss, *Theologie des Alten Testaments*, vol. 1: *Jнwн erwählendes und verpflichtendes Handeln*; vol. 2: *Israels Weg mit Jнwн* (Stuttgart: Kohlhammer, 1991–92) 1.29.

4. Ibid., 29–30.

5. See, for example, the discussion in Walter Brueggemann, *Theology of the Old Testament: Testimony, Dispute, Advocacy* (Minneapolis: Fortress, 1997) 159–64.

6. Claus Westermann, *Theologie des Alten Testaments in Grundzügen* (2nd ed.; Göttingen: Vandenhoeck & Ruprecht, 1985).

7. Ibid., 85–86.

8. Ibid., 7. See also Gerhard F. Hasel, *Old Testament Theology: Basic Issues in the Current Debate* (4th ed.; Grand Rapids, MI: Eerdmans, 1991) 92.

9. James Barr, *The Concept of Biblical Theology: An Old Testament Perspective* (Minneapolis: Fortress, 1999) 54.

10. Rolf Rendtorff, *The Canonical Hebrew Bible: A Theology of the Old Testament* (trans. David E. Orton; Leiden: Deo, 2005).

These examples are certainly not exhaustive. They point to the problems and possibilities of trying to integrate the wisdom books into OT theology from historical, thematic, and literary perspectives, respectively.

In any case, the wisdom books have come down to us not as isolated books but as part of the Hebrew Bible. The compilation of these books into a single collection invites or maybe even requires that the Wisdom Literature be integrated and that it play its part in a theology of the OT. In this article, I present a new way of addressing this challenge by using the structure of the canon as found in b. Baba Batra 14b as a road map. Using this order, I explore the interrelationship of the wisdom books and their place in the OT canon as a whole. This "structural-canonical" approach will be complemented by thematic considerations regarding wisdom theology.

On Structural-Canonical Theology and b. Baba Batra 14b

The Basic Concept of a Structural-Canonical Approach to OT Theology

First, I briefly describe the approach centered around the three concepts *canonical*, *structural*, and *structural-canonical*.[11]

By *canonical*, I mean a canonical hermeneutics as it is developed by Brevard Childs, especially in his *Introduction*,[12] focusing on the final form of the texts as their intended form, as well as on the community of faith being the transmitters of the texts and their intended reading community. This includes the notion that Scripture is made to be meaningful for the ongoing life of the community, generation after generation.

By *structural*, I refer to the literary organization of many of the OT books. It is not about reading the Bible as literature but, rather, recognizing that the Bible *is* literature.[13] All literary features, especially design structures such as concentric or parallel patterns, but also more-classical narrative plots as well as character presentations, imageries, and so on have some function in communicating what the text wants to tell the reader. These must be scrutinized according to the methods of literary study. As a result, OT theology will not be based on information taken *from* the books—as with a proof-text method—but, rather, on the meaning *of* the books, as found through the books' own literary presentation.

---

11. For a detailed presentation, see my *Ketuvim*, 75–84. The approach was first formulated by Hendrik J. Koorevaar, *A Structural Canonical Approach for a Theology of the Old Testament*, version 3.2 (Leuven: Evangelische Theologische Faculteit, 2000). See also Timothy J. Stone, *The Compilational History of the Megilloth: Canon, Contoured Intertextuality and Meaning in the Writings* (FAT 2/59; Tübingen: Mohr Siebeck, 2013) 10–33.

12. Brevard S. Childs, *Introduction to the Old Testament as Scripture* (Philadelphia: Fortress, 1979).

13. The most helpful hermeneutical reflection on the issue, in my opinion, is found in Meir Sternberg, *The Poetics of Biblical Narrative: Ideological Literature and the Drama of Reading* (Bloomington: Indiana University Press, 1987).

Finally, the compound term *structural-canonical* addresses the concept that, within the OT, structures appear not only on the level of individual books but on the larger literary horizon of small collections of books and, ultimately, the canon of the Hebrew Bible as a whole. Within this approach, OT theology is based not only on the contents but also on the structure of the canon itself. The theological position of each book is determined by its literary location in the canon.

From the point of view of literary study, the issues of context, intertextuality, order of presentation, and so forth are naturally involved in interpretation. Regarding the biblical canon, however, relating oneself to book order obviously poses some problems, especially since the tradition offers us not one order of books but many. Choosing one of them is, of course, only part of the answer.

Why Choose the Book Order of b. Baba Batra 14b?

The main objections raised to the idea of a structural-canonical approach can be summarized in the following questions:

- Since the Bible has come down to us with many different orders, how can book order play a role?
- In view of the fact that the biblical books were originally written on separate scrolls, how can we speak of an intended order?
- In view of the (alleged) fact that book order did not play a role in the history of biblical interpretation, why should we emphasize it?
- Or, to state it another way: what sort of scriptural authority could be claimed for arguments that are based on something as unreliable as book order?

I discuss all these arguments at length in my dissertation.[14] A few of them can be found in the introductory article to the present volume. In this essay, I want to give a short overview.

It is essential, in my view, to achieve a differentiated and nuanced perspective on these issues.

- Yes, the books were written on individual scrolls. Yet, at least some of the scrolls were obviously designed to be read in some order, as in the case of Genesis through Kings. Therefore, restrictions based on the length of a book do not rule out the idea of order. From the ancient Near East, we know that colophons were used for organizing clay tablets. While we do not know about this for the biblical texts, the superscriptions of the prophetic books, for example, serve a similar function by assigning all these books to a certain category. Additionally, passages at the beginning and/or ending of blocks within the canon—"canonical phenomenon"—point to an awareness of subgroups within the canon already in the age of the Bible's textual development.

---

14. Steinberg, *Ketuvim*, 84–89.

- Yes, the books were written on individual scrolls. However, whenever people thought about defining the canon—for example, writing down a list of canonical books—then surely concerning oneself with order and subgrouping was inevitable. Also, storing holy books in the sacred space of the temple may have given rise to the question of where to place the scroll vis-à-vis one another.[15]
- Yes, there are different orders. However, it is not because order did not matter but because order did matter—time and again in history, people were thinking of how best to order the biblical books. Sometimes formal criteria such as genre and chronology stood in the foreground; other times, the criteria were based on content and theology. Appreciating all these different orders means appreciating various approaches and possibilities for integrating the biblical books into a greater whole.
- Yes, there are many orders. However, they do not stand side by side undifferentiated. Rather, they can be assessed according to the criteria of age, prevalence, authority, and the rationale behind them. In the end, some orders can be shown to stand out in the sense that they are the most relevant and valuable for a theological reading.
- Yes, there is probably no "inspired" order. However, in the same way that we receive the canonical texts with certain variants and in different languages from the transmitters belonging to the different communities of faith, we also receive canonical structures from their hands. Why should it not be worthwhile studying them?

In this essay, I explore some theological implications of the book order provided in b. B. Bat. 14b. I choose this order for three reasons:

First, from the perspective of reception, the order is as worthwhile to be analyzed as any other order.

Second, the order of b. B. Bat. 14b is one of the most relevant orders from a historical point of view.

1. The source is the oldest in the Jewish tradition that explicitly deals with the order of biblical books. The tradition is identified as a baraita, which means it was reduced to writing around 200 C.E.[16]
2. The source refers itself back to the Rabbanan, Jewish authorities, and claims to present "the" order of the Nebiʾim and Ketubim. According to Brandt, in the Jewish realm there are only two other orders that claim to be authoritative; both are from the late Middle Ages.[17]

---

15. Stone, *Megillot*, 84–87.

16. Siegfried Bergler, *Talmud für Anfänger: Ein Werkbuch* (Schalom-Bücher 1; 3rd ed.; Hannover: Luther Verlag, 1995) 25; Roger T. Beckwith, *The Old Testament Canon of the New Testament Church and Its Background in Early Judaism* (Grand Rapids, MI: Eerdmans, 1985) 122, 170 n. 28; see the detailed discussion in Hermann L. Strack and Günter Stemberger, *Einleitung in Talmud und Midrasch* (7th ed.; Munich: Beck, 1982), 127–42.

17. Peter Brandt, *Endgestalten des Kanons: Das Arrangement der Schriften Israels in der jüdischen und christlichen Bibel* (BBB 131; Berlin: Philo, 2001) 149–50.

3. Baba Batra is in agreement with the early evidence regarding the tripartite structure of the canon and the number of books.[18]
4. The books of the Megillot were not yet grouped. According to the standard position, which I also follow, the grouping of the Megillot (Ruth, Song of Songs, Ecclesiastes, Lamentations, Esther) was a relatively late phenomenon, occurring only after the 6th century C.E.[19] Therefore, book arrangements that do not have this group can be considered to have a higher probability of being original.
5. Baba Batra has had significant influence on most of the other orders that are extant in the Jewish tradition. It can be said to be the mother of the family of manuscripts without a grouped Megillot, and even the orders with grouped Megillot strongly correspond to Baba Batra's principles, except, of course, for the placement of the Megillot themselves.[20]

Third, the rationale of b. B. Bat. 14b is not explicable with formal criteria but, rather, invites a theological reading. This aspect is argued in detail in the introductory article of the present volume.

Interpreting b. Baba Batra 14b as a Theological Lectionary

The order of the Ketubim given in b. B. Bat. 14b is as follows:

Ruth–Ps–Job–Prov–Eccl–Song–Lam–Dan–Esth–Ezra/Neh–Chr

Once one chooses Baba Batra and then approaches the books from a synchronic, holistic perspective—beginning with the central concerns or themes of each book—the rest is natural.[21] First, we can observe that the three wisdom books of Job, Proverbs, and Ecclesiastes stand next to each other. Second, we can observe a group of three historical books—namely, Daniel, Esther, and Ezra–Nehemiah—that deal with exile and restoration. The book of Chronicles does not belong to this group, since it does not fit chronologically. Third, in the middle between these two groups, we find the books of Song of Songs and Lamentations. To relate these two books to each other is not very rewarding. It makes much more sense to see Song of Songs as a follow-up to Ecclesiastes, especially via the connection of the call to enjoy life. On the other hand, Lamentations forms a perfect introduction to the historical series of books dealing with exile and restoration. Therefore, the Writings may be read as two series of four books each. One series is Job, Proverbs, Ecclesiastes, and Song of Solomon; and the second series is Lamentations, Daniel, Esther, Ezra–Nehemiah. The first series relates to the sphere of the individual; the second series relates to the sphere of poli-

---

18. See the sections on Ben Sira and 4 Ezra in the introductory essay of this volume.
19. Brandt, *Endgestalten*, 129.
20. For the detailed argument, see my *Ketuvim*, 144–51.
21. For the detailed argument, see ibid., 443–54.

tics and the nation. Interestingly, both series begin with suffering and end with joy: Job and Lamentations are the two books of the Bible that devote themselves fully to the topic of suffering and sorrow, whereas the Song of Songs and Ezra–Nehemiah represent topics of particular joy, which are love between man and woman on the personal level and the new beginning for the nation after the exile. This is not to say that Ezra–Nehemiah is joyful from the first to the last verse. Nevertheless, the series Lam–Dan–Esth–Ezra/Neh stretches from the destruction to the rebuilding of Jerusalem, which gives this troublesome part of Israel's history a happy ending.

Fourth, before and after these two series, there are the two large books of Psalms and Chronicles. They are both like a compendium in character regarding history and theology and can be said to form a framework around the two series. Finally, we must consider the book of Ruth. In its position, it functions as an introduction to and preparation for not only the Psalms (David) but also the whole Ketubim (motif of exile and return).[22]

Framework
The "two houses": House of David / House of God
The Torah and the "two ways"

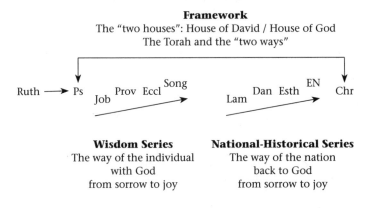

Wisdom Series	National-Historical Series
The way of the individual with God from sorrow to joy	The way of the nation back to God from sorrow to joy

On The Inner Coherence of the Four Wisdom Books

The order Job–Proverbs–Ecclesiastes–Song of Songs given in Baba Batra invites us to reflect on how these four books may belong together and form a coherent whole. I will do this by presenting some thoughts on the thematic relationships between the books as well as by looking at their specific sequence.

Thematic Considerations: Wisdom Thinking

Since at least three of the four books belong to the realm of wisdom, it is necessary to reflect on the principles of OT wisdom in order to proceed.

---

22. Regarding the hermeneutical importance of the "exile and return" model for the Hebrew Bible, see Hendrik J. Koorevaar, "The Torah Model as Original Macrostructure of the Hebrew Canon," *ZAW 122* (2010) 64–80.

There is no room in this article to interact extensively with the enormous discussion in the field. I will, rather, confine myself to some basic aspects necessary for the argument.

Principles of Wisdom Thinking

The question how to determine wisdom influence in a biblical text has been discussed extensively in the secondary literature.[23] Is it based on use of the word *wisdom*? Are the appearance of certain forms such as a "proverb" or certain topics what make up a wisdom text? In my opinion, all these may be part of it, but what is decisive is a certain way of thinking. Four aspects of "wisdom thinking" may be named—the first two of which I owe to Tomáš Frydrych's splendid analysis, especially of Proverbs;[24] the other two can be found in many introductions to OT wisdom:[25]

1. *Empirical epistemology*: The wise learn by observing nature and society. Other than the prophets and the scribes, they do not appeal to direct divine revelation ("thus says the Lord") or to Holy Scripture ("it is written") but to their own experience ("I observed"; see, e.g., Prov 7:6–7, Job 5:3, Eccl 1:14) or to that of the ancestors ("Listen, my son, to a father's instruction"; e.g., Prov 4:1). The book of Job is a possible exception since God himself speaks in Job 38–41. However, the speech argues solely by pointing to observations in creation.

2. *Paradigmatic understanding of reality*: The wise do not try to comprehend all the details and eventualities of reality but focus on what is typical. They describe patterns of behavior and derive rules and paradigms in order to make the world predictable in some sense. The principle of retribution is the most important of these paradigms. This reflection extends beyond paradigms to include examining their limitations.

3. *Connection between knowledge and life*: The purpose of the search for knowledge is to provide the reader/hearer with an orientation for conducting his/her own everyday life successfully. The limits to living life successfully are also examined.

---

23. E.g., in James L. Crenshaw, "Method in Determining Wisdom Influence upon 'Historical' Literature," *JBL* 88 (1969) 129–42.

24. Tomáš Frydrych, *Living under the Sun: Examination of Proverbs and Qoheleth* (VTSup 90; Leiden: Brill, 2002) 18, 52, 80; based on Crenshaw, "Wisdom Influence," 130.

25. E.g., James L. Crenshaw, *Old Testament Wisdom: An Introduction* (Atlanta: John Knox, 1981); Roland E. Murphy, *Wisdom Literature and Psalms* (Interpreting Biblical Texts; Nashville: Abingdon, 1983) 13–42; Christa Bauer-Kayatz, *Einführung in die alttestamentliche Weisheit* (BibS 55; Neukirchen-Vluyn: Neukirchener Verlag, 1969); Erich Zenger et al., *Einleitung in das Alte Testament* (Kohlhammer Studienbücher Theologie 1/1; 3rd ed.; Stuttgart: Kohlhammer, 1998) 329–30; for a detailed discussion and more bibliography, see my *Ketuvim*, 472–79.

4. *The "fear of the Lord" as the basis of wisdom*: This is the distinguishing feature of biblical wisdom as opposed to other ancient Near Eastern wisdom approaches. Biblical wisdom is explicitly bound to faith in Yʜwʜ via the statements, for example, in Prov 1:7 (faith as the beginning of wisdom) and Eccl 12:13 (faith where wisdom ends). On a deeper level, wisdom is bound to Yʜwʜ since the wise learn from the wisdom he has put into creation (Prov 3:19–20; 8:22ff.), and they rely on the justice with which he governs the world. This gives hope that in the end justice will prevail, as Proverbs, Job, and Ecclesiastes assert.

The Discrepancies between Proverbs and Job/Ecclesiastes

The main problem with synthesizing the OT wisdom books is the discrepancy between the "positive" attitude of Proverbs and the "negative" approach of Job and Ecclesiastes, especially regarding their differences concerning the principle of retribution. Some scholars developed the explanatory model of an older, naïve wisdom such as found in Proverbs that eventually was thrown into crisis, which resulted in the writing of the critical works Job and Ecclesiastes. To me, this seems implausible. First, the literary findings of the ancient Near Eastern cultures show that more-positive and more-skeptical works existed side by side for lengthy periods of time, long before Proverbs came into existence. Obviously, there was no linear historical development. Second, I find it difficult to believe that people in the first millennium B.C.E. could attain to a simple, retributional dogma while facing unexplainable illness or early death—even more often than we do today.

How, then, can we handle the discrepancies? In my opinion, two suggestions must be considered. The first is to recognize the aspectival approach of the old writers over against the modern perspectival approach. In aspective thinking, each aspect of a topic is presented in its own right, without relativizing it to other aspects. In Egyptian drawings, for example, the head (nose) and feet of a person are shown from the side while the shoulders are presented from the front view. Each body part is drawn in its most representative form without regard to the tensions that result for the whole picture. In the Bible, the same is true, for instance, for the two creation accounts, the successful and unsuccessful conquest of the land in Joshua and Judges, the promonarchic and antimonarchic sections in 1 Samuel, and the validity and invalidity of the dogma of retribution. The task of the modern interpreter is to recognize the aspectival thinking of the sources and transform it into a perspectival presentation of wisdom theology for today, using perspectival constructions such as "Yes, but . . ." and "on the one hand . . . on the other hand."

The second suggestion for handling the discrepancies is to understand the didactic purpose of Proverbs. Here again, I follow Tomáš Frydrych, who points out that the primary addressees of Proverbs are the פְּתִי "simple" and נַעַר "youth" (Prov 1:4). In other words, Proverbs is directed to the "beginner" in the field of wisdom. Therefore, it teaches basic principles and paradigms of wisdom. As in school, one first learns the basics, and later one differentiates. Seen this way, the black-and-white picture that Proverbs draws is not a sign of naïvité but is purposely chosen for didactic reasons.[26]

As a result, we should read the wisdom books not as contradictory but as complementary. The relationship of Proverbs to Job and Ecclesiastes is one of focusing on the possibilities versus the limits of mastering one's life, or of a beginner's book versus more-advanced teachings.

To speak about the limits of wisdom is itself part of the wisdom enterprise; it is "critical wisdom," not a "crisis of wisdom."[27]

The Song of Songs as a Wisdom Book

There is a general consensus that Job, Proverbs, and Ecclesiastes are the wisdom books. Although the subject is debated, one can add the Song of Songs to this category. Again, it is not possible to present the entire discussion here. In short, the arguments in favor of its being a wisdom book are as follows:[28]

- The Song of Songs is confined to a topic that is typical for wisdom—the relationship between man and woman (see, for example, Prov 5:15–20; 7; 30:18–19; 31:10ff.).[29] Seen from a larger perspective, the four books of Job, Proverbs, Ecclesiastes, and Song of Songs are the only books in the Hebrew Bible that do not deal with the national history of Israel and with God acting in history but, instead, with managing everyday life.

- As Childs has pointed out, Solomon is the canonical "father" of wisdom. Therefore, the superscription אֲשֶׁר לִשְׁלֹמֹה "assigned to Solomon" does not categorize the book within the realm of prophecy, speaking symbolically about the covenant between God and his people, but within the realm of wisdom, focusing on the individual in his or her everyday context.[30] In fact, the superscription has had a strong influence on

---

26. Frydrych, *Living under the Sun*, 32–35.

27. Georg Freuling, *'Wer eine Grube gräbt . . .': Der Tun-Ergehen-Zusammenhang und sein Wandel in der alttestamentlichen Weisheitsliteratur* (WMANT 102; Neukirchen-Vluyn: Neukirchener Verlag, 2004) 270.

28. For further discussion on the topic, see my "Kanonische 'Lesarten' des Hohenliedes," in *Formen des Kanons: Studien zu Ausprägungen des biblischen Kanons von der Antike bis zum 19. Jh.* (ed. Thomas Hieke; SBS 228; Stuttgart: Katholisches Bibelwerk, 2013) 164–83, 177–81; idem, *Das Hohelied* (Edition C, AT 26; Witten: SCM, 2014) 29–32. For general reviews of the Song of Songs, see Stefan Fischer, *Das Hohelied Salomos zwischen Poesie und Erzählung: Erzähltextanalyse eines poetischen Textes* (FAT 72; Tübingen: Mohr Siebeck, 2010); Meik Gerhards, *Das Hohelied: Studien zu seiner literarischen Gestalt und theologischen Bedeutung* (Leipzig: Evangelische Verlag, 2010).

29. E.g., G. Lloyd Carr, *The Song of Solomon: An Introduction and Commentary* (TOTC 17; Leicester: Inter-Varsity, 1984) 16; Murphy, *Wisdom Literature and Psalms*, 15.

30. Childs, *Introduction*, 573–75; Nicolas J. Tromp, "Wisdom and the Canticle: Ct. 8,6c–7b—Text, Character, Message and Import," in *La Sagesse de l'Ancien Testament*

the canonical arrangement. Although the canonical orders from, for example, the Greek and Latin traditions are diverse, most of them keep Proverbs, Ecclesiastes, and Song of Songs together. This is in response to their superscriptions, and they often add Sirach and Wisdom, thus supporting the notion of a Wisdom/Solomonic collection.[31] This may have been the intention for giving the book its title.

- Regarding wisdom thinking, the Song of Songs is *empirical* in that it mostly observes and describes. Interestingly, the Song does not ask what God wants but "what love wants" (Song 2:7, etc.). In other words, it reflects on the ways of love, on the inherent rules to be followed[32] in order to fully enjoy love. Its main interest is the question of the right timing—that is, when it is time to take certain steps in a love relationship.

- The Song of Songs is *paradigmatic* in that it approaches love by presenting a series of typical situations (rather than recounting a single historical event). In a way, each scene gives an example for the reader to become more conscious about how to enjoy and to handle his/her own love partnership.

- Throughout the Song, the lovers speak. However, an interpretive statement from a 3rd-person perspective summarizes things in 8:6b–7. It uses forms and vocabulary that are typical for wisdom.[33] Here, the wisdom author of the book himself has his say.

- The Song of Songs demonstrates wisdom interest in collecting items of a certain kind (see 1 Kgs 5:13). Similar to Proverbs 10ff.—which list a number of sayings regarding the pattern of act and consequence—and Job 38–41—which lists a number of phenomena demonstrating that human beings are not in control of creation—the Song collects whatever suits the speaker/writer to use as metaphors for love.[34]

The main argument *against* the Song of Songs as a wisdom book is its literary form. This results from a misunderstanding of the biblical way of handling forms, however. Today, we know that an essay or article can be used as a literary form for discussing any topic from a "critical distance."

(ed. M. Gilbert; BETL 51; Leuven: Leuven University Press, 1979) 92; Magne Sæbø, "On the Canonicity of the Song of Songs," *On the Way to Canon: Creative Tradition History in the Old Testament* (JSOTSup 191; Sheffield: JSOT Press, 1998) 274–82; Tremper Longman III, *Song of Songs* (Grand Rapids, MI: Eerdmans, 2001) 3–4; Gerald T. Sheppard, "Canonization: Hearing the Voice of the Same God through Historically Dissimilar Traditions," *Int* 36 (1982) 24.

31. Steinberg, "Kanonische 'Lesarten' des Hohenliedes," 169–77.

32. See also Othmar Keel, *Das Hohelied* (ZBK: AT 18; Zurich: Theologischer Verlag, 1986) 89.

33. Regarding the use of הוֹן in Song 8:7, see Avi Hurvitz, "Wisdom Vocabulary in the Hebrew Psalter: A Contribution to the Study of 'Wisdom Psalms'," *VT* 38 (1988) 45–46.

34. Gerhard Maier, *Das Hohelied* (Wuppertaler Studienbibel; Wuppertal: Brockhaus, 1991) 22–23; according to G. Kuhn, "Erklärung des Hohen Liedes," *NKZ* 37 (1926) 501–40; 521–72.

In the Hebrew Bible, however, the form is always closely intertwined with the content. Reflection on history, for example, is implemented by retelling history and conveying certain thematic accentuations; reflection on the character of God is done in relational contexts, such as prayer, and so on. Regarding the wisdom books,

- Proverbs deals with educational wisdom and is therefore clothed in the form of the admonitions of a father to his son.
- Job is about the controversy of righteous suffering, being presented as the story of a righteous sufferer in which a controversial debate with his friends is embedded.
- Ecclesiastes treats the problem that (among others) traditional wisdom may not apply to every individual and, accordingly, takes the form of an individual scrutinizing traditional thinking.
- The Song of Songs approaches love between man and woman but, again, not from a "critical remove"—which would be in danger of reducing love to what can be seen from the outside and of becoming voyeuristic. Instead, the form of a love song is chosen, making room for the exemplary lovers themselves to express their emotions and reflect on events.

Properly aligning the connection between form and content helps one avoid misunderstandings regarding an individual wisdom book's character. When it comes to whole books, no such thing as a wisdom form exists; wisdom is, rather, a unique way of thinking. The Song of Songs can well be understood from the empirical and paradigmatic approach to wisdom. In my opinion, it may be the best way to understand it.

A Thematic Approach to the "Wisdom Series"
For a thematic approach to all four books, I suggest the following structure:[35]

a. the fear of the Lord (as the beginning of wisdom)
b1. the possibilities of knowledge
b2. the possibilities of life
c1. the limits of knowledge
c2. the limits of life
d. the fear of the Lord (as the end of wisdom)
e. the joy of life given by God

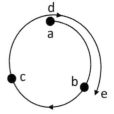

As mentioned above, wisdom is occupied with practical knowledge that helps one lead a good life. The wisdom books reflect on the possibilities as well as the limits of knowledge and life. Categories b1, b2, and c1, c2 derive

---

35. Elaborated in my "Gottes Ordnungen verstehen und leben: Eine Theologie der alttestamentlichen Weisheit," in *Freude an Gottes Weisung: Themenbuch zur Theologie des Alten Testaments* (ed. Herbert H. Klement and Julius Steinberg; 2nd ed.; Riehen: ArteMedia, 2012) 211–37.

from this principle. Again, as stated above, the "fear of the Lord" forms a framework around wisdom, appearing at the beginning of wisdom as well as at the end (a and d). While wisdom generally encourages one to lead one's life in a proactive way in order to be successful, it also concedes that true happiness is a gift of God and not the result of one's shrewdness (e).

Job, in a way, moves along all phases of the structure. After the happy beginning of the God-fearing and successful man (a, b), Job is confronted with his limits regarding life and understanding (c). In the end, he turns to an even deeper fear of the Lord, who stands above all dogmas (d), and he finally experiences new joy in life (e).

Proverbs basically moves from the fear of the Lord (a) to understanding and managing life successfully (b). Ecclesiastes, in turn, reflects on the limits of life and of knowledge (c) and gives two key instructions: "Fear the Lord" (d), and "Enjoy life" (e).[36] The Song of Songs celebrates the joy of love and gives a positive example of being happy in one's partnership (b/e).

Structural-Canonical Considerations: Walking the Way of Wisdom

From the above discussions and analyses, we might expect Proverbs to be the first book in the wisdom series, introducing the beginner to the field of wisdom. However, this is not the case in b. B. Bat. 14b, which in fact begins with Job, and for good reason. One effect of the order Proverbs–Job would be that Proverbs would present its message and then be severely attacked or even blotted out by the counterexample of Job. The sequence Job–Proverbs, however, allows Job to provide a sort of guiding framework inside which the positive message of Proverbs can fully be appreciated without overemphasizing it.

In other words: when we set foot on the path of wisdom, the first thing we must learn is to respect God. This is according to the motto of biblical wisdom, "The Fear of the Lord is the beginning of wisdom." In the beginning, Job was so righteous and even zealous that he thought he could even tell God what was right or wrong. In the end, he learned a deeper way of respecting the fact that God is God. Only after this, with Proverbs, is the "basic course" in wisdom approached: how to attain knowledge and master one's life. As argued above, Proverbs presents a simplified reality due to its paradigmatic approach and for didactic purposes. Placing Job in front of it averts the danger of misunderstanding it as an apology for a prosperity religion.

After the basic course of Proverbs, the "advanced course" follows: Ecclesiastes. Whereas Proverbs deals with the rules, Ecclesiastes focuses on the exceptions. Thus, the reader acquires a deeper, more reflective understanding

---

36. Regarding this interpretation of Ecclesiastes, see my *Ketuvim*, 319–42.

of reality. (I am not saying that Ecclesiastes was necessarily written with this specific purpose in mind, but I am describing the function it takes when placed in this position.)

At the end is the Song of Songs, which takes up Qohelet's call to "enjoy life with the wife whom you love" (Eccl 9:9) and develops it. A happy love partnership is the highlight and prime example of leading one's life successfully as God arranged it in creation; therefore, the Song forms a fitting conclusion to the wisdom series. The sometimes-stony path of wisdom leads to happiness in the end.

People who are trained to focus on the plurality of OT tradition and the discrepancies inside and between the biblical books may hesitate to accept such a smooth, straight presentation of the wisdom collection. It is not my intention to deny the internal complexity of the books under consideration. Rather, I am thinking about plurality and unity as being two poles that complement each other. Studying the overall framework should not lead to reducing the richness of the sources. On the other hand, embracing the historical complexity should not lead to forgetting that we are dealing with canonical texts that have been put together in order to be read together with a focus on their overall intention and their interrelationship. Handling the historical-theological literature of the Bible successfully involves the ability to "zoom in" and "zoom out" as may be appropriate to the task one is undertaking.

On The Placement of Wisdom in Old Testament Theology

Thematic Preparations: Wisdom and Creation Theology

From a thematic point of view, wisdom should be categorized together with creation theology and anthropology. In the Bible, the relationship is established from both sides.

On the one hand, the Wisdom Literature, especially the section on the theological foundation of wisdom, Proverbs 1–9, relates wisdom back to creation (e.g., Prov 3:19–20; 8:22ff.). Wisdom means to learn about the divine orders and structures that God laid out when creating the world and behave accordingly in order to be successful in life. In the book of Job, God's speeches use analogies between weather phenomenon, animals, and the moral order of the world to make Job understand. The argument works best when wisdom's relationship to creation theology is taken into view. The Song of Songs deals with how to handle the "flame of Yah" or "mighty flame" (Song 8:6b) of love that is placed in humankind created as man and woman. Topics laid out in Genesis 1–3, such as the relationship between man and woman or the shaping of the environment are taken up in the wisdom books.

On the other hand, the two basic categories of wisdom are accentuated already in Genesis 2–3. They are the tree of knowledge and the tree of life, symbolizing a comprehensive understanding of the world and a perfect and worthwhile life, respectively. In particular, the fact that the quest for knowledge is crucial in Genesis 2–3 reveals that wisdom is crucial to the creation story, as Gerhard von Rad, for example, has noted. After the fall, neither knowledge nor life is accessible. New perspectives emerge, however, when people start turning back to Yhwh (Gen 4:25–26). This matches the thematic structure of wisdom, as suggested above.

These hints at the mutual relationship between wisdom and creation need further elaboration, of course. Here, however, they must suffice as preparation for a structural-canonical approach to the question.

Structural-Canonical Considerations: Israelology and Anthropology

In the order presented in b. B. Bat. 14b, the series of the four wisdom books Job–Prov–Eccl–Song is placed next to a series of four works dealing with the history of Israel from the destruction of Jerusalem to its restoration, Lam–Dan–Esth–EzraNeh (see the "Framework" diagram above). Both of these series begin with a sorrowful topic (Job and Lamentations) and end with a joyful topic (Song of Songs, Ezra–Nehemiah). One could say that the wisdom books describe the way of the individual with Yhwh while the national-historical series describes the way of the nation back to Yhwh. This parallel construction invites the reader to compare the life of the individual and the life of the nation with each other and to connect them on a symbolic level. One could assess the analogies between the two series as follows: from the way that God deals with the nation, one can learn about the way that God deals with individuals and vice versa.

This idea is not too far-fetched since one can see it in other places in the Bible. One example is the Psalms. The composition techniques of the Psalter can be compared with the Ketubim, as found in Baba Batra: in both cases, there are individual units—psalms or books, respectively—that are arranged according to certain patterns in order to establish relationships and even form a unit on a higher level.[37] Admittedly, the case of Psalms is easier since its order is fixed in manuscripts already.[38]

In any case, the idea of relating the experience of the individual to the experience of the nation is an important principle in the Psalter. As is well known, Psalms 1–2 together form the introduction to the Psalter. The two

---

37. See Gerald H. Wilson, *The Editing of the Hebrew Psalter* (SBLDS 76; Chico, CA: Scholars Press, 1985).

38. In this essay, I will not enter into the discussion of the hymnic compilations found at Qumran or the variants of LXX manuscripts but confine myself to the Masoretic Text.

psalms do not have titles but are placed in front of the first Davidic psalter. Psalm 1 begins with a beatitude; Psalm 2 ends with one.[39] The two psalms prepare the reader for a double-reading perspective: that of the individual/ wisdom (Psalm 1) and that of the nation/kingdom (Psalm 2). With this double perspective in mind, the reader approaches the following psalms, understanding them as both reflections on past events in Israel's history (for example, Psalm 3, "a psalm of David, when he fled from his son Absalom") and as exemplary individual laments to God to be reused in many different situations of personal trouble.

The principle of double framing is also found in other places in Books I–III of the Psalter. Each of the concluding Royal Psalms of Books II–III is accompanied by a psalm in which an individual is reflecting on an analogous situation: Psalm 71, about an individual seeking refuge in God in old age, is placed before Psalm 72, about the kingdom's being passed on to the king's son; and Psalm 88, about an individual in utmost distress and hopelessness, precedes Psalm 89, which covers the destruction of the Davidic kingdom. The same phenomenon can be observed in the opening psalms of Books II and III: Psalm 42/43 (originally a single psalm) reflects on an individual who is being rejected by God and precedes Psalm 44, which is about the nation that is being rejected by God. Again, Psalms 73 and 74 are both about the prospering of the wicked and are connected to the temple. Psalm 73 takes the perspective of the individual; Psalm 74, that of the nation.[40]

These cases illustrate that pairs of psalms may symbolically connect the two realms of personal piety and national history. Reinhard Kratz expresses this idea in his summary on the Psalms:

> Going through the five books [of the Psalms] the reader meditates on the individual stages of Israel's history by applying them, in remembrance and confirmation, to stages of his own, individual life. He experiences them as a way from suffering and trouble to experienced or still-expected blessing, and as a way from the political condition of the kingdom and its destruction to the eternal kingdom of God. This kingdom has already become real—by way of the individual experience of deliverance, obedience to *Torah* and cult, and preservation and provision of life—but is at the same time still to come.[41]

The idea of assessing the life of the individual and the life of the nation as being related to each other on a symbolic level can further be substantiated by observations from the literary work of Genesis to Kings, with the Primeval History as its overture. Genesis 1–9, especially, focuses on the individual

---

39. See, for example, Gianni Barbiero, *Das erste Psalmenbuch als Einheit: Eine synchrone Analyse von Psalm 1–41* (Österreichische Biblische Studien 16; Frankfurt a.M.: Peter Lang, 1999) 31–41.

40. As argued in my book, *Ketuvim*, 251.

41. Reinhard G. Kratz, "Die Tora Davids: Psalm 1 und die doxologische Fünfteilung des Psalters," *ZTK 93* (1996) 27.

and at the same time prepares one for the history of Israel. Events that occur in the history of Israel are anticipated in a symbolic manner and related to the individual, as has been noticed before.

Mankind	receiving the earth	being expelled from the earth
		(Gen 1–9)
Man	receiving the Garden	being expelled from the Garden
		(Gen 2–3)
Israel	receiving the land	being expelled from the land
		(Josh–Kgs)

To the two-part pattern can be added a third element, that of new hope and new beginning. After the flood, there is the new beginning with Noah's family. After the expulsion from the Garden and Cain's murder of Abel, there is new hope when Seth and his son "begin to call upon the Lord" (Gen 4:26)—and regarding the nation, a first sign of new hope appears in 2 Kgs 25:27–30, which is about the release of Jehoiachin. The pattern of blessing, cursing, and new beginning is also established in the corresponding legal sections:[42]

	Blessings	*Curses*	*New Hope*
Leviticus 26	26:1–13	26:14–43	26:44–45
Deuteronomy 28–30	28:1–14	28:15–68; 29:1–28	30:1–11

Without having enough space here to comment on the Primeval History in detail, we can say that, to some extent, the literary work of Genesis to Kings presents its anthropology as a preparation to its "Israelology": from the story of the nation, we learn the story of the individual, and from the story of the individual, we learn the story of the nation.

Could this idea be the key to interpreting Baba Batra's Ketubim as well? As said above, the structure emerging from the book order invites us to see the wisdom series and the national-historical series as correlating to each other, connecting the realm of the individual and the realm of the nation by way of analogy. But how can this correlation be described? In my opinion, three related concepts need to be addressed in this regard:

The Idea of Correlating the Two Realms

Before approaching particular aspects of the relationship between the two series of books, the very idea of correlating the two realms must be considered.

When pastors preach on texts related to Israel's national history, they tend to interpret the historical events as symbols related to the lives of

---

42. Julius Steinberg, "Architektonische Bauformen als Mittel der literarischen Kommunikation am Beispiel von Gen 1–4," in *Sprache lieben – Gottes Wort verstehen: Beiträge zur biblischen Exegese* (FS Heinrich von Siebenthal; ed. Walter Hilbrands; Gießen: Brunnen, 2011) 51–73.

their audience. For example, the wilderness wanderings of Israel may serve them as an image for a time of "wilderness wandering" in the life of the believer. Although these pastors occasionally lapse into allegorizing, the Bible proves them basically right. In particular, Psalms, Genesis 1–11, and Baba Batra's Ketubim appear to use the same technique. Whereas the psalm pairs aim primarily at application, Genesis 1–11 builds theological teachings on the analogies. Actually, this introduces an interesting new perspective on developing Old Testament anthropology from "Israelology," by appreciating anthropology as the ongoing story between God and the individual.

The correlation runs from the nation to the individual and also vice-versa. In fact, Genesis 1–11 as well as Psalms and Baba Batra's Ketubim present the individual perspective *before* the national perspective. Especially Genesis 1–11 as the overture to the work from Genesis to Kings hints that the story of a nation depends on the stories of the individuals within that nation. In some way, this balances the collective thinking that is sometimes considered problematic by modern interpreters. When God blesses or punishes a nation, it is not that the collective is affected regardless of the attitude of the individuals; rather, it is about both the individuals and the collective.

In some instances, individuals can become symbols or representatives of the nation. For example, Hosea symbolizes idolatrous Israel, or Jonah represents Israel's arrogance. This is especially true of kings as prime representatives of the nation; individual attitudes greatly influence the fate of the nation.

Correlating the Two Realms inside the
Framework of Psalms–Chronicles

To elaborate further on the contribution of Baba Batra's Ketubim to the issue, I now consider the framework of Psalms–Chronicles.

At the risk of oversimplification, the joint theological concepts of Psalms and Chronicles can be summarized as "two houses" and "two ways" within a universalistic frame. The "two houses" are the House of David and the House of God, the kingdom and the temple, or theologically speaking, the dominion of God and communion with God as being claimed and being offered by God to all people (*Gottes Herrschaftsanspruch* and *Gottes Gemeinschaftszuspruch*).[43] The "two ways," in turn, relate to the different possibilities for human beings to respond to the will of God as laid down in the Torah, either positively or negatively (as, for example in Psalm 1 and in the portraits of the individual kings in 2 Chronicles 10ff., interpreted in the sense of "immediate retribution").[44]

---

43. See Georg Fohrer, "Der Mittelpunkt einer Theologie des Alten Testaments," *TZ* 24 (1968) 161–72.

44. See my book *Ketuvim*, 445–46.

This theological structure is presented as the literary-theological frame of the wisdom series as well as the national-historical series. In other words, in both realms, the same overarching principles apply. For example, the kingdom and the temple are not just institutions in Israel's history but are meaningful in a symbolic manner for the individual believer as well.

In the national-historical series, we see the question of the House of David or the dominion of God asked and answered, particularly in the books of Daniel and Esther, where God is working from "behind the scenes" but still in control, turning the Persian Empire upside down (Esther)[45] and setting up kings and deposing them as he pleases (Daniel).[46] The restoration of the temple and, in a wider sense, of communion with God (also by way of the Torah) are highlighted in Ezra–Nehemiah. The prayers of Lamentations 3, Daniel 9, Ezra 9, and Nehemiah 9 are about repentance and turning back to YHWH. In effect, the whole series of Lam–Dan–Esth–Ezra/Neh when read holistically describes the way for the nation to return to YHWH. The way of the pious and wise with YHWH is also exemplified by the individuals Daniel, Esther, and Mordecai.

Similarly, the theological framework of Psalm–Chronicles can be applied to the wisdom series. The notion of the "two ways" lies at the very heart of wisdom thinking. In Proverbs, turning to wisdom means turning to YHWH and turning to life, whereas turning to folly leads away from YHWH and toward death. The wisdom motto "The fear of YHWH is the beginning of wisdom" forms wise individuals' positive response to God's claim of dominion—and to his offer of communion, since the expression "fear of YHWH" is an idiom expressing the notions of respect and trust, which are part of covenant faithfulness. These principles apply to Job and Ecclesiastes as well.

While Proverbs deals with piety mainly in the sense of a prerequisite, in Job one's relationship with God receives special attention. The power and dominion of God as the creator of the world is particularly reflected in Job 38–41, and communion with God, in the sense of (Job's) personal piety is a main topic throughout the book. In this way, the book of Job is very near the Psalms.[47] Personal piety is also dealt with as a topic in Eccl 5:1–7.

Like Proverbs, the Song of Songs focuses on conducting life. Probably due to its 1st-person perspective, it does not give much of a theoretical framework to its topic, except for its general allocation to wisdom in Song 1:1 and the wisdom saying in 8:6b–7. Therefore, there is less interaction

---

45. This interpretation of the book of Esther cannot be defended here. See, for example, Michael V. Fox, *Character and Ideology in the Book of Esther* (Columbia, SC: University of South Carolina Press, 1991) 4–5; Sidnie White Crawford, "The Book of Esther: Introduction, Commentary, and Reflections," *NIB* 3.853–941; Hans-Peter Müller, Otto Kaiser, and James A. Loader, *Das Hohelied, Klagelieder, das Buch Ester* (ATD 16/2; 4th ed.; Göttingen: Vandenhoeck & Ruprecht, 1992) 219–20.

46. See, for example, John E. Goldingay, *Daniel* (WBC 30; Dallas: Word, 1989) 23–24; 331–32.

47. See the article by Will Kynes in this volume.

with the framework of Psalms–Chronicles. While the framework refers to communion between God and man, the Song of Songs reflects communion between man and woman.[48]

Understood in its context, the Song of Songs (a) celebrates love between man and woman as a vital force that God has endowed to human beings; (b) reflects on how to handle love successfully from a wisdom perspective; and (c) does so within the framework of the religious convictions expressed in Psalms and Chronicles.

To sum up, one can demonstrate that all of the books Job–Prov–Eccl–Song and Lam–Dan–Esth–Ezra/Neh function well within the framework of Psalms–Chronicles. Moreover, most of the books respond to the framework by contributing to one or the other aspect of it. This applies likewise to both of the series. Therefore, the literary-theological construction of Baba Batra helps us to understand that the life of the individual as well as the life of the nation is governed by the same principles. These are the "two houses" and the "two ways"—that is, the claim of dominion and the offer of communion on the side of God, and basically two different possible responses on the human side, each with its corresponding consequences for the progression of one's story with God.

Correlating Pairs of Books in the Two Series

The parallel makeup of the two series—each consisting of four books, beginning with sorrow and ending with joy—invites one to compare them book by book. For example, it is possible to portray Daniel as a prototype of the wise as described in the book of Proverbs, or to compare the hiddenness and incomprehensibility of God in Esther and in Ecclesiastes. However, we have to keep in mind that the person(s) responsible for the tradition in b. B. Bat. 14b did not write books in order to fit into the slots of an overall structure. Rather, he/they took books that already existed and arranged them in a pattern that probably was intended to yield the maximum possible interpretational coherence overall. Therefore, it is surely wise to be modest in one's conclusions instead of overstating the possible "intended" connections.

Regarding the two realms of anthropology and Israelology, however, I want to present some brief thoughts on Job and Lamentations, the first books of each of the series. When we compare the two books, similarities as well as differences emerge. Both begin with the utmost suffering and then allow a great deal of mourning but, when the reasons for the suffering are explained, they are strikingly distinct from each other. Lamentations is about suffering as a judgment for sin, while in Job this view of suffering is completely rejected.

This means that the interpretation of failure in Israel's history cannot simply be copied into the life of an individual. There are different standards

---

48. Both relationships appear together in Gen 1:27.

regarding the suffering of an individual and the suffering of the nation. One can even go a step further and understand Lamentations and Job as crosschecks on each other: personal sin *may* be a reason for personal suffering (Lam 3:39) but not in all circumstances (Job 1:1b, 42:7). While the fate of biblical Israel is regularly connected to its covenant faithfulness (Lam 1:18), nevertheless there is a warning not to confine God's acts in history to some simplistic pattern (Job 42:7).

And the Other Sequences of Books?

The relationships within the section of the Ketubim, based on the sequence presented in Baba Batra do not necessarily disappear when one examines other canonical arrangements. This is true for two reasons: First, while it can be said that to some extent book order creates relationships between books, for the most part it *highlights* the relationships that are already there. For example, one can compare the assessment of suffering in Job and Lamentations without recourse to b. B. Bat. 14b. Baba Batra (as interpreted in this essay) conveys the idea, however, that comparisons among the books in its particular sequence may be worthwhile.

Second, many different canonical orders for the Ketubim are cognates of the order in Baba Batra and can therefore be interpreted in a similar way. It is especially worthwhile to look at the other orders of the Jewish Ketubim that do not have the Megillot grouped. Beckwith and Brandt present 29 different orders that appear in 50 medieval manuscripts (13 of which match Baba Batra).[49]

Of the 51 manuscripts listed in table 1 below, 34 have the wisdom series and the national-historical series (nos. 1–12 above) and can therefore be interpreted in basically the same way as Baba Batra, following the idea of an analogy between the way of the individual and the way of the nation.

However, the sequence of the wisdom books among themselves varies. Of the 34 manuscripts, 19 follow Baba Batra exactly, with the order Job–Prov–Eccl–Song. Ten manuscripts have the order Job–Prov–Song–Eccl instead. In this case, the praise of the אֵשֶׁת־חַיִל, the "capable woman," at the end of Proverbs is placed face-to-face with the praise of the beautiful woman in the Song of Solomon. The two critical works of Job and Ecclesiastes provide a framework for the positive works of Proverbs and Song in the center. However, this also means losing the progression from sorrow to joy. The series ends with death and final judgment rather than with love.

Four of the manuscripts under consideration have the arrangement Prov–Job–Eccl–Song. In these sequences, the "beginner's course" of wisdom logically stands first. However, read in this order, Proverbs is in danger

---

49. Beckwith, *OT Canon*, 452–57; Brandt, *Endgestalten*, 156–58; for a detailed discussion, see my *Ketuvim*, 132–51.

Table 1. Arrangements of the Writings according to Jewish Witnesses, Megilloth Not Grouped

No.												No. of MSS	Beckwith No.	Brandt Page No.
1	Ruth	Ps	Job	Prov	Eccl	Song	Lam	Dan	Esth	EN	Chr	14[a]	I	156
2	Ruth	Ps	Job	Prov	Eccl	Song	Lam	Esth	Dan	EN	Chr	2	VI	156
3	Ruth	Ps	Job	Prov	Song	Eccl	Lam	Dan	Esth	EN	Chr	3	XIII	156
4	Ruth	Ps	Prov	Job	Song	Eccl	Lam	Dan	Esth	EN	Chr	1	IV	156
5	Ruth	Ps	Prov	Job	Eccl	Song	Lam	Dan	Esth	EN	Chr	3	III	156
6	Ruth	Ps	Job	Prov	Song	Eccl	Lam	Esth	Dan	EN	Chr	3	XIV	156
7	Ruth	Ps	Prov	Job	Eccl	Song	Lam	Esth	Dan	EN	Chr	1	VIII	156
8	Ruth	Ps	Job	Prov	Eccl	Song	Lam	Dan	EN	Esth	Chr	2	V	157t
9	Ruth	Ps	Job	Prov	Eccl	Song	Dan	Lam	Esth	EN	Chr	1	XXIII	157t
10	Ps	Ruth	Job	Prov	Song	Eccl	Lam	Esth	Dan	EN	Chr	1	(XI)[b]	157b
11	Chr	Ruth	Ps	Job	Prov	Song	Eccl	Lam	Esth	Dan	EN	2	XXII	157b
12	Chr	Ps	Job	Prv	Ru	Sng	Eccl	Lam	Dan	Esth	EN	1	XX	157b
13	Chr	Ps	Job	Prov	Eccl	Song	Lam	Dan	Esth	EN		1	XXXI	158
14	Ruth	Ps	Prov	Eccl	Song	Lam	Est	Job	Dan	EN	Chr	1	XVI	157b
15	Ruth	Ps	Job	Prov	Eccl	Song	Lam	Dan	Esth	Chr	EN	1	VII	157t
16	Ruth	Ps	Prov	Eccl	Song	Job	Lam	Dan	EN	Chr	Esth	1	XV	158

a. This is the list in b. B. Bat. 14b as well as 13 manuscripts from the 12th to the 15th centuries. Two of the manuscripts lack Ruth. In addition, Brandt cites 3 other manuscripts that are incomplete but are in accord with b. B. Bat. 14b in what we possess (p. 129).

b. The book order in the source "BM Kings 1" (14th century) differs in Beckwith and Brandt. I follow the newer edition of Brandt.

17	Ruth	Ps	Prov	Job	Lam	Song	Eccl	Esth	Dan	EN	Chr	1	IX	157b
18	Ruth	Ps	Job	Prov	Lam	Song	Eccl	Esth	Dan	EN	Chr	1	X[c]	—
19	Ruth	Ps	Prov	Job	Song	Lam	Eccl	Esth	Dan	EN	Chr	1	XII	157b
20	Ruth	Ps	Song	Prov	Eccl	Lam	Job	Esth	Dan	EN	Chr	1	XVII	158
21	Ruth	Ps	Song	Lam	Job	Prov	Eccl	Esth	Dan	EN	Chr	1	XVIII	158
22	Ruth Esth	Ps	Job	Eccl	Song	Lam	Prov		Dan	EN	Chr	1	XXI	158
23	Ruth	Ps	Job	Prov	Dan	EN	Song	Lam	Eccl	Esth	Chr	1	XXVI	158
24	Ruth	Ps	Job	Prov	Eccl	Dan	Song	Lam	Esth	EN	Chr	1	XXV	157t
25	Ruth	Ps	Prov	Job	Lam	Eccl	Esth	Song	Dan	EN	Chr	1	XXIV	158
26	Job	Ps	Prov	Eccl	Song	Dan	Chr	EN	Esth			1[d]	XXVII	125
27	Dan	EN	Chr	Ruth	Esth	Ps	Job	Prov	Eccl	Song	Lam	1	XIX	158
28	Chr	Ps	Job	Prov	Song	Eccl	Dan	EN	Ruth	Lam	Esth	1	XXX	158
29	Prov[e]	Lam	Eccl	Dan	Meg. Ant.[f]	Esth	EN	Chr				1	—	158

c. According to Beckwith, *OT Canon*, 453, not given in Brandt.

d. Jerome, *Prologus galeatus*, end of 4th century. Jerome says to refer a Jewish tradition. The internal order of the Solomonic books is not given. Brandt, *Endgestalten*, 126. Jerome also knows about a Jewish canonical structure where the books are counted as 24 and the *Ketuvim* division contains 11 books. However, he does not reproduce it. See Beckwith, *OT Canon*, 122.

e. The manuscript is incomplete. Possible there were other books before Proverbs.

f. I.e., the nonbiblical *Megillath Antiochus* (= *Megillath Bet Chaschmonai*), which was read at Hanukkah by some. Brandt, *Endgestalten*, 133.

of becoming heavily relativized or even subverted by Job and Ecclesiastes, which follow it.

Only one of the 34 manuscripts has both permutations at the same time—that is, Prov–Job–Song–Eccl—the rationale of which I find difficult to see.

Again, the arrangement of the books in the national-historical series may vary. Of the 34 witnesses that have the two series, 21 have Lam–Dan–Esth–Ezra/Neh as in Baba Batra, but 10 have Lam–Esth–Dan–Ezra/Neh instead. The exchange of Daniel and Esther, however, has hardly any effect on interpreting the national-historical series. Two manuscripts have Esther after Ezra–Nehemiah, probably for chronological reasons. The diaspora situation (even after the end of the Babylonian Exile) is highlighted for its hermeneutical effect. In one manuscript, Daniel is the first book of the national-historical series.

As said above, of the 51 manuscripts under consideration, 34 have the wisdom series and the national-historical series. Regarding the remaining 17 witnesses (nos. 13–29 above), it can generally be said that most of them are based on Baba Batra but are partly adjusted according to formal criteria such as genre (for example, placing Lamentations among the wisdom books because it is poetry) or chronology (for example, placing Ezra–Nehemiah or Esther after Chronicles), which makes them less feasible for interpretation from a theological angle.

Conclusion

In this analysis, I have shown that a structural-canonical approach offers a new perspective on how to relate the books of Job, Proverbs, Ecclesiastes, and Song of Songs to each other and within an Old Testament theology.

Regarding the inner coherence of the four books, this case can be made already from a thematic point of view. It seems important to me to reflect on the way of wisdom thinking, rather than to reduce it to a dogma of retribution. Wisdom takes an empirical and paradigmatic approach to reality. The discrepancies between the positive approach of Proverbs and the critical stance of Job and Ecclesiastes do not conflict but are complementary aspects of the same matter. I have made a case for interpreting the Song of Songs as a wisdom book. If the four books are read according to the sequence in Baba Batra, additional connections emerge. Job does not undermine Proverbs but instead prepares the reader for it, breathing life into wisdom's motto "The fear of YHWH is the beginning of wisdom." After the "beginner's course" of Proverbs, the reader approaches Ecclesiastes' more advanced wisdom. Qohelet's call to enjoy life is taken up by the Song of Songs, which celebrates love between man and woman—a highlight of managing one's personal life—thus giving the whole idea of wisdom a worthy conclusion.

Regarding the relationship between the wisdom books and the rest of the Hebrew canon, creation theology would be the appropriate starting point, as the references to creation in Proverbs 1–9 and the references to to wisdom concepts in Genesis 2–3 suggest. Regarding the structure of the Ketubim, it is striking that the way of the individual and the way of the nation are paralleled in the same way as in Genesis 1–9, where anthropology prepares one for Israelology; the same thing happens in the Psalm pairs that frame Books I–III of the Psalter (that is, Psalms 1–2, 42f.–44, 71–72, 73–74, and 88–89), where each pair complements the situation of the individual with that of the nation. This suggests that the Hebrew Bible sees the story of the individual and the history of the nation in some sort of analogy to each other.

Insights based on the order of Baba Batra are not necessarily lost when one encounters other canonical arrangements. In this sense, the structural-canonical approach to OT wisdom based on b. B. Bat. 14b is valid not only with regard to one single arrangement of books but more or less for the whole family of manuscripts of the Jewish TaNaK structure without a grouped Megillot.

Bibliography

Barbiero, Gianni. *Das erste Psalmenbuch als Einheit: Eine synchrone Analyse von Psalm 1–41*. Österreichische Biblische Studien 16. Frankfurt a.M.: Peter Lang, 1999.

Barr, James. *The Concept of Biblical Theology: An Old Testament Perspective*. Minneapolis: Fortress, 1999.

Bauer-Kayatz, Christa. *Einführung in die alttestamentliche Weisheit*. BibS 55. Neukirchen-Vluyn: Neukirchener Verlag, 1969.

Beckwith, Roger T. *The Old Testament Canon of the New Testament Church and Its Background in Early Judaism*. Grand Rapids, MI: Eerdmans, 1985.

Bergler, Siegfried. *Talmud für Anfänger: Ein Werkbuch*. 3rd ed. Schalom-Bücher 1. Hannover: Luther Verlag, 1995.

Brandt, Peter. *Endgestalten des Kanons: Das Arrangement der Schriften Israels in der jüdischen und christlichen Bibel*. BBB 131. Berlin: Philo, 2001.

Brueggemann, Walter. *Theology of the Old Testament: Testimony, Dispute, Advocacy*. Minneapolis: Fortress, 1997.

Carr, G. Lloyd. *The Song of Solomon: An Introduction and Commentary*. TOTC 17. Leicester: Inter-Varsity, 1984.

Childs, Brevard S. *Introduction to the Old Testament as Scripture*. Philadelphia: Fortress, 1979.

Crawford, Sidnie White. "The Book of Esther: Introduction, Commentary, and Reflections." Pp. 853–941 in vol. 3 of *NIB*. Edited by Leander E. Keck. Nashville: Abingdon, 1994.

Crenshaw, James L. "Method in Determining Wisdom Influence upon 'Historical' Literature." *JBL* 88 (1969) 129–42.

———. *Old Testament Wisdom: An Introduction*. Atlanta: John Knox, 1981.

Fischer, Stefan. *Das Hohelied Salomos zwischen Poesie und Erzählung: Erzähltext-analyse eines poetischen Textes.* FAT 72. Tübingen: Mohr Siebeck, 2010.

Fohrer, Georg. "Der Mittelpunkt einer Theologie des Alten Testaments." *TZ* 24 (1968) 161–72.

Fox, Michael V. *Character and Ideology in the Book of Esther.* Columbia, SC: University of South Carolina Press, 1991.

Freuling, Georg. *'Wer eine Grube gräbt . . .': Der Tun-Ergehen-Zusammenhang und sein Wandel in der alttestamentlichen Weisheitsliteratur.* WMANT 102. Neukirchen-Vluyn: Neukirchener Verlag, 2004.

Frydrych, Tomáš. *Living under the Sun: Examination of Proverbs and Qoheleth.* VTSup 90. Leiden: Brill, 2002.

Gerhards, Meik. *Das Hohelied: Studien zu seiner literarischen Gestalt und theologischen Bedeutung.* Leipzig: Evangelische Verlag, 2010.

Goldingay, John E. *Daniel.* WBC 30. Dallas: Word, 1989.

Hasel, Gerhard F. *Old Testament Theology: Basic Issues in the Current Debate.* 4th ed. Grand Rapids, MI: Eerdmans, 1991.

Hurvitz, Avi. "Wisdom Vocabulary in the Hebrew Psalter: A Contribution to the Study of 'Wisdom Psalms'." *VT 38* (1988) 41–51.

Kaiser, Walter C., Jr. *Toward an Old Testament Theology.* Grand Rapids, MI: Zondervan, 1978.

Keel, Othmar. *Das Hohelied.* ZBK: AT 18. Zurich: Theologischer Verlag, 1986.

Koorevaar, Hendrik J. *A Structural Canonical Approach for a Theology of the Old Testament.* Version 3.2. Leuven: Evangelische Theologische Faculteit, 2000.

———. "The Torah Model as Original Macrostructure of the Hebrew Canon." *ZAW* 122 (2010) 64–80.

Kratz, Reinhard G. "Die Tora Davids: Psalm 1 und die doxologische Fünfteilung des Psalters." *ZTK* 93 (1996) 1–34.

Longman, Tremper, III. *Song of Songs.* Grand Rapids, MI: Eerdmans, 2001.

Maier, Gerhard. *Das Hohelied.* Wuppertaler Studienbibel. Wuppertal: Brockhaus, 1991.

Müller, Hans-Peter, Otto Kaiser, and James A. Loader. *Das Hohelied, Klagelieder, das Buch Ester.* 4th ed. ATD 16/2. Göttingen: Vandenhoeck & Ruprecht, 1992.

Murphy, Roland E. *Wisdom Literature and Psalms.* Interpreting Biblical Texts. Nashville: Abingdon, 1983.

Preuss, Horst Dietrich. *Theologie des Alten Testaments.* Vol. 1: *Jhwhs erwählendes und verpflichtendes Handeln*; vol. 2: *Israels Weg mit Jhwh.* Stuttgart: Kohlhammer, 1991–92.

Sæbø, Magne. *On the Way to Canon: Creative Tradition History in the Old Testament.* JSOTSup 191. Sheffield: JSOT Press, 1998.

Sheppard, Gerald T. "Canonization: Hearing the Voice of the Same God through Historically Dissimilar Traditions." *Int* 36 (1982) 21–33.

Steinberg, Julius. "Architektonische Bauformen als Mittel der literarischen Kommunikation am Beispiel von Gen 1–4." Pp. 51–73 in *Sprache lieben—Gottes Wort verstehen: Beiträge zur biblischen Exegese.* FS Heinrich von Siebenthal. Edited by Walter Hilbrands. Gießen: Brunnen, 2011.

———. "Gottes Ordnungen verstehen und leben: Eine Theologie der alttestamentlichen Weisheit." Pp. 211–37 in *Freude an Gottes Weisung: Themen-*

buch zur Theologie des Alten Testaments. 2nd ed. Edited by H. Klement and J. Steinberg. Riehen: ArteMedia, 2012.

———. *Das Hohelied.* Edition C, AT 26. Witten: SCM, 2014.

———. "Kanonische 'Lesarten' des Hohenliedes." Pp. 164–83 in *Formen des Kanons: Studien zu Ausprägungen des biblischen Kanons von der Antike bis zum 19. Jh.* Edited by T. Hieke. SBS 228. Stuttgart: Katholisches Bibelwerk, 2013.

———. *Die Ketuvim: Ihr Aufbau und ihre Botschaft.* BBB 152. Hamburg: Philo, 2006.

Sternberg, Meir. *The Poetics of Biblical Narrative: Ideological Literature and the Drama of Reading.* Bloomington: Indiana University Press, 1987.

Stone, Timothy J. *The Compilational History of the Megilloth: Canon, Contoured Intertextuality and Meaning in the Writings.* FAT 2/59. Tübingen: Mohr Siebeck, 2013.

Strack, Hermann L., and Günter Stemberger. *Einleitung in Talmud und Midrasch.* 7th ed. Munich: Beck, 1982.

Tromp, Nicolas J. "Wisdom and the Canticle: Ct. 8,6c–7b—Text, Character, Message and Import." Pp. 88–95 in *La Sagesse de l'Ancien Testament.* Edited by M. Gilbert. BETL 51. Leuven: Leuven University Press, 1979.

Westermann, Claus. *Theologie des Alten Testaments in Grundzügen.* 2nd ed. Göttingen: Vandenhoeck & Ruprecht, 1985.

Wilson, Gerald H. *The Editing of the Hebrew Psalter.* SBLDS 76. Chico, CA: Scholars Press, 1985.

Zenger, Erich et al. *Einleitung in das Alte Testament.* Stuttgart: Kohlhammer, 1998.

The Search for Order:
The Compilational History of Ruth

TIMOTHY J. STONE

The word *Megillot* is anachronistic, at least if it is used to refer to a collection of biblical "books" before the 1st century C.E., and probably for 1,100 years after that. One can speak with some confidence of all five Megillot as being read liturgically only sometime after the 12th century in only some Jewish communities, even though they had not yet been labeled the Megillot as a collection.[1] Thus, to speak of the Megillot is to speak of the liturgical reception of five biblical texts in a period that was long after the time of their composition, possible redaction, and canonization. While the line between reception history and the texts' "original meaning" is blurry, if not conceptually problematic, this sort of distinction continues to be the scholarly paradigm. And within this paradigm, the study of the Megillot's reception as a collection is an unquestionably valid although seldom-observed practice. Likewise, there are few objections to ideological and reader-centered approaches to the Megillot. As soon as one steps across the line into the arena of the texts' original meaning, however, a whole host of objections arise. One may suppose that these diverse texts originated in isolation from each other and only later were brought together, when the Hebrew Bible was canonized. Their arrangement into a subcollection within the canon took place even later still, so that whatever unity or meaning they might possess as a collection comes from their appropriation by readers and communities.[2]

It is my contention in this essay that conceiving of the Megillot as books that originated in isolation and were later compiled, which in its various manifestations is much more complicated than just presented, has too often and without due argument been used to dismiss a thorough

---

1. Timothy J. Stone, *The Compilational History of the Megilloth: Canon, Contoured Intertextuality and Meaning in the Writings* (FAT 2/59; Tübingen: Mohr Siebeck, 2013) 106–12.
2. It is seldom articulated exactly like this, but this is one assumption behind the works of Albert C. Sundberg, *The Old Testament of the Early Church* (HTS 20; Cambridge: Harvard University Press, 1964); John Barton, *Oracles of God: Perceptions of Ancient Prophecy in Israel after the Exile* (London: Darton, Longman & Todd, 1986); idem, *Holy Writings, Sacred Text: The Canon of Early Christianity* (Louisville: Westminster John Knox, 1998); and Lee M. McDonald, *The Biblical Canon* (Peabody, MA: Hendrickson, 2007).

investigation into the history of the formation of the Megillot as a collection. Regardless of the many historical and conceptual problems facing this sort of investigation, it is time to examine the various possibilities.

Historical Objections

First, I will list the historical reasons that the collection of the Megillot is considered to be a late development and then posit other ways of understanding the evidence, though without providing adequate defense here, since I have addressed these issues elsewhere in detail. *Objection one*: the Megillot, as mentioned above, became a collection only after they began to be read liturgically—the Song of Songs at Passover, Ruth at the Festival of Weeks (Shavuot), Lamentations on the Ninth of Ab, Ecclesiastes at the Feast of Tabernacles (Sukkot), and Esther at Purim—in other words, at the five major festivals in Judaism. This way of grouping the texts is a post-talmudic development and is, therefore, part of their reception but has no bearing on earlier stages in this subcollection's history.[3] This point has been repeated without variation for at least the last 100 years.[4] The order of books in the Megillot is thus an anachronism.

There are, however, several problems with this view. The first and most obvious is that the order of reading the books in accordance with the festivals differs from the order of the Megillot in the Masoretic tradition since the order is Ruth, the Song of Songs, Ecclesiastes, Lamentations, Esther. Second, the Masoretic order (by *Masoretic*, I mean the family of manuscripts that follow the Aleppo Codex) most likely predates the practice of reading all five of the Megillot liturgically. According to the available evidence, Ecclesiastes only joined the liturgy sometime after the 12th century, while the Aleppo Codex probably dates to the 10th century and is the crowning achievement of many generations of work. The order of the books in this tradition is the order with which we are familiar in *BHS*—Ruth, the Song of Songs, Ecclesiastes, Lamentations, and Esther. There are other factors to consider,[5] but in my judgment it is more likely that the liturgical practices associated with these five books came about, in part, because of their prior association in the Hebrew canon rather than the reverse.

Objection two: there are many arrangements for the books of the Megillot in particular and the Writings in general, so that one cannot speak of a single or original order.[6] We possess evidence of only two orders of

---

3. Brevard Childs, *Introduction to the Old Testament as Scripture* (Minneapolis: Fortress, 1979) 501–2; see my book, *Megilloth*, 106–12.

4. See, for example, L. Blau, "The Five Megillot," in *The Jewish Encyclopedia* (ed. I. Singer and C. Adler; New York: Funk & Wagnalls, 1912) 8.429–51.

5. For more on this, see my *Megilloth*, 106–12.

6. For a more detailed discussion of this, see ibid., 103–18, and the various works cited there. Cf. Peter Brandt, *Endgestalten des Kanons: Das Arrangement der Schriften Israels in der jüdischen und christlichen Bibel* (BBB 31; Berlin: Philo, 2001), who makes the point

the Writings prior to the 12th century and then, only after this period—which coincides with the decline of the Masoretes—is there evidence of a large variety of arrangements. These two orders are the talmudic, found in b. B. Bat. 14b, and the Masoretic, found in the Cairo, Aleppo, and Leningrad codices.[7] These two arrangements differ, but it is significant (with the exception of Ruth) that their structural logic is quite similar.[8] If there was a large variety of arrangements in antiquity, then investigating the importance of the arrangements would be of little significance, but if there were only two ancient arrangements for the Writings in the Jewish tradition, this fact might open up new avenues of research. On the other hand, the concept of an original or single order is not, in my view, a prerequisite to investigating the significance of ancient arrangements. One should not prejudge the historical situation without first carefully examining the possible reasons for the various orders, which I will illustrate below in the case of the book of Ruth.

Objection three: the very idea of a meaningful order is anachronistic since it arose only after the invention and widespread use of the codex.[9] This common assertion is questionable on a number of grounds.

First, each of the great Greek codices of the 4th and 5th centuries contains a drastically different arrangement of the books. There is no evidence in the arrangements of the books within each codex or in the ways that each codex relates to the others that arrangements had now become a priority.[10]

Second, this objection presumes that there was no technological or conceptual apparatus in place in which the arrangement of scrolls was meaningful prior to the invention of the codex. The sacred space of the temple

---

over and over again that there was no original order and that the great variety of orders means that one can only approach the question from the direction of reception history. For a helpful list of almost all the different arrangements of the Writings, see Roger T. Beckwith, *The Old Testament Canon of the New Testament Church and Its Background in Early Judaism* (London: SPCK, 1985) 450–64. Stephen Chapman, "A Canonical Approach to Old Testament Theology? Deuteronomy 34:10–12 and Malachi 3:22–24 as Programmatic Conclusions," *HBT* 25 (2003) 131, concludes logically that, as the variety of orders increases, the significance of the orders decreases.

7. The order in these codices is Chronicles, Psalms, Job, Proverbs, Ruth, the Song of Songs, Ecclesiastes, Lamentations, Esther, Daniel, and Ezra–Nehemiah.

8. Compare my *Megilloth*, where I focus on the MT arrangement, with Julius Steinberg, *Die Ketuvim: Ihr Aufbau und ihre Botschaft* (BBB 152; Hamburg: Philo, 2006), who examines the logic of the talmudic arrangement. While I disagree with many of Steinberg's conclusions, we nevertheless see a similar logic in the associations of most of the books in the Writings.

9. Brandt, *Endgestalten*, 58–62, dates the codices to around 300 C.E. The comments of Schniedewind represent the consensus: "But the invention of the codex forced decisions to be made about the set order of the biblical books within the codex" (William Schniedewind, *How the Bible Became a Book* [Cambridge: Cambridge University Press, 2004] 196).

10. Stone, *Megilloth*, 95.

in Israel (and there is ample evidence of an archive of sacred texts in the temple), archival practices across the ancient Near East, and the use of catchwords or linked phrases provided meaningful ways of conceptualizing arrangements in earlier centuries, especially during the Second Temple period.[11] The vehicle for conceptualizing the order changed with the rise of the codex, but it does not necessarily follow that order was meaningless before this period.

Third, there are signs in the Hebrew Bible, in the Torah, Former Prophets, and twelve Minor Prophets, that the compilation of these texts into subcollections was, at least at some point during the history of their growth, by *design*.[12] This was true before the invention of the codex. Each of these three historical objections must be treated seriously if one wants to examine the collection of the Megillot prior to its reception.[13]

There are other supposed historical problems: The Hebrew canon was closed only after the 1st century C.E., severing the connection of authors and/or redactors to compilers and/or canonizers.[14] The Greek tradition contains many different texts and different orders and probably predates the Hebrew arrangements.[15] Conceptions of the canonical process as texts' being thrown together rather arbitrarily at some late date predominate,[16] while conceptions of the texts as growing up together in a symbiotic relationship with one other is gaining ground for other parts of the Hebrew canon but is seldom entertained for the Megillot or the Writings. If one makes it past all these historical "problems," there is a final (supposed) obstacle: the massive variety among the books of the Writings in general and the Megillot in particular makes it axiomatic that they were not composed, redacted, or compiled with a view to their interrelationship.[17]

---

11. Ibid., 80–89.

12. For a detailed defense of this see ibid., 89–94. On the links between books in the Genesis–Kings collection, see Konrad Schmid, *Genesis and the Moses Story: Israel's Dual Origins in the Hebrew Bible* (trans. James Nogalski; Siphrut 3; Winona Lake, IN: Eisenbrauns, 2010) 23–29. Schmid concludes that "Genesis–2 Kings should therefore be considered a redactional unit" (p. 23). Cf. Childs, *OT as Scripture*, 129.

13. For more on this, see the essay in this volume by Steinberg and me.

14. For a classic defense of these, see Barton, *Oracles*. Cf. McDonald, *Biblical Canon*.

15. Peter Katz, "The Old Testament Canon in Palestine and Alexandria," in *The Canon and the Masorah of the Hebrew Bible* (ed. Sid Leiman; New York: Ktav, 1974) 72–98; J. C. H. Lebram, "Aspekte der alttestamentlichen Kanonbildung," *VT* 18 (1968) 173–89. More recently, Childs (*OT as Scripture*, 667) and Stephen Chapman (*The Law and the Prophets: A Study in Old Testament Canon Formation* [FAT 27; Tübingen: Mohr, 2000] 137) both cite Katz's and Lebram's articles to defend the idea that the Greek order arose before the Hebrew.

16. While seldom explicitly stated, this view remains an implicit assumption of the work of Sundberg, *Church*; Barton, *Oracles*; McDonald, *Biblical Canon*.

17. On this, see Donn F. Morgan, *Between Text and Community* (Minneapolis: Fortress, 1990), who is the only one to give a full-length account of the nature of the Writings, but his views on the diversity of the books of the Writings are common: see, for example, Ste-

It is not my goal to respond to all of these historical objections here,[18] but in the second half of the essay, I want to chart a possible way forward by looking at one specific example. Before we proceed, however, there is an additional problem. When we consider the possibility that the Megillot and the Writings had a purposeful shape—then, by what criteria can we discern the presence or absence of such a shape? If it was designed on purpose, how would we know? Intertextual connections between books alone are not a sure guide since Ecclesiastes, for instance, refers to Genesis 3–4 more than to any of the other books in the Writings.[19] This cluster of connections does not mean that Ecclesiastes should be placed before Genesis. Or to say it another way, the textual connections between Judges 19 and Genesis 19 are significant for understanding those texts, and they may contribute to the overall unity of the Torah and the Former Prophets as a collection, but they do not tell us anything essential about the compilation of Genesis and Judges into a larger collection. What is needed is a canonical or compilational poetics that will give us a way to evaluate the presence or absence of design.

Based on research on the unity of the twelve Minor Prophets, the Psalms, and the Genesis–2 Kings complex, we can say that there are two criteria that are vital to have in place before we examine Ruth as a test case.[20] The first criterion is "catchwords or catchphrases at the seams of contiguous books." There are several instances of single words that forge links between contiguous books in The Twelve, but the link between Joel 4:16, which says, "The LORD roars from Zion and utters his voice from Jerusalem," and the repetition of the same phrase in Amos 1:2 is particularly strong. The second (and far weaker) criterion is the presence of "specific themes that are either continued in a similar manner or reversed to create a sharp contrast across contiguous books, like the Day of the LORD in the Twelve. . . . This criterion is collection conscious and may but does not necessarily ensure a particular order."[21]

The Example of Ruth

In ancient orders, Ruth appears primarily in three locations: between Judges and Samuel, between Proverbs and the Song of Songs, and before the Psalter. Here I want to examine the first two locations.[22] The Greek

---

phen L. McKenzie and John Kaltner, *The Old Testament: Its Background,Growth, and Content* (Nashville: Abingdon, 2007) 303.

18. I address each one of these objections in my *Megilloth*.

19. David M. Clemens, "The Law of Sin and Death: Ecclesiastes and Genesis 1–3," *Themelios* 19 (1994) 5–8.

20. For an evaluation of this research and more details concerning possible criteria for a compilational grammar, see my book *Megilloth*, 17–33.

21. Ibid., 33.

22. Steinberg (*Ketuvim*, 444–45) and I (*Megilloth*, 137) both explore this third position.

tradition often placed Ruth after Judges and before 1 Samuel, and this order appears to be connected to the count of 22 books, which has ancient
roots and is probably linked to the Hebrew alphabet. In this scheme, Ruth
and Judges were counted as one book, as were Jeremiah and Lamentations,
thus changing the number of books from 24, as in the Masoretic tradition,
to 22.[23] Many tentatively suggest that Ruth should be read in connection
with Judges, especially Judges 17–21, and a few even go on to connect Ruth
with 1 Samuel as well. The reasons for this, however, are not forthcoming,
and often appeals are based on salvation history or thematic resonances
alone.[24]

The chronological marker at the beginning of Ruth confirms for some
that the book belongs after Judges; but the psalms' titles, which connect
many of the psalms to David, or even the superscriptions in Proverbs that
link most of the book to Solomon are not compilational indications that
the Davidic Psalms should be placed after Samuel or that Proverbs should
be placed after 1 Kings. To use another example, in an argument for reading
Ruth as an introduction to Samuel, Tod Linafelt wonders if the structural
similarities between Ruth and 2 Sam 5:13–8:18 indicate that they were constructed by the same hand.[25] Even if one grants the validity of this obscure
structural connection, it is not clear what significance this sort of observation should have for discerning whether Ruth was placed between Judges
and Samuel by design. Can the two compilational criteria mentioned above
bring the view of Linafelt and others[26] into sharp focus?

First, all of the books of the Former Prophets have been knit together at
their seams.[27] A brief look at the connection between Judges and Samuel
will suffice. Judg 21:19 mentions the yearly festival at Shiloh, and 1 Sam 1:3
tells us that Elkanah went up yearly to sacrifice at Shiloh. The usual Hebrew
expressions, combined with the reference to Shiloh stitch these two texts
together at their seams.[28]

Second, in a similar manner, Ruth is deliberately added to this collection by breaking apart the contiguous connection between Judges and
Samuel. Judg 21:23 uses the verb נשׂא for taking a wife rather than the
more common לקח. The use of לקח for taking a wife is common in Judges
(14:3; 15:6; 19:1; 21:22). This makes the switch in Judg 21:22, where לקח is
used, to Judg 21:23, where נשׂא is used rather odd, since the two different
verbs are employed synonymously. This is the only time in Judges where

23. Stone, *Megilloth*, 68–73, 94–99, 211.

24. For the many sources on this, see ibid., 120 (for Judges and Ruth), 125 (for Ruth
and 1 Samuel).

25. Tod Linafelt, *Ruth* (Berit Olam; Collegeville, MN: Liturgical Press, 1999) xx.

26. See Kathleen A. Robinson Farmer, "Ruth," in *NIB*, vol. 2: *Numbers–2 Samuel* (Nashville: Abingdon, 1998) 889–946; Katharine D. Sakenfeld, *Ruth* (Interpretation; Atlanta:
John Knox, 1999); Christian Frevel, *Das Buch Rut* (Stuttgart: Katholisches Bibelwerk, 1992).

27. Schmid, *Moses Story*, 23–29; cf. Stone, *Megilloth*, 89–93.

28. Ibid., 90.

נשׂאis used for taking a wife. The word נשׂא also occurs once in Ruth 1:4, where Mahlon and Chilion take Moabite women as wives, but later in Ruth 4:13, the verb לקח is used when Boaz takes Ruth to be his wife. The verb לקחis known to Judges and Ruth, but the one use of נשׂא for taking a wife in each book is very near the seam between the two books. This rare use of the verb נשׂא functions as canonical "glue" to connect the beginning of Ruth to the end of Judges. In addition, the strongly contrastive scenes that take place in Bethlehem of Judah in Judges 17–21 and Ruth are consistent with the criteria of juxtaposing sharply contrastive themes across adjacent books.

Ruth has also been connected to 1 Samuel deliberately. Although Ruth 4:15 and 1 Sam 1:8 are "grammatically identical in form,"[29] the canonical implications of this fact have gone unnoticed. In Ruth 4:15, the women say to Naomi that Ruth is "better to you than seven sons," and in 1 Samuel 1:8, Elkanah says to Hannah, "Am I not better to you than ten sons."[30] The small differences between these two phrases do not negate the fact that their similarities are unparalleled in the rest of the Hebrew Bible. This link, separated by only 16 verses, binds the two books together at their seams. It is vital to note that it is not the *mere presence* of these connections at any point in adjacent books but the *location of these connections at the very edges of the book* that renders them compilationally significant. On this foundation, one could add a number of textual and thematic connections between Judges, Ruth, and Samuel—not least, the impact that Ruth's inclusion in the collection has on reframing the relationship between the cities and ancestors of Saul and David. This may be the book of Ruth's original home; it may have been the author's intent to have Ruth added to the Former Prophets in this exact position. If this is so, we can already see two different arrangements: the Former Prophets without Ruth and then with Ruth. But there is more to Ruth's compilational history because it migrates into the Writings after Proverbs.

In the two oldest arrangements of the Writings in the Jewish tradition, there are two places in the collection where Ruth is located. In the talmudic arrangement, it is found before the Psalter, where it appears to serve as an introduction to the Psalter. In the Masoretic, it is located between Proverbs and the Song of Songs. I want to examine the latter placement, and I have argued elsewhere why I think this is the older of the two arrangements, though the talmudic arrangement is the first to surface in recorded history.[31] In my view, Ruth has been deliberately stitched onto

---

29. Ibid., 126.
30. My translation.
31. For an examination of Ruth as the introduction to the Psalter, see Beckwith, *Canon*, 158; Stephen Dempster, *Dominion and Dynasty: A Biblical Theology of the Hebrew Bible* (New Studies in Biblical Theology 15; Downers Grove, IL: InterVarsity, 2003) 191–94; Brandt, *Endgestalten*, 151; Steinberg, *Ketuvim*, 444–45; Greg Goswell, "The Order of the Books in

the end of Proverbs through a number of textual connections to Proverbs' last chapter. There are many links to this last chapter, but two are particularly striking.

First, the beginning of the acrostic in Prov 31:10 asks, "Who can find a woman of substance?" The very last line of the acrostic ends with this woman being praised in the gate. Other than the reference in Prov 12:4, Ruth is the only character in the entire Hebrew Bible to be called a woman of substance, an אשת־חיל.[32] In Ruth 3:11, Boaz says to Ruth, "All the people in the gate know that you are a woman of substance."[33] In this verse, Boaz refers to the first and last line of the acrostic in Proverbs 31, which may be a shorthand way to refer to the entire acrostic.

Second, the closest lexical and thematic connections in the Hebrew Bible to Prov 31:23 (which says, "Her husband is known in the gates, when he sits among the elders of the land") are found in Ruth 4. The uniqueness and sophistication of the connections between Proverbs 31 and Ruth establish a textual link, but what makes them compilationally significant is their *location* at the very end of Proverbs.[34] In this way, the acrostic anchors Ruth to the end of Proverbs and the collection of the Writings. The location of these connections in Ruth, however, is not at its seam with Proverbs, which suggests that Ruth was not originally composed for this location but instead was moved, without redactional alterations, into the Writings. Moreover, the connections that Proverbs 31 has to Ruth are integral to the story of Ruth, and thus it is unlikely that they have been added to make the book connect with Proverbs. Nor are there textual connections between Ruth and the Song of Songs. Ruth's integration into the Writings is not as complete as was Ruth's integration into the Former Prophets.[35]

What logic, then, might have motivated this migration? There are many factors to consider, but I will make only one suggestion here. Prov 31:10–31 typifies and sums up all the ideals of wisdom found in the book of Proverbs.[36] In turn, the acrostic's textual connections to the character of Ruth make her an example of these ideals. She, however, was a Moabitess, a foreigner. In Proverbs, the son is instructed to shun foreign women and embrace Lady Wisdom.[37] The compilation of these two texts places the is-

---

the Hebrew Bible," *JETS* 51 (2008) 686. On the MT's being an older order than the talmudic, see my *Megilloth*, 105–11.

32. Within the book of Proverbs, 12:4 mentions this woman of substance.

33. My translation.

34. For more connections between Proverbs 31 and Ruth, see my *Megilloth*, 134–36.

35. For a fuller explanation, see ibid., 135–37.

36. Michael Fox, *Proverbs 1–9: A New Translation with Introduction and Commentary* (AB 18A; New York: Doubleday, 2000) 909–11.

37. Fox, ibid., 134–41, argues that there is "no stigma" attached to being a foreigner per se (p. 141). However, the foreign woman here appears parallel with the evil woman (Prov 6:24) and the prostitute (Prov 23:27), which make the stigma rather clear. See my *Megilloth*, 137.

sue of the foreigner in Proverbs in dialogical tension with Ruth, since she is both a woman of substance *and* a foreigner whom Boaz rightly marries.

Two brief notes in conclusion. First, the Megillot (if by this we mean the collection of the five smaller books of the Writings) does not appear to be an anachronism when used to refer to the collection prior to the 1st century C.E., because there is evidence of compilational activity *in the biblical texts*—possibly by authors, but more likely by redactors.[38] One result of this is that any examination of the relationship of the books of the Megillot should also consider their location in the Writings as a whole, since during this (pre–1st century) period the Megillot was not an independent subcollection.

Second, in view of the history of the compilation of the Hebrew canon, the search for an original order or single order may need to be reconceptualized. In this paper, I have tried to demonstrate the presence of three different orders (Judges–Samuel; Judges–Ruth–Samuel; Proverbs–Ruth), each configured not by mistake but by design. All three of these orders have survived in one form or another even today. Early in the history of the Hebrew canon, there was not one order or a great multitude of orders but instead a limited number of meaningful arrangements. *The reconfiguration of the earliest canonical arrangements, so far as we can track these activities, should give us reasons to reject the concept of an original order even as it highlights the importance of analyzing the canonical arrangements.* These books grew up *together* much like a forest of trees. They are all quite different, and some have been transplanted to complement others in the grove, but they still had a relationship to one another during the period of their growth before the canon was closed. They are not like a series of unrelated potted plants that are moved into the same garden, and then a fence is built around them, and the gates are locked to keep other plants out. This issue needs to be explored further, but if my analysis and conclusions point in the right direction, then the canonical process and the history of the formation of the canon need to be rethought.[39] It may also mean that the dominant historical-critical paradigm with its search for a single, original, historical setting may need to expand its historical lenses to take into account the texts' canonical history.

---

38. Although it is beyond the scope of this paper, the possible meaning of the effect created by the compilation of contiguous texts should be considered, even if there is no evidence of authorial and redactional alignment. Compilation is part of the text's history, and it may have been a meaningful rather than an arbitrary act.

39. This is not true of all works on the canon but specifically those of Sundberg, *Church*; Barton, *Oracles*; and McDonald, *Biblical Canon*.

Bibliography

Barton, John. *Holy Writings, Sacred Text: The Canon of Early Christianity*. Louisville: Westminster John Knox, 1998.

————. *Oracles of God: Perceptions of Ancient Prophecy in Israel after the Exile*. London: Darton, Longman & Todd, 1986.

Beckwith, Roger T. *The Old Testament Canon of the New Testament Church and Its Background in Early Judaism*. London: SPCK, 1985.

Blau, L. "The Five Megillot." Pages 429–51 in vol. 8 of *The Jewish Encyclopedia*. Edited by Isidore Singer and Cyrus Adler. New York: Funk & Wagnalls, 1912.

Brandt, Peter. *Endgestalten des Kanons: Das Arrangement der Schriften Israels in der judischen und christlichen Bibel*. BBB 31. Berlin: Philo, 2001.

Chapman, Stephen. "A Canonical Approach to Old Testament Theology? Deuteronomy 34:10–12 and Malachi 3:22–24 as Programmatic Conclusions." *HBT* 25 (2003) 121–45.

————. *The Law and the Prophets: A Study in Old Testament Canon Formation*. FAT 27. Tübingen: Mohr, 2000.

Childs, Brevard. *Introduction to the Old Testament as Scripture*. Minneapolis: Fortress, 1979.

Clemens, David M. "The Law of Sin and Death: Ecclesiastes and Genesis 1–3." *Themelios* 19 (1994) 5–8.

Dempster, Stephen G. *Dominion and Dynasty: A Biblical Theology of the Hebrew Bible*. New Studies in Biblical Theology 15. Downers Grove, IL: InterVarsity, 2003.

————. "An 'Extraordinary Fact': Torah and Temple and the Contours of the Hebrew Canon. Part 1/2." *TynBul* 48 (1997) 23–56, 191–218.

Farmer, Kathleen A. Robinson. "Ruth." Pp. 889–946 in *NIB*, vol. 2: *Numbers–2 Samuel*. Nashville: Abingdon, 1998.

Fox, Michael V. *Proverbs 1–9: A New Translation with Introduction and Commentary*. AB 18A. New York: Doubleday, 2000.

Frevel, Christian. *Das Buch Rut*. Stuttgart: Katholisches Bibelwerk, 1992.

Goswell, Greg. "The Order of the Books in the Hebrew Bible." *JETS* 51 (2008) 673–88.

Katz, Peter. "The Old Testament Canon in Palestine and Alexandria." Pages 72–98 in *The Canon and the Masorah of the Hebrew Bible*. Edited by Sid Leiman. New York: Ktav, 1974.

Lebram, J. C. H. "Aspekte der alttestamentlichen Kanonbildung." *VT* 18 (1968) 173–89.

Linafelt, Tod. *Ruth*. Edited by David W. Cotter. Berit Olam. Collegeville, MN: Liturgical Press, 1999.

McDonald, Lee M. *The Biblical Canon*. Peabody, MA: Hendrickson, 2007.

McKenzie, Stephen L., and John Kaltner. *The Old Testament: Its Background, Growth, and Content*. Nashville: Abingdon, 2007.

Morgan, Donn F. *Between Text and Community*. Minneapolis: Fortress, 1990.

Sakenfeld, Katharine D. *Ruth*. Interpretation. Atlanta: John Knox, 1999.

Schmid, Konrad. *Genesis and the Moses Story: Israel's Dual Origins in the Hebrew Bible*. Translated by James Nogalski. Siphrut 3. Winona Lake, IN: Eisenbrauns, 2010.

Schniedewind, William. *How the Bible Became a Book*. Cambridge: Cambridge University Press, 2004.

Steinberg, Julius. *Die Ketuvim: Ihr Aufbau und ihre Botschaft*. BBB 152. Hamburg: Philo, 2006.

Stone, Timothy J. *The Compilational History of the Megilloth: Canon, Contoured Intertextuality and Meaning in the Writings*. FAT 2/59. Tübingen: Mohr Siebeck, 2013.

Sundberg, Albert C. *The Old Testament of the Early Church*. HTS 20. Cambridge: Harvard University Press, 1964.

The Associative Effects of Daniel in the Writings

AMBER WARHURST

Daniel is a book of diversity. Fluctuating among Hebrew, Aramaic, and Greek, longer and shorter versions, hagiographic tales and symbolic visions, 1st- and 3rd-person points of view, the Babylonian and Persian empires, and the Hellenistic era and beyond—the book defies easy unification or categorization. The difficulty in classifying Daniel is further frustrated by the alternating contextualizations of the book among the Prophets in Greek, Latin, and subsequent translations of the Bible, and among the Writings in Hebrew-Aramaic versions. Even within these subcategories of the Prophets and Writings, its position is not consistent. Within the Latter Prophets, it is found sometimes before and sometimes after Ezekiel,[1] while in the Writings it usually either follows or precedes the book of Esther, and the pair is bookended on either side by Lamentations and Ezra–Nehemiah.[2]

Naturally, the literary context in which Daniel is placed—whether alongside prophetic books or in the Writings—influences the way the book is understood and interpreted. For this reason, the question of whether Daniel is more at home in the Prophets or Writings has continuously asserted itself throughout the history of the book's interpretation. The majority view has been that Daniel was located in the Prophets prior to its relocation to the Writings. This supposition is due in large measure to perceived prophet-like attributes of the book, particularly a future-oriented, predictive element. Furthermore, the earliest datable witness to the numeration and content of the Jewish canon, Josephus in *Against Apion* (ca. 100 C.E.), has frequently

---

1. Origen and Melito list Daniel before Ezekiel, while the LXX and Vulgate list Daniel after Ezekiel.

2. In b. B. Bat. 14b, the order is Lamentations, Daniel, Esther, Ezra–Nehemiah; while in the Leningrad and Aleppo codices and BHK³/BHS, the order is Lamentations, Esther, Daniel, Ezra–Nehemiah. Daniel's proximity to Chronicles is variable since it concludes the Writings in Baba Batra and BHK/BHS but opens the Writings in the Leningrad and Aleppo codices. The associations highlighted in the present investigation are derived from these more-prominent Hebrew-Aramaic orderings, which cluster Daniel together with Lamentations, Esther, Ezra–Nehemiah and, to some extent, Chronicles. However, it must be pointed out that lists which group the five Megillot together within the Writings reflect greater diversity of ordering and naturally affect the juxtaposition of Daniel. See the charts provided by Peter Brandt, *Endgestalten des Kanons: Das Arrangement der Schriften Israels in der jüdischen und christlichen Bibel* (BBB 31; Berlin: Philo, 2001) 159–64.

been interpreted as evidence of Daniel's status as a prophet. Josephus classifies the 22 books that make up the Jewish collection of Scripture according to three genres: "Five are the books of Moses. . . . the prophets subsequent to Moses wrote the history of the events of their own times in thirteen books. The remaining four books contain hymns to God and precepts for the conduct of human life" (Josephus, *Ag. Ap.* 1.38–41 [Thackeray, LCL]). Though Josephus does not mention any books specifically, he must have Daniel in mind as 1 of the 13 books written by prophets since the descriptions of the other two categories do not correspond to the genre of Daniel. One can understand how this extract from Josephus has frequently been employed to defend an early, tripartite categorization of Jewish Scripture, in which Daniel was located in the Prophets, only later to be relocated to the Writings by rabbinical groups. However, in this passage, Josephus is not directly addressing the scope and categorization of the Jewish canon but is making a case for the authority of Judean records based on their prophetic authorship (see especially Josephus, *Ag. Ap.* 1.37).[3] Josephus's testimony does not therefore provide unambiguous support for an early classification of Daniel within the Prophets.

Though the question is usually asked "Why did the rabbis move Daniel from the Prophets to the Writings?" it is just as possible from the vantage point of historical evidence to speculate about why non-Jewish readers of Daniel thought it appropriate to reclassify it as a prophetic book. Could it be that the logic of Daniel's placement in the Writings has been misunderstood? In the following investigation, I will explore, on the one hand, some of the negative attitudes, and on the other hand, some positive literary effects of Daniel's placement in the Writings. A measure of compilational intentionality is suggested by the correlation of Daniel to books containing complementary theological and literary motifs in the Writings.

Daniel's Regrettable Relocation to the Writings

A brief glimpse at the history of the interpretation of Daniel reveals that interpreters have looked askance at the book's categorization among the Writings, viewing it as an unfortunate condition attributable to regrettable historical circumstances or poorly devised compositional features of the book. Operating on the assumption that the book was transferred from the Prophets to the Writings, Theodoret of Cyrus (393–458 C.E.) in his 5th-century *Commentary on Daniel* undertakes to defend Daniel from the humiliation he perceives to be associated with its removal to the Writings, stating in his preface: "For into the far reaches of shamelessness they [the Jews] have gone as they have segregated him [Daniel] from the cho-

---

3. For a more thorough discussion, see Steve Mason, "Josephus and His Twenty-Two Book Canon," in *The Canon Debate* (ed. Lee McDonald and James A. Sanders; Peabody, MA: Hendrickson, 2002) 110–27.

rus of the prophets and withheld from it [the book of Daniel] the very title 'prophecy'" (Theodoret of Cyrus, *Commentary on Daniel, Prefatio* [PG 81.1260]). Clearly, even at this early date, Daniel's position in the Writings had come to be viewed with suspicion.

Even rabbis of the Middle Ages puzzled over the reason for the categorization of Daniel in the Writings rather than the Prophets, supposing that the book's assignment to the third section of Scripture was an indication of its inferior status. Maimonides (1134–1204 C.E.) claims that the sections of the Tanak reflect distinctions in the way prophetic revelation was received and concludes that, because Daniel was not, strictly speaking, a prophet, the book was segregated from the prophetic collection of literature. He outlines 11 degrees of prophecy and attributes the books of the Writings to the 2nd degree, in which a person speaks by the Holy Spirit: "David composed the Psalms, and Solomon the Book of Proverbs, Ecclesiastes, and the Song of Solomon by this spirit; also Daniel, Job, Chronicles, and the rest of the Hagiographa were written in this holy spirit; therefore they are called *ketubim* (Writings, or Written), i.e., written by men inspired by the holy spirit."[4]

Thus, the writers of the third section of the canon were prophets only in a general sense and were distinguished from the authors of the Prophets and from Moses, the author of the Law, who received prophecy through angelic apparitions.[5] David Kimḥi (1160–1235 C.E.) follows Rambam in distinguishing between prophecy and inspiration. Whereas inspiration by the Holy Spirit manifests itself through the employment of a person's normal faculties and words, enhanced by the power of the Spirit, prophecy is the reception of a divine message in a supernatural manner. It is because of this division of revelation into "higher and lower orders" that the books of the third section of Scripture are called the Writings—that is to say, they were written by the power of the Holy Spirit, as opposed to being received through prophetic revelation.[6] Naḥmanides (1194–1270 C.E.) furthers Rambam's thesis by attributing the distinct sections of the Tanak to the status of the individual authors and appeals to the teaching of the rabbis to establish his case. First, Moses was superior to the rest of the prophets, which is confirmed by the higher quality of his prophetic revelation: "Our Rabbis also taught concerning the difference in the degree of prophecy between Moses and the other prophets, and they said: 'What is the difference between Moses and all the prophets? The Rabbis say that all prophets saw

---

4. Moses Maimonides, *The Guide for the Perplexed* (2nd ed.; trans. M. Friedlander; London: Routledge & Keagan Paul, 1904) 242.

5. According to Maimonides, prophetic revelation is always (1) mediated through a voice, a symbolic vision, or a human-like figure (i.e., an angel) and is not a direct encounter with God; and (2) disclosed within the context of a vision or dream, since angels cannot be empirically perceived. Ibid., 243–45.

6. R. David Kimḥi, *On the First Book of Psalms* (trans. R. G. Finch; New York: Macmillan, 1919) 2–3.

through unclear vision. . . . Moses saw through a clear vision'" (Lev. Rab. 1:14).[7] As for the difference between the Prophets and the Writings, the authors of the latter were not officially prophets: "The Sages have already said concerning Daniel: 'They [Haggai, Zechariah, and Malachi] were superior to him, because they were prophets and he was not a prophet' [b. Meg. 3a]. His book, likewise, was not grouped together with the books of the prophets since his affair was with the angel Gabriel."[8] Therefore, according to medieval scholars, the distinction between the Prophets and the Writings and the explanation for Daniel's placement in the latter hinge on the prophetic nature of the material or the prophetic status of the individuals who received the revelation. Likewise, from a modern, form-critical perspective, Gerhard von Rad memorably drew attention to the formal attributes of the book of Daniel that challenged its prophetic character.[9] Daniel is called a wise man (Dan 1:3–5; 2:48–49) and not a נביא.[10] The formulaic introductions frequently observed in prophetic literature, "Thus says the LORD" and "the word of the LORD came," do not appear in Daniel. Instead, Daniel's prophetic activity is generated out of his interpretation of visions and dreams, often with the help of intermediary messengers. According to this conception, an element of inauthenticity attributed to Daniel's person or revelatory experience prevented the book from ascending to the status of a Prophet.

The exclusion of the Writings from Haftarot readings provides another common explanation for Daniel's placement in the third division of the Tanak. In the 1st century and possibly earlier, the Law and Prophets were read regularly in the synagogue every Sabbath.[11] The Writings were only used on special occasions and Psalms only in certain parts of the service.[12] The Tosefta addresses the issue of the exclusion of the Writings from the weekly lectionary: "Rabbi Nehemiah said, 'Why did they say that the Hagiographa may not be read? On account of common writings. For people will say, "The Hagiographa may not be read: how much less may common writings?"'" (t. Šabb. 13.1).[13] This statement indicates that in the same way

---

7. Ramban (Naḥmanides), *Commentary on the Torah* (trans. Charles B. Chavel; New York: Shilo, 1971) 1.229. See also Num 12:6–8, Deut 34:10, and b. Yebam. 49b, which assert that revelation to Moses differed from revelation to all the other prophets.

8. Ibid., 228.

9. Gerhard von Rad, *Old Testament Theology* (trans. D. M. G. Stalker; Edinburgh: Oliver & Boyd, 1967) 2.303–5.

10. Note Klaus Koch's observation that the more accurate title for the figure of Daniel is "man greatly beloved" (Dan 10:11, 19; also 9:23). Koch, "Is Daniel Also among the Prophets?" *Int* 39 (1985) 117–30.

11. See Acts 13:15, 27; 15:21; Luke 4:16; Josephus, *Ag. Ap.* 2.175; Philo, *Somn.* 2.127; m. Meg. 3:4.

12. J. Mann and I. Sonne, *The Bible as Read and Preached in the Old Synagogue* (Cincinnati: Jacob Mann and Hebrew Union College, 1940) 2.11.

13. The prohibition here is only on public reading of the material on the Sabbath. The context of the Tosefta makes clear that private reading of the Writings is permitted, as does the Babylonian Talmud (b. Šabb. 116b).

that common writings were unquestionably prohibited from public reading, the Writings were also excluded, apparently based on some quality that nonreligious literature and the Writings do not share with the Law and the Prophets. According to this line of reasoning, those who arranged the liturgy perceived that Daniel did not adhere to the principles required for a Haftarot reading, which resulted in its classification as a Writing rather than one of the Prophets.[14]

Another explanation for the assumed segregation of Daniel from the Prophets that captivated the scholarly majority for most of the 20th century was that the second division of the canon was "closed" prior to the composition or canonization of the book of Daniel. This view theorizes that the three sections of the Tanak attest three successive stages in the canonization process, when each collection became formally "closed" before subsequent material achieved canonical status.[15] Historical factors and innerbiblical clues provide parameters for the date of the finalization of each section: the closing of the Law was between 500 and 300 B.C.E., of the Prophets during the 2nd century B.C.E., and of the Writings in the 1st century C.E.

According to this reconstruction, the late composition and canonization of the book of Daniel accounts for its omission from the Prophets. One of the few merits of this view is that it sidesteps negative assumptions attached to the Writings and, by implication, the book of Daniel, which is the unavoidable corollary to the explanations explored thus far. On the other hand, it disallows the possibility that an associative logic contributed to the collection and arrangement of the Old Testament material, a notion that will be challenged in the examination to follow. Despite the popularity of this so-called three-stage-canon theory, it is implausible based on what we now believe about the redaction process used in the biblical text, which is that the canon developed linearly, with one section being tightly closed before another section was formed. Though this theory of the canon's formation is being increasingly rejected by modern scholars, it nevertheless persists in biblical commentaries and encyclopedias as a common explanation for the classification of Daniel as one of the Writings rather than the Prophets.[16]

A final explanation for Daniel's presumed elimination from the Prophets is the political and sociological factors in Jewish communities during the Roman era. Klaus Koch suggests that the book was downgraded from the Prophets when certain apocalyptic hopes derived from it were disappointed during the first revolt against Rome. He asserts, "Such disappointed confidence may have been the reason why the influential rabbis displaced

---

14. Robert D. Wilson, *Studies in the Book of Daniel* (New York: Revell, 1938) 2.60–61.

15. Though many scholars contributed to the rise of this theory, Herbert E. Ryle offered the fullest explanation in *The Canon of the Old Testament* (New York: Macmillan, 1892).

16. E.g., John J. Collins, *Daniel* (Hermeneia; Philadelphia: Fortress, 1993) 52.

this dangerous book, separating it from classical prophecy and placing it among the narratives of the time of the Exile like Esther and Ezra."[17] This thesis, according to Koch, provides a reasonable explanation for the "severe handling" of Daniel that is reflected in its "exclusion" from the Prophets and relocation to the Writings.

This synopsis illustrates that a primarily negative view has been attached to the categorization of Daniel in the third section of the Hebrew canon by Jewish and Christian interpreters alike throughout the history of the book's interpretation. It is assumed, based on certain presuppositions about the book's genre and thin historical evidence, that Daniel's location in the Writings reflects a demotion or exclusion from the Prophets. In what follows, two literary effects of the book's position in the Writings will be highlighted for the purpose of casting this classification in a different light. Is it possible that Daniel was assigned to the Writings because of a perceived suitability of the book for that collection? The motif of the survival of the temple vessels and the symbolic significance of the exile in Daniel and other books in the Writings will be explored as a way of inviting a reconsideration of the book's literary classification. I will show that the mutual influence of Daniel and the literary community of the third collection created a distinct hearing for these themes. The continuity and complementarity of the material challenges the assumption that the books of the Writings found themselves collected together by coincidence or by historical factors that had nothing to do with the literary and theological associations now present among the compositions. Furthermore, an examination of the themes and motifs that rise to the surface when Daniel is placed in the Writings demonstrates that the book's Hebrew categorization is anything but unfortunate.

Daniel and the Literary Community of the Writings

The backdrop of exile and the late date of the books that sit alongside Daniel in the Writings (Lamentations, Esther, Ezra–Nehemiah) tether Daniel to this subdivision. Each book, in its own way, presents the tension of the survival or annihilation of the Jewish people while being ruled by foreign kings. In Daniel, Esther, and Ezra–Nehemiah, synchronization notices to Babylonian and Persian rulers (Nebuchadnezzar, Belshazzar, Darius, Ahasuerus, Artaxerxes, and Cyrus) provide historical backdrops for the unfolding narrative and intertextual links between the accounts.

In addition, several narrative conventions in Daniel 1–6 echo features of Esther and Ezra–Nehemiah.[18] In each book, a Jew in exile is serving in

---

17. Koch, *"Daniel among the Prophets?"* 123–24.
18. For a more thorough treatment, see Timothy J. Stone, *The Compilational History of the Megilloth: Canon, Contoured Intertextuality and Meaning in the Writings* (FAT 2/59; Tübingen: Mohr Siebeck, 2013) 153–61.

the Babylonian or Persian king's court and receives special favor on behalf of the Jewish people. Each book portrays villains who conspire against the Jewish hero(es) but whose scheming is frustrated when the king issues decrees in favor of the Jews. Incidentally, this conventional scenario is also found in Lamentations, where the enemy plots the downfall of the speaker of the lament (Lam 3:52–63), but the destruction of the enemy is foreseen (Lam 3:64–66). The advocacy of foreign kings on behalf of the Jews in Daniel, Esther, and Ezra–Nehemiah (also 2 Chronicles 36) communicates an ideology of God's sovereignty over earthly kings and serves the purpose of reinforcing God's preservation of his people despite their tenure in exile. Additional intertextual links are evident between Daniel and the book of Ezra. Both books comprise Hebrew and Aramaic portions with possible structural similarities between the six episodes in Daniel 1–6 and Ezra 1–6, and the four episodes in Daniel 7–12 and Ezra 7–10.[19] For example, both Daniel 9 and Ezra 9 portray the protagonist as confessing guilt on behalf of the nation at the time of the evening sacrifice (Dan 9:21; Ezra 9:4).

One motif that becomes prominent as a result of the juxtaposition of Daniel in the Writings is the preservation of the temple vessels as a symbol of Judah's cultic continuity despite the interruption of exile. Peter Ackroyd has drawn attention to the scope and detail devoted to descriptions of the construction and preservation of the temple vessels in Old Testament and Second Temple Jewish literature.[20] Though the actual fate of the temple vessels as a result of Jerusalem's fall to Babylon is unknown, several biblical passages depict the survival of the vessels for the duration of the exile and their return to Jerusalem for use in the second temple. This creates what Ackroyd calls a "continuity theme" for the sake of bridging the gap between pre- and postexilic communities and cultic practices. He states:

> The community which sought to re-establish itself after the exile, deeply conscious of its ancestry in faith, but also aware of the problem of continuity with that faith, made use of the theme of the vessels, as it made use of other themes, to make good its claim to be the true successor . . . to be directly linked with those who stood on the other side of the exilic gulf.[21]
>
> An examination of the biblical passages detailing the history of the temple vessels bears this out.

The Motif of the Temple Vessels

The temple/tabernacle vessels are given concentrated attention in the Old Testament at key points in Israel's history, particularly as related to

---

19. Jan-Wim Wesselius, "The Writing of Daniel," in *The Book of Daniel: Composition and Reception* (ed. John J. Collins and Peter W. Flint; VTSup 83; Leiden: Brill, 2001) 2.291–310.

20. Peter Ackroyd, "The Temple Vessels: A Continuity Theme," *Studies in the Religious Tradition of the Old Testament* (London: SCM, 1987) 46–75.

21. Ibid., 60.

the tabernacle and temple: their manufacture in the preparation of the tabernacle (Exodus 25–31); the construction of Solomon's temple (1 Kings 7); the destruction of the temple (2 Kings 24–25; 2 Chronicles 36; Jeremiah 52); and the rebuilding of the temple (Ezra 1–6).[22] In the establishment of the tabernacle and the temple, the vessels are presented as essential features of God's dwelling place. Like the tabernacle and temple, the vessels are constructed in accordance with the blueprints provided by God himself (Exodus 25; 2 Chronicles 4). The vessels are not merely instruments that facilitate cultic practice but representations of cultic order according to the divine command and emblems of the divine presence associated with the tabernacle and temple.[23] The temple vessels are synonymous with the temple itself.

This is why the confiscation of some of the temple vessels in 597 B.C.E. was such a notable event (2 Kgs 24:13; 2 Chr 36:7, 10) and why the prophetic showdown of Jeremiah 27–28 concentrated on the return of the temple vessels. In 587 B.C.E., the removal of the temple vessels was again highlighted but for different reasons. This time, in the wake of the destruction of the temple, the vessels were the only surviving emblems of cultic order and divine presence.[24] Yet the biblical text does not offer a univocal account of what happened to the temple vessels when they were seized by Nebuchadnezzar. It is specifically in the Writings that the preservation and restoration of the temple vessels provides a "continuity theme" between the pre- and postexilic communities, frequently in sharp contrast to the portrayal of the temple vessels in the Prophets. The episode in Daniel that features the temple vessels plays a crucial role in the elaboration of this theme in the Writings.

The Temple Vessels in the Prophets

According to 2 Kings 25 and Jeremiah 52, the temple vessels were destroyed in 597 and 587 B.C.E. 2 Kgs 24:13 indicates that, under Jehoiachin, Nebuchadnezzar not only "carried off all the treasures of the house of the Lord" but also "cut in pieces all the vessels of gold in the temple of the Lord."[25] Similarly, 2 Kgs 25:13–15//Jer 52:17–19 describe the destruction of the vessels in the temple for the purpose of salvaging the pure bronze,

---

22. The Hebrew term used for the temple vessels, כְּלִי, occurs over 300 times in the Old Testament and is usually a general reference to containers, furnishings, tools, weapons, clothing, and baggage. K.-M. Beyse, "כְּלִי *kᵉlî*," *TDOT* 7.169–75. The word's distinct reference to the temple vessels is indicated by context and in many cases by the construct *kĕlî-bêt ywhw* or a variation on this form.

23. Ibid., 50–51; Ronald E. Clements, *God and Temple* (Oxford: Blackwell, 1965) 65–67.

24. Winfried Vogel, *The Cultic Motif in the Book of Daniel* (New York: Peter Lang, 2010) 74–76. See also Ackroyd, "Temple Vessels," 55; John Van Seters, "Solomon's Temple: Fact and Ideology in Biblical and Near Eastern Historiography," *CBQ* 59 (1997) 45–57.

25. All Scripture quotations are taken from the English Standard Version unless otherwise noted (Crossway Bibles, 2001).

silver, and gold. Based on the complete destruction of the temple and its sacred artifacts, the depiction in 2 Kings leaves little hope for restoration of the temple and cult, in keeping with the soberness of the wider DtrH in this regard.

In Jeremiah, the portrayal of cultic continuity based on the restoration of the temple vessels is ambiguous at best. In the wake of the deportation of some of the vessels during the 597 B.C.E. siege, the survival of the remaining vessels and restoration of the confiscated vessels becomes the substance of the conflict between Jeremiah and prophets who are speaking falsehood. Jeremiah not only speaks out against the prophecies that the confiscated vessels will soon be returned to Jerusalem (Jer 27:16; 28:6–9, 15); he goes on to declare that the remaining vessels will also be carried to Babylon (Jer 27:19–22). A glimmer of hope accompanies this pronouncement in the MT:

> They [the vessels] shall be carried to Babylon and remain there until the day when I visit them, declares the LORD. Then I will bring them back and restore them to this place. (Jer 27:22)

The phrases "and remain there until the day when I visit them" and "then I will bring them back and restore them to this place," though present in the MT are absent in the LXX. The shorter form corresponds to the portrayal of the destruction of the temple vessels in Jer 52:17–29, recommending the view that the notes of hope are secondary.[26] Even with the longer form of this passage, the overall presentation of Jeremiah does not foster confidence in the perpetuation of the temple vessels for the duration of the exile, ending as it does with an account of the vessels' destruction in the final chapter.

The Temple Vessels in the Writings

By contrast, the preservation and restoration of the temple vessels is a prominent motif in several books of the Writings. Chronicles contains several passages concerned with the well-being of the temple vessels during the era of the monarchy that are not recorded in Samuel–Kings (2 Chr 15:18; 24:14; 25:24; 28:24; 29:18–19). At the same time, Chronicles excludes descriptions of the total destruction of the temple vessels, implying that the vessels remained intact when they were deported to Babylon (2 Chr 36:7, 10, 18). This supposition is supported by the notice in 36:7 that the vessels confiscated during Jehoiakim's reign were stored in the king's palace—a feature that clearly alludes to the opening verses of Daniel.[27] Furthermore, in Chronicles the burning of the temple is described after the vessels have

---

26. Wilhelm Rudolph, *Jeremia* (HAT 1/12; Tübingen: Mohr Siebeck, 1968) 177; Isaac Kalimi and James D. Purvis, "King Jehoiachin and the Vessels of the Lord's House in Biblical Literature," *CBQ* 56 (1994) 449–57.

27. Whereas 2 Kings and Jeremiah present a two-stage deportation of the temple vessels during the reigns of Jehoiachin (2 Kgs 24:13; Jeremiah 27) and Zedekiah (2 Kgs 25:13–17; Jer 52:17–23), 2 Chronicles depicts a three-stage deportation in which vessels

been safely removed (2 Chr 36:18–19). This reverses the order of the portrayal in 2 Kings and Jeremiah, where the temple is burned (2 Kgs 25:9// Jer 52:13) before the plundering of the temple vessels (2 Kgs 25:13–15// Jer 52:17–19). This portrayal offer hopes for the recovery of Judah's cultic institution based on the conservation of the temple vessels. As Knoppers says of the Chronistic version of Judah's history, "The Davidic-Solomonic temple is razed, but the Davidic-Solomonic legacy does not end with the destruction of this shrine. It continues in the deported temple vessels and furnishings."[28]

The Chronistic portrayal clearly anticipates the opening verses of Ezra–Nehemiah, which describe the return of the temple vessels and exiles from Babylon to Jerusalem (Ezra 1:7–11). The link between the Chronistic portrayal of the deportation of the temple vessels intact in the final chapter of Chronicles and their safe return to Jerusalem in the first chapter of Ezra is further secured by the repetition of Cyrus's decree in 2 Chronicles 22–23 and Ezra 1:1–3, which creates a literary association between the two books. Subsequent references to Cyrus's decree in Ezra are accompanied by mention of the restoration of the temple vessels (Ezra 5:13–15; 6:3–5). Furthermore, Ezra emphasizes that the vessels that have been restored are the very same vessels that were removed by Nebuchadnezzar when the temple was destroyed (Ezra 1:7; 5:14; 6:5). Likewise, the rebuilding of the altar and temple is said to conform to the blueprints of the original constructions (Ezra 3:2, 10; cf. 6:3–4; and 1 Kgs 6:2, 36). The overall portrayal of the postexilic temple and cult in Ezra emphasizes restoration of the previous forms rather than reconstruction and renovation.

The Temple Vessels in Daniel

The book of Daniel opens with a statement of Nebuchadnezzar's siege of Jerusalem in the third year of Jehoiakim's reign (Dan 1:1). The notice corresponds to the other biblical accounts of Jerusalem's downfall in 2 Kgs 24:1 and 2 Chr 36:6 and provides the setting for the narrative material that follows. In the next several verses, the reader is provided with additional details, which set the stage for the ensuing story: the deportation of Judah's most promising youths to Nebuchadnezzar's palace (v. 3–4), the specific mention of Daniel and his three friends (v. 6), the fact that these men excelled in wisdom and knowledge (v. 4), and the assignment of a daily ration of food (v. 5). Verses 1–6 of the first chapter of Daniel were undoubtedly

---

were confiscated during the reign of Jehoiakim as well (2 Chr 36:7), thus providing a literary precedent for Dan 1:1–2.

28. Gary Knoppers, "Treasures Won and Lost: Royal (Mis)appropriations in Kings and Chronicles," in *The Chronicler as Author: Studies in Text and Texture* (ed. M. Patrick Graham and Steven L. McKenzie; JSOTSup 263; Sheffield: Sheffield Academic Press, 1999) 181–208 (esp. p. 207).

composed with Dan 1:8–6:28 in view, as a way of introducing and unifying the various tales.[29]

In this regard, mention of the deportation of the temple vessels twice at the beginning of the introduction (Dan 1:2) provides a foreshadowing of the despoliation of the vessels that occurs in ch. 5 in the account of Belshazzar (Dan 5:2, 23).[30] Nevertheless, the importance assigned to them in the introductory verses of the book seems disproportionate with their role in the wider narrative, where they do not appear again for several chapters and then are only mentioned briefly. The juxtaposition of Daniel alongside other books in the Writings where the fate of the temple vessels is pronounced illuminates the significance of the temple vessels in these opening verses of the book. That these introductory verses of Daniel were perhaps affixed as a final compositional touch further recommends the possibility that they refer to material, not only within, but also outside the book, which by that time had begun to assume an anthological identity as part of a collection of sacred literature.

Daniel presents a glimpse of the temple vessels in between the portrayals of Chronicles and Ezra–Nehemiah. Where Chronicles presents the vessels at the transition between monarchy and exile, and Ezra–Nehemiah the transition between exile and return, Daniel relates the welfare of the vessels during their tenure in exile. Chronicles and Ezra–Nehemiah are careful to report that the vessels were safeguarded in Babylon in the king's house or temple (2 Chr 36:7; Ezra 1:7; 5:14). This detail is also emphasized in Dan 1:2 with the double mention that the vessels were placed in the house of the king's god.[31] The fact that they are called "the vessels of the house of God" earlier in the same verse highlights the irony of their new location in the house of a foreign god.

This portrayal of the vessels' being stored in the house of the king's god also foreshadows the sacrilege committed in Daniel 5, where Belshazzar uses the temple vessels to serve wine to his guests during a great feast. In light of the distinct function of the temple vessels as furnishings for the house of God and instruments for the service of a sacred meal to the divinity,[32] Belshazzar's action is nothing short of blasphemy. The text makes clear that the handwriting on the wall is the immediate effect of Belshazzar's misuse of the temple vessels (Dan 5:4–5, 23–24). Belshazzar provokes God

---

29. Collins, *Daniel*, 35.

30. The Aramaic term for the vessels in Dan 5:2, 23, *māʾn*, corresponds to the Hebrew term, *kĕlî*, in Dan 1:2. See Vogel, *Cultic Motif*, 74 n. 276.

31. The first mention of "the house of his god" in Dan 1:2 is not attested in some Greek manuscripts. As the more difficult reading, the repetition in the MT is probably the better reading. See ibid., 76 n. 285.

32. Menahem Haran, "The Divine Presence in the Israelite Cult and the Cultic Institution," *Bib* 50 (1969) 255.

by disregarding the emblems of God's power and presence. His punishment correspondingly illustrates the ongoing power and divine presence resident in the temple vessels, even though they have been separated from their proper context within the Jerusalem temple and cult.

The deeper theological significance of this encounter is revolutionary for the Judean captives, who are grappling with the implications of their situation. Have they, by their persistent disregard for God's commands, invalidated his covenant relationship with them? Have they been forsaken by God? Daniel 5 demonstrates God's persistent concern for his people even in the midst of exile. Though God has abandoned his habitation in Jerusalem, he has not abandoned his people. He has accompanied them into exile, and the temple vessels serve as tangible symbols of God's ongoing presence, power, and restorative intentions for his people.

The claim of Boice that the temple vessels in Dan 1:2 are the "theme of the book and the key to everything that follows"[33] is difficult to support based on the testimony of Daniel as an isolated witness. But when combined with the other accounts of the temple vessels in the Writings (and when compared with the portrayal of the temple vessels in the Prophets), their symbolic significance in Daniel is revealed. Similarly, just as Daniel needs the other witnesses in the Writings to clarify the implications of the temple vessels, Chronicles and Ezra–Nehemiah are dependent on the depiction of the ongoing power and presence of the temple vessels in Daniel. Daniel provides the motif of cultic continuity through the preservation of the temple vessels with an indispensable image of the enduring efficacy of the sacred implements despite the interruption of exile in Babylon. In the talmudic order of the Writings, which begins with Chronicles and ends with Ezra–Nehemiah, this intervening account in Daniel is heard between the depiction of the seizure of the vessels in 2 Chronicles 36 and their restoration in Ezra 1. In the Masoretic order, Daniel, Ezra–Nehemiah, and Chronicles form a cluster of books at the end of the collection, which concentrates the motif of the temple vessels inside a smaller range of material.

The Interpretation of the Exile

Thus far, we have seen that Daniel's placement in the Writings contributes to a motif of the preservation of the temple vessels as expressed in Chronicles and Ezra–Nehemiah by illustrating God's continued presence with his people in exile. This portrayal has additional implications for the interpretation of Judah's captivity in the Writings collection.

Exile in Daniel

The events in the book of Daniel are contextualized in Judah's exile in Babylon and Persia. However, through a series of visionary depictions, the

---

33. James M. Boice, *Daniel: An Expositional Commentary* (Grand Rapids, MI: Zondervan, 1989) 15.

material speaks to events beyond the exilic purview. By attaching these future-oriented visions (especially those in chs. 2 and 7–12) to the narrative account of Daniel's tenure in exile, a correlation is created between the oppression of the Babylonian Exile and the persecution of Israel under subsequent foreign powers foreseen in the visions. The result is that the exile is portrayed as a recurring experience in Israel's history. Rather than presenting the Babylonian Exile as the negative climax of Israel's story, as in the Former Prophets, or as the decisive indicator of God's judgment and salvation, as in the Latter Prophets, the exile is one instance in a long series of oppressive encounters. A closer look at the interpretation of the book of Daniel substantiates this view.

Daniel portrays a movement through time beginning with the Babylonian era, extending through the periods of three more world powers, and culminating in the inauguration of God's kingdom. A framework of four world powers that will precede God's rule is established in ch. 2 with the vision of a man whose head, chest and arms, torso and thighs, legs and feet represent four kingdoms, beginning at the head with the Kingdom of Babylon (Dan 2:37–38). The visions in chs. 7–12 expand on Daniel's vision in ch. 2 and focus on the fourth kingdom, which will be far worse than the previous three.[34] Out of this kingdom shall arise a "little horn" (7:8; 8:9), a ruler who will exceed all other kings in blasphemy and persecution of God's people. This king will be overthrown (7:26; 8:25; 9:27; 11:45) and his demise will usher in the everlasting kingdom of the Most High (2:44; 7:27). The identity of this final earthly king is not explicitly stated in the book of Daniel, but his nation arises from the fragmentation of the Greek Empire (8:21–22). Furthermore, the biblical descriptions of his speaking out against the Most High, persecuting the saints, removing the regular burnt offering, and abominating the sanctuary (7:25; 8:11–13, 24–25; 9:27; 11:36–38) correspond to the historical reign of the Seleucid king Antiochus IV Epiphanes (175–163 B.C.E.) and probably indicate a Maccabean date for the composition of chs. 7–12.

Yet in the ongoing reception of the book, the figural potential of the book invited an expansion of meaning beyond its Maccabean context to include later periods of oppression. When the kingdom of the Most High did not materialize immediately after the death of Antiochus IV Epiphanes, the identity of the "little horn" was recognized to include subsequent kings and kingdoms at whose hands the saints were persecuted, such as the Roman Empire in the 1st century C.E. This is precisely the hermeneutical move exhibited in the reinterpretation of Daniel in 2 Esd 12:10–12. Thus, these descriptions of the Maccabean situation in Daniel were understood to contain typological meaning with reference to a future time, and the "little

---

34. Brevard Childs, *Introduction to the Old Testament as Scripture* (Philadelphia: Fortress, 1979) 616–17.

horn" signified any political power that was antagonistic to God's chosen people. Because Daniel's visions of persecution were set within the context of the exile of the Babylonian and Persian periods, the exile itself was dehistoricized and allowed to represent typical experiences of persecution for God's chosen people. Oppression under Nebuchadnezzar, Antiochus IV Epiphanes, Nero, and more are all types of Israel's exilic experience and the ultimate victory of God's people as represented in Daniel.

This understanding of the portrayal of exile in Daniel sheds light on the reference to Jeremiah's prophecy of a 70-year exile (Jer 25:11–12) in Daniel 9. The prior word of the Lord to Jeremiah is not retracted but is extended through reinterpretation; Jeremiah's 70-year exile is prolonged sevenfold (Dan 9:2, 24).[35] Without compromising the veracity of God's word or the validity of Israel's hope, the definition and extent of Israel's exile are broadened. Daniel's depiction of a recurring or protracted exile is accompanied by corroborating portrayals in other books of the Writings.

Exile in the Writings

Though Ezra–Nehemiah begins with a statement about Israel's permission to return to Jerusalem and rebuild the temple, it quickly becomes apparent that the restoration following Cyrus's decree in 538 B.C.E. is a far cry from the full-scale ingathering and national flourishing depicted in the Prophets. Rebuilding efforts are thwarted by political opposition (Ezra 4; Nehemiah 2, 4, 6), inhabitants of Jerusalem continue to pay a heavy tax to foreign rulers (Ezra 4:13; Neh 5:4–5), and failure to live up to the demands of the Law creates internal conflict (Ezra 9–10; Nehemiah 5, 9, 13). Even the rebuilding of the temple is tinged with disappointment. Though it is a cause for celebration, the shouts of joy are indistinguishable from the sounds of weeping by those who remember the glory of the former temple (Ezra 3:12–13).

Both Ezra and Nehemiah admit that, despite the return to Jerusalem, the slavery of exile continues (Ezra 9:7–9; Neh 9:36–37). Furthermore, the overview of Israel's history in Nehemiah 9 emphasizes the repeated experiences of oppression and slavery that the nation has suffered leading up to and including the Persian dominion over Jerusalem in the wake of the return (Neh 9:9, 17, 26–27, 28, 30, 36–37). According to Eskenazi, the books of Ezra–Nehemiah, though presenting the return from exile, restoration of the temple, and rebuilding of the city as the fulfillment of God's promises to his people at the same time emphasize that "the restored community will have setbacks. There is no 'once for all' resolution. . . . Tenacity, building and rebuilding by a faithful community, generation after generation:

---

35. See Michael Fishbane's discussion of this passage as an example of "mantological exegesis" or the reinterpretation and reapplication of an older oracular *traditum* by means of a subsequent *traditio*. *Biblical Interpretation in Ancient Israel* (Oxford: Clarendon, 1985) 443–46, 482–89.

this is Ezra–Nehemiah's distinctive vision of restoration."[36] Thus, Ezra–Nehemiah, like Daniel, portrays the exile as part of a larger cycle of sin, judgment, restoration, and return that neither begins nor ends with the Babylonian Exile.

A similar presentation of exile as a recurring experience is found in Chronicles. The Chronicler periodizes the history of Judah's monarchy into intervals of exile and restoration. Through the key words *seek* and *forsake* and through the evaluative assessment of each king, the author highlights correspondences between the nation's unfaithfulness and experiences resembling exile, on the one hand, and faithfulness and experiences of restoration, on the other. In this way, exile and restoration are portrayed as typical occurrences in the life of Israel.

It is clear in Lamentations that the sufferer is in the midst of exile and indeed that the shock of Jerusalem's destruction is still quite fresh. The depiction of the people's slavery in their own land in Lamentations 5 echoes the situation in Ezra–Nehemiah after the return:

> Our inheritance has been turned over to strangers, our homes to foreigners. . . .
> We must pay for the water we drink; the wood we get must be bought.
> . . .
> We have given the hand to Egypt, and to Assyria, to get bread enough.
> (Lam 5:2, 4, 6)

Furthermore, the lingering questions and lack of resolution at the end of the book imply that these conditions may continue indefinitely: "Why do you forget us forever, why do you forsake us for so many days? . . . Renew our days of old—unless you have utterly rejected us, and you remain exceedingly angry with us" (Lam 5:20–22).

Turning to the book of Esther—the portrayal of a prolonged exile is evident in the absence of any mention of a return. Though Cyrus's decree granting permission for the Jews to return to Jerusalem and rebuild their temple has already been issued when the events of Esther take place, the characters have apparently chosen to remain in Persia. The Jewish characters in Esther, though committed to preserving their national identity and well-being, seem content to remain in exile. This restoration void in the book of Esther is particularly striking since the physical and spiritual restoration of the people is a prominent theme in other Old Testament books, particularly those that are adjacent to Esther canonically and share an exilic context: Lamentations, Ezra–Nehemiah, Daniel.[37] Thus, through its silence on the issue of restoration, Esther implies a prolongation of exile.

---

36. Tamara Cohn Eskenazi, *In an Age of Prose: A Literary Approach to Ezra–Nehemiah* (SBLMS 36; Atlanta: Scholars Press, 1988) 122.

37. Stone, *Compilational History*, 119.

Two additional features pertaining to the portrayal of exile in this cluster of books are noteworthy. First, it is not a coincidence that in each of these books God's sovereignty is emphasized, despite and even by means of Israel's long tenure in exile. In particular, the foreign rulers under whom Israel is enslaved are portrayed as themselves subservient to Israel's God. Frequently, this compliance of foreign rulers with God's supreme rule is depicted through the issuing of royal decrees that either initially or ultimately correspond to God's will.[38] Rather than operating autonomously, the decrees and actions of the foreign kings are presented as according perfectly with God's intentions for his chosen people.

For example, Ezra states that "the LORD stirred up the spirit of Cyrus king of Persia, so that he made a proclamation throughout all his kingdom" (Ezra 1:1) and that this decree fulfills the word of the LORD by the prophet Jeremiah. Of the letter written by Artaxerxes in support of Ezra's return to Jerusalem, the text states that "the LORD, the God of our fathers . . . put such a thing as this into the heart of the king" (Ezra 7:27). Though the decree of Artaxerxes in Ezra 4 is in opposition to the Jews, the narrative portrayal suggests an overthrow of this ordinance by Darius in Ezra 6 (perhaps an explanation for the nonchronological arrangement of these chapters) that is not only in support of the rebuilding project but makes provision for all the necessary supplies and protection (Ezra 6:8–12).

Similarly, Esther, through a series of "coincidences" occurring in the Persian king's court, insinuates that God is at work behind the scenes securing the well-being of his people.[39] Once again, a decree issued by the king for the destruction of the Jews (Esth 3:13) is countermanded by a successive decree in support of the Jews (Esth 8:9–14).

The book of Daniel likewise contains two episodes in which decrees issued against the Jews are subsequently reversed by the king. Nebuchadnezzar's decree that all people must worship the golden image or face annihilation (Dan 3:4–6) is replaced by a decree that anyone who speaks out against the God of the Jews will be executed (Dan 3:29). So also, Darius's ordinance that petitions be made to no god but the king for 30 days (Dan 6:8–9[7–8]) is substituted by a decree that people are to tremble and fear before the God of Israel (Dan 6:27–28[26–27]). Furthermore, the book of Daniel portrays even more explicitly than Ezra–Nehemiah and Esther the submission of foreign rulers to God's authority by placing affirmations of God's power on the lips of foreign kings! Both Nebuchadnezzar (Dan 3:33[4:3]; 4:31–32, 34[34–35, 37]) and Darius (Dan 6:27–28[26–27]) worship God, pronouncing God's imperishable kingdom and enduring do-

---

38. For a thorough treatment of the role of authoritative documents in Ezra–Nehemiah, see Eskenazi, *In an Age of Prose*.

39. David J. A. Clines, *The Esther Scroll: The Story of the Story* (JSOT Supp 30; Sheffield Academic Press, 1984) 155–156.

minion (cf. Dan 3:33[4:3] and 6:27[26]). This affirmation of God's ultimate rule voiced by pagan kings articulates an undeniable theme of the book of Daniel.

It is significant that this same conviction is echoed at the end of the book of Lamentations: "But you, O LORD, reign forever, your throne endures to all generations" (Lam 5:19). While Israel's lingering experience of exile suggests that God is no longer concerned about his people or has lost control of the affairs of humanity, these books of the Writings distinctly voice God's continuing sovereignty and involvement.

A second feature of exile in these books at the end of the Writings is that the ongoing exile is closely associated with the people's continuing sin. In Daniel, the extension of Jeremiah's prophecy of a 70-year exile follows Daniel's confession of the nation's corporate guilt (Daniel 9). In Ezra–Nehemiah, declarations of ongoing slavery are contextualized within prayers confessing the people's ethnic and cultic impurity (Ezra 9:6–15; Neh 9:34–37). Lamentations repeatedly attributes the nation's exile to the people's transgressions (e.g., Lam 1:5, 8, 14; 3:40–42; 4:22). Chronicles links exilic conditions in Judah's history to periods of unfaithfulness. And in Esther, the lack of return to Jerusalem is (appropriately) combined with the absence of prayer, festival observance, or mention of God. This pervasive sin that characterizes the ongoing exile makes God's sustained power and presence all the more remarkable. In spite of the people's unfaithfulness, God remains faithful.

Conclusion

Thus, we have seen that in the cluster of books at the end of the Writings—Lamentations, Esther, Daniel, Ezra–Nehemiah, and, according to some lists, Chronicles—a distinct theology of exile is evident. On the one hand, exile is a repetitive, even continuous feature in the nation's history; on the other hand, God's sovereignty is still operating on behalf of the people in the midst of their exiles. This power is portrayed through the acquiescence of foreign kings to God's intentions, particularly the frailty of human actions and declarations that oppose God's purposes for his people. Moreover, the continued existence of the temple vessels symbolizes God's continued presence and restorative intentions for Israel as a cultic community, despite its persistent disloyalty and its current alienation from religious institutions.

Julius Steinberg suggests that the books of Lamentations, Daniel, Esther, and Ezra–Nehemiah make up a "national-historical" subcollection within the Writings.[40] According to Steinberg, the arrangement of the books

---

40. Julius Steinberg, *Die Ketuvim: Ihr Aufbau und ihre Botschaft* (BBB 152; Hamburg: Philo, 2006) 449–50.

reflects a movement from sorrow to joy, with the narratives of Daniel, Esther, and Ezra–Nehemiah providing diverse responses to the unresolved request that concludes the book of Lamentations. To be sure, the joy is tempered by an awareness of the nation's guilt—both in the past and recurring in the present—a sense of the former glory that has been lost, and a need for ongoing and more-complete restoration. However, in answer to the plea of Lamentations, the books of Daniel, Esther, and Ezra–Nehemiah reinforce the fact that God has not utterly rejected his people but is near and ready to come to their aid.

It remains unclear precisely when Daniel was assigned to the Writings. However, the thematic and literary features present in the book that coordinate with elements found elsewhere in the third collection highlight the appropriateness of the assemblage. Whether or not Daniel's assignment to the Writings was motivated by a desire to highlight these associations, the effect of the juxtaposition is significant. The addition of Daniel transposes all the components of this corpus. Now the books of the Writings are heard in light of Daniel. The distinct portrayals of the exile and Judah's hope as portrayed in Daniel influence the way these same themes are understood in other books of the Writings. Likewise, Daniel is cast in a new light when contextualized within the third section of the Hebrew canon. Elements that otherwise sound as isolated notes now harmonize with notes in the same key elsewhere in the Writings, thus creating thematic repetition and coherence. Far from detracting from the significance of the book, as assumed throughout the history of interpretation, the assignment of Daniel to the Writings promotes a distinct and crucial hearing of the material.

Bibliography

Ackroyd, Peter. *Studies in the Religious Tradition of the Old Testament*. London: SCM, 1987.

Beyse, K.-M. "כְּלִי *kᵉlî*." *TDOT* 7.169–75.

Brandt, Peter. *Endgestalten des Kanons: Das Arrangement der Schriften Israels in der jüdischen und christlichen Bibel*. BBB 31. Berlin: Philo, 2001.

Boice, James M. *Daniel: An Expositional Commentary*. Grand Rapids, MI: Zondervan, 1989.

Childs, Brevard. *Introduction to the Old Testament as Scripture*. Philadelphia: Fortress, 1979.

Clements, Ronald E. *God and Temple*. Oxford: Blackwell, 1965.

Clines, David J. A. *The Esther Scroll: The Story of the Story*. JSOTSup 30. Sheffield: Sheffield Academic Press, 1984.

Collins, John J. *Daniel*. Hermeneia. Philadelphia: Fortress, 1993.

Eskenazi, Tamara Cohn. *In an Age of Prose: A Literary Approach to Ezra–Nehemiah*. SBLMS 36. Atlanta: Scholars Press, 1988.

Fishbane, Michael. *Biblical Interpretation in Ancient Israel*. Oxford: Clarendon, 1985.

Haran, Menahem. "The Divine Presence in the Israelite Cult and the Cultic Institution." *Bib* 50 (1969) 251–67.

Kalimi, Isaac, and James D. Purvis. "King Jehoiachin and the Vessels of the Lord's House in Biblical Literature." *CBQ* 56 (1994) 449–57.

Kimḥi, R. David. *On the First Book of Psalms.* Translated by R. G. Finch. New York: Macmillan, 1919.

Knoppers, Gary. "Treasures Won and Lost: Royal (Mis)appropriations in Kings and Chronicles." Pp. 181–208 in *The Chronicler as Author: Studies in Text and Texture.* Edited by M. Patrick Graham and Steven L. McKenzie. JSOTSup 263. Sheffield: Sheffield Academic Press, 1999.

Koch, Klaus. "Is Daniel Also among the Prophets?" *Int* 39 (1985) 117–30.

Maimonides, Moses. *The Guide for the Perplexed.* Translated by M. Friedlander. 2nd ed. London: Routledge & Keagan Paul, 1904.

Mann, J., and I. Sonne. *The Bible as Read and Preached in the Old Synagogue.* Cincinnati: Jacob Mann and Hebrew Union College, 1940.

Mason, Steven. "Josephus and His Twenty-Two Book Canon." Pp. 110–27 in *The Canon Debate.* Edited by Lee Martin McDonald and James A. Sanders. Peabody, MA: Hendrickson, 2002.

Rad, Gerhard von. *Old Testament Theology.* Translated by D. M. G. Stalker. Edinburgh: Oliver & Boyd, 1967.

Ramban (Naḥmanides). *Commentary on the Torah.* Translated by Charles B. Chavel. New York: Shilo, 1971.

Rudolph, Wilhelm. *Jeremia.* HAT 1/12. Tübingen: Mohr Siebeck, 1968.

Ryle, Herbert E. *The Canon of the Old Testament.* New York: Macmillan, 1892.

Steinberg, Julius. *Die Ketuvim: Ihr Aufbau und ihre Botschaft.* BBB 152. Hamburg: Philo, 2006.

Stone, Timothy J. *The Compilational History of the Megilloth: Canon, Contoured Intertextuality and Meaning in the Writings.* FAT 2/59. Tübingen: Mohr Siebeck, 2013.

Van Seters, John. "Solomon's Temple: Fact and Ideology in Biblical and Near Eastern Historiography." *CBQ* 59 (1997) 45–57.

Vogel, Winfried. *The Cultic Motif in the Book of Daniel.* New York: Peter Lang, 2010.

Wesselius, Jan-Wim. "The Writing of Daniel" Pp. 291–310 in *The Book of Daniel: Composition and Reception.* Edited by John J. Collins and Peter W. Flint. VTSup 83. Leiden: Brlll, 2001.

Wilson, Robert D. *Studies in the Book of Daniel.* New York: Revell, 1938.

Chronicles as the Intended Conclusion to the Old Testament Canon

HENDRIK J. KOOREVAAR

Introduction: Main Problems and Presuppositions

In this essay, I will argue that the book of Chronicles was written with the intention of closing and sealing the Old Testament canon. Before making the case, I must discuss a few possible objections that could be raised:

1. Chronicles must have originated as the last book of the Old Testament Canon. If one or more books of the Old Testament had been written later, the thesis could not be sustained.[1]

2. The place of Chronicles in the so-called Alexandrian Canon (LXX, Vulgate) must be clarified. Unlike most of the Masoretic collections of the Old Testament, where Chronicles comes last, in the Alexandrian Canon it appears in the second main part, among the historical books, in the order Chronicles, Ezra, and Nehemiah. The historical books are arranged based on chronological considerations. If this order is original, the thesis could not be sustained.

3. The extent of the Chronistic work: related to point 2, Chronicles, Ezra, and Nehemiah are seen as one continuous historical work, written by an author who has been given the name "Chronicler." If

---

Author's note: This article was originally published in *Jahrbuch für evangelikale Theologie* 11 (1997) 42–76, and has been updated slightly for the present publication.

1. However, the problem is too extensive to be discussed adequately here. As an example, one could address the vulnerability of language-based arguments by which scholars date the book of Daniel (based on the Maccabean hypothesis) to ca. 150 B.C. This dating stands in strong contrast to the information given in the book itself that points to an origin around the end of the 6th century B.C. (Dan 7:1, 8:1, 9:1–2; the writing commission appears in 12:4). The dating in the 2nd century is partly based on the form of the Hebrew and the Aramaic of the book, a theory that is now outdated, as K. Koch states in his overview. According to Koch, the Maccabean hypothesis, which for 150 years was based on Aramaic-language arguments, can no longer be considered valid (K. Koch, *Daniel* [Erträge der Forschung; Darmstadt: Wissenschaftliche Buchgesellschaft, 1980] 45–46). The argument for dating the Hebrew of Daniel also seems to have been undermined. G. L. Archer, *Das Hebräische im Buch Daniel verglichen mit den Schriften der Sekte von Qumran* (Basel: FETA, 1972); idem, "The Hebrew of Daniel," in *The Law and the Prophets* (ed. J. H. Skilton; Nutley, NJ: Presbyterian and Reformed, 1974) 160–69; A. Waelkens, *De datering van het boek Daniël onderzocht* (M.A. thesis, Evangelisch-theologische Faculteit, 1991).

the theory of a Chronistic History is correct, the thesis could not be maintained.

4. The place of Chronicles in the Palestinian Canon. In some Hebrew manuscripts, Chronicles does not form the ending but the beginning of the third part of the Old Testament canon. If this placement was correct, it is doubtful that the closing character of Chronicles as given in the main thesis could be sustained.

On the other hand, if the above-mentioned thesis proves sound, further conclusions could be drawn:

1. Regarding the dating and authorship of Chronicles: the Chronicler would have been a character of high authority in his own time if he was able to write a book to which nothing more could be added by those who guarded the canon after him.
2. Regarding the theological purpose of Chronicles: if it was the intent of the Chronicler to conclude and round off the collection of Holy Scriptures as a canon, then this should be recognizable from the content and rhetorical features of the book. The theological purpose of Chronicles should correlate with the intention described above.

The Place of Chronicles in the Alexandrian Canon

In most common editions of the Bible, the books of Chronicles directly follow 1–2 Kings. This fact has long caused exegetes to question the sense of this book's being a part of the canon. In the Septuagint tradition, it is called Paralipomena, meaning "leftovers," which suggests that it was intended to be a supplement to Kings.

Over the centuries, there have been many discussions about the extent and order of the canon. The main point of discussion has been the question of whether to use the Palestinian or the Alexandrian canon. Most Old Testament scholars regard the Palestinian canon as oldest.[2]

The most important arguments in favor of the Palestinian canon over the Alexandrian canon are well known:

1. The Jews recognize only the TaNaK, the Hebrew Old Testament, as Holy Scripture.
2. Apocryphal books exist only in the Greek versions; there are only a few instances in which we have access to an original (fragmentary) Hebrew or Aramaic text.
3. The septuagintal manuscripts are far from uniform. Not all of the Apocrypha is found in all manuscripts; there is extra material as well.

---

2. E. Zenger, ed., *Einleitung in das Alte Testament* (Studienbücher Theologie 1/1; Stuttgart: Kohlhammer, 1995) 28–29.

4. The view that the "Alexandrian" canon is a Jewish canon is patently incorrect.

a. The tradition of the Septuagint reaches us not as Jewish but as Christian Scripture from the 4th–5th century C.E. It was received as a collection together with the books of the New Testament. It does not follow that the books contained in the LXX formed the canon of the Jewish community in Alexandria centuries ago; there is no evidence for this.

b. If the Letter of Aristeas is taken seriously, the impetus for the formation of the Septuagint was the Egyptian-Hellenistic authorities. Therefore, based on its origins, the Septuagint was not a Jewish undertaking but a heathen.

The question about the way that apocryphal literature entered into the Christian Codices is not answered with these arguments, however. Perhaps we can agree with Oskar Skarsaune,[3] who posits a double canon in early Christianity: (1) a shorter, more critical canon for the scholars, agreeing with the Jewish canon; and (b) a broader, less critical canon for lay believers. That the popular canon was being accepted more and more and that it was largely circulated was due to a dearth of capable biblical scholars in the 2nd century to support the churches that had a more simplistic approach.

In the Protestant realm, another problem exists. Because of its orientation to the Hebrew Old Testament, the Apocrypha was not accepted as canonical by the Reformers. However, even though the extent of the canon was different from the Alexandrian canon (or rather, the Vulgate), strangely enough, the order of biblical books even in Protestant Bibles was based on the Septuagint. This happened despite the fact that the Protestant order of books is not found in any manuscript or old canon list. It was the result of a compromise whereby on the one hand people wanted to start from Hebrew origins, but on the other hand the connection with later tradition—mainly the Vulgate—was retained. In any case, the result meant a change in the canonical structure of the Old Testament that was not without consequences for canonical Old Testament theology.

The Extent of the Chronistic Work

The thesis that the books of Chronicles, Ezra, and Nehemiah (in this order) originally formed a continuous, integrated literary work was presented in 1832 by L. Zunz.[4] Until recently, most Old Testament scholars followed

---

3. See O. Skarsaune, "Kodeks og kanon: Om bruk og avgrensing av de gammeltestamentlige skrifter I oldkirken," in *Text and Theology* (FS M. Sæbø; ed. A. Tangberg; Oslo: Verbum, 1994) 237–75; summarized by C. T. Begg in *Old Testament Abstracts* 17/2 (1994) 258–59.

4. H. G. M. Williamson, *Israel in the Books of Chronicles* (Cambridge: Cambridge University Press, 1977) 5, referring to L. Zunz, 1832, in ch. 2.

his position, and his arguments went unchallenged. People were so convinced by it that, for example, Rudolph[5] mentioned the divergent view of van den Bussche as a curiosity and then rejected it.

The most important arguments in favor of the unity of Chronicles, Ezra, and Nehemiah are as follows:

1. Chronicles ends the same way that Ezra begins (compare 2 Chr 36:22–23 with Ezra 1:1–4).
2. The apocryphal book of 1 Esdras compiles material from the last two chapters of Chronicles, the book of Ezra (but changing the order), and Nehemiah 8, supplementing it with other material. This means that 1 Esdras begins with the Feast of Passover and ends with the Feast of Tabernacles, thereby demonstrating in an exemplary manner the literary cohesion and continuity of the statements made in the books of Chronicles, Ezra, and Nehemiah.
3. The three books use the same language and style.

Recently, these arguments have been challenged. In the last two decades, the discussion has changed enough that those who posit a distinction between Ezra–Nehemiah on the one hand and Chronicles on the other cannot continue to be marginalized. According to De Vries,[6] the works that contributed most to this turn of scholarly opinion are those of S. Japhet, H. G. M. Williamson, and R. Braun. All of these scholars have seriously considered the position of a unified Chronistic Work but have rejected it as untenable. Others follow them in this. Naturally, some scholars oppose this decline of the previous consensus. R. J. Shaver,[7] for example, has made a considerable effort to refute the arguments against the Chronistic Work. Presently, scholarship seems to be divided; neither of the parties can claim to hold the majority position. The theory of a Chronistic Work is no longer a scholarly position that can be assumed. Some points of this discussion are briefly outlined here.

The Almost Identical Texts at the End of Chronicles and the Beginning of Ezra

2 Chr 36:22–23 and Ezra 1:1–4 contain the Persian king Cyrus's commission to the Jews to return to Jerusalem and rebuild the temple. In the past, the fact that this sentence appears twice was interpreted as an instruction to read the books together. At this point, the objections come along: the writer of a unified work would hardly have written the same text twice, one after the other. Against this, it can be argued:

---

5. W. Rudolph, *Chronikbücher* (HAT 1/21; Tübingen: Mohr Siebeck, 1955) iii, referring to H. van den Bussche, 1950.

6. S. J. De Vries, *1 and 2 Chronicles* (FOTL 11; Grand Rapids, MI: Eerdmans, 1990) 8–9.

7. R. J. Shaver, *Torah and the Chronicler's History Work: An Inquiry into the Chronicles References to Laws, Festivals, and Cultic Institutions in Relationship to Pentateuchal Legislation* (BJS 196; Atlanta: Scholars Press, 1989) 41–71.

1. In the original version of ChrH, the statement probably appeared only one time. After the separation of Ezra and Chronicles, the sentence was repeated to keep the connection. That this explanation is no more than speculation is perfectly obvious.
2. The doublet might have been considered a "stichic" way of structuring the text by the author or a later redactor in order to point out an important division in the text. However, it would be strange for this sort of division to occur only between Chronicles and Ezra and not in Chronicles itself. What is more, the so-called "stichic" repetition (Ezra 1:1–4) is longer than the first statement (2 Chr 36:22–23). So the question arises: which of the two versions of Cyrus's decree is original?
3. The doublet might have appeared because the scroll was full, so the writer began a new scroll. However, wouldn't the writer of such a large work have calculated the size of the work and known beforehand that it would not fit on one scroll? Wouldn't he then have chosen a division near the middle of 2 Chronicles?

The arguments in favor of an entire Chronistic Work are not ultimately convincing. 2 Chr 36:22–23 seems to be secondary to Ezra 1:1–4. The Chronicles version is shorter and ends with יְהוָה אֱלֹהָיו עִמּוֹ וְיָעַל "Yhwh his God (is) with him, and he may go up." This is an appropriate, fitting, theologically controlled final word for the book of Chronicles. On the other hand, the text of Cyrus's decree at the beginning of Ezra is longer and commissions the returnees to support the exiles. In the following chapters, the book describes this decree's accomplishment, which means that the text has an introductory function here. For the Chronicler's purposes, the commission is no longer of interest; he concentrates on the important question whether Yhwh is with his people when they return, after all that has happened.

Therefore, the writer of Chronicles confines himself to the first part of the decree, the fuller form of which is provided in Ezra. Moreover, he gives the wording a little twist.[8] While Ezra 1:3a reads, יְהִי אֱלֹהָיו עִמּוֹ וְיָעַל, "May his God be with him, and may he go up," 2 Chr 36:23b says, יְהוָה אֱלֹהָיו. The Chronicler replaces the word יְהִי "he may be" (jussive) with יהוה, which is the covenant name for God.[9] The change is very small from an orthographic point of view, but it has considerable effect: the Chronicler avoided ending with יְהִי אֱלֹהָיו עִמּוֹ וְיָעַל, which would have left open the identity of

---

8. Besides, the Chronicler always writes the name Cyrus (Kores) plene. In Ezra, the name Kores is only written plene in the first instance of the decree, in 1:1a, but it is written defectively after this. This could point to a later time for Chronicles.

9. De Vries, *1 and 2 Chronicles*, 9, uses another argument to demonstrate that the decree of Cyrus in 2 Chronicles 36 is a quotation from Ezra 1. He says that the original text of Chronicles did not have Yhwh but יְהִי "he will be." Compare the LXX.

the particular deity. By using the name Yʜwʜ, he ensured that there would be no misunderstanding about the deity who is acting here. Thereby, the Chronicler shows himself to be a theologian who closes his book with a statement of belief: Yʜwʜ surely will be with the one who is going up to Jerusalem!

Literary and Theological Differences and Similarities between Chronicles and Ezra–Nehemiah

Adherents of a Chronicler's Work point to the similarities of the two works and conclude that they have the same author; opponents emphasize the striking differences between the works, which suggest different authors. Neither position is convincing literarily or theologically; the theological differences as well as the striking similarities need to be taken into account. From the literary differences, it does not follow that there were two authors. Another possibility is that there are two distinct literary works that were written at different times; nevertheless, the author was the same.

The Genealogies in Ezra–Nehemiah and Chronicles

1. In Ezra–Nehemiah, genealogies appear that are found in Chronicles as well but with differences (for example, 1 Chronicles 9 and Nehemiah 11). This repetition does not speak in favor of a unified work. The differences point to different points of view and therefore speak against a unified concept.
2. Why would a conjectural author of the whole work put the genealogies of his own time (such as 1 Chr 3:17–23 and 9:1–34) in the front section of 1 Chronicles? If he intended a chronological approach, this information would be expected at the end, somewhere in Ezra–Nehemiah.

The Order of Ezra–Nehemiah–Chronicles

Finally, there is the question why in the Hebrew canon there is not only a distinction between Ezra–Nehemiah and Chronicles but also a different order. Rudolph presents the standard position.[10] In this view, after the Chronistic Work had come into existence, first Ezra and then Nehemiah were accepted into the canon. Chronicles seemed to be superfluous because of its parallelism with the books of Samuel and Kings. At a later stage, Chronicles was added, "auf dass nichts umkomme."[11] The full scenario that Rudolph

---

10. Rudolph, *Chronikbücher*, IV.
11. The German expression alludes to the practice of eating something just so that it does not age and need to be thrown away. See also J. M. Myers, *1 Chronicles* (AB 12; Garden City, NY: Doubleday, 1965) xvi, according to whom Ezra–Nehemiah was written as a follow-up to Samuel–Kings, which was already canonical. If Chronicles were placed before Ezra–Nehemiah, it would disturb this relationship, and then Ezra–Nehemiah would not be recognized as a follow-up to Samuel–Kings. In order to avoid this, Ezra–Nehemiah

proposes is this: (1) the hypothetically postulated Chronistic Work (2) was divided into two parts, of which (3) only the latter was considered relevant and not the first. Later, (4) the part that was originally rejected was finally recognized but was put in the canon at the wrong place. Again, sometime later (in the Septuagint), (5) the original order was restored but without reinstating the original unity.

There are several problems with this view:

1. Is it really possible to divide a large work and declare one part canonical but not the other? Wouldn't the canonical authorities be skeptical about the whole work if one part of it was clearly not canonical?
2. Didn't the objections that led to the separation remain valid? What were the new arguments that overwrote the older objections? After all, Chronicles still parallels Samuel and Kings to a wide extent. Moreover, the tradition of rejecting Chronicles must have had some authority. It seems unlikely that the newer canonical authorities would just ignore this tradition.
3. If, in a Christian codex of the Septuagint many centuries later, Chronicles appeared before Ezra and Nehemiah, would it have been considered appropriate to return to an original situation—or to come up with a new interpretation about an author's intent? For example, someone who thought in flatly historical-chronological terms would tend to see the order Ezra–Nehemiah-Chronicles as illogical and disturbing. A flatly historical reading tends to put Chronicles before Ezra, but this does not imply serious reflection on the theological intent of Chronicles in its entirety.

The Place of Chronicles in the Palestinian Canon

Today, the notion of the "normal" order of the Old Testament books is mainly shaped by Biblia Hebraica Stuttgartensia (BHS); its order is often understood as binding with regard to the canonical order of the biblical books in publications on the Old Testament—such as, for example, in the influential introduction to the Old Testament by B. S. Childs.[12] BHS ends with Chronicles. This is surprising, because it is based on the Leningrad Codex, where Chronicles is not placed at the end but at the beginning of the Writings.[13] The same is true in the important Aleppo Codex.

---

was separated (from Chronicles) and canonized, while Chronicles was not. Only later was Chronicles integrated, and therefore it was considered the last book of the Hebrew Bible, as an appendix to the Writings.

12. B. S. Childs, *Introduction to the Old Testament as Scripture* (Philadelphia: Fortress, 1980).

13. From a text-critical point of view, this is one of several weak points of BHS.

Therefore, the question of the order of the Old Testament books must be posed. Roger Beckwith,[14] in his study on the canon, presents and discusses 70 different orders for the Writings. He distinguishes four groups, the orders of which are based on literary, chronological, abnormal, and liturgical criteria, respectively. He considers the literary order to be the oldest,[15] followed by the chronological (as a late) and liturgical (as the latest development of) orders of the Holy Scriptures. In the orders dominated by literary criteria, Chronicles is often placed last. For chronological orders, Beckwith presents only 3 witnesses (2 of them based on Jerome); none has Chronicles as the last book. In the lists that are arranged liturgically, Chronicles from time to time appears at the beginning, but in the majority of instances it is the last book. In the abnormal orders, again Chronicles dominates as the last book. Consequently, it is likely that Chronicles was originally the last book of the Writings and thus of the whole Old Testament.[16]

Regarding the groupings, one must ask whether the designation *literary order* is adequate, since the theological criteria that probably played a role in creating these arrangements are excluded. The oldest Jewish witness to the order of the Writings is said to be a list in the Talmud, in the Mishnah— Tractate Baba Batra 14b–15a.[17] The order presented here is: Ruth–Psalms– Job–Proverbs–Ecclesiastes–Song of Songs–Lamentations–Daniel–Esther–Ezra (and Nehemiah)–Chronicles. It is possible that the oldest order could be original and that it may have been determined by the authorities who closed the canon.

Regarding the reason that there are different canonical orders of the Old Testament books at all, a passage on the Maccabean war in 2 Macc 2:14–15 may give a hint: "In the same way Judas also collected all the books that had been lost on account of the war which had come upon us, and they are in our possession. So if you have need of them, send people to get them for you" (RSV). The book of 2 Maccabees begins with two letters in which Jews from Palestine invite expatriate Jews in Egypt to come to Jerusalem for the Feast of Hanukkah. This information presupposes that the books of the Old Testament had been in Jerusalem before (Nehemiah is mentioned directly before 2 Macc 2:13). Judas now took care to restore the old collection. It is possible that in this process the old order was not precisely kept. In the time of the Maccabean War, the high priest had been deposed and replaced by the brother of Judas, Simon Maccabeus.[18]

---

14. R. Beckwith, *The Old Testament Canon of the New Testament Church* (Grand Rapids, MI: Eerdmans, 1985) 450–64.

15. Ibid., 210.

16. The saying of Jesus in Luke 11:50–51 and its parallels (Scripture spans from Genesis to Chronicles) can be seen as confirmation of this.

17. L. Goldschmidt, *Der Babylonische Talmud*, vol. 8: *Baba Bathra/Synhedrin* (4th ed.; Darmstadt: Wissenschaftliche Buchgesellschaft, 1996) 55–56.

18. A. R. Leaney, *The Jewish and Christian World, 200 BC to AD 200* (Cambridge Commentaries on Writings of the Jewish and Christian World 200 BC to AD 200; Cambridge: Cambridge University Press, 1984) 177–80.

The Dating of Chronicles

The discussion below regarding the dating of Chronicles is done mostly with reference to I. Kalimi,[19] because he can be regarded the most prominent scholar in this area of the study of Chronicles.[20] According to Kalimi, there are three different positions on the dating of Chronicles: an early position, a late, and an intermediary.

1. The early dating connects Chronicles to the return from the Babylonian Exile. The dates vary between 527 and 500 B.C. Scholars who hold this position, according to Kalimi, are: M. A. Throntveit with a publication in the year 1987, J. D. Newsome 1975, B. Uffenheimer 1961, F. M. Cross 1975, S. L. McKenzie 1985, A. C. Welch 1935, D. N. Freedman 1961, R. L. Braun 1986, R. B. Dillard 1987, and D. L. Petersen 1977. Cross, McKenzie, and Braun posit an additional, final redaction at a later time.

2. The late dating places the origin of Chronicles in the Hellenistic period. Different dates are given, from the beginning of Alexander the Great to the heyday of the Ptolemies and Seleucids to the beginning of the Hasmoneans. The scholars who date Chronicles to the beginning of Alexander the Great according to Kalimi are: J. Wellhausen 1878, S. R. Driver 1910, E. Bertheau 1854, S. Öttli 1889, T. Willi 1972, S. Japhet 1989, E. L. Curtis 1910, L. W. Batten 1913, R. Kittel 1902, R. de Vaux 1960, and G. Fohrer 1960. For a date in the 3rd century B.C., he lists: A. Lods 1932, W. A. L. Elmslie 1916, P. Welten 1973, L. Zunz 1832, P. H. Pfeiffer 1957, C. C. Torrey 1910, M. Noth 1943, K. Galling 1954, and O. Kaiser 1977 (according to Kaiser, however, the last redaction was in the 2nd century). For the origin of Chronicles at the beginning of the Hasmoneans, Kalimi points to B. Spinoza 1677 as the pioneer of modern biblical studies. Spinoza refers to "long after Ezra and maybe even after the reconstruction of the temple by Judas the Maccabean"—in other words, after 166 B.C.

3. Scholars who hold an intermediary position favor a dating for Chronicles around 400 B.C.—that is, between 450 and 350 B.C. Some also speak of the second half of the Persian period. Adherents to this position are: Y. Kaufmann 1960, E. J. Young 1964, E. Bickerman 1966, B. Mazar 1950, P. R. Ackroyd 1973, H. G. M. Williamson 1982, O. Eissfeldt 1956. One question to be asked is whether the so-called intermediary position should be split into two positions—namely, the time from 450 to 400 B.C., which is the time of Ezra–Nehemiah; and the period after 400.

---

19. I. Kalimi, "Die Abfassungszeit der Chronik: Forschungsstand und Perspektiven," *ZAW* 105 (1993) 223–33.

20. See, for example, idem, *The Book of Chronicles: A Classified Bibliography* (Simor Bible Bibliographies; Jerusalem: Simor, 1990).

The result of this large span in critical dating of up to 360 years is nothing short of astonishing. In his evaluation, Kalimi is all the more astonished because, in the time period under consideration, there was no uniformity but only numerous far-reaching, radical changes in the political, religious, and social realms.

If the three positions are compared with each other, it can easily be seen that the late dating, which is quite old among critical positions, still has its adherents today. However, its influence is fading. At the same time, it is surprising that the early date has been brought up again as the newest critical position. How this contradiction will be resolved and whether the new point of view will be convincing are unknown. The intermediary position is the traditional conservative position, which is shared by older and newer critical scholars as well. Kalimi distances himself from both extreme positions. In his view, the writer of Chronicles did not document events of his own time but lived after the period he was dealing with—after the time of the kings of Judah and until the Babylonian Exile. The last verses regarding Cyrus's decree are not taken into consideration. Additionally, Kalimi rejects the hypothesis of a Chronistic History consisting of Chronicles, Ezra, and Nehemiah. He sees Chronicles as a unified work, meaning that there were no later additions or redactions.

For narrowing down the date, a view on the genealogies helps. From 1 Chr 3:19–24, we may be able to infer a date *ad quem*. The verses contain the family tree of Zerubbabel, the Jewish leader who returned from exile. It is the last part of the genealogy of David. The person mentioned last, Anani, may be understood as being contemporary with the writer of Chronicles. The question how many generations are between Zerubbabel and Anani is answered differently. According to Kalimi, the Septuagint, the Peshitta, and the Vulgate attest 11 generations. Compared with the Masoretic Text, this must be seen as supplementation in order to bring the text nearer to the time of the Greek translators. The Masoretic Text follows only 6 generations.

There is a second possibility. The text may have been corrupt, and there were only 5, 4, or 2 generations. However, in my opinion this interpretation overlooks the fact that any linear-chronogical interpretation of the genealogies at all may be inappropriate. Any such interpretation also runs into trouble in other genealogies in Chronicles. Kalimi, however, uses 6 generations as the key to a date.

Now the question of the average duration of a generation must be answered. Based on the periods of office provided in the books of Kings, the average is 23–24 years. Therefore, the 6 generations after Zerubbabel would point to 382–376 B.C. as an approximate time for the writing of Chronicles.

The name Anani also appears in a papyrus from Elephantine. In the year 407 B.C., the 14th year of Darius II, the Jews of Elephantine sent a letter to the responsible leaders in Judah and Jerusalem asking to restore their destroyed temple. As one of the addressees, Ostanes, Anani's brother, is mentioned. It is possible, though not provable, that this Anani is the same person who appears in 1 Chr 3:24. If this were the case, a date of around 400 B.C. could be deduced for the writing of Chronicles. With the article of Kalimi, the trend in Old Testament scholarship is confirmed that sees Chronicles as an independent book to be dated around 400 B.C.[21]

If the position of a Chronistic History (ChrH) is held, then of course the books of Ezra–Nehemiah must be taken into consideration for the dating. Shaver points to the high priest Johanan in Ezra 10:6 and Neh 12:11, 22.[22] For him, Johanan is the high priest mentioned last. This leads to a date of 411 B.C. Although Neh 12:11–12 names his son and successor, this person is, according to Shaver, nowhere identified as a high priest. Due to the lack of external sources, we must derive the date of Chronicles from the information given in the book itself and not from Ezra and Nehemiah, but those dates must also be taken into consideration if we think that Chronicles forms the closing work of the whole Old Testament canon. In this case, Chronicles must cover the final phase of Ezra and Nehemiah as well.

It is surprising that Kalimi's argument does not deal with another passage that regularly plays a role in the discussion about the dating of Chronicles—that is, 1 Chr 9:17–18.[23] It is part of a list of the inhabitants of Jerusalem after the return from the Babylonian Exile and reads: "The gatekeepers: Shallum, Akkub, Talmon, Ahiman; and their fellow Levites— Shallum, their chief, being stationed at the King's Gate on the east, up to the present time. These were the gatekeepers belonging to the camp of the Levites." According to Keil,[24] this verse presupposes the existence of the royal palace. He sees the passage as a contemporary note. If this is correct, Chronicles must have used the passage without removing this note. This seems implausible. Roubos holds that וְעַד־הֵנָּה "up to the present time" refers to the time when the Chronicler (redactor or supplementer) made the note.[25] In this case, the rebuilding of the gates under Nehemiah would be presupposed, since the gates were given their original names. This would mean that Shallum lived in the time of the Chronicler and was still on duty.

---

21. The dating in the article of J. Kegler is typical. He thinks there was a threat to Jewish identity in the time of the writer and assumes that the development of Hellenism was the reason for this crisis. However, the gap in this assumed phenomenon is big, and the conclusion drawn is therefore speculative. J. Kegler, "Prophetengestalten im Deuteronomistischen Geschichtswerk und in den Chronikbüchern: Ein Beitrag zur Kompositions- und Redaktionsgeschichte der Chronikbücher," *ZAW* 105 (1993) 496.

22. Shaver, *Torah and the Chronicler's History Work*, 71.

23. See, for example, K. Roubos, *I Kronieken* (De Prediking van het Oude Testament; Nijkerk: Callenbach, 1969) 160.

24. C. F. Keil, *Die nachexilischen Geschichtsbücher: Chronik, Esra, Nehemia und Esther* (Biblischer Commentar über das Alte Testament 5; Leipzig: Dörffling, 1870) 117–18.

25. Roubos, *I Kronieken*, 160.

To determine the date, we must refer to Neh 12:25a–26: "Mattaniah, Bakbukiah, Obadiah, Meshullam, Talmon, and Akkub were gatekeepers who guarded the storerooms at the gates. They served in the days of Joiakim son of Joshua, the son of Jozadak, and in the days of Nehemiah the governor and of Ezra the priest, the teacher of the Law." The name שַׁלּוּם "Shallum" in 1 Chr 9:17ff. should be considered a variant form of מְשֻׁלָּם "Meshullam" in Neh 12:25. The names that follow in each of the lists are identical: in 1 Chr 9:17, they are Shallum–Akkub–Talmon (and Ahiman), and in Neh 12:25, they are Meshullam–Talmon–Akkub. These gatekeepers, according to Neh 12:26, were contemporaries of Ezra and Nehemiah. Therefore, Shallum would have been a contemporary of the Chronicler and of Ezra–Nehemiah.

The exact date is difficult to establish. As a *terminus ad quem*, the end of the period of Ezra and Nehemiah should be considered.[26] According to Shaver,[27] this would be around 411 B.C. or a little later, based on the name of the high priests in Ezra 10:6 and Neh 12:10–11:22. From Neh 12:23 ("until the time of Johanan"), we know that Johanan was the last high priest. Keil concludes that Nehemiah wrote the book of Nehemiah in his last years.[28] Therefore, he holds that 415 B.C. is plausible, although Nehemiah himself may have died around 405 B.C. If we conjecture that Shallum was older than Nehemiah, having already been on duty in the time of Joiakim, the high priest, then a dating of Chronicles around 425–420 B.C. is also possible. These thoughts on dating Chronicles seem more concrete and reliable than suggestions based on Zerubbabel's genealogy in 1 Chr 3:19–24, the interpretation of which remains indeterminate.

All of these considerations indicate that the formation of Chronicles should be dated somewhere in the last three decades of the 5th century B.C. The same can be said about the book of Ezra–Nehemiah. Is it possible that these books were edited at the same time and even in view of each other? Even if they were, they remain totally different from a literary point of view.

The Theological Message of Chronicles

The theological emphasis of Chronicles is threefold:

1. David and together with him Solomon and the Davidic Dynasty
2. The temple and, therefore, Jerusalem on Mt. Zion

---

26. Shallum must have had a long period of duty. He was alive during the reign of the (high) priest Jehoiakim, who is presented first in Neh 12:26, before Ezra, the priest and scribe. When Nehemiah arrived in Jerusalem, Eliashib, the successor to Joiakim, was already (high) priest.

27. Shaver, *Torah and the Chronicler's History Work*, 71.

28. Keil, *Geschichtsbücher*, 496 (492–99).

3. The universal frame, which indicates that David and the temple are of universal significance

Other subjects are dealt with in Chronicles: for example, "the theological norm for evaluating the kings of Judah," "the wars of Yhwh,"[29] and "the Davidic Dynasty as a paradigm for seeking God."[30] However, David and the temple define Chronicles' primary theological interest; the other topics are supplementary to this main theme.

David (with Solomon and the Davidic Dynasty)

David is significant because he is the anointed king connected to the decisive dynasty in Judah/Israel. At the same time, he is presented as the ideal king before God. He does not forget about the Ark of the Covenant but erects a tabernacle in Jerusalem and places the ark there (1 Chronicles 15). David is the founder of the orders of temple singers and temple service (1 Chronicles 16). The theology of the House of David is mainly found in 1 Chronicles 17. David wants to build a temple to replace the tabernacle. Because of his initiative, Yhwh in turn promises David that he will build a house for him. As it happens, David's son is the one to build the temple; Yhwh promises to confirm David's throne, his house, and his kingdom forever (1 Chr 17:12–14).[31] This prophetic oracle relates to Solomon in the first instance[32] but goes far beyond Solomon. In the following thanksgiving prayers, David looks forward to a "distant future" and to an "eternal blessing" (1 Chr 17:17, 27). In the same context, David mentions the release from Egypt and the redemption of Israel as the only people on earth living for the glory of Yhwh. The election of the royal House of David is therefore understood in the context of Israel's election; it is part of Israel's universal task to glorify Yhwh.

The Temple (and Jerusalem, Mt. Zion)

Next to the House of David, Chronicles devotes a lot of attention to worship, the preparation for the building of the temple, the building itself and, finally, the temple's dedication (1 Chronicles 15–17; 21–26; 28:1–29:19; 2 Chronicles 2–8). The theology of the temple is formulated mostly in 1 Chronicles 16, the praise-psalm by David for Asaph to sing; and in 2 Chronicles 6, the prayer of Solomon when he dedicated the temple.

The significance of the temple lies first of all in a special form of divine presence (2 Chr 6:1–2). The text says that the glory of Yhwh filled

---

29. A. Ruffing, *Jahwekrieg als Weltmetapher: Studien zu den Jahwekriegstexten des chronistischen Sondergutes* (SBB 24; Stuttgart: Katholisches Bibelwerk, 1992).

30. R. K. Duke, *The Persuasive Appeal of the Chronicler: A Rhetorical Analysis* (JSOTSup 88; Sheffield: Sheffield Academic Press, 1990) 150.

31. We need to understand "my kingdom" in 1 Chr 17:14 as a continuation of "my people Israel" in 1 Chr 17:10.

32. Solomon calls himself the anointed one of Yhwh for David's sake (2 Chr 6:42).

the temple, and fire from above fell down onto the burnt offerings (2 Chr 5:13–14; 7:1–3). God's dwelling place remains in heaven (2 Chr 6:18), yet God also lives among the Israelites, as seen especially in the Ark of the Covenant (1 Chr 16:6). Asaph and his brothers are to praise YHWH, first in a tent and afterwards in the temple (1 Chr 16:7). The content of their praise (1 Chr 16:8–36) is described as a commission to Israel to announce YHWH and YHWH's deeds to the nations. The Israelites must seek YHWH and remember their election and the fact that they inherited the covenant of their fathers: Abraham, Isaac, and Jacob. Therefore, the Israelites must concentrate on keeping the land of Canaan, because they stand among the nations as anointed ones—as prophets of God. YHWH, as Creator of heaven, stands uniquely above the nations. After this, the nations themselves are asked to know YHWH, to honor him. and to sacrifice to him. YHWH is the king, and he comes to rule the earth. Finally, Israel is requested to ask YHWH for the redemption of Israel, to gather it, and redeem it from the nations.

The temple in Jerusalem has a universal function. Although it is connected to the people of Israel, they are charged with calling the nations to worship YHWH as king. David's psalm for Asaph takes this point of view regarding the aim of the temple service. This universal function is also confirmed in Solomon's prayer (2 Chronicles 6) between the two theophanic manifestations—the filling of the temple with the glory of YHWH (2 Chr 5:13–14) and the falling of fire onto the altar offering (2 Chr 7:1). According to this prayer, both Israel and outsiders may come to the temple and pray for the help of God. YHWH will answer them from heaven. Whether it concerns an outside threat or judgment on sin, Israel's prayer in the temple will lead to forgiveness and help. Additionally, if the Israelites are in exile, they will find help and will return if they pray in the temple's direction. "Outsiders" coming to the temple from distant lands (having heard of YHWH's great name) may pray, and YHWH will answer them so that all nations may know and respect YHWH as Israel does. The temple plays a decisive role in Israel's task of leading the nations to worship YHWH.

The Universal Frame (of David and the Temple)

Rothstein called the first nine chapters of 1 Chronicles[33] with their extensive genealogies the *Vorhalle*, "the entrance" to the sanctuary; to him, Chronicles proper begins in ch. 10. Willi's newest commentary, however, illustrates how much the thinking on Chronicles has changed in recent decades.[34] Willi imagines the function of 1 Chronicles 1–9 differently: as the basis on which the rest is developed. 1 Chronicles 1–10 is, in fact, the real beginning—the foundation of the whole. Israel's history is embedded in and interrelated with the spread of humankind on the earth.

---

33. J. W. Rothstein, *Das erste Buch der Chronik* (KAT 18/1; Leipzig, 1927) 2–3.
34. T. Willi, *Chronik* (BKAT 24/1; Neukirchen-Vluyn: Neukirchener Verlag, 1991) 9.

Chronicles begins with Adam and ends with Cyrus, the Persian king. At the beginning of the book, Israel has its roots in the world, in humanity, in Adam with his task to govern the whole world. At the end of the book, Israel is interrelated with all the kingdoms on earth over which Yhwh has given Cyrus the right to rule. Part of this is that Yhwh commissions Cyrus to rebuild the temple in Jerusalem. Therefore, Cyrus requests that Israel go to Jerusalem. Thus, Israel's history is framed by the non-Israelite, universal ruler Adam and the non-Israelite, worldwide ruler Cyrus. This frame points to the fact that Israel, with the Davidic Dynasty and David's temple, is not the final goal but the center. As the people of Yhwh, Israel along with David and the temple have universal implications: their horizon is all of humanity.

The ending of Chronicles promises that, when Israelites travel to Jerusalem for this universal purpose, Yhwh is with them. This ending creates tension and expectation. If Yhwh travels with his people, what will happen regarding the Israelite king, the Davidic anointed one, because Yhwh the God of heaven has given all kingdoms to a non-Israelite—Cyrus, the Persian?[35] In another passage, Yhwh himself calls Cyrus his anointed one (Isa 45:1). What of the kings of Judah after Solomon? Will they have a future? Why is 2 Chronicles 11–36 presented as it is? What kind of future do these kings have, given the destruction of the temple and the exile of the Davidic king? The verses on Cyrus show that the catastrophe will end; there will be a future for Israel, the temple, and also for the House of David. Chronicles confirms that the line begun in Ezra–Nehemiah with Sheshbazzar, the prince of Judah,[36] is promised a future (Ezra 1:8, 11).

As a whole, the book of Chronicles is written from the point of view of the return from exile. According to 1 Chr 9:1, "all Israel was listed in the genealogies." The genealogies in the first part reach historically further than the book's literary ending. This does not mean that these names are a later interpolation; rather, it aims to reflect on the events described in Chronicles' closing from a later perspective. The writer and the addressees of Chronicles live with the consequences of Cyrus's decree. The Chronicler's aim in 1 Chronicles 9 is to present all Israel, even in its postexilic form, as God's people. In the preceding chapters, this happened by presenting the genealogies from Adam onward. The note "and behold, they are recorded" (1 Chr 9:1)[37] is now confirmed for the situation in Jerusalem

---

35. Together with the book of Daniel, we could say that the "time of the heathen" has begun.

36. Sheshbazzar is often identified with Zerubbabel, the Davidic prince of the (second) temple-building. Sheshbazzar may be his Persian or Babylonian name. After this, Sheshbazzar is not mentioned again, although he was the leader of the returnees. Ezra 2:2 presents Zerubbabel as the first leader to bring home the exiled.

37. It is highly possible that the important word כְּתוּבִים "Writings" in this last, closing book had become the title for the whole collection.

in the time of the writer, after Cyrus's decree. The past and the present are thereby bound together.

The Intentions of the
Chronicler in Closing the Canon

Old Testament scholars have long searched for the Chronicler's motives and intentions. Biblical writers seldom formulated goals and motives directly, but these can sometimes be inferred from the rhetoric and structure of the books themselves. G. H. Jones discusses the intentions that have been proposed for Chronicles:[38] Was the book an anti-Samaritan polemic, or the legitimization of the Davidic Dynasty (M. Noth)? Was it an apologia for Judaism (R. H. Pfeiffer) or a justification of the levitical priesthood (G. von Rad)? Jones remains skeptical about all these possibilities, looking most favorably at von Rad's proposal that Chronicles is an "interpretation of history."

In the present study, I submit that the Chronicler's primary intent was to summarize and abstract the message of the Old Testament in order to seal the collection of Holy Scriptures as the canon. This conclusion is based on theological indications from within Chronicles and in Ezra–Nehemiah, on the structural position of Chronicles at the end of the Old Testament, and on the testimony of ancient Jewish sources. I also will show that this position is based on the Chronicler's rhetorical strategy.

Theological Indications in Chronicles

The Chronicler does not intend to write anything new. While he does present *Sondergut*—"material exclusive to him"—presenting it is hardly his main goal. He pursues certain theological concerns, but they are all well formulated in other canonical books such as Samuel, Kings, and Psalms. Why would a book be added to the canon if it had nothing new to add? The repetition must be connected somehow to the Chronicler's intent.

Ackroyd's work has a section entitled "The Chronicler as Old Testament Theologian."[39] Could the Chronicler, in spite of the *Sondergut*, be considered a theologian, though he does not bring up anything new? But it is also the work of a theologian to revive existing (although perhaps neglected) messages because they are relevant to contemporary times.[40] The Chronicler, then, highlights what is of integral importance in the canon: David (and his progeny/descendants) and the temple (for all Gentiles/

---

38. G. H. Jones, *1 and 2 Chronicles* (OTG; Sheffield: Sheffield Academic Press, 1993) 98–111.

39. P. R. Ackroyd, *The Chronicler in His Age* (JSOTSup 101; Sheffield: Sheffield Academic Press, 1991) 280.

40. Childs, *Introduction*, 652, argues that that the Chronicler understands his work as a commentary on the scriptures of the Prophets. But the word *theologian* to me seems more appropriate than the word *commentator*.

nations) on the one universal world-horizon (Adam–Cyrus). Jerome picked up on the distilling nature of Chronicles by calling it a *Chronicon totius divinae historiae.*

Theological Indications in the Books of Ezra and Nehemiah

For our purposes, Ezra 7:11–26; 8:36; and Neh 2:1–9 are especially important. Here we see Ezra's and Nehemiah's status in Persia. Ezra was sent to Jerusalem in 458 B.C. by the Persian king Artaxerxes I with written orders for a spiritual administration based on the "law of the God of Heaven." He received not only the king's letter but also the necessary resources. Additionally, Ezra was mandated to create an administration; he therefore was invested with great civil and political authority that included the regulation of spiritual matters. This applies similarly to Nehemiah, who was sent to Jerusalem as a governor by the written order of Artaxerxes I in 445 B.C. (Neh 2:1–9). Ezra's and Nehemiah's reorganization policies were implemented under Persian authority to organize the community; the written law of God (in Ezra's possession) was a matter of Persian interest, creating the ideal conditions under which to formulate a binding collection of religious tradition and Scripture. Persian policy regarding Israel, begun by Cyrus, was continued and completed by Ezra and Nehemiah.[41]

According to b. B. Bat. 14b–15a, the last books of the Writings were arranged as follows: Daniel, Esther, Ezra(–Nehemiah), and Chronicles. These books, in particular, have a Persian character and might even be spoken of as having a "Persian logos" (cf. Herodotus). The last person named in this canon is the Persian king Cyrus, the liberator. Chronicles and the associated completion of Israel's authoritative religious writings partly reflect the cultural reorganization in the provinces on behalf of Persian political interests. After the Scriptures were invested with great authority, it was unlikely that anyone would disagree with the collection; it was, after all, under the

---

41. R. F. Person, *Second Zechariah and the Deuteronomic School* (JSOTSup 167; Sheffield: Sheffield Academic Press, 1993) 146–75 (esp. pp. 160–62, 164–65, 168) reveals a different point of view, which is parallel to the above-mentioned conception. He presumes that there was a group of writers who accompanied Zerubbabel out of the Babylonian Exile and back to Judah. These writers had Persian imperial orders and were responsible for the codification and preservation of religious literature that was related to the temple. This fits with the imperial strategy to restore local sanctuaries and their cults. Person refers to similar findings in Egypt. He means that the Deuteronomic School should be seen as a candidate for this school of writers and speaks of a Deuteronomistic canon that had already begun in exile and was continued by a Deuteronomistic School into the time of Deutero-Zechariah, which he dates between 520 B.C. and 458 B.C. The Deuteronomistic School must have been less popular among the Persian authorities, because Ezra arrived in 458 B.C. With him, a new stage was reached, because the Persian government was able to control the Jerusalem temple better, whereas the "true" Law of Moses was to be followed exactly. Person's work represents a trend in current research that understands the Persian Empire as a stimulating factor for the process of canonization.

authority of Persian decree. In the time following, the tradition was set and remained invariable, even once the Chronicler's goal was no longer understood.

Erich Zenger's[42] work contains a section entitled "Promulgation des jüdischen Gesetzes im Rahmen der persischen Gesetzgebung,"[43] which deals with the idea that the completion of the Pentateuch was accomplished in order to be granted approval as Persian state law. The final editing of the Pentateuch, then, was linked with the Persian state commissioner, Ezra, who promulgated the Pentateuch around 400 B.C. as the basic document of Jewish identity. The Torah, then, had *Reichsautorisation*. Zenger supports this claim by appealing to P. Frei's and R. G. Kratz's works, which consider the Persian Empire to be a compound organism of states and peoples with the Great King as its center and imperial law as its unifying element. The imperial law consisted of a variety of national and regional laws, law books, and institutions (temples) legitimized by "imperial authorization." Zenger interprets Artaxerxes I's letter in Ezra 7:12–26 as supporting the idea that the Pentateuch was Persian imperial law.

But contrary to what would reasonably be expected, the Pentateuch bears no Persian seal at all.[44] If one applies this argumentation to Chronicles instead, however, the problem disappears. Chronicles clearly indicates Persian authorization for Israel's return and reorganization. Additionally, Ezra's and Nehemiah's mission, mandate, and authority went beyond the reorganization of law texts.[45]

Ezra and Nehemiah's work entailed a conservative, restorative reform that prevailed thanks to Persian permission for the Jewish return to Judah, related to Cyrus's rebuilding commission (Ezra 1:1–4). Cyrus handed it over to Sheshbazzar (Zerubbabel), the governor of Judah (Ezra 1:5–10). He first brought a group of Israelites back to Jerusalem and rebuilt the temple (Ezra 2–6). The next step was the return of Ezra together with another group of exiles, who worked toward spiritual reform (Ezra 7–10). The climax of this restorative movement was Nehemiah's return and the reconstruction of Jerusalem's walls (Nehemiah 1–7). The movement was completed when Ezra and Nehemiah acted together on the spiritual reorganization of the nation (Nehemiah 8–13). Crowning their efforts was the binding of the religious Scriptures in a canon. Canonization per se is conservative and restorative—it is going back to what has already been—and is typified by

---

42. Zenger, *Einleitung*, 39–42.

43. ET: "promulgation of Jewish law within the Persian legislation."

44. The Pentateuch carries the stamp of the period of Israel's being in eastern Jordan and the first years of settling in Canaan.

45. See further H. Stadelmann, "Die Reform Esras und die Bibel," in *Der Kanon der Bibel* (ed. G. Maier; Basel: Brunnen / Wuppertal: Brockhaus, 1990) 65. He thinks that there are no indications in the books of Ezra and Nehemiah that Ezra's reform had anything to do with the implementation or enforcement of the Torah as canon.

the rebuilding or restoration of Jerusalem's walls. In the Old Testament, "wall" is regularly used figuratively—for protection in a general sense and for God's protection of God's people. The Jerusalem city walls symbolize this protection.[46] Completing and sealing the canon implied the completion of spiritual walls around God's priestly people. Ezra and Nehemiah accomplished this because of the mandate by the Persian Great King Artaxerxes I.[47] The Old Testament canon was therefore a Persian imperial affair. Not incidentally, then, Chronicles ends with a reference to the first Great Persian King, Cyrus.

The Structural Position of Chronicles at the End of the Old Testament

Chronicles' position has been of interest to a number of Old Testament scholars, though there is but little consensus among them.

- De Vries writes: "We do not know why Chronicles came to be placed at the end."[48] In other words, it's a "loiterer."
- Williamson notes: "The precise reason for the position of Chronicles at the end of the Hebrew Canon thus remained unexplained, but within the context of the miscellaneous collection of which the third division, the writings, is made up this occasion needs no surprise."[49] In other words, "We don't understand, but no matter: most of the Writings' order is incomprehensible."
- Myers sees the last book of the Hebrew Bible as a sort of appendix but does not explain further.[50]
- Allen asks: "Was it put last because it resembles Genesis in beginning with Adam and ending with hope of attaining the Promised Land?"[51] With reservations, he sees a possible connection between the beginning and the ending of the canon.
- De Vries assigns 2 Chr 36:22–23 to a glossator.[52] But why should the section not come from the Chronicler himself? The Chronicler is universally regarded as having lived after the return from Babylonian Exile. The so-called gloss does not relate to an event after his lifetime;[53]

---

46. See, e.g., 1 Sam 25:16; Isa 26:1, 60:18; Zech 2:5; Ps 51:20; Song 8:9–10.

47. Perhaps the prayer of Nehemiah can be interpreted in this way (Neh 13:14, 22, 29, 31). "Remember me for this, O my God, and do not blot out what I have so faithfully done for the house of my God and its services" (Neh 13:14). He prays that his work will be allowed to endure. If he also means his efforts toward (or plans) for the sealing of the canon, then God answered his prayer. The corpus of Holy Scripture was in the care of the temple (the word מִשְׁמָרִים "service/duty" literally means "preservation").

48. De Vries, *1 and 2 Chronicles*, 10.

49. H. G. M. Williamson, *1 and 2 Chronicles* (NCB; London: Pickering / Grand Rapids, MI: Eerdmans, 1982) 5.

50. Myers, *1 Chronicles*, xvii.

51. L. C. Allen, *1, 2 Chronicles* (The Communicator's Commentary Series: Old Testament; Dallas: Word, 1987) 16.

52. De Vries, *1 and 2 Chronicles*, 11.

53. Or at the beginning of his life, if we date the work as early as possible: 525 B.C.

he could write it himself. De Vries's argument works just as well in
reference to the Chronicler himself: "The man who placed the gloss at
the end of his book affirms that, according to the history as ChrH has
rewritten it, what Ezra and Nehemiah tried to do has come to reality,
and that now truly 'God is with his people.'"[54] However, this does not
relate to a glossator but to the Chronicler himself.

- Willi discusses the question of the different positions of Chronicles in
  the Writings: "Of course, the different position of Chronicles expresses
  something about how it was understood." Regarding the discussion in
  the Talmud, he writes: "In this case, Chronicles was placed at the end of
  the Hagiographa and therefore the whole Old Testament, in the sense of
  a quintessence of the entire biblical history."[55]

- Steins proposes the following: "The book of Chronicles plays an
  important role in the formation of the 'Writings' section of the
  canon; from a canon-historical point of view, it is to be seen as an
  Abschlussphänomen ["closing phenomenon"]. With this book, in the
  first half of the 2nd century B.C., a form of the 'Writings' has been
  closed; possibly the book of Chronicles was even written with this
  purpose predominantly in mind."[56] He points to the fact that its
  position at the canon's end highlights its synthesizing and integrating
  character. Chronicles recapitulates Israel's history from Adam to the
  exile, as contained within the first two sections of the canon. Thereby,
  he sees parallels to the beginning and ending of Genesis (from Adam
  to Israel in Egypt; from Adam to Israel in exile in Babylon.) For Steins,
  the historical frame is the period of restoration after the failure of the
  Hellenistic reforms and after Antiochus IV. Only later, at the end of the
  1st century A.D., was this point of view assumed by all of Jewry. Steins
  has rightly interpreted the function of Chronicles, as I am proposing
  in this article; his dating, however, is not convincing. Chronicles does
  not bear a Maccabean but a *Persian* stamp.[57] Moreover, he cannot offer
  a context that could have provided sufficiently binding canonical
  authority.

- In sum, there are some voices in Old Testament scholarship in
  recent times arguing in a similar way to understand Chronicles as
  the quintessence of Old Testament history. The relationship of the
  beginning and ending of the canon is in view, as well as the idea that it
  is about closing the Old Testament canon.

---

54. De Vries, *1 and 2 Chronicles*, 12.

55. Translated from Willi, *Chronik*, 5. He refers to A. Yellin, ה'"כתרים' בדמשק, *Mizrah Ma'arav* 1 (1919) 19–26, 117–27.

56. G. Steins, *Die Chronik als kanonisches Abschlussphänomen: Studien zur Entstehung und Theologie von 1/2 Chronik* (BBB 93; Weinheim: Athenäum, 1995) 509 (pp. 507–17: "Die Chronik—ein 'Abschlussphänomen'").

57. This was especially criticized by Zipora Talshir and Sarah Japhet: Z. Talshir, "Several Canon-Related Concepts Originating in Chronicles," *ZAW* 113 (2001) 386–403; S. Japhet, *1 Chronik* (HThKAT; Freiburg: Herder, 2002).

Old Jewish Witnesses

B. B. Bat. 15a has an interesting discussion on Chronicles' final position: "Ezra wrote his book and the genealogy of Chronicles up to his own time. . . . Who then finished it? Nehemiah, the son of Hakhaliah." This suggests a double authorship for Chronicles. Information regarding the authorship of the Old Testament books in Baba Bathra can hardly be seen as authentically representing an ancient tradition; however, it is striking how often Ezra and sometimes Nehemiah are cited as being responsible for the confirmation of the Old Testament canon.

Thus it is plausible that tradition is, in this case, reliable. External conditions were more favorable at this point than any other, and there was a need to define which traditions should be binding. The note in 2 Macc 2:13 seems to confirm this: "The same things are reported in the records and in the memoirs of Nehemiah, and also that he founded a library and collected books about the kings and prophets, and the writings of David, and the letters of kings about votive offerings" (NRSV). Beckwith[58] points out that this could not have been a general library but was, rather, a special one; a national archive. Besides the Pentateuch, this archive contained holy books of prophetic dignity but also other texts of national interest, as well as the books that were later and had been accepted into the second and third sections of the Old Testament canon, the Prophets and the Writings.[59] Nehemiah therefore is understood as a collector of literature.

The Closing and Sealing of the Old Testament

The books preceding Chronicles in the canon begin with Genesis and end with Ezra–Nehemiah. Since the Chronicler also begins with Adam and ends with Cyrus's decree, he recalls the beginning of the first book of the canon (Genesis) in his introduction and recalls the beginning of the last book of the canon (Ezra–Nehemiah) in his conclusion. This expresses his awareness of the whole Old Testament that comes before; he uses the summarizing method of "beginning and ending," presenting a concluding interpretive key to all that precedes. This obviously presupposes some existing order of Old Testament books: he *must* begin with Genesis and end with Ezra–Nehemiah. Either the order was already fixed, or it was up to him to fix it. In writing Chronicles, Ezra–Nehemiah (mostly Nehemiah) completes the task given them by God and the Persian king; Chronicles is the summation and seal of their work.

---

58. Beckwith, *Old Testament Canon*, 150–52.

59. Beckwith (ibid., 150) writes that the wording used in 2 Maccabees displays two indications of old age: the writer uses "library" instead of "holy books" or something similar. And he mentions "letters of the kings about votive offerings" instead of "the book of Ezra," in which letters of this sort were contained later.

Chronicles executes this sealing function ideally, by beginning with Adam, the human being to whom Yhwh the God of Heaven gave the task of subduing the whole earth, and then by ending with Cyrus, to whom Yhwh has given all kingdoms of the earth. Adam was there before Israel came into existence; Cyrus is, again, someone outside the covenant people. Adam and Cyrus frame Israel's call as a priestly people for the whole earth. Israel's purpose, then, does not lie within Israel but is in fact oriented toward the whole world. Cyrus, in Isa 45:1, has the same title as David, and in fact he enables Israel to carry on its task as a priestly nation. While the anointed one is understood to be an Israelite, once the Davidic kingdom is eliminated and its empire destroyed, a heathen person acquires power over all Israel and Canaan. Chronicles' main theological emphasis is on the significance of the Davidic Dynasty and the temple. However, the reader must look to the future. Thus, the book highlights certain aspects of the Old Testament without replacing it.

For Willi,[60] Chronicles brings closure to the first and second parts of the canon, the Law and the Prophets. But the Writings—the third part of the canon—should be taken into consideration as well, particularly because the beginning of the last book of the Writings (Ezra–Nehemiah) is repeated in shortened form at Chronicles' end. With this, we come to the question of the tripartite canon and the order of books in each of the blocks.[61] From a structural standpoint, the canon presents the following message to Israel:[62]

1. The *Law*. Israel's first task is to live in Canaan and to be the priestly nation for all nations. Joshua–Kings demonstrates the fulfillment of the blessings and the curses as they are formulated in the law.[63]
2. The *Prophets* have Jeremiah at the beginning and Malachi at the end.[64] Jeremiah saw at the beginning of his book that the threat would come out of the north (Jer 1:13–16). Malachi, at the end,

---

60. T. Willi, *Die Chronik als Auslegung: Untersuchungen zur literarischen Gestaltung der historischen Überlieferung Israels* (FRLANT 108; Göttingen: Vandenhoeck & Ruprecht, 1972) 176.

61. There is no direct evidence that the Chronicler was the one to give the canon its tripartite structure or that the authoritative order given in b. B. Bat. 14b–15a stems from the Chronicler. However, we need to take this into account as a possibility, since the question of totality was so important to him.

62. These observations are further developed in the "Exile and Return Model." See my essay, "3. Een structureel canonieke benadering voor een theologie van het Oude Testament als geheel," in *Theologie van het Oude Testament: De blijvende boodschap van de Hebreeuwse Bijbel* (ed. Hendrik J. Koorevaar and Mart-Jan Paul; Zoetermeer: Boekencentrum, 2013) 89–121.

63. Jewish tradition gave the books of Joshua, Judges, Samuel, and Kings the title "Former Prophets." It is questionable whether this is an appropriate designation. Actually, the four books smoothly continue the historical line from Genesis to Deuteronomy.

64. The authoritative witness in ancient Judaism about the order of the Old Testament books after the law is b. B. Bat. 14b–15a, which reveals that the prophets do not begin with Isaiah but with Jeremiah.

calls for obedience to the Law of Moses and waiting for Elijah before the great day of Yʜwʜ arrives (Mal 3:22–24[4:4–6]). The warning of Jeremiah retains significance even after Israel returns from exile to the land. Additionally Israel will lose the land if it is not different from the Israel before the exile. In the center, Malachi points to the "messenger"—the "Lord" who will come to his temple (Mal 3:1).

3. The *Writings* begin with Ruth.[65] This Moabite woman saves an Israelite family. The genealogy at the end of Ruth points to David, by whom an individual family's salvation becomes the basis for a nation's salvation. Chronicles at the end of the Writings is introduced by nine chapters of genealogies. The idea of a genealogy at the end of Ruth is borrowed by the Chronicler but put into a universal frame. David is related to the entire world and its salvation. In the Writings, David is placed between his foreign (grand)mother Ruth and the foreign king Cyrus; David and Cyrus have the same title, "anointed one," because of Isaiah.

The Purpose of Chronicles with the Old Testament as a Book

The Chronicler intends to close and seal off the Old Testament canon. By this means, the Old Testament surely has now become a book. According to Childs,[66] perhaps the most important discovery of recent scholarship on Chronicles is the fact that the Chronicler tries to interpret the history of Israel in connection with a block of authoritative writings. Even the topic of writing is mentioned relatively frequently throughout the book. The Chronicler collects genealogies, writings, and letters; his intention is to make a definitive order for the existing writings of the Old Testament.

The frequent uses of the words related to the topic of writing are as follows:

The noun סֵפֶר "book" is often used, referring to the following books: "the book of the kings of Israel and Judah" (1 Chr 9:1; 2 Chr 27:7, 35:27, 36:8); "the book of the kings of Judah and Israel" (2 Chr 16:11, 25:26, 28:26, 32:32); "the book of the kings of Israel" (2 Chr 20:34); "the annotations on the book of the kings" (2 Chr 24:27);[67] "the book of the law of the Lord" (2 Chr 17:9, 34:14), which is also called "the book of the law" (2 Chr 34:15), "the book of Moses" (2 Chr 25:4, 35:12) or "the book of the covenant" (2 Chr 34:30), and which is referred to as "the book" (2 Chr 34:15, 16, 21, 24), "a book" (2 Chr 34:18), or "this book" (2 Chr 34:21, 31).

The noun כְּתָב "writ": In 1 Chr 28:19, David speaks to Solomon about the temple to be built: "All this . . . I have in writing from the hand of the Lᴏʀᴅ upon me, and he gave me understanding in all the details of the

---

65. See, for example, b. B. Bat. 14b–15a.

66. Childs, *Introduction*, 647–48.

67. Here the word מִדְרָשׁ "explanation" is used together with "the book of the kings." The same word is used in 2 Chr 13:22 together with "the Prophet Iddo."

plan" (NIV); 2 Chr 2:11 speaks about a writing by the Tyrian king Hiram to Solomon. In it, this foreigner praises Yнwн as "God of Israel who has made the heavens and the earth." Moreover, he connects King David with Solomon, his son, and with the Temple of Yнwн; 2 Chr 35:4 asserts that the document written by David, the king of Israel, must be followed.

The noun מִכְתָּב "letter":[68] 2 Chr 35:4 is about a letter from King Solomon about the duties of the priests and Levites that have changed since the building of the temple. From this regulation, King Josiah of Judah draws his authority to begin his reforms. 2 Chr 21:12 deals with the letter of the Israelite prophet Elijah to Jehoram, king of Judah; 2 Chr 36:22–23 mentions a letter from the Persian king Cyrus to his whole kingdom regarding the rebuilding of the temple.

The verb כתב "to write" seldom appears in the Qal perfect (2 Chr 36:22; 30:1; 32:17) or Qal imperfect (1 Chr 24:6). In 2 Chr 26:22, it points to Jeremiah's writing about the life of Uzziah. The use of the Qal participle passive כְּתוּבִים, however, is striking; this form appears 19 times (1 Chr 4:41; 9:1; 29:29; 2 Chr 9:29; 12:19; 13:22; 16:11; 20:34; 24:27; 25:26; 27:7; 28:26; 32:32; 33:19; 34:19, 31; 35:25, 27; 36:8). Once, the feminine-plural Qal passive participle is used (2 Chr 34:24). Where the participle appears for the first time in the book, it has the definite article and is preceded by a demonstrative pronoun: "these (are) the (ones who are) written" (1 Chr 4:41).[69] This statement relates to the people documented in genealogies. This usage is unique at the beginning of the book; it is a form of administration language. This is characteristic for the first main part of Chronicles: the line from Adam to David. Events and people from the past are reassimilated into the larger book of Chronicles.

In most cases, כְּתוּבִים refers to already existing books (1 Chr 29:29; 2 Chr 9:29; 12:19; 13:22; 16:11; 20:34; 24:27; 25:26; 27:7; 28:26; 32:32; 33:19; 34:19, 31; 35:25, 27; 36:8). The same is true for the feminine form (2 Chr 34:24) and for the singular form הַכָּתוּב "the written" (1 Chr 16:40, 2 Chr 34:21). It is about "the book of the kings of Israel and Judah," "the book of the kings of Judah and Israel," "the book of the kings of Israel," and "the annotations on the book of the kings." But it is also about the "book of the law," which is also called "the book of the Law of the Lord," "the book of Moses," and "the book of the covenant," referred to in the words "the book," "a book," or "this book."

Finally, the expression is used in connection with a book of lamentations in 2 Chr 35:25. In sum, the Chronicler uses the word for individual Israelites who are recorded in genealogies as well as for important historical

---

68. Another word is אִגְּרוֹת "(public) writing" in 2 Chr 30:1, 6. King Hezekiah writes a "letter") to Israel and Judah. This word is only used in the late texts of the Old Testament, during the Persian period (Esther, Nehemiah, Chronicles).

69. After this, the article is used two more times, but then it only functions as a relative pronoun (2 Chr 34:24, 31).

and theological writings, with "the book of the law" as the authoritative climax.

Finally, we need to point out the masculine-singular passive participle with preposition and article: כַּכָּתוּב "as written" (lit., "as the written"). This expression is used in 2 Chr 23:18; 25:4; 30:5, 18; 31:3; 35:12, and 26 and is followed by an amplification or preceded by a noun: "in the Law of Moses," "in the law, in the book of Moses"; relating to Passover regulations: "in the Law of the Lord," "in the book of Moses." The law is the authority.

By pointing to the written past in his own book, the Chronicler emphasizes the written nature of God's will and the life of God's people. "It is written" about how Israel reacted to the will of Yнwн and about the righteous kings and priests who obeyed it. The written law was the standard according to which people lived. When people followed it, renewal and revival happened; when they did not, judgment came.

With this, the Chronicler also develops a theology of Holy Scripture,[70] by exemplifying the appropriate attitude toward the Old Testament Scriptures.[71] First, he names the Law of Moses. Second, he refers to the Prophets. Their stories, mostly about kings, are written down and must be kept (see 2 Chr 32:32). Third, he alludes to the Writings, but only in passing. (a) In 1 Chr 4:41, the genealogies from the time of Hezekiah are mentioned. The wise were especially interested in administration, both divine and human (see Prov 25:1–2, which is about documentation during the administration of King Hezekiah). When he incorporated these lists of names into Chronicles, they became part of the divine administration. (b) The second indication appears in 2 Chr 35:25: the laments of Jeremiah over the death of King Josiah; the laments "are written in the lamentations,"[72] which could be understood as a wisdom writing reflecting on judgment.

Epilogue on the Opening of the Seal

With the theological orientation of Chronicles, the Chronicler has provided a key to understanding the Old Testament. A series of individuals and events are models of character—both for the life of the community of Israel and for individuals. Examples appear in the behavior of some of the kings and the wars of the Lord. Therefore, since Chronicles encompasses the whole Old Testament, it becomes a paradigm for future generations. Although the collection of holy writings is sealed off with Chronicles, the canon is not finished in the sense that the story told in the books

---

70. See Willi, *Chronik als Auslegung*, 125. Willi says this in the context of comparing 1 Kgs 8:25 with 2 Chr 6:16. "Walk before me" now reads "walk in my law."

71. The book of Kings uses the term *book* frequently as well and has many forms relating to both the verb and the noun *writing*. Therefore, the book of Kings may have been a model for the Chronicler in developing his book's theology. In a certain sense, the book of Kings has a closing function as well, since it is the last book in the section that begins with Genesis and ends with Kings.

72. This does not refer to the book of Lamentations.

has come to an end. It is open for continuation in Israel, which is daily living within the framework of Mosaic Law; a new era with an anointed one from the House of David—and an important role for the temple—is still expected.

The New Testament begins in the book of Matthew with a genealogy (Matt 1:1–17), the genealogy of Jesus Christ, the son of David, the son of Abraham (Matt 1:1). By beginning his Gospel with a genealogy, Matthew breaks the seal of Chronicles. Chronicles, as the last book of the Old Testament also begins with a genealogy, pointing to David as the person who will lead the world. Matthew's genealogy includes Ruth (Matt 1:5). The redemption of her family (Ruth 4:13–14, 17), which was widened to a national redemption in the person of David (Ruth 4:18–22), is further widened to encompass the redemption of the world. The book of Matthew ends with Jesus' great commission (Matt 28:18–20). It begins with the words: "All authority in heaven and on earth has been given to me. Therefore go and make disciples of all nations" (NIV). There may be a parallel here to the end of the book of Chronicles, where the Persian king Cyrus says: "The LORD, the God of heaven, has given me all the kingdoms of the earth." In Jesus, the ending of Chronicles and the end of the entire Old Testament now reaches its peak and its consummation. Jesus has all power on earth—and in heaven. The word *heaven* also appears with Cyrus, but it is connected to YHWH there.

Matthew takes up the temple topic as well. Regarding Cyrus, there is a statement that YHWH had commissioned him to build for Him a house in Jerusalem. Jesus often stays in the temple; in Matt 12:6, Jesus says about himself: "One greater than the temple is here." In Matt 27:40, while Jesus is suffering on the cross, people remind him that he claimed he would destroy the temple and rebuild it in three days. In 27:51, the curtain of the temple is torn when Jesus dies.

Summary and Conclusions

1. Chronicles was written with the purpose of closing and sealing the Old Testament canon. In doing this, the Chronicler also fixes the order of the Old Testament books.
2. The Chronicler uses an inclusio to encompass the whole canon preceding Chronicles. He begins with Adam as the first human being, who received power over all the world from God; and ends with the Persian king Cyrus, who testifies that YHWH has given him power over all kingdoms of the earth. He starts with the beginning of the first book and ends with the beginning of the last book of the canon (Ezra–Nehemiah) in his possession.
3. Chronicles distills and highlights the following theological subjects from the Old Testament:

    a. David is the king anointed by God over the people of Israel. He and his dynasty therefore reign over a people that has a universal task.

    b. The temple is a place for worshiping Yʜᴡʜ, not only for Israel but also for strangers from all nations.

4. Ezra and Nehemiah achieve this work, which closes and seals the canon, in the second half of the 5th century B.C. Both were given a mandate by the Persian Empire, and acted based on an explicit commission to reorganize the social order in the area of civil administration, jurisprudence, and religion. In this context, Chronicles' function in closing the canon can be seen as part of an appointment by the Persian government, explaining why Chronicles and thus the whole canon ends by naming Cyrus as a servant of Yʜᴡʜ and mentioning his commission to them to build the temple.

5. The more-recent Old Testament scholarship on the date and function of Chronicles has paved the way for this approach in the following ways:

    a. Of the three main positions (dating the book of Chronicles around 500, 400, or 150 B.C.), 400 B.C. plays an important role in more-recent scholarship.

    b. The judicial structure of the Persian Empire formed an ideal background for canonization. So far, Old Testament scholarship has applied this to the formation of the Pentateuch; this appears too narrow. Ezra and Nehemiah's commission was not restricted to the law but encompassed all of the social and religious life of the Jewish people in Israel. This time of restoration appears to have been ideal for concluding and sealing the canon of the *whole* Old Testament.

    c. Increasingly, Chronicles is interpreted as the quintessence of all biblical history, as well as functioning to close the developing canon. As a background for this, the time of the Maccabees in the middle of the 2nd century B.C. is proposed. However, Chronicles does not bear a Maccabean but a Persian mark. This suggests that Chronicles was written with this function at the end of the 5th century B.C.

6. The seal of Chronicles and of the Old Testament is reopened by the book of Matthew at the beginning of the New Testament. Analogous to Chronicles, Matthew begins with the genealogy of Jesus as the son of David. Matthew ends with the great commission, in which all power in heaven *and* on earth is given to Jesus, just as the book of Chronicles closes by saying that Cyrus has been given power over all the kingdoms on earth from Yʜᴡʜ, the God of heaven.

Bibliography

Ackroyd, P. R. *The Chronicler in His Age*. JSOTSup 101. Sheffield: Sheffield Academic Press, 1991.

Allen, L. C. *1, 2 Chronicles*. The Communicator's Commentary Series: Old Testament. Dallas: Word, 1987.

Archer, G. L. *Das Hebräische im Buch Daniel verglichen mit den Schriften der Sekte von Qumran*. Basel: FETA, 1972.

―――. "The Hebrew of Daniel." Pp. 160–69 in *The Law and the Prophets*. Edited by J. H. Skilton. Nutley, NJ: Presbyterian and Reformed, 1974.

Beckwith, R. *The Old Testament Canon of the New Testament Church*. Grand Rapids, MI: Eerdmans, 1985.

Begg, C. T. Summary of *Text and Theology* (FS M. Sæbø, ed. A. Tangberg). *Old Testament Abstracts* 17/2. Washington D.C.: Catholic University of America Press, 1994.

Childs, B. S. *Introduction to the Old Testament as Scripture*. Philadelphia: Fortress, 1980.

De Vries, S. J. *1 and 2 Chronicles*. FOTL 11. Grand Rapids, MI: Eerdmans, 1990.

Duke, R. K. *The Persuasive Appeal of the Chronicler: A Rhetorical Analysis*. JSOTSup 88. Sheffield: Sheffield Academic Press, 1990.

Goldschmidt, L. *Der Babylonische Talmud*, vol. 8: *Baba Bathra / Synhedrin*. 4th ed. Darmstadt: Wissenschaftliche Buchgesellschaft, 1996.

Japhet, S. *1 Chronik*. HThKAT. Freiburg: Herder, 2002.

Jones, G. H. *1 and 2 Chronicles*. OTG. Sheffield: Sheffield Academic Press, 1993.

Kalimi, I. "Die Abfassungszeit der Chronik: Forschungsstand und Perspektiven." *ZAW* 105 (1993) 223–33.

―――. *The Book of Chronicles: A Classified Bibliography*. Simor Bible Bibliographies. Jerusalem: Simor, 1990.

Kegler, J. "Prophetengestalten im Deuteronomistischen Geschichtswerk und in den Chronikbüchern: Ein Beitrag zur Kompositions- und Redaktionsgeschichte der Chronikbücher." *ZAW* 105 (1993) 481–97.

Keil, C. F. *Die nachexilischen Geschichtsbücher: Chronik, Esra, Nehemia und Esther*. Biblischer Commentar über das Alte Testament 5. Leipzig: Dörffling & Franke, 1870.

Koch, K. *Das Buch Daniel*. Erträge der Forschung 144. Darmstadt: Wissenschaftliche Buchgesellschaft, 1980.

Koorevaar, Hendrik J., and Mart-Jan Paul, eds. *Theologie van het Oude Testament: De blijvende boodschap van de Hebreeuwse Bijbel*. Zoetermeer: Boekencentrum, 2013.

Leaney, A. R. *The Jewish and Christian World, 200 BC to AD 200*. Cambridge Commentaries on Writings of the Jewish and Christian World 200 BC to AD 200. Cambridge: Cambridge University Press, 1984.

Myers, J. M. *1 Chronicles*. AB 12. Garden City, NY: Doubleday, 1965.

Person, R. F. *Second Zechariah and the Deuteronomic School*. JSOTSup 167. Sheffield: Sheffield Academic Press, 1993.

Rothstein, J. W. *Das erste Buch der Chronik*. KAT 18/1. Leipzig: Deichertsche Verlag, 1927.

Roubos, K. *I Kronieken*. De Prediking van het Oude Testament. Nijkerk: Callenbach, 1969.

Rudolph, W. *Chronikbücher.* HAT 1/21. Tübingen: Mohr Siebeck, 1955.

Ruffing, A. *Jahwekrieg als Weltmetapher: Studien zu den Jahwekriegstexten des chronistischen Sondergutes.* SBB 24. Stuttgart: Katholisches Bibelwerk, 1992.

Shaver, J. R. *Torah and the Chronicler's History Work: An Inquiry into the Chronicles References to Laws, Festivals, and Cultic Institutions in Relationship to Pentateuchal Legislation.* BJS 196. Atlanta: Scholars Press, 1989.

Skarsaune, O. "Kodeks og kanon: Om bruk og avgrensing av de gammeltestamentlige skrifter i oldkirken." Pp. 237–75 in *Text and Theology.* FS M. Sæbø. Edited by A. Tangberg. Oslo: Verbum, 1994.

Stadelmann, H. "Die Reform Esras und die Bibel." Pp. 52–69 in *Der Kanon der Bibel.* Edited by G. Maier. Basel: Brunnen / Wuppertal: Brockhaus, 1990.

Steins, G. *Die Chronik als kanonisches Abschlussphänomen: Studien zur Entstehung und Theologie von 1/2 Chronik.* BBB 93. Weinheim: Athenäum, 1995.

Talshir, Z. "Several Canon-Related Concepts Originating in Chronicles." *ZAW* 113 (2001) 386–403.

Waelkens, A. *De datering van het boek Daniël onderzocht.* M.A. Thesis, Evangelisch-Theologische Faculteit, 1991.

Williamson, H. G. M. *1 and 2 Chronicles.* NCB. London: Pickering / Grand Rapids, MI: Eerdmans, 1982.

———. *Israel in the Books of Chronicles.* Cambridge: Cambridge University Press, 1977.

Willi, T. *Chronik.* BKAT 24/1. Neukirchen-Vluyn: Neukirchener Verlag, 1991.

———. *Die Chronik als Auslegung: Untersuchungen zur literarischen Gestaltung der historischen Überlieferung Israels.* FRLANT 108. Göttingen: Vandenhoeck & Ruprecht, 1972.

Zenger, E., ed. *Einleitung in das Alte Testament.* Stuttgart: Kohlhammer, 1995.

Torah-Binding and Canon Closure

On the Origin and Canonical Function of the Book of Chronicles

GEORG STEINS

Introduction

The Torah, or more precisely, the Pentateuch[1] forms the foundation and center of the Hebrew canon. It is the oldest canonical subsection as well as the point of reference for the two following subsections of the canon, the Prophets and the Writings, the canonization of which takes place in view of the Torah and with reference to the Torah.[2] Canonization is not only an outward declarative act that defines the extent and order of the normative Scriptures; it also—as newer research on the canon has revealed—can be seen in the text itself.[3] One can outline the beginning of the process of canonization, the closure of the Torah, and the second step of the process, the formation of the canonical division of the Prophets. The discussion about the formation of the third subsection of the canon, however, has not advanced as far.[4] Only the beginning of this process has

Editors' note: This essay was originally published as "Torabindung und Kanonabschluß: Zur Entstehung und kanonischen Funktion der Chronikbücher," in *Die Tora als Kanon für Juden und Christen* (ed. Erich Zenger; Freiburg: Herder, 1996) 213–56. All ET of German are ours.

1. Clarification is necessary since several meanings of *Torah* must be distinguished.

2. Cf. O. H. Steck, *Der Abschluß der Prophetie im Alten Testament: Ein Versuch zur Frage der Vorgeschichte des Kanons* (Biblisch-theologische Studien 17; Neukirchen-Vluyn: Neukirchener Verlag 1991) 167–78; N. Lohfink, "Der Begriff 'Bund' in der biblischen Theologie," *TP* 66 (1991) 170–71; C. Dohmen and M. Oeming, *Biblischer Kanon, Warum und Wozu?* (Quaestiones disputatae 137; Freiburg: Herder, 1992) 68. A helpful overview of references to the Torah from the "seam" texts "between" the canon parts can be found in E. Zenger et al., *Einleitung in das Alte Testament* (Stuttgart: Kohlhammer, 1995) 24–26.

3. Cf., e.g., Steck, *Abschluß der Prophetie*; and Dohmen and Oeming, *Biblischer Kanon*, passim.

4. Meanwhile, scholarly work on the "canon" is vast. Apart from the already-mentioned works and the references to be mentioned below, see the newer collections of essays: S. Z. Leiman, ed., *The Canon and Masorah of the Hebrew Bible: An Introductory Reader* (New York: Ktav, 1974); J.-D. Kaestli and O. Wermelinger, eds., *Le canon de l'Ancien Testament* (Geneva: Labor et fides, 1984); I. Baldermann et al., eds., *Zum Problem des biblischen Kanons* (JBTh 3; Neukirchen-Vluyn: Neukirchener Verlag, 1988); C. Theobald, ed., *Le canon des écritures: Études historiques exégétiques et systématiques* (Lectio Divina 140; Paris: Cerf, 1990); W. Pannenberg and T. Schneider, eds., *Verbindliches Zeugnis I: Kanon – Schrift –*

been explored, in what may be labeled the *Torah-binding* of the Psalter.[5] Furthermore, it may be possible to discern traces of canonization in the wisdom books.[6] Regarding the *closure* of the Writings, the issue is entirely unsettled and, consequently, so is the formation of the holy writings as a whole.

The following contribution addresses this problem by analyzing the literary-theological achievement of 1–2 Chronicles and the position of this book[7] in the third subsection of the canon. The study will lead to a reassessment of the role of Chronicles: the book plays the decisive role in the formation of the third subsection of the canon and therefore of the canon as a whole. This thesis will be developed in four steps: The *first* step examines a dominant aspect of recent research on Chronicles, which situates Chronicles on the horizon of canonical literature. As a *second* step, the reassessment of some introductory questions will be presented, in which a vital reorientation of research on Chronicles can be seen. The *third* step reveals the essential aspects[8] of the "Torah-binding" of Chronicles. And, as a *fourth* and last step, this essay proposes that Chronicles functions as a "canonical closure phenomenon" for the entire Hebrew canon.[9]

1. The Books of Chronicles in the Canonical Process

The books of Chronicles are not only part of the canon; they also draw on the canon more than any other book, and their tones are best heard within the resonance chamber of the canon. A canonical perspective is more crucial to interpreting Chronicles than any other book of the Old Testament. Therefore, the question of the formation of the canonical division of the Writings and the completion of the development of the Hebrew canon must, of necessity, be examined in light of the books of Chronicles.

Tradition (Freiburg: Herder / Göttingen: Vandenhoeck & Ruprecht, 1992). The current state of the discussion is presented by A. van der Kooij, "De canonvorming van de Hebreeuwse bijbel, het Oude Testament," *NTT* 49 (1995) 42–65; and C. Dohmen, "Der Biblische Kanon in der Diskussion," *TRev* 91 (1995) 451–60. For an introduction to the topic, see G. T. Sheppard, "Canon," *ER* (1987) 3.62–69; J. A. Sanders, "Canon," *ABD* 1.837–52; B. Lang, "Kanon," *Neues Bibel-Lexikon* (ed. Manfred Görg and Bernhard Lang; Ostfildern: Patmos, 1992) 2.440–47.

5. Cf. Steck, *Abschluß der Prophetie*, 162–63.

6. Cf. Dohmen and Oeming, *Biblischer Kanon*, 54.

7. In substance, 1 and 2 Chronicles form one book; the division into two books goes back to the LXX. Below, the expressions *Chronicles* and *books of Chronicles* will be used synonymously.

8. Within the scope of this survey, only selected aspects of the topic can be discussed. The topic deserves a monographic-length treatment.

9. Especially §§1, 2, and 4 of the current survey incorporate the results of my study, which are found in my book *Die Chronik als kanonisches Abschlußphänomen: Studien zur Entstehung und Theologie von 1/2 Chronik* (BBB 93; Weinheim: Athenäum, 1995); there, many ideas are presented and reasoned in more detail.

1.1. The "Scripture-Relatedness"
of the Books of Chronicles

> Perhaps the crucial discovery of the modern study of Chronicles is the
> extent to which the Chronicler sought to interpret Israel's history in rela-
> tion to a body of authoritative scripture. Although it is obvious that the
> Chronicler did not at any point articulate his concept of canon, he made
> use of the earlier writings in such a way as to indicate how strongly the
> consciousness of a body of authoritative writings affected him.[10]

With these words, Childs summarizes the most important result of newer
research on Chronicles:[11] elaboration on the "Scripture-relatedness" that
characterizes the whole work. This peculiarity of Chronicles becomes even
more pronounced when Chronicles is compared with the other books of
the third division of the canon. Admittedly, in every book in the Writings,
one can find references to the Scriptures of the older canonical divisions.
However, Chronicles is the most "canonical" book of the Writings. This has
led, for example, to the conclusion to define Chronicles formally as *Auslegung* ("interpretation").[12] The "Scripture-relatedness" not only concerns
the formation of Chronicles but also its reception. Chronicles not only
makes use of the rich material of the older biblical books; it also assumes
an acquaintance with these older texts by its readers.[13]

---

10. B. S. Childs, *Introduction to the Old Testament as Scripture* (Minneapolis: Fortress,
1979) 647–48.

11. Since De Wette, the books of Chronicles have frequently and emphatically been
declared of minor value as a historical source. Therefore, they have been in the slipstream
of historical-critical research for a long time. However, since the beginning of the 1970s,
they have received more attention; currently, Chronicles research is booming. This revival
of research was possible due to the relativization of the historical-critical way of questioning and to the impartial examination and evaluation of the literary and theological character of these books. Hence, research on Chronicles is participating in the general change
in trend regarding the later books and layers of the Old Testament as well as the literature
"between the testaments." Cf. J. W. Kleinig, "Recent Research in Chronicles: Currents in
Research," in *Biblical Studies* 2 (1994) 43:

> That Cinderella of the Hebrew Bible, Chronicles, has at last emerged from years of
> obscurity and scorn. Early last century she was all the rage among scholars who
> used her quite shamelessly in their battles over the reconstruction of Israelite his-
> tory. But then, when the conflict was over, Wellhausen turned on her in favor of
> her Deuteronomistic stepsister and sent her packing for her unfashionable love
> of ritual and family ties, and for allegedly playing fast and loose with the facts.
> How things have changed over the last decade! She may not yet be the belle of the
> academic ball, but she has, at least, been noticed in her own right once again and
> received long overdue attention from the scholarly community.

12. Thus T. Willi, *Die Chronik als Auslegung: Untersuchungen zur literarischen Gestaltung
der historischen Überlieferung Israels* (FRLANT 106; Göttingen: Vandenhoeck & Ruprecht,
1972); cf. P. R. Ackroyd, *The Chronicler in his Age* (JSOTSup 101; Sheffield: Sheffield Academic Press, 1991) 273–89.

13. At least, the genealogies of the so-called vestibule in 1 Chronicles 1–10 (1 Chronicles 10 belongs structurally to the vestibule; the David narrative begins in 1 Chr 11:1; for

1.2. The Books of Chronicles as Serving a Canon Revision?

At the time Chronicles was written, the "canonical process"[14] was already well advanced. Recently, Albertz published a crucial development of this idea. Albertz not only investigates the relationship of Chronicles to the older canonical works but tries to define precisely the position of Chronicles in the process of the emerging biblical canon. In his view, Chronicles served as a "canon revision"—indeed, it became the motor driving the canonization of the *second* canonical collection.[15] According to Albertz, the process of the canonical revision by the Chronicler must be understood from the perspective of the intensifying controversy with the Samaritans.

When the Samaritan community began to establish on Mt. Gerizim a competitive model to the Jewish community at the beginning of the Hellenistic period, they appealed to the Pentateuch for legitimation. Thus, for Judah it became urgent at least to maintain a claim to leadership. "This occurred at the beginning of the third century through the creation of Chronicles."[16] Since the pillars of the Judean claim—the Jerusalem temple and the Davidic Kingdom—do not appear in the Pentateuch, however, a canonical revision in the sense of an enhancement was made with the help of Chronicles, with the intention of providing official recognition for the "historical tradition of DtrH, and for the prophetic writings that enforced the salvation traditions specific to Jerusalem."[17] The Chronicler "paved the way for the canonization of the historical and prophetic traditions"[18] by means of a series of syntheses between the Torah and the historical and prophetic traditions that had been marginalized by the canonization of the Pentateuch.

Albertz describes four of these syntheses in more detail: (1) By a synthesis between the Torah and DtrH—to be seen, for example, in the explicit

---

an explanation of this demarcation, see T. Willi, *Chronik* [BKAT 24/1; Neukirchen-Vluyn: Neukirchener Verlag, 1991] 7–9; and my *Chronik als kanonisches Abschlußphänomen*, 237–39) only "speak" if the recipients are familiar with the genealogies, esp. of Genesis; cf. M. Oeming, *Das wahre Israel: Die "genealogische Vorhalle" 1 Chronik 1–9* (BWANT 128; Stuttgart: Kohlhammer, 1990) 206–7. Familiarity with the sources as a vital reception condition is valid for Chronicles altogether. An especially instructive example is the laconic phrasing "Abram, this is Abraham" (1 Chr 1:27), which refers the hearer/reader back to Genesis 17 and the whole Abrahamic story in Genesis.

14. The "canonical process" as new acquisition and actualization of the biblical traditions must be distinguished from the "canonization" that ended this innerbiblical process. Regarding the "canonical process" as the vital factor of "becoming scripture," see Childs, *Introduction to the OT*, 77–79.

15. Cf. R. Albertz, *Religionsgeschichte Israels in alttestamentlicher Zeit* (Grundrisse zum Alten Testament 8/2; Göttingen: Vandenhoeck & Ruprecht, 1992) 609ff. and the chart on pp. 466–67.

16. Ibid., 608.

17. Ibid., 610.

18. Ibid., 622.

references to the Torah and the inclusion of Priestly elements in the presentation of the king narratives—the Chronicler substantiated his purpose of writing "a history of Israel according to the rules of the canonical Torah."[19] (2) The frequent references to prophets revealed the purpose, which was "again to grant prophecy a larger role in the official YHWH-religion than the fathers of the Torah wanted to concede, for fear of an undue proportion of enthusiasm based on personal experience of the divine."[20] (3) By receiving the Jerusalem Psalms tradition, the Chronicler demonstrated "that ritual and historical reality—rightly perceived—are ultimately identical."[21] (4) "The fourth and last synthesis of the Chronicler was to intensify personal piety in the presentation of the official religion of YHWH."[22]

Albertz's description of the integrative achievements of the Chronicler provides pivotal information on the literary and theological work of the Chronicler, who "merged almost all of the religious traditions of the Old Testament that had been separate before into a unity."[23] Albertz's quest to determine precisely how Chronicles developed the canon advances the discussion in a decisive way. His specific elaboration of this new approach, however, must be firmly rejected, since—setting aside for now his appeal to the "Samaritan schism,"[24] which is problematic from the point of view of literary and religious history—Albertz in my opinion confuses the *precondition* of the Chronicler's work with its *consequences*: Chronicles was not paving the way for the canonization of the second canonical section but, to use another image, was the heir to a canonical process that had advanced beyond this point long before; it already presupposed the closure of the canonical division of the Prophets.[25]

---

19. Ibid., 612.
20. Ibid., 615.
21. Ibid., 616.
22. Ibid., 616.
23. Ibid., 622.
24. Concerning this problem, see a résumé of the newer discussion in O. Kaiser, *Einleitung in das Alte Testament* (Gütersloh: Gütersloher Verlag, 1984) 406; also H. Donner, *Geschichte des Volkes Israel und seiner Nachbarn in Grundzügen* (Grundrisse zum Alten Testament 4/2; Göttingen: Vandenhoeck & Ruprecht, 1986) 435–36. At the current state of research, it seems to be advisable not to burden the "schism" with oppressive arguments, even less so the reconstruction of Old Testament literary history, which is burdened with quite a few additional uncertainties.
25. Concerning the theological function of the books of the Prophets in 1–2 Chronicles, see H. G. M. Williamson, "History," in *It Is Written: Scripture Citing Scripture. FS B. Lindars* (ed. D. A. Carson and H. G. M. Williamson; Cambridge: Cambridge University Press, 1988) 25–38, esp. pp. 34–35. Books in the third canonical division already had a high level of authority as well. The role of the Psalter can, for one thing, be determined from the fact that the Chronicler develops the fiction of the classes of temple musicians from the psalm headings together with the Pentateuch's arrangements of the Levitical temple staff; for more detail, see my *Chronik als kanonisches Abschlußphänomen*, 254–81, 419–28. Concerning the influence of the Psalter on 1–2 Chronicles, see further W. Riley, *King and Cultus in Chronicles* (JSOTSup 160; Sheffield: Sheffield Academic Press, 1993) 33–36; and P. Welten,

Even before Chronicles was composed, the canonical "process of synthesizing" had advanced more than Albertz supposes, as can be seen in a study on the report of the building of the Solomonic temple. In the form received by the Chronicler, 1 Kings 6–8 had already been reworked with reference to the Torah—especially the description of the Sinai sanctuary in Exodus 25–40. Correspondingly, the Solomonic temple had been called האהל "the tent" in 1 Kgs 7:45. This is an old insight from literary-critical work on the books of Kings, from Stade to Würthwein.[26] Already in the pre-Chronistic period, the evident assimilation of the Torah by the following books must be taken into account. Thus, the Chronicler inherited the existing tradition of assimilation. The novelty is that the alignments made by the Chronicler were not worked into existing texts but were accomplished in an autonomous work. This presupposes that the diverging sources that the Chronicler wanted to mediate were already quite stable and independent. In a sense, there was a mature consciousness of the "unalterability" of the sources.[27]

1.3. Reorientation of the Canon Question

The above-mentioned arguments, only developed briefly here, can easily be combined with the canonical theory of Steck with regard to the question of the formation of the canonical division of the Prophets. Steck posited that

> after 240/220 B.C.E. . . . and before 180 B.C.E. (Sirach), the extent and order of the Scriptures, as it is found in the Later Prophets division of the Hebrew canon, was conceived as a literary macro unit, closed in itself and connected to the Torah, which formed a thematic and literary point of view that could not be augmented or updated (*fortschreiben*) anymore.[28]

While the thesis about the formation of the canonical division of the Prophets around 200 B.C.E. can easily be substantiated by indications within the literary corpus, by external witnesses (Sirach 44–49), and by historical considerations,[29] reconstructing the formation of the third section of the canon poses greater difficulties.[30] This lack of sources explains the success of the theory of a canonical closure at the "Synod of Jamnia"

"Lade – Tempel – Jerusalem: Zur Theologie der Chronikbücher," in *Textgemäß: FS E. Würthwein* (ed. A. H. J. Gunneweg and O. Kaiser; Göttingen: Vandenhoeck & Ruprecht, 1979) 169–83. Concerning the relationship of Ezra–Nehemiah to 1–2 Chronicles, see below.

26. Cf. B. Stade, "Der Text des Berichtes über Salomos Bauten 1 Kö. 5–7," in *ZAW* 3 (1883) 129–77; incorporated by M. Noth, *Könige I 1–16* (BKAT 9/1; Neukirchen-Vluyn: Neukirchener Verlag, 1983); and E. Würthwein, *Die Bücher der Könige* (ATD 11/1; Göttingen: Vandenhoeck & Ruprecht, 1985) ad loc.

27. See the second part of the wording about the canon: "You shall not take away anything nor shall you add anything thereto" (Dohmen and Oeming, *Biblischer Kanon*, 89).

28. Steck, *Abschluß der Prophetie*, 144.

29. Ibid.

30. See already K. Budde, *Der Kanon des Alten Testaments: Ein Abriß* (Gießen: Alfred Töpelmann, 1900) 49ff.

at the end of the 1st century C.E., which was first proposed by the Jewish historian Heinrich Graetz in 1871 but which has been dismantled in the meantime.[31]

Appeals to the tenuous body of sources or skeptical labels of *non liquet* do not need to be the last words on the issue, however. They can be taken as impetus for a reorientation "away from a historical-descriptive effort to conceptualize canonical history toward a content-related search for closure phenomena in the texts themselves."[32] That this does not, back-handedly, turn a need into a virtue can be seen by reflecting on the basis for the phenomenon of canonization: The "canonization of Holy Scripture (is) not to be conceived from the endpoint . . . as a rigid principle of distinction and selection but, rather, as a dynamic process that can even be seen in the oldest forms of dealing with those writings, when for example, older texts were not set aside as outdated but were edited and thus brought up to date."[33] The "question of the canon" is therefore—according to Dohmen and Oeming—a "question of the genealogy of the canon."[34] To be more precise, it is a question of where the breakpoints or closure phenomena may be found that show the transition from a canonical process to canonization. In this perspective, the three-part structure of the canon that evolved organically becomes the key to reconstructing a tiered canonization.[35]

Steck believes he is able to grasp the beginning of a canonization of the Writings in the book of Psalms; he sees the Psalter as the starting point for the crystallization of the collection (*Kristallisationspunkt*) that played a central role in the emergence of the Writings.[36] Dohmen sees another *Kristallisationspunkt* in the epilogue of the book of Ecclesiastes (Eccl 12:9–14).[37] In recent research, Chronicles is being appreciated as an important witness

---

31. Cf. P. Schäfer, "Die sogenannte Synode von Jabne: Zur Trennung von Juden und Christen im ersten/zweiten Jh. n. Chr.," in *Studien zur Geschichte und Theologie des Rabbinischen Judentums* (ed. P. Schäfer; Leiden: Brill, 1978) 45–64; J. Maier, *Jüdische Auseinandersetzungen mit dem Christentum in der Antike* (Erträge der Forschung 177; Darmstadt: Wissenschaftliche Buchgesellschaft, 1982); G. Stemberger, "Jabne und der Kanon," in *Zum Problem des biblischen Kanons* (ed. I. Baldermann et al.; JBTh 3; Neukirchen-Vluyn: Neukirchener Verlag, 1988) 163–74; and others. Meanwhile, this critic has dropped the broadly accepted idea of a canonical decision at Jamnia. However the *consequences* of the Jamnia theory are frequently maintained and the open-endedness of the third canonical division is presupposed for the 1st Century C.E. without new arguments.

32. Dohmen and Oeming, *Biblischer Kanon,* 57.

33. Ibid., 57.

34. Ibid., 25.

35. See additional indications of the "rank" of the three canon divisions presented by J. Maier, "Zur Frage des biblischen Kanons im Frühjudentum im Lichte der Qumranfunde," in *Zum Problem des biblischen Kanons* (ed. I. Baldermann et al.; JBTh 3; Neukirchen-Vluyn: Neukirchener Verlag, 1988) 135–46, esp. p. 138.

36. Cf. Steck, *Abschluß der Prophetie,* 157–66.

37. Dohmen proposes "that a former collection, 'wisdom' was the predecessor of a far more widespread collection of Scriptures canonized from the perspective of Torah, or that it was integrated in such a collection" (Dohmen and Oeming, *Biblischer Kanon,* 154).

to the canonical process,[38] but its role in the canonization of the third division of the canon has not been taken into consideration. Before this question can be pursued further, however, two objections must be eliminated that may result from current, well-established positions on the origin of Chronicles and the so-called Chronicler's History.

2. The Independence and Chronological Placement of the Books of Chronicles

In well-established matters (issues of introduction), there are some objections to connecting the formation of Chronicles with the final stages of the third division of the canon.[39] On one hand, many scholars accept the thesis of a "Chronicler's History" that contained 1–2 Chronicles and Ezra–Nehemiah; on the other hand, there is a relative consensus among scholars about dating Chronicles to the late Persian/early Hellenistic period. Both questions belong together given that the original connection of Chronicles with Ezra–Nehemiah is an argument against a late date for Chronicles, since Ezra–Nehemiah could not be later than the 3rd century B.C.

2.1. The Thesis of a "Chronicler's History"

The thesis of a "Chronicler's History" reaching from 1 Chronicles to Nehemiah 13 was seen as an assured result of scholarship for a long time; in a sense, it was one of the pillars of historical-critical research.[40] For the past 25 years, however, this question has been discussed extensively. Four classic arguments for a "Chronicler's History" appear in the research: (1) the linguistic relationship between 1–2 Chronicles and Ezra–Nehemiah; (2) correlations in the content; (3) the overlapping of Chronicles' conclusion with the beginning of Ezra; and (4) the testimony of the book of 1 Esdras (which runs parallel to 2 Chronicles 35–36; Ezra 1–10, and Nehemiah 8). These arguments have undergone a great deal of criticism, especially with regard to the often-neglected differences between the two books (Chronicles and Ezra–Nehemiah) and the undeniable fact that the books were passed on separately according to the oldest Jewish and Christian testimonies. Heinrich Schneider had referred to the latter fact already by the end of the 1950s (that is, a decade before the beginning of the newer debate on the "Chroni-

---

38. See above; see also Dohmen and Oeming, *Biblischer Kanon*, 95–96; W. Johnstone, "Chronicles, Canon and Context," *Aberdeen University Review* 169 (1983) 1–18; idem, "Reactivating The Chronicles Analogy in Pentateuchal Studies, with Special Reference to the Sinai Pericope in Exodus," *ZAW* 99 (1987) 16–37; and others.

39. Cf. my *Chronik als kanonisches Abschlußphänomen*, 49–83, 491–99; a short presentation of my position also appears in Zenger, *Einleitung*, 165–83.

40. Cf. M. Noth, *Überlieferungsgeschichtliche Studien: Die sammelnden und bearbeitenden Geschichtswerke im Alten Testament* (Tübingen: Max Niemeyer, 1967) 110: "However, it is certain and generally accepted that with 1–2 Chronicles and Ezra–Nehemiah we have *one* work before us. Therefore, in this case the literal affiliation does not need to be argued further, as it is the case for Dtr."

cler's History")[41] in his commentary on Ezra–Nehemiah in the "Bonner Bible" and concluded that the book of Ezra–Nehemiah should not be interpreted with respect to 1–2 Chronicles.[42]

The strongest arguments against a "Chronicler's History" are not the linguistic or thematic differences but the different composition principles in the books of Chronicles, on the one hand, and Ezra–Nehemiah, on the other. In Chronicles, the borrowed material as well as the native material are consistently arranged according to a uniform principle, which is often called the "doctrine of immediate retribution."[43] This is based on the principle that commitment to the Torah, especially regarding the main commandment, is decisive for the success or failure of each king. Sometimes the shaping of the royal histories according to the principle of retribution goes so far that the Chronicler bends the story to the constraints of his system. A prominent and characteristic example of this is Manasseh. The Chronicler explains his unusually long period of rule—55 years—by stating that the king must have converted after a time of defection from God so that in his later years of governing he did exactly the opposite of the things he did in his early years. This is not about doctrine, as the phrase about the "Chronicler's doctrine of retribution" or the like may imply; it is about a dominating literary principle of composition and about the central principle of the Chronicler's hermeneutics of Scripture. Corresponding principles are not present in Ezra–Nehemiah.[44]

The theory of the "Chronicler's History" was developed in the 1930s under premises that have lost their vitality in today's research. Both Zunz[45] and Movers[46] focused mainly on identifying the author of Chronicles. Due to criticism of the traditional opinion of Ezra as the author of Chronicles, the Chronicler was now postulated as being the author of both Ezra and Chronicles, because of the asserted correlation between the two works. Based on my observation, the latest research takes as a starting point the undisputed testimony that 1–2 Chronicles and Ezra–Nehemiah were

---

41. The impulse for this discussion is found in a survey by S. Japhet, "The Supposed Common Authorship of Chronicles and Ezra–Nehemiah Investigated Anew," *VT* 18 (1968) 330–71.

42. Cf. H. Schneider, *Die Bücher Esra und Nehemia* (Heilige Schrift des Alten Testaments 4/2; Bonn: Hanstein, 1959) 31–34, 80.

43. There are additional details presented on this subject in §3.3 below.

44. Another important difference on the level of composition is the major importance given to the speeches in 1–2 Chronicles, with their typical composition technique; see G. von Rad, "Die levitische Predigt in den Büchern der Chronik," in *Gesammelte Studien zum Alten Testament* (ed. G. von Rad; Theologische Bücherei 8; Munich: Chr. Kaiser, 1971) 248–61; M. A. Throntveit, *When Kings Speak: Royal Speech and Royal Prayer in Chronicles* (SBLDS 93; Atlanta: Scholars Press, 1987); and R. Mason, *Preaching the Tradition: Homily and Hermeneutics after the Exile* (Cambridge: Cambridge University Press, 1990).

45. L. Zunz, *Die gottesdienstlichen Vorträge der Juden* (Frankfurt, 1892) 22, and often on the following pages.

46. Cf. F. C. Movers, *Kritische Untersuchungen über die biblische Chronik* (Bonn, 1834) 14, 24, and often on the following pages.

transmitted separately. The similarities between the two works were used in the past as an argument for a single work by the proponents of the "Chronicler's History" but were also downplayed by some of its opponents; today, more-nuanced positions are posited. Either Chronicles and Ezra–Nehemiah are seen as two works written by the same author or group of authors, or literary dependencies between the two works are postulated (for example, Ezra–Nehemiah as a source for 1–2 Chronicles, or editorial activities aligning the two books).

We must adhere to separate compositions for the two works, which should not be compositionally assigned to each other as a "Chronicler's double work." The differences as well as the similarities can be explained by a twofold relationship: the oldest version of 1–2 Chronicles already presupposes a book of Ezra–Nehemiah and uses it as a source alongside others.[47] Numerous additional parallels between the works result from the fact that very late additions were made to Ezra–Nehemiah that correlate to the development of 1–2 Chronicles (especially the expansion of the explanations about the Levitical musicians).[48]

2.2. The Question of Dating

Researchers often emphasize that assured evidence for determining the age of Chronicles is missing.[49] Thus, the many suggestions for the date of the book are not surprising; they range from the late 6th century to the middle of the 2nd century B.C.E.[50] The relative consensus in current research is based primarily on three arguments: (1) the missing Hellenistic influence; (2) the image of David in Sir 47:9–10, which presupposes the Chronicler's image of David; and (3) the historian Eupolemus, who used the LXX translation of Chronicles around 158 B.C.E.[51] Thus, some conclude that Chronicles had to be written at the latest at the end of the 3rd century.

On closer examination, all three arguments prove insufficient. Against the hypothesis of missing Hellenistic influence, one may counter that Chronicles' strong interest in genealogical data is parallel to the Hellenistic interest in historiography. Even if one accepts this hypothesis, however, one must acknowledge that it is of little significance since it is an *argumentum e silentio*. The implicit presupposition that each literary work must be a mirror of the general principles and representation models in the dominant culture of its time is not satisfying from a sociological perspective. In

---

47. For example, 1 Chronicles 9 incorporates Nehemiah 11.

48. On the complexity of the problem and for an explanation of the solution, see my *Chronik als kanonisches Abschlußphänomen*, 49–82, 442–43.

49. See recently S. Japhet, *I and II Chronicles: A Commentary* (OTL; Louisville: Westminster John Knox, 1993) 25.

50. See the overview in I. Kalimi, "Die Abfassungszeit der Chronik: Forschungsstand und Perspektiven," *ZAW* 105 (1993) 223–33; additionally, my "Zur Datierung der Chronik: Ein neuer methodischer Ansatz," *ZAW* 109 (1997) 84–92.

51. This date is not undisputed; for a date around 145 B.C., see M. Hengel, *Judentum und Hellenismus* (Tübingen: Mohr, 1973) 170 n. 260.

an era of restoration, could it not just as well be true that foreign cultural influences were deliberately repressed by the author/editor's orienting himself strictly toward the main works of his own tradition?[52]

Due to missing linguistic similarities, the dependence of Sirach on Chronicles cannot be proven; a few years ago, Ben Zvi (like Noth, Ackroyd, and others before him) verified in his survey on the reception history of the books of Chronicles in early Jewish literature that Chronicles did not shape Sirach's image of the past.[53]

The idea of Eupolemus's direct dependence on LXX Chronicles seems to be questionable when both the similarities and the significant differences between the description of Solomon by Eupolemus and that by 2 Chronicles are taken into consideration. Moreover, one must remember that the Chronicler's story about Solomon had a complicated literary prehistory. In my opinion, the Chronicler's presentation of Solomon not only did not draw on 1 Kings 6–8 but also did not draw on extrabiblical material. The passage about the building of the temple is quite incoherent, and there are striking correlations with the Temple Scroll (11QT).[54] Thus, it is not easy to determine on which text Eupolemus depended.

Some authors who date the books of Chronicles to the late Persian/early Hellenistic period draw conclusions about its literary history that turn out to be problematic. In Noth, Rudolph, and (following them) Willi, the impression arises that there were—to put it pointedly—two different Chronistic works. One is a "Story of Davidides,"[55] which must be dated to the period already mentioned and which reflects, primarily, the problem of statehood. The second, extended edition is a story dated to the early Maccabean time that accentuates the subject of temple service (especially the order of the Levitical cult staff). The correlation between the two stages is not explained in more detail by Noth and the others.

In approaching this issue, one can show that the oldest conjectured stage of composition was shaped by the cult through and through and that, in this respect, there is no basic difference between the oldest stage and later revisions (Willi, by contrast, isolates extensive "additions [that were made] due to cultic influence").[56] There is no need to conjecture that

---

52. Japhet, *I and II Chronicles*, 25–26. draws attention to the fact that Persian influences can be found only marginally in 1–2 Chronicles and hence shows how low the argumentative value of general "cultural" references is.

53. E. Ben Zvi, "The Authority of 1–2 Chronicles in the Late Second Temple Period," *JSP* 3 (1988) 59–88, esp. p. 62: "Ben Sira's image of the past was not shaped by CHR."

54. The use of extrabiblical material is postulated for many positions on Chronicles; by comparison with the Temple Scroll, some more security can be obtained in the case of the report of the temple construction with the identification of *one* extrabiblical source; see my *Chronik als kanonisches Abschlußphänomen*, 373–94.

55. Willi, *Die Chronik als Auslegung*, 203.

56. This can be demonstrated by the Chronicler's concept of the covenant. The expression *covenant* is used theologically in the books of Chronicles in three contexts: in relation to the Sinai and Davidic covenants, and then in the context of the four "covenants" under

the formation of Chronicles stretched over a longer period. Even if one distinguishes between different stages of revision, these stages were so close together, considering their topics and literary technique ("exegesis of Scripture"), that the idea of a short-term literary process seems more plausible. Those responsible for this process would have been a group of scribes who probably worked closely with the leading Levitical groups of musicians and gatekeepers for the temple.[57]

There is no evidence *against* dating the books of Chronicles in the early Maccabean age.[58] A few years ago, Kellermann and Kegler presented arguments *in favor of* such a late date for the book. Both agreed that in Chronicles a polemical situation is quite evident. Based on the prophetic image in Chronicles, Kegler located the book in a historical situation

> in which the threat to the Jewish identity by foreign cults was particularly intensive. On the one hand there is a strict distinction between "Israel" and "Judah," and on the other hand there is the conception of a "true Israel" that becomes apparent in the loyalty to the Davidic Monarchy and the legitimacy of the Levitical priesthood, in ritual practices focused on fostering the temple music at its center, in relying on Yhwh alone, in a strict rejection of any kind of idolatry or adoration of foreign gods, and in the renunciation of power politics in place of relying on Yhwh alone. All these point to a historical situation in which Judahite identity has fallen into a deep crisis.[59]

For Kegler, the growth of Hellenism also reflected this crisis, although he does not mention an absolute date. Kellermann observes a remarkable analogy between Chronicles and the historical background of the books of Maccabees.

> It is striking that the deficits denounced in the Chronicler's scripture correspond in a structural sense to the massive cultic changes in Jerusalem and Judah during the peak of the Hellenistic turmoil, in 167–164 B.C.E.

---

the post-Solomonic kings (2 Chr 15:11–15; 2 Chr 23:16 // 2 Kgs 11:17; 2 Chr 29:10; 2 Chr 34:29–33 // 2 Kgs 23:1–3). In these four texts, there is a consistent, cultically dominated covenant theology; see below, §3.2.

57. Cf. my *Chronik als kanonisches Abschlußphänomen*, 415–41. Concerning the formation of the scribal class, cf. Albertz, *Religionsgeschichte Israels*, 599–600; concerning the meaning of the temple in the tradition of the biblical texts: J. Maier, *Zwischen den Testamenten: Geschichte und Religion in der Zeit des Zweiten Tempels* (NEB 3; Würzburg: Echter-Verlag, 1990) 21; and idem, *Zur Frage des biblischen Kanons*, 137–40.

58. Cf. Noth, *Überlieferungsgeschichtliche Studien*, 155: After the plea not to date the primary layer of the Chronicler's work before 300, he admits: "[A]nyone who dated Chronicles later would be unable to defend the position." In his following considerations, Noth combines the dating question with considerations about the history of the canon! Concerning the dating, see also P. R. Ackroyd, "Criteria for the Maccabean Dating of Old Testament Literature," *VT* 3 (1963) 126–27.

59. J. Kegler, "Prophetengestalten im Deuteronomistischen Geschichtswerk und in den Chronikbüchern: Ein Beitrag zur Kompositions- und Redaktionsgeschichte der Chronikbücher," *ZAW* 105 (1993) 496.

The books of 1 and 2 Maccabees correspond exactly to the Chronicler's intentions in describing this period by naming and judging its apostasy from the Torah.[60]

Observing this ideological affinity does not bring Kellermann to the conclusion that the works relate to the same chronological background. He does not use these findings to refute the usual dating of Chronicles but instead explains the remarkable analogies in such a way that the Chronicler anticipated them in his time and was apprehensive of the things that became true under Antiochus IV. This problematic recourse to the anticipation of the Chronicler becomes unnecessary, however, if these striking parallels between the books of Chronicles and the books of Maccabees are understood as reactions to the same historical situation.[61]

3. The "Torah-Binding" of the Books of Chronicles

Within Chronicles, *Torah* is not a topic alongside others but is, in many ways, the formative topic: living according to Yhwh's Torah plays a decisive role on the level of content (see 2 Chr 6:16). Moreover, the Torah determines the form of the presentation and of the Chronicler's hermeneutic of Scripture. Finally, elements of a theory of Torah interpretation can be found in the books of Chronicles. Apparently, the catchword *Torah* brings the center of the Chronicler's work and theology into view.

3.1. On the Meaning of the Expression Torah

In Chronicles, *Torah* is a homonymous word; several meanings of the word must be distinguished. First, the occurrences of the word *Torah* and related expressions and explicit references to the Torah (e.g., "Moses has said") will be registered here, as they appear in the text. This overview demonstrates the large number of occurrences. It also documents the parallel verses in Samuel/Kings (with a note about whether the relevant expressions were redactionally inserted or modified). Since there are significant correlations in terminology with Ezra and Nehemiah, these two books are also included in this overview.[62]

---

60. U. Kellermann, "Anmerkungen zum Verständnis der Tora in den chronistischen Schriften," in *BN* 42 (1988) 87.

61. This is because only during the Maccabean period can a religious crisis be taken into account that matches the "world-war dimension" of the conflict being suggested for Chronicles. With this expression, A. Ruffing, *Jahwekrieg als Weltmetapher: Studien zu den Jahwekriegstexten des chronistischen Sondergutes* (SBB 24; Stuttgart: Katholisches Bibelwerk, 1992) 36, characterizes the total threat to Judah as it appears in the war narratives; he sees the crucial trait of the Chronicler's war texts of Yahweh as being this great in dimension.

62. Based on my remarks in §2.1, these congruities cannot not be classified as arguments for a "Chronistic work." The evidence requires a nuanced explanation; on the one hand, 1–2 Chronicles and Ezra–Nehemiah are characterized by the language of their age; on the other hand, a correlation of the results with the redaction-critical insights concerning Ezra–Nehemiah shows that the majority of the parallels appear in the late complex

Table 1. *References to the Torah in Chronicles and Ezra–Nehemiah*

Passage	Hebrew Expression	Parallel Passage, if Any / Inserted or Modified
1 Chr 6:17	ויעמדו כמשפטם	—
1 Chr 6:34	ככל אשר צוה משה עבד האלהים	—
1 Chr 10:13	על־דבר יי אשר לא־שמר	—
1 Chr 15:13	כי־לא דרשנהו כמשפט	—
1 Chr 15:15	כאשר צוה משה כדבר יי	—
1 Chr 16:40	ולכל־הכתוב בתורת יי אשר צוה על־ישראל	—
1 Chr 22:12	ולשמור את־תורת יי אלהיך	—
1 Chr 22:13	לעשות את־החקים ואת־המשפטים אשר צוה יי את־ משה על־ישראל	—
1 Chr 23:31	כמשפט	—
1 Chr 24:19	כמשפטם ביד אהרן אביהם כאשר צוהו יי אלהי ישראל	—
1 Chr 28:7	לעשות מצותי ומשפטי	—
1 Chr 28:8	כל־מצות יי אלהיכם	—
1 Chr 29:19	לשמור מצותיך עדותיך וחקיך	—
2 Chr 2:3	לעולם זאת על־ישראל	—
2 Chr 4:7	כמשפטם	—
2 Chr 4:20	כמשפט	1 Kgs 7:49/inserted
2 Chr 6:16	ללכת בתורתי	1 Kgs 8:25/inserted
2 Chr 6:27	כי תורם אל־הדרך הטובה	1 Kgs 8:36/modified
2 Chr 6:31	ללכת בדרכיך	1 Kgs 8:40/inserted
2 Chr 7:17	ולעשות ככל אשר צויתיך וחקי ומשפטי תשמור	1 Kgs 9:5
2 Chr 7:19	חקותי ומצותי אשר נתתי לפניכם	1 Kgs 9:6/modified
2 Chr 8:13	כמצות משה	—

of Nehemiah 7–10 (on the redaction-critical classification, see my *Chronik als kanonisches Abschlußphänomen*, 167–208). Small differences in the use of language deserve attention too; e.g., the expression תורת האלהים (Neh 8:8, 18; 10:29–30) is not used in 1–2 Chronicles even though the Chronicler often replaces the Tetragrammaton with האלהים. Apart from this, the widespread use of standard expressions cannot be adduced as an argument for consistent authorship; only linguistic particularities or exclusive ideas appear. Given the Torah terminology, an idiolect in 1–2 Chronicles and Ezra–Nehemiah is not apparent.

In Ezra–Nehemiah, one observes an accumulation of expressions for "Torah" (Ezra 7 and Nehemiah 8–10); on the differences in the understanding of "Torah" in the two complexes, see R. Rendtorff, "Esra und das Gesetz," *ZAW* 96 (1984) 165–84; and especially T. Willi, *Juda – Jehud – Israel: Studien zum Selbstverständnis des Judentums in persischer Zeit* (FAT 12; Tübingen: Mohr, 1995) 90–117; on the historical classification of the texts, see my *Chronik als kanonisches Abschlußphänomen*, 167–208.

Passage	Hebrew Expression	Parallel Passage, if Any / Inserted or Modified
2 Chr 12:1	עזב את־תורת יי	—
2 Chr 13:11	שמרים . . . את־משמרת יי אלהינו	—
2 Chr 14:3	ולעשות התורה והמצוה	—
2 Chr 15:3	וללא תורה	—
2 Chr 17:6	ויגבה לבו בדרכי יי	—
2 Chr 17:9	ועמהם ספר תורת יי	—
2 Chr 19:10	בין־תורה למצוה לחקים ולמשפטים	—
2 Chr 23:6	ישמרו משמרת יי	2 Kgs 11:7/modified
2 Chr 23:18	ככתוב בתורת משה	—
2 Chr 24:20	את מצות יי	—
2 Chr 25:4	כי ככתוב בתורה בספר משה אשר־צוה יי לאמר	2 Kgs 14:6/modified
2 Chr 29:15	בדברי יי	—
2 Chr 30:5	כי לא לרב עשו ככתוב	—
2 Chr 30:12	בדבר יי	—
2 Chr 30:16	כמשפטם כתורת משה איש־האלהים	—
2 Chr 30:18	כי־אכלו את־הפסח בלא ככתוב	—
2 Chr 31:3	ככתוב בתורת יי	—
2 Chr 31:4	למען יחזקו בתורת יי	—
2 Chr 31:21	ובתורה ובמצוה	—
2 Chr 33:8	לעשות את כל־אשר צויתים לכל־התורה והחקים והמשפטים ביד־משה	2 Kgs 21:8/modified
2 Chr 34:14	את־ספר תורת־יי ביד־משה	2 Kgs 22:7/inserted
2 Chr 34:15	ספר התורה מצאתי . . . את־הספר	2 Kgs 22:8
2 Chr 34:16	את־הספר	2 Kgs 22:9
2 Chr 34:18	ספר נתן לי חלקיהו	2 Kgs 22:10
2 Chr 34:19	את דברי התורה	2 Kgs 22:11/modified
2 Chr 34:21	על־דברי הספר . . . את־דבר יי לעשות ככל־הכתוב על־הספר הזה	2 Kgs 22:13
2 Chr 34:24	את כל־האלות הכתובות על־הספר	2 Kgs 22:16
2 Chr 34:27	בשמעך את־דבריו	2 Kgs 22:19/modified
2 Chr 34:30	את־כל־דברי ספר הברית	2 Kgs 23:2
2 Chr 34:31	ולשמור את־מצותיו ועדותיו וחקיו . . . לעשות את־ דברי הברית הכתובים על־הספר הזה	2 Kgs 23:3/modified
2 Chr 35:6	לעשות כדבר־יי ביד־משה	—

Passage	Hebrew Expression	Parallel Passage, if Any / Inserted or Modified
2 Chr 35:12	ככתוב בספר משה	—
2 Chr 35:13	ויבשלו הפסח באש כמשפט	—
2 Chr 35:26	ככתוב בתורת יי	2 Kgs 23:28/inserted
2 Chr 36:16	דבריו	—
Ezra 3:2	ככתוב בתורת משה איש־האלהים	
Ezra 3:4	ככתוב . . . כמשפט	
Ezra 6:18	ככתב ספר משה	
Ezra 7:6	ספר מהיר בתורת משה אשר־נתן יי אלהי ישראל	
Ezra 7:10	לדרוש את־תורת יי ולעשׂת וללמד בישראל חק ומשפט	
Ezra 7:11	דברי מצות־יי וחקיו על־ישראל	
Ezra 7:12	ספר דתא די־אלה שמיא	
Ezra 7:14	בדת אלהך די בידך	
Ezra 7:21	דתא די־אלה שמיא	
Ezra 7:25	דתי אלהך	
Ezra 7:26	דתא די־אלהך	
Ezra 9:4	בדברי אלהי־ישראל	
Ezra 9:10	עזבנו מצותיך	
Ezra 9:14	להפר מצותיך	
Ezra 10:3	במצות אלהינו וכתורה יעשׂה	
Neh 1:5	ולשמרי מצותיו	
Neh 1:7	את־המצוה ואת־החקים ואת־המשפטים אשר צוית את־משה עבדך	
Neh 1:9	ושמרתם מצותי	
Neh 8:1	את־ספר תורת משה אשר־צוה יי את־ישראל	
Neh 8:2	ויביא עזרא הכהן את־התורה	
Neh 8:3	ואזני כל־העם אל־ספר התורה	
Neh 8:5	ויפתח עזרא הספר	
Neh 8:7	מבינים את־העם לתורה	
Neh 8:8	בספר בתורת האלהים	
Neh 8:9	את־דברי התורה	
Neh 8:12	כי הבינו בדברים	
Neh 8:13	אל־דברי התורה	

Passage	Hebrew Expression	Parallel Passage, if Any / Inserted or Modified
Neh 8:14	כתוב בתורה אשר צוה יי ביד־מׁשה	
Neh 8:15	ככתוב	
Neh 8:18	בספר תורת האלהים . . . כמׁשפט	
Neh 9:3	בספר תורת יי אלהיהם	
Neh 9:13–14	ותתן להם מׁשפטים יׁשרים ותורות אמת חקים ומצות טובים . . . ומצוות וחקים ותורה צוית להם ביד מׁשה עבדך	
Neh 9:16	ולא שמעו אל־מצותיך	
Neh 9:26	וישלכו את־תורתך אחרי גום	
Neh 9:29	אל תורתך . . . למצותיך ובמׁשפטיך	
Neh 9:34	תורתך . . . אל־מצותיך ולעדותיך	
Neh 10:29	אל־תורת האלהים	
Neh 10:30	ללכת בתורת האלהים אשר נתנה ביד מׁשה עבד־האלהים ולשמור ולעשות את־כל מצות יי אדנינו ומׁשפטיו וחקיו	
Neh 10:33	והעמדנו עלינו מצות לתת . . .	
Neh 10:35	ככתוב בתורה	
Neh 10:37	ככתוב בתורה	
Neh 12:44	מנאות התורה	
Neh 13:1	בספר מׁשה . . . כתוב בו	
Neh 13:3	את־התורה	

The Chronicler used a large repertoire of expressions for and explicit references to the Torah. In addition, an examination of Ezra–Nehemiah shows that other linguistic possibilities were available in the late phase of the formation of the Old Testament. That the Chronicler refers to the Pentateuch when he mentions the "book of the law" is (as far as I can tell) not controversial among researchers.[63] Obviously, 2 Chr 35:13 is an attempt at harmonizing the varying regulations for Passover preparations in Exod 12:9 and Deut 16:7.[64] "In a similar way, [the Chronicler] speaks, as does P, of 'slaughtering' the Passover (30:15; 35:1, 6, 11 . . .), and in relation to 2 Kgs 23:21 (and other times) of 'making' the Passover."[65] From these

---

63. See, for example, Lohfink, *Begriff Bund*, 170: "[A]lready in the Bible itself, the Pentateuch is considered to be תורה or νομος. When Chronicles speaks of the 'Torah of Moses,' it has already the whole Pentateuch in mind."

64. Cf. M. Fishbane, *Biblical Interpretation in Ancient Israel* (Oxford: Clarendon, 1989) 135–37.

65. J. Becker, *2 Chronik* (NEB; Würzburg: Echter-Verlag, 1988) 121.

examples—and many others might be added—it can be observed that the Chronicler does in fact use the whole Pentateuch.

The thesis of the identity of "Torah" (as a written work) and the Pentateuch is confirmed by the report about the finding of the "book" during the reign of Josiah. The first mention of this book in 2 Chr 34:14 was arranged redactionally by the Chronicler and comprehensively describes the book by its content, author, and mediator with the phrase "the book of the Torah of Yʜwʜ, given through Moses." All other references to it combine only two of these elements.[66] Minor but meaningful changes in the report of finding the book confirm the theory of its identity:

> In [2 Chr 34:18], Shaphan reads *from* it (the book). Apparently for the Chronicler it is the complete Pentateuch. In the Vorlage, 2 Kgs 22:10, he reads *it* (the book) completely; however, he himself had already read it completely in 2 Kgs 22:8 (a detail that the Chronicler omits in [34:15] considering the size of the Pentateuch).[67]

Furthermore, the proposed identification of the Torah with the Pentateuch is supported by tradition-historical research on Chronicles. While older research emphasized the similarity of Chronicles to the Priestly Source, von Rad emphasized its relationship to Deuteronomy and its close relationship to the Pentateuch.[68] The indecisiveness of the history of research is based on the blending of traditional lines that already characterized the late stages of the Pentateuch and were continued by the "hermeneutical work" of the Chronicler according to the aforementioned example of 2 Chr 35:13.

As far as I can see, there is no disagreement over the basic theory of the identity of the Torah. It is questionable, however, which Pentateuch the Chronicler had at hand. Did the Pentateuch basically correlate with the text we know, or did he have another version? For the latter option, several passages can be presented that refer to individual regulations that have no basis in the Pentateuch.[69]

> 2 Chr 30:16 intends to receive the sacrificial blood for sprinkling on the altar by the priests from the hand of the Levites—a practice that the Pentateuch does not mention and that is otherwise unknown. 2 Chr 31:3

---

66. The only comparable expression is in a similarly prominent position in Neh 8:1 (however, it uses a verbal paraphrase for the divine origin): אשר־צוה יי את־ישראל את ספר־תורת משה.

67. Becker, *2 Chronik*, 119–20; likewise, H. G. M. Williamson, *1 and 2 Chronicles* (NCB; Grand Rapids, MI: Eerdmans, 1982) 402; and Japhet, *I and II Chronicles*, 1030.

68. Concerning von Rad, see below.

69. Cf. G. von Rad, *Das Geschichtsbild des chronistischen Werkes* (BWANT 4/3; Stuttgart: Kohlhammer, 1930) 63: "If one wants to name the normative code of law, then one must think of the Pentateuch;—with this proviso that not all of the laws that the Chronicler quotes can be found there. There remains a small residue for which no reference can be found in the Pentateuch, and this fact reminds us not to act too quickly regarding the Chronicler's code of law, as though it were a known entity."

refers to royal obligations in the ritual service that the Pentateuch does not pass down. The reference to an order for the Passover in 2 Chr 30:18 cannot be identified in the Pentateuch, even though it says "as it is written." Again, for the presentation of burnt offerings during the Passover celebration "as it is written in the book of Moses" (2 Chr 35:12), no corresponding passage can be found in the Pentateuch. The regulation about the temple tax (2 Chr 24:6, 9; Neh 10:33) and the order for delivering the firewood (Neh 10:35; 13:20–21) are not found in the Pentateuch either.[70]

From the references to the Pentateuch in the Masoretic version that refer to no known source, Shaver draws the conclusion that the Pentateuch was not permanently fixed during the time of the composition of Chronicles.

> The Chronicler was not limited to the Pentateuchal legislation of the Masoretic *textus receptus*, however, since his law (he claimed) also contained stipulations not included in the Hebrew Bible. . . . [T]he Chronicler's use of the Torah canon was not yet fixed. His Torah book appears to be more than the canonical Pentateuch; others have suggested that it was less. If that is so, then at least for the Chronicler the canonization of the Torah had not yet occurred.[71]

As argued above, this thesis has a number of factors in its favor. However, the differences between the wording of the Torah according to the Masoretic Text and the references to the Torah in 1–2 Chronicles do not force us in either case to conclude that the development of the Pentateuch was not yet completed at the time of the composition of the books of Chronicles.

The term *Torah* must not be constrained to a literary work. In various places, Chronicles preserves a "dynamic" understanding of "Torah." In 2 Chr 15:3 and 19:10, "Torah" (in both places, without the article) means the will of God as communicated currently, so the Chronicler is not referring only to the past. Otherwise, an institution established for the teaching of the Torah by the priests and the Levites, which is referred to in 2 Chr 17:7–9 and obviously refers to the present time of the Chronicler, would be incomprehensible.[72] Instead, the notion of being current and new that was originally associated with the term *Torah*[73] survived even after the formation of the abstract, singular term *Torah* that referred to a literary corpus. A similar "dynamic" understanding can be supposed regarding the expression, "word of Yʜwʜ." Obviously, this expression is used in 1 Chr 15:15; 2 Chr 29:15 (pl.), and 35:6 (perhaps also in 2 Chr 36:16) as a synonym for

---

70. Kellermann, *Anmerkungen zum Verständnis der Tora*, 90.

71. J. A. Shaver, *Torah and the Chronicler's History Work: An inquiry into the Chronicler's References to Laws, Festivals and Cultic Institutions in Relation to Pentateuchal Legislation* (Ph.D. diss., Notre Dame University, 1984) 187. [*Note*: This dissertation is identical to BJS 196 (Atlanta: Scholars Press, 1989), which was not available to me.]

72. Cf. Kellermann, *Anmerkungen zum Verständnis der Tora*, 90.

73. Cf. Willi, *Juda – Jehud – Israel*, 95–99.

the Torah.[74] Finally, another stage of abstraction in the use of the word *Torah* should be considered. The expression was not only used as shorthand for the book that is a collection of the individual commandments; it also came to mean the epitome of God's will (see 2 Chr 6:16), that is, of "direction" in general (cf. 2 Chr 6:27, 31). The rabbinic tradition systematized the coexistence of different understandings of the Torah in the doctrine of a twofold Torah—the written and the oral—and in the distinction between "Torah" and "Halakah." The distinction was not a rabbinic innovation but drew on developments that were already presupposed in biblical times and were therefore relocated by the rabbis to the Torah's point of origin, Sinai, where Moses was advised about both parts during his 40-day stay on the mountain.[75]

The problem can be addressed from yet another perspective. From table 1 above, one can easily see that use of *Torah* denoted a certain sort of conduct in only about one-third of the cases.[76] Thus, the demand for and emphasis on the Torah had a programmatic character: it was the basis or framework for a self-conception and behavior with which all individual decisions and actions should be integrated. These particular norms of action, however, do not follow the Torah primarily but the given day-to-day requirements. In concretizing the will of God, the "book" plays an important but not decisive role.

> The details of legislation respond to actual historical situations, prevalent customs, legal traditions and norms, and religious concepts. At the same time, and with no sensation of incoherence, the people of the restoration regard themselves as acting according to the written book.[77]

---

74. Cf. M. Zvi Brettler, *The Creation of History in Ancient Israel* (London: Routledge, 1995) 31, who comments on the expression "according to the word of Yʜᴡʜ" in 1 Chr 15:15: "This term fits with the Chronicler's new understanding of 'the *word* of Yʜᴡʜ', which is connected to the interpretation of Torah *texts* rather than to prophetic revelation."

75. See also Willi, *Juda – Jehud – Israel*, 111.

76. In such cases, usually the wording כמשפט ("according to the instruction") or ככתוב ("as it is written") is used; see table 1 above.

77. S. Japhet, "Law and 'the Law' in Ezra–Nehemiah," in *Proceedings of the 9th World Congress of Jewish Studies* (Jerusalem: The World Union of Jewish Studies, 1988) 99–115, esp. p. 115. The important differentiation between "Torah" and "standard of acting" is worked out by Japhet on texts of Ezra–Nehemiah:

> In this respect two matters seem to have become clear thus far in the course of our discussion: that the community of Israel in the time of the Restoration, as depicted by the book of Esra–Nehemiah, was seeking to build its life in the strictest conformity with the will of God; and that the written "Book of Moses" was regarded as the embodiment of God's will in his laws. The reading and study of the Law had become a major factor in public religious life; the foundations of faith, as well as the basic demands of pious conduct, were learned from the Law, either directly or by way of midrashic interpretation. These have indeed become the foundation for the community's self-understanding. However, in the realm of actual legislation, which was to cope directly with life's changing conditions and demands, and which established detailed prescriptions for the practical conduct of the individual

It is precisely this distinction between the basic aspect of guidance and the detailed norms of action that makes the "Torah of Yʜwʜ, mediated by Moses, written down in a book" the comprehensive and ever valid order of life. At the same time there is the continuous task of mediation between both levels.[78]

From this angle, a discrepancy between a specific law in Chronicles and the wording of the Pentateuch can be understood in two ways. One can either presuppose a different text of the Pentateuch or assume the normal case of a further development of the written Torah. The question is difficult to decide but also loses importance.[79]

3.2. Torah as the Content of the Presentation

"For the Chronicler, the Torah is the main pillar of his work."[80] The meaning of the Torah can be grasped at every turn in the Chronicler's presentation. In this article, observations regarding the role of the Torah on the level of content can only be presented in the form of examples and summarizing theses; the collection is based on the preceding list of explicit references to the Torah.[81]

(1) The speeches and sermons of royal and prophetic speakers require obedience to the Torah in that they orient one toward God's will as a whole (1 Chr 22:12–13; 28:8; 29:19; 2 Chr 13:11; 14:3; 24:20). This comprehensive understanding of Torah can also be found in divine speeches (1 Chr 28:7; 2 Chr 7:17, 19; 33:8) and prayers (2 Chr 6:16, 27, 31). For obedience to Torah as well as disobedience, the Chronicler has plenty of synonymous expressions on hand that go beyond the terminology of Torah in the narrow sense, shown in the overview ("searching God/leaving God . . .").

(2) The double meaning of Torah as the epitome of God's will and as an individual regulation can be observed in Chronicles continually. In many cases, it emphasizes the fact that a certain ritual practice is or should be practiced in accordance with the Torah (1 Chr 6:16–17, 34; 15:13, 15; 16:40; 23:31; 24:19; 2 Chr 2:3; 4:7, 20; 8:13; 23:18; 29:15; 30:5, 12, 16, 18; 31:3–4; 35:6, 12–13). Explicit references to regulations in the Torah appear frequently in the report of the Passover celebration under Hezekiah and

---

and the community, no strict adherence to the details of the law was attempted. In a paradoxical way, what may be called "a religion of the book" was not in fact "a religion of the letter." (pp. 114–15)

Similarly, see T. Willi, "Thora in den biblischen Chronikbüchern," in *Jud* 36 (1980) 102–5, 148–51; and Kellermann, *Anmerkungen zum Verständnis der Tora*, 89–91.

78. See below, §3.4.

79. Texts such as 4QMMT and 11QT prove that the "Oral Torah" was also put into writing early. In view of the wide understanding of the Torah as shown above, texts such as 11QT do not appear to have been concurrent texts intending to replace or replenish the Pentateuch. See §3.4 for the role of the written texts in the transmission of God's will.

80. G. López, "תורה, *tôrāh*," *ThWAT* 8.630.

81. Concerning the role of the Torah in Chronicles, see the recent, detailed research report by Kleinig, *Recent Research in Chronicles*.

Josiah and regarding the role of the Levitical temple staff.[82] In these concrete cases, the Torah is understood as a ritual regulation rather than in the broader sense of the will of God.

> The Chronicler defines *Torah* from the perspective of temple service, which corresponds to the phenomenon that references to interpersonal regulations appear rarely—in fact, at only one point in Chronicles. Here, the term *Torah* is only used in the matter of blood guilt: 2 Chr 19:10; 21:13; 24:25; 25:3 (refer to Deut 24:16). In this case, it is almost exclusively about the case of regicide.[83]

Reference to the Torah has been intensified by a redactor's numerous small additions that regulate details of the rituals being practiced by the Aaronic priesthood: maintenance of the lampstand and the table of the Bread of the Presence inside the temple, incense offerings, and regular עלה offerings. These additions appear in 1 Chr 28:17a, 29:21aγb (from במלאכת); 2 Chr 2:3aβ (from להקדיש)–5; 13:10 (only במלאכת), 11a (until בערב); 26:16b (על מזבח הקטרת), 19b (מעל למזבח הקטרת); 29:7, 11bβ (beginning at להיות), 18b, 21b (לבני אהרן הכהנים), 35a; 30:13ba; 31:2ab (beginning at איש), 3. All these entries are related to the basic texts about priestly ritual regulations in Exodus and Numbers (Exodus 30; Leviticus 23–24; Numbers 28–29; and others).[84]

(3) Of the post-Solomonic kings, Asa (2 Chr 14:1–3), Jehoshaphat (2 Chr 17:6), Hezekiah (2 Chr 31:30f.), and Josiah (2 Chr 35:26) are the only kings who are described as faithful followers of the Torah—that is, these are the kings who receive special attention by the Chronicler. Abandoning the law is explicitly noted only in the case of Rehoboam (2 Chr 12:1).

(4) In the four covenant ceremonies under Asa (2 Chr 15:11–15), Jehoiada (2 Chr 23:16 // 2 Kgs 11:17), Hezekiah (2 Chr 29:10), and Josiah (2 Chr 34:29–33 // 2 Kgs 23:1–3), the people obligate themselves to observe the Torah, which is expressed by removing all representations of foreign cult and by renewing the Yнwн-cult in Jerusalem. The central obligation, therefore, is the central commandment to worship Yнwн alone. The making of the covenant under Asa implies, in a subtle way, the celebration of the Feast of Weeks as a remembrance of the Sinai legislation and a renewal of the Sinai covenant. The process happens "in the third month,"[85] during the pilgrimage of all the "faithful" to Jerusalem (2 Chr 15:9–10). The Feast of Weeks (שבעות) is interpreted as a "Feast of the Oath" (note the multiple uses of שבע and השבועה in 2 Chr 15:14–15), where the trombones and trumpets replace the sound of bugles (Exod 19:16, 19). At the beginning of Asa's story, there is a possible allusion to the Sinai legislation in this

---

82. On this, see §3.5 below.
83. Kellermann, *Anmerkungen zum Verständnis der Tora*, 56.
84. On this "ritual level," see my *Chronik als kanonisches Abschlußphänomen*, 430–31.
85. This dating appears elsewhere only in Exod 19:1 and Esth 8:9.

rare collocation of words: התורה והמצוה (the same expression only appears in Exod 24:12; 2 Kgs 17:37; 2 Chr 14:3; and 31:21). As a peak text in the series of narratives about the covenant, 2 Chronicles 15 states that the four covenant ceremonies or covenant renewals have the goal of enforcing the Sinai covenant.[86]

(5) The Torah is not only the epitome of the way of life for Israel but also the reference point for the parenesis and the place where specific norms of behavior can be found. The Chronicler reflects on the mediation of the Torah to the people. According to 2 Chr 17:7–9, Jehoshaphat initiated a "teaching campaign" for all of Judah (note the use of למד three times), based on the "book of the Torah of YHWH," which was carried out by the "officials of Jehoshaphat" (שׁריו), Levites, and priests; therefore, laymen were also responsible for conveying the Torah. 2 Chr 35:3 once again mentions the task of the Levites to teach (בין, *hiphil*).[87] In Neh 8:1–8,[88] the same three groups are mentioned: first Ezra, the priest (8:2; cf. Ezra 7:10), then the leading men (8:4),[89] and finally the Levites (8:7–8). This text gives no information about the competence of the laymen.

Seen from a synchronic point of view—notwithstanding all the opinions about the use of an extrabiblical source[90]—the "judicial reform" of

---

86. See my *Chronik als kanonisches Abschlußphänomen*, 455–68.

87. It is not clear whether 2 Chr 31:4b (verbatim: "that they are strong in the Torah of YHWH") belongs in this context. Usually this sentence refers to the priests and Levites mentioned before, whose study of the Torah or the correct practice of their ministry was made possible by their ensured income (e.g., Becker, *2 Chronik*, 103; and many others, often with reference to Neh 13:10–13). But compare Japhet, *I and II Chronicles*, 964, who opts for the possibility "that the purpose clause refers not to the 'priests and Levites' but to 'the people', to whom the king's command was delivered. The king's motivation is presented as directing the people to be strong in the law, in fulfilling its ordinances." See the parallel phrasing in 1 Chr 28:7.

88. See also Willi, *Juda – Jehud – Israel*, 114–17.

89. It is not about the Levites but about laity, as noted correctly by J. Becker, *Esra / Nehemia* (NEB; Würzburg: Echter-Verlag, 1990) 89; and A. H. J. Gunneweg, *Nehemia* (KAT 19/2; Gütersloh: Mohn, 1987) 111.

90. The "classic" controversy over the historicity of the "judicial reform" continues in recent research; cf. F. Crüsemann, *Die Tora: Theologie und Sozialgeschichte des alttestamentlichen Gesetzes* (Munich: Chr. Kaiser, 1992) 113–18; and Japhet, *I and II Chronicles*, 770–74, who defend the historical reliability of the message; and K. Strübind, *Tradition als Interpretation in der Chronik: König Josaphat als Paradigma chronistischer Hermeneutik und Theologie* (BZAW 201; Berlin: de Gruyter, 1991) 171–76, who rejects the idea of there being an extrabiblical source. The defenders of the historicity must admit that the old source is only present in fragments and was highly revised by the Chronicler; older parts can only be found in 2 Chr 19:5, 8a, 10a(?), and 11a. The creativity and relevance to the present times of the Chronicler and therefore the propensity to historical fiction should also not be underestimated here; therefore, also variances from the conception of the Deuteronomist (cf. Deuteronomy 17) cannot be classified as evidences of an older tradition. It is a characteristic of the vagueness of the historical reconstruction that the most recent attempt to defend its historicity can only rely on general considerations of probability (cf. Japhet, *I and II Chronicles*, 772–73).

Jehoshaphat in 2 Chr 19:4–11 must be connected to the Torah instruction
in 17:7–9. It is the same three groups of people who are entrusted with the
task of jurisdiction (v. 8). The basis of the jurisdiction can be nothing else
than the "book of the Law" mentioned in 17:9. The nationwide[91] appointment of judges and the creation of official channels institutionalize the
commitment of "Israel" (v. 8) and all aspects of life to the Torah.[92]

Summarizing these observations—the Torah has an exclusive role regarding the relationship to God (see 2 Chr 6:16) and influences the entire
history of Israel, as can be seen from the history of the kings, for example.
The Chronicler reads the canonical history from the beginning with Adam
to the new beginning under Cyrus from the perspective of the Torah and
presents it as a story of the effects (*Wirkung*) of the Torah in Israel. The
paradigms for one's relationship to the Torah are primarily the Davidic
kings; but the role of the people is also emphasized. From its contents, the
Torah is mainly perceived in ritual terms: Israel's relationship with God
takes place in the temple, Israel is a worshiping community, the temple is
the visible sign of its present connection to the Sinaitic origin of their relationship with God.[93] From the perspective of the Torah, there seems to be
a connection among the three main topics, "Israel" (cf. the "genealogical
entrance hall" 1 Chronicles 1–10), "kingdom" (1 Chronicles 11–2 Chronicles 36), and "temple." The influence of the Torah, however, cannot be
observed on the level of content only; it plays a crucial role in the composition of the book.

3.3. *Torah as the Form of Presentation*

> In Chronicles, the past is recast according to the Law; particular infringe-
> ments happen but are just exceptions to the rule. By contrast, in the
> books of Judges, Samuel, and Kings, the radical distance between the old
> practice and the Law is not denied as a whole. Even here, in individual
> cases the past has been recast according to the ideal, but as a rule the past
> is only condemned in these books.[94]

With this well-known dictum, Wellhausen appropriately describes the formal role of the Torah in the Chronicler's presentation, although it is connected with an assessment that reveals Wellhausen's historical background
and does not do justice to the parenetic intentions of Chronicles. "Yet the
Chronicler is more interested in the theological lessons reflected by the
historical events than in the historical facts themselves."[95]

---

91. Note the pleonasm in 2 Chr 19:5.

92. Cf. Strübind, *Tradition als Interpretation in der Chronik*, 172–76.

93. Kleinig, *Recent Research in Chronicles*, 58: "The law was . . . of paramount importance for Israel, since for the Chronicler Israel was basically a liturgical community whose
existence and sanctity depended on faithfulness to God's law."

94. J. Wellhausen, *Prolegomena zur Geschichte Israels* (Berlin: Reimer, 1927) 292.

95. T. Sugimoto, "The Chronicler's Techniques in Quoting Samuel–Kings," in *AJBI* 16
(1990) 70; cf. Fishbane, *Biblical Interpretation in Ancient Israel*, 394: "The Chronicler has

The Chronicler's recasting of history is oriented to the so-called "dogma of immediate retribution": a particular king's obedience to God leads to success for the ruler and for the people; disobedience leads to failure and fall. The scheme of "actions and consequences" or "blessings and curses" is based on the validity of the Torah as a principle of history. The epitome of the Torah is the main commandment, especially when interpreted from a ritual point of view. It is possible to speak of a "dogma of retribution" as one specific Chronistic *theologumenon* and still fail to understand the implications of this idea for the composition of Chronicles. It is more than an individualized doctrine of retribution, which is often misunderstood and criticized as a "rigid dogma of retribution."[96] The principle of retribution is the result of a certain type of historical thinking that is oriented toward analogies and typologies and has the purpose of recognizing basic patterns of divine action and then communicating the insights discovered.[97] It is not merely the evaluation of kings regarding their obedience to the Torah that is the basis of the doctrine of retribution. It is the fact that the doctrine serves as a principle for reading and interpreting the sources in Samuel–Kings, as a key to recasting the stories about the kings. It is *the* feature of the Chronicler's design for presenting history.[98]

The importance of this instrument of the Chronicler's hermeneutic of Scripture can be recognized in the structure of the individual kings' stories. Thus, in the "portraits of the kings," characterization is influenced by certain recurring pivotal themes or topoi that provide the overall conception of history with a schematic trait, regardless of any individual details. The constantly recurring themes that reveal the success of a king are as follows: deliverance from enemies, military success, prosperity, and building

---

taken over the 'facts' of his sources and presented them in the light of the normative piety he wished to stress and foster through David—now a teacher of Torah and no more brigand or warrior."

96. For a corrective to some of the misunderstandings of the Chronicler's "doctrine of retribution," see Kleinig, *Recent Research in Chronicles*, 61–63.

97. Cf. Childs, *Introduction to the OT*, 652:

Yet to see this feature [= the principle of retribution—G. S.] apart from the Chronicler's larger concept of scripture is to distort its significance. Actually the Chronicler's use of the motif of retribution is another aspect of his analogical thinking which is grounded in authoritative writings and is not different in kind from his use of typology. Whereas in typology, the author sought to draw patterns from history of the analogous workings of the selfsame divine reality, in his use of retribution he attempts to illustrate the continuity in God's economy between human action and its inevitable effect. Far from imposing a strange doctrine upon his material, the Chronicler was attempting to illustrate in specific events an understanding of God's ways with Israel which comprised the heart of the covenant: "If you seek him, he will be found by you, but if you forsake him, he will forsake you" (2 Chr 15:2).

98. The schema of retribution influences the narrative of the Chronicler from the beginning (cf. 1 Chronicles 10: Saul; see also 1 Chr 9:1), not just after the end of the era of Solomon (according to Kleinig, *Recent Research in Chronicles*, 61–62).

activities; the opposite of these characteristics or lack of them reveals the failure of a king.[99] Some of the rearrangements that the Chronicler makes in the sources are based on the fact that he recognizes the blessings-and-curses pattern as effective in the transmitted history and that he wants to assert this clearly in the story. Therefore, the characterization of the individual kings is not primarily oriented to chronology but to the principle of retribution, in which the theological basis of the story is revealed.[100] The contrast between piety and apostasy, and between success and failure, respectively, can structure the composition of a passage (e.g., with Manasseh, Rehoboam, and Asa). However, the pattern also informs the succession of two contrasting rulers (e.g., Saul and David, Ahaz and Hezekiah). This view of history, shaped by the principle of retribution, also leads to the removal of all negative traits from the images of David and Solomon because the negatives are not consistent with the staunch dedication of these kings to ritual service. Therefore, the Chronicler's stories about the kings play on two levels—on the steadily changing (individual) surface of the story and on the deep level of interpretation, oriented to the main commandment and the principle of retribution.

A simple manifestation of this structural principle is present, for instance, in the story of Manasseh in 2 Chronicles 33. Manasseh's story consists of two parts. An era of apostasy is contrasted with an era of piety. A king who is rated quite negatively in the 2 Kings 21 source appears in a different light: the Chronicler can only explain Manasseh's unusually long period of government (which is a sign of blessing) as a conversion (2 Chr 33:12–13).

2 Chronicles 33:1–20: Structure

33:1	accession notice
33:2–10	ritual misconduct
	especially: desecration of the temple
33:11	war and exile as punishment
33:12–13	return to God
	God's answer and deliverance
33:14–17	building activities
	military organization
	ritual reformations
33:18–20	final notice

As a foundation narrative, the story of David in 1 Chronicles 11–29 is more extensive and more complex in structure than the sections that follow it. His success appears with each of his activities in preparing for the construc-

---

99. See the overview by R. K. Duke, *The Persuasive Appeal of the Chronicler: A Rhetorical Analysis* (JSOTSup 88; Sheffield: Sheffield Academic Press, 1990) 78–79.

100. See, for example, the inclusion of 2 Samuel 5 in 1 Chronicles 14 *after* 2 Samuel 6 // 1 Chronicles 13.

tion of the temple. This begins with the conquest of Jerusalem as the first initiative of the king (see 1 Chr 11:1–5).

1 Chronicles 11–29: Structure

First Part: 1 Chronicles 11:1–22:19

11:1–12:40 *Davidic Dynasty and Jerusalem*
      11:1–9   enthronement; conquest of Jerusalem
                      overall evaluation
      11:10–12:40 documentation: support for David
13:1–16:43 *Transfer of the ark*
      ch. 13   beginning of the ark transfer to Jerusalem
      ch. 14   the greatness of David
      chs. 15–16 completion of the ark transfer
17:1–22:16 *Project planning for the temple construction*
      ch. 17   decision for construction of temple
                      promise of Nathan
      chs. 18–20 military success
      21:1–22:16 determination of the temple location
                      designation of Solomon
22:17–19 *Résumé*

Second Part: 1 Chronicles 23:1–29:25

23:1–27:34 *Israel in service to the temple and the king*
      23:1   enthronement of Solomon
      23:2   summoning an assembly of the people
      23:3–26:32 documentation: staff of the rituals
      ch. 27   documentation: Israel and the royal court
28:1–29:25 *Preparation for the temple construction*
      28:1   recapitulation of 23:2
      28:2–29:25 commissioning and enthronement of Solomon
                      collection for the temple
29:26–30 *Final notice: positive overall evaluation*

The pattern of retribution also influences the story of Solomon in 2 Chronicles 1–9. As a structural building principle, however, it is harder to recognize than other "portraits of kings." 2 Chr 1:1 and 9:29–31 form the frame to Solomon's story. This frame begins in 1:2–6 with ritual activity, followed by a report on Solomon's wisdom and prosperity. In 1:18, the announcement about intentions to construct the temple is a distinct structural signal. However, the corresponding signal of completion (of the frame) is not present in 8:16, as is often supposed, but appears in 7:22 instead. 2 Chr 8:1 has the time designation "after twenty years" and marks a distinct break, which is followed by a passage about Solomon's successful period of government. The two passages, 8:12–16 and 8:17–9:28, correlate with each other by having the same beginning, the editorial particle אז. 2 Chr 8:12–16 is not a chronological sequel to 8:1–11, since Solomon did not wait 20 years after completing the temple to pay attention to the ritual service and the staff. Instead, the story of Solomon is structured by the threefold sequence of the pattern "turning to God by caring about the ritual service leads to political success."[101]

2 Chronicles 1–9: Structure

1:1	Overall evaluation
1:2–6	ritual activities
1:7–17	success (wisdom and prosperity)
1:18–7:22	construction of the temple
8:1–11	success (wars and building activities)
8:12–16	ritual activities
8:17–9:28	success (wisdom and prosperity)
9:29–31	Final notice

In connection with Johnstone, Kleinig recently underlined the specific sacral-legal reference framework of the Chronicler's doctrine of retribution:

> What has been categorized as retribution may make better sense when considered sacrally within the framework provided by a *theology of holiness* in Chronicles. Respect for the holy things of God in the cult and the holy word of God as spoken by Moses and the prophets results in blessing and prosperity, whereas sacrilegious contempt for them brings wrath and disaster in its train. This is so because God's holiness is never neutral but always has either a positive or negative impact on those who came into contact with it. *Such "retribution" would therefore not stem from the disruption of the moral order but rather from the violation of the divinely instituted sacral order. It would be a function of God's holiness in Israel rather than of his justice in the cosmos.*[102]

3.4. Traces of Reflected Torah Interpretation

It is a frequently held view that the tradition of the Oral Torah finds expression in Chronicles: Chronicles contains hints of the developments of relevant Torah instructions; likewise, one can find hints regarding the institutions of Torah interpretation.[103] However, another aspect pertinent to this context is usually neglected: in Chronicles, one can trace a *theory of Torah interpretation*, and while there is not a systematic methodology, there are some formal aspects and approaches for the actualization of the Torah.

---

101. R. B. Dillard, "The Literary Structure of the Chronicler's Solomon Narrative," in *JSOT* 30 (1984) 85–93; idem, *2 Chronicles* (WBC 15; Waco, TX: Word, 1987) 5–7, presented an alternative proposal for the structure. He posits a parallelism between the description of Solomon's wealth in 2 Chr 1:14–17 and that in 9:25–29 and develops a concentric structure. A variation of this model can be found in S. J. De Vries, *1 and 2 Chronicles* (FOTL 11; Grand Rapids, MI: Eerdmans, 1989) 233. Dillard's proposal ignores obvious structural signals, has lopsided sections, and constructs textual equivalents between the respective sections with problematic abstractions; see also the critical remarks by P. Abadie, "Salomon dans les Chroniques," *DBSup* fascicle 61, p. 454.

102. Kleinig, *Recent Research in Chronicles*, 62–63 (italics mine).

103. See above, §§3.1 and 3.2.

Chronicles is a narrative work, not a theoretical tract; therefore, one can only extrapolate from implicit statements in searching for a theory of Torah interpretation. Traces can be found in several places scattered throughout the two books of Chronicles. The majority of the texts appear in the section that defines the role of the Levites in the Davidic-Solomonic temple.[104]

In continuity with Exodus–1 Kings, the books of Chronicles emphasize the historical connection between the Sinai sanctuary and the temple in Jerusalem. Exceeding the details in his sources, the Chronicler traces very accurately the various steps involved in bringing the ark and the Mosaic tent to the temple. The Sinai sanctuary is literally taken into the temple, as we read in the sequence of events in 1 Chronicles 13 / 15–16 / 1 Chr 21:29–22:1 / 2 Chr 1:3–5 / 5:1–10 / 7:1–8.[105] The historicization of the relationship between the Sinai sanctuary and the temple (the Mosaic sanctuary is not only the example but is in fact the predecessor to the Solomonic temple) corresponds to the emphasis on sacral-legal continuity, which is highlighted by frequent references to the ritual order in the Pentateuch.[106] Nevertheless, sacral-legal innovations in the temple of Jerusalem are not excluded. They pertain to the organization of the staff for the rituals and the description of the Levites' tasks. In some of the relevant texts, one can observe the methods used in Chronicles to develop specifications found in the Pentateuch.

(1) In the view of the Chronicler, the Levites were the appointed carriers of the ark (cf. 1 Chr 15:2 as reception of Deut 10:8 and 18:5). With the deposit of the ark in the temple, this ministry ends. The assignment of new roles to the Levites, especially their involvement in the sacrifices and the ritual music (cf. 1 Chr 6:16–17, 23:25–32; 2 Chr 35:3, 6), is on the one hand justified by the loss of their traditional ministry; on the other hand it is anchored in Deuteronomy 10 and 18 (mentioned above), as the carrying ministry was. In Chronicles, the ritual music is an essential innovation, since it is not mentioned in the Pentateuch (cf. 1 Chronicles 15–16 and 1 Chr 6:16–33).

> The argument which is implied here in Chronicles is as follows. The temporary responsibility of the Levites for the transportation of the ark was part of a larger and more permanent duty to minister to the Lord who was enthroned above it and met with his people there. This ministry, which was performed 'in' or 'with the Lord's name' (Deut. 18:5–7), was carried out by the Levites as they proclaimed that name to the people in songs of praise. So then, while liturgical song was not explicitly instituted in the

---

104. This formulation seems to be more appropriate than the usual expression "temple of Solomon," since Chronicles greatly increases the role of David in the temple construction compared with the source documents. In the Chronicler's understanding, David's role as the temple *founder* and Solomon's role as the temple *builder* complement each other.

105. See also 1 Chr 6:16–17.

106. See above, §3.2.

Pentateuch, it was held to be included in the commission of the Levites by the Lord to minister in his name.[107]

The sacral-legal innovation of the ritual music is anchored in the Torah— by specifying a general and open application of the Torah.[108] The logical structure of this use of the Torah is recognizable in 1 Chr 23:25–29 and 2 Chr 35:3: ". . . no more (אין) applies . . . , but (כי or עתה) from now on, you should do the following. . . ." This interpretation does not have the character of a comment aiming at understanding from a distance. Rather, it is about the application of the Torah to a new situation in order to master a specific task. The procedure can be described as an amplification and adaptation of the Torah. Regarding further considerations about the role of the Levites, notice that the innovations decreed by David are based on the Torah.

(2) In 2 Chr 8:13–15, Moses and David are named as legislative authorities,[109] in the same way, side by side. 2 Chr 8:13 interprets the short notice in its source, 1 Kgs 9:25, this way: during the three main annual festivals, Solomon offered עולה-sacrifices—and, in addition, during the Sabbaths and new moons, items that are not mentioned in the source. The text does not elaborate on the details; rather, it refers to the instructions of the Torah with a phrase derived from Lev 23:37: ובדבר־יום ביום להעלות כמצות משה "namely, as the duty of each day required, sacrificing according to the instruction of Moses." 2 Chr 8:14a, which has been completely revised, reports Solomon's installation of staff for the rituals in the newly constructed temple; this occurs כמשפט דויד־אביו "according to the decree of David, his father." Directly afterward, vv. 14b, 15 speak twice about the מצות דויד concerning the priests and Levites.[110] In this case, the phrase probably refers to the relationship of the Levites and the priests, which should be understood according to 1 Chr 23:25–32 as the subordination of the Levites to the priests.[111] The מצוה of Moses appear alongside the משפט and מצוה of David; the difference between משפט and מצוה is not easy to determine.[112] While

---

107. J. Kleinig, *The Lord's Song: The Basis, Function and Significance of Choral Music in Chronicles* (JSOTSup 156; Sheffield: Sheffield Academic Press, 1993) 34.

108. Kleinig (ibid., 34–39) tries to prove that additional regulations in the Torah served the Chronicler as a legal basis for the Levitical music of the cult: the Levitical music supplements the role of the priests' trumpet-playing (cf. Num 10:10) and adopts the same function; the request for ritual joy (Deut 12:6–7, 11–12, 18; 16:10–11; 26:11; 27:6–7) is understood by the Chronicler as a directive for cultic music. Kleinig's observations deserve attention even though the connections to the stated texts of the Torah can only be established by a complex argument and are less obvious than in the case of the references to Deuteronomy 10 and 18.

109. Certainly it is about derived authority.

110. There is no evidence that המלך in 2 Chr 8:15 refers to anyone other than David.

111. Concerning the redaction-critical classification and interpretation of 2 Chr 8:14–15, see my *Chronik als kanonisches Abschlußphänomen*, 288–92.

112. Probably משפט refers to the regulations of David in 1 Chronicles 23–26 and מצוה to the exact regulation about the relationship between priests and Levites in 1 Chr 23:25–

the instructions of Moses concern the practice of the sacrificial rituals, the regulations of David refer to the staff performing the rituals and, more precisely, to the musical and other ritual ministries of the Levites. Therefore, the instructions of both authorities complement each other, since David's instructions are issued on the basis of the Mosaic regulations.[113]

Only in 2 Chr 8:14 is David referred to as "man of God" in Chronicles; this is a title that belongs to Moses in 1 Chr 23:14 and 2 Chr 30:16 and identifies prophets on two other occasions (2 Chr 11:2 // 1 Kgs 12:22; 22:7, 9). 2 Chr 30:16 explains the technical details of the Passover ritual sacrifice by the priests and the Levites. It is therefore a parallel to 2 Chr 8:14. The apposition "man of God" is obviously intended to underline the authority of the legislator (cf. Ezra 3:2: Moses; Neh 12:24, 36: David). Indeed other post-Solomonic kings can issue a מצוה[114] in the Chronicler's understanding, but the title "man of God" is not used in these contexts. Again, this highlights the authority given to David. One example of a מצוה of David is the "regulation" for the Levites in 1 Chr 23:25–32, even though the term does not appear in this context. The text consists of two parts: in vv. 25–26, the new tasks of the Levites are theoretically justified;[115] vv. 28–32 name these tasks in detail.[116] The obligations of the Levites and their relation to the priests are developed in connection with Numbers 3–4 and other ritual instructions from the Torah. The מצוה amplifies and adapts older, obsolete (cf. vv. 25–26) instructions. David appears as an authorized expositor of the Torah whose interpretations are given using technical terms (משפט; מצוה).[117]

32; on the literary- and redaction-critical problems, see the analyses of the particular texts in my *Chronik als kanonisches Abschlußphänomen*.

113. 2 Chr 23:18 also mentions the regulations of David and Moses in parallel; however, the terminology is not as informed as in 2 Chr 8:13–15.

114. See 2 Chr 24:21; 29:12–25; 30:6–12; 35:10–15f.; in addition, 1 Kgs 2:43; 2 Kgs 18:36; Esth 3:3; Neh 11:23; 12:24–45.

115. Concerning the procedure, see above under #(1).

116. 1 Chr 23:27 is an addition that correlates with the internal discussion of the Chronicler about the age of entering the ministry of the Levites in 1 Chr 23:3, 24, 27; 27:23; and 2 Chr 31:16–17.

117. One way of using language that already appears here can also be found later, in the rabbinic Halakah.

The role of Moses and David with regard to the temple service is also examined by S. J. De Vries, "Moses and David as Cult Founders in Chronicles," *JBL* 107 (1988) 619–39. He distinguishes an "Authorization Formula" related to Moses from a "Regulation Formula" related to David. In my opinion, the close meshing of the two authorities (see especially 2 Chr 8:13–15) and the specific form of the development of the cultic legal material is not considered sufficiently by the distinction made between the two "formulas," which are handled too inflexibly.

E. M. Dörrfuß, *Mose in den Chronikbüchern: Garant theokratischer Zukunftserwartung* (BZAW 219; Berlin: de Gruyter, 1994), takes a "revision of Moses" into consideration, which relativizes the role of David. The redaction-critical method raises some questions: According to Dörrfuß, Moses has also been inserted redactionally into places where he already appears in the source. Even if a number of "Moses sections" are secondary, we cannot easily extrapolate from such positions to a revision that focuses primarily on Moses. In

(3) Regarding Moses and David and the actualization of the Torah, a third factor is of importance—that is, the prophets. 2 Chr 29:25 goes beyond the terminology covered so far by mentioning the מצות דויד וגד חזה־המלך ונתן הנביא "instruction of David, Gad the royal seer, and Nathan the prophet." That statement is followed by a כי with this attached explanation or explication: כי ביד־יהוה המצוה ביד־נביאיו "because by/from the hand of Yнwн [118] (is/came) the instruction through his prophets," which reveals that the מצוה is inspired. [119]

> Thus, according to the Chronicler, it is not only messages of rebuke or encouragement which are delivered in *ad hoc* situations by the prophets after Moses; the prophets after Moses also deliver the 'commandment', with its broad sense of legal obligatoriness. This general statement is linked to an institution which is presented clearly and explicitly as an innovation, established for the first time by David. This, then, represents an expression of the view that legislation did not cease with Moses; even within the sacred realm of the cult there was room for change, indicated by the Lord's continuing inspiration through the prophets. [120]

The methodological aspects of interpreting the Torah in the books of Chronicles that we have collected so far permit us to go one step beyond Japhet's interpretation. The conveying of new מצות happens in the framework and on the basis of the Torah of Moses (see above) by the inspired prophets and by David, the man of God. The interaction of the three players Moses, the prophets, and David in actualizing the Torah by amplification and adaptation, as indicated in Chronicles, is analogous to the three-part, Torah-centered structure of the canon. In my opinion, this analogy is hardly by chance and can be understood as an expression of one and the same hermeneutical concept, which on the one hand is exemplified narratively in Chronicles and on the other is imprinted in the canon as an implicit hermeneutic with regard to its structure.

Again, 2 Chr 35:15 ascribes the institution of the ritual music to a מצוה of David and several prophets. 2 Chr 35:15 substitutes the position of the prophets Gad and Nathan in 1 Chr 29:29, however, with the heads of the three classes of musicians, who are introduced as prophets. [121] This is also the context in which the striking "prophetization" of Chronicles' ritual

my opinion, literary- and redaction-critical access is too limited to draw such an extensive conclusion. In addition, the profile of the "theocratic future expectation" is peculiarly pale; furthermore, the counterpart is not profiled sufficiently.

118. The doubling of the expression ביד is surprising; probably it should be changed to ביד יהוה, which is analogous to 1 Chr 28:19; see the commentaries, ad loc.

119. Concerning the inspiration terminology, see my *Chronik als kanonisches Abschlußphänomen*, 348–49.

120. Japhet, *I and II Chronicles*, 927; cf. Kleinig, *The Lord's Song*, 32–33.

121. Instead of תודה, probably תודי should be read; see BHS; concerning the designation of Asaph as seer, see 2 Chr 29:30; Heman receives this title in 1 Chr 25:5. Concerning the redaction-critical classification of the texts, see my *Chronik als kanonisches Abschlußphänomen*, 322.

music should be interpreted. The ritual musicians do not all acquire (as many suppose) a general prophetic position.[122] Instead, only the "founding fathers" of the ritual musicians, the heads of the three tribes—that is, Asaph, Heman, and Jeduthun—are counted as prophets.[123] This function of the heads of the musicians during the time of David is meaningful with regard to the divine legitimation of music as being the ritual orders' extension.

(4) In 2 Chr 35:4, one can discern the tradition—or the beginnings of a tradition—of a written interpretation of the authoritative Torah. Josiah refers the Levites back to the order of the temple personnel, which is recorded in a "document of David" (כתב דוד) and in a "document of Solomon" (מכתב שלמה). There is no semantic difference between the terms כתב and מכתב;[124] probably the variations in the expression are meant to clarify that these are two different documents.[125]

References to the "documents" of David and Solomon should be seen in close connection to 1 Chr 28:11–19. According to v. 19, David writes down the complete plan for the future temple in a "document" (כתב), by divine inspiration.[126] It also contains the orders and tasks of the temple service staff (v. 13). In contrast to Moses, David does not look at the plan (תבנית) of the sanctuary, nor does he convert it afterwards into a sequence of oral instructions (cf. Exod 25:8ff.). Rather, the process of inspiration remains abstract, and the transmission to Solomon is done in writing. The Chronicler connects the תבנית-concept of Exod 25:9, 40 with the idea of the written plan of Ezek 43:11.[127] The regulations of David are transmitted in writing, on analogy with the Torah, and can therefore be asserted over long periods. Even centuries later, one can refer to this "document" according to 2 Chr 35:4. The existence of "Solomon's document," in a narrative sense, is not confirmed in the same way as it is for David in 1 Chr 28:11–19. Probably this idea was developed in 2 Chr 35:4 in view of the close cooperation between David and Solomon when they founded the temple. Directly before this, 2 Chronicles 34 presents the key story about the discovery of the "book of the Torah of YHWH mediated by Moses" (v. 14). The coexistence of Moses and David with regard to the exposition of the Torah that is

---

122. See the commentaries, especially on 1 Chronicles 25.

123. See 1 Chr 25:1; הנביאים is in apposition to the three previous names; on this, see my *Chronik als kanonisches Abschlußphänomen*, 325–26.

124. Cf. H. Haag, "כתב *kātab*," *ThWAT*, 4.396.

125. Other functions are supported by the writing (כתב) of Hiram (2 Chr 2:10) and the so-called letter of Elijah in 2 Chr 21:12 (see the canonical lecture about this letter in B. J. Diebner, "Erwägungen zum Prozeß der Sammlung des dritten Teils der antik-jüdischen [hebräischen] Bibel, der כתובים," *DBAT* 21 [1985] 139–99; and the edict of Cyrus in 2 Chr 36:22 [both are called מכתב]).

126. 1 Chr 28:19 does not necessarily imply that God himself is the author of this "scripture"; so H. G. M. Williamson, *1 and 2 Chronicles*, 183; cf. my *Chronik als kanonisches Abschlußphänomen*, 348–50.

127. Cf. Japhet, *I and II Chronicles*, 494.

described in the previous section is therefore complemented by another detail: not only are the two men the mediators of divine "regulations" for the temple service, but their regulations find their expression in "Scripture." More than other texts in Chronicles, the story of Josiah's Passover is filled with numerous references to legitimating authorities.[128] It is Josiah's task (vv. 10 and 16) to implement Moses' order regarding Passover as well as the instructions of David (and Solomon; see vv. 4, 6, 12, 13, and 15).[129]

Thus, one can observe several aspects of a methodology for expositing the Torah in the books of Chronicles: the exposition aims to actualize the Torah of Moses. Alongside Moses, other authoritative expositors appear whose exposition through prophetic mediation reaches back to YHWH himself. As was the Torah of Moses, the exposition is communicated in written form. Regarding this last item, a transition looms: the transition from a Torah that is continuously updated to a canonical text that is not subject to change but, instead, may be commented on externally.

3.5. Chronicles as the First Theology of the Old Testament

Ackroyd characterizes Chronicles as the "first theology of the Old Testament," with the critical awareness that, thereby, a modern systematic approach to the Old Testament has been transferred to the time of the Bible's origin.[130] The point of comparison that justifies this description lies in the Chronicler's intent "to unify, to draw together the diverse strands of Israel's thought into a more coherent whole." Ackroyd continues:

> We may be even more precise in our delineation of him as a theologian, and see him as one who aimed at presenting a unifying concept of the nature of the Jewish religious community and hence of its theology and the meaning of its rich and varied traditions.[131]

Within the literary history of the Old Testament, Chronicles is not the first attempt to join several threads of tradition. "But it is of particular significance that it is, within the Old Testament, the most comprehensive such attempt, going considerably further in its unifying endeavours than its predecessors."[132] Thus Chronicles holds a unique position in the canon of the Old Testament.[133]

---

128. See Japhet, *I and II Chronicles*, 1048.

129. Concerning the literary and redaction criticism, see my *Chronik als kanonisches Abschlußphänomen*, 221–30.

130. Ackroyd, *The Chronicler in His Age*, 280.

131. Ibid.

132. Ibid.

133. Because of the early dating of the Chronicles and the proposition of a Chronicler's work, Ackroyd cannot explore the full implications of this insight. The special position of Chronicles within the canon is also stated by W. Johnstone, "Which Is the Best Commentary? 11: The Chronicler's Work," *ExpTim* 102 (1990–91) 8–10:

> In this new climate [i.e., the sensibility toward the character of this work] the Chronicler's work comes into its own, so far from being regarded as merely bring-

The most important formal indicators of this large-scale synthesis of the disparate traditions in the older canonical books are (1) the uniform principle of presentation ("dogma of retribution"), (2) the content of the work, which contains the whole foundational story of Israel "from Adam to Cyrus," and (3) the interest in the present, which revolves around the temple and the cult as the visible pole of Israel's identity. In the underlying structure, the "Torah" is understood as the principle of history and guideline for the present. Chronicles does not recapitulate the acquisition of the Torah (see Genesis–Deuteronomy)[134] but instead conceptualizes Israel from the perspective of the Torah, thus continuing the program of the canonical section of the Prophets. Israel's identity is bound up in the Torah in the same way that the Torah identifies God for Israel. God, Torah, and Israel become a unity[135] that the narrative communicates in the theological historiography of Chronicles.

4. Chronicles as a Canonical-Closure Phenomenon

The background of the literary history and theological achievement of Chronicles for the formation of the third canonical division and the Scriptures as a whole can now be determined with more precision.

4.1. The Problem of the Closure of the Canon

In the last 20 years, a number of works have supported an early closure of the canon—that is, the formation of the Writings during the early Maccabean period.[136] The scant historical evidence that is relevant to discussions about the canon does not contradict this theory.

---

ing up the rear of the Writings, the lowest tier of the Hebrew Bible, the last gasp of waning powers, it may now be seen as summation, standing as the last part of the Hebrew Bible, so far as its normal canonical order is concerned, and by that very fact be recognized as the appropriate portal through which the study of the whole may confidently proceed. . . . It seems to me that it is only when Chronicles is interpreted, as indeed it stands as the last word in the Hebrew Bible that fully satisfactory sense can be elicited, both in the macroscopic and in the microscopic aspects.

134. Against the theory of a conscious suppression of the Pentateuch's traditions, we must state, with Noth, *Überlieferungsgeschichtliche Studien*, 163: "What Dt still had to establish historically was for Chr already self-evident and of timeless validity."

135. Cf. Crüsemann, *Die Tora*, 425.

136. Cf. S. Z. Leiman, *The Canonization of Hebrew Scripture: The Talmudic and Midrashic Evidence* (Transactions of the Connecticut Academy of Arts and Sciences 47; Hamden, CT: Archon, 1976); R. T. Beckwith, *The Old Testament Canon of the New Testament Church and Its Background in Early Judaism* (London: SPCK, 1985); S. Talmon, "Heiliges Schrifttum und kanonische Bücher aus jüdischer Sicht: Überlegungen zur Ausbildung der Grösse 'Die Schrift' im Judentum," in *Mitte der Schrift? Ein jüdisch-christliches Gespräch. Texte des Berner Symposions vom 6.–12. Januar 1985* (ed. M. Klopfenstein, U. Luz, S. Talmon, and Emanuel Tov; Judaica et Christiana 11; Bern: Peter Lang, 1987) 75:

Overall, these considerations lead to the conclusion that, at the latest around the middle of the 2nd Century B.C.E., two of the main components of the three-part corpus of Hebrew sacred Scriptures surely reached their closure in all groups of

It is methodologically important to differentiate between the following things: (1) between the historical formation of the canon and the formation of a canonical theory, which begins to become evident in Jewish sources only at the end of the 1st century C.E.; (2) between the fact of the formation of the canon by a group/party and the general reception of this canon; and (3) between the stabilization of the scope and order of the books and the fixing of the textual shape.[137]

The preface of Ben Sira (generally dated to 132 B.C.E.) describes a tripartite canon three different times by using the triad "the law, the prophets, and the other 'scriptures.'"[138] The use of the open term *scriptures* is not evidence per se for the incompleteness of the third canonical section. Instead, it describes this third division precisely in its literary specialty as a collection of disparate works. The disparity of this collection, based on its form and content, contrasts with the first and second canonical divisions, in which the individual books (in different ways) are more connected to each other.[139] Anyone who argues for an open canon based on the word usage of Sirach's preface must also explain why this terminology was continually used in the subsequent period (see Philo and Josephus),[140] and even later it was obviously still in use, in case one posits a later date for the closure of the canon.[141]

Furthermore, rabbinic discussions about the canonicity of individual scriptures should not be taken to indicate that the third canonical division was basically open at least until the end of the 1st century C.E.[142] It seems

---

contemporary Judaism. . . . Beyond that, it can be stated that this item [the third section] of the three-part corpus was constituted as the last one. Nevertheless, reports in the rabbinic literature that deal with the books in the כתובים indicate that also this part of the canon was de facto completed in the early Hellenistic era.

137. Maier, *Zwischen den Testamenten*, 18: "Interest in the shape of the text increased with the amount of authority that was assigned to the text. When it eventually was considered sacred Scripture, the exact shape of the text certainly became important."

138. Cf. F. Vattioni, *Ecclesiastico: Testo ebraico con apparato critico e versioni greca, latina e siriaca* (Naples: Istituto Orientale di Napoli, 1968) xvii–xviii.

139. Does not the stereotypical wording require a clear concept of "the Scriptures" by the hearers?

140. Philo, *Contempl. Life* 25; Josephus, *Ag. Ap.* 37ff.

141. Otherwise, for example, see Diebner, *Erwägungen*, who considers the Ben Sira prologue to be a Christian fiction from the 2nd Century C.E. However, he cannot argue for a corresponding interest, especially since the Christian orientation is toward the LXX. Highly problematic as well is Diebner's method of reconstructing a steady progression of the "sanctification" of more and more books in the later Hebrew Bible, by way of referring to the OT quotations in the NT and the chronology of the NT books.

142. See G. Wanke, "Bibel I," *TRE* 6.1–8, esp. p. 6: "[D]enials of the canonicity of particular books of the hagiographa by tannaitic and amoraic rabbis in the 1st to the 3rd century are not evidence of an open canon in the 1st century C.E. Instead, they call into question a matter of fact already mandatory for Judaism but without being successful." And the fact "that the number of canonical Scriptures is evidenced relatively late in rabbinic literature should likewise not be interpreted too strictly, since nearly all refer-

that—in the context of the theory that the canon was closed at Jamnia—
these discussions have been burdened with conclusions that are far too
weighty. Talmon sees in them, for example, "scholastic exercises" without
factual consequences.[143] In view of recent research, Hennings comes to this
conclusion regarding the dispute between Augustine and Jerome on the
canon of the Old Testament:

> [R]abbinic discussions about the canon of the Hebrew Bible were not
> about the selection of various scriptures but about the fixation of an al-
> ready existing tradition. The existing tradition limits the range of the
> texts to be discussed and provides at the same time the criteria for the
> decision. Therefore, the existing tradition itself is the criterion for the He-
> brew Bible, not the fact that it is written in Hebrew, as is often supposed.
> During difficult times, near the turn of the second century, the rabbis
> achieved an agreement concerning the delineation of what already ex-
> isted. This is one of the measures that was taken after the Jewish War
> and that served to defend Jewish unity against all deviations. A reaction
> of distinction, however, especially against the Septuagint or Christianity
> does not appear in the rabbinic discussion. It is not about excluding cer-
> tain scriptures but about making an inventory of the traditional stock
> and establishing it as a normative entity.[144]

Leiman observes three indicators of a closure of the canon at the latest
in the middle of the 2nd century B.C.E.:[145] (1) the collection of sacred Scripture that was assigned to Judas Maccabeus (see 2 Macc 2:13–14); (2) the
canonization of the early Maccabean form of the book of Daniel. "There
is no evidence that normative Judaism ever thought again about adding
a book to the canon. Since no books were added to the canon anymore,

---

ences originate from different intentions than from the discussion about the extent of
the canon."

143. See Talmon, *Heiliges Schrifttum und kanonische Bücher*, 79.

144. R. Hennings, *Der Briefwechsel zwischen Augustinus und Hieronymus und ihr Streit um
den Kanon des Alten Testaments und die Auslegung von Gal. 2,11–14* (Vigiliae Christianae:
Supplement 21; Leiden: Brill, 1994) 135–36. Similarly, Wanke, "Bibel I," 7: "What is generally said to be the closure of the canon appears not to be a binding decision of an authorized institution. Rather, it is the attempt to explain from a dogmatic point of view what
is already there by way of tradition. A dogmatic decision did not made the canon; rather,
the canon gave rise to a subsequent dogmatic interpretation."

Given all the differences in the details (e.g., the counting of the books) between the
"canon theories" of Josephus, *Ag. Ap.* 37–43, and 4 Ezra 14, it is still clear that the criteria
of canonicity invoked in each case were not themselves making canonical decisions, but
each clearly reflected a situation already established by the tradition. According to C. Macholz, "Die Entstehung des hebräischen Bibelkanons nach 4 Esra 14," in *Die Hebräische Bibel und ihre zweifache Nachgeschichte: FS R. Rendtorff* (ed. E. Blum et al.; Neukirchen-Vluyn:
Neukirchener Verlag, 1990) 379–91, esp. p. 388, 4 Ezra 14 already assumed the canonicity
of the books of the Hebrew Bible; 4 Ezra 14 was a "legitimation etiology of the apocalyptic
literature," not of the biblical books.

145. Leiman, *The Canonization of Hebrew Scripture*, 131–32.

it was completed." And (3) the proto-Lucan recension of the Greek Bible, which presupposes the formation of a normative Hebrew text.[146]

4.2. The Formative Role of Chronicles

The original sequence of scriptures in the third canonical division cannot be reconstructed precisely. According to Beckwith, the order found in the b. B. Bat. 14b is the oldest; however, this is controversial.[147] In this order, Chronicles appeared at the end—after Ezra (= Ezra–Nehemiah). Orders such as those in the Leningrad Codex and Aleppo Codex are much more recent than the talmudic order.[148] The idea that Chronicles' original position was at the end of the Writings is often derived from Matt 23:35 // Luke 11:50–51.[149] The passage refers to the blood of all the righteous ones/prophets, and mentions Abel and Zechariah as examples. Hence the Q-source seems to be referring to 2 Chr 24:20–21, which is the report about the murder of the prophet and priest Zechariah (the last reported murder of a prophet in the Old Testament), and to be embracing the whole story enclosed in the Old Testament ("all the blood since the beginning").

Observations on the formation of the first two canonical subsections call attention to the fact that the canon grew from within and that a closing phenomenon can be found in the text itself,[150] rather than understanding the formation of the canon in the sense of an external declarative act. From this, the question arises whether there could have been an analogous process for the third canonical section. For the third section, the problem of closure is particularly difficult: how should such a disparate collection be closed? For the canonization of the second canonical

---

146. See also the summary of recent discussion in B. S. Childs, *Biblical Theology of the Old and New Testaments: Theological Reflection on the Christian Bible* (Minneapolis: Fortress, 1993) 59–60.

147. According to b. B. Bat. 14b, Ruth is located at the beginning of the Writings. Is this not due to a historiographical understanding: Ruth as the genealogy of David, the creator of the Psalms? See the remarks on Ruth in b. B. Bat. 14b! It is more likely that originally the Psalms were at the beginning; note the formula "law, prophets, and David/Psalms" (2 Macc 2:13; Luke 24:44).

148. These orders connect historiographical and liturgical aspects. The outer frame is formed by historiographical works in a broader sense: at the beginning is Chronicles (for the era up to the exile); at the end is Daniel (during the exile) and Ezra–Nehemiah (after the exile). At the same time, Chronicles is the "introduction" (virtually a "macroheading") to the Psalter, because Chronicles celebrates David as a poet, composer, and founder of the ritual music. From the fact that the number of Megillot (themselves again in "historical" order) has grown to five, we can establish the late date of this order (after the 8th century); cf. Beckwith, *The Old Testament Canon*, 202–3.

149. Ibid., 115, 211–22.

150. The fact that *canonization* does not mean only a "selection and collection of authoritative Scriptures" but is also reflected "in the text" is not taken into consideration often enough (cf. Steck, *Abschluß der Prophetie*; and Dohmen and Oeming, *Biblischer Kanon*, passim).

division, Steck considered its "factual as well as literary connection to the Torah"[151] to be decisive. That the end of Chronicles in 2 Chr 36:22–23 contains references to the Torah and the prophets is easy to see. But even more than that, Chronicles as a whole can be understood as a "closure phenomenon."

From this perspective, the exposed position of Chronicles at the end of the Writings as well as the synthesizing and integrating character of this work appear in a new light. The difficult task of closing the canon by shaping the collection of the Writings as a third canonical division is solved by Chronicles in an impressive way: Chronicles recapitulates the whole history of Israel, from its beginning until Cyrus—focused on the definition of Israel (thus the "genealogical vestibule," 1 Chronicles 1–10) and on the period of the First Temple (thus the main part 1 Chronicles 11–2 Chronicles 36). Theologically, the *relecture* of history is dominated by the topic of the *Torah*; this matches the principle of "canonizing by Torah-binding," as Steck observed. Therefore, the last book of the third section connects this section to both preceding sections and establishes a Torah-centered overall view of the tripartite canon. Several features that are unique to Chronicles—such as its interest in shaping history, the intensity with which the traditions are joined together, and the dominance of the Torah topic—are appropriately explained as being due to the concluding character of Chronicles.[152]

A fitting period for the closure of the canon would have been during the restoration era after the failure of Hellenistic reformation attempts under Antiochius IV. During this time, the radical questioning of Jewish identity may have awakened the "need for criteria for determining one's identity." By means of canonization, the community "retreat[ed] . . . to the tradition."[153] The momentum to establish this identity led to a zenith

---

151. Steck, *Abschluß der Prophetie*, 144.

152. Other conceptions of the third canonical division as they manifest themselves in the book orders of the versions work well with this thesis. The disparity of the texts in the third division only permitted an "outer" closure of the section, by placing a specific book at the end. As long as the books are allowed to coexist within the section, the possibility for regrouping them is not excluded. Such modifications can also be observed in the second canonical division, which was more well-developed (see the ranking of Isaiah according to b. B. Bat. 14b and the LXX). Concerning the problem of a formation of the disparate collection of "scriptures," see also Talmon, *Heiliges Schrifttum und kanonische Bücher*, 75:

It has already been emphasized that in contrast to the תורה and נביאים, the books in this [third] section do not have characteristics that are obvious and common to all [of the books]. With good reason, it was therefore labeled with the vague term כתובים or *Paralipomena*. Therefore, it is understandable that this partial collection of the canon was exposed more than the others to the danger of being invaded by 'sectarian' or at least questionable texts.

153. Wanke, "Bibel I," 2.

that corresponded to the depths of the crisis.[154] I am not implying that, with this development, the formative phase of the Hebrew Bible was generally finished.[155] Even though during the Maccabean restoration, *one* group brought its canon to a close, this canon did not immediately meet with universal approval. The examples of Qumran and the Samaritans, what we know about the formation of "religious parties" from the 2nd century B.C.E. on, as well as the Greek tradition (even though speaking of the "Alexandrian Codex" has its own problems)[156] require us to differentiate when we discuss the formation of the canon. Without naming a "reference group," we cannot speak about a canon;[157] discussion of *the* canon of Judaism appears to be possible, at the earliest, only at the end of the 1st century C.E.[158]

Conclusion

If these reflections are correct, then an important biblical- and systematic-theological result appears: the canon of the Hebrew Bible is older than Christianity and is thus a prerequisite to it.[159] The implications of this insight would need to be explored and appropriated theologically.

---

154. S. Talmon, *Heiliges Schrifttum und kanonische Bücher*, 52, brings the "endeavor of canonization" to the formula: "The more profound the impact of the turmoil was that negatively influenced the social-religious-political construct of Israel, the stronger the determination became to counter this development by creating positive, stabilizing values. The canon is one of these values."

155. See Steck, *Abschluß der Prophetie*, 139–40, for analogies to the second canonical division.

156. See already Budde, *Der Kanon des Alten Testaments*, 11; Hennings, *Der Briefwechsel zwischen Augustinus und Hieronymus*, 140–42; D. Dorival, "L'histoire de la Septante dans la judaïsme antique," in *La Bible Grecque des Septante: Du judaïsme hellénistique au christianisme ancien* (ed. G. Dorival, M. Harl, and O. Munnich; Paris: Cerf, 1988) 31–125, esp. pp. 112–19; and especially M. Hengel, "Die Septuaginta als 'christliche Schriftensammlung', ihre Vorgeschichte und das Problem ihres Kanons," in *Die Septuaginta zwischen Judentum und Christentum* (ed. M. Hengel and A. M. Schwemer; WUNT 72; Tübingen: Mohr Siebeck, 1994) 182–284.

157. See Childs, *Biblical Theology of the Old and New Testaments*, 59, who speaks of a "stability within certain circles of Judaism." Analogous differences were common for a long period of time in cases of text-formation.

158. Cf. Josephus, *Ag. Ap.* 37ff.; and 4 Ezra 14.

159. For a contradictory view, see the consequential position of A. Sundberg, "The Bible Canon and the Christian Doctrine of Inspiration," in *Int* 29 (1975) 352–71, esp. p. 356: "[T]he church received 'scriptures' from Judaism, but not a canon." The importance of this conclusion is increased by the fact that the widespread opinion that the church adopted the LXX canon is only partly true; numerous church fathers adhered to the extent (though not the textual form) of the Hebrew Bible. The LXX did not just replace its prototype; cf. Hennings, *Der Briefwechsel zwischen Augustinus und Hieronymus*, 140–45. On this complex historical and theological problem, see Hengel, *Die Septuaginta zwischen Judentum und Christentum*.

Bibliography

Abadie, P. "Salomon dans les Chroniques." Pp. 450–56 in vol. 61 of *DBSup*.

Ackroyd, P. R. *The Chronicler in His Age*. JSOTSup 101. Sheffield: Sheffield Academic Press, 1991.

———. "Criteria for the Maccabean Dating of Old Testament Literature." *VT* 3 (1963) 113–32.

Albertz, R. *Religionsgeschichte Israels in alttestamentlicher Zeit*. Grundrisse zum Alten Testament 8/2. Göttingen: Vandenhoeck & Ruprecht, 1992.

Baldermann, I., et al., eds. *Zum Problem des biblischen Kanons*. JBTh 3. Neukirchen-Vluyn: Neukirchener Verlag, 1988.

Becker, J. *Esra/Nehemia*. NEB. Würzburg: Echter-Verlag, 1990.

———. *2 Chronik*. NEB. Würzburg: Echter-Verlag, 1988.

Beckwith, Roger T. *The Old Testament Canon of the New Testament Church and Its Background in Early Judaism*. London: SPCK, 1985.

Ben Zvi, E. "The Authority of 1–2 Chronicles in the Late Second Temple Period." *JSP* 3 (1988) 59–88.

Brettler, M. Zvi. *The Creation of History in Ancient Israel*. London: Routledge, 1995.

Budde, K. *Der Kanon des Alten Testaments: Ein Abriß*. Gießen: Alfred Töpelmann, 1900.

Childs, B. S. *Biblical Theology of the Old and New Testaments: Theological Reflection on the Christian Bible*. Minneapolis: Fortress, 1993.

———. *Introduction to the Old Testament as Scripture*. Minneapolis: Fortress, 1979.

Crüsemann, F. *Die Tora: Theologie und Sozialgeschichte des alttestamentlichen Gesetzes*. Munich: Chr. Kaiser, 1992.

De Vries, S. J. *1 and 2 Chronicles*. FOTL 11. Grand Rapids, MI: Eerdmans, 1989.

———. "Moses and David as Cult Founders in Chronicles." *JBL* 107 (1988) 619–39.

Diebner, J. B. "Erwägungen zum Prozeß der Sammlung des dritten Teils der antik-jüdischen (hebräischen) Bibel, der כתובים." *DBAT* 21 (1985) 139–99.

Dillard, R. B. "The Literary Structure of the Chronicler's Solomon Narrative." *JSOT* 30 (1984) 85–93.

———. *2 Chronicles*. WBC 15. Waco, TX: Word, 1987.

Dohmen, C. "Der Biblische Kanon in der Diskussion." *TRev* 91 (1995) 451–60.

Dohmen, C., and M. Oeming. *Biblischer Kanon, Warum und Wozu?* Quaestiones disputatae 137. Freiburg: Herder, 1992.

Donner, H. *Geschichte des Volkes Israel und seiner Nachbarn in Grundzügen*. Grundrisse zum Alten Testament 4/2. Göttingen: Vandenhoeck & Ruprecht, 1986.

Dorival, G. "L'histoire de la Septante dans la judaïsme antique." Pp. 31–125 in *La Bible Grecque des Septante: Du judaïsme hellénistique au christianisme ancien*. Edited by G. Dorival, M. Harl, and O. Munnich. Paris: Cerf, 1988.

Dörrfuß, E. M. *Mose in den Chronikbüchern: Garant theokratischer Zukunftserwartung*. BZAW 219. Berlin: de Gruyter, 1994.

Duke, R. K. *The Persuasive Appeal of the Chronicler: A Rhetorical Analysis*. JSOTSup 88. Sheffield: Sheffield Academic Press, 1990.

Fishbane, M. *Biblical Interpretation in Ancient Israel*. Oxford: Clarendon, 1989.

Gunneweg, A. H. J. *Nehemia*. KAT 19/2. Gütersloh: Mohn, 1987.

Haag, H. "כתב *kātab*." Pp. 386–98 in vol. 4 of *ThWAT*.

Hengel, M. *Judentum und Hellenismus*. Tübingen: Mohr, 1973.

————. "Die Septuaginta als 'christliche Schriftensammlung', ihre Vorgeschichte und das Problem ihres Kanons." Pp. 182–284 in *Die Septuaginta zwischen Judentum und Christentum*. Edited by M. Hengel and A. M. Schwemer. WUNT 72. Tübingen: Mohr Siebeck, 1994.

Hennings, R. *Der Briefwechsel zwischen Augustinus und Hieronymus und ihr Streit um den Kanon des Alten Testaments und die Auslegung von Gal. 2,11–14*. Vigiliae Christianae, Supplement 21. Leiden: Brill, 1994.

Japhet, S. *I and II Chronicles: A Commentary*. OTL. Louisville: Westminster John Knox, 1993.

————. "Law and 'the Law' in Ezra–Nehemiah." Pp. 99–115 in *Proceedings of the 9th World Congress of Jewish Studies*. Jerusalem: The World Union of Jewish Studies, 1988.

————. "The Supposed Common Authorship of Chronicles and Ezra–Nehemiah Investigated Anew." *VT* 18 (1968) 330–71.

Johnstone, W. "Chronicles, Canon and Context." *Aberdeen University Review* 169 (1983) 1–18.

————. "Reactivating the Chronicles Analogy in Pentateuchal Studies, with Special Reference to the Sinai Pericope in Exodus." *ZAW* 99 (1987) 16–37.

————. "Which Is the Best Commentary? 11: The Chronicler's Work." *ExpTim* 102 (1990–91) 7–11.

Kaestli, J.-D., and O. Wermelinger, eds. *Le canon de l'Ancien Testament*. Geneva: Labor et fides, 1984.

Kaiser, O. *Einleitung in das Alte Testament*. Gütersloh: Gütersloher Verlag, 1984.

Kalimi, I. "Die Abfassungszeit der Chronik: Forschungsstand und Perspektiven." *ZAW* 105 (1993) 223–33.

Kegler, J. "Prophetengestalten im Deuteronomistischen Geschichtswerk und in den Chronikbüchern: Ein Beitrag zur Kompositions- und Redaktionsgeschichte der Chronikbücher." *ZAW* 105 (1993) 481–97.

Kellermann, U. "Anmerkungen zum Verständnis der Tora in den chronistischen Schriften." *BN* 42 (1988) 49–92.

Kleinig, J. W. *The Lord's Song: The Basis, Function and Significance of Choral Music in Chronicles*. JSOTSup 156. Sheffield: Sheffield Academic Press, 1993.

————. "Recent Research in Chronicles, Currents in Research." *Biblical Studies* 2 (1994) 43–76.

Kooij, A. van der. "De canonvorming van de Hebreeuwse bijbel, het Oude Testament." *NedTT* 49 (1995) 42–65.

Lang, B. "Kanon." Pp. 440–47 in vol. 2 of *Neues Bibel-Lexikon*. Edited by Manfred Görg and Bernhard Lang. Ostfildern: Patmos, 1992.

Leiman, Sid Z., ed. *The Canon and Masorah of the Hebrew Bible: An Introductory Reader*. New York: Ktav, 1974.

————. *The Canonization of Hebrew Scripture: The Talmudic and Midrashic Evidence*. Transactions of the Connecticut Academy of Arts and Sciences 47. Hamden, CT: Archon, 1976.

Lohfink, N. "Der Begriff 'Bund' in der biblischen Theologie." *TP* 66 (1991) 161–76.

López, G. "תורה, *tôrāh*." Pp. 598–637 in vol. 8 of *ThWAT*.

Macholz, C. "Die Entstehung des hebräischen Bibelkanons nach 4 Esra 14." Pp. 379–91 in *Die Hebräische Bibel und ihre zweifache Nachgeschichte. FS R. Rendtorff.* Edited by E. Blum et al. Neukirchen-Vluyn: Neukirchener Verlag, 1990.

Maier, J. *Jüdische Auseinandersetzungen mit dem Christentum in der Antike.* Erträge der Forschung 177. Darmstadt: Wissenschaftliche Buchgesellschaft, 1982.

———. "Zur Frage des biblischen Kanons im Frühjudentum im Lichte der Qumranfunde." Pp. 135–46 in *Zum Problem des biblischen Kanons.* Edited by I. Baldermann et al. JBTh 3. Neukirchen-Vluyn: Neukirchener Verlag, 1988.

———. *Zwischen den Testamenten: Geschichte und Religion in der Zeit des Zweiten Tempels.* NEB 3. Würzburg: Echter-Verlag, 1990.

Mason, R. *Preaching the Tradition: Homily and Hermeneutics after the Exile.* Cambridge: Cambridge University Press, 1990.

Movers, F. C. *Kritische Untersuchungen über die biblische Chronik.* Bonn, 1834.

Noth, M. *Könige I 1–16.* BKAT 9/1. Neukirchen-Vluyn: Neukirchener Verlag, 1983.

———. *Überlieferungsgeschichtliche Studien: Die sammelnden und bearbeitenden Geschichtswerke im Alten Testament.* Tübingen: Max Niemeyer, 1967.

Oeming, M. *Das wahre Israel: Die "genealogische Vorhalle" 1 Chronik 1–9.* BWANT 128. Stuttgart: Kohlhammer, 1990.

Pannenberg, W., and T. Schneider, eds. *Verbindliches Zeugnis I. Kanon – Schrift – Tradition.* Freiburg: Herder / Göttingen: Vandenhoeck & Ruprecht, 1992.

Rad, G. von. *Das Geschichtsbild des chronistischen Werkes.* BWANT 4/3. Stuttgart: Kohlhammer, 1930.

———. "Die levitische Predigt in den Büchern der Chronik." Pp. 248–61 in *Gesammelte Studien zum Alten Testament.* Edited by G. von Rad. Theologische Bücherei 8. Munich: Chr. Kaiser, 1971.

Rendtorff, R. "Esra und das Gesetz." *ZAW* 96 (1984) 165–84.

Riley, W. *King and Cultus in Chronicles.* JSOTSup 160. Sheffield: Sheffield Academic Press, 1993.

Ruffing, A. *Jahwekrieg als Weltmetapher: Studien zu den Jahwekriegstexten des chronistischen Sondergutes.* SBB 24. Stuttgart: Katholisches Bibelwerk, 1992.

Sanders, J. A. "Canon." Pp. 837–52 in vol. 1 of *ABD.*

Schäfer, P. "Die sogenannte Synode von Jabne: Zur Trennung von Juden und Christen im ersten/zweiten Jh. n. Chr." Pp. 45–64 in *Studien zur Geschichte und Theologie des Rabbinischen Judentums.* Edited by P. Schäfer. Leiden: Brill, 1978.

Schneider, H. *Die Bücher Esra und Nehemia.* Heilige Schrift des Alten Testaments 4/2. Bonn: Hanstein, 1959.

Shaver, J. S. *Torah and the Chronicler's History Work: An inquiry into the Chronicler's References to Laws, Festivals and Cultic Institutions in Relation to Pentateuchal Legislation.* Ph.D. Dissertation, Notre Dame University, 1984. [Repr. BJS 196. Atlanta: Scholars Press, 1989.]

Sheppard, G. T. "Canon." Pp. 62–69 in vol. 3 of *ER* (1987).

Stade, B. "Der Text des Berichtes über Salomos Bauten 1 Kö. 5–7." *ZAW* 3 (1883) 129–77.

Steck, O. H. *Der Abschluß der Prophetie im Alten Testament: Ein Versuch zur Frage der Vorgeschichte des Kanons.* Biblisch-theologische Studien 17. Neukirchen-Vluyn: Neukirchener Verlag, 1991.

Steins, G. *Die Chronik als kanonisches Abschlußphänomen: Studien zur Entstehung und Theologie von 1/2 Chronik.* BBB 93. Weinheim: Athenäum, 1995.

————. "Zur Datierung der Chronik: Ein neuer methodischer Ansatz." *ZAW* 109 (1997) 84–92.

Stemberger, G. "Jabne und der Kanon." Pp. 163–74 in *Zum Problem des biblischen Kanons.* Edited by I. Baldermann et al. JBTh 3. Neukirchen-Vluyn: Neukirchener Verlag, 1988.

Strübind, K. *Tradition als Interpretation in der Chronik: König Josaphat als Paradigma chronistischer Hermeneutik und Theologie.* BZAW 201. Berlin: de Gruyter, 1991.

Sugimoto, T. "The Chronicler's Techniques in Quoting Samuel–Kings." *AJBI* 16 (1990) 30–70.

Sundberg, A. C. "The Bible Canon and the Christian Doctrine of Inspiration." *Int* 29 (1975) 352–71.

Talmon, S. "Heiliges Schrifttum und kanonische Bücher aus jüdischer Sicht: Überlegungen zur Ausbildung der Grösse 'Die Schrift' im Judentum." Pp. 45–79 in *Mitte der Schrift? Ein jüdisch-christliches Gespräch. Texte des Berner Symposions vom 6.–12. Januar 1985.* Edited by Martin Klopfenstein, Ulrich Luz, Shemaryahu Talmon, and Emanuel Tov. Judaica et Christiana 11. Bern: Peter Lang, 1987.

Theobald, C., ed. *Le canon des écritures: Études historiques exégétiques et systématiques.* Lectio Divina 140. Paris: Cerf, 1990.

Throntveit, M. A. *When Kings Speak: Royal Speech and Royal Prayer in Chronicles.* SBLDS 93. Atlanta: Scholars Press, 1987.

Vattioni, F. *Ecclesiastico: Testo ebraico con apparato critico e versioni greca, latina e siriaca.* Naples: Istituto Orientale di Napoli, 1968.

Wanke, G. "Bibel I." Pp. 1–8 in vol. 6 of *TRE.*

Wellhausen, J. *Prolegomena zur Geschichte Israels.* Berlin: Reimer, 1927.

Welten, P. "Lade – Tempel – Jerusalem: Zur Theologie der Chronikbücher." Pp. 169–83 in *Textgemäß: FS E. Würthwein.* Edited by A. H. J. Gunneweg and O. Kaiser. Göttingen: Vandenhoeck & Ruprecht, 1979.

Willi, T. *Chronik.* BKAT 24/1. Neukirchen-Vluyn: Neukirchener Verlag, 1991.

————. *Die Chronik als Auslegung: Untersuchungen zur literarischen Gestaltung der historischen Überlieferung Israels.* FRLANT 106. Göttingen: Vandenhoeck & Ruprecht, 1972.

————. *Juda – Jehud – Israel: Studien zum Selbstverständnis des Judentums in persischer Zeit.* FAT 12. Tübingen: Mohr, 1995.

————. "Thora in den biblischen Chronikbüchern." *Jud* 36 (1980) 102–51.

Williamson, H. G. M. *1 and 2 Chronicles.* NCB. Grand Rapids, MI: Eerdmans, 1982.

————. "History." Pp. 25–38 in *It Is Written: Scripture Citing Scripture. FS B. Lindars.* Edited by D. A. Carson and H. G. M. Williamson. Cambridge: Cambridge University Press, 1988.

Würthwein, E. *Die Bücher der Könige.* ATD 11/1. Göttingen: Vandenhoeck & Ruprecht, 1985.

Zenger, E., et al. *Einleitung in das Alte Testament.* Stuttgart: Kohlhammer, 1995.

Zunz, L. *Die gottesdienstlichen Vorträge der Juden.* Frankfurt, 1892.

"A Threefold Cord Is Not Quickly Broken"

Interpretation by Canonical Division in Early Judaism and Christianity

STEPHEN B. CHAPMAN

Is Canonical Interpretation Novel?

One of the main charges leveled against a canonical approach to biblical interpretation is that it pretends to do something old while in reality doing something new.[1] Early on, James Barr characterized the holistic thrust of Brevard Childs as trading on exactly this confusion:

> The feeling for literary genre and its relation to meaning, which goes along with the full form of a book at any stage of its formation, was still alive in the literary redaction of the books, but the process of canonization, far from preserving that feeling, did much to destroy it. Canonization as holy scripture, given the ideas of inspiration that both Judaism and, later, Christianity then held, led not to the heightened appreciation of literary genres but to the loss of that appreciation; it led not to the high evaluation of the shape of books as a whole but to the neglect of it.
> . . . Thus, both in traditional Judaism and in traditional Christianity, law or doctrine could be proved from individual scripture passages without anyone worrying in the slightest that these passages, if read in the light of their actual literary genre and total shape as a literary work, did not mean at all what people understood them to mean.[2]

Yet in framing this critique Barr appeared to concede that biblical books do have a literary shape, a "shape of books as a whole." His argument was not in fact that biblical books lacked a "total shape" but that this shape had been actively disregarded in traditional modes of interpretation.

Barr offered midrashic exegesis as a telling example:

---

1. An earlier version of this essay was delivered as a paper for the "Exile (Forced Migrations) in Biblical Literature" Consultation at the 2011 Annual Meeting of the Society of Biblical Literature in San Francisco, California. I am grateful to Daniel Stulac for his help in preparing the manuscript for publication.

2. James Barr, *Holy Scripture: Canon, Authority, Criticism* (Philadelphia: Westminster, 1983) 80.

One of its chief mechanisms was that whereby a linguistic item, occurring in a particular context, can be read with the senses appropriate to
that item in other contexts. In other words, it works by means of a massive decontextualization. It relied to a high degree upon the canon, in
that the scriptural canon was the field from which many of the senses
were selected . . . but the canon did not fix the context, it provided freedom from the constraints of context. What controlled midrashic exegesis
was not the canon, but the religion.[3]

Here again, Barr did not argue for the sheer incoherence of Scripture within
traditional interpretation. Instead, he relocated the markers of such coherence, moving them from structurally based, intertextual cues to the
extratextual concepts and practices brought to bear on Scripture by its
interpreters. Thus, Barr argued that "the church has always read the Bible
in pericopes," explaining: "One can indeed and should read the Bible as
a whole but for purposes of worship, liturgy and preaching rather limited
passages have been used since ancient times."[4] So Barr actually took a normative stance with respect to the "wholeness" of Scripture; such wholeness
is real, and it should apparently be used as a guide in contemporary interpretation. Indeed, from Barr's perspective one of the chief problems with
traditional biblical interpretation was the fact that it had ignored Scripture's holistic dimension.

Yet, despite the claim of canonically oriented approaches to represent
a more theological manner of engagement with Scripture, Barr concluded
that they are actually less theological than they need to be because they do
not grapple with ultimate questions of truth, such as whether the portrayal
of God in Nahum is true or adequate: "Canonical criticism, as it has worked
out so far," Barr summarized, "appears to be not a particularly theological operation but a sort of literary-historical reading of a novel and unusual kind."[5] One wonders how Barr might respond to the suggestion that
much traditional, premodern interpretation did not really "grapple" with
truth either but simply assumed the truth of what it related. It must also
be remembered that Barr's book on canon appeared well before Childs's
magnum opus, *A Biblical Theology of the Old and New Testaments*, in which
Childs did explicitly address the nature of truth in relation to biblical-
theological claims.[6]

John Barton has strongly maintained Barr's position within the ongoing
debate:

Now it is in their holism, it seems to me, that theological and literary
interpretation in our day fail to make good their claim to be recovering

---

3. Ibid., 80–81.
4. Ibid., 91.
5. Ibid., 102.
6. Brevard S. Childs, *A Biblical Theology of the Old and New Testaments* (Minneapolis:
Fortress, 1993) 80–90.

the scriptural vision of the Fathers, the rabbis or the Reformers. It is true that pre-critical interpretation regarded books of the Bible as a unity, in the sense that they did not think they were composed from pre-existing fragments or even longer source-documents: Isaiah was by Isaiah, not by First, Second and Third Isaiah together with a whole heap of other contributors. But it is not true that they therefore interpreted the biblical texts holistically, as having a beginning, a middle, and an end, a plot, a shape, a *Gestalt*. Rabbinic exegesis, for example, often sees no divisions in the text where critical commentators find dislocation—they do not find any disjunction between Isaiah 39 and 40. But at the same time they do find it possible to break the text down into verses and half-verses and to comment on each as if it were a text in its own right. The Midrashim are apparently serial comments on biblical books, proceeding verse by verse. But any reader of these texts knows that it is folly to try to find any progression of thought within a midrash, still less any progression which is an attempt to mirror the "ductus" of the book being commented on. The principle that "there is no before and after in the Torah" justifies any amount of jumping from text to text, in a way that negates any idea of plot, the development of arguments, or narrative shape. It is rather as though every biblical book were like Proverbs, and like the sentence literature of Proverbs 10–29 at that: isolated atoms of communication, each to be interpreted in its own right. Where rabbinic exegesis *is* holistic is in its interpretive framework, which is provided by the whole tissue of rabbinic assumptions about theology and ethics.[7]

Here Barton goes so far as to characterize the traditional religious use of Scripture as "atomistic,"[8] a "collection of innumerable fragments . . . in which every pericope, indeed every sentence or even every word, had a meaning independent of its context."[9] On this reading of the tradition, any kind of literary structure or genre designation was simply irrelevant

---

7. John Barton, "Canon and Old Testament Interpretation," in *In Search of True Wisdom: Essays in Old Testament Interpretation in Honour of Ronald E. Clements* (ed. Edward Ball; JSOTSup 300; Sheffield: Sheffield Academic Press, 1999) 44 (his italics). Cf. idem, "Intertextuality and the 'Final Form' of the Text," in *Congress Volume: Oslo 1998* (ed. A. Lemaire and M. Sæbø; VTSup 80; Leiden: Brill, 2000) 33–37; esp. p. 34: "Rabbinic reading, like 'final form' exegesis, is innocent of sources or underlying documents, but it is not at all interested in the biblical text as a communicative unity. On the contrary, its approach is commonly atomistic, and it plucks texts from anywhere in Scripture without regard to their context in order to assemble its garlands of proofs for this or that disputed point of halakah"; idem, "Canonical Approaches Ancient and Modern," in *The Biblical Canons* (ed. J.-M. Auwers and H. J. de Jonge; Leuven: Leuven University Press, 2003) 199–209; idem, "What Is a Book? Modern Exegesis and the Literary Conventions of Ancient Israel," in *The Old Testament: Canon, Literature and Theology* (Society for Old Testament Study Monographs; Burlington, VT: Ashgate, 2007) 137–47; esp. p. 141: "[I]t is as though all of Scripture, Torah and Prophets and Writings alike, were conceived as being like Proverbs 10–22—aphorisms applicable quite apart from their literary context."

8. Barton, "Canon," 45.

9. Idem, *Oracles of God: Perceptions of Ancient Prophecy in Israel after the Exile* (Oxford: Oxford University Press, 1986) 150.

to the interpretation and use of the biblical books, both in Judaism and Christianity.

Was Traditional
Scriptural Interpretation "Atomistic"?

This sort of characterization of the tradition requires renewed scrutiny. While not wholly inaccurate, the view that traditional religious use of Scripture was exclusively "atomistic" is seriously one-sided. I believe that further work in the history of biblical interpretation is needed in order to examine the adequacy of this view, especially for the Second Temple period and the first few centuries of the Common Era.[10] I cannot hope to be comprehensive in this present essay, but I do intend to offer sufficient examples for sketching an alternative construal.

The first point to make is that Barr and Barton have a strong case, and it deserves a considered response. In my exegesis courses, I like to use sermons and other sorts of examples from the history of interpretation in addition to academic commentaries. But I have learned to my chagrin that it can be challenging to find sermons exclusively or even primarily on a single biblical chapter or story, particularly in the premodern period. In this sense, "narrative interpretation" indeed does not appear to predomi-

---

10. More work is needed on the Jewish sources in particular. But even with regard to the Christian sources, which have been investigated to a greater degree, prior treatments have not always asked the right sorts of questions. For some of the most important previous work in this area, see especially Georg Aicher, *Das Alte Testament in der Mischna* (Freiburg: Herder, 1906); Victor Aptowitzer, *Das Schriftwort in der rabbinischen Literatur* (Library of Biblical Studies; repr., New York: KTAV, 1970); M. Boertien, "Einige Bemerkungen zu Bibelzitaten in der Mischna," in *History and Form: Dutch Studies in the Mishnah* (ed. A. Kuyt and N. A. van Uchelen; Publications of the Judah Palache Institut 4; Amsterdam: Amsterdam University Press, 1988) 71–81; E. Earle Ellis, *Paul's Use of the Old Testament* (5th ed.; Grand Rapids, MI: Eerdmans, 1991); idem, "Biblical Interpretation in the New Testament Church," in *Mikra: Text, Translation, Reading and Interpretation of the Hebrew Bible in Ancient Judaism and Early Christianity* (ed. M. J. Mulder and Harry Sysling; Compendia rerum iudaicarum ad Novum Testamentum 2/1; Assen: Van Gorcum / Philadelphia: Fortress, 1988) 691–719; Joseph Fitzmyer, "The Use of Explicit Old Testament Quotations in Qumran Literature and in the New Testament," *Essays on the Semitic Background of the New Testament* (London: Chapman, 1971) 3–58; Arnold Goldberg, *Mystik und Theologie des rabbinischen Judentums: Gesammelte Studien I* (ed. Margarete Schlüter and Peter Schäfer; Tübingen: Mohr Siebeck, 1997); idem, *Rabbinische Texte als Gegenstand der Auslegung: Gesammelte Studien II* (ed. Margarete Schlüter and Peter Schäfer; Tübingen: Mohr Siebeck, 1999); Martin S. Jaffee, *Torah in the Mouth: Writings and Oral Tradition in Palestinian Judaism, 200 BCE–400 CE* (Oxford: Oxford University Press, 2001); Bruce M. Metzger, "The Formulas Introducing Quotations of Scripture in the New Testament and in the Mishnah," in *Historical and Literary Studies: Pagan, Jewish, and Christian* (New Testament Tools and Studies 8; Grand Rapids, MI: Eerdmans, 1968) 52–63; Alexander Samely, *Rabbinic Interpretation of Scripture in the Mishnah* (Oxford: Oxford University Press, 2002); Aharon Shemesh, *Halakhah in the Making: The Development of Jewish Law from Qumran to the Rabbis* (Berkeley: University of California Press, 2009).

nate in the tradition. In his Bampton Lectures, H. P. Liddon described traditional biblical interpretation in terms much like those of Barr and Barton:

Scripture was believed to contain a harmonious and integral body of
Sacred Truth, and each part of that body was treated as being more or less
directly, more or less ascertainably in correspondence with the rest. This
belief expressed itself in the worldwide practice of quoting from any one
book of Scripture in illustration of the mind of any other book. Instead of
illustrating the sense of each writer only from other passages in his own
works, the existence of a sense common to all the Sacred Writers was rec-
ognised, and each writer was accordingly interpreted by the language of
the others.[11]

This description does bring to mind the rabbinic dictum that "there is
no before and after in the Torah,"[12] just as Barton suggests. So I am willing to stipulate that narrative approaches to biblical stories and holistic
considerations of a single biblical book may well be relatively exceptional.
There are, of course, significant examples of narrative-oriented interpretation, such as many of Origen's sermons, which often track the biblical text
line by line even as they simultaneously employ extensive figuration; or
Joseph Hall's *Contemplations upon the Principall Passages of the Holy Storie*
(1612–26) and *Contemplations on the New Testament* (1662). Even though
Hall characteristically shuttles back and forth continually between text and
application, he nevertheless masterfully attends to the literary details of
particular passages of Scripture in their broader narrative context. Yet Hall's
lasting importance may finally stem from the relative rarity of his more
literary approach to the biblical text, as well as from his impressive narrative sensitivity.

So where might we look in order to make the case that early Jewish and
Christian interpreters did attend to the literary integrity and the narrative features of Scripture? Was there really no attention to narrative-literary
(or canonical) context at all? The famous illustration of Irenaeus comes
quickly to mind: in his debate with the Valentinian Gnostics, he likened
their use of Scripture to the rearrangement of a well-crafted mosaic of a
king into a poorly executed picture of a dog or a fox:

Such, then, is their system, which neither the prophets announced, nor
the Lord taught, nor the apostles delivered, but of which they boast that
beyond all others they have a perfect knowledge. They gather their views
from other sources than the Scriptures; and, to use a common proverb,
they strive to weave ropes of sand, while they endeavor to adapt with
an air of probability to their own peculiar assertions the parables of the
Lord, the sayings of the prophets, and the words of the apostles, in order
that their scheme may not seem altogether without support. In doing so,

---

11. H. P. Liddon, *The Divinity of Our Lord and Saviour Jesus Christ: Eight Lectures Preached
before the University of Oxford, in the Year 1866* (6th ed.; London: Rivingtons, 1872) 45–46.
12. E.g., b. Pesaḥ 6b; Mek. Rab. Ish. Beš. 4; Sipre Num. 64; Eccl. Rab. 1:12.

however, they disregard *the order and connection of the Scriptures*, and so far as in them lies, dismember and destroy the truth. By transferring passages, and dressing them up anew, and making one thing out of another, they succeed in deluding many through their wicked art in adapting the oracles of the Lord to their opinions. Their manner of acting is just as if one, when a beautiful image of a king has been constructed by some skilful artist out of precious jewels, should then take this likeness of the man all to pieces, should re-arrange the gems, and so fit them together as to make them into the form of a dog or of a fox, and even that but poorly executed; and should then maintain and declare that *this* was the beautiful image of the king which the skilful artist constructed, pointing to the jewels which had been admirably fitted together by the first artist to form the image of the king, but have been with bad effect transferred by the latter one to the shape of a dog, and by thus exhibiting the jewels, should deceive the ignorant who had no conception what a king's form was like, and persuade them that that miserable likeness of the fox was, in fact, the beautiful image of the king. In like manner do these persons patch together old wives' fables, and then endeavour, by violently drawing away from *their proper connection*, words, expressions, and parables whenever found, to adapt the oracles of God to their baseless fictions.[13]

Irenaeus's point is that Scripture must be read through the church's "rule of faith"—the summary content of orthodox Christian belief, which itself grows out of Scripture and serves to identify Scripture's proper plot or story form.[14] In other words, Scripture must be read with an eye toward its larger narrative context and within an interlocking web of Christian theological convictions in order to be read rightly.

However, this example does not yet successfully meet Barr and Barton's objections. Irenaeus's illustration does speak of the importance of context for scriptural interpretation (Scripture's "order" [*taxis*] and "connection" [*hiermas*]), but the narrative character of this context is mediated through the "rule of faith." The way to argue with the Gnostics might seem to entail not pointing them to the details of the biblical text per se, which are in fact conceded to be rearrangeable, but to view these details according to Scripture's plot as the church has traditionally understood it. Barr and Barton, I suspect, would actually view Irenaeus's stance as in line with their argument that "religion" controlled the traditional interpretive context rather than the biblical canon. But Irenaeus also describes the "beautiful image" of the king as constructed by "some skilful artist" and the rearranged "miserable likeness" as "poorly executed." In this regard, Irenaeus

---

13. Irenaeus, *Against Heresies* (ed. A. Roberts and J. Donaldson; Ante-Nicene Fathers 1; Grand Rapids, MI: Eerdmans, 1986; orig. 1885) 1.8.1 (italics mine).

14. Robert W. Wall, "Reading the Bible from within Our Traditions: The 'Rule of Faith' in Theological Hermeneutics," in *Between Two Horizons: Spanning New Testament Studies and Systematic Theology* (ed. Joel B. Green and Max Turner; Grand Rapids, MI: Eerdmans, 2000) 88–107.

does acknowledge something like the literary logic and artistry of Scripture as it is[15] and simultaneously the way that Gnostic interpretation not only operates with a different conceptual framework but violates Scripture's inherent aesthetic form.[16] So it seems we do find here an initial warrant for the notion that the evident freedom we encounter within premodern interpretation—which moves with great abandon throughout the canon, mixing together all kinds of things that look like apples and oranges to historical-critical eyes—may nevertheless have gone hand-in-hand with literary sensitivity and keen awareness of how various biblical books and traditions fit together within the wider scriptural story.[17]

As strange as it may seem to say it, there is still much we do not know about the actual use of Scripture in early Judaism and Christianity, particularly in worship and preaching. Nevertheless, I want to argue that we can discern an alternative understanding of Scripture's internal differentiation and even a sense of its literary-theological "shape" by considering the sources available to us.[18] For the remainder of this essay, I offer two sets of

---

15. Christopher R. Seitz, *The Character of Christian Scripture: The Significance of a Two-Testament Bible* (Studies in Theological Interpretation; Grand Rapids, MI: Baker, 2011) 195–96. Cf. Everett Ferguson, "Factors Leading to the Selection and Closure of the New Testament Canon: Some Recent Studies," in *The Canon Debate* (ed. Lee Martin McDonald and James A. Sanders; Peabody, MA: Hendrickson, 2002) 314.

16. This observation also articulates my hesitation with regard to the thoughtful reappraisal offered by Nathan MacDonald, "Israel and the Old Testament Story in Irenaeus' Presentation of the Rule of Faith," *JTI* 3 (2009) 281–88. I believe that MacDonald ultimately overstates Irenaeus's sense of the Old Testament's "pluriformity" and underplays Irenaeus's commitment to the Old Testament's narrative coherence. I agree with him that Irenaeus's rule of faith is not identical with Scripture and that the rule of faith was not simply a narrative summary of Scripture. But neither, I stubbornly maintain, did it exist apart from Scripture as an "extra-canonical framework," as Frances Young wants to understand it; see her *Biblical Exegesis and the Formation of Christian Culture* (Cambridge: Cambridge University Press, 1997) 18. In my view, the rule of faith was not *itself* the plot but, rather, it was something like the "gist" of Scripture. For a sense of the larger discussion, now see Tomas Bokedal, "The Rule of Faith: Tracing Its Origins," *JTI* 7 (2013) 233–55; Leonard G. Finn, "Reflections on the Rule of Faith," in *The Bible as Christian Scripture: The Work of Brevard S. Childs* (ed. Christopher R. Seitz and Kent Harold Richards; Biblical Scholarship in North America 25; Atlanta: Society of Biblical Literature, 2013) 221–42.

17. This is precisely why, by way of offering a solution to the problem of the false scriptural *hypothesis*, Irenaeus *does* point to the text per se. Irenaeus does not exclusively or even primarily appeal to baptism and church/public tradition (contra Young) but instead describes how the true believer "takes each verse and restores it to its *proper* context" (Irenaeus, *Against Heresies*, 1.9.4; my italics). Baptism therefore does not provide a theological "framework" but a hermeneutical preunderstanding, insight or "hunch," which must then be sought in and confirmed by the logic and coherence of the Bible itself.

18. For a description of early modern interpretation as attentive to the "design" of biblical books, see Gerald Sheppard, "Between Reformation and Modern Commentary: The Perception of the Scope of the Biblical Books," in William Perkins, *A Commentary on Galatians* (ed. Gerald T. Sheppard; Pilgrim Classic Commentaries; New York: Pilgrim Press, 1989) xlviii–lxxvii. See the accounts of interpretive "context," "subject-matter," and "scope" in Thomas Hartwell Horne, *An Introduction to the Critical Study and Knowledge of*

examples: first, briefly, the early titles used for Scripture; and, second (at greater length), the manner in which scriptural passages were sometimes cited according to their literary genre and/or canonical division.

Canonical Titles in Early Judaism and Christianity

Even if not entirely uniform, the earliest titles known to us for the Hebrew Bible identify *constituent parts* of the biblical collection and appear to have generic connotations, although it is difficult to know exactly what those connotations may have been. So the phrase "the law and the prophets and the other ancestral books" appears three times in the Prologue to Sirach; the expression "the law of Moses and the prophets and the psalms" is found in Luke 24:44; a reference to "the laws, and the oracles given by inspiration through the prophets, and the psalms" is made by Philo (*Contempl.* 25); the formula "the law and the prophets" is used in 2 Macc 15:9, 4 Macc 18:10 and on multiple occasions in the New Testament (e.g., Matt 5:17–18; 22:40; Luke 16:16; Acts 13:15; 28:23). Variants of the expression "Moses and the prophets" also appear more than once at Qumran (e.g., 4QMMT C 10, "the book of Moses and the books of the prophets and the writings of David"; 1QS 8:15–16, "the law which He commanded by the hand of Moses . . . and as the prophets have revealed by His holy spirit"; cf. 1QS 1:3; CD 5:21–6:1, "Moses and all his servants the prophets")[19] and in the New Testament (e.g., Luke 16:29, 31; 24:27; John 1:45; Acts 26:22).

To be sure, the whole of the Hebrew Bible can also be designated simply as *torah* or "law" in both Jewish and Christian tradition (e.g., 1 Macc 2:67;

---

the Holy Scriptures (9th ed.; 2 vols.; New York: Carter, 1853) 1.336–40. In the course of his discussion, Horne cites (p. 338 n. 3) a "Sermon on the Duty and Means of Ascertaining the Genuine Sense of the Scriptures," by the Rev. H. P. Burder:

> How unfair, how irrational, how arbitrary, is the mode of interpretation which many apply to the word of God! They insulate the passage; they fix on a sentence; they detach it from the paragraph to which it belongs, and explain it in a sense dictated only by the combination of the syllables or the words, in themselves considered. If the word of God be thus dissected or tortured, what language may it not seem to speak, what sentiments may it not appear to countenance, what fancy may it not be made to gratify? But would such a mode of interpretation be tolerated by any living author? Would such a method be endured in the commenting on any of the admired productions of classical antiquity? Yet in this case it would be comparatively harmless, although utterly indefensible; but who can calculate the amount of injury which may be sustained by the cause of revealed truth, if its pure streams be thus defiled, and if it be contaminated even at the very fountain head?

19. Eugene C. Ulrich, "The Non-Attestation of a Tripartite Canon in 4QMMT," *CBQ* 65 (2003) 202–14, has argued that this reconstruction of 4QMMT is too uncertain to be used as evidence. James C. VanderKam, *The Dead Sea Scrolls and the Bible* (Grand Rapids, MI: Eerdmans, 2012) 64–66, discusses Ulrich's argument and agrees with him, although VanderKam nevertheless believes that "a functional collection of authoritative texts" did exist at Qumran (p. 55).

7:17; John 10:34; 15:25; 1 Cor 14:21; Rom 3:10–19). Or in line with pro-phetic tradition, it can be called "oracles" (= *chresmoí*; e.g., Philo, *Conf.* 143) or "words" (*lógia*; e.g., Rom 3:2; Heb 5:12; 1 Clem. 53.1) or "word" (*lógos*; e.g., Philo, *Sacr.* 55; Josephus, *J.W.* 6.2.1; 1 Clem. 62.3). The terminology of "writings" (*grámmata*; e.g., Philo, *Contempl.* 28, 75, 78; Josephus, *Ag. Ap.* 1.10, 18; 1 Clem. 53.1) or "holy scriptures" (*graphaì hagíai*; e.g., Rom 1:2) or "scriptures" (*graphaí*; e.g., Philo, *Abr.* 236; Matt 21:42; Rom 15:4) or "scrip-ture" (*graphé*; e.g., Philo *Spec.* 1.1; John 20:9; Gal 3:22) can be used as well.[20] But the designation of the biblical canon by the names of its main divisions appears to be the older usage.[21]

Thus the names for the biblical canon in antiquity themselves connote not only a sense of the canon's internal differentiation but distinctive scrip-tural subcollections (or divisions or genres).

Canonical Divisions and Genre Designations in Early Judaism

In addition to their use as canonical titles, genre designations are regu-larly invoked in interpretive discussions in intriguing ways. One parade example comes from a rabbinic discussion of the last two words of Exod 15:11, "doing wonders," in the Mekilta of Rabbi Ishmael.[22] In order to elucidate this final phrase, the rabbis offer other biblical verses, in effect interpreting Scripture by Scripture:

---

20. For these and other titles, see Roger T. Beckwith, *The Old Testament Canon of the New Testament Church and Its Background in Early Judaism* (Grand Rapids, MI: Eerdmans 1985) 105–9. Beckwith acknowledges the view that in the New Testament *graphé* is always used to refer to an individual portion of Scripture rather than being used as a term for all of Scripture, but against this position he cites B. B. Warfield, "The Terms *Scripture* and *Scriptures* as Employed in the New Testament," in *Inspiration and Authority of the Bible* (ed. Samuel G. Craig; Philadelphia: Presbyterian and Reformed, 1948) 21; and G. Schrenk, *"gráphō, graphé,"* TDNT 1.754–755. Schrenk cites in particular Gal 3:8; John 2:22; 10:35; 17:12; 20:9; 1 Pet 2:6; 2 Pet 1:20. Cf. VanderKam, *Scrolls*, 56: "It seems as if the word is a collective term denoting a known body of literature."

21. VanderKam (ibid., 57) notes that the Hebrew equivalent of "the scripture" does not appear in the Dead Sea Scrolls, although the expression "as it is written" occurs already in the Old Testament (Neh 8:15). Beckwith, *OT Canon*, 108 n. 10, observes that the expression "holy writings" (*hierà grámmata*) was known already from the 4th cen-tury B.C.E. outside Jewish tradition; cf. Johannes Leipoldt and Seigfried Morenz, *Heilige Schriften: Betrachtungen zur Religionsgeschichte der antiken Mittelmeerwelt* (Leipzig: Harras-sowitz, 1953) 21–22.

22. Mek. Rab. Ish. Shir. 8 (ed. Horowitz-Rabin), 144.14–22. I owe this example to Wil-liam Scott Green, "Writing with Scripture," in Jacob Neusner with William Scott Green, *Writing with Scripture: The Authority and Uses of the Hebrew Bible in the Torah of Formative Judaism* (Minneapolis: Fortress, 1989) 17–18. Green notes that using verses from all three canonical divisions "makes scripture itself seem naturally and ubiquitously to articulate a single message about God's persistent devotion to Israel." However, he does not com-ment on the pattern of these citations or the direction of movement from one division to another.

"Who among the gods is like you, Lord? Who is like you, majestic in holiness, awesome in praises, doing wonders?" **[Exod 15:11]**

"Doing wonders"—"Did wonders" is not written here, but "doing wonders"—in the Age to Come. As it is said, "Therefore, says the Lord, the time is coming when men shall no longer swear, 'By the life of the Lord who brought the Israelites up from Egypt,' but, 'By the life of the Lord who brought the Israelites back from a northern land and from all the lands to which he had dispersed them'; and I will bring them back to the soil which I gave to their forefathers" **[Jer 16:14–15]**.

Another interpretation: "Doing wonders"—He did wonders for us and he does wonders for us in each and every generation. As it is said, "I will praise you, for I am filled with awe; you are wonderful and your works are wonderful; and you know my soul very well" **[Ps 139:14]**. And it says, "You have done many things, Lord my God, your wonders and your thoughts towards us" **[Ps 40:6]**.

Another interpretation: "Doing wonders"—He does wonders for the fathers, and in the future for the sons. As it is said, "As in the days of his going forth from the land of Egypt, I will show him wonders" **[Mic 7:15]**. "I will show him"—what I did not show to the fathers. For, look, the miracles and mighty acts that in the future [I will] do for the sons, they [will be] more than what I did for the fathers. For thus scripture says, "To him who alone does great wonders, for his mercy endures forever" **[Ps 136:4]**. And it says, "Blessed is the Lord God, God of Israel, who alone does wonders, and blessed be his glorious name forever, and may the whole earth be filled with his glory. Amen and Amen" **[Ps 72:18–19]**.

Notice that first an interpretation of the source text (from the Pentateuch) is offered in which the verb is treated as a participle with a future-tense expectation; this interpretation receives biblical support from Jeremiah 16, which refers to the future work of God. This interpretation is then followed by an interpretation of the phrase as referring both to God's past and his present work on behalf of Israel, a view that receives supports from two verses in two different psalms. Finally, a third interpretation of the phrase is mentioned in which the past works of God are said to be the same as the works of God expected in the future, which will nevertheless be even more impressive. This third interpretation in turn cites a prophetic text in Micah 7 and, again, two verses from two different psalms.

In this example, the consideration of various interpretations moves *through* the biblical canon. A pentateuchal text is interpreted with reference to texts from the Prophets and the Writings, and the direction of interpretation moves in the same general pattern—twice—from Pentateuch to Prophets to Writings. The pattern exhibits a specific style of movement rather than a random association of texts. In other words, I think we can observe in this instance the logic of what Samuel Davidson once charmingly called the "triplicity" of the Old Testament.[23] Although I will not at-

---

23. Samuel Davidson, *The Canon of the Bible: Its Formation, History, and Fluctuations* (2nd ed.; London: King, 1877) 59.

tempt an exhaustive study, this sort of logic is said to be commonly at work within rabbinic discussions.[24] The fact that it exists at all demonstrates that traditional Jewish interpretation did at times operate with a notion of internal differentiation within the canon and that the genre of a particular biblical text (that is, its canonical location) could make a difference in how it was understood and used.[25]

Another example can be found in Pirqe Rabbi Eliezer. In this case, a triple citation appears in which verses from the Prophets, the Pentateuch, and the Writings are again used in concert:

> [W]hatever the Holy One, blessed be he, created in his world, he created but for his glory, for it is said, Every one that is called by my name: for I have created him for my glory. I have formed him; yea, I have made him **[Isa 43:7]**, and again it is said, The Lord shall reign for ever and ever **[Exod 15:18]**. The Lord has made everything for himself **[Prov 16:4]**, and heaven and earth, angels and planets, waters and trees and birds and beasts, all join in the great chorus of praise to God.[26]

Here, the prophetic citation precedes the quotation from the Pentateuch, but the rhetorical effect is quite similar. Producing a witness from each part of the canon clinches the argument.

The famous response of Rabbi Gamaliel, when asked for scriptural proof for the resurrection of the dead, provides another example of the phenomenon. He too cites three texts, one each from the Pentateuch, Prophets, and Writings. The way they represent canonical divisions is even made explicit:

> Sectarians [*minim*] asked Rabbi Gamaliel: "How do we know that the Holy One, blessed be He, will resurrect the dead?" He answered them from the Torah, Prophets, and the Hagiographa, yet they did not accept it: "From the Torah: for it is written, 'And the Lord said to Moses, Behold you shall sleep with your fathers; and this people will rise up' **[Deut 31:16]**. From the Prophets: as it is written, 'Your dead men shall live, together with my dead bodies shall they arise. Awake and sing, you that dwell in the dust; for your dew is as the dew of herbs, and the earth shall cast out its dead' **[Isa 26:19]**. From the Writings: as it is written, 'And the roof of your mouth,

---

24. See the (unsigned) note on "Tanakh" in *EncJud* 15.790. I owe this reference to Tal Ilan, "The Term and Concept of TaNaKh," in *What Is Bible?* (ed. Karin Finsterbusch and Armin Lange; Contributions to Biblical Exegesis and Theology 67; Leuven: Peeters, 2012) 219.

25. In what follows, I will also not attempt to offer a historical reconstruction of the way that this practice of triple citation may have originated and developed over time; I am more concerned simply to provide examples of the pattern at work. For a historically oriented presentation that covers some of this same ground, see ibid., 219–34. Ilan does not discern explicit allusions to the Ketubim as such in the Mishnah and therefore suggests that the threefold nature of the biblical canon only became established in the Talmud. As will be obvious from my discussion, I do not want to exclude the possibility that such allusions began earlier than that.

26. Pirqe Rab. El. 3; as cited in Solomon Schechter, *Aspects of Rabbinic Theology* (New York: Schocken, 1961) 80–81.

like the best wine of my beloved, like the best wines that goes down sweetly, causing the lips of those who are asleep to speak'" **[Song 7:9]**.[27]

Because the rabbi shows that all three canonical divisions support the notion of resurrection, the biblical canon is understood to give its united support.

An additional example addresses the significance of Sabbath observance in relation to other commandments:

> We find in the *Torah*, in the *Nevi'im* and in the *Ketuvim* that the Sabbath is a counterweight to all the other commandments. In the *Torah* as it is written: "How long will you refuse to obey My commandments and my teaching" and it is written: "Mark that the Lord has given you the Sabbath" **[Exod 16:28–29]**. In the *Nevi'im* as it is written: "For they had rejected my rules, disobeyed my laws" and it [*sic*] written "and [they] desecrated my Sabbaths" **[Ezek 20:16]**. In the *Ketuvim* as it is written: "you came down on Mount Sinai and spoke to them from heaven" and it is written: "You gave them right rules and true teachings, good laws and commandments. You made them know your holy Sabbath" **[Neh 9:13–14]**.[28]

In this case, the citations also move through all three canonical divisions in canonical order: Pentateuch–Prophets–Writings. The priority of Sabbath observance is strengthened considerably by illustrating how it is based on and supported by the scriptural witness of the Prophets and the Writings as well as the Pentateuch. Of interest—especially in light of the later tradition that religious rulings (or Halakah) were to be reached on the basis of pentateuchal Scripture alone—is the way this example may betray worry that pentateuchal Scripture might not be sufficient.

Certainly, this kind of threefold movement was not always employed by rabbinic interpreters of Scripture. Some cases of multiple scriptural citation instead exhibit double citations from the Prophets, or the pairing of a pentateuchal verse with another from the Writings, or a doubled Torah reference:[29]

> [Akiba] used to say: Beloved is man that he was created in the image [of God]; greater abundance of love is that it was made known to him that he was created in the image, as it is said, "[F]or in the image of God he made the man" **[Gen 9:6]**.

> Beloved is Israel because they are called children of God; greater abundance of love is that it was made known to them that they were called children of God, as it is said, "You are children to the Lord your God" **[Deut 14:1]**.

---

27. B. Sanh. 90b.

28. Y. Ned. 3:9, as cited in Ilan, "Term," 231. I have adjusted the form of the biblical references in this citation to match the pattern I have adopted in the other examples.

29. For other such examples, see Samely, *Rabbinic Interpretation*, 276 (e.g., m. Moʻed Qaṭ. 3:9 with Jer 9:19 and Isa 25:8) and 332 (m. Sanh. 10:3 with Num 14:35 and Ps 50:5).

Beloved is Israel because given to them was the instrument with which the world was created; greater abundance of love is that it was made known to them that to them was given the instrument with which the world was created, for it is said, "For a good teaching have I given you; my Torah do not forsake" **[Prov 4:2]**.[30]

Nevertheless, the threefold pattern appears to be the ultimate expression of this interpretive impulse, and it is hard to escape the way in which all of these patterns evoke the totality of the canon's witness.

Another rabbinic text imagines a scene in which the various canonical divisions are personified and interrogated one by one about the proper nature of punishment for sin. First Wisdom is questioned, and it responds with the words of Prov 13:21, and then Prophecy is asked, and speaks using Ezek 18:14, and so on:

They asked Wisdom (Hagiographa), "What is the punishment of the sinner?" Wisdom answered, "Evil pursues sinners" **[Prov 13:21]**. They asked Prophecy, "What is the punishment of the sinner?" Prophecy answered, "The soul that sinneth, it shall die" **[Ezek 18:4]**. They asked the Torah, "What is the punishment of the sinner?" Torah answered, "Let him bring a guilt-offering and it shall be forgiven unto him, as it is said, 'And it shall be accepted for him to make atonement for him'" **[Lev 1:4]**. They asked the Holy One, blessed be he, "What is the punishment of the sinner?" The Holy One, blessed be he, answered, "Let him do repentance and it shall be forgiven unto him, as it is said, 'Good and upright is the Lord: therefore will he teach sinners in the way'" **[Ps 25:8]**.[31]

The implication behind this passage also seems to be that a particular theological notion can be strengthened by demonstrating its presence throughout the biblical canon. It may also be suggesting that, in order for a theological position to be adequate and accurate, it needs to demonstrate its "triplicity" in Scripture. In this case, the pattern of citations follows the order Writings–Prophets–Law–Writings.

Rabbinic traditions register difficulties, too, in reading the divisions together, and sometimes they relate discussions in which the various canonical divisions are either harmonized or used against each other. Yet even these difficulties indicate a kind of "canonical" awareness on the part of the rabbinic tradents. If "religion" had been the sole "control" for interpretation, as Barr suggested, then "outlier" views would simply have been rejected as being out of conformity with tradition or current practice. On at least some occasions, however, the problem is also understood to involve the apparent contradiction of one part of the scriptural witness with

---

30. M. 'Abot 3:15, as cited in Samely, *Rabbinic Interpretation*, 172.

31. Y. Mak. 31d, as cited in Schechter, *Aspects*, 293 (except that he misidentifies Ps 25:8 as Prov 25:8). As Schechter also notes, the version of this passage in Yal. Mach. contains the order Torah–Prophets–Writings–God, with an additional reference to David (Ps 104:35) between the Prophets and the Writings (p. 294).

another. So, for example, the rabbis attempted to reconcile the description of the temple in Ezekiel 40–48 with descriptions of it in the Pentateuch.[32] They also acknowledged the contradiction between Isa 6:1 ("I saw the LORD") and Exod 33:20 ("No one shall see me and live").[33]

Another passage reports the collision of two views on personal responsibility and punishment, one from the Torah and one from the Prophets:

> Moses said, "God visits the sins of the father upon the children" **[Exod 34:7]** but there came Ezekiel and removed it and said, "The soul that sins, it shall die" **[Ezek 18:34; but see also Deut 24:16; 2 Kgs 14:6]**.[34]

Interestingly, on this point it is the prophetic view that becomes "the one generally accepted by the Rabbis," according to Solomon Schechter.[35] This kind of outcome indicates that the relationship between the divisions was at least sometimes viewed as more mutual—in other words, that pentateuchal texts did not always trump nonpentateuchal texts. Indeed, texts from the Prophets and the Writings are understood to be torah in the broad sense (Dan 9:10; Ps 78:1; ʾAbot 6.7; cf. John 10:34; 12:34; 15:25; 1 Cor 14:21),[36] although they retain their own character as canonical divisions. Part of the reason that the prophetic view of individual responsibility won out, at least for some rabbis, was precisely the possibility that prophecy could offer an update or "improvement upon the words of the Torah."[37] In this fashion certain apparent contradictions within Scripture could be explained and resolved through their genre designation or association *within* the canonical corpus.

M. Yad. 4:4 provides a fascinating instance of the kind of "generic interpretation" I am attempting to describe:[38]

> Judah the Ammonite proselyte appeared before [the scholars] in the academy and asked them: "Am I permitted to enter the congregation [i.e., to marry a Jew]?" Rabbi Galamiel replied, "You are not." Rabbi Joshua replied, "You are."

---

32. B. Šabb. 13b; Menaḥ. 45a.
33. B. Yebam. 49b.
34. B. Mak. 24a.
35. Schechter, *Aspects*, 188.
36. As pointed out in Metzger, "Formulas," 57, m. ʾAbot 6:7 also introduces six quotations from Proverbs as torah. See the additional rabbinic authorities cited in Richard Campbell Leonhard, *The Origin of Canonicity in the Old Testament* (Ph.D. diss., Boston University, 1972) 120 n. 2; and Ephraim E. Urbach, *The Sages: Their Concepts and Beliefs* (trans. I. Abrahams; Cambridge: Harvard University Press, 1987) 287–88. Verses from the Prophets and the Writings are sometimes cited in response to the question "Where do we prove this from the Torah?"
37. Schechter, *Aspects*, 187.
38. For this example, see Bleddyn J. Roberts, "The Old Testament Canon: A Suggestion," *BJRL* 46 (1963–64) 164–78. Roberts mistakenly cites Jer 30:2 as the final verse.

Rabbi Gamaliel retorted: "Scripture says, 'No Ammonite or Moabite shall enter the congregation of the Lord; even to the tenth generation, etc.' **[Deut 23:4]**."

Rabbi Joshua said to him: "And are Ammonites and Moabites still in their homelands? Long ago Sennacherib king of Assyria came up and mixed all the peoples, as it says, 'I have removed the boundaries of the peoples' **[Isa 10:13]**."

R. Gamaliel retorted: "But Scripture says, 'But afterwards I will restore the fortunes of the Ammonites' **[Jer 49:6]**, and they have long since returned."

Rabbi Joshua said to him: "Scripture also says, 'I will restore the fortunes of my people Israel' **[Jer 30:3]**, and they have not yet returned."

So they permitted him to marry.

In this case, the Pentateuch and the prophetic corpus are employed in debate; not only is the genre difference between them recognized, it also becomes itself a part of the argument. The issue concerns the status of an Ammonite proselyte. Rabbi Gamaliel cites a commandment from the Pentateuch (Deut 23:3) as a warrant for rejecting the Ammonite, but Rabbi Joshua uses a prophetic text (Isa 10:13) to dispute the continuing applicability of the commandment. Gamaliel then counters with another prophetic text (Jer 49:6), arguing that the Prophets in fact support his position by demonstrating this applicability eschatologically. Joshua, however, argues from Jer 30:3 that the eschaton is not yet fulfilled and therefore that the commandment still does not apply. This argument somewhat surprisingly leads to the acceptance of the Ammonite! In this example, then, prophetic texts are used to argue the relevance of a pentateuchal injunction, again contrary to the later rabbinic position that Halakah can be derived from the Pentateuch alone.

This generic pattern of biblical interpretation is perhaps most beautifully expressed in the words of Ben Azzai, Rabbi Akiba's disciple. He describes his study of the Bible in this way: "I thread words of the Torah onto the Prophets and words of the Prophets onto the Hagiographa, and the words of the Torah are as joyful as when they were given at Sinai."[39] Not only is the combination of testimonies from all three witnesses lifted up here as a model for interpretation, the Prophets and Writings explicitly function to actualize Torah teachings from the past.

Thus, there are good reasons to reject Barton's judgment that, "Though it is assumed throughout the Talmud that Scripture is threefold, no practical consequences of any kind seem to follow from this."[40] To the contrary, at

---

39. Lev. Rab. 16:4. Urbach, *Sages*, 300, cites this text and the story about Elisha b. Abuyah in t. P. Ḥag. 2.1, 77b as examples of how Akiba's circle prized the intertwining of verses from the Torah, Prophets, and Writings.

40. Barton, *Oracles*, 41; cf. idem, *Holy Writings, Sacred Text: The Canon in Early Christianity* (Louisville: Westminster John Knox, 1997) 154: "Jewish tradition seems to discourage the quest for the 'meaning' of the way the Bible is arranged."

least some rabbinic traditions demonstrate a concern to build interpretive arguments using verses from all three of the canonical divisions, even recognizing and taking advantage of the differing perspectives that the three divisions offer. This triple reflex is already present within the Hebrew Bible itself in verses such as Jer 18:18 and Ezek 7:26. While it does not appear that these two biblical verses have written collections of Scripture in view, they do acknowledge standardized genres of professional insight ("instruction" from the priest, "counsel" from the wise, "word" or "vision" from the prophet), and they testify to the importance of consulting all three modes of revelation. In fact, it is likely that these genre expectations regarding religious revelation *preceded* the stabilization of the biblical canon and helped give it its tripartite literary shape. [41]

The interpretive playfulness resulting from generic differentiation and canonical association can be clearly glimpsed in the later use of *petiḥtot* or "opening verses" found in homiletical *midrashim* and the sermons known as *yelammedenu*. [42] The *petiḥtah* was a verse taken from the Writings or the Prophets and used to introduce the homiletical treatment of a pentateuchal text, as can be seen repeatedly, for example, in Genesis Rabbah. [43]

Here is an excellent example of the technique from Exodus Rabbah:

> Our Rabbis commenced this Pārāšâ with the verse: "They have dealt treacherously against the Lord, for they have begotten strange children; now shall the new moon devour them with their portions" **[Hos 5:7]**. This teaches that when Joseph died, they abolished the covenant of circumcision, saying "Let us become like the Egyptians." You can infer this from the fact that Moses had to circumcise them on their departure from Egypt. As soon as they had done so, God converted the love with which the Egyptians loved them into hatred, as it is written: "He turned their heart to hate His People, to deal craftily with His servants" **[Ps 105:25]**, to fulfill that which is said: "Now shall the new moon devour them with their portions." Therefore it is written: "there arose up a new king" **[Exod 1:8]**. [44]

---

41. For a detailed argument about how such shaping might have worked with regard to the first two canonical divisions, especially as they exercised increasing influence on each other, see my book *The Law and the Prophets: A Study in Old Testament Canon Formation* (FAT 27; Tübingen: Mohr Siebeck, 2000). For an investigation into the canonical shaping of the Writings, see Timothy J. Stone, *The Compilational History of the Megilloth: Canon, Contoured Intertextuality and Meaning in the Writings* (FAT 2/59; Tübingen: Mohr Siebeck, 2013).

42. Charles Perrot, "The Reading of the Bible in the Ancient Synagogue," in *Mikra: Text, Translation, Reading and Interpretation of the Hebrew Bible in Ancient Judaism and Early Christianity* (ed. M. J. Mulder and Harry Sysling; Compendia rerum iudaicarum ad Novum Testamentum 2/1; Assen: Van Gorcum / Philadelphia: Fortress, 1988) 158.

43. See Ben Zion Wacholder, "Prolegomenon," in Jacob Mann, *The Bible as Read and Preached in the Old Synagogue* (2 vols.; New York: Ktav, 1971) 1.xxxv.

44. As cited in Avigdor Shinan, "Sermons, Targums, and the Reading from Scriptures in the Ancient Synagogue," in *The Synagogue in Late Antiquity* (ed. Lee I. Levine; Philadelphia: American Schools of Oriental Research, 1987) 101. Here again, I have adjusted the form of the biblical references.

In this instance, a verse from Hosea is used to introduce a Torah reading that begins at Exod 1:8. However, a verse from the Writings is also introduced in order to thread the two verses together by providing a linguistic and conceptual bridge. With this kind of interpretive practice, the artfulness of the commentator was shown by his ability to reveal the connections between the surprise "opening" verse and the Torah text under consideration. The link is established through wordplay involving "moon" (*ḥōdeš*) in Hos 5:7 and "new [king]" (*ḥādāš*) in Exod 1:7. In such a fashion, the Writings and the Prophets were brought into interpretive "play" with the pentateuchal synagogue portions.

In fact, the main point of Jacob Mann's comprehensive study on the use of Scripture in the synagogue was to emphasize how strongly the prophetic lections (or *haftarot*) had influenced these homilies.[45] Thus, the typical progression was the Torah reading, the *haftarah*, and a sermon that began with a verse from the Writings. As Mann pointed out, "In this manner the preacher demonstrated to his audience *the union of the three divisions of the Bible.*"[46] Isaiah Sonne reached a similar conclusion:

> The underlying idea was to stress the unity of the three parts of Scripture: that there is nothing in the Prophets and the Hagiographa that could not be found in the Pentateuch, that all three parts are but one and the same expressed in different forms, various modes of the same substance. This is a unifying principle which links the Torah reading, the Haftara (Prophetic reading) and the homily, beginning with a verse from the Hagiograph, together.[47]

This formal canonical unity thus provided a source, framework, and goal for traditional homiletical interpretation in the synagogue.[48]

A related phenomenon can be seen at work in the *ḥatimah* at the conclusion of the sermon.[49] This rhetorical move takes the first or last verse of the

---

45. As Wacholder also notes in Mann, *Bible*, 1.xx, the frequent assumption that passages from the Writings were never read within the synagogue service cannot be sustained: "The mishnaic prohibition notwithstanding, certain psalms, or other Hagiographic selections, considered apt for a particular Sabbath used to be recited, evidently preceding the Prophetic portions. We know that this was so from the New Year liturgy, from lists of Hagiographic portions found in works such as the Pesikta Rabbati, the Tractate Soferim, and Aggadat Bereshit, as well as from manuscript collections." Beckwith, *Canon*, 144, notes how b. T. Šabb. 116b makes explicit mention of a *haftarah* reading from the Writings in Nehardea. Does this instance reflect an earlier practice, increasingly discouraged, or simply a local aberration from what was the standard practice? Here again, further work is needed.

46. Wacholder in Mann, *Bible*, 1.12 (emphasis his).

47. "Isaiah Sonne's Preface to Volume II," in ibid., 2.xxxi.

48. For other indications of unifying features within traditional Jewish interpretive practice, see Alexander Samely, "Scripture's Implicature: The Midrashic Assumption of Relevance and Consistency," *JSS* 36 (1992) 167–205.

49. See further Doris Lenhard, *Die rabbinische Homilie: Ein formanalytischer Index* (Frankfurter Judaistische Studien 10; Frankfurt: Gesellschaft zur Förderung Judaistischer Studien, 1998).

Torah lesson and then adds a prophetic verse expressing consolation. Frequently, an eschatological note is sounded by drawing a contrast between
things as they now are and things as they will be.[50] Sometimes the *haftarah*
or prophetic lesson from the lectionary is also cited in the process. At the
heart of these homiletical practices was a concern to explore and exemplify
the unity of Scripture.[51]

Citation by Division in Early Christianity

The triple scriptural reflex in Judaism is also evident in the New Testament. For example, in Romans 3, Paul cites from the Psalms (14:1–2 [Rom
3:10–12]; 5:9 [Rom 3:13]; 10:7 [Rom 3:14]; 36:1 [Rom 3:18]) and Isaiah
(59:7–8 [Rom 3:15–17]) in order to make a point about the "law." Of course,
New Testament sermons such as Paul's in Acts 13 can take a salvation-
historical form that combines verses from all three divisions of the canon—
with arguably less attention to their genre and more attention to the way
in which they relate successive episodes within the overarching story of the
work of God.[52] But this kind of biblical interpretation is not "atomistic"
either. The last words of the mother of seven in 4 Macc 18:10–18 provide
an example of the way that salvation-historical and generic impulses could
in fact be combined: she relates that her husband would teach the Law
and the Prophets by telling the stories of past heroes of the faith—yet the
verses quoted in the process come from Genesis, Numbers, Daniel, Isaiah,
Psalms, Proverbs, and Ezekiel, concluding with Deuteronomy, thus once
more combining the three canonical divisions.

When Christians began to recognize the New Testament writings as
Scripture, they also compiled them according to genre and used the genre
designations as titles, on analogy with Jewish tradition. The persistence of
this practice underscores the remarkable continuity between Jewish and
Christian interpretive practice.[53] Thus, already in 1 Clement, the author

---

50. Samely, *Rabbinic Interpretation*, 277.

51. See further Michael Graves, "The Public Reading of Scripture in Early Judaism,"
JETS 50 (2007) 483–84. Interestingly, there may be a distinction observable at this point
with regard to halakic *petiḥtot*, which discuss matters of normative religious practice and
appear to do so, at least sometimes, on the basis of pentateuchal Scripture only; for an
example of this type, see Shinan, "Sermons," 103.

52. On the Jewish background to Acts 13, see Larry W. Hurtado, *At the Origins of Christian Worship* (Grand Rapids, MI: Eerdmans, 1999) 33. On the wider phenomenon, see Jan
Willem Doeve, *Jewish Hermeneutics in the Synoptic Gospels and Acts* (Assen: Van Gorcum,
1954).

53. Behind this practice was most likely the liturgical reading of texts from both the
Torah and the Prophets during synagogue services even prior to 70 B.C.E. See further Dirk
Monshouwer, "The Reading of the Scriptures in the Early Church," *Bijdragen* 54 (1993)
57–71; Lawrence Schiffman, "The Early History of Public Reading of the Torah," in *Jews,
Christians, and Polytheists in the Ancient Synagogue* (ed. Steven Fine; New York: Routledge,
1999) 44–56.

makes reference to "the blessed Moses . . . [who] has set down fully in the sacred books the instructions which he himself received; and the other prophets also, who came after him, [who] all bear their witness to the ordinances which he laid down" (1 Clement 43). Similarly, in his letter to the Philadelphians, Ignatius of Antioch writes of the "Apostles" in parallel with the "Prophets" (Ign., *Phld.* 5). While it seems likely that written materials are here in view, it is admittedly a matter of debate whether in this instance "Apostles" refers to the figures of the apostles, the New Testament Epistles, or the entirety of the New Testament.[54] The letter to Diognetus offers a tantalizing description of what early Christian worship might have been like: "A chant celebrates the fear of the Law, / The grace of the Prophets is made known, / The faith of the Gospels is implanted, / The tradition of the Apostles is secured, / And the grace of the Church waxes jubilant" (Diogn. 11).[55] Tertullian's later reference to "the Law and the Prophets together with the Gospels and apostolic Letters" (*Praescr. Haer.* 36.5) appears to acknowledge the same sort of traditional worship practice.

Such linguistic usage also appears in the New Testament writings themselves, which can refer to the entirety of Jewish Scripture as "the law" (e.g., John 10:34; 12:34; 1 Cor 14:21) or simply "[the] prophets" (Rom 1:2; cf. Eph 2:20) or even "the wisdom of God" (Luke 11:49). The concept of "prophets and apostles" as a means of summing up the entire biblical legacy is apparently still developing during the period of the New Testament canon's formation. At first, such terms seem to refer to individuals and groups, both the historical (e.g., Matt 23:34; 1 Thess 2:13–15) and the contemporary (1 Cor 12:28–29; Rev 18:20). But over time, the terms are increasingly employed more broadly (e.g., Eph 2:20), eventually being used as a combined reference both to historical figures and to the scriptural reports containing accounts of those figures. By the late 2nd century, the phraseology of "prophets and apostles" becomes a standard way of indicating the biblical witness as a whole (Diogn. 11:5–7; 2 Clem. 14:2).[56]

In addition to such "generic" titles and references for Scripture, there was also similarity at times between the way the rabbis adduced supporting scriptural verses from all three divisions of the canon and the way early Christian writers gave multiple scriptural attestations. In 1 Clement 28–29, a citation from Ps 139:7–8 is followed by one from Deut 32:8–9, which is in turn followed by another citation that has long represented an

---

54. Maxwell Staniforth, ed., *Early Christian Writings: The Apostolic Fathers* (New York: Penguin, 1968) 115 n. 2.

55. See ibid., 185 n. 12: "It is tempting to see in these lines a glimpse of the early Church's worship, with psalms, Bible-reading, and a sermon."

56. For an effort to reconstruct this linguistic development, see Dennis Farkasfalvy, "'Prophets and Apostles': The Conjunction of the Two Terms before Irenaeus," in *Texts and Testaments: Critical Essays on the Bible and Early Church Fathers* (ed. W. Eugene March; San Antonio, TX: Trinity University Press, 1980) 109–34.

interpretive crux: "Behold, the Lord takes a people for himself out of the midst of the nations, as a man takes the first-fruits of his threshing floor; and it is out of that people that the Holy of Holies shall come." Although some interpreters have wanted to claim this verse as evidence that Clement at times quoted noncanonical sources, most investigators have viewed the verse instead as a composite citation in which several different biblical verses are combined, a situation made even more difficult to analyze because Clement may have been quoting from memory. Among possible biblical source texts, frequently mentioned are Num 18:27; 2 Chr 31:14; and Ezek 48:12, possibly with cribbing from Deut 4:34 and 14:2 as well. Given the threefold pattern of such citations in Judaism, one might easily expect Clement to reach for a prophetic text in this sort of instance (Ezek 11:17 is also suggestive).[57] But even without being able to identify Clement's source text(s) precisely, the same kind of impulse toward comprehensive canonical citation pattern appears to be present as was evident in Judaism.

In the New Testament itself, John 19:36–37 suggests a similar effort to provide a comprehensive appeal to the tripartite Hebrew tradition, even if in its present form the text styles its appeal as double rather than triple in form.

> These things occurred so that the scripture might be fulfilled, "None of his bones shall be broken" **[Exod 12:10, 46; Num 9:12; Ps 34:20]**. And again another passage of scripture says, "They will look on the one whom they have pierced" **[Zech 12:10]**.

Interpreters have picked up on the global scope of these invocations of Jewish Scripture, particularly since they conclude a section of the Johannine Passion Narrative that turns on the question of proper legal observance (John 19:31–35). Even though the Old Testament texts are conflated and presented as only two citations, a threefold pattern is nevertheless still apparent, following the order Pentateuch–Writings–Prophets.[58]

---

57. It is also possible that Clement knew an apocryphal version of Ezekiel; see Donald Alfred Hagner, *The Use of the Old and New Testaments in Clement of Rome* (NovTSup 34; Leiden: Brill, 1973) 66–72, for this and other proposals.

58. For recent studies, see William Randolph Bynum, *The Fourth Gospel and the Scriptures: Illuminating the Form and Meaning of Scriptural Citation in John 19*:37 (NovTSup 144; Brill: Leiden, 2012); Maarten J. J. Menken, "The Old Testament Quotation in John 19:36: Sources, Redaction, Background," in *The Four Gospels, 1992: Festschrift Frans Neirynck* (ed. Frans Van Segbroeck; BETL 100; 3 vols.; Leuven: Leuven University Press, 1992) 2.101–18. Bynum in particular observes that "[t]he two final scriptural citations of 19:36 and 37 which close both the crucifixion episode and the entire Passion Narrative demonstrate that in the piercing of Jesus, Jewish leaders and Roman authorities, unbeknown to either group, together fulfilled the Law, as well as the Prophets and the Psalms, to the letter" (p. 180). However, both studies largely overlook the threefold pattern of Jewish interpretive practice under investigation in this essay. I suspect this oversight has occurred because of the narrowly text-critical orientation of these studies. Rather than focusing on the precise textual form of a single quotation or the exact manner of its importation, there is a

An even clearer New Testament example is found in Rom 10:18–21:

> But I ask, have they not heard? Indeed they have, for "Their voice has gone out to all the earth, and their words to the ends of the world" **[Ps 19:4]**. Again, I ask, did Israel not understand? First Moses says, "I will make you jealous of those who are not a nation; with a foolish nation I will make you angry" **[Deut 32:21]**. Then Isaiah is so bold as to say, "I have been found by those who did not seek me; I have shown myself to those who did not ask for me." But of Israel he says, "All day long I have held out my hands to a disobedient and contrary people" **[Isa 65:1–2]**.

Here the pattern of citation moves from the Writings to the Pentateuch to the Prophets. This particular complex of allusions is also introduced by additional quotations from Moses (Rom 10:5 → Lev 18:5; Deut 30:12–14), and the Prophets (Rom 10:11–12 → Isa 28:16; Rom 10:13 → Joel 3:5[2:32]; Rom 10:15–16 → Isa 52:7; 53:1). Sometimes such chain citations are constructed on the basis of a catchword connection or common theme as well as attending to the canonical location of the individual citations.[59] In Romans 10, the crucial word is thus "all" (*pas*).[60]

Rom 15:8–12 illustrates the same technique quite nicely:

> For I tell you that Christ has become a servant of the circumcised on behalf of the truth of God in order that he might confirm the promises given to the patriarchs, and in order that the Gentiles might glorify God for his mercy. As it is written, "Therefore I will confess you among the Gentiles, and sing praises to your name" **[Ps 18:49 = 2 Sam 22:50]**; and again he says, "Rejoice, O Gentiles, with his people" **[Deut 32:43]**; and again, "Praise the Lord, all you Gentiles, and let all the peoples praise him" **[Ps 117:1]**; and again Isaiah says, "The root of Jesse shall come, the one who rises to rule the Gentiles; in him the Gentiles shall hope" **[Isa 11:10]**.

---

pressing need to explore more fully how such quotations work together literarily in the received form of the New Testament writings.

59. E. Earle Ellis, "Quotations in the New Testament," in *ISBE* 4.18–25.

60. On the use of Scripture in Romans 10, see further James W. Aageson, "Scripture and Structure in the Development of the Argument in Romans 9–11," *CBQ* 48 (1986) 268–73; James D. G. Dunn, "'Righteousness from the Law' and 'Righteousness from Faith': Paul's Interpretation of Scripture in Romans 10:1–10," in *Tradition and Interpretation in the New Testament* (FS E. E. Ellis; ed. Gerald F. Hawthorne and Otto Betz; Grand Rapids, MI: Eerdmans, 1987) 216–28; Dietrich-Alex Koch, *Die Schrift als Zeuge des Evangeliums: Untersuchungen zur Verwendung und zum Verständnis der Schrift bei Paulus* (Beiträge zur historischen Theologie 69; Tübingen: Mohr Siebeck, 1986); J. Ross Wagner, *Heralds of the Good News: Isaiah and Paul "in Concert" in the Letter to the Romans* (NovTSup 101; Leiden: Brill, 2002). As observed by Stanley E. Porter, "Paul and His Bible: His Education and Access to the Scriptures of Israel," in *As It Is Written: Studying Paul's Use of Scripture* (ed. Stanley E. Porter and Christopher D. Stanley; SBLSymS 50; Atlanta: Society of Biblical Literature, 2008) 122–23, Romans 9 also displays a broad movement from pentateuchal to prophetic citations.

Here the obvious catchword connection is the term *Gentiles*. Yet the need to include scriptural warrants from all three sections of the Hebrew canon helps to explain the number and distribution of the Old Testament citations, which otherwise might appear random and redundant.[61] After an introductory reference to the Writings, the citations proceed in the order Pentateuch–Writings–Prophets.

Another compound example is found in Heb 1:5–13:

> For to which of the angels did God ever say, "You are my Son; today I have begotten you?" **[Ps 2:7]**. Or again, "I will be his Father, and he will be my Son"? **[2 Sam 7:14]**. And again, when he brings the firstborn into the world, he says, "Let all God's angels worship him" **[Deut 32:43]**. Of the angels he says, "He makes his angels winds, and his servants flames of fire" **[Ps 104:4]**. But of the Son he says, "Your throne, O God, is forever and ever, and the righteous scepter is the scepter of your kingdom. You have loved righteousness and hated wickedness; therefore God, your God, has anointed you with the oil of gladness beyond your companions" **[Ps 45:6–7]**. And "In the beginning, Lord, you founded the earth, and the heavens are the work of your hands; they will perish, but you remain; they will all wear out like clothing; like a cloak you will roll them up, and like clothing they will be changed. But you are the same, and your years will never end" **[Ps 102:25–27]**. But to which of the angels has he ever said, "Sit at my right hand until I make your enemies a footstool for your feet?" **[Ps 110:1]**.

This set of Old Testament citations is generated as part of an argument involving divine sonship.[62] Yet even here, a threefold awareness is evident amidst heavy reliance on the Psalms, with Scripture once again included from all three sections of the Old Testament canon.

---

61. See also Douglas J. Moo, *The Epistle to the Romans* (NICNT; Grand Rapids, MI: Eerdmans, 1996) 878: "Paul cites every part of the OT—the 'writings' (vv. 9b and 11), the 'law' (v. 10), and the 'prophets' (v. 12)—to show that the inclusion of Gentiles with Jews in the praise of God has always been part of God's purposes." Cf. William M. Greathouse and George Lyons, *Romans 9–16: A Commentary in the Wesleyan Tradition* (New Beacon Bible Commentary; Kansas City, MO: Beacon Hill, 2008) 234: "In rabbinic style, Paul selects texts from each of the three main canonical divisions of Israel's Scriptures: the Law (LXX Deut 32:43 in Rom 15:10), the Prophets (LXX Isa 11:10 in Rom 15:12), and the Writings (LXX Ps 18:19 [= 2 Sam 22:50] in Rom 15:9b and Ps 117:1 in Rom 15:11). Such representative quotations of Scripture allow him to assert the unanimous biblical witness to God's intent, through the ministry of the Messiah—**the Root of Jesse**—to extend his **rule** to include **the Gentiles**" [bold-face type in original].

62. As Moo, *Romans*, 105, notes, 4QDeut 32 confirms that the quotation identified as Deut 32:43 is in fact from Deuteronomy 32, although this verse is actually missing from the MT. See further Arie van der Kooij, "The Ending of the Song of Moses: On the Pre-Masoretic Version of Deut 32:43," in *Studies in Deuteronomy* (FS C. J. Labuschagne; ed. Florentino García Martínez; VTSup 53; Leiden: Brill, 1994) 93–100. On Hebrews 1, see also Gareth L. Cockerill, "Hebrews 1:6: Source and Significance," *BBR* 9 (1999) 51–64; Susan E. Docherty, *The Use of the Old Testament in Hebrews: A Case Study in Early Jewish Bible Interpretation* (WUNT 2/260; Tübingen: Mohr Siebeck, 2009) esp. pp. 197–98.

The existence of this phenomenon in these particular examples means that it is all the more necessary to attend to the possibility of formal patterns in other cases of compound biblical citations in the New Testament, and not only to explore individual citations in a narrowly text-critical fashion.[63] Early Jewish and Christian interpreters frequently display an awareness of the *canonical location* of the biblical texts they cite. Most likely, both this awareness and its interpretive implications have their roots in the liturgical practice of the ancient synagogue, a practice that appears to have carried over into the early church.

Things Old and New

I doubt that I have completely dislodged the view set out so forcefully by Barr and Barton, but I hope that perhaps I have suggested why a challenge to their view is needed and on what terms such a challenge might be mounted. Another related matter that would need to be taken up in greater detail is the alleged novelty of *book-oriented* readings. On the one hand, as I have already conceded, these kinds of readings are sometimes conspicuous by their absence from sermons and other interpretive works in the Christian tradition. Indeed, Karel van der Toorn has recently challenged the very idea of biblical "books," arguing that their "book" character is not original:

> The books of the Bible were not designed to be read as unities. . . . A biblical book is often like a box containing heterogeneous materials brought together on the assumption of common authorship, subject matter, or chronology. Whatever literary unity these books possess was imposed by the editors and is, to some extent, artificial. The editors could rearrange, expand, or conflate the separate units at their disposal in such a way as to achieve the illusion of a single book with a single message.[64]

However, the fact that the book-character of the biblical books is not "original" is not by itself a sufficient reason to ignore it. To the contrary, one could just as easily argue that it makes sense to read the biblical books as they have been shaped by their editors and their tradition of transmission on the basis that these tradents likely understood the texts better than we do. Even more significantly, the later biblical commentary literature does tend to read the biblical books *as books*, and this prominent stream within the history of interpretation provides an important counterweight to the use of isolated verses or pericopes in preaching.[65]

---

63. For an effort to treat the entire book of 1 Peter as unfolding according to a threefold canonical pattern, see Hans van Nes, "Traces of a Three Part Canon Underlying 1 Peter," in *Das heilige Herz der Tora* (FS H. Koorevaar; ed. Siegbert Riecker and Julius Steinberg; Aachen: Shaker, 2011) 183–97.

64. Karel van der Toorn, *Scribal Culture and the Making of the Hebrew Bible* (Cambridge: Harvard University Press, 2007) 16.

65. For an illuminating example in the early modern period, see Gerald T. Sheppard, "Interpretation of the Old Testament between Reformation and Modernity," in William

But to what extent were the biblical books really considered "books" by early Jews and Christians? Benjamin Sommer has offered a needed corrective to easy assumptions about the existence of "books" in ancient Israel.[66] However, I still see more literary and historical evidence in favor of the biblical writings' having been perceived as possessing a basic book-shape than I do against it. One of the most important indications is simply that the biblical writings were in fact transmitted as book-oriented scrolls, as is evident not only at Qumran but also in the rabbinic rules for copying biblical texts. As these copying rules indicate, for example, the twelve books of the Minor Prophets were treated as individual "books," even though they were routinely transmitted together on a single scroll.[67] It seems clear that the literary structure and proportions of a biblical book as a particular literary composition or "work" were not simply determined by or perceived as identical to the scroll onto which the work was copied.

In the end, I am still willing to grant that holistic readings of individual biblical books, especially of the type we have seen since the emergence of the "new" literary criticism toward the end of the last century,[68] do not predominate when viewed against the horizon of the entire history of biblical interpretation. But I am not willing to concede that traditional use of the Bible in Judaism and Christianity was "atomistic," unconcerned with any kind of literary, narrative, or canonical context, treating Scripture only as a random assortment of proverbial proof-texts. Even from the few examples produced in this essay, that point of view appears to be demonstrably false.

Instead, an established sense of Scripture's "triplicity" is evident in the pattern of interpretive judgments frequently rendered by early Jewish and Christian interpreters. As the writer of Ecclesiastes perceptively observed in the course of making another point, they knew that "a threefold cord is not quickly broken" (Eccl 4:12).[69]

Perkins, *A Commentary on Hebrews* 11 (1609 Edition) (ed. John A. Augustine; Pilgrim Classic Commentaries; New York: Pilgrim Press, 1991) 46–70.

66. Benjamin D. Sommer, "The Scroll of Isaiah as Jewish Scripture, Or, Why Jews Don't Read Books," in *Society of Biblical Literature: 1996 Seminar Papers* (ed. Eugene H. Lovering; SBLSP 35; Atlanta: Scholars Press, 1996) 225–42.

67. See *b. B. Bat.* 13b; cf. *Sop.* 2:4. For further discussion, see Ehud Ben Zvi, "Twelve Prophetic Books or 'The Twelve'? A Few Preliminary Considerations," in *Forming Prophetic Literature: Essays on Isaiah and the Twelve in Honor of John D. W. Watts* (ed. Paul House and J. W. Watts; JSOTSup 235; Sheffield: Sheffield Academic Press, 1996) 125–56. Contra Barton, *Holy Writings*, 154: "[T]he book of the Twelve is a seamless fabric and it hardly matters whereabouts a text is taken from." If it were "seamless," it would not have been transmitted as *twelve* in one—just one.

68. For a detailed presentation of this recent development in scholarship, see David M. Gunn, "Hebrew Narrative," in *Text in Context: Essays by Members of the Society for Old Testament Study* (ed. A. D. H. Mayes; Oxford: Oxford University Press, 2000) 223–52.

69. Such an application of Eccl 4:12 is not altogether fanciful but is in keeping with the same traditional impulse as explored throughout this essay. See Rashi's interpretation of the reference to "threefold" counsel in Prov 22:20–21 (reading with several ancient versions), which he takes as a reference to the Torah, Prophets, and Writings.

Bibliography

Aageson, James W. "Scripture and Structure in the Development of the Argument in Romans 9–11." *CBQ* 48 (1986) 268–73.

Aicher, Georg. *Das Alte Testament in der Mischna.* Freiburg: Herder, 1906.

Aptowitzer, Victor. *Das Schriftwort in der rabbinischen Literatur.* Library of Biblical Studies. Reprinted, New York: KTAV, 1970.

Barr, James. *Holy Scripture: Canon, Authority, Criticism.* Philadelphia: Westminster, 1983.

Barton, John. "Canon and Old Testament Interpretation." Pp. 37–52 in *In Search of True Wisdom: Essays in Old Testament Interpretation in Honour of Ronald E. Clements.* Edited by Edward Ball. JSOTSup 300. Sheffield: Sheffield Academic Press, 1999.

———. "Canonical Approaches Ancient and Modern." Pp. 199–209 in *The Biblical Canons.* Edited by J.-M. Auwers and H. J. de Jonge. Leuven: Leuven University Press, 2003.

———. *Holy Writings, Sacred Text: The Canon in Early Christianity.* Louisville: Westminster John Knox, 1997.

———. "Intertextuality and the 'Final Form' of the Text." Pp. 33–37 in *Congress Volume: Oslo 1998.* Edited by A. Lemaire and M. Sæbø. VTSup 80. Leiden: Brill, 2000.

———. *Oracles of God: Perceptions of Ancient Prophecy in Israel after the Exile.* Oxford: Oxford University Press, 1986.

———. "What Is a Book? Modern Exegesis and the Literary Conventions of Ancient Israel." Pp. 137–47 in *The Old Testament: Canon, Literature and Theology.* Society for Old Testament Study Monographs. Burlington, VT: Ashgate, 2007.

Beckwith, Roger T. *The Old Testament Canon of the New Testament Church and Its Background in Early Judaism.* London: SPCK, 1985.

Ben Zvi, Ehud. "Twelve Prophetic Books or 'The Twelve'? A Few Preliminary Considerations." Pp. 125–56 in *Forming Prophetic Literature: Essays on Isaiah and the Twelve in Honor of John D. W. Watts.* Edited by Paul House and J. W. Watts. JSOTSup 235. Sheffield: Sheffield Academic Press, 1996.

Boertien, M. "Einige Bemerkungen zu Bibelzitaten in der Mischna." Pp. 71–81 in *History and Form: Dutch Studies in the Mishnah.* Edited by A. Kuyt and N. A. van Uchelen. Publications of the Judah Palache Institut 4. Amsterdam: Amsterdam University Press, 1988.

Bokedal, Tomas. "The Rule of Faith: Tracing Its Origins." *JTI* 7 (2013) 233–55.

Bynum, William Randolph. *The Fourth Gospel and the Scriptures: Illuminating the Form and Meaning of Scriptural Citation in John 19*:37. NovTSup 144. Leiden: Brill, 2012.

Chapman, Stephen B. *The Law and the Prophets: A Study in Old Testament Canon Formation.* FAT 27. Tübingen: Mohr, 2000.

Childs, Brevard S. *A Biblical Theology of the Old and New Testaments.* Minneapolis: Fortress, 1993.

Cockerill, Gareth L. "Hebrews 1:6: Source and Significance." *BBR* 9 (1999) 51–64.

Davidson, Samuel. *The Canon of the Bible: Its Formation, History, and Fluctuations.* 2nd ed. London: King, 1877.

Docherty, Susan E. *The Use of the Old Testament in Hebrews: A Case Study in Early Jewish Bible Interpretation*. WUNT 2/260. Tübingen: Mohr Siebeck, 2009.

Doeve, Jan Willem. *Jewish Hermeneutics in the Synoptic Gospels and Acts*. Assen: Van Gorcum, 1954.

Dunn, James D. G. "'Righteousness from the Law' and 'Righteousness from Faith': Paul's Interpretation of Scripture in Romans 10:1–10." Pp. 216–28 in *Tradition and Interpretation in the New Testament: FS E. E. Ellis*. Edited by Gerald F. Hawthorne and Otto Betz. Grand Rapids, MI: Eerdmans, 1987.

Ellis, E. Earle. "Biblical Interpretation in the New Testament Church." Pp. 691–719 in *Mikra: Text, Translation, Reading and Interpretation of the Hebrew Bible in Ancient Judaism and Early Christianity*. Edited by M. J. Mulder and Harry Sysling. Compendia rerum iudaicarum ad Novum Testamentum 2/1. Assen: Van Gorcum / Philadelphia: Fortress, 1988.

———. *Paul's Use of the Old Testament*. 5th ed. Grand Rapids, MI: Eerdmans, 1991.

———. "Quotations in the New Testament." Pp. 18–25 in vol. 4 of *ISBE*.

Farkasfalvy, Dennis. "'Prophets and Apostles': The Conjunction of the Two Terms before Irenaeus." Pp. 109–34 in *Texts and Testaments: Critical Essays on the Bible and Early Church Fathers*. Edited by W. Eugene March. San Antonio, TX: Trinity University Press, 1980.

Ferguson, Everett. "Factors Leading to the Selection and Closure of the New Testament Canon: Some Recent Studies." Pp. 295–320 in *The Canon Debate*. Edited by Lee Martin McDonald and James A. Sanders. Peabody, MA: Hendrickson, 2002.

Finn, Leonard G. "Reflections on the Rule of Faith." Pp. 221–42 in *The Bible as Christian Scripture: The Work of Brevard S. Childs*. Edited by Christopher R. Seitz and Kent Harold Richards. Biblical Scholarship in North America 25. Atlanta: Society of Biblical Literature, 2013.

Fitzmyer, Joseph. *Essays on the Semitic Background of the New Testament*. London: Chapman, 1971.

Greathouse, William M., and George Lyons. *Romans 9–16*: A Commentary in the Wesleyan Tradition. New Beacon Bible Commentary. Kansas City, MO: Beacon Hill, 2008.

Goldberg, Arnold. *Mystik und Theologie des rabbinischen Judentums: Gesammelte Studien I*. Edited by Margarete Schlüter and Peter Schäfer. Tübingen: Mohr Siebeck, 1997.

———. *Rabbinische Texte als Gegenstand der Auslegung: Gesammelte Studien II*. Edited by Margarete Schlüter and Peter Schäfer. Tübingen: Mohr Siebeck, 1999.

Graves, Michael. "The Public Reading of Scripture in Early Judaism." *JETS* 50 (2007) 467–87.

Green, William Scott. "Writing with Scripture." Pp. 17–18 in Jacob Neusner with William Scott Green, *Writing with Scripture: The Authority and Uses of the Hebrew Bible in the Torah of Formative Judaism*. Minneapolis: Fortress, 1989.

Gunn, David M. "Hebrew Narrative." Pp. 223–52 in *Text in Context: Essays by Members of the Society for Old Testament Study*. Edited by A. D. H. Mayes. Oxford: Oxford University Press, 2000.

Hagner, Donald Alfred. *The Use of the Old and New Testaments in Clement of Rome.* NovTSup 34. Leiden: Brill, 1973.

Hurtado, Larry W. *At the Origins of Christian Worship.* Grand Rapids, MI: Eerdmans, 1999.

Ilan, Tal. "The Term and Concept of TaNaKh." Pp. 219–34 in *What Is Bible?* Edited by Karin Finsterbusch and Armin Lange. Contributions to Biblical Exegesis and Theology 67. Leuven: Peeters, 2012.

Irenaeus. *Against Heresies.* Edited by A. Roberts and J. Donaldson. Ante-Nicene Fathers 1. Grand Rapids, MI: Eerdmans, 1986. [orig., 1885]

Horne, Thomas Hartwell. *An Introduction to the Critical Study and Knowledge of the Holy Scriptures.* 9th ed. 2 vols. New York: Carter, 1853.

Jaffee, Martin S. *Torah in the Mouth: Writings and Oral Tradition in Palestinian Judaism, 200 BCE–400 CE.* Oxford: Oxford University Press, 2001.

Koch, Dietrich-Alex. *Die Schrift als Zeuge des Evangeliums: Untersuchungen zur Verwendung und zum Verständnis der Schrift bei Paulus.* Beiträge zur historischen Theologie 69. Tübingen: Mohr Siebeck, 1986.

Kooij, Arie van der. "The Ending of the Song of Moses: On the Pre-Masoretic Version of Deut 32:43." Pp. 93–100 in *Studies in Deuteronomy: FS C. J. Labuschagne.* Edited by Florentino García Martínez. VTSup 53. Leiden: Brill, 1994.

Leipoldt, Johannes, and Seigfried Morenz. *Heilige Schriften: Betrachtungen zur Religionsgeschichte der antiken Mittelmeerwelt.* Leipzig: Harrassowitz, 1953.

Lenhard, Doris. *Die rabbinische Homilie: Ein formanalytischer Index.* Frankfurter Judaistische Studien 10. Frankfurt: Gesellschaft zur Förderung Judaistischer Studien, 1998.

Leonhard, Richard Campbell. *The Origin of Canonicity in the Old Testament.* Ph.D. Diss. Boston University, 1972.

Liddon, H. P. *The Divinity of Our Lord and Saviour Jesus Christ: Eight Lectures Preached before the University of Oxford, in the Year 1866.* 6th ed. London: Rivingtons, 1872.

MacDonald, Nathan. "Israel and the Old Testament Story in Irenaeus' Presentation of the Rule of Faith." *JTI* 3 (2009) 281–88.

Menken, Maarten J. J. "The Old Testament Quotation in John 19:36: Sources, Redaction, Background" Pp. 101–18 in *The Four Gospels: FS F. Neirynck,* vol. 2. Edited by Frans Van Segbroeck. BETL 100. 3 vols. Leuven: Leuven University Press, 1992.

Metzger, Bruce M. "The Formulas Introducing Quotations of Scripture in the New Testament and in the Mishnah." Pp. 52–63 in *Historical and Literary Studies: Pagan, Jewish, and Christian.* New Testament Tools and Studies 8. Grand Rapids, MI: Eerdmans, 1968.

Monshouwer, Dirk. "The Reading of the Scriptures in the Early Church." *Bijdragen* 54 (1993) 57–71.

Moo, Douglas J. *The Epistle to the Romans.* NICNT. Grand Rapids, MI: Eerdmans, 1996.

Nes, Hans van. "Traces of a Three Part Canon Underlying 1 Peter." Pp. 183–97 in *Das heilige Herz der Tora: FS H. Koorevaar.* Edited by Siegbert Riecker and Julius Steinberg. Aachen: Shaker, 2011.

Perrot, Charles. "The Reading of the Bible in the Ancient Synagogue." Pp. 137–59 in *Mikra: Text, Translation, Reading and Interpretation of the Hebrew Bible in Ancient Judaism and Early Christianity.* Edited by M. J. Mulder and Harry Sysling. Compendia rerum iudaicarum ad Novum Testamentum 2/1. Assen: Van Gorcum; Philadelphia: Fortress, 1988.

Porter, Stanley E. "Paul and His Bible: His Education and Access to the Scriptures of Israel." Pp. 122–23 in *As It Is Written: Studying Paul's Use of Scripture.* Edited by Stanley E. Porter and Christopher D. Stanley. SBLSymS 50. Atlanta: Society of Biblical Literature, 2008.

Roberts, Bleddyn J. "The Old Testament Canon: A Suggestion." *BJRL* 46 (1963–64) 164–78.

Samely, Alexander. *Rabbinic Interpretation of Scripture in the Mishnah.* Oxford: Oxford University Press, 2002.

———. "Scripture's Implicature: The Midrashic Assumption of Relevance and Consistency." *JSS* 36 (1992) 167–205.

Schechter, Solomon. *Aspects of Rabbinic Theology.* New York: Schocken, 1961.

Schiffman, Lawrence. "The Early History of Public Reading of the Torah." Pp. 44–56 in *Jews, Christians, and Polytheists in the Ancient Synagogue.* Edited by Steven Fine. New York: Routledge, 1999.

Schrenk, G. "*Gráphō, graphé.*" Pp. 754–55 in vol. 1 of *TDNT* 1.

Shemesh, Aharon. *Halakhah in the Making: The Development of Jewish Law from Qumran to the Rabbis.* Berkeley: University of California Press, 2009.

Sheppard, Gerald. "Between Reformation and Modern Commentary: The Perception of the Scope of the Biblical Books." Pp. xlviii–lxxvii in William Perkins, *A Commentary on Galatians.* Edited by Gerald T. Sheppard. Pilgrim Classic Commentaries. New York: Pilgrim Press, 1989).

———. "Interpretation of the Old Testament between Reformation and Modernity." Pp. 46–70 in Williams Perkins, *A Commentary on Hebrews* 11 (1609 Edition). Edited by John A. Augustine. Pilgrim Classic Commentaries. New York: Pilgrim Press, 1991.

Shinan, Avigdor. "Sermons, Targums, and the Reading from Scriptures in the Ancient Synagogue." Pp. 97–110 in *The Synagogue in Late Antiquity.* Edited by Lee I. Levine. Philadelphia: American Schools of Oriental Research, 1987.

Seitz, Christopher R. *The Character of Christian Scripture: The Significance of a Two-Testament Bible.* Studies in Theological Interpretation. Grand Rapids, MI: Baker, 2011.

Sommer, Benjamin D. "The Scroll of Isaiah as Jewish Scripture, Or, Why Jews Don't Read Books." Pp. 225–42 in *Society of Biblical Literature: 1996 Seminar Papers.* Edited by Eugene H. Lovering. SBLSP. Atlanta: Scholars Press, 1996.

Staniforth, Maxwell, ed. *Early Christian Writings: The Apostolic Fathers.* New York: Penguin, 1968.

Stone, Timothy J. *The Compilational History of the Megilloth: Canon, Contoured Intertextuality and Meaning in the Writings.* FAT 2/59. Tübingen: Mohr Siebeck, 2013.

Toorn, Karel van der. *Scribal Culture and the Making of the Hebrew Bible.* Cambridge: Harvard University Press, 2007.

Ulrich, Eugene C. "The Non-Attestation of a Tripartite Canon in 4QMMT." *CBQ* 65 (2003) 202–14.

Urbach, Ephraim E. *The Sages: Their Concepts and Beliefs.* Translated by I. Abrahams. Cambridge: Harvard University Press, 1987.

Young, Frances. *Biblical Exegesis and the Formation of Christian Culture.* Cambridge: Cambridge University Press, 1997.

VanderKam, James C. *The Dead Sea Scrolls and the Bible.* Grand Rapids, MI: Eerdmans, 2012.

Wacholder, Ben Zion. "Prolegomenon." Pp. xx–xxxv in Jacob Mann, *The Bible as Read and Preached in the Old Synagogue.* 2 vols. New York: Ktav, 1971.

Wagner, J. Ross. *Heralds of the Good News: Isaiah and Paul "in Concert" in the Letter to the Romans.* NovTSup 101. Leiden: Brill, 2002.

Wall, Robert W. "Reading the Bible from within Our Traditions: The 'Rule of Faith' in Theological Hermeneutics." Pp. 88–107 in *Between Two Horizons: Spanning New Testament Studies and Systematic Theology.* Edited by Joel B. Green and Max Turner. Grand Rapids, MI: Eerdmans, 2000).

Warfield, B. B. "The Terms *Scripture* and *Scriptures* as Employed in the New Testament." Pp. 229–41 in *Inspiration and Authority of the Bible.* Edited by Samuel G. Craig. Philadelphia: Presbyterian and Reformed, 1948.

Response

JOHN BARTON

The canon of the Old Testament/Hebrew Bible has moved to the center of attention in recent years, and the present volume is a welcome addition to this burgeoning field, with its concentration on the Writings in particular. All of us who have written on the canon will need to weigh it carefully. There seem to me to be at least seven themes that emerge and need evaluation. After presenting them, I shall make a few general comments.

1. There is the question of the formation of the canon as a whole, without which of course there would be no division called the Writings. This has been investigated in huge detail in the last few decades, and it would be hard to find a better summary of this work than in the introduction to this volume by Steinberg and Stone. They deal fairly with all the contributions to the debate (including my own!). Their conclusion, that the canon of the Writings was decided already by the time of Ben Sira, tends in the more conservative direction, as the field is now understood, but is clearly defensible. Very important, it seems to me, is their suggestion that the canon may not have been the same for all Jews in the period of its formation: thus Josephus and the Dead Sea Scrolls may give us different impressions, not because one represents a "more developed" version of the contents of the canon, but because contemporaneous groups in Judaism may have seen the matter in different ways. But since this volume is specifically about the Writings, this is not the place to discuss the formation of the canon in general except as it bears on them. In practice, most of the contributors are concerned with the Writings once they existed as a discrete division, and debate about how that came to be may continue without affecting most of what is said in the other essays.

2. Inside the Writings, as it were, there is a question to be asked about the internal arrangement of given books, especially the more apparently anthological ones, such as Psalms and Proverbs. This issue surfaces, however, only in the piece by Hossfeld and Zenger on the composition of the Psalter, and I will set it aside. Study of the composition of the Psalter now forms an industry in its own right.

3. Much more central to most of the writers' concern is the question of the historical development of the Writings as a whole. It is well known that the order of these texts varies between different manuscripts and different listings: Beckwith has identified at least 70 different sequences.

Many scholars (including me) have argued that in a time before the codex the idea of "order" is somewhat nebulous, and so it was unlikely to have played a role in the formation of this division (unlike the Torah and Former Prophets, where we are dealing with a continuous story). It is a theoretical rather than a practical question, and it is not clear why anyone would have asked it. But it can be suggested that it is not in fact an anachronistic question (Dempster, p. 99) because, even in the time before the codex, some care may have been given to how the scrolls were stored. Particularly with the copies kept in the temple, there is likely to have been a concern for the arrangement of the scrolls on shelves or in jars (Steinberg and Stone, p. 40), and thus a concern for order could go back much further than the earliest discussion known to us, which is in b. B. Bat. 14b. This seems to me a reasonable point, though it should not be pressed too far, as though some standardized order is likely to have been followed in every physical collection of biblical scrolls. But in any case, Baba Batra dates to before the time when Jews began to use codices yet is interested in the order of the books, so it cannot have been a matter of indifference even in the 2nd century C.E. (if the text really is reproducing a baraita). And of course, even in Greek codices of the Bible, the order is by no means standardized (Stone, p. 177), which might further undermine the idea that thinking in terms of order is a problem only with scrolls.

On the other hand, one might argue this point differently. If even codices, which unquestionably must be arranged in some order or another, differ in the order that they contain, then this could mean that scribes were not very concerned about the issue but treated the Writings as an anthology that they could rearrange at will. We should then have to distinguish actual practice from the theoretical interest in the sequence that we find in b. B. Bat. 14b, which may have had some other purpose than to instruct scribes or librarians. One could see the question as an entirely theoretical one, or as concerned with something like a mnemonic purpose, rather than as focused on the realities of storage or library classification—so, at least, one might argue. It is certainly possible to exaggerate the variation in order: as Brandt has shown, the various sequences group together in families, with one major variation being between the orders that segregate the five Megillot and those that do not. There are eastern and western traditions for arranging the Writings (Brandt, pp. 70–73), each of which contains minor variations, rather than a free-for-all.

Dempster (p. 89) and Steinberg (p. 151) both argue that the existence of so many orders is actually evidence for how important order was. At first sight, this seems counterintuitive: if so many manuscripts and lists have a different order, one might think that order did not matter very much but could be varied at will. At the same time, I can see the point in arguing that people were at least very *interested* in the order of the Writings; it mattered to them in some way. And this means, as we shall see, that it at least could have had some importance for interpretation. This is made clear not only in the present volume but in three important works by contributors to it: Peter Brandt's *Endgestalten des Kanons*, Julius Steinberg's *Die Ketuvim*, and Timothy Stone's *The Compilational History of the Megillot* (see Dempster, p. 90)—which together build a detailed case for attending seriously to sequence in the study of the Writings.

4. Most scholars think that the Writings is a collection of previously existing books that have been grouped together. The idea that any of them was written specially for the collection is, I think, a novel one and emerges in the pieces by Koorevaar and Steins on Chronicles, which both of them see as being written for its function within the Writings—or even within the Bible as a whole—as a summary or key to the entire collection. Evaluating this requires a high degree of expertise in the study of Chronicles, but on the face of it seems rather improbable. Koorevaar's argument (p. 232) that Chronicles is then "opened" in Matthew belongs to a theory of pan-biblical theology and is surely not a historical point about the composition of the Writings.

5. More plausible to most, I think, will be the idea that the individual books may have been "tweaked" to make them fit their place among the Writings. Where there are catchwords (Stone, p. 178) connecting the end of one book to the beginning of another, these could have been added to facilitate the link—though one would need in every case to show that they are indeed additions and were not required anyway by the logic of the books in which they appear. But some such tweaking does seem to be implied when Steinberg and Stone suggest that the books have been "shaped" in the process of becoming part of the canon. Thus, in orders where Ruth precedes Samuel, one may point to the parallel between the chorus of women's words to Naomi, "your daughter-in-law who loves you, who is more to you than seven sons" (Ruth 4:15) and Elkanah's to Hannah, "Am I not more to you than ten sons?" (1 Sam 1:8), as linking the books. Yet it would surely be hard to argue that these lines were added to one book or the other to make the link, especially because there are other orders (indeed, the normative order now of all Hebrew Bibles) in which Ruth is located among the Writings and is not linked to Samuel at all. Sometimes I am not quite clear what is being asserted about the "shaping" of the individual books to make them fit into the canon: does this mean actual changes to the text, or is it more a matter of how they were read?

6. We turn now to interpretive issues. To what extent was the arranging of the Writings important to their interpretation? "Naturally, the literary context in which Daniel is placed—whether alongside prophetic books or in the Writings—influences the way the book is understood and interpreted" (Warhurst, p. 187). It is true that the question of whether Daniel is a prophet or not is linked in some interpreters' minds to the issue of whether the book appears among the Prophets or the Writings, and Warhurst cites an important remark by Theodoret on this topic (Warhurst, p. 188). This is important and shows that the divisions of the canon did have some

interpretational importance. Chapman shows that the rabbis often seek to find proof texts from all three divisions and that this may even be observed in the New Testament, and this seems to me plausible and important.

But is this also true of books' place in the sequence *within* the Writings? Steinberg argues that the compilers "took books that already existed and arranged them in a pattern that probably was intended to yield the maximum possible interpretational coherence" (Steinberg, p. 166). But as a matter of historical fact, it is hard to find examples where this was definitely the case. Writers do not cite the juxtaposition of certain books within the Writings and draw out theological implications from this.

At this point, it may be right to refer to the discussion of traditional Jewish and Christian interpretation of the texts as "atomistic," which both James Barr and I have done. Chapman seeks to counter this with the argument that sometimes citations are assembled with an awareness of where they come from: it is not as though the Scriptures were treated simply as a random collection of aphorisms. To an extent this is true, but even in the cases he cites, there is seldom any attention to the meaning of the texts chosen within the books they are taken from: rather, they are treated as *obiter dicta*, out of context. And sometimes, in both Talmud and midrash, subsemantic items such as individual features of the spelling of words are appealed to in interpretation. I think the word *atomistic* is fair as a description of this sort of approach.

The study of the arranging of the Writings belongs to the history of the reception of the biblical texts, mainly in the Middle Ages. We have no evidence for any order older than b. B. Bat. 14b, and though there are many theories in the present book about why one order or another was preferred by the rabbis, explicit references to an order are few and far between. Apart from b. B. Bat. 14b, the many orders identified by Beckwith are all posttalmudic and surely throw little light on the intentions of the actual compilers of the Writings. The variation confirms that there was no "original" order: the Writings are an anthology that can be plausibly arranged in various ways, by genre, theme, date, or catchword, and no one order is definitive or authoritative. What the various arrangements are evidence for is how Scripture was regarded in medieval Judaism, but even then only if we can be sure that the order was intentional and not random. This is, I believe, seldom the case. Given a juxtaposition of two books, it is always possible to deduce a rationale for the juxtaposition, but in the absence of explicit comments by contemporary interpreters it is almost never possible to know that one is reading the sequence rightly. Ruth may precede Psalms because Ruth was the ancestor of David, the psalmist, or it may follow Proverbs because Ruth is an example of the "woman of worth" with whom Proverbs ends; both are plausible theories; neither is necessarily the case. It may be true that we need a "canonical or compilational poetics" (Stone, p. 179); but are we likely to get one?

7. The other interpretive question is this. Whatever may historically have been the case, *should* the order of the Writings influence our interpretation of them now? Will Kynes argues that it is important to read Job, not just in the light of Psalms, but *after* Psalms, so that a canon with the books in this order does best justice to both books and is somehow mandatory or at least advisable (Kynes, p. 131). This statement sees the order of the books as determinative for our own interpretation, whether or not it corresponds to historical reality. I am reminded of Jack Miles's *God: A Biography*,[1] which takes the normal, modern, Hebrew sequence of the books of the Bible as a framework for constructing a "biography" of the biblical God. He argues, for example, that God never speaks again after his words to Job in the voice from the whirlwind. As a literary reading of the Hebrew Bible that we now happen to have, this seems to me unimpeachable and highly interesting. It makes no historical claims at all, of course, about how the canon came to be constructed but simply reflects on it as it lies before us in a printed Hebrew Bible.

I sense, however, that for many contributors this essentially literary approach is not enough and that they are looking for a "canonical" reading more in the manner of Brevard Childs. It is interesting in this connection that Childs himself did not say much about the *order* of the canon. Dempster identifies this as a defect in Childs's approach (Dempster, p. 89); one may guess that © would have cited the variation in order that we have already discussed as a reason not to go down this road. It is perhaps Dempster who comes closest to a Childs-like interpretation, however, when, for example, he suggests that the order of the Writings in which Ruth comes before Psalms emphasizes the non-Jewish ancestry of David and so implies a reading of Psalms as pointing forward to the universal scope of the reign of the Messiah: he even calls attention to the much-disputed "kiss the Son" [*sic*, with capital] in Ps 2:11 as part of this. Here we have a panbiblical, indeed, a Christian reading of the canonical order, perhaps going further than Childs himself would have gone. Is it wrong to see in Dempster's interpretation an implication that the canonical order is in some way providential for those with eyes to see?

I conclude with a few general remarks. The order of the canon, and especially of the Writings as the most "anthological" division of the canon is a fascinating topic, well aired in this welcome volume. The papers assembled here show that, although there are many different orders, certain patterns emerge: most obviously in later orders that keep the Megillot together, but generally in the placing of "wisdom" books next to each other. There are also puzzles: why, as a matter of historical fact, does Ruth so often begin the Writings, and why does Chronicles often appear at the beginning or end and apparently without regard for its evident continuity with Ezra–Nehemiah? I

---

1. Jack Miles, *God: A Biography* (London: Simon & Schuster, 1995).

do not find most of the suggestions about these details very convincing on the historical level—not because the explanations offered are impossible but because they fall short of proving what, perhaps, simply cannot be proved. Too often a given juxtaposition was made plausible, but I felt that a different placement could have been argued for equally well, as with the variant locations of, again, Ruth. But to me, it is on the literary level that canonical "readings" work best, when scholars ask not how the Writings were in fact read—which we can seldom know—but how we *could* read them. Much of what is presented here is reception history, but much goes even beyond that and is, in effect, reader-response criticism. *Given* this or that canonical order, this is how we might interpret the texts that make up this order—without implying that no other order is possible. This is probably the best we can do in interpreting the shape of the canon, in light of the variety of sequences in which we encounter it.

The problem is that a reader-response approach is hard to square with the kind of theological interpretation that many people interested in the canon tend to be looking for, including at least some of the contributors to this volume. As soon as one has a high theory of scriptural inspiration, the apparent randomness of the arrangement of the Writings may seem to be a problem, and it will not be felt adequate to say that any given order *can* be read as having theological significance for us, since this seems to make the meaning of the text altogether too dependent on human ingenuity. I do not see the way out of this dilemma.

Perhaps there is an analogy with the approach that I earlier called "midrashic," that is, attention to subsemantic elements such as parts of words, and the taking of texts altogether out of context. Could there be, in canonical reading of the sort represented here, a kind of supersemantic interest? Could it be that finding meaning in complete collections of books—especially when these collections are anthologies rather than natural sequences (as are, say, the Former Prophets)—is improper in the same way, although on a macro- rather than a micro-level? It is like asking about the meaning of the complete plays of Shakespeare. One could order the plays in many ways—chronologically, generically, or thematically—and then find different implications in the various juxtapositions that resulted. But probably no one would take this very seriously. I wonder if trying to find meaning in the order of the Writings is that kind of enterprise. Perhaps to say this is to do no more than repeat the old cliché that the Bible is not a book but a collection of books, but this is an important truth: there comes a point beyond which some collections do not constitute a unity of any kind, and I am inclined to think that this is true of the Writings. Biblical theologies can proceed in many ways to synthesize the material in the collection, but I have my doubts whether attention to canonical order is the best one. That said, the study of how the texts were in fact sequenced is a fascinating and rewarding one, and this volume represents a high-water mark in discussing and elucidating it.

Response

TAMARA COHN ESKENAZI

The canonical shape of Scripture is anything but trivial, given the authority granted to the Bible in both Judaism and Christianity. The extensive contribution to the subject that this volume offers, especially to the canonical shape of the Writings/Ketubim, is therefore most welcome. The comprehensive introductory essay "The Historical Formation of the Writings in Antiquity," in particular, is already a milestone in providing an up-to-date review of the evidence and highlighting key points of the on-going debates. Julius Steinberg and Timothy Stone are to be congratulated and thanked for this work. Most of the essays that I read indeed enlarge our understanding. While uncertainties remain, this book sheds important light on the issues and enables readers to appreciate both the diverse opinions and the complexities that account for them. Roger Beckwith's observation that there are 70 different orders for the Writings[1] illustrates some of the challenges, even as it nicely echoes the rabbinic dictum that there are 70 faces to the Torah.

The authors in this volume are mostly European and emphasize European scholarship. As such, the book helpfully introduces resources that are sometimes overlooked in American circles, even as it does not always reflect some current American scholarship (I was surprised, for example, not to find engagement with the important work of Gary Knoppers in the several essays on Chronicles).[2] By focusing on European scholars, this volume opens the door to a richer intercontinental dialogue, especially when some essays introduce larger studies from which they derive.

My original goal was to include responses to the articles by Peter Brandt ("Final Forms of the Writings: The Jewish and Christian Traditions"), Stephen Dempster ("A Wandering Moabite: Ruth–A Book in Search of a Canonical Home"), and Timothy J. Stone ("The Search for Order: The Compilational History of Ruth"), all of which make important contributions, and to that of Hendrik J. Koorevaar ("Chronicles as the Intended Conclusion to the Old

---

1. R. Beckwith, *The Old Testament Canon of the New Testament Church* (Grand Rapids, MI: Eerdmans, 1985) 450–64. Cited by H. J. Koorevaar, p. 214.

2. The cultural or religious background of many of the scholars may account for the prevalence of using the term *Old Testament* when exploring the Writings/Ketubim, an oddity given that, technically, the corpus labeled Writings/Ketubim, does not exist as such in the Old Testament.

317

Testament Canon") which I find quite problematic, especially because of the Christianization of Chronicles.[3] But considerations of time and space lead me to concentrate on only two essays (Steinberg and Stone's "Historical Formation of the Writings in Antiquity" and Georg Steins's essay on "Torah-Binding"), and in the case of the Steinberg and Stone, I focus primarily on one aspect. In both cases, I consider my comments to be part of an ongoing conversation generated by this important volume—a conversation that will continue fruitfully, I trust, thanks to this book.

Steinberg and Stone's "Historical Formation of the Writings in Antiquity" is (as noted above) a particularly rich and helpful review of the state of the question and a superb introduction to the data and the scholarship. Section 2 of the essay examines the question of the order of the books in the Writings/Ketubim. It demonstrates that a great variety of options have been developed over the millennia. Steinberg and Stone's review of the issues and positions is most helpful. Their attempt in this part to establish that the order of the Ketubim was meaningful before the advent of the codex, however, is less successful. It is here where categories and conclusions seem to me to drift away from demonstrable support for arguments. Their first point, that "order could be significant . . . before the use of the codex" (p. 37) is plausible indeed. But the following discussion does not show that a commonly agreed-upon order existed or that it was, in fact, a *significant* issue before the ascendance of the codex.

Looking at b. B. Bat. 14b, one can readily concur with Steinberg and Stone that b. B. Bat. 14b depicts a tripartite canon of 24 books. Steinberg and Stone identify the passage dealing with the canon as a Baraita (on the basis of Strack and Stemberger) and thus belonging to the mishnaic period—that is, "reduced to writing around 200 C.E." (p. 41). As such, it is the earliest evidence for a concern with a sequence. As Brandt (p. 70) notes in his essay, and as Steinberg and Stone mention in support of the claim about this passage's influence (p. 40), 13 of the 51 extant MSS follow this sequence. It seems that Steinberg holds the widespread view that the grouping of the five Megillot as a unit, which is a relatively constant feature of the Writings/Ketubim in more-recent MSS, "is a relatively late phenomenon occurring only after the 6th century C.E." (p. 41). Stone, however, explicitly challenges this position, concluding that, "while the MT order comes into our purview in the late 8th century C.E., it had ancient roots"

---

3. The problems include assertions such as this: the "Chronicler highlights what is of integral importance in the canon: David (and his progeny/descendants) and the temple (for all Gentiles/nations) within one universal world-horizon (Adam–Cyrus)" (pp. 222–223). Such a recasting of Chronicles' central agenda and the goal of the canon itself is markedly a Christian interpretation. It is one thing to suggest that Chronicles can be appropriated for Christian theology (for which David, a temple "for all Gentiles," and a "universal world–horizon" are to be valued). It is another thing to claim this theology as Chronicles' main intention, to be recognized as central to the canon of the Hebrew Bible as a whole.

(p. 51). In either case, the order of the Megillot in various MT versions continues to change, which complicates conclusions about early versions.[4]

The introduction suggests that the list in b. B. Bat. 14b is probably the "mother of the family of manuscripts" (p. 42), then attempts to decipher its rationale. After reviewing diverse positions on the subject, Steinberg and Stone conclude that "genre and chronology cannot be the primary key to the rationale of the TaNaK structure" (p. 43) and proceed to offer an alternative.

My reading of the talmudic text leads me to conclude that chronology is more relevant than Steinberg and Stone acknowledge. I am also not as convinced that the order of the books was as central for an early period as they suggest. If Brandt is correct that, "[f]or the transmission of the Bible, until the 5th or even the 8th century A.D., Jews used scrolls exclusively" (p. 62), then the order is not likely to have been significant until such a late date. And the prevalence of the grouping of the Megillot in these later MSS together with the fact that most of the documents do not match b. B. Bat. 14b would count as evidence against the prominence of b. B. Bat. 14b as the "mother of the family of manuscripts" (p. 42).

Furthermore, in the case of the Ketubim, I question the validity of the conclusion that "there is internal evidence in the OT that the sequence of the books was not arbitrary but meaningful" (p. 37). Of course, some sequences were important. As for internal evidence, the examples that Steinberg and Stone marshal are forms of intertexuality, which they use as markers for sequences. Their analysis may imply that authors or redactors intended a particular sequence at the stages of composition or redaction. At the very least, they suggest that the decided order was influenced by this sort of intertextuality. But the variety of possible arrangements on the basis of intertextual features as well as the legacy of different arrangements show the opposite when it comes to the Ketubim.

Take the book of Ruth. Stone regards "they married" in Ruth 1:4 as implying that Ruth belongs after Judges, given Judg 21:23. The verb serves as "canonical glue" that points to Ruth as belonging with Judges (p. 181). However, this connection is hardly as effective as the first verse of Ruth, which explicitly places the narrative in the time of the judges. Which of these links should be regarded as the canonical glue? Leading words disclose intertextuality (note, perhaps, in this connection *ʾēšet ḥayil* "woman of valor," which is unique to Prov 31:10 and Ruth 3:11), not markers for

---

4. The most obvious examples are the different JPS versions, each claiming to be reproducing the MT. See also some standard Hebrew-language "Rabbinic Bibles" in which the Megillot are interspersed in the Pentateuch. For example, a widely used edition in Orthodox Jewish communities, the *Ḥumaš miqraʾot gedolot*, published by "Holy Books Publishers" (Israel; alas, no date is listed) places the Megillot in the following order: Esther follows Genesis. Song of Songs follows Leviticus. Ruth Follows Numbers, and Lamentations and Ecclesiastes follow Deuteronomy.

a sequence. The intertextuality that the biblical books display can indeed point to a dialogue among texts, but it is able to generate a variety of sequences, as in fact the variety in extant MS arrangements amply shows. One might be able to argue that Judges or Joshua seeks to fill in a lacuna and is thus subject to original considerations of "order." But this logic does not hold equally for the books in the Ketubim.

I think that a discussion of intertextuality needs to be explored more fully in this connection and differentiated from claims about canonicity. I fully concur with the view that Stone, for example, holds that texts in the Ketubim grew in conversation with each other as well as with other literary works. The evidence of cross-fertilization, however, cannot be used uncritically and without additional facts as proof of canonization.

Looking for catchwords as markers of intended sequence is highly speculative, given the variety of arrangements that can be proposed. Catchwords seem to dictate that Chronicles should come just before Ezra–Nehemiah (given the overlapping sentences of 2 Chr 36:22–23 and Ezra 1:1–3), as it does in the LXX, but this is not the case in the Leningrad Codex or b. B. Bat. 14b. Webs of intertextuality are very likely at work, but they are too elastic to yield or justify one arrangement over another and cannot support an intended arrangement or even presumed canonicity, unless we have evidence to support it.

I also remain unpersuaded that interest in the arrangement of books was prompted or influenced by the "archival " storage in the temple. There is next to no evidence that these writings were part of the temple "library." In fact, texts such as 2 Macc 2:13 that mention a "library" do not connect it with the temple (Nehemiah, we read, founds a library; he does not collect and place books in the temple; moreover, the writer of 2 Macc 2:14–15 offers to send these books to the addressees, a sign that the "library" was not deemed the only place for these books). Josephus makes it quite clear that sacred books were to be found in a variety of places, including his own private possession (Ag. Ap. 2.175). See, for example, "but if any be caught stealing their holy books, or their sacred money, whether it be out of the synagogue or public school, he shall be deemed a sacrilegious person, and his goods shall be brought into the public treasury of the Romans" (Ant. 16:164/16.6.2). See also J.W. 2:229/2.12.2; 7.150; Ant. 12:256/12.5.4).

Looking at b. B. Bat. 14b in the larger context of the talmudic corpus, we see that the first striking feature of this discussion of "a canonical order" is its uniqueness.[5] That such a discussion appears only once in the Talmud is itself an indication that the issue of sequence was not prominent in rabbinic discourse. One might attempt to excuse the silence by claiming

---

5. The mishnaic discussions about the Song of Songs and Ecclesiastes (for example, m. Yadaim 3:5) concern inclusion as sacred writings, not sequence.

that there was tacit consensus and therefore no need to discuss the matter further. However, the lack of a stable order, when evidence does surface, suggests the opposite of a consensus, even when 13 versions of 51 are the same. Moreover, when we look closely at b. B. Bat. 14b and its context, the passage shows a lack of uniformity.

In seeking a "holistic way" of dealing with scripture, Steinberg (p. 43) looks for a theological message for the order in b. B. Bat. 14b. What is missing from the discussion is a closer look at Baba Batra itself.[6] It seems to me that this rabbinic text actually offers early interpretations of a rationale as well as "proof" of fluidity—both of which stand in tension with the proposal made by Steinberg and Stone when interpreting the evidence of b. B. Bat. 14b.

We can begin with the rabbinic discussion of the prophets. Contrary to the order that eventually prevailed, b. B. Bat. 14b places Isaiah after Ezekiel. We can imagine some reasons for this arrangement: although Isaiah begins in the 8th century, it extends to the postexilic period as its point of termination and thus reaches past the events in Ezekiel. The pericope, however, includes rabbinic opinions on the matter and thereby enables us to see the rabbinic sages' rationale.

> Rabbis taught: The order of the Prophets is, Joshua, Judges, Samuel, Kings, Jeremiah, Ezekiel, Isaiah, and the Twelve Minor Prophets. Let us examine this. Hosea came first, as it is written, God spake first to Hosea. But did God speak first to Hosea? Were there not many prophets between Moses and Hosea?[7]

Chronology, we learn, is the first issue that the sages address, indicating that it is a norm they expect. But they then struggle to account for the oddity of the location of Hosea:

> R. Johanan, however, has explained that [what it means is that] he was the first of the four prophets who prophesied at that period, namely, Hosea, Isaiah, Amos and Micah. Should not then Hosea come first? — Since his prophecy is written along with those of Haggai, Zechariah and Malachi, and Haggai, Zechariah and Malachi came at the end of the prophets, he is reckoned with them.

Chronology continues to be considered the first organizing principle in this explanation. But as the argument develops, length becomes a consideration and provides an explanation: "But why should he not be written separately and placed first? — Since his book is so small, it might be lost [if copied separately]."

---

6. I understand that Steinberg's *Ketuvim* includes a longer discussion, but it is not reflected here. My comments are confined to the case made in the present introduction.

7. This quotation and all the other Baba Bathra quotations come from the online Soncino version: http://www.come-and-hear.com/bababathra/bababathra_15.html.

Having given one rationale for "extenuating circumstances" that override chronology, the writer picks up the challenge of Isaiah in the next sentence:

> Let us see again. Isaiah was prior to Jeremiah and Ezekiel. Then why should not Isaiah be placed first? — Because the Book of Kings ends with a record of destruction and Jeremiah speaks throughout of destruction and Ezekiel commences with destruction and ends with consolation and Isaiah is full of consolation;[14] therefore we put destruction next to destruction and consolation next to consolation (b. B. Bat. 14b).

We learn from this discussion that, in the earliest extant reflection on the subject, chronology seems to be at work as the first criterion but with the themes as an intersecting criterion that takes priority in certain situations. The same type of argument seems to account for the order in the Ketubim, which immediately follows:

> The order of the Hagiographa [Ketubim] is Ruth, the Book of Psalms, Job, Proverbs, Ecclesiastes, Song of Songs, Lamentations, Daniel and the Scroll of Esther, Ezra and Chronicles. Now on the view that Job lived in the days of Moses, should not the book of Job come first? — We do not begin with a record of suffering. But Ruth also is a record of suffering? — It is a suffering with a sequel [of happiness], as R. Johanan said: Why was her name called Ruth? — Because there issued from her David who replenished the Holy One, blessed be He, with hymns and praises. (b. B. Bat. 14b)

Here too the consideration of chronology seems to be assumed as primary but with an adjustment to account for the messages of Job and Ruth.[8] This passage is directly followed by a discussion of authorship. The discussion deserves a close look for the light it sheds on sequence, and thus I cite the lengthy pericope here in full:

> Who wrote the Scriptures? [lit. "Who wrote them?"]— Moses wrote his own book and the portion of Balaam and Job. Joshua wrote the book which bears his name and [the last] eight verses of the Pentateuch. Samuel wrote the book which bears his name and the Book of Judges and Ruth. David wrote the Book of Psalms, including in it the work of the elders, namely, Adam, Melchizedek, Abraham, Moses, Heman, Yeduthun, Asaph, and the three sons of Korah. Jeremiah wrote the book which bears his name, the Book of Kings, and Lamentations. Hezekiah and his colleagues wrote (Mnemonic YMSHK) Isaiah, Proverbs, the Song of Songs and Ecclesiastes. The Men of the Great Assembly wrote (Mnemonic KNDG [*sic*]) Ezekiel, the Twelve Minor Prophets, Daniel and the Scroll of Esther. Ezra

---

8. We should note that Job is regarded here as living at the time of Moses; contrast with Brandt's suggestion that he was a contemporary of the Queen of Sheba (Brandt, p. 71, based on b. B. Bat. 15b). The date for Job fluctuates heavily from Moses to the time of Ahasuerus and several points in between (b. B. Bat. 15b). But, while his date continues to be discussed in a variety of connections, no such discussion recurs about the order of the books or their dates.

wrote the book that bears his name and the genealogies of the Book of Chronicles up to his own time. This confirms the opinion of Rab, since Rab Judah has said in the name of Rab: Ezra did not leave Babylon to go up to Eretz Yisrael until he had written his own genealogy. Who then finished it [the Book of Chronicles]? — Nehemiah the son of Hachaliah. (b. B. Bat. 14b–15a)

Two things in this passage about authorship are noteworthy for the present discussion. First, the chronological order of attribution and, second, the attributions themselves. The sages here attach Proverbs, Song of Songs, and Ecclesiastes—in that order!—to Hezekiah and his court, Solomonic ascriptions not withstanding. The chronology of the presumed authors seems to be at work for the Ketubim in this earliest interpretation of the list's rationale (again, attesting that Moses is connected to Job). Moreover, the order is already inconsistent for the Solomonic books: the order in this discussion is "Proverbs, Song of Songs, Ecclesiastes." It diverges from the order of the list itself, which has Proverbs, Ecclesiastes, Song of Songs. At the very least, one must conclude that this sequence was not regarded as fixed, decisive, or of primary significance.

As for the general correspondence between claims of authorship and the earlier list in Baba Bathra 14a, one may ask: Is the authorship discussion merely a derivation from the list that precedes it? This may be the case, but it nevertheless gives us the earliest traditions about the rationale for the sequence: it indicates that chronology is the primary concern, subject to other overriding exigencies as in the case of Ruth and Job. It also seems that the order was not so precisely established even in this earliest of discussion, since (as noted) the sequence about authorship lists Proverbs, Song of Songs, and Ecclesiastes differently from the passage about the list.

Uncertainty and inconsistency about the order of the Ketubim persists in our time, as Brandt's review of the evidence shows. In the 20th century, as we know, BH and BHS, while reproducing the Leningrad Codex, chose to move Chronicles from its position as first in the Ketubim, to the end. Brandt's lists for the Jewish Bible also show current, 21st-century diversity. The online version of JPS that he lists (p. 60) differs from that of most Jewish printed Bibles, including the most recent JPS, all of which keep the Megillot in the liturgical sequence, not as the online JPS version has it.

Turning back to the discussion of b. B. Bat. 14b in Steinberg and Stone, one could agree with Steinberg that certain theological meanings emerge from a "holistic reading" of the Ketubim as they appear in the Talmud. I myself find "holistic readings" to be of great value when interpreting inherited traditions. But that sort of conclusion needs to be distinguished sharply from the claim that one has thereby uncovered the rationale for the sequence.

A similar point can be made in regard to Georg Steins's fine essay on Chronicles, to which I now turn.

In his well-argued and compelling essay "Torah-Binding and Canon Closure: On the Origin and Canonical Function of the Book of Chronicles," Steins rightly notes three sets of distinctions that need to be differentiated in the discussion of canon:

> (1) between the historical formation of the canon and the formation of a canonical theory, which begins to become evident in Jewish sources only at the end of the 1st century C.E.; (2) between the fact of the formation of the canon by a group/party and the general reception of this canon; and (3) between the stabilization of the scope and order of the books, and the fixing of the textual shape. (p. 272)

There is every reason to concur with Steins that, as J. Maier states in *Zwischen den Testamenten*: "Interest in the shape of the text increased with the amount of authority that was assigned to the text."[9] We can also surely agree on the basis of Josephus and 4 Ezra that a canonical process, or canonical thinking, is evident at the end of the 1st century C.E.[10] But we also learn that no uniformity had been reached, given that the only two sources disagree. Moreover, we also cannot be so sure that Josephus's 22 books correspond to our books, with Ruth and Lamentations attached to Judges and Jeremiah, respectively. Josephus, after all, reports that Ezekiel wrote two books (Ant. 10:79/10.5.1) and that Daniel, likewise, had more than one (Ant. 10:267/10.11.7).

Steins effectively illustrates how Chronicles anchors some of its distinctive views in the Torah. Note, for example, the new function of the Levites as musicians in 1 Chr 23:25–32, which Steins sees as "the application of the Torah in a new situation in order to master a specific task" (p. 266).[11] Steins shows how well Chronicles integrates Mosaic and Davidic traditions as joined sources of authority (see, e.g., p. 267) and how much the Torah infuses Chronicles. Let me note, however, that surprisingly the word *torah* is not very frequent in Chronicles; it appears 19 times, which is not much more than the 11 times in Kings and is considerably less, proportionately, than the 25 times in the much shorter Ezra–Nehemiah. Yet, as Steins shows, other terms and formulations embed various forms of Mosaic authority in Chronicles. Steins's review of examples is illuminating. I am grateful to him for highlighting these features of Chronicles, even though my conclusions about the functions of these references differ from his: I would not have been alert to all the variations and forms of Chronicles' use of the Torah were it not for Steins's meticulous analysis.

---

9. J. Maier, *Zwischen den Testamenten: Geschichte und Religion in der Zeit des Zweiten Tempels* (NEB 3; Würzburg: Echter-Verlag, 1990) 18; cited by Steins, p. 272 n. 137.

10. If this is what Steins considers "a canonical theory," then we do not agree.

11. Interestingly, this passage does not mention the Torah or allude to it, but the point may stand given a larger context.

Nevertheless, I think it is a great leap to claim on the basis of available data that the goal or even the consequence of the work (intended or not) is to serve as the closing document. Such a view would require a notion of a closed canon at a very early date—that is, the time of the writing of Chronicles. Not only is there no evidence to support this concept (especially in light of the use of the scroll, not the codex, until centuries later), but there is nothing in Chronicles itself that speaks to a notion of closure. Indeed, the entire book is more overtly open-ended than any other biblical book: its partial quotation points to an open-ended future as well as (in the received material) to another text. The book ends mid-sentence, as it were.

Instead of Chronicles' having an intention to close the canon, it seems to me that it used the Torah consistently in the service of the temple and as a validation for it and its functionaries—perhaps especially when the later practices diverged from those in the Pentateuch. This harmonizing of the Torah and the temple was essential in an age when the Torah was coming to the fore as an authoritative source for communal life, something that Ezra–Nehemiah establishes. A reconciling of Torah and temple is needed, given the limits of the pentateuchal teachings, which in any case applied to the tabernacle, not a temple. Chronicles' interest and primary concern, then, is the temple, not the canon.

It is noteworthy that the word *torah* is used only twice in 1 Chronicles (1 Chr 16:40 and 22:12). In that era, David seems to have sufficed. It is when it comes to succession that the Torah serves as the guiding principle. The instructions to Solomon, which mention the Torah, are especially illuminating. This lengthy speech (1 Chr 22:7–19) begins and ends with references to the temple, which is to be expected. But the contrast between this version and the one in the book of Kings, upon which it is based, throws into a sharper relief the subordinate role of the Torah in Chronicles, where it is a "handmaiden" of the temple.

Here's how Chronicles records the messages of David to Solomon: having recalled God's messages about the temple (1 Chr 22:7–10), David instructs Solomon:

> Now, my son, may the LORD be with you, and may you succeed in building the House of the LORD your God as He promised you would.
>
> Only let God give you sense and understanding and put you in charge of Israel and the observance of the Teaching [*torah*] of the LORD your God.
>
> Then you shall succeed, if you observantly carry out the laws and the rules that the LORD charged Moses to lay upon Israel. Be strong and of good courage; do not be afraid or dismayed. (1 Chr 22:11–13, JPS)

Compare these words with David's final words in 1 Kings 2, where *torah* also appears and where it indeed occupies the primary message (in contrast to the parallel in 1 Chronicles):

I am going the way of all the earth; be strong and show yourself a man.
Keep the charge of the LORD your God, walking in His ways and following His laws, His commandments, His rules, and His admonitions as recorded in the Teaching [*torah*] of Moses, in order that you may succeed in whatever you undertake and wherever you turn.

Then the LORD will fulfill the promise that He made concerning me: "If your descendants are scrupulous in their conduct, and walk before Me faithfully, with all their heart and soul, your line on the throne of Israel shall never end!" (1 Kgs 2:2–4, JPS).

In 1 Kings, God's teaching and the Torah stand as the starting point and as David's central message, before he instructs Solomon to settle accounts with friends and foes. In 1 Chronicles, David's focus on the Torah is more limited, both in terms of the number of words used in this longer speech and in the use that is made of the Torah. These details combine to show a lesser focus on the Torah in 1 Chronicles than in 1 Kings.

As others have shown, the story of Josiah in 2 Chronicles 34 likewise alters the role of the Torah from its source in 2 Kings 22. Whereas 2 Kings positions the Torah as the basis for Josiah's reforms, 2 Chronicles renders its presence a result.

Thus, as Steins rightly points out, Chronicles' interest "revolves around the temple and the cult as the visible pole of Israel's identity" (p. 271). Chronicles' use of the Torah aims to underscore this perspective.

Rather than concluding that Chronicles seeks to close a canon, Steins marshals evidence that testifies to the canonical status of the Torah in its time and to the eagerness of Chronicles' author to attach his work to it. There is indeed, "Torah-binding" at work. And this is of great importance. However, it is not convincing to conclude that the book was written in order to be the last word or as a conclusion, when neither of these concepts appears as a category of concern in the book itself or in pre-Christian sources. To make this claim is also to suggest that the earliest recorded readers—some of whom placed the book at the beginning of a collection and even (in the LXX) in the middle—failed to understand the book's key message. Such a claim can be valid at times; works can be misunderstood by early readers or deliberately reframed to undercut their messages; but we need stronger evidence before concluding that we, who are millennia removed, can better grasp an author's main goal.

As for the conclusion of Chronicles, Steins's statement is both a puzzle and an example of the difficulty with the arguments he presents. Moving toward his conclusion, Steins writes: "That the end of Chronicles in 2 Chr 36:22–23 contains references to the Torah and the prophets is easy to see" (p. 275). But here are the concluding words, and the presence of Torah is hard to find:

And in the first year of King Cyrus of Persia, when the word of the LORD spoken by Jeremiah was fulfilled, the LORD roused the spirit of King Cyrus of Persia to issue a proclamation throughout his realm by word of mouth and in writing, as follows: "Thus said King Cyrus of Persia: The Lord God of Heaven has given me all the kingdoms of the earth, and has charged me with building Him a House in Jerusalem, which is in Judah. Any one of you of all His people, the Lord his God be with him and let him go up." (2 Chr 36:22–23, JPS)

The mention of Jeremiah indeed appears. But in what sense do we find the Torah in these verses? Rather, the final sentence, which partly quotes the beginning of Ezra–Nehemiah, points to an open future in which individuals will go up to build God's house. This lack of closure, this incompleteness, which is generated by ending mid-sentence, I suggest is an important feature of Chronicles and perhaps the decisive clue to what the book seeks to communicate.

Response

CHRISTOPHER R. SEITZ

Above all, the achievement of this book is successfully to move beyond two-dimensional views of the canon in general and the Writings in particular that have been popularized recently. I note three major advances before undertaking a review of the contents chapter by chapter.

1. The significance of orders in the canon or the Writings does not turn on successfully determining which can hold title to being the "original"; such a quest may only point to a genetic fallacy in the conception of how the association of individual writings emerged over time and was preserved (sometimes with creative diversity).

2. The fact that diverse orders exist cannot any longer be reduced to mere randomness, which in turn recent theorists held was tidied up either by the mechanical expedience of a codex or the decisions of an institutional body ("councils which rule books in or out" or otherwise dictated material sequence due to mechanical necessity); this conclusion is anticipated as well by the perennial problem with determining the existence of said councils at all when it comes to the canon of the Scriptures of Israel; just how such councils might have done their work; or why, with the emergence in time of a codex, diversity did not cease but was creatively sustained after all;

3. The idea that there was a tripartite order that was Jewish in character or represented a Jewish position—the logic of which was revealed via comparison with a Christian position of a four-part order, which is now familiar in English printed Bibles—is shown by the evidence never to have been an accurate way to consider the matter.[1] The orders that emerge in Christian and Jewish circles both are diverse and represent a wide, though limited, range of creative associations. The Writings show this especially to be true, since books like Ruth, Chronicles, and Ezra–Nehemiah creatively migrated for a host of nonhistorical reasons. This migration happily overrides threefold or "other-fold" orders, as we can see their rough

---

1. A particularly weak popularization is to be noted in M. Sweeney, "Tanak versus Old Testament: Concerning the Foundation for a Jewish Theology of the Bible," in *Problems in Biblical Theology: Essays in Honor of Rolf Knierim* (ed. Henry T. C. Sun and Keith L. Eades; Grand Rapids, MI: Eerdmans, 1997) 353–72. See also my book *The Goodly Fellowship of the Prophets: The Achievement of Association in Canon Formation* (Grand Rapids, MI: Baker, 2009) 48.

contours in reception history. The reasons that can be adduced for their movements and their associations are manifold but are chiefly theological and hermeneutical in character.

The strongest feature at work in this book, a feature that marks the contributions of each of the authors, is the thoroughness and sobriety with which each faces the evidence. No stone is unturned in the extremely complicated terrain of canonical lists in Jewish and Christian reception. No effort is made to strong-arm the diverse evidence into simple or two-dimensional systems of significance, which can so often be the case in studies of a similar kind, from both sides of the spectrum. There is diversity in the listings, but there is also ample evidence of associative principles at work that can be organized and evaluated in careful ways.

One typical pitfall is avoided entirely: the sort of concerns that animated the formation of the NT canon are not unconsciously allowed to infiltrate the examination of the Scriptures of Israel in their own integrity as a witness.[2] This is all the more critical in the light of their subsequent reception history within specifically Christian circles in new translational forms in which they are located alongside a second canonical achievement (the New Testament). All too often the specifics of the canonical process of the books that preceded the NT have been folded into a subsequent set of decisions and formational actions that are said to embrace both testaments at one and the same time. This is both historically inaccurate and literarily and hermeneutically confusing or anachronistic. One must respect the integrity of the formative moves that mark the development and stabilization of the canon of Hebrew Scripture, even when the reception history that demonstrates a measure of diversity in sequence and association is one that is manifested in Christian circles, where a wider Christian Bible—OT and NT—is in view. In a word, however we understand the formation of the NT canon—closure, order, exclusion—this latter phase in the coming-to-be of a twofold Christian canon must leave untouched the antecedent and unique dimensions of the finalization of the first testament. This is important even when, reaching back into that phase, one may discover diverse canonical associations that persist or are enriched in subsequent listings— for Jewish and Christian communities treasuring these books for similar and for different reasons in the lived life with them of preaching, teaching, edification, Christological hearing, or talmudic extension. The differences in the testaments extends to their formational and associative aspects—no less so when a later Christian Bible including the first testament manifests diversity in listings and orders.[3]

---

2. So Craig Allert, *A High View of Scripture? The Authority of the Bible and the Formation of the New Testament Canon* (Grand Rapids, MI: Baker, 2007). See my evaluation in *Goodly Fellowship*, 120–22. See also S. Chapman, "The Canon Debate: What It Is and Why It Matters," *JTI* 4 (2010) 287–88.

3. In the view of Barton, Barr, McDonald, Allert, and others, "The determination of the OT canon, such as it was, was not made until some time after the NT and was caught

Steinberg and Stone rightly point out at the very beginning of their overview both an impasse over canon and the one-sided way that certain projects have handled the discussion. *The Canon Debate* (2007) is a parade example. As they note, "[O]nly one side of the debate was included in the volume" (p. 2). One might stay with this observation a bit longer and probe the reasons for it. The example they give of Childs's remarks concerning Barr ("ships passing in the night") was actually not made with reference to the canon debate at all but, rather, to issues of historicism and Childs's exchange with Barr over allegory and typology. Furthermore, I do not think the example of 1 Jude is, strictly speaking, relevant either. The account that Barr gives of Jude/Enoch in his *Holy Scripture* book (1983) is fairly breezy, and he never states flatly that Jude is cited as Scripture. Instead, in a speculative and roundabout way, he refers to 2 Tim 3:15 ("sacred writings") and wonders what might have been in the library of the author (actually, it is the author's audience: "how from childhood you have been acquainted with the sacred writings"). Enoch is "apparently familiar to the writer of Jude"—a statement wholly uncontroversial. It is "likely to have been among the sacred letters . . . on which Timothy was brought up"— not exactly a very strong claim, though a curious one. When Childs "flatly asserted that Jude does not cite it as Scripture" (see above, p. 2), Barr is never mentioned. Childs means by "cited as Scripture" what is usually meant by that, "as it is written in Book of Enoch," and Barr is not able to make that kind of claim or does not choose to, in any event.[4]

Childs's training in historical-critical methods is a far better explanation. For him, canon was always a theological-hermeneutical conception built upon proportional or otherwise convincing diachronic findings.[5] Canon was in many ways an extension of OT form-criticism and redaction-criticism, with their attendant theological concerns, now operating at the level of the final form of a text.[6] Lee McDonald is simply not conversant with these same methods or their theological rationale.[7] Childs made the point fairly clearly in a later essay, where he compared the canon

up in the selfsame struggle of the NT to achieve its own canonical status, order, shape, and a logic of authority and apostolicity" (*Goodly Fellowship*, 32).

4. See the far-more exegetically sophisticated discussion of R. Bauckham, in *Jude and the Relatives of Jesus in the Early Church* (Edinburgh: T. & T. Clark, 1990).

5. See the essay by Neil MacDonald ("Theological Interpretation, the Historical Formation of Scripture, and God's Action in Time") in *The Bible as Christian Scripture: The Work of Brevard S. Childs* (ed. C. R. Seitz and Kent H. Richards; Atlanta: Society of Biblical Literature, 2013) 85–102. I have repeatedly sought to make this point, most recently in "The Canonical Approach and Theological Interpretation," *The Character of Christian Scripture: The Significance of a Two-Testament Bible* (STI; Grand Rapids, MI: Baker, 2011) 27–91.

6. Childs could of course argue against what he saw as atomistic deployments of distinctive species of redactional evaluation (Kratz, Steck). See "Critique of Recent Intertextual Canonical Interpretation" *ZAW* 115 (2003) 173–84.

7. His review of *Goodly Fellowship* likewise shows no indication of the historical-critical issues at stake. Instead, he simply rehearses yet again the views that he has recycled for many years now. See L. McDonald, "Review of *Goodly Fellowship*," *Int* 64 (2010) 427–28.

discussion in Germany and in Anglophone discussion.[8] One will search in vain in *The Canon Debate* for any engagement with the work of Janowski, Rendtorff, Oeming, Steins, Lohfink, Dohmen, Söding, Zenger, Gross, or Frankenmoelle. It is to the credit of the present volume that both sides of the debate are presented and also that the contributors represent continental and Anglophone scholarship. When Childs wrestles with the final form of Genesis and the combination of sources, he plows terrain that von Rad himself anticipated was going to be important to consider.[9] The same can be said of the Deuteronomistic History and its present reconfiguration into Torah plus Former Prophets. One wonders whether any of this discussion is remotely under control by Lee McDonald and the contributors he assembles, because it never forms any sustained discussion in a volume purportedly on canon. Even the work of J. Jeremias on the mutually associative editing of Amos and Hosea is very much relevant to the question of canon, because it suggests that the historical particularities of each prophet were maintained while also being brought into coordination—not as extrinsic acts by canonical editors, but within the very growth to final form of the works themselves.[10]

This may also explain why Barton's conception of Law plus "a wide religious literature without definite bounds" seems so implausible to those with long acquaintance with German critical methods and their extension in Anglophone circles.[11] The Deuteronomistic History has already been mentioned. The DtrH is reflective of a major effort to produce an associative work of sustained theological importance beginning with the transitional book of Deuteronomy (which now forms the conclusion of the Torah) and concluding with the exiling of Israel's monarchy. Von Rad and Noth disagreed over the final theological point being made in this work but not over its association and editorial coherence as such. They accepted on historical-critical grounds that these moves were intrinsic to the literature's coming-to-be and were not the work of canonical editors tidying up a wide religious literature without definite bounds or shape at some late date. The present volume can puzzle over the position of Ruth within the DtrH/ Former Prophets—or introducing the Psalter or following Proverbs—pre-

---

8. B. S. Childs, "The Canon in Recent Biblical Studies: Reflections on an Era," in *Pro Ecclesia* 14/1 (2005) 26–45.

9. See my "Prophecy and Tradition-History: The Achievement of Gerhard von Rad," *Prophecy and Hermeneutics: Toward a New Introduction to the Prophets* (Grand Rapids, MI: Baker, 2007) 155–88.

10. Idem, "Scriptural Author and Canonical Prophet: The Theological Implications of Literary Association in the Canon," in *Biblical Interpretation and Method: Essays in Honour of John Barton* (ed. Katharine J. Dell and Paul M. Joyce; Oxford: Oxford University Press, 2013) 176–88.

11. The original phrase is that of A. Sundberg, *The Old Testament of the Early Christian Church* (Cambridge: Harvard University Press, 1964) 102. On Barton's questioning even the stability of the law itself, see my *Goodly Fellowship*, 54.

cisely because the stability of certain basic blocks is taken as given on good historical-critical grounds, without requiring one to posit a single exemplar that will account for all the books in question as we know them to exist in subsequent lists. Precisely because significant progress has been made in understanding the Psalter as a whole work—or the relationship of Ecclesiastes to Proverbs, or the logic of the DtrH—one is able to see how adjustments emerged due to associative moves of different kinds in their wake. Ruth exists as a single work but also one in interpretive relationship to David in the Psalms, the virtuous woman of Proverbs, and the barren Hannah of 1 Samuel. Close historical-critical observations about the Psalter (Psalms 1–2 within the canonical shape of the whole), the Solomonic literature (Proverbs–Ecclesiastes–Song and its variants), and the Deuteronomistic History enable one to grasp the significance of Ruth in a variety of orders. In light of this, to speak of a "wide religious literature without definite form" simply introduces wide-scale confusion from the start.

The same can be said of additional associative work elsewhere within the Nebi'im. The parade example at present is The Book of the Twelve. In spite of the fact that one might think of scroll length as an expedience only, which allowed one to arrange the 12 individual works in any order ("wide religious literature without definite shape"), the overwhelming evidence from Qumran is of a single order, the order that we have come to recognize as that of the MT.[12] In the history of interpretation, in spite of working with a Greek translation, Theodore, Didymus, and Cyril all followed this same order. So to point out the existence of minor variations is simply to acknowledge a curious footnote in history.[13] One might even say that, if it could be shown that an alternative order existed before the one familiar to us in the MT and virtually unrivaled in reception history, it would still not be indicative of a wide religious literature without definite scope, but would be precisely the opposite: the production of a 12-book collection that proved durable through all the vicissitudes of listing variation. If the basic building blocks of the DtrH, the Twelve, and the Three end up being amenable to movement and reassociation as blocks, this is still reflective of something very different from a conception in which all one can say is that the Torah was fixed in form. Tripartite and fourfold are not hard rivals created to bring about an order that was never there among

---

12. Almost all scholars now reject the idea of Jonah after Malachi as being based on meager evidence that is capable of alternative readings. We have no evidence of a Hosea–Amos–Micah sequence at Qumran. See F. Watson's recent, thorough investigation of the Qumran evidence for the sequence of the Twelve (*Paul and the Hermeneutics of Faith* [London: T. & T. Clark, 2004]). And even if an order like this were to surface, it would be the proverbial exception establishing the rule.

13. To my knowledge, the only modern Bible that represents an order of Hosea–Amos–Micah to open the Twelve is the Orthodox Bible, and yet I am unaware of any reception-historical evidence of its being commented on in that form or with something like a significance to be set in contrast to the standard order.

individual works but are reclassifications of associated blocks amenable to our evaluation as such. The fourfold form we associate with modern English Bibles does not exist in precisely that form in ancient lists anyway. Rather, what we see is the maintenance of these basic blocks in a variety of creative reclassifications (DtrH with kindred histories; the Twelve before Isaiah–Jeremiah–Ezekiel or after Jeremiah–Ezekiel–Isaiah; even Josephus and his "five" plus "thirteen" plus "four").

If one is not sufficiently conversant with diachronic scholarship in the field of OT studies, the dimension of the development and growth of the literature—as revealed by source, form, tradition, redactional, and canonical methods—will not form the proper field of focus for assessing canonical dynamics extending all the way from incipient developments, through medial phases, to a variety of creative final listings and arrangements. In its place will come instead a concern with external factors: the number of books, institutional forces in selection and stabilization, bald comparisons of lists, or citation statistics of OT verses as they appear in the NT or reception history. And these are frequently made worse by conflating OT and NT distinctives into one externalized grid. The distinction between a fixed fivefold Torah "canon" and a wide range of religious literature is exactly the kind of confusing alternative that tilts the investigation in the wrong way from the start. It suggests on the one hand a stable association with canonical authority, the alternative of which would then have to be individual, discrete, unassociated writings on the other hand (the total number of which is not fixed, and the shape of each in relation to others is of a consistently indeterminate character). But the very idea of incipient-to-medial association, identified by close diachronic work, is a signal that posterity and the afterlife of the literature beyond an "original audience" are already in view. Instead of a library of discrete works of indeterminate number and form, whose final character will be given by committees or institutional bodies, we are witnessing the growth of that character within the literature's own development, which stamps it at early, medial, and final stages alike. So it is no small thing to distinguish between the stable Torah and the remaining works and thereby to gloss over the achievements of association in the non-Torah writings that are kindred in character and are far more likely to point to a reciprocal process in which the "Law and the Prophets" came into being. The very existence of a DtrH that has "lost" its programmatic beginning to the final form of the same Torah means that we are dealing with a false distinction at the outset. Diachronic reading derives its purpose from avoiding this error by refusing to focus on only one or the other end of the wider historical, developmental spectrum. The building blocks that lie at the root of the various listings we now possess are the best signs that such a distinction (Torah + remaining works) is faulty and must be set aside. Chief among these is the Deuteronomistic History, which overlaps with what will in time be called "The Former Prophets." The massive prophetic achievement of The Book of the Twelve stands alongside this narrative accomplishment. The close editorial relationship between Isaiah and the Twelve has frequently been noted and helps explain the tendency to place them next to one another in many listings. This comprehensive prophetic testimony covers the same temporal range as the Twelve. Flanking it are the major prophetic books of Jeremiah and Ezekiel, each with its own editorial history of development and finalization. The tendency toward large-scale accomplishment and literary integration is one ingredient in the way the major blocks have begun to form.[14]

It is within this context, then, that the most difficult canonical evaluation, that of the Ketubim, must take place if progress is to be made. Here is where the success of the present project can in large measure be identified. In my own work, I have distinguished between the achievements of association that one can spot in the Torah and the Prophets as compared with the Writings. This general view holds, moreover, whether we are speaking of the present order of the MT or of alternatives—in light of the discussion above. That is, one can explain the differences between the tripartite order of the present MT and similar threefold orderings (b. B. Bat. 14b)—as compared with alternatives in which the Ketubim conception has been differently cast—once one has a clearer sense of the logic of incipient associations testified to in the literature of both arrangements. The fact that Steinberg and Stone identify in the Ketubim a historical sequence and a poetic sequence is hardly surprising. Behind it lies the explanation for why recastings occur such as we can identify even in a very modern organizational structure such as the English printed Bible.[15] My own view (insofar as genetics are useful heuristically) is that the peculiar association resulting in the category Nebi'im—whereby two very different blocks of material (DtrH and four prophetic "books"; or "Former and Latter Prophets" as they will come to be known) now exist side by side—led to the rearrangement of them into prophetic and historical writings in other listings. Extracting the "historical writings" from the Ketubim (if this is the correct way to conceive of it genetically) leaves behind the poetic books, which in turn must be classified or reclassified.

Other things might be noted quickly in passing, because these surface in the opening review chapter. I have already mentioned the fact that even

---

14. As I write in the conclusion to my contribution to the Barton FS,

In this chapter my point is that the language of 'scripture' and 'canon' cannot be tidily distinguished, and that far from being an external valorization, the prophetic legacy was from its inception about canonical association, and the reasons for this are theological. The prophetic word was a divine word, and so could be heard in association, and indeed pressed for just that hearing. ("Scriptural Author," 186–87)

15. On the lateness of this particular form, see Brandt's essay. He speaks of a "scholarly cliché" whereby the prophets are thought to be a final section of the OT particularly suited to Christian Bibles.

when in Greek dress, Christian authors do not necessarily work with orders and associations that are different from that of the MT. Ellis has further noted that, in Christian writings where Deutero-Canonical works are cited by the authors, if these same authors are asked to provide an account of canonical biblical texts that they agree are authoritative, they advert to the 24/22-book canon.[16] One can also note the frank admission that difficulties can emerge in dogmatic exegesis (Prov 8:22–31 is a prime example) precisely because the church is working with a translation that can obscure things.[17] The point here is that, when the Christian Church possesses books in number and order that differ from the narrower canon of the Jews, it nevertheless is aware of a conservative estimate that it must take into consideration. The alternative would be to concede the point that the main difference between Christian and Jewish interpretations of the Old Testament and the reason for disagreement is textual factors and not more-substantive interpretive differences regarding the character of the literal sense of the one testamental witness shared by both groups, even in a different translation or final order.

The exhaustive account of all extant arrangements is provided in the chapter by *Peter Brandt* entitled "Final Forms of the Writings: The Jewish and Christian Tradition." At the outset, the author makes clear that "linear sequencing" was a necessity for the editors and that the long history in Christian and Jewish circles shows multiple ways of resolving this. But equally he is at pains to show that one ought not understand this as an adventure in producing variety due to lack of principles. As he states it economically, "there is only a limited number of multidimensional arrangements" (p. 59). One question not taken up is the degree to which what he terms "editors," especially in early orders, inherited preexisting arrangements, such as the "Torah and Prophets." His chapter is not, however, a diachronic investigation of the emergence of Jewish and Christian orders. This also means that early Christian orders that deviate from an early tripartite form need not be regarded as "a conscious rejection of the Jewish canon." As noted above, departures from the tripartite order could equally be viewed as simple rearrangements, creating new categories such as historical and poetic books, given the mixed character of the Nebi'im as this section emerged in association with the DtrH and the Three and the Twelve.[18]

---

16. E. Ellis, *The Old Testament in Early Christianity* (WUNT 54; Tübingen: Mohr Siebeck, 1991) 10–36. Melito's list is consistent with Baba Batra; Epiphanius, Origen, Jerome, Augustine, and Athanasius are examined as well. When asked to list authoritative books, they provide the conservative listing as constituting a genuine, undisputed canonical witness.

17. See the illuminating review of *qanah* in Greek translation by C. F. Burney, "Christ as the ARXH of Creation," *JTS* 27 (1926) 160–77. Several church fathers reckon that the Arian problem turns in no small part on lack of access to the Hebrew text of Proverbs, leading to confusion over "create" and "make" with reference to the eternal wisdom of God.

18. See my discussion in *Goodly Fellowship*, 77–104.

It was mentioned at the outset that moves to classify "Christian" and "Jewish" orders as tripartite and quadripartite, respectively, and to speak of the theological distinctives of each is a faulty conception, without any warrant in the reception history of the OT/HB.[19] Brandt's thorough review makes this abundantly clear; Jewish and Christian orders are internally manifold in character and do not follow a simple three- versus fourfold form. The idea that the final section of a Christian Old Testament consists of "Prophets" and so anticipates the NT is misleading and a scholarly "cliché" (p. 75). The evidence that he provides could appear to suggest that such a Bible in Christian circles first emerged with Luther's rearrangement of the Paris Vulgate. By extracting the "Apocrypha" and placing those books in a special category, the Paris Vulgate in Luther's hands would then conclude with the Twelve. In all the preceding listings in Christian circles, the Twelve never took up final position, and the idea of a standard quadripartite form is equally unattested.

With respect to the Writings themselves, Brandt offers a conclusion at the close of his remarks that bears further reflection: "[T]he books attributed to the 'Writings' in the Jewish Bibles seldom appear in a unified collection" (p. 83). A corollary of this would be the observation that this marks the Writings as distinctive vis-à-vis the "Law" and "Prophets" groupings in Jewish circles. I have made this same point, as has Georg Steins, and concluded that the character of the Writings is simply different. The moves toward association that we find in the Law and Prophets are not there to the same degree. The point of the present volume is to remind us that we can nevertheless account for the variety as (1) not unlimited, (2) subject to certain logical principles, and (3) not being evidence of late decisions to provide closure to an unstable Hebrew canon *tout court*. The Writings constitute a kind of library. This is why they can migrate and do. To translate this fact into major declarations about the status of the Hebrew canon as a totality is a category error. As Chapman has recently noted, and as this volume makes clear, it is semantically meaningful to speak of an "open canon" and mean by that: a core canon with accompanying writings whose sequence and precise number is more fluid. This is the "Law and Prophets" and the "Writings." So Brandt continues, "A historical reason for this [different status for the Writings as a 'unified collection'] may be that the 'Writings' were not yet considered a fixed canonical concept in those circles propagating the reception of the Jewish Bible in early Christianity" (p. 83). And of course, to speak of the Writings as not yet being a "fixed canonical concept" does not translate into any grand statements about the character of the Hebrew Bible as a total canonical achievement but is only a statement about the character of the Writings within that achievement. That the Writings have a different character from the Law and Prophets is simply a recognizable

---

19. Pace Sweeney, "Tanak versus Old Testament."

fact and is unrelated to the canonical authority of the Hebrew Bible that now consisted of two main parts—the Torah+Prophets and the Writings—as it emerged in the Second Temple context.

In my own work, I have probably overstated the individuality of the witnesses in the third division as being what characterizes this division, given the thorough evaluation provided in the present volume for the different arrangements and associations.[20] That said, I do believe that the associations that mark the main canonical section (Torah+Prophets) are of a thicker nature than what we see in the Writings. It is the achievement of the present volume to stay with the diverse evidence that we have in Jewish listings and to probe the significance of the arrangements that they set forth all the same.

Stephen Dempster provides a thorough and closely argued evaluation of the three different placements of Ruth in the canon (before Psalms; between Proverbs and Song of Songs; between Judges and 1 Samuel). The details of these three arrangements need not be reviewed here, except to say that all three have a high degree of exegetical logic and interpretive potential. Dempster does an excellent job of displaying this. It is important to note that the essay plays itself out against what is perceived as a danger to be avoided, which is that the presence of different orders indicates that no "original order" was held in sufficient esteem that it could not be departed from (the view of L. B. Wolfenson, as cited by the author).

It should be noted that Wolfenson draws this conclusion precisely because he believes he knows what the actual order of change was, from the "first" listing (the talmudic, with Ruth before Psalms) to that of the Masoretes (Ruth after Proverbs). Precisely because he is committed to the theory of an "original order," he draws the conclusion that gives Dempster concern: "When . . . it was convenient to depart from this order, there was evidently no scruple about doing this" (p. 91). Only in the context of claiming to be able to plot the precise movement from a "first" to subsequent arrangements does Wolfenson issue his evaluative judgment. When Dempster therefore writes "Diversity need not preclude canonical order but may well have assumed it," I understand his concern with the evaluation of Wolfenson but cannot see different starting premises at work. Both Dempster and Wolfenson hold that there is a "first" or "original list." Dempster appears to operate with an assumption that "certainty of order" is what allows for "freedom to experiment with various orders" (p. 91). Wolfenson believes the second conclusion is possible merely by knowing which list is prior to another, and it is hard to know why he is wrong and Dempster right based on the terms of the argument. Moreover, does one genuinely need to be able to posit original canonical order, strictly speaking, in order to account for freedom to rearrange?

---

20. "The Accomplishment of the Writings," in my *Goodly Fellowship*, 105–25.

I mention this because the obvious subplot of Dempster's contribution is the search for original canonical order as crucial to interpretation. In Wolfenson's conception, there is an original order, but it is presented only to show that it does not have any controlling status. This seems to be too insouciant for Dempster. The business of finding the "original canonical order" (p. 92) is one, then, of high seriousness. Here is the apparent point of concern and where Dempster wants to distinguish his project. After showing compellingly how the three different orders all have important exegetical integrity, his main concern is showing that the talmudic order is the original one. This is done by examining all the other options for development and rejecting them in favor of his own position. Knowing the beginning of the journey of the "wandering Moabite" is what enables one to appreciate the subsequent developments. So when Stone is cited at the close it is to question his conclusion. Dempster regards Stone's statement that "Ruth's compilational history reveals its deliberate and meaningful contextualization in multiple places during the canonical process" as being congenial with his survey of the journey; but not the following: "This may reveal that the search for an 'original' order—as well as the rejection of the significance of order if there are multiple arrangements—may be misguided."

I wonder whether here we are touching on a particular methodological problem. Dempster wants to acknowledge that, in the particular case of Ruth, "canonization allows for flexibility of arrangement in the interests of hermeneutical creativity," yet it is crucial to him that one be able to identify an "original canonical order" (p. 92), which in his judgment is that of the Talmud. I believe that here we enter into an important debate regarding the Bible in reception history, as measured against something to be classified as "history as origins." The relationship between these two things is clearly a symbiotic one.[21] The Bible exists as a book in time and space, and because of its particular canonical character, in relationship to communities. The Bible is not less than that which is claimed about it in the history of reception, but the latter cannot be dismissed as without its own historical character. To make a hard claim—even with flexibility given to the case of Ruth—about "an original order" that nowhere exists as a predominant reading or order (Ruth before Psalms) introduces us to a kind of history that makes it hard to join up with the reality of reception history as having its own significance. When Jerome and Augustine sparred over the status of the Hebrew verity, as this was beginning to make its force felt in new renderings that departed from the received text, it was finally necessary for Augustine to acknowledge that inspiration must cover both text

---

21. On the delicate relationship between history (origins) and history (reception), see the penetrating study of Andrew F. Gregory and C. Kavin Rowe, eds., *Rethinking the Unity and Reception of Luke and Acts* (Columbia: University of South Carolina Press, 2013).

forms. The surpluses that exist due to translation and reception lead us on a "search for the Christian Bible" in every age.[22]

In the case of Ruth, then, only relative value could ever be placed on an "original order," given the richness displayed in all three locations where the book now finds itself—two of which emerge in time as far more prominent than the talmudic location, which is held out as being "original." The significance of our knowledge of that order cannot be gainsaid, and these newer studies of the diverse orders of Ruth helpfully remind us of this fact. At question is the character of the value that is being placed on it via a claim regarding its historical originality lodged within a modern debate. One conclusion to be drawn is that precisely because of its rich hermeneutical and theological potential it was a book always seeking the widest field of *association in the nature of the case and all along the way.* If search for an original order were to find priority over the associative theological potential, I would question its true gain. In the specific case of Ruth, it is the very success with which one can comprehend its interpretive logic and significance in three places at the same time that reconfigures the significance of an alleged "originality" for one or another order. The fact that we are aware particularly of two of these places, given the reception history of Bibles in Jewish and Christian circles, is surely a gain and not a puzzle requiring sequential explanation. That newer studies of the Writings are able to think through the implications of diversity in listings without thereby declaring orders as being without meaning is of inestimable value for our interpretative day.

The essay by *Hossfeld and Zenger* belongs in the context of recent work on the editorial coherence of the Psalter, to which they are of course major contributors. Their attention to the motif of "Davidization" as a means to perceive the diachronic development of the five books of the Psalms raises an important question that they do not address. At the close of the chapter, they speak about interconnectedness as well as individuality in respect to the Psalter, though their own contribution really focuses on matters internal to the Psalms as a "small library" (p. 129). More importantly, the literary relationships that they do posit as useful for describing the Psalter's development (setting aside the details and success of the reconstruction) are not those within the Writings predominantly. Indeed, one implication to be drawn is that the editorial frame of the Psalter (Psalms 1–2 and 146–50) remains virtually untouched vis-à-vis the neighboring books in the Ketubim (Job and Proverbs).[23] The frame's contribution belongs to the

---

22. See Childs's use of this term, in *Biblical Theology of the Old and New Testaments* (Minneapolis: Augsburg Fortress, 1992). He writes, "One of the purposes of this attempt at a Biblical Theology is to apply these hermeneutical guidelines in working theologically within the narrow and wider forms of the canon in search both for the truth and the catholicity of the biblical witness to the church and the world" (p. 67).

23. On Ruth and the Psalter, see the remarks preceding. Note as well that the order Job–Psalms is not the order being investigated by Kynes. He wants to think through the

"individuality" of the Psalter and not to its "interconnectedness" to neighbors in the Writings.

Though the essay of *Kynes* wants to understand the significance of the juxtaposition of Job and Psalms, this is a different task from work that is based on dedicated intertextual and editorial accomplishments. It assumes that decisions have purposely been made to encourage "reading Job following the Psalms" (as the title of the essay makes clear). In other words, both Job and the Psalms exist individually with their own complex internal developments. Some of this is an obvious implication from their large size (and the comparison with Proverbs is also relevant at this point). Job's internal structure and coherence would require a dedicated treatment of its own,[24] and Kynes does not replicate what Hossfeld and Zenger seek to do on this front; the task he pursues is different and more in line with the larger goals of the book. He simply undertakes to think through the fact of their placement next to one another, with Psalms following Job. My point here is that Job and Psalms exist principally as individual works in the Writings. The editorial associations one can identify among the works of Proverbs, Ecclesiastes, Song of Songs, and for other reasons, Ruth are signs of a different kind of relationship than what obtains for Job, Psalms, and Proverbs. I call attention to this fact for other reasons in my own account of the significance of the Writings, vis-à-vis the main canonical achievement of the Law and Prophets.

Kynes is careful to argue that the order he is inclined to follow is not a claim on his part to normativity. This is because his inquiry is more at the level of basic comparisons: the character of David and Job; form-critical observations about shared genre in Psalms and Job; and allusions within Job to several psalms, most notably Ps 8:5[4] in Job 7:17–18. At the close, he speaks of a dialogical relationship between the two books.

One place where he is concerned to register caution is with the now-typical association of Job with so-called "wisdom books" (variously, Proverbs, Ecclesiastes, Sirach, sometimes Song of Songs, and certain wisdom psalms or narratives—the Joseph Saga and the Succession Narrative). In this popularized, widespread model, Job is to be plotted on a movement from conservative-school wisdom to skepticism and revolt (Qohelet), and indeed the book of Job is said to contain something of this movement within its own editorial history. Since the particular group called "wisdom books" does not appear anywhere in canonical form, Kynes is right to question whether this label exhausts what can be said of our interpretation of

---

order found in b. B. Bat. 14b—that is, Psalms–Job. He correctly notes that the usual order in Jewish lists is Psalms–Job and that the English printed Bible order was "not normative" at an allegedly earlier period (Kynes, p. 132 n. 3). This strengthens my comments here on the individuality of the two books, since no editorial strategy had been deployed to create a distinct order; instead, Kynes speaks more generally of the "hermeneutical value" in reading the two together.

24. C. Seitz, "Job: Full Structure, Movement, and Interpretation," *Int* 43 (1989) 5–15.

Job, as is Steinberg in his own essay on the topic. Here we see how recourse to canonical form—even a form that itself is not monolithic—provides a very different lens on the interpretation of a book such as Job. To read Job in the light of the Psalter is compelling for all the reasons Kynes helpfully points out, no matter how one then returns to the context implied by a modern critical category such as "wisdom literature" and seeks to integrate its history-of-religion conceptualization. I will say more about this question when I discuss Steinberg's chapter.

One question related to the individuality of these two major witnesses needs further reflection in my view. Though it has been noted that Job's placement next to the Psalms of David has been explained in some sources as pointing to a chronological index (Job as a contemporary of David), the book itself operates with its own very distinctive frame of reference. Job is not an Israelite, as is Israel's king. The temporal perspective of the book is markedly pre-Torah, if not antediluvian. The great age of Job and the characterization of his setting resemble those of the patriarchs (see Ezek 14:14, where he Job ranged alongside Noah and the Canaanite Dan'el). The revealed name of God is almost entirely avoided in the book of Job. It is used by the frame-narrator to tell the reader who it is we are dealing with, and only a single time by Job himself (1:21).[25] Job is a sheik from the "land of Uz," and the friends who come to visit him likewise are not Israelites.

Form-critical comparisons of the Psalms and Job can operate within a diachronic conceptuality wherein the actual declared setting of the book evaporates before the historical-critical logic that makes fruitful genre comparisons possible. The same can be said of dating the author of Job in a postexilic setting and forgetting thereby that an author can meaningfully operate within the conceptual framework of the work he is constructing (in the case of Job; likely with older sources as well), just as can the author of King Lear, or a postexilic author of Qohelet, to choose an example closer to home. The point here is that Job's specific dilemma—as the book sets that forth as an ingredient of its proper interpretation—is both comparable with David's and quite distinctive. It is more akin to a "patriarchal temptation," to use Luther's characterization of the world of the patriarchs, in which highly individualized figures operated before the giving of the Law vis-à-vis the divine *Urgewalt*. The kind of hermeneutical "dialogic" required to ensure that we properly grasp the difference between Job and David and thus grasp the theological significance of works wherein they are the main protagonists is surely a desideratum of any approach calling itself a canonical reading.

How one relates to the David of the Psalms—King and Everyman—is the subject of the Hossfeld and Zenger essay in this volume. One might

---

25. Compare issues related to the revelation of the divine name in Genesis. On this, see "The Call of Moses and the 'Revelation' of the Divine Name," in my *Word without End: The Old Testament as Abiding Theological Witness* (Waco, TX: Baylor University Press, 2004) 229–50.

equally say that how one relates to the character of Job is revealed as much in the contrast between his situation and David's as in what is arguably comparable. The assault on Job belongs to a single serious question posed by the satan: can a mortal serve God for naught (Job 1:9)? It is not obvious that anything like this serves to organize the dramatic movement of David and the monarchy that he represents in the flow of the five-book Psalter. Job will forever operate "in the dark" in key ways that distinguish him from the king under Torah, such as the Psalter sets that out. If reading Job following the Psalms is to be governed by the claim of Bloom with which Kynes's essay opens ("There are no *texts*, but only relationships *between* texts"), the juxtaposition of Job and the Psalms in the Writings will operate best by noting that they have simply been set astride one another without any canonical clues for what this might mean. Their absence is crucial to appreciating the distinctive character of each work, by themselves or juxtaposed with one another.

It is difficult to summarize the contribution of *Steinberg*, in part because of its ambition. In many ways, his assumed subtext is a calling into question the popular categorization of "wisdom literature" such as we confront it in most standard textbooks. These present "wisdom" according to an evolutionary principle and range the books in a way that establishes this point: "an older, naïve wisdom such as found in Proverbs that eventually was thrown into crisis, which resulted in the critical works of Job and Ecclesiastes" (p. 155). Steinberg provides good empirical and comparative grounds for rejecting this model. But given his interest and that of the volume at large in understanding the various canonical lists available for our evaluation, one can see right away that the standard textbook model has rejected altogether any serious hermeneutical advice that the final shaping of the canon/s might be providing. That is, Job usually precedes Proverbs, and when Proverbs does come first, only rarely is it in a series replicating the standard textbook idea, and even then, the final "voice" of wisdom is Song of Songs. I know of no standard treatment of wisdom, moreover, that would seek to find corroboration via available canonical lists.

Though Steinberg allows the order of b. B. Bat. 14b to guide his reflections (Job–Proverbs–Ecclesiastes–Song), he does so in the spirit of other chapters in the volume. He accepts that other lists exist. But he insists that a (limited) variety of orders is in itself a testimony to why order is decisive after all: "[T]ime and again in history, people were thinking of how best to order the biblical books" (p. 151). Farther along in the essay, he speaks of many different derivations of the talmudic orders for the Ketubim that could be interpreted in a similar way but could also permit creative alternatives (pp. 167ff.). It might have been useful to explain this in more detail, though one sympathetic with the general approach will likely take the point.

The order he works with obliges him to explain why the Song of Songs ought to be included as a wisdom book, since it is frequently omitted from standard accounts and yet now follows Ecclesiastes and precedes what he labels "the national-historical series" (Lamentations–Daniel–Esther–Ezra/ Nehemiah). One should note in passing that Steinberg is not disputing the classification we are accustomed to referring to as "wisdom" but is instead (1) identifying it in a fresh way in accordance with orders of the Writings, and (2) seeking better to integrate it into Old Testament theology as a whole—a perennial challenge. The chapter opens with just this concern clearly set forth. The path of integration, then, he assumes may likewise be provided by the structure of the Writings. The fate of the individual (often held to be a hallmark of wisdom) is discussed in the "wisdom series" but also juxtaposed with the fate of the nation in the "national-historical series," thereby suggesting where wisdom "fits" in larger OT thought. The frame consisting of Ruth–Psalms and Chronicles in b. B. Bat. 14b reinforces this integrative principle, according to Steinberg.[26]

All in all, Steinberg offers a refreshingly suggestive approach to re-thinking the category "wisdom literature" and how it fits into the larger thought-world of the Old Testament. This brief review cannot explore all the details of his argument, some stronger and more persuasive than others. The movement he describes from Job to Proverbs may strike many as contrived, since why one would begin the exploration of wisdom through the lens of Job is harder to explain than why Job's following Proverbs might take the wind out of wisdom's sails and was therefore to be avoided. I agree that the message of Job is not chiefly one of skepticism, for reasons I mention above, and like Steinberg I do not think OT "wisdom" is best comprehended through a history-of-religions evolutionary grid. Steinberg speaks of Job as "breathing life into wisdom's motto, 'The fear of Yhwh is the beginning of wisdom'" (p. 170) and, while the claim is possible, it would require more development. Far more probable is the significance of the movement from Proverbs to Ecclesiastes, or their coexistence as opening onto Song of Songs. Modern scholarship and the history of reception (especially in Christian circles) both have seen importance in the innerrelationship of these works. Might Job's precise location in a sequence be a more low-flying matter of less-interpretive significance? It is less connected to Proverbs via identifiable editorial linkage than Ecclesiastes is to Proverbs as a paired text, and one would likely see that association even if the two books were not side by side, as they sometimes are not.[27] The joyous re-

---

26. It would have been interesting to see engagement with the recent monograph by Jennie Barbour (*The Story of Israel in the Book of Qohelet: Ecclesiastes as Cultural Memory* [Oxford: Oxford University Press, 2012]) since she makes the strong case that Ecclesiastes is fundamentally a book about Israel's history.

27. See G. Wilson, "'The Words of the Wise': The Intent and Significance of Qoheleth 12:9–14," *JBL* 103 (1984) 175–92; and the recent discussion of Katherine Dell in *Interpreting Ecclesiastes: Readers Old and New* (Critical Studies in the Hebrew Bible 3; Winona Lake, IN: Eisenbrauns: 2013).

frains of Qohelet are more integrative and positive if the movement toward Song of Songs is intending to pick up on them and develop them further. In my view, this is precisely what the juxtaposition accomplishes, should we be in any doubt.[28]

I have already referred to aspects of *Stone's* work in the evaluation of Dempster above. Stone sits much easier with the need to establish an original order for the proper interpretation of Ruth.[29] In this essay, he begins with the phenomenon of the Megillot (which includes Ruth). He rejects the idea that the Megillot cannot serve as a lens onto an ancient order and is only a liturgical device from after the 12th century. His argument is fairly simple: "[I]t is more likely that the liturgical practices associated with these five books came about, in part, because of their prior association in the Hebrew canon" (p. 176), that is, in the Aleppo Codex, which he describes as "the crowning achievement of many generations of work." The fact that the order there (Ruth–Song–Ecclesiastes–Lamentations–Esther) is different from the liturgical order (Song/Passover–Ruth/Weeks–Lamentations/Ninth of Ab–Ecclesiastes/Booths–Esther/Purim) signals to Stone that the books were already assembled and were only re-sequenced to correspond to a (slowly developing) liturgical calendar.

Two methodological points that he makes before turning to Ruth call for attention. He cautions that intertextual connections between books "are not a sure guide" to order, since Ecclesiastes refers to Genesis more than any book in the Writings (where it appears). I think the arguments associating Ecclesiastes with Proverbs on intertextual grounds are quite compelling and leave untouched the fact that a later book may likewise allude to Genesis. Second, the arguments for editorial coherence in The Book of the Twelve extend far beyond the two examples he gives and serve as an outstanding example of what he calls "canonical or compilational poetics" (p. 179). One thinks of the work of J. Jeremias on the mutual editing of Amos and Hosea and the present location of Joel; the place of Obadiah in light of earlier references to Edom; the call for repentance at the close of Hosea and its being taken up in Joel; the wisdom refrains noted by R. C. Van Leeuwen in the first six books, which only work with the MT order; the evidence of contiguous books in the vast array of 12 witnesses at Qumran, confirming the MT order; the significance of the precise middle of the collection now found at Mic 3:12 and 4:1; the *maśśaʾ* units that close off the collection (Zech 9:1; 12:1; Mal 1:1); and the final book that operates with an "authorial voice," which bespeaks the "messenger who is

---

28. Compare the commentary treatment by Tremper Longman and others, who regard the refrains as resigned "carpe deim" expostulations, exposing the cynical force of the book as a whole, and certainly not related to Song of Songs (*The Book of Ecclesiastes* [NICOT; Grand Rapids, MI: Eerdmans, 1998]).

29. As Stone puts it: "[T]he concept of an original or single order is not, in my view, a prerequisite to investigating the significance of ancient arrangements" (p. 177).

to come" (Mal 3:1). This list could be extended further, as recent work on the Twelve shows. I was surprised not to see fuller reference to that work here—instead, Stone only cites of one page from his own thesis (where the discussion is much more comprehensive)—since the Twelve gives superb evidence of a wide range of "canonical poetics" extending well beyond catchwords or thematic generalities.

The main finding that Stone wishes to set forth entails the linkages in the individual books of the DtrH and the way that Ruth's inclusion in that collection occasioned a subtle alteration of verb forms so that it would better fit with what precedes (the end of Judges) and would also anticipate 1 Samuel ("better than X sons" in Ruth 4:15 and 1 Sam 1:8). Yet at the same time, the logic of Ruth's following the carefully composed acrostic of Proverbs 31 is also compelling, in Stone's view (the *ʾēšet ḥayil* is Ruth, according to Ruth 3:11). For all that, Stone does speak of Ruth's "migration" from the Former Prophets to the Writings as being "not as complete" (p. 182). Obviously, this is a close-run affair, and one may wonder how or why it is necessary to declare for one option or the other. I found less persuasive the idea of "dialogical tension" between Proverbs' concerns with the foreigner and Ruth as a Moabitess "woman of valor." Ruth clearly opts to come fully into the bosom of God's chosen people, indeed at the risk of her own life and against the cautions of her mother-in-law. Proverbs itself contains wisdom from the foreigner (22:17ff.; 30:1ff.) without cavil or need for explanation, and indeed the final poem probably presents itself in this form. The full unity of Ruth and Naomi is the theme at the finale of the book (4:17), and Boaz and Ruth give rise to King David (4:22).

Still, this is not a crucial factor in Stone's larger argument, which in regard to Ruth might be summed up in this way: "Early in the history of the Hebrew canon, there was not one order or a great multitude of orders but instead a limited number of arrangements" (p. 183). Indeed, one can note that different arrangements, translational options, scope, lectionary presentations, and so forth persist to this day. If canonical authority and logic turned on the determination of a single order and scope, once upon a time, it certainly did not persist through time—and this without damage to the claims of the material to be Holy Scripture all the same. Childs notes this in his own remarks about the perennial "search for the Christian Bible."[30]

One of the real plusses of the treatment of Daniel by *Amber Warhurst* is the careful way she turns the typical procedure for assessing Daniel's location in Greek and Hebrew orders on its head. The intriguing survey of earlier Jewish and Christian reactions to Daniel in the Writings shows that the issue is not a modern historical-critical one alone, though the terms of the discussion are very different. The basic idea is that Daniel's location in the Writings somehow amounts to an intentional demotion or is best con-

---

30. Childs, *Biblical Theology of the Old and New Testaments*, 67.

ceived as a moving of Daniel away from his true association with the Prophets. Von Rad and others had long noted that Daniel is in fact never called a prophet and indeed is depicted far more like the shrewd sage, consistent with what we know of main themes of the Writings. Given the attention being paid in this volume to matters of sequence and arrangement, one could add to this other formal observations, given the character of (what has come to be called) the Latter Prophets. This group is a stable unit of four books, relatively indifferent to precise sequence. We have three main prophets whose books are of approximately equal length, and a fourth collection of Twelve Prophets, the verse count of which as a whole is similar in size. Daniel is about one-fourth of this length. Including the book would make an "odd man out," given the symmetry of the collection in Hebrew lists. One wonders, if we had the book only unto itself and knew nothing about the possibilities for classification, whether we would have reflexively located it alongside the Three and the Twelve.

Warhurst goes well beyond these sorts of considerations, however, in her reading of Daniel within the Writings. Her observations concerning the themes of (1) temple vessels and (2) the persistence of exile demonstrate clear associations among "the cluster of books at the end of the Writings—Lamentations, Esther, Daniel, Ezra–Nehemiah, and, according to some lists, Chronicles" (p. 203). She picks up on the idea from Steinberg of a "national-historical" grouping. This includes the idea that Lamentations poses a question that the following books reflect on from different angles, thus representing a movement from sorrow to joy, "tempered by an awareness of the nation's guilt" (p. 204). In sum, the location of Daniel in the Writings "transposes all the components of that corpus" (p. 204). It is where it belongs. Though she does not say it explicitly, this amounts to a rejection of the idea of a movement out of a prior location, with all the attendant reflection that this change created in its wake. I have described the three major prophets as independent works whose order, because of this, is less critical to their individual interpretation—hence, different orders in the reception history. I am less sure this would translate into an argument for the suitability of arrangements in which Daniel now sits alongside these prophets, though this has certainly happened. In my view, this simply shows that the individual character of the Writings is of a different kind than what we find in the Law and the Prophets, and because of this, books could migrate and did. Some found their place in a logical but different canonical location (Ruth is the parade example). One must suppose that Daniel's capacity to migrate functioned in something of the same way.

The chapters of *Koorevaar* and *Steins* might well have rounded off the volume, illustrating thereby a central premise that they share about Chronicles as the last book of the Hebrew Bible/Old Testament. Not only do they believe Chronicles is the final book of the canon (as in b. B. Bat. 14b), its entire purpose is to summarize and recapitulate for the last time all that precedes literarily (it is canon-conscious of the "law and prophets" as genuine divisions) in the form of a final historical roundup, confirming the view of Jerome, *Chronicon totius divinae historiae.* They both agree that the older argument for a unified Chronistic Work, including Ezra–Nehemiah, is no longer tenable. It is belied by the coherence and particular overarching style of the Chronicler, who is wrapping things up for all time (and is enclosing Ezra–Nehemiah within its final ambit as well). Chronicles is replete with citations of earlier writings, and this is in some sense its signature theological purpose. It tells the story of humankind from Adam to Cyrus and sets before Israel for all time a paradigm for living in a sacral vocation under Torah/Prophets on behalf of the whole world: the first theme is central to Steins's thesis and the latter to Koorevaar's. Both are thoroughly versed in Chronicles scholarship and broker that in evenhanded ways. Their main disagreement is over the dating of this final canonical accomplishment. The detailed character of their treatments is not easily summarized, and my point here is only to set out the basic contours of their arguments.

I share with Steins a sense that a feature of the Writings is (1) the individual character of the works in this division and (2) their relationship to books in the prior two divisions as particularly decisive to their sense-making (in a way that is not true of the Law and the Prophets themselves).[31] This can also explain why the final position of Chronicles—if indeed that view is correct—was corrigible of rearrangement, such as we see it in other listings (and in English printed Bibles). The individuality of the works and their relationship to works in the first two sections was sometimes the cause of their reassignment. So long as the general conception of this fact is kept before us, the argument for Chronicles' final position as a historical datum ("this is the original sequence") does not, in my view, have to overreach.

I was intrigued by the comment of Koorevaar that, during the Reformation, the humanist and theological instinct to prioritize the MT (justified by recourse to Jerome) did not extend to matters of order and sequence.[32] On his view, it belongs to the narrative purpose of Chronicles as a theological accomplishment in its own right to come last in canonical position— what Steins refers to as its *Abschlussphaenomen.*[33] This purpose is obscured if the work does not come last or if it is ranged before Ezra–Nehemiah (sometimes in an earlier division altogether). Of course, it would be fascinating to know what effect it would have in our modern discussion if the more popular order of Malachi–Matthew (virtually absent in antiquity) was instead represented by Chronicles–Matthew—an order that Koorevaar views as crucial to Matthew's own narrative unfolding and theological purpose.

---

31. See *Goodly Fellowship,* 105–25.

32. See Brandt's essay in this volume regarding Luther and the Paris Vulgate (p. 79).

33. From Steins's 1995 publication, *Die Chronik als kanonisches Abschlussphaenomen: Studien zur Entstehung und Theogie von 1/2 Chronik* (BBB 93; Weinheim: Athenäum, 1995).

Matthew "breaks the seal" on the final summative history and inserts his own final denouement, as consistent with and as extending the original vision of Chronicles. Can this reading still be maintained as critical to understanding Chronicles and Matthew, and the NT and the OT as canonical accomplishments for that matter, without the concomitant of insisting on an original historical order or one reinforced by fresh Bible publications, where Chronicles is purposefully and necessarily the last word? Again I am reminded of Childs's comments regarding the "search" for the Christian Bible. His concern here is the acknowledgment of a history of reception throughout wider Christendom in which the Bible's order was not held in one fixed form but, for reasons we may not be able to track, was flexibly recast.

This seems to me one of the major successes of the present volume, and one senses it in the present two essays under review. The variety of orders is nowhere denied. The quest for canonical significance does not require a maximal or totalizing theory of "original order," though the search is allowed its place all the same. Sometimes one has a sense that the determination of original order is more decisive for one contributor than another, and this is certainly true of the essays by Koorevaar and Steins. One is trying to track the logic of the orders in their variety, and a diachronic theory here can be useful. In the case of Chronicles—and this is important to underscore—we are talking about a canon consciousness that arises within the work itself and is fully distinct from an external declarative act. Chronicles is last because that is its own view of the matter, not because an institutional decision declared this place for it. My own view is that what is exposed thereby is not so much a plea for a single printed edition that reinforces the theory—who can bring that about anyway?—but greater sensitivity to and critical appraisal of just what the variety bespeaks. Chronicles' position elsewhere than at the close of the Hebrew Bible need not rob it of certain crucial features that Steins and Koorevaar are at pains to set forth as consistent with this location.

The final essay, by *Chapman*, is a creative exploration of the effects of a tripartite sensibility, as one can note this in reception history. It is an intriguing and creative contribution. What was far less clear to me was his starting point and how what he has developed might satisfy the concerns of those who hold that the history of reception defeats a canonical sensibility as Childs and others have argued for this in the modern period. That Christian reading of the Bible ignored its book form strikes me as an indication of a deep unfamiliarity with reception history as such. Origen, Didymus, Diodore, Theodore, Theodoret, Cyril, Basel, Nyssa, Jerome, Augustine, Cassiodorus, Aquinas, Erasmus, Luther, and Calvin all wrote commentaries on biblical books as books. Aquinas frequently comments on structural movement in the Psalter, and the observations about the initial psalms' purpose via-à-vis the whole is never absent from the tradition. The order of the Twelve is frequently discussed. Chrysostom had a distinctive theory regarding the sequence of the letters of Paul. One could multiply the point endlessly.

What Chapman's essay may provoke is a keener awareness of the significance of the macrostructure of the Old Testament, operating at a kind of lower consciousness in the subsequent effective history. We see this reflected of course in the standard nomenclature of the New Testament, "Law and Prophets" and "Law and Prophets and Psalms," in referring to Israel's sacred literature. The first, more-common expression, far from pointing to an "open canon," simply points to the closed and stable main units of the OT at the time, with which a third, more-flexible library of individual works circulated. Alternatively, the "Prophets" could simply refer to any non-Torah works, even as a rough distinction was probably already at work of the sort that Chapman helpfully tracks, in the threefold category distinction he collates here. None of this would make any sense whatsoever if the concept of a book were as foreign to the ancient world as Barr and Barton sought to claim. The entire weight of the present volume on the Ketubim exposes the weakness of this claim, and indeed its eccentricity. One also reads the essays of Steins and other European contributors and realizes immediately that an entire discourse on canon as a hermeneutical and theological achievement has simply not filtered through much British and North American scholarship (see Steck, Dohmen, Oeming, Lohfink, Zenger, van der Kooij, Albertz, and Wanke).

One observation, yet to be stated, is worthy of further reflection at the conclusion of this review. How is that those who claim a kind of presupposition-less stance on canon and are disinterested in its theological and hermeneutical dimension end up with a curious set of religious claims all the same? These take the form of the following, in part or in whole:

1. The Bible receives its authority because someone/some institution says so;[34]
2. The Bible makes no effort on its own part in effecting coherence and innerrelationship; the reader is in charge of this, or a churchly authority;
3. The two parts of the Bible can be effectively collated into one when it comes to thinking about canon and closure; there is no precedent

---

34. Contrast the Roman Catholic position from *Dogmatic Constitution on the Catholic Faith* (1870), which reads, "These books the church holds to be sacred and canonical not because she subsequently approved them by her authority after they had been composed by unaided human skill, nor simply because they contain revelation without error, but because, being written under the inspiration of the Holy Spirit, they have God as their author, and were as such committed to the church" (quoted from Chapman, "The Canon Debate," 289).

authority inherited from Israel in the form of a canon or core-canon;[35]

4. The New Testament only accidently quotes as Scripture—repeatedly and with the rarest exception, in the form of allusion—the Hebrew-language books of the OT and nothing else;[36]

5. The organizational achievements of the Law and the Prophets, if acknowledged to be such, ought to extend in equal measure to the Writings; instead of this, the third division is "open" or "random literature without definite bounds" because it does not formally mirror the first two parts; it cannot have its own character and also be "canonical" in the same sense;[37]

6. The Christian religion can appeal to its authorizing center ("the man Jesus"; "Jesus Christ"; "God") as in some sense independent of the scriptural testimony to this reality, or its own canonical letter and shape as a whole.[38]

When Barton dismisses the work of Beckwith on the grounds that he is a "fundamentalist," with no actual engagement with his arguments, a conclusion we might draw is that Barton's own position is, by contrast, free of religious presupposition.[39] This is incorrect. The six items above constitute a strong religious stance, and one may rightly conclude that the "neutral

---

35. See n. 2 above.

36. There is no real distinction to be made between allusions, milieu awareness, and the formal citation of Scripture as such. Yet even a distinction between the citation of Scripture (OT) and reference to NT writings in the earliest church fathers is quite obvious. See Hans von Campenhausen, *The Formation of the Christian Bible* (Philadelphia: Fortress, 1972).

37. Compare Seitz, *Goodly Fellowship;* and G. Steins, "Zwei Konzepte—Ein Kanon: Zur Gestalt und Gestaltung des TeNak" (Vienna, SBL 2007 paper).

38. After many centuries of monotheism, understood from a philosophical rather than scriptural perspective, it is today more likely to be assumed that if there is a God, there is only one God, and that while Scripture speaks about him, it is also possible to be in independent or direct relationship with him; that one can believe in God *before* he is encountered through Scripture; and the one already known (or thought to be known) is *then* identified with the God of Abraham, Isaac, and Jacob, the Father of Jesus Christ. (John Behr, *The Way to Nicaea: The Formation of Christian Theology* [Crestwood, NY: St. Vladimir's Seminary Press, 2001] 1.19)

39. After failing to deal with any of the details of Beckwith's actual argument, Barton transitions thus: "It is a thousand pities, therefore, that such a book should turn out, when read closely, to be essentially a very sophisticated piece of fundamentalist apologetic" (p. 64). And: "The problem is really much more insidious, and comes down to that peculiar failure in historical perception which afflicts all fundamentalists like a colour-blindness" (p. 64). It is a shame to have this sort of in-house dismissal of "fundamentalists" run interference for any serious evaluation of the work itself, which lends further support to the perception that this is simply two religious positions on collision, rather than a sober and sustained historical evaluation as such. Barton's review appears in *Theology* 90 (1987) 63–65.

examination of the evidence" quite logically lines up with the religious convictions animating the examination from the outset.[40]

The point is that there is always a reciprocating relationship between what one seeks to find and what one finds in fact. Good scholarship is scholarship that is capable of adjustment and constant review. What one finds in the European discussion is an awareness that the concept of canon is ineluctably hermeneutical and theological and that this arises in the light of the material being assessed itself, with its press for a hearing in conjunction with other scriptural testimony. There is no "scripture" here and "canon" there, because the Scriptures by their very character insist on a permanent hearing, beyond the circumstances of their origin (Deut 5:3; 6:20–25; Zech 1:6; John 20:31; Rom 15:4; 2 Tim 3:14–17). That is what makes them what they are. This means that the "yes" of ensuing generations is caught up in the providential purposes of the God who inspired the origins, development, and association of the Scriptures in their full coming-to-be. It is not an external "yes" but a deference to the claim already being asserted by the character of the testimony, that here God is speaking with full authority to a community in which we know ourselves in Christ to have been caught up. In Luther's apt phrase, *Ecclesia non facit Verbum sed fit Verbo.*

This particular *theological* conviction about the priority of the word of God finds it *material* correlate in the existence of a First Testament prior to the evolved Christian Scripture, containing now Old and New Testaments. The existence of a canonical authority at the time of the formation of the Gospel testimony reminds the church of how it is birthed by the word—a fact testified to in the New Testament, rooted in the dominical consciousness itself: "You search the scriptures . . . and it is they that bear witness to me" (John 5:39). The present volume makes several cautionary points about the character of this material witness: its outer limits may await final resolution, and its internal order is capable of rearrangement. Neither of these historical observations touches on the critical point that the Scriptures of Israel—including the Ketubim—are doing the full canonical work of bearing witness to the One God in a completely sufficient way and that sufficiency lies at the root of the later creedal assertion, grounded in the NT, that the work of God in Christ was "in accordance with the scriptures."

---

40. Chapman quite correctly notes religious bias in the work of Allert and McDonald, from which Barton and Barr and others are likewise not immune: "[T]he theological anxiety driving their presentations of canon history has to do with the perceived excesses of those on their theological right" ("Canon Debate," 289).

Index of Authors

Index of Scripture

Deuterocanonical Literature

New Testament